Contemporary Society

An Introduction to Social Science

Twelfth Edition

John A. Perry

Emeritus, Cuyahoga Community College

Erna K. Perry

PEARSON

Boston   New York   San Francisco
Mexico City   Montreal   Toronto   London   Madrid   Munich   Paris
Hong Kong   Singapore   Tokyo   Cape Town   Sydney

Executive Editor: Jeff Lasser
Editorial Assistant: Lauren Macey
Senior Marketing Manager: Kelly May
Production Supervisor: Roberta Sherman
Editorial-Production Service: Nesbitt Graphics, Inc.
Composition Buyer: Linda Cox
Manufacturing Buyer: Debbie Rossi
Electronic Composition: Nesbitt Graphics, Inc.
Interior Design: Nesbitt Graphics, Inc.
Photo Researcher: PoYee Oster, Photoquick Research
Cover Administrator: Kristina Mose-Libon

For related titles and support materials, visit our online catalog at www. ablongman. com.

Between the time website information is gathered and then published, it is not unusual for
some sites to have closed. Also, the transcription of URLs can result in typographical errors.
The publisher would appreciate notification where these errors occur so that they may be
corrected in subsequent editions.

Cataloging-in-Production data unavailable at press time.

Printed in the United States of America

10 9 8 7 6 5 4 3 2 1   RRD-VA   12 11 10 09 08

Contents

Preface

We are pleased to be in the enviable situation of having a book published in its twelfth edition. We are confident that both new and previous users of the text will agree that its longevity is an indication that we have been doing something right.

The course in Social Science, for which this book is intended, is directed at entering college students with different educational backgrounds and needs. The course itself is not meant for those who plan to specialize in a specific social science. Rather, the course is designed to offer an overview of the social sciences for those students who intend to specialize in other fields. A textbook for such a course, therefore, must offer a panorama, or a perspective, on how the social science disciplines perceive and interpret the world around us. The text should not be mired in details or be overly weighted down by references and definitions. It should not offer too much too soon. Above all, it should not present a compendium, or a list, but an integrated social science view of the world.

In this twelfth edition of *Contemporary Society*, we have retained the basic outline of the text, as we believe that the chapters flow in a rational, self-explanatory order. Recent editions have included new findings in the areas of astronomy and paleoanthropology. This knowledge is important because it throws new light on the age of the universe and of humans. We also discuss other contemporary issues, such as: the research on the human genome; the ethical considerations revolving around the issues of cloning and stem cell use; campaign reform; presidential power; the perceived divisions of the American electorate into red and blue states; the war in Iraq; and global warming. In this edition, new material has been added on terrorism, the global and U.S. economy, the rising inequality in wealth and incomes, immigration, education, and the status of religion in the United States.

An innovation we have retained in this edition are the boxes, usually several per chapter. The intent of the boxes is to illustrate certain points, to add material for which there is no room within the chapter, to generate discussion, and at times just to break up the material with a bit of informative humor. Some of the boxes from the preceding edition have been retained, others have been deleted, and a number have been added. Among the topics discussed in the boxes are books, such as *Consilience*, and articles from the educated person's press, such as those dealing with the attempts of scientists to create life, how astrophysicists view the cosmos, how groups form around traits that people share, how the maternal bond impacts on personality, why humans kill, global inequality, how women fare around the world, change in the United States, arranged marriages, the conflict between science and religion, communism in China and in the USSR, values in politics, globalization and its foes, and so on.

In this edition, as in the previous one, we have also added lists of web sites that may be of interest to students. These appear at the end of each chapter. We urge instructors to point them out to students, because some of them could add much to the students' understanding and general knowledge, as well as provide a bit of humor.

The focus of the book remains centered on change, which is the pervasive reality of our era. We try to bring home the idea that the transition from an industrial to a postindustrial order is fraught with difficulties, as was the previous transition, from an agricultural to an industrial order. The increasing fragmentation of the social order, which leads people away from community and a common purpose to conflict and disunity, is shown in this framework.

Students who enroll in a social science course may well wonder whether familiarity with the social sciences will help them solve life's problems. Of course, education in general has not proved to be a panacea either for personal or for social problems. But the search for rational solutions, learning to see preconceptions and prejudgments for what they are, and seeing the possibility of working for positive change without having to resort to violent or self-destructive behavior are sufficient justification for presenting a social science perspective. We will consider ourselves successful if students become aware that they need not accept the world as it is but can act to change it and that the social sciences can provide them with some of the instruments of change.

For the instructor, we offer an *Instructor's Manual/Test Bank*. It includes more than 70 multiple-choice questions, 25 true/false questions, and several essay questions for each chapter. A computerized version of the test bank is available in both Windows and Mac versions.

For the student, we have prepared a comprehensive Study Guide. It includes learning objectives, chapter outlines, chapter summaries, and fill-in-the-blank and multiple-choice practice tests for each chapter.

Finally, no book can see the light of day without the TLC and constant supervision of editors, photo researchers, and other support personnel. To them we extend our sincerest thanks.

As always, our reviewers have offered invaluable advice and suggestions; therefore, we would like to thank: Ann Creighton-Zellar, Virginia Commonwealth University; and Margaret Tseng, Marymount University.

John A. Perry and Erna K. Perry

Through the Lens of Science

IN THIS CHAPTER, YOU WILL LEARN

■ *of the existence of the external world, which we inherit, and the social world, which we create;*

■ *that the analysis of the social world with the tools of science is a fairly recent innovation;*

■ *the basic differences between the social and the natural sciences;*

■ *the elements and steps of the scientific method;*

■ *which disciplines constitute the social sciences;*

■ *the various research methods used in the social sciences.*

Life on our planet has undergone tremendous changes since its beginning, both in the natural world into which we are born, and the social world we have created and to which each generation contributes. What do we mean by the **natural** and the **social** worlds? Clearly, at birth all living things enter a physical world that is not of their own making. Plants and animals either adapt to this ready-made environment or die out. They cannot change the nature of their habitat, for on planet Earth all living organisms exist in an environment shaped by forces and governed by laws that are only partially and imperfectly understood and only minimally amenable to change or control. Early humans did not understand this world and attributed many phenomena to spirits and supernatural beings. Today, the natural world is studied by the methods of science in such disciplines as biology, physics, chemistry, ecology, and so on. These disciplines are the so-called exact sciences and are not within the realm of our inquiry in this text.

Each newly born **human** being, however, also enters a social world that has been shaped by those born previously and is continually reshaped by each new generation. The existence of this **social** world, while taken for granted by the majority of people, is of tremendous importance to humans. It is what distinguishes them from other animals. Animals, aside from certain biological adaptations to new environments or climates, retain an essentially unchanged lifestyle from the moment of their emergence. Humans, on the other hand, have manipulated their social world to the point of affecting their lifestyles dramatically (although their biological and physical characteristics have scarcely changed in the last 20,000 years). This social world was not always well understood, either, but in the last 200 years, disciplines have originated with the goal of examining it with the same scientific methodology that the exact sciences use. These disciplines are collectively called the **social sciences**.

The social sciences were born in a period of social turmoil, when new ideas and beliefs were causing conflict and fragmentation in European societies. They represented an attempt to make sense of a social reality that had become too difficult to grasp with the old tools. They offered the hope that the social world could also be examined in a dispassionate, objective way that would yield specific rules of behavior for people to follow to improve their individual and collective lives. Perhaps the expectations for the social sciences were too high: in spite of efforts, few grand theories have been developed or secrets of social life have been uncovered. Nonetheless, the social sciences and their methodology remain effective—and probably unique—tools for rationally examining our social world.

■ The Social Sciences

The purpose of the social sciences is to study systematically all aspects of the human condition and of human behavior, using a methodology borrowed from the physical sciences wherever possible. This insistence on systematic and methodical study is what distinguishes the social sciences from philosophy, art, and literature, which also comment and reflect on all facets of the human condition. In fact, insights into the nature of human behavior and the characteristics of societies have been expressed by artists, poets, and philosophers since time immemorial. Artists, poets, and philosophers avail themselves of such tools as intuition, imagination, authority, tradition, rational thought, and common sense, tools available to all of us and which we still use every day.

Technology marches on! Social scientists have another tool at their disposal—the ubiquitous computer—to help them in researching how people interact even in the remotest societies.

Galileo Galilei, an Italian astronomer and physicist (1564–1642) theorized, after looking at the sky with a telescope, that it was the earth that moved around the sun, and not the other way around as was commonly believed in his time. Many theories in the social sciences also dispel some widely held, but incorrect, beliefs.

Unfortunately, however, these tools have a major shortcoming: they are not always accurate and thorough, and they are often colored by individual or societal prejudices. For instance, for centuries people believed that the earth was flat and, thus, one could fall off its edge. That was a reasonable deduction if one used only one's senses: the earth does look flat when we look only as far as our eyes reach. It was also accepted knowledge that the earth was the center of the universe and the sun went around it, and that too was a logical conclusion if all one did was look with the naked eye. However, when instruments were invented that could measure and see beyond the human senses, the knowledge that up to then had been accepted as truth needed to be modified; and that did not happen without a fight. The Polish astronomer Nicolaus Copernicus (1473–1543) and the Italian Renaissance astronomer Galileo Galilei (1564–1642) were ostracized and nearly lost their lives when they tried to convince their compatriots that it was the earth that circled the sun, not the other way around, thus challenging the ancient wisdom of such authorities as Aristotle and the Catholic Church. These astronomers had not trusted their senses alone but attempted to arrive at the truth by using a new tool of inquiry: science.

■ The Social World Seen through the Lens of Science

Science may be briefly defined as a method using a system of rational inquiry dependent on the empirical testing of facts. It is this method, rather than a particular body of content, that gives scientists a unique way of looking at things. The purpose of the scientific method is to obtain evidence that is verifiable and subject to replication and to make no judgment about even the most seemingly obvious "facts" until original suppositions are overwhelmingly supported by proof.

The social sciences emerged when some social philosophers determined to use the scientific method to study specific aspects of human behavior in the social world. Initially, social philosophy differed little from philosophy in general, but certain ideas prevalent in the eighteenth century, during the era commonly called the Enlightenment, led to the division of social philosophy into a number of separate disciplines. This historical period was characterized by an increase in people's faith in the power of reason. Scholars and philosophers became convinced that, just as universal laws of nature had been discovered by natural scientists through the use of the scientific method, similar laws would become apparent if human behavior could be examined by the same approach. Once the principles of social life were uncovered, they theorized, a more perfect society could be attained.

As usually happens, the need for a new approach to the analysis of human social behavior was prompted by dramatic societal changes. The conditions brought about by the Industrial Revolution and the movement of people to cities encouraged thinkers to seek solutions to the many new problems faced by individuals in these changed societies. With the rise of industry, in fact, two new social classes emerged: the owners of manufacturing machinery and the industrial workers who operated it. There were vast discrepancies in the standards of living between these two social classes, with the workers laboring for long hours in difficult conditions and suffering frequent layoffs. As people kept moving to cities in search of factory jobs, cities became places in which conditions of overcrowding and lack of hygiene were rampant. Soon, cities became breeding grounds of poverty and crime. It was primarily these problems that the early social scientists attempted to address by applying the scientific method to human behavior, in this way giving rise to the social sciences. These include cultural anthropology, economics, geography (including demography and ecology), political science, psychology, sociology, and those dimensions of history that go beyond the strictly narrative recounting of events.

What do the social sciences study today? Following are some examples of what contemporary social science examines. An economist at Georgetown University is one of four authors of a report that concludes that childhood poverty costs the United States about $500 billion a year because poor children become less productive adults, earn less money, commit more crimes, and have more health problems that are paid for by taxpayers. Consequently, the authors suggest that the United States would be well served to invest significant resources to poverty reduction (Eckholm, 2007, A15).

A physicist at the University of Maryland, who calls himself an "econophysicist," maintains that present patterns of economic inequality are "as natural, and unalterable, as the properties of air molecules in your kitchen" (Shea, 2005, 67). Econophysicists use the tools of physics to study markets and other economic phenomena. Thus, in studying wealth distribution in the United States, these researchers maintain that the dispersion of income is similar to the distribution patterns of the energy of atoms in gases that are at thermal equilibrium. Moreover, this is a pattern that many closed, random systems tend to follow.

Stanford University psychologists and economists designed a study to find out which part of the brain is active when a person decides to spend money at a shopping mall, and what produces the urge to buy (Tierney, 2007, D1). A Columbia University sociologist tries to decode social interactions to discover why people give themselves reasons for actions and attitudes (Gladwell, 2006, 80).

Finally, more and more the social sciences are combining with the exact sciences to discover findings in the areas of medicine and climate, findings that will affect and possibly benefit people and societies.

In defining the social sciences, the key words are *systematically* and *methodically*. Because the social world is subjected to scientific scrutiny, the knowledge that has accumulated about how humans live in their world is organized according to definite concepts, theories, and research and not according to random, subjective, and possibly biased observation.

■ The Scientific Method

Although the social sciences are considered scientific disciplines, they cannot employ exactly the same methodology as the natural or physical sciences. They do, however, share with all sciences the use of the scientific method. The basic technique of the scientific method is a special kind of observation called *scientific observation*. This kind of observation differs from simply looking around. Those of us who have the use of our vision look at things all the time, but we seldom arrive at scientific conclusions. We obtain evidence from our senses, but for such evidence to be reliable, it must first be confirmed by the scientific method. That is, scientific observation must proceed *systematically*. Scientists must select and define a problem and then make an organized plan for collecting data. Scientific observation must be *accurate and precise*. In collecting data, scientists must subject them to careful checking, rechecking, and cross-checking, as well as to careful measurement. Scientific observation should take place under *controlled conditions*, although that is frequently impossible. Researchers should be able to make particular features of the environment remain constant, so that when other features change, they can be sure which specific cause is determining which effect. This requirement is difficult to achieve in the social sciences, because research on people cannot always be performed in a laboratory. Control is difficult even in the natural sciences, because many phenomena can only be observed at a distance. Finally, scientific observation must be made by a *trained observer*. Only such a person knows which data are relevant and which are only peripherally important. The vocabulary of science includes concepts, theories, and research.

Concepts

Concepts are generalized, abstract ideas that symbolize whole categories of people, objects, and processes. They are ways of classifying things that are in the same category. For instance, the concept of "chair" includes all those objects made for people to sit on, although there is an infinite variety of such objects, from gilded Louis XIV antiques to the chrome-and-vinyl kitchen variety. Concepts are used to simplify the way people think and communicate. Society, nation, art, education, and voting are only some examples of concepts.

Concepts are used by social scientists to generalize about some aspects of human interaction. They are guidelines that direct the interpretation and analysis of reality. Concepts are the technical vocabulary of the social sciences, and they have precise meanings that may differ considerably from the generally understood versions.

Theories

Theories are sets of concepts and generalizations so arranged that they explain and predict possible relationships among phenomena. In the social sciences, theories are formulations of principles of behavior through which scientists try to increase their knowledge of human interaction. Theories are founded on observation and analysis using the vocabulary of concepts. Without theories, the accumulation of knowledge would be impossible, just as the formulation of theories would be impossible without concepts. A theory does not have the force of a law. A law is an explanation of unchanging relationships among events. According to the law of gravity, an object always falls in the same direction under given conditions. The social sciences have no laws because they deal with people rather than with inanimate objects, and people have intelligence and will that are not subject to unchangeable laws. Theories are always open to change and even to total rejection if new evidence is presented to challenge them. Finally, when people speak of "theory" in casual conversation, they mean nothing more than a guess. In scientific terminology, a theory carries much more weight because it is based on supporting evidence.

Research

Research tests and bolsters, or refutes, theories. Research may be defined as systematic scientific inquiry conducted under controlled conditions in which data are carefully observed for the purpose of determining the relationship between one factor (for example, income) and one or more other factors (for example, child-rearing techniques).

Variables.   The factors whose relationship social scientists try to uncover are called *variables*. These are characteristics that differ (vary) in each individual case—from person to person, from group to group, from time to time, from place to place, and from situation to situation. In explaining what variables are, one social scientist adds that "A variable is a name for something that is thought to influence (or be influenced by) a particular state of being in something else...in addition, [it is] a special kind of concept that contains within it a notion of degree or differentiation" (Hoover & Donovan, 1995, 21–22). Age, education, income, religion, and political affiliation are some of the most frequently used variables in social scientific research. Social scientists use measurements, usually of a statistical nature, to determine the value of a variable in a specific case.

Marie Curie, a French-Polish physicist and chemist and the first woman scientist to win a Nobel Prize, working in her laboratory. Scientific research is conducted systematically, under strictly controlled conditions in which data are carefully observed and accurately noted, to be able to determine relationships between one factor and one or more other factors.

Variables, then, are concepts that vary, and they are used in the social sciences to uncover how change in one phenomenon can explain change in another one. Variables are of two kinds: *independent* or *dependent*. **Independent** variables are those that exert influence on **dependent** variables. The relationship between variables may be one of **cause and effect,** in which case the independent variable is the cause and the dependent variable receives its effect. The relationship between variables may also be one of **correlation,** meaning that two or more variables are simply related in some way. Correlation and causation are distinct phenomena and should not be confused. *Correlation* occurs purely by chance and the variables change together, whereas in *causation*, one phenomenon is responsible for another. Sometimes the correlation among two or more variables turns out to be *spurious*, meaning that it is false—that in reality the association is caused by another factor that scientists have not even considered and did not intend to measure. It is, therefore, imperative that scientific research be carefully controlled. Variables must be clearly stated and must be measurable; the relationship between variables must be equally clear and measurable; and the pursuant hypothesis (that the variables are related) must be testable (Hoover & Donovan, 1995, 35).

Steps of the Scientific Method

The steps in the scientific method, illustrated in Figure 1.1, may be summarized as follows.

Selecting and Defining a Topic.   First, an investigator must have a clearly defined idea of what should be investigated. A topic for investigation is usually prompted by curiosity; thus, it tends to be in the form of a question. For instance, are children of first-generation immigrants more successful in attaining upward mobility than children of native-born citizens? The researcher should also specify whether a causal relationship is suspected (one variable causing the occurrence of another). Because it is difficult to prove causal relationships and distinguish cause from effect, researchers are often satisfied with proving that a correlation between two or more phenomena exists.

Reviewing the Literature.   After selecting the topic, the researcher must review all the existing literature on the subject to ensure that it has not already been investigated. If it has, the researcher might have to alter the topic, perhaps focusing on a facet of it that has not been investigated previously. A review of the literature is an important step in the scientific method. It connects new research with old, allows the accumulation of ideas, and directs scientists to the right variables to pursue. Libraries are now equipped with computerized systems that make the job of reviewing books and articles much less time consuming than it was in the past.

Forming a Hypothesis.   The hypothesis is a tentative statement of the selected topic that is subject to testing and verification. The hypothesis must, in clearly expressed terms, predict a relationship between two or more variables. Hypotheses may be based on a researcher's mere hunch or educated guess; for instance, a researcher may speculate that religion influences the way a person votes. The remaining steps of the scientific method may prove the hypothesis valid (yes, religion affects voting behavior), may cause it to be reformulated (yes, but only if the voter is in a specific age bracket), or may contradict it altogether (no, religion has nothing to do with voting behavior). A hypothesis may also derive from common-sense deductions, curiosity, or traditional wisdom; it may emerge from existing theories and previous research; or it may originate from a review of the literature on an issue that interests a researcher.

Developing a Research Design (Collecting, Classifying, and Analyzing Data).
The research plan that is developed after the hypothesis is stated must specify from what

The Steps of the Scientific Method

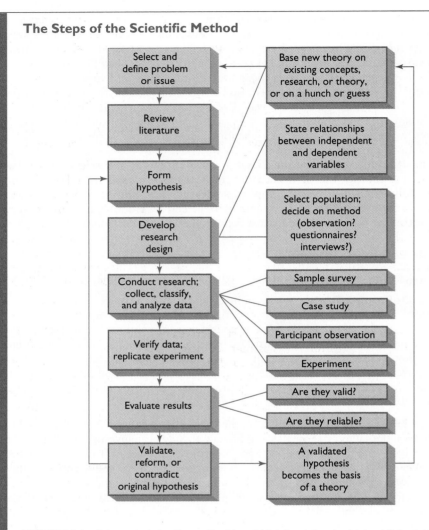

FIGURE 1.1 Science includes the method by which information is obtained. Scientists in all scientific disciplines, therefore, must follow the steps of the scientific method with rigor and objectivity.

group(s) and in what manner data are to be collected. Decisions must also be made about how best to obtain the data (direct observation, questionnaires, interviews, or a combination of research methods).

After data have been systematically collected, the researcher must classify, organize, and record them. Data must also be made public so that others may have access to both the findings and the procedures. In most scientific disciplines, including the social sciences, computers are used to classify and organize data.

The data are then analyzed. In this step, the researcher subjects the previously classified data to various statistical methods to see whether relationships are substantial or so small that they may be due to chance. Statistical computation determines whether the data support the hypothesis.

Verifying. Because most research is subject to error—of which the researcher may or may not be aware—another important step in the scientific method is verification. This step consists of repeating the research project (replication) and may be done either by the scientist who conducted the original research or by another scientist. For research to be considered successful, it must be capable of being repeated by another scientist with the same results.

Generalizing. Finally, conclusions must be drawn from the analysis of data. Do the data substantiate the original hypothesis? Do they refute it? Are alterations to the hypothesis in order? A cautious researcher tends to make undergeneralizations, which may keep his or her research from being useful to others. An overconfident researcher tends to make overgeneralizations, which may lead to false hypotheses and wrong conclusions.

Conclusions are usually summarized in reports, sometimes published in professional journals or as monographs. The researcher attempts to relate the conclusions to existing theories or current research and makes suggestions about the necessity of altering some accepted theoretical assumptions or the need for new hypotheses that have emerged from the research.

The Scientific Spirit: Skepticism, Objectivity, Relativity

Underlying the scientific method is an attitude best described as the *scientific spirit*. The most important principle of the scientific spirit is that scientists approach everything with great *doubt and skepticism*, taking nothing for granted. This attitude must be displayed even with regard to their own findings, which are always subject to change after further analysis.

Another principle is that of *objectivity*. Scientists must try to rid themselves completely of personal attitudes, desires, beliefs, values, and tendencies when confronting data intended to support a finding. They must try to be totally dispassionate, allowing no individual biases to affect their judgment. Of course, such a degree of objectivity is only an ideal to which scientists aspire; no human can be objective all the time. The issue of objectivity has been especially polemical in the social sciences, which deal with the relationships and behavior of people.

Closely related to objectivity is the third principle of the scientific spirit: *ethical neutrality*. According to this principle, scientists must not make value judgments about their findings; they must not pronounce their conclusions to be good or bad, right or wrong. They must be concerned only with whether the findings are true or false.

Finally, scientific conclusions must never be considered final, absolute, or universal truths. Rather, they should be considered as *relative* to the time and place in which they are obtained and always subject to change or revision.

■ The Social Science Disciplines

The boundaries among the social sciences are artificial in the sense that they all study the same thing: human behavior in the social environment. Each discipline, however, focuses on specific facets of that world and behavior, in effect allowing social scientists to specialize. Social scientists are aware of the overlapping nature of their disciplines, and they often borrow from one another. The differences, in short, are a matter of emphasis.

Anthropology

Anthropology combines a natural science—biology—and information gathered from the social sciences to uncover the relationships between human biological traits and traits acquired socially, that is, by living in groups. The discipline is divided into *physical anthropology*, which is concerned principally with human biological origins and the variations in the human species, and *cultural anthropology*, which has traditionally dealt with the study and comparative analysis of preliterate societies.

Physical anthropologists deal with traits that appear in specific populations and with characteristics that populations develop as a result of adaptation to particular environments. The variety of "racial" groupings among human populations is a subject of research for anthropologists, as are fossil studies and research on living primates. Additionally, physical anthropologists use *genetics*, the science that analyzes heredity, in an attempt to uncover how the genes of living organisms determine the characteristics of their offspring. Genetics is particularly useful to social scientists as they try to untangle the complex issue of how much of human behavior is learned and how much is inherited. Another way of putting it is that physical anthropology is divided into three branches that frequently overlap: *paleoanthropology*, meaning the study of fossils, of human and of related species; *primatology*, or the study of primates; and *genetics*, or the study of modern human variability and adaptability.

Cultural anthropology concerns itself with all facets of human culture: kinship forms, linguistics, material artifacts, economic structures, music, and folklore. In addition, cultural anthropologists today are likely to include the study of subgroups within contemporary societies and apply their methodology to new settings. An examination of the gay and lesbian community in a large metropolitan area, for instance, or a description of the lifestyles of prostitutes or the homeless are examples of studies that could be carried out by cultural anthropologists.

Anthropological research includes much dirty work as researchers dig and sift through many layers to find the fossils that provide clues to the history of the human race.

Anthropologists have developed a gamut of theories, some of which are discussed in the text. For an overview of these theories, see the Web site of the University of Alabama, **http://www.as.ua.edu/ant/faculty/murphy**, and of Indiana University, **http://www.mnsu.edu/ emuseum/cultural/anthropology/theories/html.**

Anthropology also includes the field of *archeology*, which is concerned with unearthing fossilized bones and artifacts of humans and other species to furnish dates and historical data about past societies, both those that left no written records and those whose records may have been lost or are incomplete. Anthropological concepts are used to describe the physical development of humans as well as to delineate their chief feature, culture.

Economics

The economy is a human institution, that is, an ingrained habit through which people have attempted to facilitate their survival in the face of scarcity of resources. Economics is the discipline that studies the systems that societies construct to help them in this endeavor. Economists attempt to understand the activities of people in the production, distribution, and consumption of goods and services necessary to sustain life. They examine the value of work, of natural resources, and of money as a medium of exchange; they define the concepts of supply and demand, savings and investments, cost and price, and economic fluctuations; and they describe the principles used by political systems to justify their methods of distribution of goods and services.

Economics attempts to explain some social processes (such as "who gets what and why"), the origins of some social problems (such as poverty), the importance of work as a source of identity, occupational status, increases or decreases in the standard of living, the effects of rising expectations, and so on.

Economists, too, have availed themselves of a number of theories—classical, neoclassical, Keynesian, monetarist, and others—that will be addressed in upcoming chapters. Two Web sites that offer clear descriptions of both the theories and the scholars who espoused them are: **http://www.bized.ac.uk/virtual/economy/library/theory** and **http://www.frbsf.org/ publications/education/greateconomists.**

Geography

Geography is primarily a natural science concerned with the planet we inhabit, that is, the land, bodies of water, mountains, valleys, types of vegetation, and animal habitats. These subjects are in the area of physical geography, which draws most of its knowledge from the disciplines of astronomy, botany, ecology, geochemistry, geology, meteorology, oceanography, and so on. However, geography is also concerned with the ways in which people use the natural environment: why they settle in some locations rather than others, which types of land are good for agriculture and which for mining, what routes of transportation people choose to follow and why, and where people establish their industrial centers. These matters are in the realm of human/cultural geography and depend on information obtained from such social sciences as anthropology, history, political science, psychology, sociology, urban studies, and so on. Of special importance to the social sciences are several disciplines that are offshoots of geography. *Demography* is the study of populations, including increases and decreases in size, composition, age grouping, and future trends. *Ecology* is the science that studies the relationship between all living organisms and their natural environment. It includes *biodiversity*, or the study of the variety and interdependence of species. Geography and its related fields are clearly described online at **http:// en.wikipedia.org/wiki/geography.**

Box 1.1   **Fur or Nakedness, Tools or Diet?**

Have you ever wondered why almost all animals have some kind of furry covering and humans, who are also animals, are naked? Or whether it was what we ate in the early stages of human existence that caused our brains to develop to a greater complexity than those of other animals? Or what came first, the chicken or the egg?

These are not the primary concerns of anthropology, but they are subjects of research in paleoanthropology. This discipline, a subfield of anthropology, is seldom mentioned in the media, and the results of its research are often considered esoteric and of interest only to other researchers in the same discipline. Yet, the findings are not only fascinating in themselves, but they also tell us much about our ancient forebears, about our ancient environment, about how we, as well as many of our traditions, have evolved through the millions of years of our existence on planet Earth.

Because mammals need to keep warm, most of them have fur or hair. Some mammals lost their fur as their environment changed; thus, whales and walruses lost it when they began to live in the sea. Elephants and rhinoceroses developed a very thick skin and, besides, are very big, so they do not lose much heat during cold nights. But humans continue to live in climates that are very cold; why did they lose their furry covering? A number of theories try to answer this question.

First, some researchers believe that when hominids split from the common ape ancestor, some five million years ago, they became bipedal. This allowed them to walk out of the dense forests they had inhabited earlier and be subject to the hot sun on the treeless African savannah. To keep a bit cooler, they gradually lost their hairy or furry covering.

This explanation is not totally convincing, however, because naked skin would not have been ideal in the heat of the day or in the cold of the night. Other researchers have proposed a different theory, which seems to be a better explanation for the mystery of human hairlessness. They maintain that humans lost their fur to rid themselves of external parasites—blood-sucking lice, fleas, and ticks—that not only tormented them but also transmitted a number of diseases. Moreover, these scientists add, once hairlessness had evolved through natural selection, it became a method of sexual selection, that is, it became a sign that the individual was free of parasites, therefore sexually attractive. Why are men hairier than women? Because there is more pressure on women to be sexually attractive to men than vice versa. Why have we retained pubic and armpit hair? Because those are humid areas replete with sweat glands, which give off pheromones, or airborne hormones, which in turn are thought to send sexual signals in mammals. Complete hairlessness in the climate of Africa led to the acquisition of dark skin. Studying the evolution of a gene that determines skin color, researchers determined that humans became hairless about 1.2 million years ago.

Unfortunately, the planet was in the grip of an ice age from 1.6 million years ago to only 10,000 years ago. This meant that people had to cover themselves. And how did scientists determine the date of this event? They studied the DNA of human head and body lice, which evolved from the original louse as soon as humans began to use body coverings. It seems that people have been wearing clothes since between 42,000 and 72,000 years ago. Finally, the invention of clothing probably was a factor in the spread of humans around the globe, especially in the colder northern climates. So, by researching a seemingly frivolous subject, we discover many facts of human history (Wade, 2003, D1 and D4).

Similarly, researchers have found the earliest known stone tools, mixed with fossilized animal bones. They have dated this find to almost 2.6 million years ago and have deduced from this combined find that the primal technology was used to butcher animal carcasses for meat and marrow. Such an enriched, high-protein diet probably led to a larger brain, which in turn enabled these hominids to adapt to their environment better—to make better tools, to find better shelter, to hunt more or bigger animals (Wilford, 2003, D3).

As to which came first, the chicken or the egg, that has not been resolved yet!

History

History is not universally considered a social science, because its primary objective is to record human events for future generations. In fact, historians often cannot use the scientific method. The discipline, however, does attempt to study systematically a sequence of related events—or a number of such sequences—for the purpose of learning about, verifying, and establishing meaningful relationships among them. Because history provides a context in which to study human relationships systematically, it may be considered a social science. Historical facts are interspersed in discussions of every facet of the social sciences, because it is impossible to interpret the present and speculate about the future without reference to the past.

Political Science

The chief concern of political science is the study of power. The discipline probes the need for an institution to maintain order, make decisions, and provide for defense. It also analyzes the forms the institution takes and the processes that emerge. The discipline includes such concepts as the state, politics, power, and ideology. Historically, political science has had a strong philosophical, legal, and administrative orientation. More recently, the discipline has taken a turn toward the social sciences in that it is concerned with the effect of government and its processes on individuals and groups in society. An important part of political science is *international relations*, which tries to uncover patterns of behavior among the nations of the world. The University of Michigan website contains a wealth of resources on the subject: **http://www.lib.umich.edu/govdocs/polisci/html.**

Psychology

Psychology focuses on the forces that shape and motivate individuals, forming their minds and personalities. The discipline, especially in its medical form, *psychiatry*, draws on the natural sciences for information concerning the physical structure of humans, their nervous system, their physical development and maturation, and other physical processes. It draws on the social sciences for input in the areas of behavior that originate from social interaction. Because psychology deals with human beings, who are complex mixtures of biological and social elements, the discipline is wide-ranging and the most experimental of the social sciences. Psychologists must be familiar with human biology as well as with social processes and their effects. For instance, in trying to explain the human capacity to blush, psychologists must understand how the body undergoes certain biologically caused organic changes—blood rushes into the veins and capillaries of our face and chest area. They also must be aware of the social pressures that trigger these changes—someone stares at us, or compliments us, or, on the contrary, scolds us in front of someone whose respect we crave. The embarrassment we feel is expressed by blushing.

Social psychologists specialize in studying socialization, emotions, memory, perception, and intelligence. They also examine such issues as language acquisition, motivation, learning, adjustment and maladjustment, the effects of heredity and environment, problem solving, and others. The Encyclopedia of Psychology online offers more than 2,000 links on psychological subjects: **http://www.psychology.org.**

Sociology

Sociology is the newest of the social sciences, having emerged long after the other social science disciplines were already established. Contemporary sociology may be defined as the systematic and scientific study of human social relationships and of all the social systems that such relationships engender. In more popular terms, sociology is said to be the study of human groups in interaction, or the scientific study of human society and human group behavior. While psychology also analyzes human behavior, its focus is the individual. The focus

Box 1.2   Psychology: How Much of a Science?

Researchers in the social sciences, because they deal with human behavior in a variety of circumstances, cannot avail themselves of the scientific method to the same extent as researchers in the exact sciences do. Humans are characterized by intelligence and will, and do not follow exact rules of behavior—they are influenced by numerous variables, both biological and social. In spite of this, adopting the scientific method has advanced enormously our knowledge about what makes humans tick.

One of the most glamorous of the social sciences has been psychology (and its medical portion, psychiatry, which depends on medical research for its findings). Psychology has appealed to large numbers of people because it delves into the mysteries of human behavior. Why are some people antisocial? Why do some become mass murderers and others become people of good will, engaged in service to others? What makes some marriages happy and others full of conflict? Why do some parents raise children who become respectful and respected citizens, and others raise children who grow up to be juvenile delinquents? These and myriad other, similar questions have been tackled by psychologists, beginning with the famous Viennese researcher Sigmund Freud, who developed theories of the unconscious mind and childhood stages of development.

More recent theories and methods of treatment have depended on the Rorschach inkblot test to explain some facets of personality, have assumed the existence of multiple personalities, have theorized about repressed memories of sexual abuse, have posited that some individuals are subject to sexual addiction, have accused members of an addict's family of facilitating that individual's behavior by codependency, and have used such therapies as "critical incident" debriefing for trauma victims, as well as eye-movement desensitization and reprocessing techniques. Some of these theories have created conflicts between practicing psychologists and academic psychologists (those who do research). The latter have accused mental health practitioners of using faddish, unproved techniques that on occasion may be harmful and have challenged them to prove that such treatments are valid. The conflict stems from the academics' dependence on controlled trials and other statistical methods to determine whether a specific treatment works, whereas mental health practitioners tend to base their techniques on clinical experience, and sometimes intuition, instead of scientific evidence.

Some academic psychologists—a number of whom have split from the dominant professional organization, the American Psychological Association, and have formed a separate organization—claim that clinical psychologists have been out of touch with scientific research findings. They cite surveys that show that many clinical psychologists, busy with patients, fail to read even one scientific journal article a month and that many doctoral programs in clinical psychology do not require research training. Such failures allow untested and possibly damaging treatments to be used, according to the academics, who have founded journals with the specific mission to use "objective investigation of controversial and unorthodox claims in clinical psychiatry, psychology, and social work."

Clinical practitioners are not taking this criticism lying down. Some maintain that their work with troubled patients cannot be based on experimental trials and that science has little relevance in the consulting room. They say that problems presented by some of their patients are much more complex than anything researchers have studied. Such conflicts in the discipline bode well for its future because they will eventually force clinicians to become more aware of what science has to offer and will soften the attitudes of academic researchers to accept the notion that sometimes science is not the only answer (Goode, 2004, D1 and D6).

of sociology, on the other hand, is the individual in interaction with others or as he or she moves in the social environment.

The climate for a science to study human groups did not arise until nearly the middle of the nineteenth century, when the French philosopher Auguste Comte coined the name "sociology" in his *Positive Philosophy* (1838). In this treatise, Comte repudiated authority and speculation in favor of systematic observation and classification as the bases of all scientific inquiry. He was followed most notably by the French social philosopher Emile Durkheim. Durkheim demonstrated the use of scientific methodology in the new discipline by outlining how he studied suicide by planning a research design, collecting masses of data on suicide

The patient on a couch and the therapist sitting behind him or her with a notebook has been a symbol of psychology ever since Sigmund Freud used it. It has also been ridiculed and used as a source of humor by comedians. However, psychologists use many other situations to help patients.

rates in a number of societies, and using the data to derive a theory suggesting that social factors—conditions of upheaval in society and the extent of integration of people in the social order—affect even such personal choices as committing suicide (*Suicide*, 1897).

Today, sociology studies an enormous variety of subjects, in particular human groups of every stripe, organizations, and institutions. The discipline looks at the environment, religion, politics, the economy, deviance, criminality, change, demography, industry, technology, medicine, urban and rural areas, and so on. It focuses especially on the organization of complex industrial societies, such as the United States, analyzing data and events through a number of theoretical models, the foremost of which are functionalism, conflict theory, and symbolic interactionism. In addition, research is undertaken within the framework of newer theories, such as feminism, exchange theory, and postmodernism. Most of the social sciences share some of these theoretical approaches.

■ Research Methods in the Social Sciences

In the search for meaningful facts to test and bolster their hypotheses, leading to valid theories, social scientists use a number of research methods (Table 1.1).

These methods may be *historical*—that is, they may include a perusal of documents such as public records, newspapers, legal codes, court records, minutes of various committees, and annual reports of corporations; they may be comparative and *cross-cultural*, in which comparisons of different societies—or specific segments of them—are made for the purpose of tracing cultural patterns to determine either their universality or their uniqueness (these methods are especially used in anthropology); or they may be *mathematical*, based on complicated calculations using mathematical and statistical principles to express

TABLE 1.1   Common Methods of Social Science Research

Method	Subject of Research	Procedure	Used for	Criticism
Sample survey	Statistically valid sample of a population.	Collect data; have sample fill out questionnaires; conduct personal interviews; obtain factual information; probe attitudes; establish relationships among variables.	Establishing facts.	Not always 100% accurate in reflecting attitudes and opinions.
Case study	Total behavior of a particular unit of people.	Gain confidence of members; obtain biographies of members; learn each member's views; establish hypothesis or relationships that can be tested by other means.	Studying a particular unit (family, gang, ethnic group) in depth or several units for comparison.	Most useful when events under consideration are rare; often cannot be used as a basis for generalization; expensive and difficult to compute quantitatively.
Participant observation	Members of a specific group.	Researchers take part in life of group members, sometimes without revealing their identities.	Studying all or some aspects of a group's culture from the inside out.	Depends on personality of researcher; researchers may be biased; researcher may try to overgeneralize.
Experiment	In the laboratory, people volunteer or are paid to be subjects. In the field, researcher studies an existing group.	Subjects undergo a number of tests, and their responses are recorded. Researchers control of hold constant one variable and systematically observe or measure the results.	Establishing facts that cannot be established in any other way.	Very expensive if many people are involved; physical safety and dignity of people must be considered; people change their behavior when they know they are being observed.

ideas. In fact, the mathematical and quantitative approaches in the social sciences have been gaining ground. In the last several decades, the computer has become a staple in social scientific research. Frequently, a combination of methods as well as sources is used: public and private documents are analyzed, the artistic output of a specific historical period is scrutinized, the literature is studied, and statistical information—birth and death rates, for instance—is compiled. Most social scientists shy away from research methods that are subject to personal interpretation. They prefer methods that appear to be more objective, that is, in which personal biases are kept out as much as possible. This does not mean that descriptive, subjectively interpreted work is not being produced, nor that such work lacks meaning. The research methods most commonly used by social scientists today are as follows.

Sample Survey

The sample survey research design consists of two separate features, the sample and the survey. The researcher decides to study a specific group, which is called the *population*, a statistical concept referring to the totality of the phenomenon under investigation. For example, the population might consist of middle-aged professionals, newly registered voters, or college students enrolled in four-year private schools. Because it is impossible to study every individual who is a member of the chosen population, researchers select a statistically valid sample. There are procedures that allow researchers to select such a sample. Only if the sample is truly representative of the total population can generalizations about the results of research be made.

The next step is to survey the sample population. Surveying involves collecting data by means of questionnaires, personal interviews, statistical information, or probing of attitudes. Most important, relationships among variables are analyzed. If a broad spectrum of the population is being surveyed at a specific point in time, the study is called *cross-sectional*. Preelection polls are a familiar example. Major magazines and news organizations are constantly polling people to probe their attitudes on current events.

If the survey continues over a longer period, engaging in contrasts and comparisons, it is referred to as a *longitudinal* study.

The sample survey is a useful research design, yielding accurate results for some investigative questions but not for others. It is comparatively easy to establish factual information with the sample survey technique, but there is a greater margin for error in surveying attitudes and opinions.

Case Study

The case study research design is especially helpful when it is necessary to study a particular unit in depth or to study several units for purposes of comparison. The unit may be a person, a family, a group of residents of a retirement community, employees of a particular corporation, members of a religious movement, and so on. The researcher must obtain a complete, detailed account of the behavior of the unit under consideration. In the case study, the entire population of the unit is surveyed.

Case studies are most valuable not so much because of their accuracy, but because they often suggest hypotheses that can then be tested by other methods. They are most valuable when the unit being analyzed is relatively rare, such as a group of brainwashed prisoners of war or a group of converts to an authoritarian religion.

Participant Observation

Somewhere between the case study and the sample survey techniques, we find a method called *participant observation*. Here the researcher tries to take part in the lives of the group members being studied. The researcher associates with group members as closely as possible and attempts to share in their experiences and lifestyles, sometimes without revealing his or her purpose. A number of sociologists and anthropologists have used this technique, developed by anthropologists to study preliterate cultures, to analyze ethnic and black street-corner cultures.

The participant observation technique has its shortcomings. Much depends on the personality of the researcher, who must develop trust in, and friendship with, the subjects. Thus, there is the danger of the researcher becoming too involved with the subjects and thereby losing objectivity, as well as the danger of overgeneralizing in the belief that the findings obtained from the group studied are true of all similar groups. At the same time, this method, like the case study, has given researchers many useful insights that can be tested and verified later by more quantitative techniques.

Box 1.3   **Consilience**

Scientific knowledge has expanded so rapidly that today any lay person knows much more about how things work than a nineteenth-century physician did. Harvard naturalist Edward O. Wilson believes that such expansion of knowledge is due to the scientific method. Moreover, Wilson argues in his book, *Consilience: The Unity of Knowledge*, that human behavior and human affairs can only be interpreted through biology and the other natural sciences. He maintains that social scientists, by ignoring the natural sciences, have handicapped their efforts at expanding the knowledge of their own disciplines. The reason for the success of the natural sciences, according to Wilson, is consilience, by which the author means a linking of insights from a number of different disciplines into a system of explanation that is coherent. As an example, modern medicine is based on the knowledge gathered from molecular and cell biology, which in turn are based on genetics, which ultimately obey the laws of physics. The social sciences, on the other hand, often seem to operate as if they inhabited a separate universe. Wilson insists that to gain self-awareness, "we must accept that human life is a physical phenomenon, generated and sustained by the same principles as bugs, trees and fishes" (Cowley, 1998, 59).

These ideas are not new. In a preceding book, *Sociobiology: The New Synthesis*, Wilson posited that certain tendencies in human behavior—status seeking, altruism, nepotism—have a biological basis. A number of critics on the left, however, panned the book, accusing its author of social Darwinism (because life is competitive, winners are superior and rise to the top, and losers are inferior and eventually disappear). Nonetheless, the author continued to elaborate on sociobiology, and today a number of psychologists and sociologists are beginning to test his idea that human behavior has a biological component. For example, psychologists and neuroscientists have shown that the mind—a social concept—is the product of the brain—a physical organ. Because the brains of contemporary humans have evolved in the process of natural selection (see the next chapter), certain aptitudes, biases, and abilities of humans that affect their behavior exist because they facilitated survival in some previous environment. In fact, studies have shown that people everywhere have an innate ability to acquire language, to recognize faces and the meaning of facial expressions, and that they avoid incest. It turns out that many of these abilities are located in specific areas of the brain, which neuroscientists are now tracing.

Neuroscientists are also beginning to understand what dreams are, and here too they have found that certain areas of the brain are responsible for them. In the same way, Wilson believes that some day, using the combination of natural and social sciences, social scientists will find the reasons for war, inflation, and religion. They could settle the question of which social arrangements best accommodate the universal features of human nature, or which environmental conditions bring out the best or the worst in human beings.

Ultimately, Wilson hopes that through consilience, humans, who have become the greatest destroyers of life, will come to realize how dependent they are on other earthbound organisms. In Wilson's own words, "Most of the issues that vex humanity daily—ethnic conflict, arms escalation, overpopulation, abortion, environmental destruction, and endemic poverty, to cite several of the most persistent—can be solved only by integrating knowledge from the natural sciences with that from the social sciences and the humanities. Only fluency across the boundaries will provide a clear view of the world as it really is, not as it appears through the lens of ideology and religious dogma, or as a myopic response solely to immediate need. . . . A balanced perspective cannot be acquired by studying disciplines in pieces; the consilience among them must be pursued" (Wilson, 1998, 62).

Wilson's ideas are being followed by other scientists. As noted earlier, some economists are beginning to use some tools of physics to study markets and other economic phenomena. These so-called econophysicists point out that incomes and wealth behave very much like atoms. The distribution pattern of upper-middle-class incomes (approximately $150,000) in the United States, in fact, follows a pattern called "exponential," which is the same pattern of the energy of atoms in gases that are at thermal equilibrium. This pattern is also one that is used by many other random systems. The incomes of the wealthiest 3 percent follow what is called in physics a *power law:* a very long distance between their high income and the income of the next layer. Most other developed nations follow a similar pattern of income distribution. Therefore, the econophysicists say, even though individuals have a will and governments try to redistribute wealth, neither will succeed because "large, complex systems have their own statistical logic that trumps individual, and state, decisions" (Shea, 2005, 67).

Behavioral economists, teamed with psychologists, have also developed a "Tightwad-Spendthrift" scale intended to predict whether a person will spend a lot of money on things they do not necessarily need, or forgo the purchase and keep the cash. They positioned volunteers in an MRI machine, gave them an amount of money they could spend, and showed them images of a variety of objects. When a subject saw something of interest, one specific area of the brain lit up, showing activity there. If the object held no interest for the volunteer, another area of the brain became active. It was thus possible for the researchers to see, before the volunteers made their decision, whether they were going to buy the object or not (Tierney, 2007, D1 and D6).

The Experiment

The experimental method is used in all scientific disciplines. In the social sciences, the experiment may take place either in a laboratory or in the field. In the laboratory experiment, people are recruited to serve as subjects who can be volunteers or paid by the researcher. The scientist conducts a number of tests and records the subjects' responses. In the field experiment, the researcher goes out among the people instead of bringing them to the laboratory. In both the field and the laboratory, one variable is controlled (by setting up control groups), and the results are systematically observed and measured. Every scientific experiment consists of (1) keeping all variables constant except one, (2) changing that one variable, and (3) discovering what happens.

Obviously, experimentation under controlled conditions is not possible in all social science disciplines and is also subject to shortcomings. Wide-ranging experiments in which thousands of people are involved are very expensive and difficult to organize. The physical safety and the dignity of people must be safeguarded. It is impossible to force people to act as subjects in an experiment, and the ethics of tricking them into acting as experimental subjects are certainly questionable. Finally, when people are aware that they are the subjects of an experiment, their behavior tends to change from the usual. This tendency can ruin the experiment and make results invalid. Experiments on people are most reliable when the subjects are not aware of the true goals of the experiment but do know that some type of experiment is being conducted. Nevertheless, even harmless deception sometimes leads to intellectual dishonesty in interpreting results, and so the technique is not widely used.

Statistical Analysis

By whatever method data are gathered by social scientists, one of the most favored manners of analyzing them is with statistics. **Statistics** are methods in the form of numbers used to process the information obtained by research. Statistics simplify the communication of information and help researchers make decisions about the meaning of their research. Statistics that communicate information in a clear manner are called *descriptive* statistics. Descriptive statistics convey the *central tendency*—what is typical—of a group of numbers by calculating the mean, the median, and the mode.

The **mean** is obtained by adding all of the figures and dividing them by the number of cases. This is what an instructor does when she reports on the average exam grade obtained by students. If the mean is 95, it is assumed that the central tendency of that particular population (class of students) is to study very hard. Central tendency can also be measured by the **median**, which is the number in the middle of the distribution of scores (so that roughly half of the students would have higher scores than the median, and half would have lower

Box 1.4 Collecting Data with a Human Face

Certain subjects do not lend themselves easily to social science research. People who have undergone traumatic experiences, whether in a war, in a revolution, during a famine, or in other disasters, are not always willing to talk about the pain they experienced. Yet, the insights social scientists gather from such experiences are invaluable in showing how humans respond to specific situations.

The experiences of European Jews who survived the Holocaust are especially difficult to extract without causing psychological harm to the victim. One social scientist who specializes in interviewing Holocaust survivors describes his methodology:

After almost 25 years of interviewing survivors of the Holocaust, my own technique has evolved through a series of variations. I began using an interview schedule—a questionnaire—that was divided into four sections: prewar life, life during the war and Holocaust, postwar experiences, and later experiences. That worked fairly well, but I found myself veering off from the questionnaire because it was not only confining but also distracting to some interviewees. From the beginning I tried to do as much research as possible. In a preliminary phone conversation I would learn the hometown or city of the survivor and where he or she was during World War II. Eventually, I would bring street maps of the cities and the ghettos and even maps of some of the camps and initiate the interview (after, "Please tell me where you are from and where you were during the war") with "Can you show me the street where you lived," and then ask questions about where the schools were, the synagogues, places of work, and so forth. Questions about religion, family life, frequently get as specific as food on the Sabbath, soccer games, school schedules and curricula, to relationships with non-Jews and details about daily routines. Over the years, I have found it productive to engage in the interview to the point of asking clarifying questions, depending on the flow of the narrative, and interrupting as surreptitiously as possible to explicate more carefully. Critical to a productive interview were gaining trust and conveying a

sense of at least basic knowledge of the history and geography of the Holocaust. (Survivors frequently seem convinced that an American barely knows where Poland is, much less Lodz or Rosisz.) It is fundamental, then, that the interviewer subtly conveys a sense of familiarity with that history and geography. There is no question that survivors believe that no interviewer can completely understand or appreciate the nature of the experience of the Holocaust. They are correct, of course, and yet somehow an interviewer must convey at least a minimal sense of that appreciation and a knowledge of that vital stumbling block. Perhaps the most significant and painfully problematical element of many survivor interviews has to do with silence. Elie Wiesel once noted that "the silences also speak." My feeling about this has remained from the start: the silences must be allowed to persist, even if they are accompanied by tears. It behooves the interviewer to permit the silence to be resolved by the interviewee, if only to protect the survivor's integrity. What is happening during those silences? Is the survivor searching for a correct word? Overwhelmed with the memory? Wondering why he or she is revealing these anguished stories? Convinced that no language can properly convey the real meaning or a thorough description of the experience? Is there a language that can completely communicate what went on from minute to minute in a place like Auschwitz? Is there an Auschwitzese to convey to an outsider the simultaneous internal and external actions of those times and places? Such questions of simultaneity and the difficulties of serial language to describe it have plagued writers from James Joyce to Sigmund Freud, from Louis Carrol to Franz Kafka, from Primo Levi to Thaddeus Borowski. The literary questions assume horribly depressing consequences in survivor testimonies and produce frustration and silence. A good interviewer ought to be aware of such seemingly esoteric yet central issues.

(*Source:* Personal communication with Sidney Bolkosky, William E. Stirton Professor in the Social Sciences, Professor of History; Director, Honors, University of Michigan.)

scores). Although it is the least frequently used measurement, central tendency can be measured with the **mode**, the number that appears most frequently in a group of numbers—in this case, the one single score obtained by the largest number of students.

Statistics are also *inferential*, providing techniques researchers use to decide whether they can make valid statements about a specific population based on a particular sample of it. Statistical tests exist that allow researchers to calculate percentage statements of probability;

The methods of science have become essential in contemporary postindustrial societies. In analyzing scientific research, statistics are a dominant tool. The decennial census that counts individuals residing in the nation provides a multitude of other information.

the higher the percentage of probability, the more assurance that what was true of a sample is true of the population at large.

The Scientific Method in the Social Sciences

In summary, none of the research methods available to social scientists is 100 percent effective or error proof. Conducting research is difficult in all sciences, but in the social sciences the difficulty is compounded by the problems of subjectivity, logistics, and the unpredictability of human behavior, and by the great number of variables that must be controlled.

As a result, social scientists often use whatever technique seems to best fit the needs of their research designs. The *historical* or *impressionistic* study, which consists of describing and analyzing observations according to informal but coherent and purposeful guidelines, is still popular. The *demographic* method is also used with good results. This is the method used by the Census Bureau to report population and urbanization trends. Demographers, sociologists, and economists all look at demographic facts and come to some conclusions as to what they indicate.

It should be stressed again that in spite of the use of the scientific method, social scientists have more difficulty obtaining verifiable data than do physical scientists. Examining fossil remains in the laboratory is very different from examining people as they relate to one another. Not only do people not lend themselves to many of the experiments that can be performed on the inert fossil, they also evoke a reaction from the researcher, which the fossil does not. Researchers cannot help reacting to people—they find an individual likable or disagreeable, good-looking or ugly, intelligent or dense—whereas in analyzing a fossil such judgments do not even enter the researchers' minds. Much as they wish to further objectivity, the conclusions of social scientists may be tinged by bias. In the social sciences, then, there are no absolute conclusions and no absolutely objective interpretations.

The Chapter in Brief

Social science disciplines evolved from social philosophy to study scientifically how people behave in the social world that is of their own making (as opposed to the physical world into which they are born). The disciplines are fairly new, although their subject matter has occupied philosophers for thousands of years. What is really new about the social sciences is that they attempt to use the scientific method to formulate generalizations and theories about human behavior in society.

The social sciences use the scientific method as a tool for theory building. The scientific method implies that researchers do their work with a set of attitudes that includes doubt, objectivity, and ethical neutrality. The scientific method also involves a specific technique based on precise and systematic observation and recording of data. This technique includes the selection and definition of problems and a plan for the collection of data; a statement of hypothesis; the actual collection of data, their classification, analysis, and verification (replication); and generalization. Controlled conditions and trained observers are also essential. The scientific method uses concepts (abstract ways of classifying things that are similar), theories (sets of concepts arranged so as to explain and predict possible and probable relationships among phenomena), and research (which tests and bolsters theories or refutes them).

Social scientific research includes the following methods: the sample survey, the case study, participant observation, and field and laboratory experiments. In addition, the historical or impressionistic methods and the demographic method are used.

The scientific method, although it is vastly superior to gathering information by superficial observation, insight, or other traditional methods, is especially difficult to apply in the social science disciplines because of the need for objectivity, skepticism, and ethical neutrality.

Terms to Remember

case study A method of research consisting of a detailed, long-term investigation of a single social unit.

concept A generalized idea about people, objects, or processes that are related to one another; an abstract way of classifying things that are similar.

cross-section A survey of a broad spectrum of a population at a specific point in time.

ethical neutrality An attitude of the scientific method in the social sciences, requiring that scientists not pass moral judgment on their findings.

experiment A method of research in which the researcher controls and manipulates variables in one group to test the effects of an independent variable on a dependent variable.

hypothesis A tentative statement, in clearly defined terms, predicting a relationship between variables.

longitudinal A survey that continues over a long period, engaging in contrasts and comparisons.

objectivity A principle of the scientific method, especially in the social sciences, requiring researchers to divest themselves of personal attitudes, desires, beliefs, values, and tendencies when confronting their data.

participant observation A method of research in which researchers try to take part in the lives of the members of the group under analysis, sometimes without revealing their purposes.

population In the social sciences, a statistical concept referring to the totality of phenomena under investigation (e.g., all college students enrolled in four-year private universities).

research An aspect of scientific methodology that bolsters and complements theories. In the social sciences, four fundamental formats are used: the sample survey, the case study, the experiment, and participant observation.

sample survey A method of research consisting of an attempt to determine the occurrence of a particular act or opinion in a particular sample of people.

theory A set of concepts arranged so as to explain and/or predict possible and probable relationships.

variables Factors whose relationships researchers try to uncover; characteristics that differ (vary) in each individual case.

Suggested Readings

Babbie, Earl. 2001. *The Practice of Social Research*, 9th ed. Belmont, CA: Wadsworth. How research in the social sciences is done—a comprehensive and readable text.

Best, Joel. 2001. *Damned Lies and Statistics: Untangling Numbers from the Media, Politicians, and Activists*. Berkeley: University of California Press. This book suggests how statistics can be misused by politicians, administrators, the media, and other activists for their own agendas.

Ericksen, Julia A. 1999. *Kiss and Tell: Surveying Sex in the Twentieth Century*. Cambridge, MA: Harvard University Press. An evaluation of the methodology used by social scientists in the many surveys of human sexuality.

Hoover, Kenneth, and Todd Donovan. 1995. *The Elements of Social Scientific Thinking*, 6th ed. New York: St. Martin's Press. A concise introduction to the vocabulary, concepts, and methods of the social sciences. Mainly jargon-free, this small book leads students through the complex path of social scientific thinking.

Ross, Dorothy. 1991. *The Origins of American Social Science*. Cambridge, NJ: Cambridge University Press. A historical look at the development of the social sciences in the United States.

Tilly, Charles. 2006. *Why?* Princeton, NJ: Princeton University Press. A Columbia University scholar attempts to decode the structure of social interactions. Why do we give the reasons we do to explain our behavior? According to the author, people rely on four categories of reasons: conventions, stories, codes, and technical accounts. An interesting sociological argument.

Web Sites of Interest

http://www.academicinfo.net/subsoc.html
Offers descriptions and definitions of the various social sciences and links to other sites of interest.

http://en.wikipedia.org/wiki/social_sciences
Another source of information about the social sciences.

http://www.abacon.com/sociology/soclinks/mega.html
Allyn and Bacon's own sociology Web site.

http://www.top20sociology.com
Links to the top 20 sociology sites.

In addition to these sites, each individual social science has sites on the Internet.

2

In the Beginning . . .

IN THIS CHAPTER, YOU WILL LEARN

- *what the natural sciences have discovered concerning the origin of the universe and the planet on which we live;*
- *what the natural scientists know about how life on earth began;*
- *the basic premise of the theory of evolution, as well as its principal concept, natural selection;*
- *the importance of genetics as a tool of natural science;*
- *the historical stages of human evolution as shown by the fossil record;*
- *the appearance of agriculture and its consequences;*
- *the biological foundations of human culture.*

"In the beginning God created the heaven and the earth. And the earth was without form, and void; and darkness was upon the face of the deep. And the Spirit of God moved upon the face of the waters." So begins the Judeo-Christian Biblical account of the creation of the earth. The narrative goes on to recount how God made its first inhabitants, fashioning them out of clay and breathing life into them. Those brought up in Western societies, or at least within the Judeo-Christian religious tradition, are familiar with this introduction to Genesis and comfortable with it. The narrative is appealing because it presents the events of creation in terms that all can understand. Other societies, with different cultures and in other regions, have similar explanations of the origin of the world and of life.

The physical sciences tell a different story, one that is more difficult for people to grasp. According to astrophysicists who study the early universe, the earth, which is our home, is a fairly small and insignificant planet in the Milky Way galaxy. In turn, the Milky Way is only a minor galaxy in a universe that is unthinkable in its vastness. The exact age of the universe is still being debated, but scientists at the National Aeronautics and Space Administration (NASA), using its Wilkinson Microwave Anisotropy Probe (WMAP), pegged the age of the universe at 13.7 billion years (NASA/Goddard Space Flight Center, 2003). This research is

Box 2.1 An Astrophysicist Views the Cosmos

In an interview with Sir Martin Rees, one of the world's leading theorists on cosmic evolution, the following points emerged, giving us an interesting illustration of how an astrophysicist views the evolving cosmos:

■ Astronomers try to understand "how our universe evolved from simple beginnings to the complex cosmos we see around us, of which we are a remarkable part ourselves."

■ It is important to be aware of astrophysics because if we are to understand where the atoms we are made of come from, we must understand the stars. For instance, we know now that "all the atoms were once inside a star. When our Milky Way galaxy was first formed about 10 billion years ago, it contained the simplest atoms: hydrogen and helium. Then, the first stars were formed and the nuclear fuel that kept those stars shining converted hydrogen into helium through nuclear fusion and then converted helium into other atoms: carbon, oxygen, and the rest of the periodic table. Later, the stars ran out of fuel, they exploded, threw back all that debris into interstellar

space and it all eventually condensed into new stars. One of which was our sun."

■ "We are the dust of long dead stars. Or, if you want to be less romantic, we are nuclear waste."

■ "The most wonderful thing we know about in the universe is life, and that's the most complicated emergent phenomena we know of."

■ Studying astrophysics "gives one a slightly different perspective on time scales...we are still at the beginning of cosmic evolution, not the culmination. Even our sun is less than halfway throughout its life. That makes me feel we should regard ourselves as part of the natural order, rather than the culmination of it."

■ There have been remarkable discoveries in the last few years, and all indications are that we must consider all our knowledge provisional and subject to alteration.

■ "We are trying to decide if our universe will continue expanding forever, or if the firmament will eventually crash together in a big crunch. The evidence strongly favors perpetual expansion." (Dreifus, 1998, B15)

part of cosmology, the study of the origin and evolution of the universe, a pioneering science that holds the promise for scientists to converge toward truth, in spite of limits.

Current thinking, supported by the discoveries of NASA's Cosmic Background Explorer (COBE) satellite, paints a scenario in which the universe begins with a primeval explosion, commonly called the Big Bang (this is where cosmology begins its quest; before this moment the force involved lies beyond known physics). The explosion was the result of a submicroscopic, infinitely dense, and unimaginably hot knot of pure energy that flew outward in all directions, eventually giving rise to radiation and matter. Gravity then drew the matter to denser regions that, over billions of years, became galaxies, stars, planets, and everything that exists. The evidence supporting the theory includes observations that the universe is expanding; the detection of electromagnetic radiation, called microwaves, presumably left over from the initial explosion; and the relative abundance of chemical elements in the universe. The COBE satellite recorded minute temperature variations in the blanket of radiation, which were interpreted as remains from the Big Bang, and the discovery of those fluctuations helped explain how the seemingly homogeneous fabric of the early universe had arranged itself into the clusters of galaxies and giant voids of space that are known today. The NASA/WMAP team suggests that the Big Bang and Inflation theories appear to be supported by its new portrait of the cosmos. They add that the contents of the universe include 4 percent atoms, 22 percent an unknown type of dark matter, and 74 percent a mysterious dark energy, which acts as a sort of antigravity (NASA/WMAP Science Team; **http://map.gsfc.nasa.gov/m_mm.html**).

A graphic illustration of the Big Bang theory would show the expansion of the universe from less than the size of an atom to about the size of a grapefruit, an event that occurred in less than a trillionth of a second after the Big Bang and was dominated by a single super-force. Then, as the universe cooled and expanded, the original force broke into four forces that are observable today: gravity, electromagnetism, and the weak and strong nuclear forces, which work inside the atom (Broad, 2003, D4). Over the next 13.7 or so billion years, gravity created galaxy-like structures, stars formed in the galaxies, and the universe continued to expand (**http://usatoday.com/tech/science/space/2006-03-16-big-bang-expansion-x. html**). It is still unknown whether the cosmos will expand forever or whether gravity will eventually slow and reverse the expansion, causing the universe to collapse. The information gained from the COBE satellite seems to indicate that the universe is at critical density, that is, it will continue to expand but ever more slowly, so that eventually its growth will be hardly perceptible. A new NASA satellite, called the Microwave Anisotropy Probe, or MAP, as mentioned earlier, will study the various kinds of matter in the universe. (For more on this fascinating subject and what MAP is doing right now, check out the NASA website at **http://www.nasa.gov**).

■ The Beginnings of Life

The study of the origins of the universe is in the province of the physical sciences, particularly in astrophysics, a discipline that is continually expanding as scientists probe ever deeper into space. We offer here only a superficial overview of the subject. Social scientists, on the other hand, are interested in the social world, which humans have created and continue to create.

Two views of how life began.

Yet, to understand life, particularly human life, as well as the structures that humans have erected to simplify their existence on earth, we should be aware of the physical framework within which the earth and humans exist (see also Box 1.3 in Chapter 1 regarding consilience). Therefore, it is important to clarify our physical nature and the kind of natural environment we have traditionally inhabited. It is the biological makeup of humans, in fact, and the experiences of the species that have made the present-day culture-bearing, symbol-using social animal possible.

There is no one model, or theory, that describes the origins of life on Earth with certainty. Scientists have suggested that some essential components of life could have been created by the interaction of simple chemicals that were in existence in the "primordial soup" that was the Earth after having been bombarded by a rain of meteors. Current models also posit that the components of molecules and cells needed for life were present in the early environment of Earth. Experiments have shown that organic molecules could have originated spontaneously from inorganic forms. More detailed information about the origins of life may be obtained by visiting the following web site: **http://www.resa.net/nasa/origins_life.htm**, as well as by "googling" the phrase "origins of life." The point is that fossilized imprints of a thriving microbial community have been found between layers of rock that was estimated to be 3.5 billion years old. This means that life was already established a billion years after the formation of the planet, a much faster evolution than had been previously believed. Therefore, life apparently originated on a planet still racked by volcanic eruptions and constantly menaced by comets and asteroids. Some researchers even believe that life did not begin only once; rather it tried to come into existence several times before it finally "took" and spread all over the planet (Nash, 1993, 70).

Eventually, protoplasm, simple one-celled microorganisms that were neither plants nor animals, somehow acquired the ability to reproduce themselves. Like some bacteria we know today, these organisms floated in the waters, living on minerals and other substances that were present there. Gradually, some of these organisms developed the ability to make chlorophyll. Using this substance in combination with carbon dioxide and sunlight, the organisms were able to build their own organic substances. They survived so well that eventually they became plants. Other organisms, which had not developed chlorophyll, began feeding on the plants and eventually emerged as animals.

Ultimately, some pioneers did venture out of the safety of the sea to try to survive in the rocky, bare, and harsh environment of dry land. This is thought to have happened about one billion years ago, although researchers discovered microbes that lived near volcanic vents formed 3.2 billion years ago (Wade, 2000, D1). One of the earliest creatures to try this adventure is believed to have been an arthropod, a predecessor of crabs, lobsters, and insects. The scorpion-like creature eventually became half terrestrial and half aquatic. Another such creature was a kind of salamander whose fossil remains (in the shape of an arm bone) indicate to researchers that it had been a transitional species between fish and amphibian. Originally a fish, its fins became adapted as arms, which at some point became strong enough to allow the fish to lift its head out of the water and, eventually, to push itself out of the water altogether. This, according to the researchers, would have happened 365 million years ago. Without plants, however, the dry land was indeed inhospitable. It was not until some plants also abandoned their homes in the sea, learning to survive in the coastal lowlands that were frequently flooded and drained, that life on the dry continents became possible. In a way, dry land became a testing ground for life. A large number of plants and animals came into being: some adapted to existing conditions and lived; others could not and perished. Plants developed through a succession of mosses, ferns, and seed plants. Terrestrial animals included huge reptiles, flying birds, and small mammals.

■ The Emergence of the Theory of Evolution

By what processes did simple one-celled organisms become immensely complex animals and plants? We know that the processes occurred extremely slowly, in a span of time so great that it is difficult for us to grasp. During this span, a large number of species appeared and later became extinct, and many social mechanisms that developed as an aid to survival also disappeared without a trace. However, scientists have been able to reconstruct the milestones: the appearance of primates among mammals, leading eventually, through apes and hominids, to modern humans; the emergence of cultural traits, contributing to the development of agriculture; and, within the past 5,000 years, the emergence of urban societies and the concept of the state.

The reconstruction of events so far in the past has been painful and painstaking. It began only when scientists, basing their studies on scientific theories and using the scientific method, took advantage of the fossil record to support the hypotheses these theories suggested.

Curiosity about the vast variety of animal species in existence, as well as the diversity in the physical appearance of the human species, led thinkers long ago to speculate that both animals and humans had undergone changes to adapt to different environments. The ancient Greeks and Romans thought so, but as the societies of the West embraced Christianity, they tended to discount any explanation that went against the teachings of the Bible. Working within Biblical limits, scholars contented themselves with classifying and describing. For instance, the Swedish naturalist Karl Von Linné (Carolus Linnaeus, 1707–1778) classified plants and animals according to their similarities and arranged them in hierarchical categories, with *Homo sapiens* (humans) at the top and invertebrates such as worms at the bottom.

Another naturalist, the French Baron Georges Cuvier (1769–1832), compared the structures of one animal with those of another, thus giving origin to a major field of biology, comparative anatomy. When confronted with the mineralized bones and teeth of animals that were not currently living, Cuvier had to admit that these were the fossil remains of extinct species. This belief, however, went against the religious beliefs of the West. A strict interpretation of the Bible fosters the belief that God had created humans and all other living creatures that were inferior to humans at the same time, and none of these had changed since the moment of creation. One reason people believed in static, immutable creation was that the political and social orders of Europe were static and appeared unchangeable at this time, too.

The seventeenth and eighteenth centuries saw an increase in critical thinking and relatively free inquiry, and the nineteenth century brought dramatic changes of a social and cultural nature because of the Industrial Revolution. The rising middle class, whose members were generally well educated, were unwilling to accept the idea that the status quo was the only proper condition of a society. The climate was favorable to the notion of change. In France, a country torn by a revolution that saw the monarchy supplanted by a republic, scholars began to speculate openly that living organisms were probably subject to changes that were passed on to succeeding generations. They based this idea on the visible changes that forces of elements such as rain, wind, sun, and tides wrought on the appearance of the earth. Thus, Baron Jean Baptiste de Lamarck (1744–1829) wrote that it was obvious that animals were not fixed in appearance but changed in response to certain requirements of their environment. Furthermore, those changes were passed on to the offspring, which were then better suited to life in their environment. (By the way, the reason why so many aristocrats wrote on the subject was that anthropology was considered a gentleman's hobby, because people could see no practical use from pursuing information about the origins of species.) Their claims were reinforced by findings of fossils, including some of species no

Earth is only a small planet in the Milky Way Galaxy, but miraculously it possesses all the ingredients to sustain life as we know it.

longer living, which were being discovered at about that time during excavations for industrial purposes. However, although they speculated, they could not produce sufficient evidence to make their case.

A Revolution in Thought: Darwin and His Theory

In 1830, a Scottish geologist, Charles Lyell (1797–1875), published a book, *Principles of Geology*, in which he maintained that natural forces operating in a uniform manner had transformed the topography of the world into its present appearance. In other words, the earth was continually being altered by the forces of wind, rain, and temperature as well as by the flooding of rivers and volcanic eruptions. These changes, he thought, occurred very slowly, so the planet had to be very old—many millions of years old, and not the few thousand years that the Bible and the Christian establishment attributed to it.

Lyell's book came into the hands of amateur naturalist Charles Darwin (1809–1882), who was able to observe the flora and fauna, as well as the peoples of various continents, during his tenure as a ship's naturalist during a five-year voyage. That voyage, on a ship called the H.M.S. *Beagle*, which surveyed the coasts of South America, Australia and Asia, and the South Seas, led him to develop a revolutionary theory. In 1859, Darwin published his famous *On the Origin of Species* (preceded by a preliminary paper that Darwin presented with a young colleague, A. R. Wallace). In it, Darwin maintained that species are not immutable, as was previously thought; on the contrary, species belonging to the same category are lineal descendants of some other species likely to be extinct. Darwin also posited that the changes occurred as a reaction to environment. Most important, Darwin offered proof by describing the *mechanism* of evolutionary change: namely, natural selection.

Natural Selection

Natural selection is a process that, in simplified form, works this way: some individuals, out of the total population of a particular territory, are born with a random feature—let us say, a thumb that can be opposed to the rest of the fingers on the hand. These individuals do better in an environment in which they have to grasp objects than individuals who lack this feature. Thus, they survive longer and have a chance to reproduce, passing the feature on to some of their descendants. Individuals who lack the opposable thumb are less likely to survive long enough to reproduce. Eventually they disappear altogether from the population.

Darwin deduced the process of *natural selection* from his observations that among both plants and animals more offspring in each generation are born than can possibly survive. In nature, there is competition for living space, resources, and mates. Some individuals are more successful in competing than others because of specific traits that they possess in a particular environment. This fact is usually referred to as "survival of the fittest," but this phrase may be misleading. A "fit" organism is one that survives and reproduces in a particular environment at a particular time. When the environment changes, as it frequently does, a new trait may be required, and organisms possessing the new trait will become the "fittest." In this way, the natural environment selects which genes are preferable, and those genes become more frequent in a given population, at least until there is a change in the environment.

A frequent example of how natural selection works is the explanation for the long necks of giraffes. Among the entire giraffe population at a certain period of time, individual giraffes were born with necks of varying proportions. The giraffes with longer necks were able to reach higher into the trees and, thus, were better fed and healthier. As a result, they lived longer and had more offspring, some of which inherited the trait for long necks. Gradually, there came to be more long-necked giraffes than short-necked giraffes, until finally the whole giraffe population had longer necks than the giraffes of previous times. Had the environment in which the giraffes lived changed to one in which plants grew in the form of grass and shrubs only, the long necks would have become liabilities. The giraffes that by chance were born with a short neck would then have had the advantage and would have eventually become the norm.

The Role of Heredity

Some points of the natural selection process puzzled Darwin, however. One was how the beneficial trait was transmitted if individuals possessing it mated with others who did not possess it. In Darwin's time, it was believed that offspring inherited a blend of their parents' traits, but there was not sufficient evidence to support the idea.

An answer to this puzzle came through the work of an Augustinian monk, Gregor Mendel (1822–1884), who had been crossbreeding plants. Mendel concluded from his experiments that traits are not blended, nor do they disappear completely. Rather, some traits are dominant and tend to be expressed; others are recessive and tend to remain hidden. A recessive trait, hidden by a dominant trait, may disappear for a generation but may reappear in a later generation.

Mendel's work remained obscure until the beginning of the twentieth century, when the combination of Darwinian evolutionary theory and Mendelian genetics, now termed the **modern synthesis**, was validated by a number of researchers. The latter were able to prove mathematically that even minute differences in the ability to survive and produce offspring could result, in a long enough span of time, in substantial change. Their work laid the groundwork for contemporary evolutionary theory, which is best understood in the context of genetics.

■ Genetics

The relatively new science of genetics is divided into three subfields: chromosomal or Mendelian genetics, concerned with how chromosomes transmit genes across generations; cytogenetics, which focuses on biochemical and cellular events; and population genetics, which deals with natural selection and other reasons for genetic variation and changes in populations. To understand how humans evolved and why they exhibit such a wide variety of physical traits, we must become acquainted with some of the mechanisms of heredity.

Population Genetics: Factors for Change

The structural traits of plant and animal—what the plant and animal will look and be like—are transmitted by hereditary units called *genes*. Genes contain a blueprint with instructions to the reproductive system about how a specific plant or animal should appear and function: what color eyes, hair, and skin it should have; what height and body type it should be; and whether it should have four legs and a tail or two legs, two hands, and no tail. This blueprint, or code, is dependent on the arrangement of the DNA molecules, which make up the content of genes. DNA stands for deoxyribonucleic acid and is the basic building block of all life. Each type of gene has a DNA of a slightly different chemical structure, and this is what determines the inheritance of specific traits. In turn, each organism has a different kind and number of genes, varying from a very small number for simple organisms, such as viruses, to a very large number for complex organisms, such as humans.

Genes, each containing a section of DNA with an identifiable structure or function, are arranged in a linear order and packaged in units called *chromosomes*. Humans normally

Each newborn inherits 46 chromosomes, 23 from its mother and 23 from its father. Therefore, each person resembles each parent but is not a copy of either.

Box 2.2 The Revolution in Evolution

It has always been the dream of scientists to create life in the laboratory. It is not a new idea: we all have seen movies about the Frankenstein monster created from body parts and brought to life by an electric charge. But contemporary scientists are trying to approximate the creation of the first living thing, as it may have occurred in reality, in a thimble-size test tube. They believe that a molecule that has evolved in their lab with the capacity of reproducing may have been the precursor of the current RNA. In turn, the RNA together with the DNA, carries the genetic code in all living creatures. Although the scientists do not know what causes the transition from nonliving to living, they do know that at some point the distinction between the two blurs and disappears. Should they succeed in creating a "living" molecule, then the question to be tackled next will be whether life was a unique one-time event, or whether it results from a common chemical process, making the creation of life continuous.

Experiments such as these are becoming widespread, so that the discipline of biology is continually expanding. The genomes of more than 300 species have been decoded, with more in the works, and new scientific findings seem to be appearing on a daily basis. In fact, many science writers are beginning to refer to biology as the new science of "evo devo." This name, which sounds like the title of a band, is the shortened form of *evolutionary developmental biology*, the term for a discipline that offers a new way of looking at how life evolved. Evo devo contends that organisms undergo two types of changes through time. One change occurs during the lifetime of an animal, the other in the historical evolution of a species, and the two types of changes are connected.

The idea that evolution and development are related had occurred to scientists before. Even before Darwin's work, scientists opined that the development of an organism from a single cell—the ovum—into an embryo and finally into a living individual echoes the history of life. We know that, as an embryo develops, rudimentary forms of a former being appear, only to disappear when a new, better mechanism develops. The embryo develops gills, for instance, but they soon give way to lungs, which work better when the individual must breathe in the air and not in water. The appearance of the gills during the embryo's development indicates to scientists that an ancestral form of the individual lived in water at some point in the distant past.

Evolutionary developmental biology has begun to explain more exactly the processes that turn a formless egg into a complex adult. The explanations revolve around the manner in which DNA builds organisms. As is noted in the text, DNA's function is to command cells to make proteins, and specific stretches of DNA, called genes, make specific proteins. In short, a specific sequence of DNA tells a cell to build a specific kind of protein, which yields a specific organ. Not all genes are expressed, however, and species look different because they use the same bits and pieces of DNA in different combinations. Living beings still must adapt to their environment through natural selection, but the adaptation does not occur by the creation of new genes. Rather, it occurs by genetic "switching," that is, by combining existing genes, with some alterations, in different ways. Thus, a small number of primitive genes has yielded, through the millennia, wings and fins, arms and legs.

The evo-devo discipline, in other words, supports the Darwinian and the Mendelian theory of genetics, which posit that all life forms on the planet derive from one or a few common ancestors (Carroll, 2005).

---

have 46 chromosomes arranged in matching pairs. Each individual inherits one set of 23 chromosomes from its mother and another set of 23 from its father. Chromosomes are located in the nucleus of every cell.

The Human Genome Project.   Scientists have in the recent past uncovered the order, or sequence, of the human genetic code. The cracking of the genetic code of human life has been called a pinnacle of human self-knowledge, because in effect, scientists have deciphered the hereditary set of instructions that defines the human organism. This is the script by which, millions of times, an egg meets a sperm and the resulting individual is born with all its parts in place, ready to function in the myriad ways in which a human being functions.

The script consists of more than three billion base pairs—the rungs between the strands of the double helix of the DNA. The bases are adenine (A), cytosine (C), guanine (G), and thymine (T). In the future, scientists hope to locate all genes and uncover their function. This would lead to practical applications in the area of health. The sequencing, in fact, is expected to revolutionize the practice of medicine. The knowledge gathered from the sequencing of the genome is already being used to direct the communication system of the body to act in specific ways: for instance, ordering cells to repair damaged tissue or fight off invaders. Eventually, scientists expect to develop a variety of diagnostic tools and treatments that may be tailored to individual patients. They also hope that the sequencing will be helpful in taking advantage of the body's ability to self-repair.

Gene Frequency. Within each inbreeding population—a group of individuals who breed with one another because they live in the same general territory—genes occur in specific proportions. That is, such a population might contain individuals with 30 percent of gene X, 20 percent of gene Y, and 50 percent of gene Z. This condition is called *gene frequency*. As long as gene frequency remains constant, the population will have a specific appearance. If gene frequency changes—if the proportion of a given gene increases or decreases—the population is undergoing evolution. Eventually, changes will occur in some aspect of the population's appearance or structure.

Mutation. How does gene frequency change? Normally, the DNA is a stable structure not subject to change. On occasion, however, a slight change in DNA does occur; then the information content of the gene is changed, and the change is transmitted to later generations. Permanent change in genetic material is called *mutation*. Mutation is rare (mutant

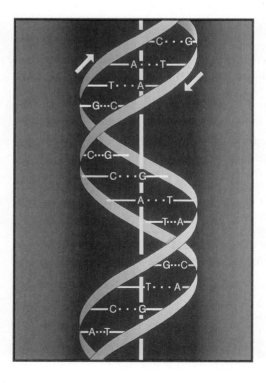

Much knowledge about the mechanisms of heredity has been provided by research into DNA, the basic building block of life.

genes have been calculated to run from a low of about five mutations per million sex cells to a high of about 100 per million, in the human population), but it is constant, and it is the source of the variations characteristic of humans. Sometimes mutations produce obvious abnormalities, such as Down's syndrome, but the large majority of them produce more subtle effects (Haviland, 1995, 63). Scientists have speculated that some forms of mutation are caused by radiation, certain chemicals, and heat, but it is likely that we are ignorant of many other causes.

It should be stressed that what happens when an offspring is born with the inherited genes from its father and mother—which make the offspring appear distinct from either parent—is *not* mutation: it is a reshuffling of existing genes. Mutation is a random, chance occurrence that sometimes has positive results, enhancing an organism's chance of survival, and at other times has harmful consequences, causing disease or malformation. A harmful mutation that leads to the organism's death has no consequences for the process of evolution. A positive mutation contributes to the genetic variation within a population (the reason for differences in skin coloration, for instance) and is a necessary condition for natural selection.

As an example, geneticists have recently speculated that a mutation in a gene that occurred around 2.4 million years ago was probably responsible for reshaping the human face. The mutation took place in a gene responsible for developing strong jaw muscles for chewing and biting. Other primates, like chimpanzees and macaques, still have such strong jaws, as well as the gene responsible for producing them. In humans, however, a mutation inactivated this gene. As a result, human jaws became smaller, less protruding, and weaker. At the same time, this led to the development of a larger brain. Jaw muscles apparently limit the growth of the skull, so smaller jaw muscles left more space in the skull to be filled by the brain.

Genetic Drift. In addition to mutation, the balance of a gene pool may be upset by genetic drift. (A *gene pool* consists of all the genetic material available to a specific population to be inherited by the next generation.) Genetic drift is the effect of chance events on the gene pool of small populations. In particular, it affects small populations that are isolated for several generations. In these circumstances, a random trait will tend to become so common in the span of a few generations that the group will begin to look distinct from the original group.

Gene Flow. On the other hand, some breeding populations exchange genes with members of different gene pools (members of some societies are required to choose mates from a different population group). *Gene flow* is the term that denotes the movement of genes from one genetic pool to another. Gene flow results in hybridization (the offspring look different in some respects from either parent). It is theorized that such matings result in *hybrid vigor*, or offspring that are better specimens than either parent. (Modern Hawaiians, a hybrid population that is a mixture of Polynesian, European, and Asian populations, are noted for their size, good health, and general vigor.) One effect of gene flow has been the establishment, in the last 400 years, of a new **phenotype** (the physical, or outward, appearance of an organism, as opposed to the **genotype**, which is the actual genetic composition of an organism) in Central and South America. This phenotype was formed when the gene pool of the native populations mixed with genes of the Spanish colonists as well as with those of the Africans whom they imported as slaves.

Speciation. The ultimate form of variation is the evolution of one species into another. The development of a new species, or *speciation*, occurs when two or more groups of an original species become isolated from one another and, in time, adapting to their separate environments, develop such profound genetic changes that they can no longer breed with one another. (Only members of the same species can exchange genes through reproduction. Members of different species can mate, even reproduce, but the offspring will either die or be infertile.) Speciation was used by Darwin to explain the fact that humans, monkeys, and apes descended from a common primate ancestor.

It should be pointed out here that the variations among humans we call races are not separate species but slight variants of a single species. Differences in appearance are due to gene flow, genetic drift, and migrations. It is clear that some human groups do not interbreed because of geographic and cultural reasons, but all human groups *can* interbreed.

Natural Selection and Adaptation. The processes we have enumerated produce changes in gene pools and, thus, changes in specific populations, but change in itself is not necessarily advantageous to the population. Changes must fit a specific environment, or be adapted to it. **Adaptation** is a process that intervenes to ensure that organisms achieve an adjustment to their environment that is beneficial, and it does so through the process of natural selection. As we saw earlier, **natural selection** is the name given to the evolutionary process in which certain factors present in the environment of a specific location exert pressure in such a way that they select some individuals for survival and reproduction of the next generation, while others are not so favored. Natural selection, then, is not a random process but one that leads to an organism's adaptation to the environment. The process may take the form of *directional selection*, in which change in gene frequencies is promoted (because an adaptation to a new environment is needed), or it may take the form of *stabilizing selection*, in which natural selection promotes the status quo rather than change (because change would be detrimental to the organism's adaptation to its environment).

Box 2.3   Human Evolution Designed by Humans

For millions of years human—as well as plant and animal—evolution proceeded according to the mechanisms of nature, totally outside human control. Today, however, this is no longer the case. It is now within the reach of scientists to make genetic changes in people, plants, and animals that persist through the generations. In effect, humans can now manipulate evolution. This process, called *germline genetic engineering*, differs from the simple genetic engineering that has already produced better-quality grains and faster racehorses. Now it appears that molecular biologists and geneticists will be able within a short time to intervene by giving people genes that will prevent them from getting certain diseases, cure them of others, confer superior intelligence, or rid people of the unpleasantness of aging. In addition, unlike genetic therapies that are in existence now (in which genes are inserted into specific body tissues), the genetic changes being considered by the scientists will be capable of remaining permanent and

being passed on to subsequent generations. "We are talking about intervening in the flow of genetic information from one generation to the next. We are talking about the relationship of human beings to their genetic heritage," as one scientist put it (Kolata, 1998, 12).

The ethical conundrum that such capabilities engender will be the next obstacle facing scientists. However, it is obvious that today's scientists use evolutionary knowledge to help humanity. For example, it is well-known that hospitals are often the environments in which bacteria flourish and adapt by evolving resistance to the powerful antibiotics used against them. One researcher has been following 12 initially identical populations of the bacterium *Escherichia coli* that kept adapting to the conditions in their separate test tubes. The researcher hopes to be able to find a way to slow adaptation in the bacterium or to select for a milder version of the bacterium that would prove easier to counteract (Hayden, 2002, 48).

A number of important conclusions can be drawn from this simplified review of the theory of evolution. First, human evolution is not just a matter of highly complex biochemical events carried on by the DNA genetic code; it also involves cultural patterns of behavior such as occur in mating practices, migrations, isolation, wars, and so on. Second, by providing two sources of genetic material (from the mother and the father), the sexual reproduction system ensures the existence of a balanced range of variation in genetic traits. Offspring resemble their parents and ancestors in many ways but are never identical copies of them. Third, the processes of natural selection and adaptation through mutation, genetic drift, and gene flow are responsible for constantly changing the genetic composition of a population through a progressive weeding out of some characteristics while passing on others. Finally, it should not be assumed that every feature of every population is the result of adaptation and selection. Some of the visible differences among populations may be due to accidental genetic drift.

■ The Long Trek: Human Evolution

The long evolutionary journey of humans begins with the appearance of mammals. These initially small, insignificant animals made their appearance on earth during the Paleocene epoch, or 65 to 55 million years ago (Table 2.1; see also websites dealing with the geological history of the earth: **http://paleontology.esmartstudent.com/physicalhistory.html**; and **http://faculty.vassar.edu/mehaffey/academicanimalstructure/outlines/history.html**). They fed at night on plants, insects, eggs, and worms (they were flesh eaters) to stay out of the way of the gigantic reptiles that dominated life during the day. Night feeding accustomed them to being

Box 2.4 Evolution: Theory or Fact?

Evolutionary scientists are still facing a bitter controversy. People who follow a literal interpretation of the Bible do not accept the theory of evolution, and parents in a number of states have lobbied school districts not to teach it or to teach a variant of the Biblical explanation alongside it. Scientists, on the other hand, are so convinced of its veracity that they want the word *theory* deleted altogether. They have probed the fossil record, deciphered genomes, and scrutinized the details of plant and animal development. In addition, they have experimented in laboratories and are able to confirm almost everything that Darwin postulated. For instance, one researcher at Stanford University has been able to demonstrate natural selection in action. He found that in a hot environment, butterflies that have a metabolic gene that confers tolerance to high temperatures reproduce at higher rates than butterflies that lack that gene. Eventually, all butterflies in the hot environment had that gene; butterflies that functioned better at lower temperatures disappeared from that environment. Moreover, paleontologists working in the hills of Pakistan have recovered fossils that illustrate, step by step, how a hairy, doglike creature wandered off into the sea and eventually took the form of the first whales.

Scientists are also speculating that not all evolutionary change happens gradually. Sometimes catastrophes occur that change the environment dramatically and wipe out entire species. Any survivors that are able to adapt to the new environment may give rise to a new species altogether. This is what is thought to have happened when an asteroid impact with the earth killed off the dinosaurs some 65 million years ago. The mammals that had coexisted with the dinosaurs for about 150 million years were small, ratlike creatures. When the dinosaurs disappeared, however, they had the opportunity to evolve new features, which eventually led to the development of humans (Hayden, 2002, 43–50).

TABLE 2.1 Major Milestones in the Evolution of Mammals

Years, in Millions	Periods	Epochs	Life Forms
345	Carboniferous		
			Earliest reptiles
280	Permian		
			Reptiles with mammal-like traits
230	Triassic		
180	Jurassic		Earliest mammals
135	Cretaceous		
65		Paleocene	Earliest primates or primate-like mammals
55		Eocene	
			Earliest monkey-ape ancestors
34		Oligocene	
23		Miocene	
5		Pliocene	Earliest hominids
2		Pleistocene	

active in cooler temperatures and eventually led to their developing warm blood. In turn, with warm blood they could survive in a wider range of climates and temperatures than could the cold-blooded reptiles. This ability became invaluable when great changes in the geology of the earth resulted in a cooler and drier climate and the disappearance of swamplands: the large reptiles could not adapt and eventually disappeared, but the small mammals adjusted and survived.

One order of mammals, the *primates*, appeared during the Eocene epoch, about 55 to 50 million years ago, and took to the trees in the forests that covered most of the earth. Primates are an order of mammals to which monkeys, apes, and humans belong (Table 2.2 and for further details: **http://en.wikipedia.org/wiki/mammal**). They gradually developed brains, sense organs, limbs, and reproductive systems (at which point they are called prosimians), and their adaptation to the environment and living conditions of the forest prepared them for the next evolutionary step.

This highly successful group of tree-dwellers began, about 35 million years ago, to evolve first into monkeys, larger in size than their predecessors and fond of plants, and a little later into apes. The apes were still larger than their forebears were and more adept at hanging from branches with three limbs while picking fruit with the fourth. Eventually, some apes came down from the trees to attempt survival on the ground. The reason for this change of environment was probably climatic: the earth was changing once more, with forests giving way to open woodlands and later to grassy savannas.

These apes are referred to as *hominoids*, that is, they belong to the superfamily *hominoidea* (Table 2.2). Of those, the *ramapithecines* were more terrestrial and adapted to the open country. Because they also had a rather human-like appearance, some scholars assumed that their fossil remains, named *Ramapithecus*, were those of *hominids*, that is, that they belonged to the family *hominidae*, to which only humans belong. This view is no longer held today. Hominids differ from other primates in that they are bipeds (they walk on two

TABLE 2.2   The Place of Humans in the Animal Kingdom

Kingdom	Animalia	Consists of living creatures with a limited growth period and the ability to move. Includes animals from amoebas to mammals.
Phylum	Chordata	Beings with an internal stiff structure, such as a spinal cord.
Subphylum	Vertebrata	Animals from the phylum Chordata with a segmented spinal column.
Class	Mammalia	Animals with these features: warm blood, hair, sweat glands, four-chambered heart, breasts for feeding the young, diaphragm for breathing.
Subclass	Eutheria	Placental mammals who bear their young after a full-term pregnancy.
Order	Primates	Placental mammals with grasping hands, two breasts on the chest, a small number of offspring per birth, long pregnancies, and long periods of infancy. Monkeys, apes, and humans are primates that share good vision and a bony eye socket.
Suborder	Anthropoidea	Includes monkeys, apes, and humans.
Superfamily	Hominoidea	Primates defined by dental traits. Includes apes and humans.
Family	Hominidae	Modern humans and their closest ancestors, *Australopithecus* and *Homo erectus*.
Genus	Homo	Includes *Homo erectus*, Neanderthals, and modern humans.
Species	Sapiens	Neanderthals and modern humans.
Variety	Sapiens	All modern humans, i.e., all living races.

feet), they have large brains, smaller and nonprotruding faces, and smaller teeth arranged in a curve on the jaws. Based on molecular analysis, it appears that the split between hominoid and hominid occurred between 7 and 5 million years ago (Relethford 2000, 312). An even more recent finding of fossils in Spain points to an ape species dating to about 13 million years ago. Paleontologists believe that this species may have been the last common ancestor of all living great apes, including humans (Wilford, 2004, A8).

The evolution of hominids from that split to the appearance of *Homo sapiens*, the scientific name of modern humans, is the subject matter of physical anthropology, paleontology, and archaeology. A great number of scientists have been involved in research in this area, and the fossil record has often been corrected when new fossil finds occur. This fascinating subject has been exhaustively presented in a number of web sites. Modern humans may have developed independently in various parts of the world from successive hominid and *Homo* ancestors. In fact, the issue of whether *Homo sapiens* has a single African origin or a multiregional origin has not yet been resolved. The latest fossil research seems to indicate that for at least three million years of recorded history the human line was confined to Africa, that it consisted of at least two major subdivisions, and that eventually the line dispersed throughout the globe. (Follow the work of paleontologists, anthropologists, and archaeologists on these web sites: **http://archaeologyinfo.com/evolution.htm; http://www.geocities.com/soho/ atrium/1381/hominids1.html; http://www.pbs.org/wgbh/evolution/humans/humankind/index. html; http://www.talkorigins.org/faqs/homs/species.html#moderns;** and **http://anthro.palomar. edu/hominid/australo_1.htm.**)

Split between Chimpanzee and Human Lines

The evolutionary line of development from hominids to modern humans is in the realm of prehistory, and thus our view of it is based on speculation and educated guesswork about fossilized remains. All that seems to be apparent is that 10 million years ago, the world was full of apes, whereas 5 million years ago, records show that hominids appear (Gee, 2002).

Paleoanthropologists now think that modern humans did not evolve in a straight line from their ape-like precursors. Rather, it seems more likely that more than one group of hominids lived side by side. For instance, there is evidence that several hominids (*Australopithecus robustus*, or "robust southern ape"), *Australopithecus boisei*, and *Australopithecus africanus*, related to the other australopithecus but smaller—barely 4 feet tall—coexisted by exploiting different resources. By approximately one million years ago, only one type of hominid remained, giving scientists reason to believe that something happened to destroy their coexistence. In short, researchers who once believed that only one hominid species existed at one time now tend to believe that the human family tree looks more like a bush, with many branches pointing in different directions. This belief is fueled by more refined analyses of fossils and a number of new discoveries.

Newer findings have concluded that the differences between chimps and humans lie most especially in the genetic activity of their respective brains. In fact, whereas scientists

Box 2.5   From Fossil to Fossil

In 1999, Dr. Meave G. Leakey, excavating on the western side of Lake Turkana, discovered a skull that was dated at 3.5 million years old. This skull appeared to belong to a totally different species than did the Lucy species, which was a contemporary. Dr. Leakey assigned the new discovery the name *Kenyanthropus platyops*, or flat-faced man of Kenya (Wilford, 2001, 3). The importance of this discovery lies in the fact that at least two lineages of hominids existed as far back as 3.5 million years. Until this particular discovery, scientists had evidence that multiple species of hominids had existed simultaneously only from 2 million years ago.

By 2.4 million years ago, the evolution of the genus *Homo* was proceeding in a different direction from that of *Australopithecus*. Another skull fragment found near Lake Baringo in Kenya was determined to be the earliest known fossil of a member of the *Homo* line of human ancestors. The dating supports the theory that modern humans appeared about 2.5 million years ago in a period of dramatic climate changes (Wilford, 1992, A8). In the Olduvai Gorge, a deep valley running between the volcanic highlands and the Serengeti Plain of East Africa, for instance, anthropologists have found the fossilized remains of a creature (*Homo habilis*, or "handy man," considered to be the first true member of the human family) who was between 4 and 5 feet tall, stood upright, and had

a large cranium. Although *Homo habilis* differed little in appearance from the australopithecines, there is evidence of an increase in brain size and a reorganization of brain structure, so that it is believed that the mental abilities of the new species were probably greater than that of the australopithecines. *Homo habilis* is thought to have existed 1.85 million years ago.

Since no complete fossils of the early members of the genus *Homo* have been found, the origin has been described as "one of the most intriguing and intractable mysteries in human evolution" (Wilford, 2007, D1). Fossil discoveries are constantly being made throughout the world, but they consist of a few skulls and bones, so that a final date for the origin has been impossible to state. The latest find has been in the former Soviet republic of Georgia, and has been dated to 1.8 million years. This indicates to the researchers that these human ancestors had evolved enough to enable them to travel long distances, from Africa to temperate Europe. The discoverers of these fossils hope that the find will "lead to a breakthrough in the critical evolutionary period in which some members of *Australopithecus*, the genus made famous by the Lucy skeleton, made the transition to *Homo*. The step may have been taken more than two million years ago" (Wilford, 2007, 20).

have long been aware that chimp DNA is 98.7 percent identical to human DNA, what they could not determine was the origin of the differences. At first, researchers focused on language, which is the defining difference between the two species. However, research showed that the area in the left hemisphere that mediates language was equally large in both chimp and human brains. When they began to probe differences on the genetic level, however, researchers found that human and chimp genes show very different patterns of activity in operating brain cells. ". . . the gene activity levels in the evolution of human brain genes have been five times faster than that of the chimp brain genes. This finding fits well with other evidence suggesting that an explosive evolutionary development took place, at least in the human lineage, after the comparatively recent split between the common ancestors of chimps and people some five million years ago . . ." (Wade, 2002, A18).

■ Modern Humans: The Road to *Homo Sapiens*

New studies based on genetic and archeological data support the hypothesis that behaviorally fully modern humans originated in sub-Saharan Africa. These humans had made important cultural improvements: they had language, some type of boats or rafts, and more sophisticated stone implements. At this point, they began to move out of Africa, reaching Europe and Asia between 65,000 and 25,000 years ago and probably closer to 45,000 to 35,000 years ago for Europe (Wilford, 2007, 1–3). The researchers believe that these humans had become meat eaters and were searching for a wider area in which to hunt animals (Wilford, 2000, 1, A28).

Remains in England and Germany point to close precursors of modern humans as having appeared some 300,000 to 250,000 years ago. Definite fossils of *Homo sapiens sapiens* (the species label for modern humans) date back only 75,000 years, but in early 2005 researchers

The United States is a heterogeneous society now, containing people from all over the globe. The differences in the outward appearance of people, however, derive from their former genetic isolation and from the effects of genetic drift and gene flow.

uncovered evidence that bones found in Ethiopia's Lake Turkana are roughly 195,000 years old. The best known of these are the fossil remains of the Neanderthals, of whom some inhabited Western Europe as recently as 36,000 years ago (the classic Neanderthals), while others were found in Asia, Africa, and Europe. It is from the Neanderthals that we derive the stereotype of the "caveman," for they had thick skulls, heavy brow ridges, broad noses, low foreheads, and not much chin. These features, as well as a short, stocky, and muscular body build, may have been adaptations to the glacial climate of Western Europe at the time. Neanderthals used much more sophisticated tools than their predecessors, lived in fairly settled communities, used caves for shelter, and buried their dead with ceremonies and flowers, indicating the development of ritual and the possibility that they believed in an afterlife. They probably used a primitive type of language to communicate with one another. Archeologists and anthropologists at Duke University have recently probed the brains of humans and compared them with casts of brains from ancient human fossil skulls. This analysis has convinced them that vocal capabilities like those of modern humans could have evolved more than 400,000 years ago. This would mean that earlier species, even before the appearance of the Neanderthals, had the use of speech (Wilford, 1998, A1, A17, 4).

Scientists do not agree as to whether the Neanderthals are the ancestors or precursors of modern humans. On the one hand, genetic material (DNA) from the bones of a 30,000-year-old Neanderthal seems to indicate that Neanderthals did not interbreed with modern humans, even though the two species may have coexisted. The test, in fact, prompted the scientists who performed it to say that Neanderthals "diverged away from our line quite early on, and this reinforces the ideas that they are a separate species from modern humans" (Wade, 1997, A14). On the other hand, paleontologists have recently examined the 24,500-year-old skeleton of a young boy discovered in Portugal, and their conclusion was that he was a hybrid. This discovery has prompted scientists to hypothesize that Neanderthals and

These cave paintings date back at least 20,000 years. They were made by the Cro-Magnon people, using a kind of oral spray—saliva mixed with pigment—and blowing it on the wall.

modern humans coexisted for thousands of years, and moreover, that they cohabited and interbred with modern humans. They suspect that Neanderthals and *Homo sapiens* were not two separate species or subspecies, but two groups that thought of each other as appropriate mates. "They intermixed, interbred and produced offspring," as one paleoanthropologist states (Wilford, 1999, A1, A21). This discovery may undermine the out-of-Africa hypothesis of modern human origins, and bolster the regional continuity theory, discussed above. The fact remains that Neanderthals stopped flourishing and seem to have disappeared abruptly around 28,000 years ago (Wade, 2000, A16).

The next fossil remains, found at a site in south central France and dating from about 35,000 to 30,000 years ago, are those of Cro-Magnon humans. These are definitely classified as belonging to *Homo sapiens sapiens*. The Cro-Magnon were tall and light-boned and had high foreheads, smaller faces and jaws, definite chins, and slight or no ridges over the eyes and in the back of the head. They were also hunters and gatherers, but they must have been more efficient at providing a constant food supply because their numbers seem to have increased. The beautiful paintings they left on the walls of their caves indicate a certain sensitivity to their surroundings and an early attempt at art, perhaps in the service of religious beliefs. According to population geneticists, today's Basques of France and Spain are very likely the most direct descendants of the Cro-Magnon people, the first really modern humans (Subramanian, 1995, 55).

The Cro-Magnons and other groups of *Homo sapiens* were well established in the Old World (Europe, Africa, and Asia) from 40,000 B.C. to 12,000–8,000 B.C. Some of the *Homo sapiens* appear to have arrived in the New World about 40,000 years ago, during the Ice Age, probably via a land bridge across the Bering Strait. However, the earliest hard evidence of a human presence in this hemisphere goes back only 14,000 years (Rincon, 2004). We share most of our physical features with these distant ancestors. Their activities bring us to the last period of prehistory, which ends with the invention of agriculture.

■ Agriculture: Cultivation and Domestication

During what is called the Neolithic, or New Stone Age, which began about 12,000 to 10,000 years ago, a transition from foraging for food to domesticating plants and animals occurred. This slow transition eventually transformed hunting, gathering, and fishing peoples to food producers, representing a dramatic change in the manner of subsistence and the economy. Actual farming was preceded by the domestication of plants and animals, an evolutionary process in which humans, intentionally or unintentionally, alter the genetic makeup of certain plants or animals, so that the latter are finally unable to survive or reproduce without human intervention.

Domestication was certainly facilitated by the ending of the Ice Age. The retreating glaciers left the planet warmer and wetter, favoring the spread of vegetation, including such grasses as wild wheat and barley. This type of vegetation attracted herds of animals, which in turn attracted hunters and gatherers, who found a ready supply of food and so may have abandoned their nomadic ways.

The domestication of certain plants changed them from wild to cultivated and resulted in larger size of the edible parts. It also led to a reduction, or a total loss, of the means of seed dispersal and of protective devices—such as thorns, husks, or toxins—events that were advantageous to humans. Domestication resulted in a better-tasting plant and a more secure source of food.

The Fertile Crescent

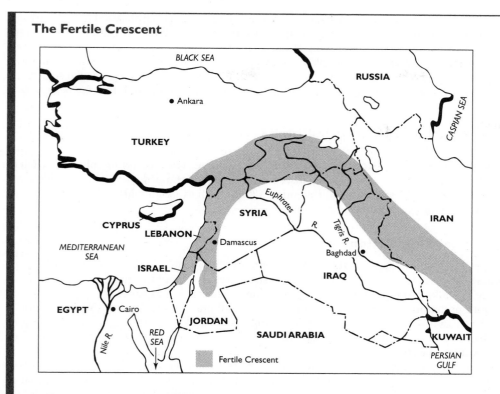

FIGURE 2.1 This 2,000-mile-long area extending from modern Israel and Jordan to Iran and the Persian Gulf is called the Fertile Crescent. It is considered to be the birthplace of agriculture.

Domestication eventually led to agriculture—the deliberate growing of food—which is thought to have appeared in several areas independently, although perhaps not at the same time. The world's very first farmers were probably inhabitants of the Near East, in the region called the Fertile Crescent (Figure 2.1), a 2,000-mile arc that includes parts of Israel, Lebanon, Jordan, Syria, southern Turkey, Iraq, all the way to the head of the Persian Gulf. Among the chief crops were wheat, barley, legumes, grapes, melons, dates, pistachios, and almonds. The first domesticated animals—sheep, goats, pigs, and cattle—also appeared in this region (Wilford, 1997, B9). Some of these crops spread from the Fertile Crescent across Europe and Asia between 7000 B.C. and 2500 B.C., but it was several thousand more years before maize or corn became a cultivated crop in the Americas. This was because there was no native wild wheat or barley here, and the domestication of maize requires a more sophisticated biological reorganization.

The Fertile Crescent was an area in which natural living conditions were very favorable, and it soon attracted large concentrations of people. Eventually, the region became so overpopulated that some people were forced to leave and retreat to locations where food was less abundant. To supplement their more meager supplies of plants, these emigrants transplanted some of the seeds of the wild wheat and barley near seasonal streams, where they flourished. In this manner, agriculture spread to other areas.

With agriculture came permanent settlements as well as surpluses. Here begins the dichotomy of human nature: when a definite advantage to survival emerges, a disadvantage also appears almost concurrently. One of the results of surpluses, in fact, was warfare, as some groups tried to appropriate the surpluses of others. Populations grew at phenomenal rates and cities came into being, requiring the development of ever more sophisticated social structures. Eventually, writing appeared and the recorded portion of the history of humanity began.

■ The Evolution of Human Nature

Long before recorded history, our ancestors were honing what we commonly call "human nature." That is, they were evolving customs and habits that aided survival in specific environments and, at the same time, differentiated them from other animals. This differentiation usually had *biological* origins but *social consequences*.

Biological Foundations

Even at the hominid stage, certain evolutionary developments in the physiology of humans became the precursors of some of the social structures that were to come into existence. For example, walking on two legs may have developed because it was easier for the hominids to see both predators and prey as they walked in the tall grass of the savanna. Walking upright also freed two of the limbs for carrying things, food and their young, from one place to another. Having the use of hands may also have led to the use of tools for digging roots or transporting objects.

In turn, thinking about how to use tools and improve chances for survival led to enlargement of the brain. A bigger-brained infant that had to pass through the birth canal of an upright-walking female had to be born small in body, thus still immature. Such an infant had to remain dependent on its mother for a long time, and a mother saddled with a helpless infant was herself not a very effective provider. Hence, a division of labor according to sex became a necessity for survival. Females were able to forage for plants and roots even with an infant in their arms, but both depended on males for occasional meat, the product of the hunt. The distinctively human habit of food sharing, as well as the institution of the family, may be traced to these beginnings.

Many other social processes and constructs resulted from mechanisms of biological adaptation. Human females lost their estrus (periodic sexual receptivity) and began to be sexually receptive all the time. This helped them forge stronger bonds with specific males, lessened competition among males for females (each male and female could form a pair), and benefited the children, who had the protection of two adults. Rudimentary moral systems based on reciprocal altruism ("do unto others as you would have them do unto you") came into being, as did the incest taboo, designed to force individuals to choose their sexual partners outside their own family or troop, thus minimizing hostilities among troops. Feelings such as gratitude, sympathy, and friendship may have emerged, as well as guilt, shame, and moral indignation, all necessary social tools for keeping groups together and making the individual loyal to the group.

When groups had grown to fairly large size and complexity, some type of organization was needed. It is a characteristic of most primates that they organize themselves into troops, choosing leaders and hierarchies of dominance. Humans followed this tendency and soon there were tribal unions and confederations of various sorts. In a group setting, more rules have to be developed and followed, and thus remembered. Natural selection would favor the

Box 2.6 Using Biology to Interpret History

Although history is considered only partially a social science, of late the tools of biology have been used to arrive at some explanations of human behavior and cultural traditions. The field of biohistory is new, but it is being touted as a new way of understanding the human experience.

A case in point is the example offered by Robert S. McElvaine in his book *Eve's Seed: Biology, the Sexes and the Course of History*, (McGraw-Hill, 2000). Having observed that certain values in Western society are perceived as either masculine or feminine—aggression and competitiveness as masculine, compassion and cooperation as feminine—the author proceeded to research the reasons for these differences between the sexes. What he found was that originally, biological differences between the sexes had few social consequences. In early hunter and gatherer societies, men and women shared power equally to a great extent, because the labor of both was equally important to the survival of the group. When agriculture was invented, however—and the author believes that this invention was mostly the merit of women—the product

of the hunt was no longer as important. The group could survive on the harvest of the fields and the meat of domesticated animals. Because men could not bear or nourish children, they found their roles diminished—they were basically out of a job. This would have occurred around 8000 B.C.

Looking for a new role, men began to take over agriculture, in the process developing the values of aggressiveness and competition. This "maladaptive strategy" eventually led to the tradition of patriarchy, or dominance over women and children, as well as war. What had worked to the advantage of the group on the African savannah—aggressive male hunting behavior—got redirected toward other males and the subjugation of women. The stereotypes we observe now are the result—after thousands of years—of males trying to compensate for the loss of roles for which biological evolution had prepared them, but which a historical accident had taken away from them (Eakin, 2001, A15–A17).

individuals who learned best and remembered longest, as well as those who could inhibit violent impulses.

Progress in social organization and the development of social systems were greatly enhanced by the discovery of fire. The domestication of fire allowed humans to wander farther into colder climates, to keep predators away from campsites, and to inhabit caves, all elements helpful to survival. Fire also encouraged the cooking of food, and the softer food reshaped the contours of the human face. Fire may have promoted personality changes, leading to sociability, an increase in conversation, and thus the further development of language. Finally, fire probably played a distinct role in advancing religious practices.

In the period following the advent of big game hunting, the discovery of fire, and the invention of agriculture, early humans began to resemble modern people to an extraordinary extent. These humans had already evolved a considerable culture, as well as many of the patterns of behavior by which we live today. From then until the present, the social world, with its complexities and contradictions, has been the subject of evolution.

The Chapter in Brief

According to scientific research, the universe is around 13.7 billion years old. The currently dominant theory assumes that it began with a gigantic explosion (the "big bang") that was the result of a submicroscopic, infinitely dense and unimaginably hot knot of pure energy that flew outward in all directions, eventually giving rise to radiation and matter. The force of gravity then drew the matter to denser regions, which, over billions of years, became galaxies, stars, planets, and everything that exists in the universe. The universe is still expanding, although we do not know whether expansion will continue forever or whether eventually it will reverse and collapse.

Life is thought to have originated in the form of microorganisms capable of surviving in an extremely hot environment, and later in the oceans, where simple one-celled organisms developed and acquired the ability to reproduce. Growing in complexity, these organisms eventually gave rise to plants and animals. When plants could survive on dry land, the environment was ready to house living things such as huge reptiles, flying birds, and small mammals. Mammals were the most insignificant of the animals, but they were adaptable and survived great climatic changes. One order of mammals, the primates, took to a life in the trees of the thick forests that were covering the earth and began an evolutionary process that culminated in the emergence of humans.

Evolution functions through a process of natural selection in which individuals who possess a feature that is successful in a given environment multiply and those who lack that feature eventually die out. The study of genetics has clarified how this process works. Mendel found that inherited traits are either dominant or recessive. Traits are never blended, nor do they disappear completely. The dominant ones are expressed, and the recessive ones may wait several generations before reappearing. Variation in species is caused by mutation, gene flow, genetic drift, and migration.

Evolutionary adaptations prompted by climatic changes led the tree-dwelling primates to come down from the trees, become bipedal, and hunt small game. Between 6 and 4 million years ago, primates began to diverge into precursors of modern monkeys and apes, and ancestors of humans. It is believed that a number of prehumans, or hominids, coexisted at one time, but by 1 million years ago, only one, *Homo erectus*, seems to have survived. In the interval between *Homo erectus* and the appearance of *Homo sapiens*, "wise man," such social phenomena as big game hunting, rudimentary families and troops, a division of labor between males and females, and the fundamentals of a moral system appeared. Technology was greatly improved by the discovery and taming of fire. The Neanderthals and the Cro-Magnon were two species that preceded somewhat the emergence of modern humans, the latter being almost indistinguishable from them. The appearance of agriculture some 8,000 years ago closed the long period of human prehistory. Agriculture brought with it a population explosion, the establishment of permanent settlements and cities, warfare, and writing, with which the recorded portion of human history begins.

Terms to Remember

adaptation A process that intervenes to ensure that organisms achieve an adjustment to their environment that is beneficial.

Australopithecus A prehuman who lived from about 4.5 million to 1 million years ago. Some researchers maintain that this type of prehuman is not a direct ancestor of modern humans but rather is a contemporary of an upright-walking, meat-eating, large-brained species that survived; others insist that *Australopithecus* is on the human ancestral line.

chromosomes Carriers of genes, or the hereditary blueprints of organisms. Each human inherits a set of 23 chromosomes from each parent.

Cro-Magnon The closest predecessors or perhaps contemporaries of modern humans, who lived about 35,000 years ago. They were expert toolmakers and artists, and they lived in tribes that displayed evidence of rules and kinship systems.

directional selection Change in gene frequencies is promoted because an adaptation to a new environment is needed.

DNA Deoxyribonucleic acid. A complex biochemical substance that is the basic building block of life. It determines the inheritance of specific traits.

estrus Period of sexual receptivity and ability to conceive.

evolution A theory that explains change in living organisms and variation within species. Evolution functions according to processes of natural selection, mutation, genetic drift, gene flow, and speciation.

gene flow The movement of genes from one gene pool to another. It results in new combinations of genes in the offspring.

gene frequency The proportion in which the various genes occur in an inbreeding population.

gene pool All of the genetic material available to a population to be inherited by the next generation.

genes Hereditary units that transmit an individual's traits. They are contained in the chromosomes and made up of DNA.

genetic drift The fluctuations in frequencies of specific traits in a small, isolated population, so that visible differences between an isolated population and the population from which it broke away become obvious.

genetics The science of heredity.

genotype The actual genetic composition of an organism, which is not necessarily expressed.

hominids Prehuman creatures who walked on two feet.

Homo erectus The upright hominid thought to be a direct ancestor of modern humans.

Homo sapiens A species whose fossils date back 75,000 years (or perhaps 195,000 years) and includes Neanderthals. The species label for modern humans is *Homo sapiens sapiens*, whose fossils date back 30,000 years and include Cro-Magnon.

mutation A permanent change in genetic material.

natural selection A process of evolution in which random traits are tested for their survival value; the successful traits are passed on, while organisms possessing less successful traits eventually become extinct.

Neanderthal A subspecies of *Homo sapiens* (but some consider them hominids) whose fossil remains date from 70,000 to 35,000 years ago. They are known to have buried their dead.

phenotype The physical, or outward, appearance of an organism.

primates An order of mammals to which monkeys, apes, and humans belong.

Ramapithecus A hominoid having hominid-like features, dated between 14 and 8 million years ago.

stabilizing selection When natural selection promotes the status quo rather than change, because change would be detrimental to the organism's adaptation to its environment.

Suggested Readings

Angier, Natalie. 2007. *The Canon: A Whirly-gig Tour of the Beautiful Basics of Science.* New York: Houghton Mifflin. A frequent contributor to the *New York Times* Science pages, the author intends to remedy Americans' ignorance of the basics of science.

Boaz, Noel T. 1997. *Eco Homo: How the Human Being Emerged from the Cataclysmic History of the Earth.* New York: Basic Books. The author maintains that human evolution was spurred by changes in climate, a claim not universally accepted. The human–chimp split, bipedalism, and the development of culture are written about interestingly.

Brace, C. Loring. 1995. *The Stages of Human Evolution,* 5th ed. Englewood Cliffs, NJ: Prentice Hall. A physical anthropology text, in paperback, that offers easily understood, up-to-date facts and principles of the discipline.

Cavalli-Sforza, Luigi Luca. 2001. *Genes, People, and Languages.* Berkeley: University of California Press. A well-known geneticist describes the migrations of our forebears for the last several hundred thousand years. A provocotive survey of human evolution.

Fagan, Brian M. 1992. *People of the Earth: An Introduction to World Prehistory,* 7th ed. New York: HarperCollins. A worldwide look at the findings of archaeologists that reveal some aspects of our prehistoric past.

Haviland, William A. 1994. *Anthropology,* 7th ed. Fort Worth, TX: Harcourt Brace. An anthropology text, in paperback, that includes all the basic divisions of anthropology and presents the concepts and terminology relevant to each.

Stringer, Christopher, and Robin McKie. 1997. *African Exodus: The Origins of Modern Humanity.* New York: A John Macrae Book/Henry Holt & Company. The authors argue for an "out of Africa" theory, that is, that hominids emerged in Africa about a million years ago and spread to the Middle and Far East.

Wells, Spencer. 2003. *The Journey of Man: A Genetic Odyssey*. Princeton, NJ: Princeton University Press. The author is a geneticist who used DNA to identify genetic markers that record the spread of humans around the world. Small mutations in the Y chromosome are passed on from father to son, so that descendants of a single individual can be traced through many generations. Also a PBS documentary.

Web Sites of Interest

http://www.astro.ucla.edu/~wright-cosmology_faw. html
A tutorial in cosmology from the University of California.

http://www.galacticsurf.com/cosmolGB.htm
Offers "cool" sites for amateurs.

http://www.ucmp.berkeley.edu/history/evolution.html
Explores the theory of evolution.

http://www.becominghuman.org
View a documentary, ask questions, surf links.

http://www.talkorigins.org
Explores the creation/evolution controversy.

http://ghr.nlm.nih.gov
A guide to understanding genetics.

http://www.mnh.si.edu/anthro/humanorigins/ha/a_tree. html
The Smithsonian Institution's web site about human origins.

3

Culture: Product and Guide to Life in Society

IN THIS CHAPTER, YOU WILL LEARN

- *what makes humans unique;*
- *the importance of symbols, especially language;*
- *the importance of shared meanings;*
- *why culture is responsible for human progress and the social evolution of societies;*
- *what is the content of culture;*
- *why norms are vital to societies;*
- *the difference between the attitudes of ethnocentrism and cultural relativity;*
- *of the existence of subcultures and countercultures.*

Though all modern humans belong to the same species, *Homo sapiens sapiens*, and are all the result of the same physical evolutionary development, it is obvious to any observer that they differ among themselves. The physical differences are slight: some groups have darker skin or hair, some have mostly blue eyes, some have prominent cheekbones and almond-shaped eyes. All, however, are recognizably members of the group called "humans," both in their physical appearance and especially in their genetic makeup. A group of population geneticists summarized the variation among humans at the level of their chromosomes in this way: with the exception of genes for surface traits such as skin coloration and height, all humans are remarkably alike. In fact, the variation from individual to individual is so much greater than the differences among groups that it makes no sense to speak of "races" at the genetic level. "What the eye sees as racial differences—between Europeans and Africans, for example—are mainly adaptations to climate as humans moved from one continent to another" (Subramanian, 1995, 54). Anthropologists who use genetics in their research also support this finding, noting that external differences are genetically inconsequential. They are small variations that evolved in response to the environment. For instance, the fair skin of northern Europeans, a result of a change in just one gene, may have developed to better absorb sunlight in areas where it was rare and to synthesize vitamin D (Shute, 2001, 40).

The differences among humans are much more apparent in the languages they speak, in the gods they worship, in the governments to which they profess loyalty, and in the traditions they follow. These differences are often quite dramatic, and their causes have aroused curiosity and interest. When they occur within groups that occupy the same territory, they are also often a source of conflict.

In a very basic sense, the differences arise from the fact that people are scattered in different parts of the planet, where they live in groups of all sorts, the largest of which are called societies (see Chapter 4). Within these societies, people mate with partners much like themselves, until through the centuries specific biological traits become characteristic of a group—straight, blond hair and blue eyes, for instance, or dark, curly hair and brown eyes. Similarly, because they interact most frequently with members of the same group—their society—the people of each group come to share similar values, beliefs, and patterns of behavior: in short, they come to share a *culture*.

Culture is extremely important to people and becomes so much a part of individual personality and group characteristics that it has often been mistaken for having a biological origin. The fact is that people who live in groups, close to one another, end up looking and eventually thinking very much alike, whereas those farther removed develop slight or great differences in appearance, customs, languages, religions, and life-styles. In heterogeneous societies, in which members have been drawn from a variety of locations, different groups may be characterized by distinct traits.

It cannot be stressed enough, however, that in spite of the variety we encounter among the peoples of the world and in our own midst, all humans share more qualities than they differ on. In part, the similarities derive from our biological nature, as pointed out by the

Women in Muslim countries subscribe to an extreme cultural interpretation of Islam, which exhorts them to maintain a modest appearance.

research of geneticists. No matter how widely we travel in the world, we observe that all people must eat, although what they eat and when and how they eat may vary tremendously from place to place. All people must sleep, though some do it in beds with thick mattresses and others on thin mats or on bare floors. All people build some sort of shelter for themselves, though some weave their homes out of palm fronds and mud, others from lumber and bricks, and still others, with the help of objects available in their environment, from blocks of ice to sheets of tin. All people classify themselves according to some sort of kinship system, although in some places first cousins are considered the best source of marriage partners and in other places they are taboo for such a purpose. All people develop some kind of social system, with rules for behavior, values, attitudes, customs, and traditions, and all make decisions for survival according to some type of economic system. In short, though people are infinitely different, they are also infinitely alike. If people's common humanity unites them, the differences in cultures tend to divide them. In a society in which a number of cultural groups coexist, therefore, tensions are common. In such societies (and most industrial and postindustrial societies are heterogeneous), people are being pulled in myriad directions, and they do not follow a monolithic set of values, beliefs, behavior guides, and traditions.

■ Culture: Concept and Importance

The term *culture* is one of the most important concepts in the social sciences, for culture is the most easily observed and most distinctive product of our group way of life. While it may be a source of division, it is also what makes us uniquely human. As a term, *culture* is often misunderstood and misused. In everyday conversation, people tend to refer to well-educated persons with good manners or to those who attend concerts of classical music and art exhibits as being cultured. In reality, every individual who was brought up in a social group is cultured, because culture is what results whenever a group of people lives together for any period of time. It becomes the way of life of a people, and whoever learns that way of life absorbs the culture of the group.

Culture is the *product* of a social group—and the group that is generally considered today is society, the largest group in which people live (see Chapter 4). It should be stressed, however, that society and culture are two aspects of the same phenomenon. We are looking at culture in this chapter and at society and other social groupings in the following chapter; but in fact the two are interrelated and interdependent. Society, culture, and the individual form a triangle within which human life is acted out from beginning to end. Culture cannot exist apart from society because it is its product, and it is inconceivable that a society would fail to produce a culture.

What is more, humans cannot exist outside of a social group for very long, at least not until they are self-reliant, when exposure to the group's culture has already taken place. An individual who has not undergone such exposure can hardly be called human. Quite a few instances of infants isolated from human interaction exist. In all cases, these "feral" ("savage; wild-animal-like") individuals either die in childhood or survive as animal-like creatures, without the ability to walk or communicate in a human way. They are not truly human, for they fail to learn how to act as humans do. An individual, then, is dependent on his or her social group for physical survival and for learning how to be human. What individuals learn is precisely the culture of the society into which they are born and more specifically of the social group to which they belong.

Culture is not only an outgrowth of interaction; it becomes itself a pattern for further interaction. The relationship of culture to society may be better understood in a theatrical context. Society may be compared to a group of actors who play roles befitting their characters according to the position they occupy in the play. The script used by the actors is comparable to culture. Just as a script is written by a playwright for actors to perform, so culture has been established by generations of humans for their descendants to live by; but the creation of culture is a much less deliberate act than the creation of a play. However, just as a playwright edits the script, changing some roles and expanding others, so, too, each generation adds, deletes, changes, and modifies some parts of culture.

Biological Predispositions to Culture

Although biology is responsible for our ability to speak and symbolize—and thus, indirectly, for our ability to create culture—it is also very limiting. In many respects the human biological makeup has made it difficult for people to survive on earth. Because humans cannot breathe in water, vast parts of the earth are uninhabitable to them. Because they have a thin layer of skin with very little hair on it, they need protection from the elements. Because they lack the claws and fangs and poisons of many animals, they must develop other means of defending themselves.

These biological shortcomings are more than made up for, however, by the qualities humans *do* possess. These include: (1) a grasping hand with a thumb that can be opposed to the other four fingers, enabling them to handle the most delicate of objects; (2) an upright posture, freeing the forelimbs to handle and carry objects; (3) stereoscopic (two-eyed, with overlapping fields) vision, enabling them to focus far or near; (4) highly complicated vocal equipment, making it possible for them to speak; and (5) an extremely well-developed brain, part of a complex nervous system that coordinates the functioning of the whole human machine.

It is this biological equipment that has made it possible for humans to create culture. In turn, culture has been a tool for adapting to the environment in those instances where physical qualities were lacking. And the fact that language made it possible to communicate information made the process that much easier and faster.

The Birth of Culture

No doubt there was evidence of culture even among small groups of hominids able to communicate with one another. Anthropologists generally maintain that ever since *Homo erectus*—that is, between 100,000 and 40,000 years ago—cultural evolution has been more important than biological evolution. In other words, human populations began to depend on the development of appropriate tools, food production, clothes, shelter, and weapons to counter certain environmental problems, rather than depending on the alteration of their genetic makeup through natural selection to reach the same goal. This was not, of course, a conscious choice, but rather the result of interaction based on the human ability to communicate. It may be said, then, that human groups began to rely on brainpower, or their cognitive capacity, for survival. What is meant by brainpower is not limited to intelligence but includes other skills: the ability to learn, to form concepts, to be creative, self-aware, and reliable, to be able to evaluate oneself and others, to perform under stress, and so on.

The first evidence of an explosion of culture, usually termed the Middle/Upper Paleolithic transition, included the following major developments (thought to have originated between 40,000 and 30,000 years ago):

1. change in stone-working technology from flakes to blades, including the technique of attaching blades to handles.
2. widespread manufacture and use of tools and weapons made from bone, antler, and ivory, including the techniques of grinding and polishing.

3. appearance of ornamentation of the body by means of jewelry made of pierced teeth, as well as beads and perforated shells.

4. the first representational art forms, such as engravings on bone and stone, as well as ivory sculptures.

5. reliance on a specific animal, such as reindeer in Western Europe, for food.

6. a shift from living in small, dispersed groups to a pattern of several large groups occupying large sites in addition to many smaller sites.

7. higher population densities and expansion in previously uninhabited zones, such as Australia and the Americas.

8. during the Upper Paleolithic period, rapid and continuous technological change and innovation, as well as the first evidence of variation in forms of artifacts from region to region (Jolly and White, 1995, 368).

Anthropologists are still debating the reasons for the occurrences outlined above. Many suggest that they resulted from climatic changes and from the appearance of language as a form of symbolic communication. Others believe that language had been present prior to the emergence of *Homo sapiens*, at least in a rudimentary form. There is agreement that for the first time all elements of what we call culture were present: language, art, religion, technology, and so on.

Another dramatic change in human cultures occurred around 10,000 years ago as a result of the end of the last glacial era. Areas that had been covered by ice became available for human settlement; grasslands changed into deciduous forests; and rivers and seas were teeming with aquatic life. These changes in the physical environment required changes in the way of life of people. As some of the large animals that had been objects of the hunt became extinct, people turned to hunting smaller animals and depending more on seafood and other

The most important element of culture is language. Each language, however, reflects a specific culture. Therefore, it is very difficult to communicate across cultures. This American soldier, speaking through a translator, is trying to question an Iraqi man. Although the words are translated, their meaning and the way they are spoken will undoubtedly be misunderstood.

In industrial and postindustrial societies weaving was long ago taken over by machines. In traditional societies, however, much weaving is still done by hand, and young weavers are taught the skill by their elders.

China is a rapidly industrializing society, entering the twenty-first century with giant steps. This is the way textiles are produced today.

local resources. Finally, this is the time in which the domestication of plants and animals, and ultimately agriculture, emerges, evoking yet again dramatic changes in culture: a sedentary life-style, population increases that may have forced people to move to new areas, bringing their culture with them, the beginning of trade, increased manufacture and use of pottery, indicating a settled way of life in agricultural villages, the building of permanent housing, and the weaving of textiles. An agricultural way of life marks the beginning of civilization. New archeological discoveries on the border between Syria and Turkey have yielded clay tablets with cuneiform writing, indicating that an early urban civilization and literacy were present more than 5,000 years ago in the region (Wilford, 1993, B7).

The agricultural era, rendered more sophisticated by the founding of numerous cities, and eventually states, endured for a very long time. It was supplanted only around the middle of the eighteenth century by a system called industrialism. That system is only now being pushed aside by one based on artificial, computer-driven intelligence.

Cultural Evolution and Sociobiology

Darwin's theory of evolution, discussed in the preceding chapter, was enormously influential not only in the biological sciences but also in the social sciences. A number of social thinkers began to adapt Darwin's ideas to the social world, speculating, for instance, that the reason humans, dispersed in a variety of environments, have nonetheless remained similar in appearance is due to the fact that they evolved through culture rather than biological adaptation. This view came to be called *cultural evolution* because it maintained that the most successful cultural adaptations were handed down to the next generation, while the least successful disappeared. An English social philosopher, Herbert Spencer (1873), coined the phrase "survival of the fittest," by which he meant that those who were most successful at adapting in a particular society—those who prospered—had the best chances of surviving the longest and passing on the successful traits to their children. These ideas, known later as *social Darwinism*, were interpreted to mean that Western societies, having become the wealthiest and most powerful in the world with their adoption of capitalism and adaptation to the industrial system, were superior to all others. This interpretation was rejected by later social scientists, who concluded that cultural evolution did not result from superior individuals but rather from other social factors. (See **http://en.wikipedia.org/wiki/cultural_ evolution.**)

The idea that some human behaviors depend on biology and not strictly on culture has continued to reappear, however. The discipline of *sociobiology*, a term coined by the Harvard biologist Edward O. Wilson (1980), attempts to apply genetic factors to social behavior. Such factors exist in relation to animals, but it is a matter of controversy whether they also exist in human societies. For instance, sociobiologists maintain that some human behaviors, particularly aggression, homosexuality, and even religious feelings, are genetically programmed and not simply learned through socialization. Although a number of studies have claimed to have found genes responsible for certain behaviors (especially in the case of homosexuality), it is safe to say that behavior is the result of the interaction between culture and biology. Several web sites discuss sociobiology in greater detail: **http://www.ship.edu/ ~cgboeree/sociobiology.html** and **http://www.psych.ucsb.edu/research/cep/index.html**.

What, Then, Is Culture?

We have been speaking of culture, its origin and importance, without actually ever defining it. **Culture** is everything that humans make, use, learn, know, and believe. It is how they behave and what they share with each other and transmit to each new generation in the attempt to deal with the demands their common life makes on them. Culture is something that humans create and have done so for thousands of years. It is what each generation inherits from the preceding one and to which each generation adds its own touch. It is uniquely human (though this is subject to argument, because studies of nonhuman primates indicate that they too are capable of some forms of communication and the use of simple tools). It includes all the accumulated knowledge, beliefs, ideas, values, goals, as well as all the material objects that groups of people have ever invented or used. Culture is learned during the process of socialization—learning to be human—through *symbolic interaction*, that is, language and gestures with which we communicate. Culture evolved to allow humans to adapt to their various environments without waiting for genetic alterations. Culture provides each individual with ways of satisfying biological and emotional needs in the best manner possible, without having to personally do so by trial and error. While each society develops a culture that is distinct from other cultures—because it is a response to a specific environment—all cultures share similarities because they are reactions to universal human needs. Cultures, just like the groups that create them, are in a constant state of flux.

■ The Symbolic Nature of Culture

The most important quality of culture is its symbolic nature. Humans are called the "culture-bearing" animals because of their ability to create and use symbols. One reason animals other than humans lack a rich culture is that they lack this ability.

Animals communicate through a system of *signals* that are biologically determined and genetically transmitted responses to outside stimuli. Animals yelp in response to pain, run in response to fear, and kill in response to hunger. Of course, animals can also be taught to act in ways that are not instinctual: dogs can be taught to sit, to stay in one place, to stand on their hind legs, to come close, and to fetch the paper. However, a dog so trained will not be able to teach its newborn puppy to behave similarly; a human will have to perform this training (although some types of learned behavior are apparently passed on by some animals). Human parents, on the other hand, teach their offspring by showing them or telling them, that is, by using symbols. The advantage of this system is clear: if you can tell your child how to do something that will aid in his or her survival—or comfort—then your child does not have to waste time finding out this information by trial and error. In short, the wheel does not have to be reinvented in each generation; instead, people can refine and build on the inventions of their forebears and, therefore, have time to think about new inventions.

The Necessity of Sharing Symbols

Because we communicate through symbols, we can teach our children and have, in fact, taught them through an endless chain of generations. Symbols are arbitrary signs that can be used in an abstract manner and whose meanings are communally agreed upon, that is, shared by the group. All English-speaking people, for instance, agree that the sound of the word *bread* stands for a type of food made with the basic ingredients of flour, water, and yeast. The word "bread" is not the object bread; it only symbolizes, or stands for, the food. The point is that the sound means nothing to someone who does not understand English, nor does it mean anything to someone in a society in which there is no such food. Symbols must be understood and shared by members of a society, or they are meaningless. Consequently, symbols vary from culture to culture. In Japan, one bows to be polite; in the United States, bowing is an expression of inferiority or submission, so it is not done except perhaps in church. To an American, a baseball bat is something used in a popular sport; to an inhabitant of the Amazon who has no access to television, it is a piece of wood, a thick tree branch shaped in such a way that it can be used to hit someone or something. Every American child knows what the red, white, and blue cloth means when it flutters in the wind in front of a school or federal building. If, however, someone were to visit from a society in which there was no state, unaware of the symbolism inherent in a flag, the object would simply be perceived as a piece of multicolored fabric.

■ Language: The Most Important System of Symbols

Language is the most effective system of symbols used by humans, but it is not the only one. Gestures—including body language of which people may not be consciously aware—music, and the visual arts are other symbol systems used to communicate. These too must be shared with members of one's social group; otherwise, they are misunderstood or not understood at all. For instance, in the United States we nod our heads when we mean yes and shake it from side to side when we mean no, but in other societies the reverse is true or some other symbolic system prevails.

Different societies also vary in the use of space in communication. In North America and northern Europe, people stand about three feet away from one another when conversing, particularly if they are strangers or mere acquaintances. South Americans stand much closer to one another in similar circumstances. Thus, a North American might consider

Although language is the most important system of symbols humans use, each society uses many other symbols. All Americans know, for example, that our flag stands for our country.

a South American pushy or fresh for standing so close, whereas the South American might think the North American cold and unfriendly for standing so far away.

In language, symbols are employed to name things, individuals, and categories. The fact that every object and even intangible abstractions have a name seems natural and commonplace to us, but to someone who has not been taught the shared symbols, it is not necessarily so apparent. Helen Keller, blind and deaf from shortly after birth, describes the moment when she realized that everything had a name as a revelation that literally began life anew for her:

> Suddenly I felt a misty consciousness of something forgotten—a thrill of returning thought; and somehow the mystery of language was revealed to me. I knew then that "w-a-t-e-r" meant the wonderful cool something that was flowing over my hand. That living word awakened my soul; gave it light, hope, joy, set it free! (Keller, 1903)

Language plays a particularly important role in the development and transmission of culture. There cannot be a flourishing culture without language because language makes possible a wide range of communication, which in turn allows people to engage in coordinated group activities that help them to survive. Historically, language facilitated cooperation in hunting ventures. Successful hunting meant fairly constant food supplies, which led to the establishment of permanent communities (cities and nations) and a more efficient division of labor.

While it is itself the most significant invention or product of culture, language is the foundation on which culture is erected and by which it is transmitted. The social life of humans is dramatically affected by language. Their range of knowledge is infinitely expanded because it is not necessary for each individual to experience events personally. Instead, countless experiences can be told to countless people, countless times.

Language goes far beyond the signal systems that other animals use. It allows humans to create the dimensions of time and space so that events that occurred long ago (history, tradition) and far away (geography) may be related. With language, it is possible to project what might happen, or what a person wishes would happen, in the future. One can share individual thoughts and feelings, as well as information. Although the words of each language stand for, or symbolize, real objects or activities or events, they can also be made to symbolize abstractions and feelings, such as loyalty or love. Language can even be used to express things people have not experienced, such as God, as long as people agree that God can be experienced. People invent words to express everything that emerges in their culture and find new words to fit new cultural patterns as they appear. There were no such words as "groupies" or "hippies" before the 1960s, expressions such as "user friendly" before the late 1970s, "videos" and "cyberspace" before the 1980s, "the Internet" and "web site" before the 1990s, or "texting" before 2000, and words such as "obesogenic" in the twenty-first century, an era in which obesity has become endemic in the West.

Because of language, knowledge spreads and accumulates. Knowledge accumulation is greatly speeded up and expanded when writing is added to the spoken word; but even in societies in which writing has not been invented, special individuals are designated to preserve and pass on orally certain kinds of knowledge deemed necessary or desirable for the members of the society to know. Again, transmitting culture means that each generation does not need to rediscover things; each new generation can build on the experiences of previous generations. In fact, it is significant that cultures survive the societies in which they originate. Ancient Greece and Imperial Rome ceased to exist thousands of years ago, yet their cultures have left profound marks on all of Western civilization. The literature and art of the ancient Greeks and Romans are still read and admired today. Language, then, is a most important social tool.

Does Language Create Reality?

Because of the interrelationship of language and culture, some social scientists have maintained that the very structure of language shapes people's reactions and attitudes toward reality. As an example, they cite the fact that in some languages there is no way to express the idea of past or future because the societies in which the languages developed did not focus on any time but the present. In the native language of the Sioux tribe of Native Americans, for instance, the idea of being late or of waiting cannot be expressed. For them these ideas do not exist; they view the world from the perspective of the present. The Hopi do not differentiate between the past and the present; you cannot express the idea that you went somewhere yesterday but you are home today. In other languages, certain phenomena can be expressed with an infinite number of nuances. Filipinos have 92 different ways of describing rice, a staple of their diet. In English, we recognize a distinction between the words "fear" and "shame," but to some Australian Aborigines, the two words are one and can also mean shyness, embarrassment, or respect. The Chinese say that their language is simply not a language for lovers: the expressions "I love you," and "kiss" sound so foreign and formal in Chinese that those who know English use that language to express their feelings in their intimate relations rather than using their native tongue. Chinese also has no equivalents of "dear," or "sweetie," or "honey," so that in dubbing American movies, rough approximations have to be coined that prompt explosions of giggles in viewers. The reason such words are lacking in Chinese is that Chinese culture is one in which people are reluctant to express emotions openly, and the Chinese are restrained and shy when it comes to expressing love. Dating was for years prohibited in high school and discouraged in college, and to kiss in public or in the view of others is still considered shameful, although these customs are giving way in the wake of China's embrace of the free market. The language in fact has more words describing rice than love (Kristof, 1991). Finally, in the fictional work *1984* by George Orwell, the newly created language Newspeak did not contain a word for freedom.

Consequently, people could not think about or desire freedom. Think of the consequences of such an absence!

Two anthropologists who became linguistic experts, Edward Sapir and his student and later colleague Benjamin L. Whorf, wrote that languages are not simply a matter of attaching labels to things and thoughts (Sapir, 1960; Whorf, 1956). On the contrary, languages are a reflection of people's thoughts, feelings, and actions, and in turn they shape the way people think, feel, and act. In short, it is our language that tells us what is real and true; it is our language that shows us how to interpret the external world. We can know the world only as far as our language permits it—if there is no word for something, that something does not exist for us (this is known as the Sapir-Whorf hypothesis). That is why every language has some words or expressions that have no counterpart in another language, making the work of a translator very difficult. Sapir concluded that, in effect, members of different societies may be said to live in "distinct worlds, not merely the same world with different labels attached" (Sapir, 1949, 162). A more recent study by Peter Gordon of Columbia University supports the Sapir-Whorf hypothesis. The researcher studied an isolated Amazon tribe whose members—only 200 people—do not count beyond the number two. Anything larger than two is referred to as "many." The researcher wanted to know whether this limits their perception of larger amounts. In a test in which they were asked to match small groups of items according to how many there were, they performed well when there were only two or three items but always answered incorrectly when there were more than three objects to match. The conclusion of the researcher was that language indeed affects perceptions of reality, although he added the caveat that his study may reflect only a unique situation (Graham, 2004, www. sciam. com/ article). Indeed, the Sapir-Whorf hypothesis should not be interpreted as meaning that language restricts or limits a person's perception of reality forever. The fact is that language and culture give rise to each other: language changes in response to changes in the content of culture, but at the same time, it is an important factor in shaping cultural content.

■ The Content of Culture

A society's culture is taken for granted by the people who make up that society. They believe their culture is the only "right" one and that things are done, were always done, and ought to be done as they are in their society. That is the reason for the "culture shock" people experience when they first encounter a society in which things are done differently than in their own. People generally accept their culture because they have been socialized to accept it—they have grown up with it and have not been encouraged to examine it dispassionately. When culture is analyzed, it becomes clear that it consists of a large number of elements.

Material Culture

First, a good portion of culture is visible and tangible, because it consists of the huge number of products conceived and manufactured by humans. All material objects, from the primitive stone ax of our prehistoric ancestors to the complex computer on which these words are being written, belong to the category of material culture. Material objects are created to fill a shared need of the society. They come into being when one individual has an idea that is seized upon by others, who may add to, modify, and change the idea, and put it to use.

The automobile, for instance, was the foremost symbol of industrial society, just as the computer is of contemporary postindustrial society. The automobile was the result of an idea that took hold and continued to be developed throughout countless generations of people. No doubt, an ancient human honed a stone into a circular shape or found one ready-made and noticed how rapidly it rolled down an incline. Someone else, faced with the necessity of dragging a heavy boulder, thought of the possibility of having the round stone—wheel—do most of the backbreaking labor of moving it. Later, after animals had been domesticated, other ingenious (or lazy?) individuals experimented with attaching wheels to a cart, placing heavy objects inside, and letting oxen or horses pull it, again easing the hard work of agriculture and speeding up the transportation of people and things. Much later still, when the steam engine and the internal combustion engine were invented, wheels were attached to these machines and people could ride in comfort and speed in boats, on railroad trains, and finally in automobiles. The originators of the automobile industry, then, simply applied the finishing touches to an idea born of the human brain and produced by human hands many thousands of years ago. Incidentally, the knowledge needed to put elements of material culture together to obtain new products is a function of **technology**, a practical application of knowledge. Technology includes material objects and the rules and procedures that govern them. Thus, it spans material and nonmaterial culture. (Technology is discussed in the context of sociocultural change, Chapter 10.)

Nonmaterial Culture

The other component of culture consists of abstractions that include knowledge, beliefs, values, and rules for behavior. This part of culture is the nonmaterial part, but the material and nonmaterial parts are not distinct entities. For instance, for the automobile to be built, not only did raw materials have to exist but also ideas about the necessity for rapid and comfortable transportation. Finally, the knowledge of how to make the different parts of the vehicle work had to be present. Social scientists, as may be expected, are concerned chiefly with the nonmaterial aspects of culture, because most of human life is shaped by and carried out in the context of beliefs, values, and behavioral rules.

■ The Components of Nonmaterial Culture: Cognitive and Normative

Nonmaterial culture consists of cognitive and normative components (Figure 3.1). The cognitive component includes the definitions that people give to everything that exists, or to everything they think exists. More specifically, it includes *knowledge, beliefs*, and *technology* (in the sense of knowledge of procedures for completing tasks). The normative component consists of *values, norms* (further divided into folkways, mores, and laws), *institutions*, and *sanctions*. The normative component is, if possible, an even more important feature of culture because it includes rules for behavior, and human societies could not exist if people did not follow rules.

The Normative System

The *normative system* deals primarily with *rules* (norms) that specify what ought, or ought not, to be. Norms "designate any standard or rule that states what human beings should or should not think, say, or do under given circumstances" (Blake & Davis, 1964). Norms, however, are derived from values.

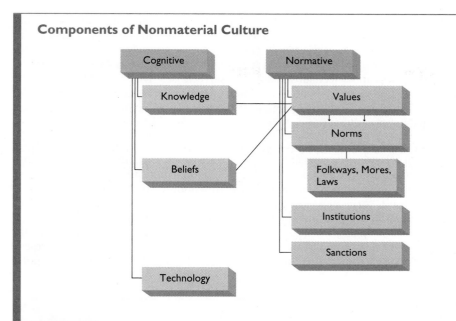

Components of Nonmaterial Culture

FIGURE 3.1

Values. *Values* are abstract evaluations that certain kinds of behaviors, actions, or systems are good, right, moral, beautiful, or ethical—and, therefore, that these items are desirable. For instance, the sociologist Robin Williams (1970) has listed the following values that are recognized in American society: equal opportunity, achievement and success, activity and hard work, efficiency and practicality, progress, science, material comfort, morality, freedom, democracy, humanitarianism, individualism, external conformity, in-group superiority, and patriotism. He could have added other characteristics valued by Americans: optimism, sociability, honesty, and romantic love. Decades later, some of these values are just as valid, although there has been a slight change of emphasis. Americans value freedom over equality, self-reliance over government intervention, and education for the sake of upward mobility over education for the sake of expanding one's knowledge and understanding. Some American values, moreover, may be in the process of change: while many Americans are materialistic, some express a willingness to stop the race toward material acquisition to spend more time with their families.

Values are not often spelled out specifically but rather can be inferred from the way people behave. When we see superthin young women modeling clothes and magazine after magazine displaying diets and exercise programs on their covers, we may safely guess that thinness is a value in our society. Moreover, values are often contradictory. To achieve success in business, it may be necessary to forgo some elements of honesty or morality. We value individualism but also require a degree of conformity. Our belief in equality does not preclude our feeling superior to groups who differ from us in race or religion or from attempting to obtain advantages for the group to which we belong.

Values are also often in a state of flux, although some of our values have remained stable throughout our existence as a society. One often hears the accusation that Americans have lost their work ethic—that the "me" generation of the 1960s and 1970s, unlike their predecessors, was interested in fulfilling the self. On the other hand, the value of monogamous sexual relationships seems to be regaining some of its former preeminence after a period of "sexual revolution." The so-called family values, that is, a strong belief in marriage, fidelity, and bearing and raising children within the family circle, are being strongly espoused by certain segments of our society. Of course, because we are a highly heterogeneous society nowadays, not all segments of American society subscribe to the same values, which itself is a matter of much controversy. A good example is provided by the proposition that homosexual couples should be allowed to marry. While one portion of the population favors this idea, another portion is so strongly opposed that it recommends a constitutional amendment to forbid it.

Norms.   *Norms*, which have been defined as rules or standards prescribing how one ought to act, think, or even feel on given occasions, cover a wide range of circumstances. They dictate conduct in formal and informal situations as well as in significant and less significant ones. They cover everything from when, how, and with whom to shake hands to when it is permissible and when it is forbidden to kill another person.

Norms are internalized by the individual, becoming part of that individual's personality and belief system. So thoroughly are most norms internalized by most people that they are obeyed not simply out of fear of punishment but because people believe that norms represent the "right" or correct way to act. Breaking norms produces guilt feelings in most people.

The normative system of culture consists mainly of rules of behavior that societies have established for the good of their members. If these rules are couched in religious terms—God says you must do this and refrain from doing that—they are much more likely to be followed, particularly by the believers. In Judeo-Christian societies, the Ten Commandments, which the Old Testament in the Bible says were given to Moses by God, are still widely observed.

In short, the cultural norms that originate in each society are essentially a set of *behavioral expectations*, a system that tells a member of a society how that society expects the individual to behave in a wide range of circumstances.

All cultural components are intimately interrelated. The normative system provides rules and standards of behavior, based on values, but these derive from the cognitive component of culture. We can say, then, that **beliefs** are what most people *think* is true about the reality of the world around them, while **values** are what most people think is *good and right*. **Norms** are how most people think they and others *should* behave, and how they in fact *do* behave most of the time. Norms are reflections of values, which in turn are reflections of beliefs.

Imperfect Agreement. The various components of culture are never in perfect agreement. Especially in heterogeneous societies, people accept conflicting norms, values, and beliefs. For instance, although Americans maintain that they believe in the equality of all people, they also believe in the value of competition, which leads to the success of some and the failure of others and, as a consequence, to inequality of income and life-styles. Individualism is another important value in American society, having gained a foothold when the early settlers thought of the New World as a place where the individual could get ahead on his or her own initiative, without the shackles of class and status that prevailed in the Old World. Since then, individualism in one form or another has persisted as an important value of American culture. Critics charge that individualism, in the sense of obsession with the self, has harmed public life and the public good (by which is meant the good of the society), but others believe they are seeing a reversal of this untrammeled individualism in the number of people who express a need for coherence and meaning in their lives, as well as commitment to others rather than sheer personal achievement.

Social Integration. When norms, values, and beliefs are in agreement, the society in which that culture exists is considered to be well integrated. *Social integration* is never total, but a degree of cultural integration is a must. The United States is an example of a society that is only *loosely* integrated. For instance, there is a wide array of beliefs on almost every issue: abortion, the death penalty, affirmative action, drug testing, and so on. A loose form of integration is true of all urban industrial and postindustrial societies, particularly those that consist of more than one cultural group.

On the opposite end of the continuum we find *closely* integrated societies, such as that of Japan. Japan will probably not continue to remain so closely integrated for very long, but for the moment, having been isolated for many centuries and having cultivated a homogeneous citizenry, the Japanese agree on most of the important values and beliefs of their society, displaying the characteristics of an extremely well-integrated social order.

Categories of Norms: Folkways, Mores, Taboos, and Laws

Norms are classified by social scientists according to their importance and functions. One category of norms consists of *folkways*, which are norms that specify expected behavior in *everyday* situations.

Norms that guide human behavior in areas of life that are considered of extreme importance are called *mores*. (*Mores* is a Latin word, the plural of *mos*, meaning custom.) Mores define for people whether a specific act is right or wrong, or its morality or immorality. A person who consistently violates some folkway, such as by becoming drunk at a dinner party, may be excluded by the hostess in the future; but a person who violates mores, such as killing another dinner guest, is punished in the name of society (that is, by some legal action).

The violation of mores is considered a crime against the whole society. Mores that are expressed in negative terms ("thou shalt not") and that deal with acts considered extremely repellent to the social group are categorized as *taboos*. In most societies, taboos include incest and cannibalism.

Taboos are deeply etched in the conscience of most members of a society. Some people are physically incapable of performing an act that is forbidden so strongly, but other influences on the personality may weaken the hold of taboos and mores in general. To prevent this, or to clarify and strengthen the effect of mores and taboos, societies pass laws that prohibit specific acts under penalty of imprisonment and even death. *Laws* are formal codes of behavior that are binding on the whole society. They specify both the behavior that is considered deviant and the punishment appropriate for each kind of deviation. The punishment is meted out by official representatives of the society.

Laws are particularly necessary in a complex, heterogeneous society that is experiencing rapid social change, because many norms are not clear enough for so many different groups of people to understand or accept. In simpler societies that have stronger kinship ties, a smaller number of norms is sufficient to prevent much deviation. Unlike norms, laws are not internalized by the individual (they do not become part of his or her personality) but are learned and obeyed by a majority of people because they are based on rational ideas that are understood and accepted by most. The more closely laws reinforce mores that are universally accepted in a society, the more successful the laws are.

An advantage of laws over folkways and mores is that they can be repealed or modified if they do not work. Folkways and mores, on the other hand, tend to persist as habits and customs long after their usefulness in society has passed. That is one reason why laws are sometimes passed in a society with the hope that the folkways and mores will eventually follow.

The Need for Social Control

Do normative systems have a purpose in societies? Most emphatically, they do. Every group must ensure that its members conform to most of its expectations most of the time. If they do not, anarchy and disorder prevail and the business of the group, the reason for which it was formed, cannot go on. This is especially true if the group in question is society, because the business of society concerns the health and welfare of a large number of people. Consider what would happen if we could not trust other drivers on the road to stop at a red light. Rush-hour traffic, bad as it is when most drivers obey the rules of the road, would be a total nightmare, leaving in its wake many dead or maimed every day. Society, therefore, must have ways of exerting a certain amount of control over its members to make them obey at least the rules that are vital to the survival of the group.

A society exerts this social control in a number of ways. The ultimate form of control is physical force. Physical force is at the core of political power and authority. A person who represents such power and authority may use physical force against an individual who breaks the law. Thus, a police officer may knock to the ground an alleged perpetrator of a crime who is trying to escape and may even shoot if the individual does not heed the officer's request to halt. However, a society that depends on force alone to exert social control is a harsh one, characterized by much conflict or oppression.

More frequently, societies depend on more subtle methods of social control. Social control can be exerted by economic pressure: the need to get and keep a job has most workers toeing the line as far as company regulations are concerned. Occupational pressures have the effect of making a majority of individuals perform their duties appropriately

Box 3.1   **From Folkways to Laws**

The larger and more heterogeneous societies become, the more likely it is that folkways and mores give way to laws. When large numbers of people became automobile drivers, a whole list of laws had to be enacted to regulate what was, and was not, permissible to do while driving a car. A more recent example, and one that is likely to have people exclaim, "What's this world coming to!" is taking place in Great Britain. That country has long had a reputation for its polite ways. The last couple of decades, however, have seen a large influx of immigrants from other cultures. In addition, Great Britain has undergone some of the same changes that have been endemic in the West: the breakdown of traditional families, large-scale drug abuse, lesser deference given to older persons and people of high status, a system of social welfare that sometimes creates in its beneficiaries an attitude of entitlement without the need for responsibility, and a philosophy popularized in the 1960s of "letting it all hang out" and the importance of the individual rather than of the social group.

One of the results of this has been a deterioration of standards of behavior, to the point where the government has had to step in and enact a number of laws, collectively known as "antisocial behavior orders." Since the passage of those laws, about 1,600 Britons have been served such orders and have been fined, jailed, or evicted from public housing for such things as truancy, vandalism, drunken brawling, defacing public property, or harassing neighbors. Some recipients of these orders can be banned from entering specific neighborhoods or maintaining a

relationship with—even visiting—specific people. If an individual is caught stealing from a store, for instance, he or she is banned from entering that store again. Individuals in gangs who are caught committing burglaries, threatening neighbors, or committing acts of vandalism are jailed, and on leaving jail they are not permitted to see their former colleagues in crime for a certain period of time.

Not everyone agrees that such laws are necessary. Most Britons, however, maintain that a lack of respect for others is an increasing component of life in crowded central cities and in the vast housing projects where many people live. They add that parents no longer set boundaries for children and that people no longer recognize that living in civil society requires a mutuality of duty and a reciprocity of respect. They believe, therefore, that the government must step in and tell offenders what they can and cannot do (Lyall, 2004, 1, A6).

Great Britain is certainly not the only society experiencing a loosening of the rules of a civil society. Persons of a certain age in the United States are equally horrified at the language many young people use; at the aggressive manner in which people drive, cutting in and out of traffic to gain a minute without regard for other drivers; at the profanities that are heard on radio and television; and at the general lack of manners on the part of service persons. We have not yet made use of laws to reverse this trend, nor is it clear whether laws can do so, but it would certainly make for a more pleasant life if some of the old folkways were still followed!

in or out of their place of work; a minister, priest, or rabbi, therefore, is not likely to be seen at the corner tavern on Saturday night, though some of the parishioners may spend their time this way.

Sanctions.   Perhaps the most effective pressures exerted by societies come in the form of *sanctions*. Sanctions may be negative or positive, official or unofficial. *Negative sanctions* consist of punishment, while *positive sanctions* represent rewards. For instance, being named to the Supreme Court after a distinguished career in law is an official positive sanction; it is a reward offered in the name of the whole society. Being told by an instructor that one's paper shows brilliant insights is an unofficial positive sanction; it is a reward received within a small group. A person who is jailed as a result of breaking a federal, state, or local law receives an official negative sanction; the individual is punished in the name of society. The theater patron who is asked to leave because of noisy, rude behavior receives an unofficial negative sanction; the individual is being punished, but more informally because the infraction is less severe and damages a small group, not the society as a whole.

Suprisingly, the unofficial sanctions, those that appear to be less severe, have the most impact on individuals. The reason for this is that we value members of our primary groups, our family and friends, more than we do the official representatives of the larger society, even though the latter have more power to affect our lives negatively. In other words, we would rather get a speeding ticket from a police officer than be told by our fathers that we are lousy drivers.

In the final analysis, social control through the enforcement of norms works because individuals are so anxious to be accepted by the group. Researchers have found that, even in group discussions, individuals tend eventually to change their minds to conform to the consensus of opinions expressed by other individuals. In a group of 20, if 15 argue one point and 5 argue the opposite point, chances are good that in time the 5 opponents will come to agree with the majority. In society, too, people yearn for acceptance; thus, many more are conformists than nonconformists.

Overt and Covert, Real and Ideal Norms

Before leaving a discussion of norms, a few more points should be noted. First, although the norms of their culture are firmly embedded in the personality of most individuals, this is not true of each and every individual. There is always a minority of people in every society who ignore some of the norms, but no one who ignores or rejects all social norms can continue to live in a social group. Second, in every society some norms emerge that are not officially accepted as proper behavior but that are widely practiced by people anyway. So it is possible to speak of an *overt* culture, which describes the officially accepted patterns of behavior, and of a *covert* culture, according to which some people actually behave. For instance, a person who publicly subscribes to a high moral system of sexual behavior may be found to engage in promiscuous sexual behavior privately.

The fact is that we can recognize in each society an *ideal* culture, consisting of the formal, approved folkways, mores, and laws, and the real culture, consisting of what people actually do and how they really behave. Although this situation may be considered hypocritical, the existence of the ideal culture provides a model of behavior toward which people may aspire.

Traits, Complexes, and Institutions

For purposes of analysis, culture is further classified into traits, complexes, and institutions. *Traits* are the smallest element, or unit, of culture. In material culture, every single object that people in a society use is a trait. In nonmaterial culture, every single idea, symbol, or belief existing in a society is a trait. A nail, a brick, and a house are all traits of material culture; saluting the flag (denoting patriotism), kissing (a symbol of affection), voting (a belief in a particular political system), and praying (faith in a transcendent life) are all traits of nonmaterial culture.

A number of related traits that accumulate around an activity form a *culture complex*. Football is a culture complex consisting of material traits (the pigskin itself, uniforms, helmets, a field, etc.) and nonmaterial traits (the ability of the players, a set of rules, a belief in winning, team spirit, etc.). All areas of human life display numerous culture complexes.

When a number of culture complexes cluster around a central human activity, an institution emerges. *Institutions* are formal systems of beliefs and behavior composed of interrelated norms and culture complexes. In the example above, sport is the institution of which football is a culture complex.

■ Pivotal Institutions

What is important about institutions is that they emerge around some fundamental human *need* that must be filled for the individual to survive and the society to prosper. The five basic (or pivotal) institutions, which arose from the five most fundamental human needs, are the family (need to replenish society with new members, regulate sex, and care for the helpless newborn); the economy (need to procure food, shelter, and clothing); government (need to maintain peace and order); education (need to transmit culture and train new generations); and religion (need to overcome fear of the unknown and find explanations of the meaning of life).

These five basic institutions are common to all societies. However, the forms they assume and the traits and complexes they display differ from society to society. In later chapters, each of the pivotal institutions of American society is discussed in some detail. For now, it is well to note that institutions are cultural instruments designed to show people how to behave in such a way as to benefit them and the society and fulfill their biological needs in the best possible manner. Cultural institutions are entrenched so well in societal members that they come to believe that their needs cannot be fulfilled in any other way. In fact, those who fail to behave according to the precepts of one institution or another are ostracized and often believe themselves to be failures in life. The high rates of remarriage after divorce prove that individuals are ready to try and try again to succeed in the cultural institution of marriage.

■ Ethnocentrism and Cultural Relativity

Statements to the effect that "there is no place like home" are echoed by members of every society about their own country or region. And though we may all be Americans, many of us belong to groups that are distinct from one another by reason of race, or ethnic origin, or religion; within these groups, we refer to ourselves as "us" and to the others as "them." The reason for such feelings is that we feel comfortable in the place in which we were born and brought up and among people much like us. So comfortable, in fact, that whatever we internalize from the culture of a specific place and group seems right and proper to us. The other side of the coin, of course, is that the customs of other places and groups seem to us wrong and inferior. Western travelers to some Asian countries in which dogs are considered a perfectly normal part of the diet are shocked and nauseated to see skinned bodies of what they consider pets hanging in the markets. However, an Indian traveler to a Western European or North American country would be similarly sickened to see a side of beef hanging in a butcher shop, because cows are considered sacred animals and are allowed to wander freely in India. It is easy, and natural, for such travelers to express their disgust with the "barbaric" habits of the country they are visiting. In doing so, they are displaying **ethnocentrism**, a belief that one's own society is superior to others based on judging other societies with the standards of one's own. This attitude, though often irrational, reflects our cultural indoctrination that all customs that differ from our own are somehow abnormal—strange at best, uncivilized at worst.

As noted, all societies and, for that matter, all groups display a certain amount of ethnocentrism; in moderation, ethnocentrism has the positive effect of promoting unity and loyalty within the group that exhibits it. In excess, however, ethnocentrism leads to conflict with groups that are dissimilar, or, when one group is more powerful than another, to oppression and sometimes to genocide. This was the case in Nazi Germany when the government determined to annihilate groups it considered inferior: Jews, Gypsies, homosexuals, the mentally and physically impaired, and others. Today, it is happening in other societies. In the former Yugoslavia, Serbs, Croats, and Muslims have been for years engaged in "ethnically" cleansing their respective regions of each other. In Rwanda, the Hutu and the Tutsis committed genocidal acts against each other. In short, tribalism is still deeply embedded in people, in spite of the fact that most societies long ago abandoned tribal life in favor of divisions according to political states.

To counter the negative effects of ethnocentrism, anthropologists, aware that the early practitioners of the discipline were especially guilty of ethnocentrism, have suggested that the concept of **cultural relativity** be popularized. Proponents of *cultural relativity* assert that cultures must be analyzed on their own terms, in the context of their own societal setting. No society has the right to use its own values and norms to judge the traits of another society. In this view, there are no universal norms or moral absolutes when it comes to cultures: cultures are neither better nor worse, only different. This does not mean that in looking at other cultures we agree with or approve of certain behaviors, or that we discard our own cultural or moral values. It merely means that other cultures should be approached with attitudes of tolerance, respect, and understanding.

Box 3.2   Different Strokes for Different Cultures

Would you pay $10,000 for a "lucky" license plate? Many motorists in China do.

In a country where the average farmer earns one-twentieth of that amount per year, and where the yearly per capita income is about $5,300, newly rich Chinese attend auctions in which license plates with what are considered lucky numbers are sold. In one day, one such auction sold $366,500 worth of license plates, and the top price of one was $10,000. This expensive plate was APY888, which explains its high cost. In fact, numbers are very important in Chinese society, serving almost as a second language. The most unlucky number is 4, pronounced "si," which also means "death." This number is so feared that many buildings omit the number entirely in their address or in designating the floor. The luckiest number is 8, pronounced "ba," which rhymes with "fa," the Chinese character for "wealth." The symbolism of numbers may be traced to Confucianism and Taoism; however, it is being misinterpreted by people and exploited by those who want to make a fast profit.

So potent is the superstition in this culture that although license plate numbers are distributed randomly, as everywhere else, people absolutely refuse to accept any plate with the number 4: motorists state that it might as well read "death," and there is enough death occurring on Chinese roads without this bad omen. As a result, for $2,000 one can buy a cell phone with a "lucky" number,

for $140,000 the plate A88888 may be purchased from a private individual who offered it on the Internet, and one Chinese airline paid around $300,000 for an 888-8888 phone number.

Numerology in China is becoming even more popular as the country experiences increasing wealth. Not only are some numbers considered lucky and others unlucky, but the holders of lucky numbers have a very high status as opposed to the less fortunate who cannot afford to spend such sums on luxuries. This fact, too, leads to injustice, as motorists sporting lucky license plates are often allowed to break driving laws, even committing vehicular homicide, because their plates advertise their high status (and possibly their connection to the Communist Party) (Yardley, 2006, A4).

Of course, superstitious beliefs are not limited to Chinese culture. In our own society many people fear the number 13, especially if it falls on a Friday. Here, too, the 13th floor is omitted in many buildings. This is not the only superstitious belief: children know that if you "step on a crack, break your mother's back," and that one should not walk under a ladder. Many also fear seeing black cats crossing the streets, and many more have equally fantastic beliefs. These superstitions tend to have long histories and are preserved as folk tales. It is interesting that although they differ from society to society, they are universally present in all societies.

■ Cultural Differences and Universals

When early explorers, missionaries, and adventurers first came in contact with foreign societies, they of course judged them according to their own ethnocentric standards. In some of the more exotic societies, they could not help experiencing what we now call "culture shock." They explained the dissimilarities of foreign cultures by speculating that they were due to racial, geographic, and even religious causes. However, while all of these influences have a bearing on the course of cultural development—obviously, the natural environment influences culture in the sense that no igloos can be built in the Amazonian jungle, nor palm huts become the customary dwellings of Alaskans—no one reason can be found to explain perfectly what makes one culture dissimilar from another.

As striking as some differences appear to be, cultures have many more similarities than differences. Pivotal institutions, as already stated, are present in all societies. Further, many norms, values, and beliefs are also unexpectedly similar. All people enjoy adorning themselves, whether with a ring through the nose, on an earlobe, or on a finger; all people have some food taboos, whether it is against eating cows or pigs or dogs. All people have some form of music and dancing and some form of art or handicraft.

Social anthropologist George P. Murdock (1949, 1965) compiled a long list of elements that are common to all known cultures. The list includes such widely different elements as play, hospitality, and weather control. Similarities common to all cultures are called *cultural universals*. They are general themes on which each culture develops its own variations. The conclusion we draw from the fact that so many cultural universals exist is that we truly share common human bonds.

Box 3.3 The Aarial of Kenya

Although it has become progressively more difficult to find isolated societies whose cultures differ significantly from our own, anthropologists occasionally do find such a society. A small enclave of people living in a remote desert area of Kenya, the Aarial tribe has been a source of research for anthropologists, to the tribespeople's great amazement. In fact, the Aarial, who have not been affected by the media since only one television showing CNN was found in a small urban center nearby, cannot imagine why anthropologists would be plucking hairs from their heads or asking indelicate questions such as how often they have sexual relations, what they consider to be a positive body image, and even how frequently they suffer from diarrhea.

The information gathered by anthropologists and tribal members is reciprocal: each group undergoes a bit of a culture shock. The Aarial wonder why white persons would spread a white lotion on themselves for protection from the sun; why they would wear shorts, leaving their legs unprotected, but then wear heavy boots on their feet, why they drink water out of bottles and eat strange foods wrapped in plastic; and, mainly, why they are interested in such questions as whether the tribesmen have satisfactory sex lives and how many times a day they urinate. The anthropologists, on the other hand, find it exciting to uncover the way of life of a seminomadic society that has had few encounters with modernity. Among the anthropologists' findings are the facts that the Aarial eat mainly meat, milk, and blood; that their wealth consists in owning much livestock; that their women work harder than the men; that prospective husbands buy their wives by exchanging livestock for them; that wedding days are painful for the brides because they undergo cutting of their genitals before the ceremony, so that marriages cannot be consummated until some time later.

Members of the tribe, in short, believe the anthropologists ask dumb questions. The anthropologists, on the other hand, are convinced that the life, diet, and cultural practices of a society that has been isolated from much of the rest of the world can tell us much about what all societies have historically experienced (Fratkin, 1997).

Over time, cultures undergo change. Change may be fast and dramatic or slow and imperceptible. The kinds and the processes of change, as well as its results, are discussed in Chapter 10.

Subcultures and Countercultures

Variation and uniformity, as noted earlier, are characteristic not only of societies but also of groups within each society. This is especially true of contemporary technologically advanced societies, which tend to be heterogeneous (made up of dissimilar groups) not only because they attract people from all over the world to their superior economies but also because many societies have been created as political units by uniting a number of separate ethnic groups.

Subcultures. In the United States, the native inhabitants and the original settlers who came from England have been augmented, through the centuries, by numerous people from all over the globe. Today, groups exist on the basis of the members' race, ethnicity or country of origin, religion, and numerous other distinguishing features. Even in more homogeneous societies, people form groups based on the region in which they live (Northerners or Southerners), their occupation (musicians, circus acrobats, doctors, lawyers), their social class

Adorning oneself is a cultural universal, that is, in every culture people adorn themselves. In American society, and in Western societies in general, tattoos and nose piercings are not a type of adornment used in the mainstream. However, they are common in subcultural or countercultural groups as shown in this photo of men at a tattoo convention in England.

(WASPS or Yuppies, middle class or working class), their religion (Roman Catholics, Muslims, Protestants, Jews), their sexual preference (gay persons, transvestites, bisexuals), even their age (teenagers, golden-agers). Sociologists refer to these subdivisions, these groups within the larger group of the society, as **subcultures.**

Subcultures have distinctive features that set them apart from the general culture of the society, yet they retain the principal features of that culture. (The word *subculture* never implies any inferiority to the larger culture—it refers only to its being a segment of that larger culture.) Teenagers are a good example of a subculture. They certainly identify with the goals and values of the larger societal culture and are guided by this culture's behavioral patterns. At the same time, many of their interests and some aspects of their behavior are peculiar to their age group: teenagers seem to have a special language, a distinctive manner of dress, a taste for special kinds of music, and a fondness for specific foods and forms of recreation.

Teenagers are a temporary subculture; that is, as people grow older, they abandon it. Some subcultures are much more permanent, however. Although the United States was at one time considered a melting pot—or at least it was the alleged goal of the society to become a melting pot—in reality a large number of subcultural groups based on race and ethnicity exist among us. Whereas historically such groups preferred to be absorbed into the mainstream culture, the last several decades have seen a reversal, with most members of subcultural groups choosing to maintain a degree of cultural distinctiveness. This desire has produced some controversy, particularly when such groups are vocal in their refusal to blend into the mainstream and when their traditions clash with the laws of the society. One instance of subcultural goals clashing with mainstream values and laws is represented by the Amish, who are concentrated principally in the rural areas of Pennsylvania and Ohio. The religious beliefs of the Amish include a refusal to embrace modern technology of any kind, and they deem eight years of education sufficient for their members. All states, however, have laws requiring their residents to remain in school until they are 16 years old. Which should have preeminence, the law of the state or the religious freedom of the subcultural group?

Countercultures. Sometimes groups emerge in a society that have a faddish quality, in the sense that they come and go rather quickly. A *counterculture* differs from a subculture in that it is a group within the larger society whose members adopt a value system and goals that are in *direct opposition* to those of the wider societal culture. In the twentieth century, the United States witnessed the emergence of the "beatniks" in the 1950s, and of the "hippies" a generation later. These groups shared many goals that differed from those of the wider society, chief among them antimaterialism, rejection of conventional morality in the areas of sex, drug use, and the need to work. The hippies and "flower children" also stood in opposition to the Vietnam war and were fierce supporters of individual freedom as opposed to the norms superimposed, in their view, by the "establishment." A lengthy period of economic recession, among other things, put an end to all but a small residue of countercultural lifestyles. Many of the countercultural ideas, however, were absorbed by the mainstream culture, just as its outward symbols—the long hair, the colorful unisex attire, and the music—had been. It may be argued that the very success of the counterculture spelled its doom, but its real goals were never achieved.

A rejection of conventional norms and folkways is also displayed by "punkers," identified by their colorful if bizarre hairstyles and clothing, and "bikers," such as the Hell's Angels, whose life-style apparently centers around motorcycles, alcohol, and drugs.

Some criminal groups are countercultural, although not all are; most criminals accept the goals of their society and reject only the means of attaining them. A gang of delinquent youths is usually considered countercultural because its set of values and standards of behavior are distinct from, or run counter to, those of the wider culture. Members of organized crime, however, or criminals who engage in theft and fraud, are not countercultural; for them, crime is simply a shortcut to attaining the material success that others must work for (or inherit).

Almost every historical period, as well as most societies, has had its counterculture, although in some periods societies were too rigid to tolerate a counterculture and suppressed any attempts at nonconformity. Today, we have become much more tolerant of nonconforming life-styles, although, of course, when such life-styles endanger the lives or property of the majority, they must be proscribed. Terrorist groups, and paramilitary groups proclaiming their hatred for the federal government or for specific minority groups (the "Skinheads"), crop up periodically, with such tragic outcomes as the bombing, with enormous loss of life, of the Oklahoma City Federal Building. The attacks perpetrated by al Qaeda and similar groups against Western targets is the work of a global terrorist group that may be described as countercultural in a global, rather than a societal, sense.

The Chapter in Brief

The most important product of the interaction that occurs in groups, especially in societies, is culture. Culture may be superficially defined as the way of life of a specific people, but it is much more than this. At the very least, it acts as a guide for further social interaction—it is a blueprint for living. The most basic element of culture is language, a system of symbols that allows people to accumulate knowledge and transmit it without relying on personal experience. The sharing of symbols is a much more effective tool for survival than are the genetically inherited signals with which animals other than humans cope with life and communicate with each other.

Culture has both material content (tangible products and objects) and nonmaterial content (ideas, values, knowledge, beliefs, rules for behavior, and institutions). Much of a society's nonmaterial culture is made up of norms; rules of behavior that are learned and shared by each member of the society through interaction. Norms include folkways, mores, taboos, and laws.

The structure of culture consists of traits (the smallest unit of culture), culture complexes (a number of related traits), and institutions. Institutions are formal systems of beliefs and behavior, composed of interrelated norms and culture complexes. Institutions primarily center on and help fill universal human needs. Five basic (pivotal) institutions are common to all human societies: the family, the economy, education, government, and religion.

The culture of each society is both different from and similar to the culture of other societies. To members of a specific society, a foreign culture may appear irrational or silly, but that impression is biased because the culture is judged by the standards of those who are doing the judging (ethnocentrism). It is more just to use cultural relativity to judge foreign cultures, because then each culture is analyzed in its own societal context and on the basis of how well it fills its members' needs.

Cultural differences among societies are partly the result of geographic and other factors, of which little is yet known. The similar characteristics displayed by cultures arise because all cultures must help to fulfill universal human needs, both biological and emotional. Characteristics common to all cultures are called cultural universals.

Because societies are made up of various groups, culture also varies within single societies. Groups within a society may be differentiated on the basis of geographic location, social class, occupation, race, ethnicity, religion, and so on. Such groups may produce a distinctive culture, including a separate language or jargon, customs, traditions, and rituals. If the principal values of such a group are the same as those of the general culture of the society, the group is called a subculture. If the principal values are in direct opposition to those of the larger culture, the group is called a counterculture.

Terms to Remember

counterculture A group that possesses a value system and goals that are in direct opposition to those of the larger society.

cultural relativity An attitude of judging each culture on its own terms and in the context of its own societal setting.

cultural universals Similarities common to all cultures (example: the existence of pivotal institutions).

culture The way of life of people in a society. The totality of what is learned and shared by the members of a society through their interactions. The product of social interaction and a guide for further interaction. Culture includes material and nonmaterial aspects.

culture complex A number of related traits that accumulate around a specific human activity.

culture trait The smallest element or unit of culture. In material culture, it is any single object. In nonmaterial culture, it is any single idea, symbol, or belief.

ethnocentrism The attitude that one's own culture is right and that cultural patterns different from it are wrong.

folkways Norms that direct behavior in everyday situations; customary and habitual ways of acting.

institution A number of culture complexes clustering around a central human activity.

laws Formal codes of behavior. Laws are binding on the whole society; they outline behavior that deviates from the norm and define prescriptions for punishing it.

mores Norms that direct behavior considered either extremely harmful or extremely helpful to society.

They define the rightness or wrongness of an act, its morality or immorality. Violation of mores is punished by society.

normative system A system of rules regulating human behavior.

norms Behavioral standards that dictate conduct in both informal and formal situations; a set of behavioral expectations.

sanctions Rewards (positive) or punishments (negative) directed at individuals or groups by either legal and formal organizations (official) or the people with whom one interacts (unofficial) to encourage or discourage specific types of behavior.

signals Biologically determined and genetically transmitted responses to outside stimuli.

social control The process by which order is maintained within society through obedience to norms—folkways, mores, taboos, and laws.

subculture A group that has distinctive features that set it apart from the culture of the larger society but still retains the general values of mainstream society.

symbols Genetically independent responses to stimuli in the form of representations: a word or image standing for an object or a feeling. Symbols are learned and can be changed, modified, combined, and recombined in an infinite number of ways. Language, music, and art are common symbol systems.

taboos Mores stated in negative terms. They center on acts considered extremely repellent to the social group.

Suggested Readings

Barber, Benjamin R. 1995. *Jihad Vs. McWorld: How Globalism and Tribalism Are Reshaping the World*. New York: Random House. The author analyzes the cultures of the capitalist West and those of local, traditional cultures, noting that they are in conflict. Conflict is particularly evident between global capitalism and some of the fundamentalist Islamic cultures.

Bellah, Robert N., Richard Madsen, William M. Sullivan, Ann Swidler, and Steven M. Tipton. 1986. *Habits of the Heart: Individualism and Commitment in American Life*.

New York: Harper & Row. An examination of American culture, focusing on the conflict between the values of individualism and achievement on the one hand and a desire for close relationships and community on the other.

Brown, Donald E. 1991. *Human Universals*. New York: McGraw-Hill. A survey of anthropological literature focusing on cultural universals found in human groups.

Chagnon, Napoleon A. 1983. *Yanomamo: The Fierce People*. 3rd ed. New York: Holt, Rinehart and Winston. A fascinating account of a culture truly unfamiliar to

Americans, as well as of the methods of research involved in this anthropological project.

DeVita, Philip B., and James D. Armstrong, eds. 1998. *Distant Mirrors: America as a Foreign Culture.* 2nd ed. Belmont, CA: West/Wadsworth. American culture as seen by scholars from Europe, Africa, Asia, and Latin America.

Weinstein, Deena. 2000. *The Music and Its Culture.* Cambridge, MA: Da Capo. An examination of the subculture formed by those engaged in "heavy metal" music.

Zellner, William M. 1995. *Countercultures: A Sociological Analysis.* New York: St. Martin's. The Unification Church, the Church of Scientology, Satanists, skinheads, survivalists, and the Ku Klux Klan examined as examples of countercultural groups.

Web Sites of Interest

http://www.wsu.edu:8080/~dee
An anthology of world civilizations in a classroom setting.

http://www.thebritishmuseum.ac.uk/world/world/html
Every region of the world is represented in these histories of cultures.

Group Interaction:
From Two to Millions

IN THIS CHAPTER, YOU WILL LEARN

- *that humans are group animals who survive and become true human beings as a result of being members of groups;*

- *that within each group, individuals are assigned statuses and carry out roles, a condition that makes each group a social system;*

- *that a social system has structure, which gives life a pattern of predictability;*

- *that of the multitude of groups, primary groups are those most important to the individual;*

- *that the largest group to which people belong is society;*

- *that there has been a trend away from the small, traditional societies of the past (Gemeinschafts) to the large associational societies of the present (Gesellschafts);*

- *that the interaction that occurs within all social groups is based on the processes of cooperation, competition, exchange, and conflict;*

- *that the way to manage life in large, complex societies is through the establishment of formal organizations that depend on bureaucracy to function.*

"United we stand, divided we fall," "In unity there is strength," "E pluribus, unum." All these sayings attempt to bring home an ancient truth that has become a cliché by virtue of so much repetition: people are *social* animals. Being a social animal means that humans do not live in isolation. From the moment of birth as fragile, helpless creatures, humans depend on others, at first for sheer survival and later for protection, companionship, affection, reproduction, and economic survival—in short, for everything.

A group way of life is not only a necessity for humans but also an advantage in the difficult task of survival. It is much easier to exist in a family group than alone: the newest born is fed and protected, and all eat better when two or three adults work to provide for the group instead of each individual working alone. It is also easier to defend one's home or belongings (or territory from predators) in a group setting; thus, there is much truth in the sayings about the importance of the group.

In spite of all its advantages, a group way of life lends itself to disorder and chaos, because whenever people live in close proximity to one another there is a potential for conflict. Individuals differ in temperament, in likes and dislikes, in goals and desires. When the groups that live in close quarters are many, the problems of coexistence multiply. Therefore, a group way of life requires the development of some sort of organization, or system, to ensure a fairly smooth coexistence. Individuals must know what is expected of them and, in turn, what they can expect of others. They must agree on their duties and responsibilities to the group, and what the group members owe them. They must know what to expect from the behavior of group members, and how they themselves should behave toward them. They must ensure that no social encounter is a complete surprise in terms of what members of the group say and do, but on the contrary, that the encounter be predictable to a great extent. Otherwise, groups cannot function adequately.

An organizational system does in fact develop within groups, though we are not consciously aware of it. It emerges thanks to the repeated interaction of individuals with other individuals, and of groups with other groups. The system is structured because people behave according to the statuses they hold in each group and to the roles those statuses oblige them to play. Moreover, it is obvious that interaction takes place in the framework of specific social processes. Social life, in short, is organized into a system with its own definite structure.

The presence of a system does not guarantee harmony, but it does guarantee a certain amount of predictability. This makes our group way of life much easier.

■ How Is the Social System Organized and Structured?

Social scientists who analyze group life do so at two levels: the interpersonal or **microsocial** level and the group or **macrosocial** level. On the microsocial level, they focus on the way individuals relate to one another based on the position that each holds in relation to the other: husband to wife, father to daughter, teacher to student, employer to employee, and so forth. On the macrosocial level, they examine relationships between and among groups that make up the largest group, society, and focus on the values and rules for behavior that emerge when people live in a society. The social system that emerges from such interactions is, of course, an abstraction, a model that illustrates how social relationships work. It is important to remember that every group, whether it consists of only two people or many millions of people, is basically a social system. As is characteristic of systems, each part is connected to, and dependent on, every other part. It follows that the way each individual in a group behaves influences every other individual in the group. This interconnectedness and interdependence eventually result in shared patterns of behavior that members come to expect of each other.

The orderly and fairly predictable patterns of interaction that emerge in a social system give that social system structure. *Social structure*, also referred to as *social organization*, is the foundation underlying the network of organized relationships among the component parts of a social system. It is the patterned and recurring way in which individuals and groups interact.

Social structure should not be viewed as a fixed set of rules. Rather, it is a dynamic process in which stable and predictable patterns are continually redefined and altered to fit the changing conditions of each situation. The members of a musical band are an example of a group that exhibits a social system with a structure and organization. These members meet every afternoon, Monday through Thursday, from 1:00 to 3:00, for the purpose of rehearsing a program they will perform Thursday through Saturday nights at a downtown hall. The musicians are there for a specific goal, and to achieve that goal they behave according to regular and predictable patterns. Most come in carrying their instruments; they take their assigned seats; they tune their instruments; they stop chatting when their lead musician appears; they begin to play when he or she gives them a signal. Each member of this social system knows what to do, and each expects the other members to know what to do and to do it. As long as they do this, the social system of the band is stable and enduring, and the group can function. If one or more members begins to be consistently late for rehearsals, or some members fail to bring their instruments; if they continue to talk when they should be playing; if they question the leader's right to tell them how to play a passage; if they take out sandwiches and begin eating in the middle of a number—if any of these things should happen with any frequency, the organization of this system will inevitably be destroyed, and the group will eventually have to disband because it can no longer function as a group with a specific purpose. As you know, many bands have in fact broken up and ceased to exist or have been reconstituted with other members because the original system had become unworkable.

Elements of Social Structure: Statuses and Roles

In the example above, the social structure became ineffective because some members failed to follow the **norms**, did not behave according to their **statuses**, and did not perform their expected **roles** in the situation of the rehearsal. In their simplest definition, *norms* are rules for behavior, *status* is a position in a social group, and *role* is the carrying out of the status. People have such statuses as mother in a family group, teacher in an occupational group, plumber in a work group. The dynamic aspect of that status, or what the mother, the teacher, and the plumber *do*, is the role. The theatrical term *role* is very appropriate. It may be said, in fact, that each individual is handed a script by society. Individuals are like actors who perform assigned roles throughout their lives. When we say that society assigns roles, we are of course speaking figuratively. We are not really handed a script, but we are born with some statuses, and we acquire others because of what we do or fail to do. Statuses are ranked; that is, they are value-rated according to the prevailing values of the group. In American society, the teacher has a higher status than the plumber, and both have a lower status than a famous musician.

A person who occupies a specific status is expected to behave in a way befitting that status. We do not expect the plumber to give us a lecture on the English literature of the Middle Ages, nor do we expect the teacher to fix our leaky faucet. (Of course, the teacher may in fact be able to fix faucets, just as the plumber may be an expert in literature.) When you enter a classroom at the beginning of a term, you expect one individual, man or woman, to come and stand in front of the class, write his or her name on the board, and proceed to tell you what textbook to buy, how many exams you will take, how many papers you will write, how many times you will be allowed to be absent. You assume that this person is an instructor—even though you have no absolute proof—and so you find it natural to follow his or her instructions. If a child came into your classroom and attempted to give you similar instructions, you would be outraged, and rightly so. Similarly, if you go for a job interview, you recognize that the interviewer has a right to ask you fairly personal questions about your past performance or about your salary requirements, questions that you would not tolerate from a stranger you had just met while waiting for a commuter train. Or, should you find yourself

Societies and their cultures do not change at the same pace. India, for instance, is still largely preindustrial and agricultural. Statuses in such a society are mostly ascribed, that is, people are born into a particular status, such as these women planting rice in a flooded rice paddy.

in the emergency room of a hospital, you would find it natural to address the woman with the stethoscope as "Doctor," even though she might call you John, and to remove your clothes and let yourself be examined. Because you are the patient and she the doctor, you do not address her as Jane, nor do you expect to give her orders. As a student, a prospective employee, and a patient, you accept as a given the behavior of your instructor, your future employer, and your doctor in certain situations; in other situations, or with people of different statuses, you would not abide it.

Statuses and roles evolve out of the need of each group to perform its tasks efficiently. In a society, a great many functions must be performed each day if the society is to operate well. Food must be produced and made available for consumption, shelter must be built, the sick must be healed, children must be educated, and so on. In time and through experience, it has become clear that efficiency is much improved when tasks are allocated to particular individuals who specialize in performing them. Such an allocation of tasks is what we call *division of labor*, which is the origin of most, though not all, statuses (some statuses are allocated on the basis of gender or age).

Statuses and the roles that grow out of them are not static. They are continually subject to change, growth, and replacement. Change within each group and change in society, as well as daily interaction, constantly redefine statuses and roles.

Statuses: Ascribed and Achieved

Some statuses and their roles are ours at birth; that is, we cannot avoid having them. A child is born either male or female; it is either white, African, Asian, Hispanic, or a mixture of these; its parents are either working-class, middle-class, or upper-class—or somewhere along the social class continuum—and they may claim allegiance to a given ethnic group and religion. These statuses of the newborn child are **ascribed** to it; they are not attained through any individual effort or merit or fault. *Ascribed* statuses are involuntary, being based on gender, age, race, ethnic background, and the social position and religious affiliation of one's family.

Most other statuses, however, are **achieved** by individuals through their own effort and choice, or conversely, through lack of effort, apathy, or poor choices. We become college graduates, wives, or bank managers because we want to, and we put some effort into it, or we remain unemployed or end up in prison because we failed to obtain a skill or made unwise decisions.

In preindustrial societies, ascribed status is more prevalent than achieved status. For instance, in feudal Europe, society was divided into estates—a kind of permanent and rigid social class—and mobility from one estate into another was almost impossible to achieve. In India, too, until recent times people were divided into castes based on occupation. In such societies, the scope of individual choice is small. Even with ability, talent, or hard work, individuals cannot rise above the occupation and social class of their parents. In industrial societies, on the other hand, there is a commitment to individualism and personal achievement. Freedom of choice is jealously defended, and the accomplishments of the individual are ardently applauded. As a result, achieved status is valued, although the ascribed status that comes from belonging to a family that has enjoyed a high status for a few generations is also highly valued.

In most postindustrial societies, and especially in the United States, the past several decades have seen much upheaval as a result of people's dissatisfaction with their ascribed statuses and the consequent roles they have been forced to fulfill. Thus, women and racial and ethnic minorities have fought to change certain discriminatory practices to which they were subjected as a result of their ascribed statuses. Although the problematic aspects of their roles have not been eliminated entirely, progress has been made in that direction.

The status of women in India has undergone a dramatic change since that country began to industrialize its economy.

Describe this photo. What is the status of the man looking at some records? Is that his master status? What role is he playing? What about the woman? What is her role? Whose status is higher in our society? What is the status of the man lying in bed? Is that his master status? What is his role?

■ The Multiplicity of Statuses and Roles

As must be quite obvious by now, each person has many statuses and performs many roles in his or her lifetime. The CEO of Hot Dogs, Incorporated, is best known by his status of corporation president, which becomes his *master status*, but he also has the added statuses of son, husband, father, brother, lawyer, regent of the state university, member of a country club, elder in the Presbyterian church, and fund raiser for the Republican Party. On an occasional basis, he also occupies the statuses of patient (when he sees his doctor), client (when he visits his stockbroker), customer (when he goes shopping), and driver (when he drives his car).

Not all of these statuses are equally important. The importance of the statuses is determined by the values of the group that is involved in ranking them. On a macrosocial level, the individual described above would be ranked as having a high status because of his position as a corporation president. On a microsocial level, however, he may be ranked low by his wife and children, in whom he takes little interest. His status may be ranked equal with that of the other elders in the church, though the volunteers in the Republican Party may consider him an upstart.

Clearly, if there is a multiplicity of statuses, there is an equally large number of roles that people must perform. No one performs all roles well. The corporation president in the example above must be good at performing his master role or he would not remain in his position for very long. As was noted, however, he may leave much to be desired in his roles of husband and father. Generally, people select the roles they consider most important and perform these roles best. There is a relationship between a person's self-image and the role he or she chooses to perform best. The chief executive in the above example may see himself as a great American business leader and consequently performs his role of CEO well, whereas he may feel that he was forced to marry because of pressure from his pregnant girlfriend and her family, and so performs the role of husband and father badly.

Real and Ideal Roles

Groups frequently prepare their members to fill roles they then never have the opportunity to fill, or they teach their young ideal patterns of behavior that are seldom or never really followed. In Sunday school, for instance, children learn that people should love their neighbor and turn the other cheek; but their football coach tells them to "murder" the opposing team and take revenge for a previous loss. Such contradictory teachings do not necessarily constitute hypocrisy. Ideal patterns of behavior serve a necessary function, acting as a brake on real patterns that may decline to an undesirably low level.

Conflict, Strain, and Confusion in Roles

When the real differs substantially from the ideal, however, confusion follows. Young people are disillusioned when they come in contact with the "real" world; they feel betrayed. In some instances, the disparity may have positive results, as individuals resolve to bring the real more in line with the ideal and work to reach a social goal; in other instances, stresses and strains result from the discrepancy.

Rapid social change, on the other hand, contributes to a situation in which future lifestyles are unpredictable, and thus it is impossible to prepare for them. In industrial societies, many tasks are performed outside the home, and children grow up without knowing exactly what their parents do when they "go to work." Some roles, then, are not learned at all, or are learned improperly in childhood, and have to be picked up as one goes along. Again, these problems do not arise in preindustrial societies, but in technological societies they are very common.

Strain. Often, playing one's role well produces strain. For instance, a supervisor must uphold discipline to ensure that a work group reaches its goals. In the process, however, the supervisor may have to be severe, even unfriendly, or drive workers too hard, and so become disliked by the subordinates. The alternative is to be a "good guy" and be well liked at the expense of attaining group goals. A leader must constantly weigh his or her behavior in terms of the role of leading.

Role strain can also occur when entrenched statuses become altered as a result of changes in the social system. Women traditionally occupied the statuses of wives, mothers, and homemakers, which were considered undemanding tasks requiring little intellectual acumen or talent, and they were consequently ranked low. Men, on the other hand, held the statuses of providers, which, although ranked according to the prestige and financial rewards their particular job brought, were generally considered to require superior capabilities. As a result, all the positions of real power in society were held by men. As women achieved more education, however, they began to compete with men in the labor market. In turn, as they became financially independent, their roles within the family strengthened. Many men were not able to adjust to their changed roles, and conflicts between marital partners frequently led to divorce. Divorced women were forced to compete for jobs as a matter of survival, theirs and the children of the failed marriage (angry fathers frequently shirk their financial responsibilities toward their children). The consequent shift in statuses and roles that follows social change, then, has created a situation that necessitates adjustment both within the family institution and in the society at large. As we are constantly reminded by the media

Because of the high number of women in the workforce, it has become necessary for families to avail themselves of babysitters to take care of their small children. This situation often creates strains in the role of mother: many women are conflicted about whether it is best to remain at home with their children and give up career opportunities or a better standard of living with the extra income, or to leave their children for many hours a day with strangers.

and politicians, the institution of the family is in a period of crisis. Eventually, people will learn to adjust to new roles, or adapt old roles to new circumstances, but the transitional period is very difficult for both individuals and the society.

Conflict.   Having to fulfill multiple roles can produce conflict. A corporation president's role demands spending an unusually large proportion of time on business connected with the corporation. To be a good spouse and parent, however, enough time should also be spent in family activities, so that intimate interaction can take place. Each individual must choose which of these roles should take precedence, and the difficult decision is sure to create conflicts for individuals, frequently leading to the breakup of families.

Confusion.   Finally, roles may create confusion, particularly when a person in a specific status must suddenly abandon the corresponding role and embrace a new one. An accountant pushed out of employment because of mandatory retirement, for instance, may feel a loss of identity and may refuse to accept the role of retiree, particularly if interests always revolved around the job and he or she cannot fill the hours of leisure. College-educated women, especially those on the threshold of promising careers, may also experience confusion if an unplanned pregnancy pushes them into the roles of mothers and full-time housekeepers.

Roles that are performed poorly according to societal judgments may cause individuals not only confusion and strain but also mental illness, maladjustment, or a condition of constant frustration. For many reasons—sometimes simply by chance—people fail in the roles for which they have been prepared. In a highly competitive economic system, people frequently fail in their professions and businesses. The high incidence of divorce shows that large numbers of people fail in their marital roles. It is obvious, however, that most people cannot fill all roles equally well, and sometimes a person may fail in one role while succeeding in a conflicting one.

■ Groups

As noted in the preceding section, all social interactions take place according to an abstract social system in which individuals have specific statuses and play the roles that go with those statuses. The interactions, of course, take place within groups. In turn, groups are not what they seem to be.

The word *group* is commonly understood to mean a number of people congregated at the same time in the same place. However, 15 students cramming for an exam in a student lounge are not necessarily a group in the sociological sense. Twenty commuters on the morning train into Manhattan are not necessarily a group, either. These people, who are merely in the same place at the same time, are *aggregates*, not groups.

Many people also share a certain characteristic: they may have red hair in common, for instance, or may have been born on the Fourth of July. These people do not make up a group either; instead, they form a *category*.

Suppose, however, that 3 of the 15 students cramming in the student lounge have been studying there since the beginning of the school year. Suppose, further, that they have an English class together, and they eat lunch at the same time. Because they are human and, therefore, social beings, these students, after the first exchange of greetings, begin to sit together in English class and in the cafeteria and stop to chat every time they pass each other in the hall. Of an aggregate of 15, then, 3 have formed a group. By the same token, if all the redheads in the United States who were born on the Fourth of July of 1945 decided to organize a club, if they corresponded regularly and met periodically, they too would have ceased to be a category and would have become a group.

For a number of people to constitute a group, these conditions must be met:

1. Symbolic interaction among the members should be taking place. (*Symbolic interaction* is communication by means of speech, gestures, writing, or even music. Members are

These people crossing an intersection in New York do not constitute a group in sociological terms because they do not interact; they just happen to be in the same place at the same time.

aware of one another, respond to one another, and behave in such a way that they influence one another.) Group members expect interaction to continue indefinitely, but many groups form and disperse within short periods of time.

2. There should be recognition by each member that he or she is part of the group and recognition by the group that each person is a member. Group membership gives members a feeling of identity.

3. A certain amount of agreement or consensus among the members about the rules of behavior, values, and goals they share should exist.

4. The group should have structure; that is, members should be aware of their statuses, roles, rules of behavior, duties, and obligations, as well as the privileges that result from group membership.

In other words, what constitutes a group is a matter of degree; it depends on how much members interact with one another, how strongly they feel their "we-ness," and to what extent group norms affect their behavior.

Groups are extraordinary in number and diversity. In size, groups may vary from two to several hundred million or even a billion—from a couple to a whole society. In fact, there are more groups in a society than there are individuals, because each person is a member of more than one group at any one time. The factors that are considered in classifying groups are size and special characteristics.

Group Size

The smallest of groups consists of two members and is called a **dyad**. The dyad is the most elementary social unit and is a very fragile one: the unit ceases to exist as a group when one of the members withdraws (Simmel, 1905/1956). The **triad**, or group consisting of three

These seniors playing bridge do make up a group because symbolic interaction is taking place. Each person recognizes that he or she is a member of the group, they agree on how to play, and each is aware of his or her status, of rules of behavior, of their duties and obligations, as well as of the privileges of belonging to the group.

Even two people are considered a group—a dyad—by social scientists. This group is also organized according to a social system, and because it consists of two young lovers, it is a primary group.

members, is a more stable social unit because one of the members may withdraw without destroying the group. Thus, triads are considered more important to the structure of societies (Caplow, 1968).

Size in general has a definite impact on members. With each additional member, the number of possible relationships increases and with it the probability of new coalitions forming. Rapid increases in membership may also prove disruptive: if there are more than 10 or 12 persons in a group, a leader becomes necessary to ensure that each member contributes equally to the group. The addition of new members tends to be discouraged by the original members who feel comfortable with the status quo.

Small groups—families, close friends, a clique within a large organization, a committee formed to solve a problem—share common characteristics. Relations among members tend to be face-to-face, and members generally hold similar values. The small group is quite durable, as members identify with it and are loyal to it. Small groups are influential in the impact they make on the behavior of their members, and they are more accepting of democratic leadership than are large groups.

Large groups, of course, display the opposite features. Above all, they tend to be highly organized. The largest group to which people belong is society, but large groups also include formal organizations (such as corporations) and their bureaucracies, which are discussed later in the text.

■ Primary and Secondary Groups

A very important classification of groups is that into primary and secondary groups. The term **primary group** was coined by Charles Horton Cooley, who designated as primary groups those in which members engage in intimate interaction and cooperation of the sort that is basic to the development of an individual's personality (Cooley, 1909/1910). Additional characteristics that distinguish primary from other groups include: (1) relatively small size, (2) physical nearness of members, (3) intense interaction among members, and (4) group stability and relatively long duration. The family is the foremost example of a primary group.

If primary groups were put at one end of an ideal continuum (a conceptual model representing a hypothetical ideal type to which reality may be compared in analyzing phenomena), the opposite end would be occupied by secondary groups. **Secondary groups** tend to be large, and people's interaction within them is formal, role-based, utilitarian, specialized, and temporary. The transaction that takes place between a salesperson and a customer, no matter how friendly, is of a secondary nature (unless the two happen also to be personal friends). Of course, many secondary relationships eventually develop into primary ones, as when people who were just acquaintances discover they have a hobby in common and start to see each other on a regular basis; and occasionally a primary relationship slides into a secondary one, as when two good friends quarrel and from then on exchange only icy greetings upon seeing each other.

Primary groups are universal and are of tremendous importance to individuals. It may even be said that they are necessary to the well-being of most people. It is easy to break the spirit of a person who is totally removed from primary relationships. Such a person's mental health may be severely affected. That is why isolation is often used as a method of brainwashing or torture. If primary relationships are lacking in what we would generally consider a "natural" primary group—the family, for instance—people go out of their way to create such relationships in other groups. The frequency of gangs created by teenaged youths to take the place of a broken or nonexistent family is one example of the need for primary groups. Even so, not all primary relationships are of a harmonious nature, nor are they always satisfying to the individual. They may involve a large amount of conflict or the enforcement of conformity, which stifles individuality.

Urban postindustrial societies such as the United States have increasingly become characterized by secondary relationships. Many of the functions that at one time were performed by primary groups are now carried out by secondary groups. For example, in the past, the sick were cared for by the family at home rather than by paid nurses and doctors in a hospital. Doctors and the hospital staff are much more capable of healing than members of the family and their home remedies. They undoubtedly help cure many more people than families did in the past, but they cannot have the same feelings for their patients, nor their patients for them; hence, the alienation and impersonality that is experienced by many people confined to hospitals and nursing homes. This is not to say that primary-type relations do not flourish in secondary-type groups. The fact that people live in neighborhoods, some of which are based on national origin (Chinatown, Little Italy, Spanish Harlem, Little Vietnam) has long been acknowledged as a source of community even in the largely anonymous urban environment. In fact, such neighborhoods have been characterized as "urban villages," meaning that, for all practical purposes, people live in them as if they were small villages. Moreover, even when they do not live in close-knit communities, urban residents can easily find a number of people with whom they are compatible, simply because a city, with its large number and variety of people, offers a wide choice of friends and acquaintances. People do not need to be neighbors of place; they become neighbors of taste (they come together because they have talents or interests in common). In an often-quoted description of New York, the author E. B. White maintained that many a New Yorker spends a lifetime within the confines of an area smaller than a country village, and that such a person feels ill at ease even a few blocks from his familiar corner (White, 1949).

Additional Classification of Groups

In addition to their size and primary or secondary nature, groups are classified according to other features. **In-groups** and **out-groups** are based on the distinction between *us* and *them*, probably one of the oldest distinctions people have made and one with which we can all identify, whether we belong to the Avondale Country Club or the Purple Sharks. **Reference groups** provide us with standards we use to evaluate our own status against that of others. They serve as points of comparison and affect people's values, goals, attitudes, and behavior. **Membership groups** are either formal or informal organizations to which individuals belong; for instance, the YWCA is a formal membership group, whereas one's friends from high school constitute an informal membership group. Finally, some groups are of a **voluntary** and some of an **involuntary** nature. A person's family (which cannot be chosen) and a branch of the armed services into which a person is inducted during a war are examples of involuntary groups. Conversely, there are thousands of groups, ranging from fraternities to political parties, from fan clubs to bridge clubs, that individuals may join entirely of their own free will or for reasons of social and economic expediency. Such groups are voluntary.

■ Society

Society is defined as the largest group of people inhabiting a specific territory and sharing a common way of life (culture). The people in a society share this common way of life as a result of interacting on a regular, continuous basis and because they have acquired patterns of behavior on which all more or less agree. Society differs from many other large groups because within this group people can live a total, common life, whereas in smaller groups a person lives only one facet of her or his life. In short, society is not an organization limited to a specific purpose, as is, for example, the American Medical Association. Rather, it is the most self-sufficient group, and its independence is based on the techniques developed for fulfilling the needs of its members.

Classification of Societies

Throughout history, societies have assumed a number of different forms. One way of classifying societies is according to their chief mode of subsistence (Lenski, 1970, 1987, 18–142). Another type of classification is according to basic patterns of social organization.

Classification According to Chief Mode of Subsistence

In classifying societies according to the way they provide their members with food, shelter, and clothing, we find that the most commonly occurring types include the following:

The **hunting and gathering society** is one of the earliest and least technologically complex forms of societies. It is characterized by a small (around 40 individuals), nomadic population, uncomplicated technology, little division of labor or specialization, and particular stress on the importance of kinship ties.

For most of the approximately 2 million years of human existence on the planet, people have lived in hunting and gathering societies. Hunters and gatherers are nomadic by necessity: they must forever search for better hunting grounds and new areas where naturally occurring fruits and vegetation are more abundant. As a result, they cannot accumulate belongings, as everything each person owns must be carried to the new food source. A few

Box 4.1 A Glimpse into the Human Past

Although most humans today live in technologically advanced, sophisticated, industrial, and postindustrial societies, some remnants of our distant past remain. One area that is fairly rich in isolated hunting and gathering societies is the Amazon rain forest, much of which is located in Brazil. Anthropologists believe that this area is the last place on Earth where hunting and gathering tribes still exist; in fact, they think that about 55 such uncontacted Indian groups may be secluded in remote areas of this jungle.

While flying over such a tract, an official in charge of Brazil's federal Department of Isolated Indians caught sight of a village of about 200 members that heretofore had been unknown to modern civilization. Such finds, although they still do occur, are becoming less frequent. It is thought that when Portuguese navigators reached the coast of South America around 1500 A.D., there were between 1 and 11 million native peoples living there (to whom they gave the name "Indians" because, as you recall, the Europeans thought they had reached India). Today, around 500 years later, only 300,000 such natives remain, victims of their invaders' greed, which subjected them to slavery, war, starvation, and disease.

The government of Brazil, to make up for past mistakes, has been attempting to leave any remote tribes alone, demarcating their territories and protecting them from farmers, loggers, gold miners, poachers, and other outsiders by posting guards. Nearly 200 million acres of the national territory have been promised to the remaining natives. However, this policy has many opponents, who want the government to return to its former policy of assimilation. For the tribes, assimilation has sometimes been disastrous, and sometimes beneficial and welcome.

A group of such hunters and gatherers is still living in the deep jungle of the Amazon basin in both Venezuela and Brazil. These are the Yanomamo, well known to anthropologists because of books that have been written about them. This group is believed to be the most culturally intact people in the world. Despite some interaction with the modern world, their culture reflects that of a Stone Age tribe, with characteristics dating back more than 8,000 years. The Yanomamo have not yet discovered the wheel. The only metal they have comes from outside their society. Fire is still often made by using fire sticks. Their numbering system consists of one and two and more than two—in short, they cannot describe three or more items specifically. Their economy is hunting and gathering, although they also tend small gardens. Women weave and decorate baskets, some of which are carried by a strap around the forehead. Men carry quivers that contain carved wooden spear and arrow points. They hunt with bows and arrows or blow guns made with pieces of cane and mouthpieces cut or carved from wood. They sometimes use poisoned darts with the blow guns. The poison is derived from the poison dart frog and can bring down the largest game. Young boys begin practicing archery skills at an early age, sometimes with a lizard tied to a string (**http://indian-cultures.com/cultures/yanomamo.html**. Accessed 4/12/2004).

It is difficult to believe that such societies still exist, but in conditions of extreme isolation, they do. As we will see in Chapter 10, when societies come in contact with one another and their cultural content is diffused, material and nonmaterial culture thrives and grows.

small hunting and gathering societies still exist in the rain forest of Brazil as well as in the Philippines and in Central America (Headland & Reid, 1989).

The **pastoral**, also called the **herding society**, has tended to develop in areas ill suited to the cultivation of land but containing animals amenable to domestication and use as food sources. This subsistence strategy leads to a more secure food supply and a possible surplus of animals. A surplus raises the standard of living of all, resulting in larger populations; but it also leads to ranking people according to their possessions, leading to social classes, conflict, and warfare. Pastoral societies still exist, at least as parts of industrial or industrializing societies.

The **horticultural society** appeared when people discovered how to cultivate grains, and the **agrarian society** was firmly established with the invention of the plow at around 3000 B.C. In the horticultural society, small garden plots are cleared with digging sticks and

Our earliest ancestors existed in hunting and gathering societies. Most of the world has since moved on to other types of societies; however, a small number of hunting and gathering societies still exist. These are Borra Indians from a village along the Amazon River in Peru.

gradually with sticks tied to stones, bison shoulder blades, and much later to metal objects, eventually resulting in a hoe. Although hoe gardening produces surplus food, the amount is minimal and the soil becomes depleted very rapidly, forcing people continually to cultivate new gardens. Once the use of the plow becomes established, however, large areas of land can be cultivated.

In both the horticultural and agrarian societies, ever greater surpluses are produced, and a settled lifestyle predominates. Some of the side effects of the shift from horticulture to agriculture are negative: people become differentiated, principally into landholders and landless peasants; and a bureaucracy develops to oversee an increasingly complex economy. Finally, some societies are predominantly **fishing** and **maritime societies** because of their location on rivers and seas.

Industrial Societies

The most revolutionary change in the form of societies, however, comes with the emergence of the **industrial society**. Most societies in the world today are already industrial, trying to become industrial, or postindustrial. Industrial societies are characterized by (1) urbanization, or growth of cities at the expense of rural areas; (2) massive mechanization and automation, or the substitution of machines for human labor and intelligence; (3) a complex bureaucracy, or organization into formal groups for greater efficiency; (4) separation of institutional forms, that is, the development of schools, hospitals, stores, and factories to perform functions formerly filled by the family; and (5) the substitution of impersonal, secondary relations for primary relationships. The transition from agrarian to industrial societies has been accompanied by disorganization and disruption.

Increasingly, a form of society that has been described as *postindustrial* is emerging. Sociologist Daniel Bell has commented that while the first technological revolution of 200 years ago brought steam-powered transportation and factory machine production, the second technological revolution, which occurred 100 years ago, spread electricity and chemistry, permitting the production of synthetics and plastics. The third technological revolution, which is still underway, has joined computers and telecommunications to produce television imagery, voice telephone, digital computer data, and facsimile transmission (Bell, 1987). These products are changing contemporary societies, because they have become not simply geographic places but global networks accessible with the push of a button. Power in postindustrial societies belongs to those who have the ability to respond speedily and flexibly to new information; thus, the old organizational structures are in the process of being dismantled, and new ones will have to be instituted. These new organizational structures are more fully explored in later chapters, but it is instructive to point out that, of course, such a transformation is disruptive to social organization. First of all, the statuses of certain individuals must be permanently altered, and new statuses are often acquired at the cost of great sacrifices. Transitional periods between different economic systems are always conflict producing and painful, as the many victims of "downsizing" and outsourcing can testify.

Classification According to Social Organization

A more important classification of societies, and manner of analysis, is according to their basic patterns of social organization. In small, homogeneous societies, members interact with one another on an informal, personal, face-to-face basis, and behavior is dictated by tradition. This kind of society is called a **Gemeinschaft**, which is roughly translated from German as a "communal or traditional society." In societies that are large and heterogeneous, such as modern industrial societies, relationships among members are impersonal, formal, functional, and specialized. Furthermore, they are often contractual (dealings are spelled out in legal contracts rather than by word of mouth or tradition). This society is called a **Gesellschaft**, or "associational society" (Tönnies, 1887/1957). It is obvious that Gemeinschafts are characterized by primary relationships, whereas Gesellschafts more commonly display secondary relationships.

In the modern world, there has been an easily observable shift from Gemeinschaft to Gesellschaft societies. The large size of societies and the complexities of a technological economy require secondary groups, which are dedicated to efficiency rather than sentiment.

■ Interaction and Social Processes

Societies, and the various kinds of groups that exist within them, are not static entities. They are in constant flux, undergoing change and modification. Interaction among the members of a group and among the many groups is continually taking place. **Interaction** refers to behavior or action that is symbolic; that is, words and gestures that have meaning. It is also behavior that is directed toward others, in the sense that each person is aware of how others will probably respond, and is reciprocal, in the sense that each person is conscious of and responsive to the actions and reactions of others.

Although interaction is not governed by rigid rules, it is not haphazard, either. Interactive behavior is repeated sufficiently often that it creates a pattern capable of predicting future behavior when similar situations arise. Following behavioral patterns established by others long ago is a way of simplifying our lives.

A number of key patterns of interaction are present and at work whenever interaction takes place. They have been called the "microelements of the social bond, or the molecular cement of society" (Nisbet, 1970). These patterns of interaction are the social processes.

Social interaction, whether it occurs on a primary or a secondary group level, involves a great many social processes. We focus on four primary social processes: exchange, cooperation, competition, and conflict. All other processes, among which are accommodation, assimilation, and coercion, are really combinations of, or derivations from, the primary processes.

Exchange is a transaction in which one of two individuals—or groups, or societies—does something for the other with the expectation of receiving something of equal value in return. If you type a paper for a fellow student, you expect him or her to take good notes for you when you are absent. When the doctor clears up your skin infection, you are expected to pay the bill. When you are hired to work for a corporation, it is expected that you will receive a salary in exchange for your labor. In short, exchange is a pervasive process in groups of all sizes, and it is generally found in the context of the norm of *reciprocity*, which requires that you do something in return for what someone has done for you. When social exchanges are fair and equal, the social structure of the group tends to be solid, but when exchanges are perceived as one-sided, eventually the social structure suffers, leading to a disintegration of the group involved.

Cooperation is a primary social process involving two or more persons or groups working jointly in a common enterprise for a shared goal. It is often considered the most basic of the social processes because without it life would be difficult, if not impossible.

Competition is a form of interaction that occurs when two or more individuals try to take possession of the same scarce object, whether it be tangible, such as a precious gem, or intangible, such as someone's love. Competition is a basic process because most living organisms must compete for limited resources necessary to their survival; plants, for instance,

---

Box 4.2   A Social Process with a Biological Facet

Are the social processes that underlie social interaction, and thus social structure, learned behavior, or are we born with some of them?

There are no definite answers to such a question, but research seems to point to the biological roots of some of these processes. We have said that cooperation is a necessary process in a social system because it aids people in survival. Beyond simple cooperation is altruism, a behavior in which a person helps another person without direct benefit. Why do some individuals, like a Mother Teresa, dedicate themselves to aid the lives of unfortunates while forgoing most of the pleasures of life, whereas others tend to think only of themselves, even doing harm to others for their own advantage or pleasure? Perhaps it is merely because one area of the altruistic individuals' brains are better developed than a similar area in the brains of selfish individuals. This at least is the finding of scientists from the Duke University Medical Center, who subjected a number of students to a magnetic resonance imaging (MRI) scanner while they answered questions as to how often they engaged in helping behavior. They also had the students play computer games in which they were told that winning earned cash either for themselves or for a charity.

The MRI scanner took images of participants' brain activity. An area of the brain called the posterior superior temporal sulcus lit up when students related instances of altruism or when they won for a favorite charity.

The researchers summed up their experiment by stating that altruistic behavior could be predicted. In addition, because altruism is beneficial to a group, they wondered if the region of the brain could be developed early in life by educating young people. In short, understanding the function of this region of the brain may give us clues to how important social behaviors originate (BBC News, 2007).

Box 4.3 Civil War: The Ultimate Group Conflict

Civil war is on our minds of late as the two rival sects of Islam, Sunni and Shia, engage daily in violent acts in Iraq, with a dramatic loss of life. War, of course, is the ultimate step in the social process of conflict. But what exactly brings a society to be divided by such extreme conflict?

Common sense suggests that it is the presence of a number of groups that differ from one another that causes violence between and among them. A study by two political scientists from Stanford University, however, points out that the presence of various groups is not the only or the predominant cause of civil wars (*civil war* is defined as internal conflict in which at least 1,000 deaths per side occur). James D. Fearon and David D. Laitin analyzed 127 civil wars that broke out between the end of World War II and the end of the twentieth century. Their findings are that civil wars break out in countries that are politically unstable and poor and that have a large population and a rough terrain. The fact that they are multiethnic, multiracial, or multireligious may be one reason for conflict, but it is not the main reason. The main reason is

that in such countries it is easy to organize an insurgency. Insurgent groups rise up to fight the government for control or to separate from it.

The researchers report that in the time frame they examined, civil wars have broken out at a rate of 2.3 per year, and that by 1992, more than one-quarter of the states in the world were experiencing civil war, of which two-thirds had an ethnic rivalry cause, one-half had secessionist goals, and the rest were provoked by rebels who wanted control of the government. These civil wars saw a minimum of 16 million people killed. Many civil wars, moreover, last a long time when insurgents are able to finance them by profits from the sale of arms, drugs, or diamonds.

The researchers' findings may be reassuring to countries such as the United States and others containing many ethnic and religious groups but with stable political systems and good economies. But it foreshadows many years of conflict for countries such as Iraq, which has neither (Fearon and Laitin, 2002).

compete for sunlight, water, and nutrients. Animals, including humans, compete for food, shelter, and sexual gratification. But whereas plants and animals limit their competitiveness to things needed for survival, people also compete for things that they have learned to need but which are not necessary for survival.

Conflict is diametrically opposed to cooperation; that is, conflict is a hostile struggle between two or more persons or groups for an object or value that each prizes. Conflict is also the process in which opposing parties attempt to injure, harm, or destroy one another to achieve a specific goal. Like cooperation and competition, conflict is also present in most facets of life. It was believed at one time that conflict was a universal characteristic of humans, but the discovery of societies in which conflict is kept at an absolute minimum largely disproved this belief.

It should be clear that although the four foremost social processes are discussed separately, in reality they are not so distinct and they often occur in the same interactive situation. When two gas stations on opposite corners of the street agree to charge the same price for gasoline, they are cooperating and competing at the same time. Two opposing teams compete for victory, but the members of each team cooperate among themselves. Cooperation sometimes deteriorates into conflict, and history has shown many instances of conflict evolving into cooperation.

To recapitulate, human life is lived in a large variety of groups. People interact within these groups, and groups interact with one another according to social processes, the most important of which are exchange, cooperation, competition, and conflict. Interaction, in turn, crystallizes into distinct patterns of behavior that give each group structure and organization.

Box 4.4   **All the Lonely People**

Despite the fact that humans are social animals, that they live and can survive only in groups, there have always been individuals who have been pushed to the margins of society. For some persons, the reasons are to be found in a physical or psychological abnormality. For many others it does not lie in personal flaws but, rather, in the fact that the social structure undergoes changes. In the 1950s, for instance, individuals unwilling or unable to conform to the prevailing conservatism of the society were described as "the lonely crowd." The 1970s and 1980s produced a countercultural group that stood in contrast to the anxieties and angst of individuals driven by climbing the career ladder. The 1990s produced another breakdown of social connections, sometimes described as "bowling alone."

The twenty-first century has brought with it a further escalation of such a breakdown. Not only do Americans bowl alone, but now their circle of friends and extended family has tightened to a point where it may include only the nuclear family or only a spouse or, increasingly, no one. According to a fairly recent sociological survey, 25 percent of people say they have no one to confide in.

The survey, conducted by the National Opinion Research Center at the University of Chicago, looked at results from 1985 to 2004. Additionally, sociologists from Duke University and the University of Arizona found that there has been a dramatic drop in the number of people who are considered close confidants. These researchers describe the drop as being nearly one-third, resulting in a trend toward smaller, closer social networks limited to spouses or partners. Even contacts through clubs, neighbors, and organizations outside the home are dwindling. The conclusions drawn by the researchers are that such a trend is detrimental to the society: it tears away a safety net and lessens people's interest in civic and political activities.

As for the reasons for the drop in confidants on whom one can count for social support and help, the researchers only speculate that people, especially women, are working longer hours, which keeps them from interacting with others in the community. Moreover, the Internet as a form of communication may also be at fault; in fact, although e-mailing and text messaging may keep us in contact with family and friends, it seems to lessen the need for face-to-face interaction, which is a more intimate connection. The hope is that the Internet will be a tool for strengthening our connections in the future (McPherson, 2006; Smith-Lovin, 2006; Putnam, 2000).

■ Formal Organizations

Organization, in the sense of "order," is characteristic of most enterprises in which humans participate. Communication in the form of speech is organization of sounds. Music is organization of tones. Teams are organized players. All human interaction, in fact, acquires some structure (organization) because of constant repetition. In urban, industrial societies characterized by large numbers of anonymous individuals with only loose loyalties to the state and to each other, organization is of the essence. We have seen that the coming of the information society was preceded by the transition to secondary groups that are prevalent in Gesellschaft-type societies. These types of societies contain a maximum number of formal organizations, groups in which a system of organization, or organization seen as a process, is brought to its highest point.

Formal organizations are associations that are deliberately brought into existence to enable people who do not know each other to carry on complicated relationships for the purpose of attaining specific *goals*. It is through these formal organizations that most necessary activities are carried out in large, complex societies. For example, the business of governing is carried out by a network of formal organizations called "the government." Educating each new generation is the task of formal organizations called "schools." Production, distribution, and trade occur through countless formal organizations called "corporations."

Formal Organizations and Institutions Distinguished

An important distinction must be made between formal organizations and institutions (see Chapter 3). An **institution** is a procedure, an established way of doing things, a pattern of behavior, a deeply ingrained societal custom that becomes part of the social structure. Institutions are *not* groups of people. One cannot join an institution; one can merely do things in an institutionalized way. When two people marry, they carry out a human activity—establishing a paired relationship for the purpose of propagating the species—in an institutionalized way. If a couple simply live together, they carry out that activity in a noninstitutionalized way.

On the other hand, formal organizations *are* groups of people. One may join formal organizations or have dealings with their members or employees. When speaking of government as an institution, what is meant is the regular and established way in which political decisions are made, laws are enacted, and order is maintained in society. When speaking of a particular government (such as the government of the United States), what is meant is the formal organization consisting of large numbers of highly structured and hierarchically ranked people who are elected, appointed, or hired to carry out the activities involved in the governing process (Figure 4.1).

Characteristics of Formal Organizations

Formal organizations display the following characteristics. First, they have a **formal structure**; that is, goals and how to carry them out are stated formally in policy guidelines, constitutions, and other bylaws. They include a body of officers whose relations with one another and with other members of the organization are specified in writing.

Second, formal organizations are meant to be relatively **permanent**. Some of them, especially those established for profit making, may prove to be temporary; but, the expectation is that the formal organization will last as long as it performs the tasks it set for itself.

Third, authority is organized in a **hierarchical order**, giving rise to a bureaucracy. The leadership of the organization is assumed by individuals, who are ranked from high to low. The high-ranking individuals make decisions and give the orders, and each lower rank executes them.

Fourth, formal organizations have a **formal program**. Those who are part of the organization use the program as a guide to attain their goals. Relationships among individuals in the organization are systematic and complex, following bureaucratic principles (see below) and the guidelines specified in the program.

Types of Formal Organizations

Formal organizations are of all types: private and public, local or national or global, voluntary and involuntary, focusing on special interests or on universal needs. One distinction among them is made on the basis of how control is exerted over people, or how members relate to the organization. Sociologists identify three types of formal organizations on this basis: normative, coercive, and utilitarian (Etzioni, 1975).

Normative Organizations. Some formal organizations are joined by choice, because individuals feel that their goals are worthwhile. These formal organizations are called *voluntary associations*. They consist of members who are spare-time volunteers, although most also have a core of full-time, paid, professional employees. Examples of voluntary associations are church organizations, professional groups such as the American Medical Association, and recreational associations such as the American Contract Bridge League.

Organizational Chart of the U.S. Department of the Navy

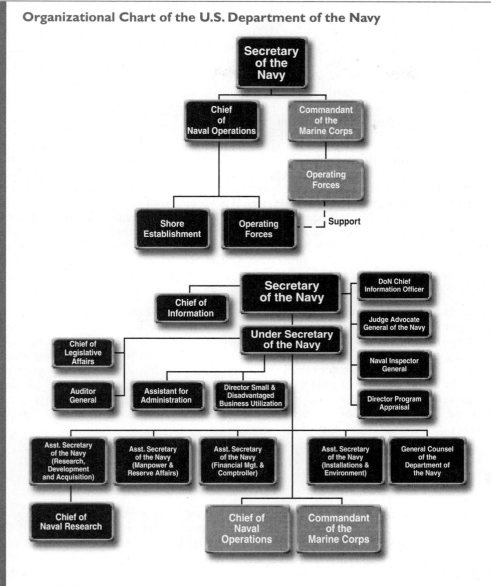

FIGURE 4.1

Americans are known as "joiners," and there are a great many voluntary associations. In reality, however, only a minority of people are active in voluntary organizations. The latter are usually urban residents in their middle years, married and with children, socially and economically upwardly mobile or already at a high socioeconomic level, residentially stable, and well educated.

Voluntary associations bring together people whose particular interests are not shared by the whole society; for instance, not everyone agrees that a woman should be able to obtain an abortion in the United States, but a good number of people do agree that she should. The supporters of legal abortion are better able to work for the cause effectively when they organize into a voluntary association. They may even be able to convince an indifferent or hostile majority of the value of their goal. Thus, voluntary associations are often testing grounds for social programs that are still too controversial to be handled by institutional organizations. They also provide a channel through which the private citizen can share in the decision-making process of society. This facet is particularly important to interest groups, political parties, and social movements, all important voluntary organizations that are examined in later chapters.

Coercive Organizations.   Organizations that people are compelled to join with the threat of force include prisons, mental hospitals, and the military when there is a draft. Naturally, members of these organizations do not join voluntarily and have no commitment to them. In the United States, the military services have become voluntary associations, but during previous wars they had been coercive. Prisons, hospitals, and the military are illustrative of an extreme type of coercive organization, the *total institution,* which isolates inmates from the rest of society, providing an all-encompassing social environment in which special norms and distinctive physical features prevail. The goal of coercive organizations is to change the attitudes and behavior of the inmate or patient—in particular, to change an individual's sense of self, or personality (Goffman, 1961).

Utilitarian Organizations.   People join some formal organizations out of necessity to gain material benefits. For instance, if they want a job, they may have to become employees of a corporation. Businesses of all types, and all the various industries, are examples of utilitarian organizations. Utilitarian organizations do not coerce their members as coercive organizations do, but they do not offer them as much personal freedom as normative organizations. In short, people join utilitarian organizations because they have to make a living, and not because they especially enjoy participating in them. As a result, particularly at the lower end of the organization, workers are not too committed to the goals of the organization: they do what they must to get paid.

■ Bureaucracy

All formal organizations, when they attain a certain size, are administered according to the principles of bureaucracy. **Bureaucracy** is a hierarchical system (or an organizational model) for rationally coordinating the work of many individuals through a division of labor and a chain of authority. In other words, a bureaucracy is a system for organizing a group of people in a pyramid fashion. The purpose is to administer large-scale organizations in the most efficient and intelligent manner. It is an attempt to obtain the desired goals by the best possible means.

In its ideal form, as set forth by Max Weber, a pure bureaucracy *ought* to be characterized by (1) specialization, or division of labor; (2) a chain of command, or a hierarchy of authority; (3) a body of rules covering both rights and duties of all members at all ranks; (4) another set of rules outlining procedures for carrying out all tasks; (5) impersonality in the relationships among members; (6) selection based on merit and job tenure (seniority); and (7) the norm of efficiency (Weber, 1925/1947, 334).

Weber believed that a bureaucratic form of organization made social life more "rational" because it was a system in which goals could be attained efficiently and with a minimum of conflict among people. In a bureaucracy, individual personalities do not matter to the organization because each position consists of activities that remain the same no matter who fills the position. This formality gives the organization stability, predictability, and continuity. Bureaucratic organization works equally well for private and public associations—in fact, for all kinds of associations designed to serve people.

Weber knew that bureaucracy would not work as well in reality as in the ideal form he described, and it does not. The worst thing that can be said about bureaucracy is that while it is supposed to serve people, it often frustrates them instead. Bureaucracies are resistant to change, and bureaucrats somehow start to believe that rules are ends in themselves. Blind loyalty to rules results in the familiar "red tape" phenomenon, as well as in the stifling of personal initiative on the part of bureaucrats. Bureaucrats often want to "pass the buck" because it is easier to shift the responsibility for decision making to someone higher in the hierarchy—then that person can be blamed if the decision turns out to be wrong. Bureaucracies also have a nasty habit of becoming devoted to their own welfare and perpetuation simply because employees want to hang on to their jobs.

Dynamic Quality

In spite of its several failures, bureaucracy has a certain *dynamic* quality that enables it to respond to changing conditions in society. In some respects, in fact, bureaucracies may be instrumental in promoting innovation in a society. Blau and Meyer (1971, 105) suggest that the ideas of scientists alone could not lead to the inventions that in turn trigger social change. In today's complex societies, bureaucratic machinery is needed to translate the ideas of scientists into products and to furnish scientists with laboratories and environments in which they can collaborate on new developments. The authors conclude that the "deliberate introduction of a social innovation . . . depends on bureaucratic methods of administration."

Although hospitals are organized in a hierchical, formal, and structured bureaucratic fashion, an informal side also exists, as illustrated by this group of nurses and doctors eating lunch in a cafeteria.

Informal Side of Bureaucracy

Finally, alongside the formal and structured side of bureaucracy there exists an informal side made up of networks of personal relationships that develop among employees. These networks are occasionally responsible for getting things done through the influence of individuals instead of the regular channels of authority. Sometimes the informal structure, in getting around the rules of the formal structure, actually defies the purpose of the formal bureaucratic organizations. In the long run, however, it may help to reach the goals of the formal organization.

The development of bureaucracy in the private and public sectors, and current alterations in corporate forms of bureaucracy, are discussed further in later chapters that deal with various facets of the economy.

The Chapter in Brief

People are group animals who spend the best parts of their lives in groups of one kind or another. Life in groups acquires a certain pattern through repetition; each group is a social system with a structure and an organization. The structure consists of shared and repeated patterns of behavior that emerge as a result of the interaction of group members. People interact by using a number of social processes and by relating to others from the standpoint of their own position (status) in the group while carrying out the behavior befitting that position (role). Some positions (statuses) within the group are ascribed; that is, people have no control over them (such as gender, age, race, or ethnic origin). Other statuses are achieved as a result of personal effort or merit or lack of it.

Because of the multiplicity of statuses that each person holds in a large variety of groups, people are faced with role confusion, conflict, and strain, as well as failure. In general, people attempt to fill the role attendant on their master status best.

A group is defined by (1) symbolic interaction among the members; (2) members' awareness of membership; (3) members' awareness of the roles, duties, obligations, and privileges resulting from group membership; and (4) members' agreement on shared values.

Groups are classified into dyads (groups consisting of two individuals) and triads (groups consisting of three individuals), which are the basic social units, and according to their size. Groups are also classified as to whether they are primary or secondary, in-groups or out-groups, reference groups, formal or informal groups,

and voluntary or involuntary groups. Of these, the most important classification is that into primary and secondary groups. Primary groups engage in intimate, intense, informal, and spontaneous interaction on a personal and total basis; secondary groups tend to be large, temporary, formal, utilitarian, and specialized. Although primary relationships are very satisfying and important to the individual, industrial societies are increasingly characterized by secondary groups.

The largest group to which people belong is society. Societies are classified according to either their chief mode of subsistence (hunting and gathering, pastoral or herding, horticultural, agrarian, fishing or maritime, and industrial) or their basic patterns of social organization (traditional or communal—Gemeinschaft; modern industrial or associational—Gesellschaft). Gemeinschaft societies are relatively small, with a homogeneous membership; behavior is dictated by tradition, and members interact on an informal, face-to-face basis. Gesellschaft societies tend to be large and heterogeneous, and relationships among members are impersonal, formal, functional, contractual, and specialized. The trend historically has been a transition from a Gemeinschaft to a Gesellschaft type of society.

The reciprocal relationships that occur within and among groups are called interactions. Interaction takes place through a number of social processes, the most basic of which are exchange, cooperation, competition, and conflict. Whatever the type of relationship—primary or secondary—one or more of these social processes is at work.

All human activities are somewhat organized and structured. In complex societies, organization is on a large scale; that is, groups of people who are not personally related must carry on complicated relationships to attain some specific goals. Most of the activities of modern societies are performed in these groups, which are called formal organizations or associations. Some of these organizations are normative, or voluntary; others are coercive, such as prisons, mental hospitals, and the military, and still others are utilitarian, such as business companies. Formal organizations have a formal structure, a degree of permanence, a hierarchical order of authority, and fixed relationships among members. Most are highly organized in an administrative pattern termed a bureaucracy.

Bureaucracy is a hierarchical arrangement based on division of labor and a chain of authority for the purpose of rationally coordinating the work of many individuals. Bureaucracy in its ideal, or pure, form, seldom corresponds to its real functioning: it tends to resist change, its rules become rigid and ends and means become confused, it stifles personal initiative, and it makes employees indecisive. At the same time, bureaucracy is dynamic enough to respond to change and promote innovation in society.

Terms to Remember

achieved status   A position attained through individual effort or merit.

aggregate   A number of people who are in the same place at the same time, but who do not interact with one another.

ascribed status   An inherited position—one that is not attained through individual effort or merit.

bureaucracy   The hierarchical system of administration prevailing within a formal organization. The hierarchy depends on job specialization, a set of rules and standards to promote uniformity, and an attitude of impersonal impartiality.

category   (referring to people) A number of people who have some characteristics in common but who do not interact with one another.

competition   A social process (form of interaction) that occurs when two or more individuals try to obtain possession of the same scarce object or intangible value using rules and limits.

conflict   A social process (interaction) consisting of a hostile struggle in which two or more persons engage for an object or value that each prizes, possibly to the point of destruction.

cooperation   A basic social process (interaction) involving two or more individuals or groups working jointly in a common enterprise for a shared goal.

dyad   The smallest type of group, consisting of two members.

exchange   A social process (interaction) consisting of a transaction in which one of two individuals—or groups or societies—does something for the other with the expectation of receiving something of equal value in return.

formal organizations   Large-scale associations of people in which most of the activities of complex societies are handled. They are highly organized groups displaying a formal structure, a body of officers, the expectation of permanence, and a hierarchical organization of authority (bureaucracy).

Gemeinschaft   A small, homogeneous, communal, and traditional society. Relationships among members are personal, informal, and face-to-face, and behavior is dictated by tradition.

Gesellschaft   A large, heterogeneous society, typified by the modern industrial state. Relationships among members tend to be impersonal, formal, contractual, functional, and specialized. Also called an associational society.

group   A number of people who engage in symbolic interaction; who are mutually aware of and influence one another; who recognize their membership in the group and are in turn recognized as members by the group; who are aware of the roles, duties, obligations, and privileges of membership; and who agree to a point about the behavioral guidelines, values, and goals they share.

in-group   Group to which the individual belongs and which confers on the individual a social identity.

organization   A formal process that deliberately brings into existence a group of people to perform tasks directed at achieving a specific goal. It allows people who are unacquainted with each other to cooperate effectively on complex projects.

out-group   Group to which others belong, excluding the individual defining group membership.

primary group   A relatively small group of people who live physically near one another and who interact intensely. Characteristics include stability, relatively long duration, informal and spontaneous interaction, and individual, personal, and total types of dealings.

reference group   A group providing individuals with standards against which to measure themselves.

role   The carrying out of a status. A way of behaving that befits a status and is transmittable as well as fairly predictable.

secondary group   A group that is in general larger and of shorter duration than a primary group. Interaction among members is formal, role-based, utilitarian, specialized, and temporary.

social organization   The network of patterned human behavior that is the product of interaction and, at the same time, guides interaction.

social processes   Key patterns of interaction common to all human societies (cooperation, competition, exchange, and conflict).

social structure   The content of the social system, consisting of statuses, roles, groups, norms, and institutions.

social system   A conceptual model of social relationships in which each part is interdependent and interconnected to every other part.

society   The largest social group. An interrelated network of social relationships that exists within the boundaries of the largest social system.

status   A ranked position in a social group. Statuses are rated according to their importance in a social group.

symbolic interaction   Communication through speech, gestures, writing, or even music.

total institution   An extreme type of coercive organization that isolates individuals from the rest of society, providing an all-encompassing social environment in which special norms and distinctive physical features prevail, with the goal of changing the individual's attitudes, behaviors, and personality.

triad   A group consisting of three individuals. A more stable social unit than a dyad.

Suggested Readings

Hall, Richard H. 1991. *Organizations: Structures, Processes, and Outcomes.* Englewood Cliffs, NJ: Prentice Hall. An overview of how sociologists analyze the various types of organizations.

Janis, Irving L. 1989. *Crucial Decisions: Leadership in Policymaking and Crisis Management.* New York: Free Press. The author originated the expression "groupthink" meaning an individual's diminished capacity for critical thinking because of the conforming influence of the group.

Kephart, William M. 1991. *Extraordinary Groups: An Examination of Unconventional Life-Styles.* New York: St. Martin's Press. A collection of essays about groups that are unconventional and out of the mainstream, such as self-help groups, unusual occupational groups, and ethnic groups.

Kottak, Conrad P. 1999. *Assault on Paradise: Social Change in a Brazilian Village.* 3rd ed. New York: McGraw-Hill. The transition from a Gemeinschaft to a Gesellschaft type of society is described by an anthropologist who records the transformation of a fishing village into a tourist attraction.

Lenski, Gerhard, Jean Lenski, and Patrick Nolan. 2001. *Human Society: An Introduction to Macrosociology*, 9th ed. New York: McGraw-Hill. A detailed account, from a sociological perspective, of different types of societies and the role technology plays in each of them.

Moss-Kanter, Rosabeth. 1989. *When Giants Learn to Dance: Mastering the Challenges of Strategy, Management, and Careers in the 1990s.* New York: Simon and Schuster. This well-known sociologist, specializing in formal organizations, applies sociological concepts to problems of corporate organization.

Putnam, Robert D. 2000. *Bowling Alone: The Collapse and Revival of American Community.* New York: Simon and Schuster. The author maintains that participation in voluntary organizations has been declining in American society, which has resulted in a consequent decline in shared cultural values.

Woolsey Biggart, Nicole. 1989. *Charismatic Capitalism: Direct Selling Organizations in America*. Chicago: University of Chicago Press. Some organizations, for instance, Amway and Mary Kay Cosmetics, foster a type of bureaucracy based on emotional intensity among its members in the hope of motivating them to excel in sales.

Web Sites of Interest

http://www2.pfeiffer.edu/~lridener/DSS/formorg.htm
Links to a number of web sites discussing bureaucracy and formal organization.

http://www.umsl.edu/~keel/010/groups.html
A sociology course that offers clear definitions of the subject of groups.

5

Becoming a Person: The Birth of Personality

IN THIS CHAPTER, YOU WILL LEARN

- that human infants must learn how to become human beings;
- that personality is based on a delicate interplay of heredity and environment;
- that the acquisition of personality occurs through the process of socialization;
- the various theories of socialization;
- who are the agents of socialization;
- that socialization occurs throughout a person's life;
- that one has to become resocialized to each new role in life.

If one were to look into a hospital nursery almost anywhere in the world, the picture would be similar: rows of cribs or baskets containing infants of indeterminate gender, some of whom are squirming and crying while others are sleeping peacefully. A closer look will reveal differences in appearance, but at first glance, all the babies look very much alike. Should one meet the same babies 20 years later, the differences among them would no doubt be dramatically obvious: not only would these individuals be distinctive in looks but also, if engaged in conversation, they would display a variety of attitudes, opinions, beliefs, and values. Moreover, they would differ in the manner in which they expressed them.

The infants met in the hospital have been subjected to two unavoidable processes. One is maturation, or the physical development of the body, which proceeds at approximately the same rate for everyone. The other is socialization, or the process of becoming human, learning societal norms and values while developing a personality unique to each individual.

The question may be asked at this point whether it is necessary to *become* human, whether in fact people are not *born* human. The answer, based on a large number of instances

Box 5.1   The Isolated and/or Feral Child

People have long been fascinated with the question of how children who are not socialized by the example of other humans turn out. Myths and legends abound about human babies left to be suckled by a she-wolf (Romulus and Remus, the founders of the city of Rome), about little boys abandoned in the jungle to be raised by apes (Tarzan), about the "wild boy of Aveyron," found in a forest in France and believed to have survived without human contact (this last story is based on a true event). It is said that even King James of England isolated some babies to see if they would grow up speaking Hebrew, the language of the Bible. He must have been sorely disappointed. The so-called "feral" children—thought to have been raised by animals—or those isolated from most human contact fail to develop into full human beings.

The first reliable information about such children in the twentieth century comes from the work of sociologist Kingsley Davis (1940–1947), who studied a six-year-old born illegitimately to a mildly retarded woman. The child, Anna, had been discovered living in pitiful conditions in the attic of her grandfather's house. The child's mother had kept her alive physically but had neglected her in every other way. When found, she was sitting with her arms tied above her head to prevent any movement. Davis found her frail and emaciated to the point of being unable to use her arms and legs. She did not smile, laugh, speak, or show any emotion, as if she were unaware of the world around her. Eventually, after much intensive therapy, she learned to walk, to feed herself, to play with toys, and to respond with something approaching human emotion. However, it was obvious that she would never catch up to children her age: she did not begin to use language before her tenth birthday, and she died soon thereafter.

Another case that came to Davis' attention also involved an illegitimate child, known as Isabelle, who had been kept isolated under very similar conditions, but with a deaf-mute mother. This six-year-old displayed some of the same symptoms as Anna: she could not speak, walked only with great difficulty, and seemed more animal-like than human. When she was first tested, psychologists concluded that she was retarded and probably uneducable. However, they worked intensively with her, and she soon began to thrive. By the age of eight, she had attained the development of a normal six-year-old, and at fourteen she was attending sixth grade. Davis concluded that social isolation is extremely damaging, that it hinders development even in cases where later socialization is undertaken intensively, and consequently that the socialization process is necessary for becoming fully human.

The latest known instance of social isolation that took place in the United States involved a girl, born to a psychotic father and a blind mother, who was kept strapped to a potty chair in a secluded room from the age of two to eleven. Genie, as she is called by researchers, was in a similarly emaciated physical condition, and although she outwardly looked normal, she tested as having the mental development of a one-year-old. She knew a few words, which she babbled, but she had absolutely no social skills, continually spitting and masturbating in public. Researchers were at first unsure whether her retardation was due to prenatal physical causes or resulted from her isolation. In time and under constant guidance, Genie learned many more words than the average retarded person acquires. However, she never mastered the complexities of grammar, which the normal child acquires as a matter of course by imitation. The researchers concluded that Genie had missed the critical period in her development when she was ready to learn language and, thus, would probably never totally master it. In fact, though she seemed to exhibit traits pointing to a high intelligence in some areas, her language skills never went beyond those of a third grader. Genie is still alive, but she has never become a fully social being who is able to interact with others and show human emotions. Those in charge of her case conclude that the absence of parental love has damaged her so that she is unable to express her feelings and thoughts and live a full life (Rymer, 1993; see also **http://www.feralchildren.com**).

of social isolation, seems to be that, indeed, one must learn from others to become human. That is, the infant is basically a creature capable of a few bodily functions but little more. Infants who have been left alone without any human companionship, even if their biological needs are attended to, either die or fail to develop normally. It is only in the process of relating to others of our species and learning from them that we become unique individuals with distinctive personalities who fit into a particular social structure.

■ Personality

It is frequently said of a person that he or she either has a nice personality or no personality at all. The first description is only partial and vague, and the second one is impossible, for every person has a personality. People tend to use the term *personality* imprecisely.

Personality may be defined as a complex and dynamic system that includes all of an individual's fairly consistent behavioral and emotional traits—actions, habits, attitudes, beliefs, values, goals, and so on. It is, of course, an abstract term. It is *dynamic* because personality continually changes and adjusts to events that affect the person or in accordance with how the person perceives these events. Personality may also be seen as a *circular* system: while the roles people fill in society affect their personalities, personalities also influence the way roles are seen and accomplished. Finally, personalities are *distinctive* because each individual is born with a specific set of inherited traits and potentials and then has experiences that are exclusively his or her own. Even identical twins, with the same biological heredity, may display personality differences based on different life experiences.

Personality: A Social Product on a Biological Basis

The study of personality has involved a number of scientists—psychologists, sociologists, anthropologists, and ethologists (scientists who study animal behavior in natural surroundings). Much of the research concerns, first, the issue of what proportion of personality is made up of *inherited traits* and what proportion consists of *learned behavior*—are people predominantly biological or predominantly cultural creatures? Unfortunately, no easy answer can be given. Research to date seems to indicate that personality development occurs

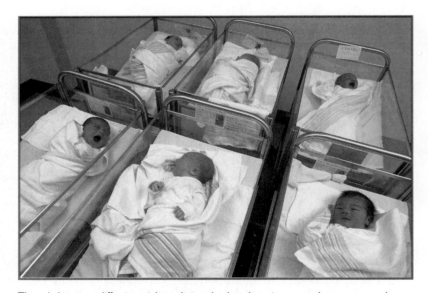

These babies may differ in weight or hair color, but there is not much one can say about their character or personalities. Those traits will emerge after a process of socialization.

as a consequence of the interplay of biological inheritance, physical environment, culture, group experience, and personal experience.

The biological inheritance that all humans share is one that, in some respects, predisposes them toward accepting learning from others, in the process of which they acquire a personality. Humans lack strong instincts; thus, to a great extent they must *learn* how to act to their best advantage. (While they lack instincts, humans do have biological drives, such as self-preservation, hunger, thirst, and the need for sex. Some also add the drive toward exploration, experimentation, and analysis. These drives are perceived as tensions or discomforts in the organism that must be relieved. How best to relieve the discomfort is the function of culture, which represents the accumulated learning of countless preceding generations of people.)

Biology is also responsible for the universal human need for social and physical contact, which humans share with a number of animals and which may be interpreted as a need to receive and give love. As noted above, it has been shown repeatedly that infants deprived of loving human contact—those institutionalized because of being orphaned, those isolated because of being illegitimate or having been born to mothers with mental illness, or those simply badly neglected—do not develop normally, either physically or mentally. Some fail to thrive and die in infancy. Others grow up to be mentally or otherwise damaged (Spitz, 1964). Although the reasons are not clearly understood, it seems that absence of body contact and stimulation in infancy inhibits the development of higher learning functions. In this need, humans are not alone: our close biological cousins, members of the ape family, show a need for similar closeness and body contact. In a well-known experiment involving rhesus monkeys, researchers found that rhesus infants, separated from their biological mothers, preferred a soft and cuddly "mother" made of terrycloth, even though "she" did not feed

In a classic experiment, rhesus monkeys who were fed by a wire "mother" substitute ran to embrace the soft, terrycloth "mother" when frightened or anxious.

them, to a surrogate mother made of wire from which they did receive food. The infants ran to the soft "mother" in times of stress and preferred to spend most of their time near "her" (Harlow, 1966). In the wild, many animals engage in grooming behavior, which is thought to be an expression of bonding and the need to share an activity with others—to interact socially.

A more recent study supports the idea that parent–infant bonding has a biological basis and has a profound impact on later development. A team of researchers reports that in a group of mice, those individuals who lack a gene that allows them to obtain relief from pain also have difficulty establishing bonds with their mothers. In the first few days after birth, mice are very vulnerable, and when separated from their mothers, they cry out in distress. Cries for help are instrumental in cementing mother–child attachment. Such attachment is fundamental to survival, but the mice lacking the specific gene do not engage in the attachment behavior. "The study provides strong evidence that the same brain chemicals that control physical pain also regulate the psychological ache of loss and separation" (Carey, 2004, D7).

The biological fact that human infants are born helpless and must depend on adults for sheer survival also predisposes them to accept learning from adults and leads to the formation of strong bonds between them. Finally, the biologically based potential for learning and using symbol systems makes it possible and probable that humans accept the culture into which they are born. In turn, the capacity for language is what makes the creation of culture and social structure possible, as we have seen in Chapters 3 and 4.

Heredity and Environment

In addition to having these general effects on humans as a species, biology also affects people as individuals, accounting for some of their uniqueness in appearance and personality. Just as each individual inherits from each parent specific genes that determine whether the individual is short or tall, has blue or brown eyes, and has straight or curly hair, so too heredity determines many personality characteristics, including intelligence, sociability, timidity, and basic temperament (Horn et al., 1976; Juel-Nielson, 1980; Herbert, 1982). Other personality traits, such as leadership abilities, control of impulses, attitudes, and interests, however, depend to a much greater extent on the environment in which a person is raised. These two factors, heredity and environment, are so interrelated as they act on the personality that it is impossible to measure exactly the influence of either. All that can be said with certainty is that whether a person's full potential is developed depends on that person's social experience or the environment in which life is spent.

Social scientists have pondered the mystery of why siblings, who share 50 percent of their genes, can at times be so dissimilar. Two professors of human development have stated in their book, *Separate Lives: Why Siblings Are So Different*, that siblings are also 50 percent different genetically. Those differences, when measured by tests of personality, attitude, belief, and temperament, explain why the same environment is perceived differently by siblings, in spite of sharing the same parents, social class, and most daily experiences. These idiosyncratic responses mold characters in different directions. For example, a child who is genetically shy reacts differently to having a social butterfly for a mother than his or her outgoing sister. The research reported by these writers has been replicated in studies of thousands of children in Sweden, England, and Colorado (Dunn & Plomin, 1990).

Biological inheritance determines personality in another way also. People respond to certain physical traits in a particular way—favorably to some, negatively to others—and their reaction influences an individual's personality. A fat person is considered beautiful in some societies and, thus, develops a positive self-image, which in turn may result in a self-confident, pleasant, outgoing personality. In our own United States, on the other hand, fatness is not considered a positive attribute. As a consequence, such a person may have a low self-image and be withdrawn, shy, self-conscious, and unpleasant in interaction with others (though this unpleasantness may be in self-defense). In short, it is not biological inheritance per se that necessarily affects personality; rather, it is the way a society and culture interpret biologically inherited traits that has a bearing on an individual's personality.

As to the physical environment, although it is not true that personality types correspond to climatic or geographic areas, as was once believed, it is true that certain conditions caused by the physical environment may influence some dominant personality traits. One example from the not-too-distant past concerns the Ik. These inhabitants of a region of Uganda lost their traditional hunting grounds because of the country's political partition. They then began to suffer profound deprivation to the point of starvation. A previously friendly and outgoing people, the Ik became incredibly selfish and greedy, lacking compassion toward the old, whom they encouraged to die, and taking the last morsel away from their own children so that they themselves might eat (Turnbull, 1973).

Culture too has a definite impact on personality, in the sense that every society subjects its members to unique experiences that differ from the experiences of members of other societies. Because of this commonality of social experiences, most members of a specific society share a particular configuration of personality traits. This so-called *modal* personality is thought to be representative of that society. People speak of the Latin lover, the hard-drinking Irish, the "keep-a-stiff-upper-lip" British, the punctual German, and the arrogant French. Although these descriptions of personality types have become stereotypes that do a disservice to their respective societies, it remains true that each society, by virtue of the values and beliefs that are dominant in it, develops one or more personality types that reflect the society's culture. In a complex, heterogeneous society, moreover, there may be as many personality types as there are subcultures; witness the "Southern belle" and "urban cowboy" familiar to Americans, in addition to stereotypical portraits of minority groups. Ultimately, however, even in the most conforming of societies, human personality retains a great amount of individuality.

■ Becoming Human: Socialization

A just-born infant is completely unaware of self. The infant at this point is a living bundle of drives that create tensions demanding to be satisfied. Most theorists agree that the infant does not know that it is human or even that it exists. In fact, the creature cannot distinguish between itself and other objects in its environment. It is only when others act toward the infant in a manner that is distinct from the way they act toward other people and objects that the infant begins to recognize that he or she is a separate entity. This awareness of one's distinctiveness, or separateness, of having borders between oneself and others, is the first step in the emergence of the self—and it occurs as a result of interaction with others.

The emergence of self, in turn, is a first step in socialization. **Socialization** is the process that teaches individuals how to become functioning human beings who must fit into a number of groups and be productive members of a society. Sociologists maintain that a distinctive personality is acquired during the process of socialization.

Goals and Functions of Socialization

From the point of view of society, socialization has specific goals. First, it teaches the basics of life in the society. Second, it transmits skills that are important to survival in the society. Third, it instills in new members of society a desire to work toward some goals that the society considers important. Fourth, it teaches members how to fulfill social roles, for only if a majority of people does so can the social system continue to exist (see Chapter 4). Finally, it provides each individual with his or her identity, because people need to know who they are so that they may act accordingly.

The process of socialization is not limited to infants and children. Rather, it continues throughout an individual's lifetime, as there are always new roles to be learned and new circumstances to which to adjust. However, socialization is different for children and for adults. Children must, first of all, learn how to regulate their biological drives in socially acceptable ways. They must learn to develop values that are in accordance with the aims of their society. They must develop a self-image. Adults, on the other hand, must primarily learn new roles as they enter the labor force or as they change their statuses—as they get married or become parents or grandparents. The experience of socialization is also different for the two groups. Children tend to be emotionally involved with those who socialize them, which makes the process much more effective. Adults are usually socialized voluntarily, but the involvement with their socializers is secondary in nature (see Chapter 4): they deal with professors or supervisors instead of mothers and fathers. This type of socialization is less effective and easier to resist, and the results are more superficial.

Socialization occurs on both a conscious and an unconscious level. Children are deliberately taught certain behaviors, attitudes, and values, but others are picked up unconsciously, from overheard conversations or observed actions of adults. Behavior, attitudes, and values picked up unconsciously are usually much more difficult to shed.

Finally, socialization must take into consideration the feelings, or emotions, that humans display. Three of the most fundamental of human emotions are love, anger, and anxiety.

Love is needed to ensure normal development. Unloved children become unloving adults, who may display psychological disturbances. Rejecting parents who deny their children love, respect, and self-esteem risk causing serious maladjustment and stunted development in their children.

Anger is the reaction to deprivation and frustration. One of the chief aims of socialization is to channel anger in such a way that it does not result in aggression. Parents who are unable to direct their children's anger often put up with temper tantrums, which are the child's way of attempting to control others in a destructive and disruptive form, and they may leave themselves open to antisocial behavior throughout their offspring's adolescence.

Anxiety, unlike anger, is not a definite, sharply defined emotion. Rather, it is a diffuse state of mind in which the individual feels uneasy but is not aware of exactly why. In this respect, anxiety differs from fear, which is a response to a definite threat. Anxiety has been considered the hallmark of modern Western societies; in fact, some of our values are very anxiety-producing.

If socialization is to be successful, these emotions must be manipulated in such a way that they do not become destructive to individuals or to society. The process of socialization functions to the advantage of both society and the individual. Society profits because each new generation learns how to behave as a member of it, and the individual profits because he or she acquires a self and a unique personality in the bargain.

The socialization process, which turns bundles of flesh and blood into human beings, begins when a significant other interacts with the newborn.

■ Theories of Socialization

Exactly how the self emerges during socialization has been the subject of numerous theories, both in sociology and in psychology. The most widely accepted theories from the sociological perspective are those of the "looking-glass self" and symbolic interactionism. Psychologists, on the other hand, have viewed the acquisition of personality in the process of becoming human from the perspective of the unconscious, the rational, the moral, and the transitional self.

The Looking-Glass Self: Cooley

Charles Horton Cooley (1864–1929) and his colleague George Herbert Mead (1863–1931) were two American sociologists who formulated the original interactionist theories based on the finding that the self is the result of a learning process that occurs when individuals interact with those around them. Cooley speculated that the development of a socially defined self begins in the early stages of life. In interaction with their immediate family and later with peer groups, maturing individuals learn that they are distinct from others and that their needs are satisfied because they are loved. Essentially, they learn how they stand in particular relationships to others and how others feel about them. Each individual senses the opinions of others from their reactions to him or her. Cooley called this process the **looking-glass self**, because it resembles looking into an imaginary mirror that reflects back to the looker his or her image as others see it (the others, of course, are society in general; thus, society is internalized by the individual). If the reflected image is good (as society says it should be), the person is satisfied. If the image is bad, the person feels ashamed and dissatisfied with himself or herself.

The Self in Society: Mead

The theory that social, and particularly symbolic, interaction is the basis of the emergence of self and personality was further developed in the work of George Herbert Mead. Many complex ideas are embodied in **symbolic interactionism**, but they all center around the interrelationship of **mind** (the abstract whole of a person's ideas), **self** (the individual's self-concept or self-awareness), and **society**.

Symbolic interaction is the first prerequisite for personality formation, according to Mead. Such interaction is at first nonverbal—the infant cries and the parents respond to it. This sets the stage for more meaningful communication through language. Once language is present, mind and self can emerge and actions can be replaced by ideas. Mind and self are social products because individuals internalize, or make their own, the attitudes of those around them through language. Thus, individuals become capable of thinking about themselves as they think about others: they become objects to themselves. They begin to realize the distinctions among I, me, and you, and they begin to treat themselves as they treat others. This enables them to learn to control their own behavior and direct it into meaningful channels. People become self-critical because others are critical of them. In this manner, society begins to control individuals.

This uniquely human quality of being able to get outside oneself and view oneself as others do is possible because of the human ability to take on various roles. Role-playing is learned by children in the course of play. At first, the others whose roles children take are members of their family and of their peer group or, as Mead called them, the **significant others**. Later, individuals learn to take the role of society as a whole or, in Mead's terms, to take into account the **generalized other**. The change from taking the role of significant others to taking the role of the generalized other is complete when the child, in considering some action, no longer thinks, "Mommy says I must not do it," but rather, "It's not right to do it." At that point, the child has internalized—made a part of herself or himself—the folkways, mores, values, and other norms of society, thereby acquiring a conscience.

Although the self that emerges as a result of internalizing the attitudes of others is principally of a social nature, it has another more creative and spontaneous element. Mead called this element the **I**, positing that it emerged before the social element, which he called the **me**. The I is the subjective, acting, natural, uninhibited part of the self. The me, in contrast, is the objective representative of cultural and societal expectations that have been made part of personality by the individual. The I is unique to each individual; the me is conventional in that it is shared with others.

■ The Self and the Unconscious: Freud

The best-known personality theorist—and widely regarded as the founder of modern psychology—is Sigmund Freud (1856–1939). Freud attempted to explain the structure of personality in the light of biological drives. The theories that he and some of his followers espoused, called **psychodynamic theories**, used a sophisticated definition of the word *instinct*. They also assumed that culture and society had a definite effect on human behavior.

Freud's **psychoanalytic theory** presupposed the existence of unconscious, as well as conscious, processes. The unconscious processes resulted from repression of painful experiences and revealed themselves in dreams or in analysis. Freud also speculated about the existence of the **libido**, an instinctual drive toward pleasure whose representative within the personality was the **id**. Social learning, according to Freud, caused the development of the **ego**, a part of the personality that functioned to restrain the primitive, irrational actions of the id. Finally, the **superego** emerged as a result of having internalized the values and norms of one's culture. The superego operated subconsciously, whereas the ego functioned on a conscious level.

Freud also insisted that personality developed according to a fixed number of psychosexual stages in the period from infancy to adolescence. Each stage represented the individual's attempts to gratify the libido at different periods of physical maturation. The success of the ego and superego in channeling the energy of the id into socially approved activities depended on how well an individual has resolved the conflicts at every stage. The stages are:

1. *oral*, in the first year of life;
2. *anal*, in the second and third years;
3. *phallic*, or *Oedipal*, in the third through fifth year;
4. *latency*, from age five to the beginning of adolescence;
5. *genital*, during puberty and into adulthood.

Freud further maintained that dysfunctions of personality—that is, behaviors that society labeled abnormal or deviant—were caused by lack of harmony between the id, the ego, and the superego. The disharmony created anxiety, and anxiety in turn led to the development of defense mechanisms. **Defense mechanisms** are the frequently unconscious actions that individuals use to ward off anxiety. Some of the more common ones include repression, regression, projection, and displacement. These mechanisms hide from individuals their real motives and goals and thus protect them from loss of self-esteem. However, overreliance on defense mechanisms can cause individuals to show disturbed behavior of varying intensity. It is such overreliance, as well as other forms of "abnormal" behavior, that Freud set out to cure with the therapy he called *psychoanalysis*, which is designed to delve into a person's subconscious to uncover causes of specific behaviors.

Freud's influence has extended far beyond the field of psychology, and his theories have given us valuable insights into the human personality. Today, however, psychoanalytic theory is accepted by most behavioral scientists only with reservations. The most serious criticism involves the importance Freud assigned to the early years of life. He maintained, in fact, that personality was fixed by the age of 5 and difficult to change without psychoanalysis. More contemporary theories tend to stress that personality development does not stop after infancy, childhood, or even puberty but, on the contrary, is a never-ending process, changing to respond to changing demands.

■ The Transitional Self: Erikson

Freudian thought has given origin to numerous theories that have enlarged and modified some of its basic assumptions. Among the neo-Freudians, Erik Erikson (1968) contended that human personality development takes place in eight psychosocial stages that closely parallel Freud's psychosexual stages. Erikson's stages, however, encompass the entire life of the individual and, thus, are more compatible with contemporary thought.

Erikson maintained that at each of the eight developmental stages, the individual is faced with an identity crisis in which the self must try to redefine itself. (Erikson's eight stages are infancy, early childhood, play age, school age, adolescence, young adulthood, adulthood or middle age, and maturity.) If the individual is successful in redefining the self, that is, if the challenges presented by a new stage of the life cycle are conquered—he or she is

Box 5.2 The Impact of Freud on Psychology

Sigmund Freud is considered a giant in the discipline of psychology. Although today the discipline has taken other directions, the impact of his theories has been widespread. Freud's essential idea was that by observing patients' symptoms their cause could be discovered by searching their unconscious. Of course, even today most therapies attempt to do the same, that is, discover the cause of problems with the hope of overcoming them.

In addition to the theories mentioned in the text, theories and therapies based on Freud's thought include some of the following.

An early collaborator of Freud's was Carl Jung, responsible for the so-called analytical psychology. Jung broke away from Freud because he disagreed with him concerning the importance of early sexuality. Jung classified people as introverts or extroverts and posited that the unconscious is not present only in individuals, but that all of humanity exhibits similar fears, thoughts, and behaviors, which he called a collective unconscious. It is this collective unconscious that influences personality (see **www.allpsych.com/personalitysynopsis/jung.html**).

Discounting the function of the unconscious was B. F. Skinner's operant conditioning, a therapy based on his predecessor, John Watson, who preferred an empirical method of overcoming psychological problems. Skinner focused on observable behaviors and posited that behavior changed as a result of responses to stimuli (that is why this approach is also called the stimulus-response theory) backed up by reinforcements (see **http://www.bfskinner.org/operant.asp**).

Quite well known to most of us is group therapy, which utilizes the shared experiences of the group and is used in such rehabilitating institutions as Alcoholics Anonymous; the interpersonal psychotherapy of Harry Stack Sullivan, who focused more on the social and cognitive aspects of personality and developed a method of guiding and supporting patients (see **http://www.allpsych.com/personalitysynopsis/stack_sullivan.html**); and the social psychoanalysis of Karen Horney and the psychoanalytic feminism of Nancy Chodorow, both of whom focused on gender as determinant of personality, the first in response to Freud's notion that women have "penis envy," the other basing personality on gender identity (see **http://www.answers.com/topic/feminism-and-psychoanalysis**).

Cognitive therapy is an effort to change a person's troubling or self-destructive behavior by manipulating the content of his or her thoughts. This therapy is the prevalent one today and is used mostly in trying to deal with depression and posttraumatic stress disorder but also for a number of other mental illnesses and problems. It is sometimes combined with behavioral therapy in an attempt to change negative thoughts or behavior. It was developed by Aaron Beck and is still run by the therapist and his daughter from the Beck Institute for Cognitive Therapy and Research (see **http://www.habitsmart.com/cogintro.html**).

As popular as this therapy is, psychology marches on. A former collaborator of Aaron Beck's, Steven Hayes, is proposing that persons afflicted with depression, anxiety, panic attacks, and so on not try to change their negative thoughts but accept them. Hayes believes that suffering is a part of life, that happiness is not normal, and that rather than changing one's thoughts, one ought to examine them dispassionately, or "disidentify" from them, so they no longer control one's behavior. The name given to this therapy is acceptance and commitment therapy (ACT), and it is currently the most divisive therapy in the discipline. The adherents are termed third-wave psychologists; the second wave are the cognitive psychologists, who turned away from the first wave, or the behaviorism of B. F. Skinner (see **http://www.acceptanceandmindfulness.com/authhayes.htm**).

able to progress to the next stage, thereby achieving increasing maturity. If the individual is unable to satisfy the new demands of a particular stage, psychological problems may develop, preventing the person from progressing to the next stage and from reaching a higher level of maturity. For instance, at the stage of adolescence, the individual is faced with rapid physical growth and sexual maturity and must learn to fill new roles related to a future occupation, as well as to a functioning sexuality. Young people at this stage are plagued by role confusion and absence of a definite identity. According to Erikson, this is why young people tend to overidentify with cliques and popular culture and why they "fall in love" so often.

What they call and perceive as "love" for another person is in reality an attempt to project their own image on another and see it reflected back and thus clarified (Erikson, 1963, 262). Successful young individuals eventually come to know who they are and what they want to do. Those who have not resolved these questions remain at a loss, not knowing what kind of person they are or what they should do in life. Socialization, then, never ends, according to Erikson, and the self must constantly meet new crises and learn new roles until death.

■ Developmental Theories: Piaget

Developmentalists, whose chief proponent was the late Swiss psychologist Jean Piaget (1896–1980), stress the importance of individual interpretations of situations according to moral values and intellectual skills. Intellectual and moral development can proceed only in stages, however. In turn, these stages can develop only according to an individual's physical maturation. For instance, Piaget insisted that a child of 3 could not understand the concept of speed, and no amount of conditioning would make the child understand it.

Piaget designated the stages of cognitive development as:

1. the sensory-motor stage, from birth to 2 years, in which children cannot understand societal rules;
2. the preoperational stage, from 2 to 7 years, in which rules are learned but not questioned, although they may be disobeyed;
3. the concrete-operational stage, from age 7 to 11, in the course of which such concepts as numbers, weight, cause and effect, and other cognitive skills needed for everyday life are mastered;
4. the formal-operational stage, from age 11 to 16, in which the capacity for rational and abstract thinking is fully developed and education becomes the best vehicle for exploring the mind.

Developmentalists also assert that people are essentially active organisms, who are capable of judging, interpreting, defining, and creating their own behavior, provided they have reached a specific stage of physical maturation. Thus, although it will prove fruitless to force a child of 5 to reason abstractly, there is no reason why an adolescent of 14 or 15 cannot do so to the same extent as an older adult.

■ Moral Development: Kohlberg

Expanding on Piaget's ideas that children's intellectual development proceeds in stages, American psychologist Lawrence Kohlberg (1963, 1981) theorizes that their moral development, their sense of what is right and wrong, proceeds similarly. Moreover, he posits that children's sense of morality develops from within themselves rather than being superimposed by society. He arrived at this conclusion by doing research in a number of countries and noting that, even though societies differ on the specifics of what is considered right and wrong, the same basic values are taught in every society. In short, morality seems to be a cultural universal: although certain foods may be forbidden in one society but allowed in another, such values as concern for others (empathy) and desire for equality and reciprocity (justice) appear to exist in all societies. Individuals do not all have equally developed systems of moral values because they are at different levels of maturity.

Kohlberg claims that there are three levels of moral development, each more complex than the preceding. All children reach every level as they mature, but not all children absorb it, so not all progress to the next level equally equipped. Young children define right and wrong in terms of obedience and disobedience to authority, their concern being the consequences of an act and not the intention behind it; they have a *preconventional* morality. Adolescents adopt a morality based on socially approved values, trusting in a higher authority to define right and wrong; they are at a *conventional* level of development. Some, but not all, adults reach a *postconventional* level, in which the existence of conflicting values is acknowledged and the attempt is made to resolve the conflict in a rational manner or according to what are perceived as higher principles. An individual at this level may consider breaking the law if the law is perceived as unjust.

Kohlberg has been criticized on several counts. First, the fact that an individual recognizes that an act is immoral does not prevent the individual from committing the act. Second, Kohlberg has been accused of focusing on the way men and boys perceive ethics and justice; had he included women and girls, he might have obtained a different view. And finally, Kohlberg's assumption that his theory is applicable to all cultures has been questioned; in particular, the postconventional stage is thought to be more characteristic of liberal, technologically advanced, democratic societies than of authoritarian, agrarian, or undemocratic ones (Gilligan, 1982; Snarey, 1987).

■ Agents of Socialization

Specific people, groups, and organizations are chiefly responsible for transforming a raw bundle of tissues and nerves into a functioning human being, knowledgeable in the ways of society, competent in enough skills to survive and sometimes to thrive and excel in the society, and with features and traits familiar to others yet still recognizably unique.

The Family

The foremost socializers are the people who raise the newborn. Barring unusual circumstances, in most societies these people are generally the infant's parents. Thus, most socialization occurs within the family.

The role of the family in socialization is crucial. First, the family influences the child in its earliest stage of development, when the child is most receptive. It meets all of the child's needs, both physical and emotional. It is a constant influence because most people maintain family relationships from infancy into adulthood. The family is also a primary group, and the personal and emotional ties are conducive to effective socialization. The family, finally, provides the new individual with his or her first identity, as the infant is born into a particular racial group, religion, and social class.

Although parents try to teach, guide, influence, and control the behavior of their children, the latter are not mere clay in parental hands. Socialization, in fact, is reciprocal. The way infants look and act has a bearing on how parents feel and act toward them. And even the most helpless infant can initiate interaction simply by crying. Infants who obtain a positive response to the crying—who are picked up, cuddled, and comforted—receive a different view of the world and their position in it than infants whose crying is ignored.

Parental behavior varies in each family. It also has been shown to vary according to social class and even to race and ethnicity (Kohn, 1977; Harrison, 1990; Starrels, 1992). For

The father plays a very important role in socializing a child.

instance, in African-American families and among Afro-Caribbean immigrants, child rearing appears to be the responsibility of a wider range of relatives than among white families. In addition, because of the changing nature of the family, many children are being reared by single parents or in households that combine children from previous marriages or by same-sex parents. As a result, socialization experiences are varied.

The School

Second to the family, the school acts as a powerful agent of socialization. It is the first formal agency charged with the task of socializing children and represents the first link to the wider society. In school, children must learn not only basic skills needed in the society but also the hidden curriculum of how to cope successfully in a competitive environment. American schools have often been hotbeds of controversy (school prayer, the decline in standards), probably because they are recognized as being such important socializing agents.

Day Care Centers

Many children are becoming acquainted with a type of school much earlier than children did in the past. Day care centers have become necessities as increasing numbers of women have joined the workforce. Such centers are by no means sufficiently numerous to meet demand, nor are they free from controversy. Many Americans are against them on the basis that a child's own mother is the best socializing agent for the child. That has not always been found to be true: many women are, in fact, better mothers when their lives are focused on things other than house and family exclusively. In addition, research has shown that when children from stable families attend high-quality day care centers (in which the ratio of staff

Box 5.3   Humans: The Social Animals

We have seen that children brought up in isolation, whether they are abandoned by parents and survive in forests with the aid of animals or are neglected and raised with little human contact, do not fare well. Even when they are rescued and taught to behave as humans behave, they never quite catch on. From observation of feral, isolated, or neglected children, scientists have deduced that there is a physical reason for the inability of these individuals to join the human race. With progress in disciplines that study the brain, answers are slowly emerging.

One study followed adopted children who had been neglected as infants in foreign orphanages. Even two or three years after adoption, these children produce two important hormones in different patterns from children who have been raised in a loving environment. These hormones are oxytocin and vasopressin, small proteins produced by the pituitary gland. Researchers have discovered that these hormones, in addition to having physical functions in the body, affect social behavior. In particular, they promote positive interactions with other persons, especially the social bonds between mother and child and sexual bonds between men and women.

In children who have developed positive relationships with their mothers, oxytocin levels increase after about half an hour of physical interaction with her. Previously neglected children, however, do not show this rise. In addition, when in need of comforting, children with a secure parental bond seek out a parent, whereas the formerly neglected children run to the nearest adult. The adopted children, unfortunately, also have difficulties in forming and maintaining relationships even in adulthood.

The researchers speculate that there is a period during the first two years of life in which strong relationships are developed between infant and care giver, and when this occurs, later relationships are easier to attain. The oxytocin acts as a kind of reward. It provides a positive feedback about social interactions. Possibly, this development occurs during a critical window of time, and the neglected children may have missed it.

As the discipline of neuroscience progresses, scientists are able to unravel the molecular pathways that allow individuals to feel, think, dream, and so on. It is becoming clear, for instance, that our brains are wired to connect with one another; therefore, one person's mood affects another's. This happens even among strangers (that is why it is probably true that if you smile, the whole world smiles with you). But it is especially true between people who are close to each other. In his book entitled *Social Intelligence*, Daniel Goleman maintains that the brain itself is social and that we connect with others all the time, sensing moods and feelings and reacting to them. He also notes that oxytocin is secreted during positive interactions, whereas cortisol is secreted during stressful occasions. The first hormone boosts the immune system, whereas the latter interferes with some immune cell functions.

Goleman speculates that throughout human history people lived in extended families, including young and old members, and this fact is responsible for our need for others and for the manner in which others affect our own personalities. In spite of being born with a distinct temperament, our connections with others can temper and shape our personalities in other directions—anger-prone individuals, say, can spend time with mellower, calmer individuals and absorb less aggressive behavior. This, in fact, is the essence of what the author means by "social intelligence." Social intelligence, or the ability to experience others, leads to empathy (feeling what the other person feels), which is the antidote to cruelty. We are wired for kindness because survival is much more dependent on helping one another than on killing one another (Goleman, 2006).

to children is one to three for infants and no higher than one to six for toddlers), their intellectual development is neither helped nor hindered to any great extent, though their ability to interact with others is increased (Belsky & Steinberg, 1978).

One of the researchers of this study, however, has more recently changed his mind on the effects of child care. In the largest long-term study of child care in the United States, the results indicated that children who spend most of their time (30 hours per week) in child care are three times as likely to exhibit such behavioral problems as aggressiveness, disobedience, and defiance as those who were cared for primarily by their mothers (Stolberg, 2001, A18). Dr. Jay Belsky, a principal investigator in this research study, said that such children scored higher on such things as "[getting in] fights, cruelty, bullying, meanness as well as talking too much" and demanding that their needs be tended to immediately (Stolberg, 2001, A18). However, the study has not yet undergone a rigorous scientific evaluation or peer review.

The National Institute of Child Health and Human Development is carrying on an ongoing study of early child care and youth development. Its findings, summarized year by year, may be found on their web site, **http://www.nichd.nih.gov/news/releases/child_carel. cfm?renderforprint=1**. Its findings regarding child care, however, are frequently politicized. From a conservative point of view, findings would be skewed to show that day care is detrimental to children. From a more liberal point of view, day care allows mothers to pursue careers that might be considered more fulfilling than being strictly mothers and housekeepers, and, most importantly, in most American families, it is a financial necessity for a mother to work, especially in homes where the mother is the chief, or the only, wage earner.

Schools are also used as socialization agents for the labor market. In that function, they are expected to teach manners, respect for authority, and the development of basic social skills. At the same time, schools manage to stress certain cultural values (such as competition) and disseminate the idea that the society of which students are a part is superior to others. This is the *hidden curriculum* that schools impart above and beyond basic skills. Of course, how well schools perform any of their responsibilities has become a controversial point, discussed later in the text.

The Peer Group

Of increasing importance in American society, where school-age children spend more time with their friends than they do with their parents, is the peer group. Socialization within the peer group takes place informally and unintentionally, that is, most effectively. In addition, activities within the peer group tend to be strictly pleasurable, unlike those in school and in the family, which involve work as well as fun. Membership is voluntary, again unlike the situation in the family or school, and members treat each other as equals without having to

The peer group is second only to the family as the most effective socializer of children.

answer to those higher in authority. All these factors explain the attraction of the peer group and its great influence on the individual. Finally, the peer group offers a source of identification: adolescents especially turn to their peers to learn what kinds of people they are.

According to one theory, peers are *the* most influential shapers of a young person's personality (Harris, 1999). The author of this theory maintains that, contrary to the current notions in psychology, parents really matter very little. The type of person we become is determined by two things: (1) our genetic inheritance and (2) the kinds of peers with whom we associate outside the home. The theory demolishes almost every tenet of the child development discipline inasmuch as it is based on existing research used in a new way. For instance, a number of comprehensive studies, particularly those by behavioral geneticists, have shown that about 50 percent of the personality differences among people is attributable to genes, which means that the other 50 percent is due to one's environment. When researchers try to find causal links between a child's social environment created by parents and how that child eventually turns out, however, they cannot find them. On the contrary, according to a large and rigorous study, when adopted children and their adoptive parents were closely followed for several years and given extensive personality and intelligence tests, the results showed that the adopted children had very little in common with the adoptive parents. In fact, they were no more similar to one another than if the children had been compared with strangers off the street (Gladwell, 1998, 57). A control group of 250 parents and their biological children, subjected to the same tests, on the other hand, showed that the children were fairly close to their parents in intellectual ability and other aspects of personality. This particular study concluded that the only reason we resemble our parents is that we share their genes and there is no similarity when there is no genetic inheritance.

Nature versus Nurture

The "nature versus nurture" question has been answered by maintaining that personality consists of both, though in unknown quantities. According to the new theory, however, researchers have been looking in the wrong places. The nurture is not so much a function of the home, but of the neighborhood, the school, and the people with whom the growing child associates. The author provides more examples: it is true that children who are treated with affection turn out to be nice people who treat others with kindness, and those who are beaten and mistreated at home turn out to be people who are cruel and unpleasant to others. But is the reason for such an effect the behavior of the parents, or the temperament of the child who induces the parent to treat him or her one way or another? In other words, is it not possible that a parent feels like hugging a child that is well behaved and nice, and finds it more difficult to hug one that is nasty and frequently misbehaves? This proposition—that a child's temperament evokes the style of parenting—has also been thoroughly tested recently by behavioral geneticists. Contrary to all predictions, one study showed that although differential parental treatment relates to differences in adolescent adjustment, the negativity of parents does not cause the negative adjustment in their children: It merely reflects it (Gladwell, 1998, 58). Parents are hostile because their children are hostile.

The other point made by the author of the peer-important theory is that children behave differently among their peers, in the outside world, than they do at home. While admittedly a parent's behavior toward a child influences how the child behaves in the presence of the parent, or in the context of home, this behavior does not necessarily carry over outside the home. Again, a number of studies purport to prove this point. The importance of the peer group was exemplified by a sociologist who asked a number of students to write an autobiographical sketch describing the event in their lives that made them most unhappy. More than a third of the respondents described something that a peer did to them, and only 9 percent attributed the hostile act to their parents. The author concludes that whatever our parents do to us is overshadowed by what our peers do to us (Gladwell, 1998, 59). In short, this theory "calls for neighborhoods, peers, and children themselves to share the blame—and the credit—for how children turn out" (Gladwell, 1998, 62).

The Media

One of the most powerful sources of socialization, equaling the socializing influence of the peer group and in many instances surpassing that of school and family, is the influence of the *mass media*. Newspapers, magazines, radio, the Internet, and most especially television have infiltrated every American home to the point where characters from the innumerable TV shows are much more familiar to people, especially to children, than any other heroes or villains past or present. The amount of time spent watching television and the quality of the entertainment presented (centering on sex and violence) have been blamed for inciting criminal and delinquent behavior as well as for the decreasing level of taste and general knowledge of the population. However, no simple cause-and-effect relationships have ever been unfailingly established, although there are definite factors pointing to the negative influence of television as a socializing agent.

Television does not reproduce reality as most of us experience it but selects specific areas, themes, topics, and interpretations for presentation. Even in a newscast not everything that occurred on a certain day is reported; only news items of a certain level of importance and/or judged to have wide appeal are selected. Thus, children may derive a false idea of what the world and our life in it is all about. Television also popularizes norms that may be prevalent only among a small number of people, again giving the young and unsophisticated a wrong impression of how the majority of people in the society live (Bierman, 1990; Donnerstein et al., 1993). Even the incidental learning—what the audience unintentionally learns as a side effect of entertainment—may lead to distortions and stereotyping. Television, however, has been shown to be a very effective teaching tool; in fact, its very effectiveness has many thinking persons frightened.

The computer is causing controversy as well, because it too has enormous educational potential alongside possibly deleterious effects. At the moment, children who have access to the Internet can find hard-core pornographic material not intended for them at the same time that they can garner an encyclopedic amount of information with the click of a mouse.

Occupational Groups

The role of occupational groups or organizations as socializing agents cannot be ignored. The experience provided by such groups is termed *specialized* or *occupational* socialization, and it consists, basically, of training to fit a particular occupational role: that of clergyman or labor-union public relations official or corporate executive. The successfully socialized individual eventually displays personality traits that reflect the needs of the occupational role: conformity, cooperation, team orientation, and so on.

Reverse Socialization

In urban, industrial societies, the younger generation often transmits knowledge and skills to the older generation—a turnaround from what took place in the older, traditional, agricultural societies. In the United States, for instance, this is often the case in immigrant families, in which the children who were born here understand and feel more at ease in American culture and often find themselves explaining the way things are done to their parents and grandparents. When social change is very rapid, the same thing can happen even to the native born: young children may know more than their middle-aged parents about the functioning of digital cameras or computer software or the way certain mind-expanding drugs work.

Resocialization

Personality development continues throughout a person's life. Because life is a succession of changes in which people constantly assume new statuses, it is necessary for people to keep learning new roles. Some changes are so profound that they require almost total *resocialization*, a radical alteration of formerly held values and behavior. This process of role transition—shedding old roles in favor of new ones—may be quite dramatic. Resocialization in general refers to situations in which entirely new sets of norms and values must be learned—and old ones forgotten—because people are suddenly thrust into different cultures or subcultures, are isolated from their former primary groups, become handicapped as a result of an accident or illness, or embrace a new religion or political ideology. Some situations requiring resocialization are entered into voluntarily; most are not. In either case, a radical redefinition of one's self-concept and a rethinking of values and beliefs are usually in order.

The most dramatic instances of resocialization occur when individuals are forced, either by an organization or by representatives of society, to alter their former identity. This may happen when a foreign power "brainwashes" prisoners of war to inculcate the superiority of their own political system. It also happens when society, to protect itself, isolates certain individuals and denies them freedom of movement by containing them in prisons or mental hospitals.

Prisons and long-term hospitals, as well as all branches of the military service, convents and monasteries, prisoner-of-war or refugee camps, and similar places, are called *total institutions* (see Chapter 4). In total institutions, individuals live in groups that are cut off from the rest of society for a period of time, residing and working in a controlled, rigidly structured environment. Total institutions attempt to resocialize their inmates to give them totally new identities and behavior patterns: former criminals are expected to become productive citizens, drug addicts are expected to become drug free, and converts to a cult are expected to develop blind loyalty to their new religion.

■ Socialization through the Life Cycle

Other changes, less dramatic but no less important, require an adjustment of socialization to accommodate new values and modes of behavior. Certain periods of the life cycle—such as adolescence and old age—and specific crises—such as divorce, death of a spouse, loss of a job, or becoming disabled—also force the individual to submit to resocialization to become reintegrated into the social system and continue to live a productive life.

Childhood

Childhood is defined as roughly the first 12 years of life. Not until societies became industrialized was childhood perceived as a separate stage. The concern of parents was for the survival of children (infant mortality rates were very high), and children who survived were considered little adults, with the same duties and responsibilities.

Today, in the technologically advanced societies, children are expected to enjoy freedom from adult responsibilities. They dress differently from adults and are socialized to behave differently. Of late, however, it has been noted that strong pressures exist to have children

grow up faster. The media expose children to graphic violence and sex as well as other problems—financial and marital—that were previously considered totally out of their sphere. In
addition, the increasing number of working mothers and latchkey children forces the latter
to degrees of independence and responsibility unheard of a generation ago. Finally, parents
and schools pressure children to learn skills early because such achievement reflects well on
them. These factors have resulted in what some call the "hurried child" pattern (Elkind,
1981). Such a pattern is probably detrimental to children who are presented with issues and
problems they are not equipped to solve.

Adolescence

The years of puberty and adolescence were similarly never considered a separate stage of
life until societies became industrialized. Until then, children barely past infancy were
forced into menial labor on farms, in mines, on board ships, and as apprentices to artisans.
One need only read fictional accounts of life in nineteenth-century England, as in the works
of Charles Dickens, to realize that the lives of children were not carefree, unless they
belonged to the upper classes. This situation changed in the United States with the introduction of child labor laws and compulsory education, which kept children out of the labor
force until they turned 16. The need for an ever more skilled labor force has also extended
the period of adolescence in this century by encouraging greater numbers of young people
to attend college.

Adolescence has been characterized as a stage of life rife with emotional and social
turmoil. The adolescent is said to be in limbo, neither child nor adult. The search for identity
is exacerbated by physical changes and contradictory messages from socializing agents.
Adolescents reach sexual maturity and become capable of reproduction. The message they
receive from the media is that they should be sexually active. At the same time, they are
strongly urged to refrain from such activity by adults, who realize that they lack the psychological maturity—not to mention the financial means—to support a family (pregnancy being
a frequent outcome of sexual activity). Similarly, adolescents are expected to become increasingly self-reliant and responsible, but they lack the skills to obtain jobs that would make
them financially independent of their parents. There is, therefore, much anxiety, conflict,
and bewilderment on the part of adolescents regarding the nature of their new roles: they
are asked to abandon their roles of children, but they are not allowed to acquire the roles
of adults. The result may be rebelliousness toward authority, running away from home,
dropping out of school, or withdrawing into moody silence. The last decade has also seen
a marked increase in suicide in this age group.

Because adolescents share a number of values and attitudes that differ from those of the
mainstream culture, they are considered a subculture, as noted in Chapter 3. The so-called
youth culture, perceived by adults as irresponsible and concerned mainly with having a good
time, is familiar to all Americans. Each generation has its own version of this culture—from
bobbysoxers to hippies—but the culture is not equally strong in all periods. In the 1950s,
young people differed little from their parents in values or goals; at most, they differed in
superficial ways, such as in the way they dressed and the kind of music they favored. In the
1960s and 1970s, the young subculture differed substantially from adult culture. In the
1980s and into the new century the young were once again concerned with issues of financial
stability and political conservatism, thus resembling adults.

Of course, in every generation there are some individuals who remain uninterested in
the youth culture. Conversely, some adults embrace this lifestyle with gusto. And, although
most young persons grow out of their "youth culture" stage, some never do. Aging hippies,
middle-aged dropouts, and adult delinquents are also part of our societal panorama.

Adulthood

Adulthood, too, has had to be redefined as a stage of life in industrial societies. Whereas in agrarian societies most of a person's life was spent as an adult—since children began to work as soon as they could fend for themselves, and the old worked until they died—technology and medicine have wrought so many changes that adulthood has a number of steps.

Erik Erikson divides adulthood into three stages: *young adulthood*, in which the individual must resolve the dilemma of committing to another person or remaining self-absorbed (intimacy versus isolation); *middle age*, in which one must decide whether to establish and guide the future generation or fail to meet the need to be needed (generativity versus stagnation); and *old age*, in which one either accepts in a mature way how one has lived one's life or is disillusioned with life and afraid of death (ego integrity versus despair).

The years of young adulthood are spent in forming a family, learning parenting, and solidifying career goals. All of these events can be very trying. Intimate relationships require adjustments that some individuals are unable or unwilling to make. People are generally not taught the parenting role, and the arrival of a child can be perceived as traumatic to unprepared parents. Careers often demand of people sacrifices—such as leaving the area of the country where one was born or having to travel extensively—and are particularly difficult for women, who have to make choices concerning the roles they want to fill. The situation is made even more difficult when choices are not available and young mothers must work for financial reasons.

Later adulthood, after the age of 40, is often marked by crises. Men can feel trapped in jobs or careers they never really liked. Marriages can begin to feel stale. Mothers who raised children may suddenly feel unneeded, and job opportunities are scarcer for those over 40. Both sexes must begin to accept their physical decline, a difficult proposition in a society that

Some adults, particularly after the age of 40, experience crises as a result of unhappiness with careers or marriages and because of the beginning of their physical decline. Many deal with these "midlife crises" by divorcing, changing occupations, or acting as if they were still young, as this elderly gentleman is doing.

prizes youth and attractiveness. These factors are responsible for the widely recognized "midlife crisis" that impels many to divorce or to make radical changes of occupation. At this point, too, old roles must be unlearned and new ones learned. Society offers little support for these older adults in crisis; thus, the crisis sometimes becomes catastrophic. Divorced women of this age group are hit particularly hard: their income is drastically lowered, and their chances of remarriage are slim.

New research into this phase of life refutes the notions delineated above, however. Sociologist John Clausen, in a study of a group of 300 people who passed through middle age and did not encounter any "crisis," concludes that there are many turning points in people's lives, but most of them come before the middle years. Most people specify marriage, divorce, a death in the family, or career choices as turning points, and success or failure in high school as predictive of future stability (competence in high school was credited for nearly half the stability of men over the next 40 years of their lives and one-third of the stability of women). In addition, it turns out that some individuals have a number of crises, and others have very few. The crisis-prone individuals frequently were divorced long before age 40 and changed jobs frequently (Irving, 1990).

Old Age

Old age is defined as beginning at 65 and is, of course, the stage that culminates in death. As life expectancy increases, an ever larger number of Americans live well past this age; in fact, the percentage of 65-year-olds in this society has risen threefold since the beginning of the last century, and now seniors surpass teens in number. (Currently, 75 percent live past age 65 and the oldest old—those 85 and over—are the most rapidly growing group. The elderly population will double between now and 2050 to 80 million and by 2030 one in five Americans will be elderly; U.S. Bureau of the Census, 2006.) Nonetheless, the elderly in an industrial society do not enjoy the respect and influence that they do in traditional societies (see Chapter 8). Moreover, rather than leaving old roles for new, the elderly must abandon former roles that gave them a social identity and provided meaningful activities and prepare for the ultimate role: facing death. Because this prospect is anything but pleasant, and because many elderly people are also burdened by lack of funds and physical and mental deterioration, the resocialization process is not smooth. Many elderly people are left feeling dejected, useless, and confused as their principal obligation becomes that of disengaging from former social roles. Though more support groups are springing up to help the elderly and the dying to cope, this stage of the life cycle continues to be the most problematic.

■ Some Conclusions

The socialization process clearly does not always work perfectly: some individuals fail to be properly socialized, or perhaps the socialization process is not strong enough to overcome certain temperamental anomalies. Yet, societies cannot exist in chaotic circumstances. They must have a degree of order. In turn, order in society is promoted by adhering to norms and fulfilling roles, thereby making the social system work smoothly (see Chapter 4). And, of course, roles and norms are learned in the process of socialization. Is it a failure of socialization that some individuals refuse to follow common norms? Is it an inborn defect in some individuals? In attempting to answer such questions, we broach the subject of deviance and deviants, which is the topic of the next chapter.

The theories of personality formation represent only the major directions in which social scientists have sought answers to the basic questions regarding what makes people become what they are and the roles played by nature or nurture. The discipline of psychology has produced many theories in an attempt to answer these questions. The theories stressing self-concept and self-actualization, for instance, emphasize what we can become instead of what we are and how individuals can improve their self-concept and therefore fulfill their potential, instead of dwelling on how they got to be the way they are. Carl Rogers (1961) and Abraham Maslow (1968) are two American psychologists associated with these theories. The school of Gestalt psychology, founded by German theorist Max Wertheimer (1880–1943), maintains that behavior has to be viewed as a whole rather than being reduced to parts that can be examined (in German, *Gestalt* means "whole" or "entire figure"). The individual perceives reality as a whole, and that whole is more than the sum of its parts. Gestalt psychologists stress not only that behavior must be considered in its entirety but also that behavior depends on how the individual perceives the situation. The existence of these and many more theories that have not been mentioned should suggest the complexity of the subject as well as the absence of definite answers to the puzzle of human personality. Each theory emphasizes a different aspect of the individual and consequently reaches somewhat different conclusions. Clearly, however, people do not mature into productive human beings unless they interact with others, and the quality of such interaction is of utmost importance.

The Chapter in Brief

Personality is an abstract term denoting a dynamic system that includes all of an individual's behavioral and emotional traits—attitudes, values, beliefs, habits, goals, actions, and so forth. Personality develops on the basis of certain biological factors common to all humans as well as according to a unique genetic heredity. On this basis are superimposed a unique physical environment; socialization into a shared culture; common, or group, experiences; and unique, or individual, experiences.

Biology plays an important role in personality formation. Each individual is born with specific inherited physical and temperamental traits to which others in the society react. All humans are also born with certain biological drives and needs that they must learn to satisfy in socially approved ways. Socialization is the process in which they learn to do so. In the bargain, people develop a self and a personality.

Humans are predisposed toward accepting socialization by biology. They need to be physically touched and loved by others. They are totally helpless as infants, needing the ministrations of others for sheer survival.

Socialization is a process that is advantageous to both the individual and society. As to how socialization occurs, Cooley maintains that it is a process in which others supply a mirror image of the individual who then judges himself or herself accordingly. Mead also insists on the need for symbolic interaction with others and on the necessity of learning a variety of roles and seeing how complementary they are.

Other theorists view personality formation from other perspectives. Freud stresses the importance of the psychosexual stages of development from infancy to adolescence and the resolution of the struggle between the id, the ego, and the superego. Piaget speculates that intellectual and moral development proceeds in stages according to the individual's physical maturation. Kohlberg focuses on moral development.

The principal agents of socialization include the family, the school, the peer group, and, increasingly, the mass media. In traditional societies, the family is the most important socializing agent. In technologically advanced societies, the peer group usurps this function, particularly during adolescence.

The danger of the mass media as socializing agents is that they present an unrealistic and selective view of the world.

Socialization is a continuing process as individuals learn to fulfill new roles befitting new statuses acquired at different times of the life cycle. In some cases, the new roles require that old patterns of behavior and the old identity be completely abandoned. This process is called resocialization and is used most frequently when the individual enters a total institution such as the military services, a prison, or a mental hospital.

Resocialization is at work at every stage of the life cycle. In adolescence, the individual must relinquish childish roles and acquire adult ones, though society is ambiguous as to the identity of the adolescent. Hence, the rebellious and nonconformist behavior of adolescents and their clinging to a youth subculture. Adulthood generally consists of three stages, but it is being suggested that with the lengthening of human life, this stage is in the process of change.

Some theories eschew explanations. Rogers and Maslow are concerned with acquiring a positive self-concept and attaining self-actualization regardless of how or why a specific personality developed. Gestalt theorists stress the totality of behavior and individual perceptions of reality as they affect personality.

Terms to Remember

developmental theories A school of thought in modern psychology whose chief exponent was Jean Piaget. Developmentalists hold that personality development proceeds in stages that are dependent on physical maturation (sensory-motor, preoperational, and concrete- and formal-operational).

ego (Freud) A part of the personality that functions on a conscious level. It attempts to force the id to satisfy its instinctual needs in socially acceptable ways.

generalized other (Mead) The individual's perception or awareness of social norms; learning to take the role of all others with whom one interacts or of society as a whole.

id (Freud) The representative of the libido in the personality, existing on an unconscious level and making up the primitive, irrational part of the personality.

instincts Genetically transmitted, universal, complex patterns of behavior.

libido (Freud) The instinctual drive toward pleasure, which is the motivating energy behind human behavior.

looking-glass self (Cooley) The process of personality formation in which an individual's self-image emerges as a result of perceiving the observed attitudes of others.

midlife crisis What many people in middle adulthood experience when they reflect on their personal and occupational roles and find them wanting.

mind (Mead) The abstract whole of a person's ideas.

personality A complex and dynamic system that includes all of an individual's behavioral and emotional traits, attitudes, values, beliefs, habits, goals, and so on.

psychoanalytic theory A theory of personality developed by Sigmund Freud. It assumes the existence of unconscious as well as conscious processes within each individual.

psychosexual stages (Freud) The manner in which individuals attempt to gratify the force of the libido at different periods of physical maturation. The phases are oral, anal, phallic (or Oedipal), latent, and genital.

resocialization A process in which the individual's existing self-concept and identity are erased in favor of a new personality or are altered to fit new roles.

self (Mead) The individual's self-conception or self-awareness.

significant others (Mead) Important people in an individual's life whose roles are initially imitated.

socialization The learning process by which a biological organism learns to become a human being, acquires a personality with self and identity, and absorbs the culture of its society.

superego (Freud) A final element of personality, existing largely on an unconscious level and functioning to impose inhibition and morality on the id.

symbolic interactionism   A school of thought founded by George Herbert Mead whose theories center around the interrelationship of mind, self, and society and include the belief that society and the individual give rise to each other through symbolic interaction.

total institution   An organization or a place of residence in which inmates live isolated from others and where their freedom is restricted in the attempt to resocialize them with new identities and behavior patterns.

Suggested Readings

Adler, Patricia A., and Peter Adler, eds. 1986–1989. *Sociological Studies of Child Development: A Research Annual*. 3 vols. Greenwich, CT: JAI Press. A number of essays focusing on child development from a sociological perspective.

Arana, Marie. 2001. *American Chica: Two Worlds, One Childhood*. New York: Random House. A common experience for immigrants is growing up in two cultures, in which socialization expectations are sometimes contradictory. This book portrays such a socialization experience.

Craig, Grace. 1995. *Human Development*. 7th ed. Englewood Cliffs, NJ: Prentice Hall. A textbook in human development embracing the entire life course.

Dennis, Everette, ed. 1996. *Children and the Media*. Rutgers, NJ: Transaction. Readings in this anthology examine such issues as how the media treat children as news, the content of educational programming, and how the media deal with issues that affect children.

Gilligan, Carol. 1982. *In a Different Voice: Psychological Theory and Women's Development*. Cambridge, MA: Harvard University Press. A colleague of Lawrence Kohlberg analyzes moral development during the process of socialization, focusing on differences between males and females.

Harris, Judith. 1998. *The Nurture Assumption*. The author presents a radical new theory, discounting the influence of family and positing that heredity and experiences outside the home shape personality.

Kenny, Lorraine Delia. 2000. *Daughters of Suburbia: Growing Up White, Middle Class, and Female*. Brunswick, NJ: Rutgers University Press. A study of teenage girls from suburban Long Island focuses on a seldom-explored population: the average American young woman.

Sheehy, Gail. 1995. *New Passages: Mapping Your Life Across Time*. New York: Random House. The arrival of the Second Adulthood stage of life is celebrated by this author, who had examined the stages of the life cycle in a previous book.

Web Sites of Interest

http://www.personality-project.org
Issues in personality theories and research, academic and nonacademic.

http://www.ship.edu/~cgboeree/perscontents.html
A table of contents with links to the most important personality theorists, who they were, and what they said.

http://www.personalityresearch.org
The web site deals with scientific research programs in personality psychology. It has links to personality tests, glossary, journals, and more.

Deviance and Criminality: The Need for Social Control

IN THIS CHAPTER, YOU WILL LEARN

- *what is meant by the term* deviance;
- *the functions and relative nature of deviance;*
- *the various explanations of deviance furnished by the social sciences;*
- *the nature, extent, and classification of crime;*
- *the inadequacies of the criminal justice system.*

The media overwhelm us daily with the horrible deeds of some people. A baby is found strangled and thrown into a garbage bin; a man confesses to having killed and dismembered a large number of young men; another individual goes on a killing spree in a small-town restaurant. A battered wife shoots her husband dead with his hunting rifle; a stepfather stabs his teenage stepdaughter to prevent her from testifying at his rape trial, at which he stands accused of having molested her since she was a little girl. There is no need to go on with examples; every newspaper in the country, every local television newscast, every radio news program includes a number of such events every day, and many, many more, so that a reader or viewer or listener some days feels overcome with revulsion at the world. Why do some people commit such atrocious acts? What should society do to keep such persons from doing further harm? What can be done to prevent such acts from ever happening?

These questions have been asked a great many times, and neither theologians, nor philosophers, nor scientists have been able to answer them satisfactorily, though each has tried. The presence of "evil"—which is the term applied by religion and philosophy to acts deemed damaging to others and to the social group as a whole—was acknowledged long ago and has been experienced in all societies of the world. The extent and frequency of "evil," however, is not the same everywhere. Nor is the effect or the result of "evil" the same everywhere (the result of evil that science *can* discuss is crime). In societies that are homogeneous and well integrated, such as Japan or Finland, although crime exists, it does so to a much lesser extent than in multiethnic, heterogeneous societies. The reason is that a great majority of Japanese and Finns hold the same values, follow the same norms, honor the same traditions, and aim for the same goals. Moreover, in Japan the social group is more important than the individual, and individual wishes and desires are always subjugated to the needs of the group. Finally, the idea of individual freedom and individual rights—on which our entire political system is predicated—has a very short tradition in Japan. Finland, too, is a relatively classless society, in which people are convinced that the state is benevolent, and they display a trust in its civic institutions, As a consequence, street crime is low and law enforcement officials receive support from a majority of the public.

When the United States was a society of English settlers, originating from the same places in Europe and bound together by an authoritarian religion, it is quite possible that crime was less frequent but certainly not altogether absent. Today, however, the United States has become tremendously heterogeneous, consisting of people from all parts of the globe, with all sorts of traditions and norms. The United States that evolved from the generations of settlers' descendants has given Americans a common character, and there are still values and issues that unite us. But there are also as many issues that divide us. We are divided racially, religiously, linguistically, and on a great many other bases. The information explosion and its wide diffusion to the masses have overwhelmed us, so that many of us are not quite sure what to believe. These factors, and many more, of course, have rendered our social cement—what holds us together—brittle, and when the social bond is broken, when the society is fragmented, it is easier to act without considering one's neighbor.

Of course, even with the abundance of acts that are against law and morality, we must realize that only a small portion of the population is involved. The majority is still law abiding. Driving down the street, most of us still stop for a red light and proceed on green. That we do this regularly is symbolic of two important aspects of life in society: one, that people in a society share common norms; and two, that people (or at least most people) obey those norms and, most important, they trust others to obey them. In this case, the common norm is the command (transmitted by a symbol, the traffic light) to stop on red and proceed on green. The norm is so well ingrained in most people that they stop on red even when the streets are deserted and they are not being observed by another living soul. And the shared expectation is the trust exhibited by those motorists who proceed with the green light, as well as by pedestrians who cross the street when the signal says "Walk." Both are certain that motorists who have the red light will unfailingly stop. When this trust is betrayed and a motorist fails to stop at a red light, the predictable result is that either a collision occurs or a pedestrian is hit. In either case, the orderly flow of cars and people is disrupted, giving way to temporary chaos.

◼ Deviance

The word *deviance* has an immediately negative connotation. That is, we think "bad" when we hear "deviant." However, that is an erroneous perception of the word, for the term refers simply to a departure from social norms or behavior that does not conform to social norms. In this definition, Joan of Arc was certainly deviant, for it was surely against the social norms of the time for women to lead armies into battle. Yet she has come down through history not as a villain but as a heroine and a saint (even though the French refer to her as *la fou* or "the crazy one").

"Departure from social norms," then, is too broad a definition of deviance. There are many gradations of social norms, and while a violation of a folkway may be informally sanctioned (see Chapter 4), it would make little sense to call the violator a deviant. To make matters even more confusing, even in instances of universally held mores, deviance is relative. Thus, killing is a universal taboo, prohibited by both secular governments and religions. Yet there are exceptions to the proscription: in time of war, as self-defense, or in defense of one's family, killing is not only allowed but ordered and encouraged, and people receive medals and commendations for it.

Other types of departure from social norms also do not fit our perception of deviance. Some individuals are able to do calculus at 6 and graduate from college at 14. Mozart was writing splendid music before he was out of his teens. Such people are statistical rarities whom we admire; they are not deviants. On the other hand, individuals who may also be statistically rare because of defects or disabilities—people afflicted with dwarfism or those born with obvious malformations or physical and mental abnormalities—tend to be considered deviant. Thus, it is the departure from social norms that is *perceived negatively* by a majority of people that defines deviance.

The same act sometimes may be considered deviant or not, depending on who performs it. A small child might find a gun and discharge it at a passerby, killing him, but we would hardly call the child a murderer. And a banker who is found to have embezzled funds may be condemned but is punished much more lightly, and the crime is considered less serious than had the act been committed by an unemployed drifter.

Distinctions must also be made between *nonconforming* behavior, which may be prompted by ideological convictions, and *aberrant* behavior engaged in for personal gain or out of greed. A person who is arrested for obstructing access to a nuclear power plant is not in the same category of deviance as the one arrested for shooting an elderly man to steal his Social Security check.

■ The Relative Nature of Deviance

The preceding discussion should have made it amply clear that deviance can neither be easily defined nor pointed out with assurance. Of course, in the past—and in some cases even today—people tended to subscribe to much more absolutist views. They believed that social norms were clear-cut and, thus, certain types of behavior were obviously deviant. Moralists among the population still cling to the idea that deviants are immoral, antisocial, or sinners.

Social scientists, and those who incline toward a scientific approach to human behavior, admit the ambiguity of the term and stress its *relativity*. Deviance is relative because it varies according to the circumstances, time, place, age, mental health of the individual, and even according to the social status of both the deviant and the person who does the defining. The relative nature of deviance is particularly apparent in societies such as that of the United States, which is extremely heterogeneous, made up of large numbers of subcultural, and occasionally countercultural, groups.

The terms *deviant* and *deviance* are used here in preference to *normal* and *abnormal*, which tend to be value-laden (that is, one makes an even harsher value judgment when one defines a person as "abnormal"). However, the terms are, for all practical purposes, interchangeable. Defining normality and abnormality presents the same problems as defining

Killing is forbidden in all societies, by secular laws and religious tenets. However, there are exceptions: in time of war, soldiers are permitted, even ordered, to kill those they consider the enemy. In addition, the state and its government can use death as punishment for a capital crime in societies in which the death penalty is not prohibited by law.

deviance and the lack of it. In the social sciences, sociologists prefer to speak of deviance rather than abnormality, whereas psychologists use the other term. Similarly, sociologists tend to see deviant behavior as a failure of socialization, or of factors in the environment, whereas psychologists incline toward the medical view, which speculates that societies, like individuals, are healthy, and deviance is evidence of disease. Both views are discussed here.

Functions of Deviance

It seems odd to attribute functions to deviance, yet it appears that it is not entirely disruptive to society. It has been said, in fact, that if there were no deviants, societies would have to invent them. To begin with, deviants become examples of the kind of person *not* to be, and their behavior a model of behavior that is *not* condoned by society. Thus, deviants help define what the boundaries of permissible behavior are. The example of deviants and the punishment that is meted out to them reaffirm the existing norms of the group, serving as a warning not to stray from the straight and narrow. Group cohesion is enhanced as members reassert the values of the group and are reassured in the conviction that they are worth preserving. As paradoxical as it seems, deviance may add to the stability of society: "deviance cannot be dismissed simply as behavior which disrupts stability in society, but may itself be, in controlled quantities, an important condition for preserving stability" (Erikson, 1964).

Another important function of deviance is its contribution to social change. The learning of new norms and the abandonment of some old ones become imperative in all societies. Some of these new norms may actually emerge from the deviant activities of a minority of people. The first individual who challenges the status quo is usually considered deviant, as is the one who attempts to do something in a new way. For example, women who picketed the White House and staged demonstrations in an attempt to gain the right to vote at the beginning of the twentieth century were no doubt considered deviant, yet had they not acted in this deviant manner, the women of the current generation probably would still not be able to vote.

■ Explaining Deviance

It has often been said that good and evil are two sides of the same coin, existing equally in all humans. Because what is considered "good" is understood by most to ultimately benefit the individual and group, acting in conformity with group norms is not generally questioned. What is questioned is why some individuals break the rules. Thus, attempts to explain deviance have existed from the earliest times, couched in the idiom and philosophy of the times. Most religions approach deviance as sin, the breaking of God's commandments. In modern times, psychologists search for the reasons for deviance within the individual. Sociologists look for explanations in the interaction of people.

The treatment of deviants depends on how deviance is explained. Throughout history, people who behaved in a manner other than that prescribed have been accused of being witches or of being possessed by the devil. To free them of their affliction, they were regularly hanged, burned, or put to death in other horrible ways. Even when, in fifteenth-century Europe, the idea appeared that perhaps such people were ill, they were still beaten, locked away, chained, and treated like subhumans. The English word *bedlam*, meaning confusion and uproar, comes from the name of a well-known "madhouse" in England.

Early Biological Explanations

Explanations of a more scientific nature have been offered from the points of view of biology, psychology, and sociology. The instinctive fear inspired by someone who looks threatening was given expression in the theories of the Italian criminologist Cesare Lombroso (1911), who held that some individuals become deviant because of inborn and genetically transmitted traits. Lombroso was convinced that his ideas could be supported by scientific research: he described and measured traits that he attributed to a "criminal" type, such as a jutting jaw, red hair, a sparse beard, and insensitivity to pain. In spite of the initial popularity of Lombroso's theories, it later became apparent that these traits appeared almost as frequently among the noncriminal population as among the criminal population.

In the United States, psychologist William Sheldon revived a version of the theory by claiming that body structure was related to personality. Sheldon classified people into *endomorphs*, with soft, round bodies and a social, easygoing, and self-indulgent personality; *mesomorphs*, with muscular, agile bodies and a restless, energetic, and insensitive personality; and *ectomorphs*, with thin and delicate bodies and an introspective, sensitive, nervous, and artistic personality (1940, 1949). In a later study, Sheldon concluded that mesomorphs were disproportionately represented among a sample of delinquent boys, a finding that was subsequently expanded in another research project by behavioral scientists Sheldon Glueck and Eleanor Glueck (1956). The latter, however, were careful to add that body type *in addition* to other traits and experiences probably predisposed certain people to deviance.

This is a very important qualification. In fact, it is very probable that it is not the body type per se that predisposes one to specific behavior. Rather, it is how others react to a

Those who are deviant as a result of psychological dysfunctions have never fared well among the rest of societal members. Mental hospitals tend to be very depressing places.

person's body type, and how that individual comes to perceive himself or herself, that may cause specific kinds of behavior. A short person, called "Shorty" in a ridiculing and denigrating way, may well acquire a poor self-image and may choose to strike back in ways that may be termed deviant. On the other hand, it is unlikely that a thin, fragile youth would be invited to join a juvenile gang, or that an overweight person would become a cat burglar. Thus, body type is only very indirectly responsible for behavior.

Another biological explanation of deviance focuses on sex chromosomes. In a normal male, these consist of an X and a Y, while a normal female has two X chromosomes. Some persons are born with more than their share of chromosomes, however: XXY, XYY, and so on. In a study of male patients who had an XYY chromosome configuration, it was shown that the latter were taller than average males, tended to be mildly retarded, and appeared more often in criminal than in noncriminal groups (Owen, 1972). Here, too, however, it is possible that the deviance is caused more by being an extremely tall, ungainly-looking male than by the extra chromosome; at any rate, the theory came into disfavor. Research on the topic of possible genetic causes in violence and aggression continues to generate controversy. On the one hand, criminality is such a complex form of behavior that to assign a single, biological cause to it is extremely shortsighted. On the other, some researchers maintain that such traits as impulsiveness and the inability to defer gratification—which may, if unchecked, lead to criminal behavior—are essentially genetically transmitted and so could possibly be tracked in affected individuals. A study conducted by a psychologist that compared more than 14,000 men who had been adopted with their biological fathers found that there was a correlation: the biological fathers of adopted men who had convictions for theft were also likely to have had similar convictions (Goleman, 1992, B5, B8). This research, however, did not find any direct inherited tendency for violence.

Box 6.1   Why Are Humans Killers?

A widely believed "fact," even among scientists, is that only humans kill members of their own species. However, two anthropologists report in a book that they observed a number of chimpanzees travel, on purpose, to the border of their range, enter neighboring territory, attack and kill a male from that territory, and then return home (Wrangham & Peterson, 1996). Although this was the first recorded instance of such behavior, it was not the only one. As a result of improved observation techniques, students of primate behavior began to notice that killing others of their own species was part of a pattern of ape behavior. Such behavior includes raids in which victims are murdered, battering and raping females, and infanticide.

The recording of the observed violence was important not only because it debunked the myth that only humans kill one another but also because chimpanzees happen to be the species closest biologically to humans. DNA analysis has shown that chimps are closer to humans than they are to gorillas, leading to speculation that the common ancestor to both humans and chimpanzees existed as recently as 5 million years ago (Lehmann-Haupt, 1996, B6). In addition, anthropologists have recently shown that a system of male-initiated territorial aggression is widespread and consistent throughout human civilization. This system includes lethal raids into

neighboring territory in which males look for vulnerable victims to attack and kill. Therefore, in spite of descriptions of utopian societies, violence is *not* an invention of Western civilization. Rather, the two anthropologists conclude, humans are killers universally.

Why this is so is a question to which the scientists do not know the answer. Some form of violence may be beneficial to the group and may convey advantages to future generations, but other forms appear to be senseless. The anthropologists stress the importance of culture as a way for humans to overcome the instinctual baggage they may have inherited. However, they point out that nature (biology) and nurture (culture) are not two distinct elements: chimps put a lot of thought into apparently instinctive behavior, and some apparently rational human behavior is dictated, or impelled, by biological drives. In their opinion, it is pride, in the sense of achievement of high status, that motivates both humans and chimps.

Humans, then, find themselves in an evolutionary bind. On the one hand, the lust for high status and the taste for meat helped us evolve into humans. On the other, we are burdened with the instinct for violence to attain them. It is a classic dilemma, one that will be overcome only with a rigorous application of human intelligence.

■ Personality Disorders Caused by Physical Conditions

A major form of disorder is caused by a malfunction in the brain. Such a malfunction may be organic, acute, or chronic in form. Another is mental retardation, which may result from poor prenatal care, from the mother having contracted rubella during pregnancy, or from a genetic cause (as in Down syndrome, in which the individual has 47 chromosomes instead of 46). These mental disorders are physical in origin and are not necessarily considered examples of deviance. However, emotional disturbances and deviant behavior may develop either from the symptoms (in the form of disturbed thinking processes) or from the way people react to the symptoms.

Another form of disorder is *psychosomatic*, meaning that the individual suffers physical symptoms of disease that do not arise from a physical cause. The physical symptoms result from emotional tension or anxiety and can take the form of colitis, migraine headaches, gastritis, asthma, skin disorders, ulcers, hypertension, anorexia, and impotence or frigidity. Although people who suffer psychosomatic disorders are often not taken seriously, it is important to stress that the symptoms are in every way as real as if there were an organic cause. In addition, as our medical knowledge increases, physical causes are often found for these symptoms.

Neuroses, also called *anxiety disorders*, are considered to be mild personality disorders that do not prevent the affected individual from functioning in society. Nonetheless, they may be debilitating for the neurotic person and for those around him or her.

Almost all of us have neurotic tendencies, and neuroses have been so widely discussed in the popular press that we are at least familiar with them. The most common ones include *anxiety reaction* (feeling anxious without reason), *phobias* (unreasonable fear of heights, the dark, tunnels, bridges, enclosed places, open places, snakes, or bugs), *depression* (feeling that life is not worth living), *obsessive-compulsive reaction* (being unable to stop fixed ideas from occurring or repeating certain activities without being able to stop), *hypochondria* (believing oneself ill or always about to acquire a disease), and *dissociative reaction* (amnesia and multiple personality, both of which are attempts to repress an idea or experience). Most of these disturbances rarely require institutionalization, but some do require treatment. In severe cases of depression, phobia, and dissociation, institutionalization may be prescribed. In less severe cases, treatment is provided on an outpatient basis. Going to one's analyst, or "shrink," has become a cliché in some circles, particularly among well-to-do professionals. The rest of the population copes as well as it can with the occasional disruptions caused by their neuroses.

Next in severity are the personality disorders that result in well-ingrained maladaptive behavior. Persons suffering from these personality disorders include *sociopaths* (who engage in antisocial behavior without anxiety or remorse), sexual deviants (transvestites, necrophiliacs, bestialists, and pederasts, the last being the most dangerous to others because they use children to obtain sexual gratification), and addicts.

Finally, *psychoses* are serious mental disorders that cause those affected to be hospitalized because of their inability to function in society. The three major psychoses are schizophrenia, paranoia, and manic-depression or bipolar disorder.

Schizophrenia is a label applied to people for whom there seems to be no other label. Schizophrenics vary in the intensity of their disturbance. Some are totally withdrawn, unable to interact with other people. Others can function in society but are severely limited in certain areas. All, however, fail to function at the level of their capabilities. The disturbance appears to run in families, but it is not known precisely whether it is inherited or is a genetic predisposition that expresses itself in a specific environment. If the cause of onset is diagnosed correctly and institutionalization is brief, treatment has been known to be possible and effective.

True **paranoia** (which exhibits links to schizophrenia) is rare, but paranoid tendencies are frequent. Persons who are paranoid feel that the world is against them and that people around them spy on them and intend to do them harm. Some also believe themselves to be great and famous personages ("delusions of grandeur") and attribute their persecution by those around them to envy.

Any of the above forms of psychosis may cause the affected person to hallucinate. Such a person may be certain of hearing voices where there are none, which is a wrong perception of reality, or may have delusions about themselves or others, which is a misinterpretation of reality. Some live for years in an imagined world. In short, for them the distinction between the real and the imagined becomes so blurred that they fail to distinguish one from the other.

Anxiety and severe depression, on the one hand, and unprovoked happiness or euphoria, on the other, characterize *manic-depression*, formally called **bipolar disorder**. These mood swings can occur from one moment to the next. People with bipolar disorder represent a threat mainly to themselves: in their depressed states they may attempt suicide, whereas in their manic states they may take on tasks beyond their capacity. Fortunately, there are drugs that stabilize this psychosis fairly well.

Treatment of Physically Caused Disorders

There have been dramatic improvements in the treatment of mental disorders in this century, as people have become more aware of the nature of these disorders and as medicine and the disciplines of psychology have attained more knowledge. However, a great many of those afflicted by mental disorders are not being helped, either because treatment is not within their means or because it is ineffective. The following are the major forms of treatment:

1. *Psychotherapy.* This includes psychoanalysis, group therapy, family therapy, transactional analysis, and various other forms of analysis. All these forms have in common the fact that nothing physical goes on, nor are drugs given. The therapies are simply verbal exchanges between patient or patients and therapist.
2. *Behavior therapy.* Based on the principle of conditioning, this kind of therapy stresses the modification of behavior through rewards and punishment.
3. *Psychopharmacology.* Sometimes used in conjunction with other therapies, this form uses drugs and chemicals to treat symptoms of mental disorders.
4. *Hypnotherapy.* This treatment uses hypnosis—subconscious suggestions—to deal with mental disorders.
5. *Electroconvulsive shock therapy.* This type of treatment, which is very painful and can cause loss of memory and learning disabilities, has been popularized in the movies and in literature because unethical therapists have used it to punish patients. However, it has lost much credibility and is not used as frequently as in previous years. It consists of subjecting patients to severe jolts of electricity to the cranial area. The method works by suppressing neuron activity, and it has been effective in some cases of severely depressed patients.

In the 1930s and 1940s, *psychosurgery* in the form of frontal lobotomy was hailed as a method for treating severe mental disorders, but it often left patients totally dysfunctional and at other times increased aggressive behavior. As a result, the operation is no longer performed for psychological disorders.

■ Psychological Explanations

Psychological explanations of deviance have become very popular in this century as a result of Sigmund Freud's work (see Chapter 5). Freud assumed that people are born with tendencies toward aggression and sexuality, drives that are potentially destructive and thus must be inhibited. Inhibition occurs through the development of the ego, which directs people to solve physical needs in socially approved ways, and of the superego, a kind of conscience that prohibits behavior that the individual has learned to consider wrong.

In the Freudian scheme, deviant behavior occurs when the superego is not sufficiently developed to be able to impose its will on the other component of the personality, the id, which is uncivilized and primitive. Deviance may also be the result of an over-developed superego, in which case people act in a deviant way to bring punishment on themselves for the drives they feel they should never have experienced, even if they inhibited them successfully.

Psychological theories resemble biological theories and follow a medical model in that they assume that deviance is caused by mental defects, abnormality, or illness. But they are more sophisticated in that they recognize that one cannot separate the cause from its effect. There is little doubt that mental illness may cause behavior easily perceived as deviant. But mental illness is also used as the rationalization for deviant behavior. Alcoholism, drug addiction, child abuse, and crimes committed for reasons other than greed or financial gain are often attributed to mental illness. In fact, the judicial system uses this rationalization to exonerate certain criminals from punishment.

■ Explaining Deviance from a Sociological Perspective

As is becoming clear, not all deviants are mentally ill, nor are all mentally ill persons deviant. The psychological theories and their variants—that deviance is caused by aggression triggered by constant and profound frustration, or that it originates in unconscious processes having to do with an improperly developed superego or conscience, or that it is a form of disease or birth defect—are very difficult to test empirically. They fail to take into account the relative nature of deviance and the role played by social interpretations of deviance. They focus too exclusively on the act—deviance—and the actor—the deviant—and not enough on the stage—society—on which the actor performs. At least, this is so in the opinion of sociologists.

There is no single-factor explanation for human behavior. It is always the result of a variety of factors, some of a genetic and some of a social nature. Sociologists, who focus on human interaction, maintain that all human behavior, including deviant behavior, is a product of the type of social organization in which people live, of the social structures they erect, and of the social processes in which they are involved. The focus here is not only on the act and the actor, then, but also on the set, the scenery, the script, and the audience.

Social Integration and Anomie: A Functionalist View

One of the earliest attempts to explain deviance from a sociological perspective was put forth in the work of Emile Durkheim (1897, 1951, 1966). This nineteenth-century social philosopher introduced the concept of *anomie*, which he defined as a condition of normlessness that pervades individuals when the established rules of behavior are no longer valid, are conflicting, or are weak. Such conditions develop in times of crisis or when rapid social change takes place in a society. At such times, people are confused because old norms that formerly gave structure to their lives no longer have this effect. Individuals in such societies are said to be loosely integrated culturally and socially, because they fail to agree on norms and values and are consequently confused as to behavior. Obviously, in these circumstances, individuals are vulnerable to deviance. For instance, it is possible to notice a great disparity in crime rates when we compare the crime rates of homogeneous and highly culturally integrated societies—for instance, Finland—and those of heterogeneous and loosely integrated ones, such as the United States.

A society with a high degree of anomie is in danger of falling apart because the cement that holds it together loses its ability to bond people. People no longer share goals and values. They do not agree on what constitutes right and wrong. They do not impart similar values to their children—in fact, many do not impart any values at all, leaving children to grow up directionless. One of the results of such neglect is the increase in violent behavior on the part of the young, particularly in violent action that seems to have no provocation and that makes little sense.

The high rates of crime in the inner cities may also be attributed to anomie, coupled by the pervasive presence of drugs and their high profitability, as well as the ease of obtaining guns in our society. Additional causes that have been suggested include poverty, social tension, and hopelessness, conditions that have afflicted inner cities for many generations. The tendency to form gangs to take the place of dysfunctional or nonexistent families and a street ethic that requires young men to act tough to prove their manhood are also cited as causes of violence.

Which theory of deviance best explains gang membership?

Merton's Classification of Deviant Behavior

The concept of anomie has been expanded by Robert Merton (1938, 1968), who has applied anomie theory to a variety of forms of deviant behavior. Merton sees deviant behavior as the consequence of a lack of balance in the social system, as a gap between what the society sets up as goals for its members and the means that it puts at their disposal for reaching them. This gap produces strains that can result in deviant behavior.

An obvious example may be found in American society, which sets up as one of its most important goals the achievement of success, usually translated into economic terms as the attainment of wealth. The socially accepted ways of satisfying that goal are either to be born into a wealthy family or to obtain the type of education or skills that will guarantee employment in a profitable enterprise where one can, by dint of hard work and innovative thinking (or just plain good luck), rise to the top.

Obviously, the first way is strictly up to chance, and only a very small percentage of families in the society are in a high social class. The second way of attaining success is also difficult. Higher education is expensive and requires intellectual ability that is not universal. And even the best education and training do not guarantee success. As a consequence, a substantial segment of the population who wants to be successful is denied access to success through the acceptable ways. Such people may experience anomie and, in frustration, may turn to various forms of deviance—socially unacceptable means—to achieve the desired societal goals that they have internalized (see Table 6.1).

Merton's classification of behavior is based on people's acceptance or rejection of either the cultural goals or the means of achieving them. Merton's theory is quite general, but it has been very influential and has given origin to many more specific theories. Albert Cohen (1955), for instance, asserts that gangs are usually made up of lower-class youths to whom the middle-class means of achieving success are not available. Youth gang members achieve success among their peers by deviating from society's norms to follow gang norms.

TABLE 6.1 Robert Merton's Theory of Deviance

Mode of adaptation	Cultural goals	Institutionalized means	Deviant?	Examples
Conformists	Accept	Accept	No	Study and attain professional status
Deviants				
Innovators	Accept	Reject	Yes	Gang member, member of organized crime, embezzler, bank robber
Ritualists	Reject	Accept	Yes	Low-level bureaucrat, missionary, government worker, worker with the poor (individuals not interested in money or power)
Retreatists	Reject	Reject	Maybe	Drug addict, dropout, alcoholic, street person
Rebels	Reject/Accept	Reject/Accept	Yes	Revolutionary, terrorist

Criminologists Cloward and Ohlin (1960) also use anomie theory to suggest that gangs supply their members with a respectable status that they cannot obtain through socially approved means. The researchers classify juvenile gangs into three subcultural groups: the criminal, interested in material benefits; the conflict, involved in territorial squabbles; and the realist, using alcohol and drugs to bind its members together. In all three types, the members feel that they are achieving success in spite of what others in the society think of them.

The anomie theory, however, does not explain *all* forms of deviance. It focuses on society as the source of deviance, rather than on the individual. It assumes that there is an agreement on values in the society that does not exist, in reality, to quite the extent Merton implied.

Cultural Transmission (Differential Association): Interactionist Perspective

The *cultural transmission* theory, also called the *differential association* theory, is a kind of learning theory, as it is based on the proposition that deviance is learned through symbolic interaction, much as all other human behavior. Again, as is true of learning in general, the learning of deviance occurs most effectively in small, intimate primary groups such as the family, the peer group, and the neighborhood. The individual interacting with people who are themselves deviant learns deviant techniques and rationalizations for deviant acts, as well as conceptions of law, property, and human rights from a deviant perspective.

According to Edwin Sutherland (1949, 1961), the following factors influence an individual's becoming deviant:

1. The intensity of association with others—whether they are friends and relatives or merely acquaintances.
2. The age at which interaction takes place—children and adolescents are more impressionable than older individuals.
3. The frequency of association—the more one associates with deviants, the more one is influenced by them.

4. The duration of contact—the longer the association with deviants, the better the chance of acquiring deviant tendencies.
5. The number of contacts—the more deviants an individual knows, the better the chance of becoming deviant in turn.

Becoming deviant, however, is not simply a matter of having "bad companions." Rather, it is a matter of the choices an individual makes in response to his or her needs.

One implication of this theory is that a society with a number of subcultures (a heterogeneous society) has higher rates of deviance because people do not share the same values, norms, and goals. Members of subcultures may also feel a greater loyalty to their own group than to the majority group or dominant culture, while members of the dominant culture may perceive some subcultural values and norms as deviant.

The focus of the cultural transmission theory, that deviance is learned, is important. However, it overlooks the possibility that some forms of deviance may be learned not only from people but also from ideas. Some individuals may join such groups as the American Nazi Party after reading works by authors who espouse the Nazi ideology. On the other hand, people such as lawyers and social workers who have frequent dealings with deviants seldom learn deviant behavior from their clients, or at least they seldom act on it. And finally, it is also known that knowledge gained from associating with nondeviants can be used in a deviant way. A pharmacist who sells drugs illegally for gain is engaging in deviant behavior that he or she did not learn from deviants. Thus, the theory explains only partially why some people learn deviance and others do not, and it does not touch on the reasons for specific behaviors being defined as deviant.

Labeling Theory

A different conception of what constitutes deviant behavior and how people are defined as being deviant is represented by the *labeling* theory. This approach places an emphasis on the process by which an individual is labeled as deviant and on how the individual is treated as a consequence of having been so labeled, rather than on the behavior of the person. Some of the questions asked by labeling theorists are: How does the group come to define a specific individual as deviant? How do the members of the group modify their reactions and interactions with an individual defined as deviant? What are the effects of the changed behavior of group members on the deviant individual?

Howard Becker (1963), a sociologist who was instrumental in developing the labeling theory, maintains that all of us are guilty of deviant behavior at one time or another. This *primary deviance* is temporary, unimportant, prompted by curiosity, and easily concealed. Examples of primary deviance are a junior executive who pads an expense account somewhat, a guest who takes a towel from a hotel room, or a youth who has one homosexual experience or tries an illegal drug. Such behavior is usually not discovered by others, and the perpetrators do not consider themselves deviant.

In some circumstances, however, the act is discovered, perhaps by parents, friends, employers or employees, school administrators, teachers, or the police. The perpetrators are then on the way to becoming labeled as deviants. They are accused, sermonized, and often punished in what Becker calls a "degradation ceremony." They are made to feel that they are morally inferior to their accusers and are called by such unflattering labels as "nuts," "weirdos," "queers," and so on. Other people, in response to these labels, react to the labeled individuals as if they were in reality what the labels indicate. Eventually, the labeled individuals come to accept these labels, altering their self-concepts to fit the reaction of others to themselves, and they begin to act them out. Now their behavior is *secondary deviance* and becomes habitual.

Crimes against persons are often dramatic. In recent years, our society has witnessed a number of killings by young students. Which theory of deviance do you think best explains such killings?

At this point, after being labeled as deviants and accepting the label, the offenders' lives take a new turn. They are stigmatized (pointed out, isolated, avoided) by non-deviants and forced to seek the company of other deviants, which reinforces their behavior. Lacking a way out, they are well on their way to a deviant career, inasmuch as being deviant becomes their master status. The labeled person's life becomes a self-fulfilling prophecy. This is in keeping with the view that socialization is a process in which the self emerges and is characterized by the reflected reactions of others: the symbolic-interactionist perspective.

The labeling theory has been helpful to students of deviance because it shows that only certain people or actions are selected for labeling as deviant, but the theory has its shortcomings. Labeling is not always involved: many persons who are never discovered nevertheless continue to act in a deviant fashion. Are they any less deviant because others do not know about their deviance? The theory also overlooks the fact that some deviants may actually be jolted out of their behavior by the labeling process and as a consequence may be moved to change their behavior to conform to norms (Liazos, 1972).

■ Crime: Deviance That Hurts

Most people equate deviance with crime, but of course the two are not the same, as the foregoing discussion should have made clear. Everyone is deviant to some extent or other, at one time or another, but not everyone is a criminal. Criminals represent only a small minority of people in society, but the acts they perpetrate are very damaging, so that crime and criminals are very much on the public's mind.

In most contemporary societies, informal social control is not sufficient to contain deviance. Therefore, formal social controls must be instituted. One type of formal social control is the enactment of statutes, or laws, that define the actions that are prohibited to members because they are too destructive to the society. The prohibited actions are termed crimes and are punished by the society through its judicial system.

Crime, then, is any action that violates the law. Laws, in turn, are passed at a variety of governmental levels: local, state, and federal. Laws differ from the unwritten societal norms in that (1) they are put into effect by political authority, (2) they are specific rules instead of informal understandings, (3) they are applied uniformly, (4) they carry specific punitive sanctions, and (5) they are administered through official agencies of the society.

Even though crimes and punishments are specifically defined, they too are relative, varying in kinds and extent. One distinction is made between criminal behavior on the part of adults as opposed to juveniles under 18 years of age. The distinction is based on the belief that minors are not yet fully socialized (but if they commit an especially serious crime, juveniles may be treated as adults by the criminal justice system). Another distinction is between the so-called index crimes and actions that are considered crimes by the legal codes but not by a majority of people. The *index crimes* involve the violation of mores and include murder (including homicide, voluntary manslaughter and involuntary manslaughter), rape, robbery, aggravated assault, burglary, larceny, arson, and auto theft. Crimes that most people ignore range from the regional prohibition to serve alcohol by the glass, although one can buy bottles, to the 55-mile-per-hour speed limit, which was a federal law for a few years and was observed only when a police car was in sight.

Classification of Crimes

Criminal behavior ranges over a very wide spectrum and is perpetrated by individuals belonging to a large variety of groups. Most crimes fit into one of the following categories.

Crimes against Persons. These crimes almost always involve violence and the use or threat of force to injure victims and are, therefore, the ones most feared by people. Violent crimes include murder and non-negligent homicide, forcible rape, robbery, and aggravated assault.

Crimes against Property. These crimes do not involve the threat of force or injury to victims; rather, the goal of perpetrators is to gain possession of, or to destroy, property by unlawful means. Property crime includes burglary, larceny-theft, motor vehicle theft, and arson.

Juvenile Delinquency. This refers to violations of the law by minors. In the last decade, we have witnessed a number of violent crimes perpetrated by ever-younger persons. Not only have there been several instances of teens killing teachers and fellow students, but 10- and 12-year-olds have brutally murdered younger children. Juveniles have also been engaged in criminal behavior as members of gangs.

As we have seen, most sociologists tend to assign social factors to the causes for crime. Their research shows that children who become juvenile delinquents tend to have experienced harsh and erratic discipline three to four times more often than children who do not become delinquent. Such children tend to have, on average, a verbal IQ eight points lower than the norm, because of prenatal factors, such as a mother who abuses drugs and alcohol during pregnancy, a fact known to damage the central nervous system of the fetus, or because they were exposed to high levels of lead from peeling paint and auto fumes. The latter factors are known to lower IQ and impair concentration, predisposing children to hyperactivity, a pattern predictive of crime in adolescence. When they arrive in first grade, such children are unprepared to learn. "They are more aggressive than other kids, have conduct problems, and low

Box 6.2   What Contributes to Crime? How Can We Prevent It?

Because crime is so damaging to society, social scientists continue to probe ways to prevent it, which means that first they have to determine its causes. The myriad theories presented by psychologists and psychiatrists, sociologists, biologists, and other scientists have never yielded a concrete and all-encompassing result, and so social scientists must press on.

In an article first published in 1982, researchers maintained that crime and disorder in a community are inextricably linked. "Social psychologists and police officers tend to agree that if a window in a building is broken and is left unrepaired, all the rest of the windows will soon be broken" (Wilson & Kelling, 1982, 30). The researchers offered a number of examples to support that where communal barriers are lowered by a feeling of "no one caring," vandalism and crime are the inevitable result. They suggested that when behavior is disorganized, or "untended" in their words, community controls break down. "A piece of property is abandoned, weeds grow up, a window is smashed. Adults stop scolding rowdy children; the children, emboldened, become more rowdy. Families move out, unattached adults move in. . . . Fights occur. Litter accumulates. People start drinking in front of the grocery; in time, an inebriate slumps to the sidewalk and is allowed to sleep it off. Pedestrians are approached by panhandlers." At this point, even if there is no increase in violent crime, residents begin to think that serious crime is on the rise and begin to behave differently. They try not to use the streets often, they move quickly and without looking at others, they attempt to remain uninvolved, and they start to consider their neighborhood as the place where they live, rather than as their home. This is an instance of atomization and alienation (Wilson & Kelling, 1982, 31). If order is not improved in such a neighborhood, serious crime is sure to follow.

This theory about the roots of crime became immensely popular and was the basis for the crackdown on quality-of-life crimes in New York City under Mayor Rudolph Giuliani. The authors had suggested in the initial article that in addition to fixing "broken windows" residents had to become involved in their community, volunteering to walk the streets, get to know one another, take care of one another's children—including scolding them for rude behavior—in short, they had to care. However, the lead researcher of this study does not consider this a theory but merely speculation.

Another study, very carefully set up in Chicago, somewhat contradicts the broken window notion. In their 1997 paper, the authors maintained that most major crimes were linked to two variables in a neighborhood: concentrated poverty and a lack of collective efficacy. This last term refers to the necessity of people in a neighborhood to intervene in the affairs of their neighborhood. Allowing people from the outside—government agencies, the police—to clean or fix up their neighborhood does not work. Community meetings, held in local churches or schools, is much more likely to result in a solution to the community's problems. As an example, the rate of homicide in Boston had decreased drastically during the mid 1990s. The researchers attributed the drop to a group of black ministers who began to walk the streets, engaging kids and working with other adults to develop after-school programs. During those activities, and because of the relationships developed between the young adults and those in charge, details came out about who were the gang leaders or criminals in the community. This information in turn helped the police department arrest the offenders and thus rid the area of much crime.

This study is continuing and has garnered the collaboration of researchers from a number of important universities. The researchers feel that it would be a great contribution to social science if the study could show that where one grows up is more important than, or just as important as, one's temperament or IQ (Sampson, Raudenbush and Earls, 1997, 918–924; Hurley, 2004, D1–D2).

reading achievement, a pattern that solidifies by third grade, at which point these youngsters get marked as problems and put in special education classes. As early as third grade, they are stigmatized, and at a social disadvantage" (Goleman, 1992, B5, B8). The labeling theory, in this case, may explain their criminal proclivities. Subsequently, they may prefer to associate with others like themselves (differential association theory), or they may use illegal means to reach the societal goals that become impossible to reach by legal means (anomie theory).

Because of the increase in senseless, savage murders resulting from the easy availability of guns, juvenile crime has been subjected to additional scrutiny. It appears that while in the past unimportant conflicts used to be settled with a fistfight, today they are settled with firepower, which often results in death. Over and over, however, research shows that lessons in cruelty start at home and are simply facilitated by the presence of weapons. In *Kids Who Kill*, psychologist Charles Ewing reports that many young people who commit seemingly motiveless crimes have themselves been sexually or physically abused, even though they seldom admit to having once been a victim. It seems that to abuse another human being, a youngster has to have been abused first. Abuse, neglect, instability, a sense that no one cares are almost certain to create individuals who focus on their own immediate gratification no matter who suffers as a result. The ease with which guns are available in our society helps to transform anger and frustration into murder and mayhem. According to a lobbying organization called Handgun Control, in 1996 handguns were used to murder only 2 people in New Zealand, 15 in Japan, 30 in Great Britain, 106 in Canada, 213 in Germany, and 9,390 in the United States (Herbert, 1999, A31). The point has been made repeatedly that if young people could not obtain guns, they would use their fists or other less lethal weapons to express their feelings and avoid the frequent massacres at American schools that we have sadly witnessed.

Social Order Crimes or Crimes against Morality

Criminal acts such as gambling, prostitution, illegal drug use, vagrancy, and public drunkenness do not impose physical suffering on others but offend the moral sensibilities of the majority. These crimes are often referred to as **victimless crimes** because no other person is allegedly hurt. However, it is obvious that such crimes make victims of the perpetrators and, very often, their families. Drunken drivers can become killers, and alcoholics frequently expose their families to poverty as a result of losing jobs or to physical abuse while intoxicated. Drug addicts can rob, burglarize, and kill in pursuit of their next fix, and they certainly get in trouble with the law if they also sell drugs. Women who abuse drugs while pregnant make victims of their babies who are often born addicted or with physical and behavioral problems. Prostitutes subject themselves to dangerous situations, can easily acquire venereal diseases, including AIDS, and are likely to experience a lifestyle in which drug and alcohol abuse are rampant, leading to self-destruction. Family life for such women is nonexistent, and if they have children, they are forced to live in an unhealthy environment.

White-Collar Crime. Criminal acts committed by respectable persons, often of high status, in the performance of their occupational roles are listed as white-collar crimes. The FBI categorizes these crimes as illegal acts that are characterized by deceit, concealment, or violation of trust but that are not dependent on force or threat of force. The acts include false advertising, copyright infringement, swindling, stock manipulation, price fixing, tax evasion, embezzlement, forgery, and fraud. These acts are committed by individuals and/or organizations to obtain money, property, or services; to avoid payment of taxes or money owed; to prevent a loss of money or services; or to secure a personal or business advantage. Such crimes are tolerated more than others because they seldom involve violence and are not committed by seasoned criminals. However, in sheer numbers of dollars, white-collar crime costs society three times more per year than the four other major categories of property crimes. In recent years, the American public has been made aware of corporate crime with the examples of Enron, Adelphia, Martha Stewart, and so on, but there are thousands of cases involving health care fraud, government fraud (e.g., contractors overcharging government agencies for work,

White-collar crime does not evoke the same repulsion as other crimes because it seldom involves violence. Nonetheless, such crime costs the society not only in terms of money, but also because of ethical concerns.

services, or manufactured items), financial institution fraud (e.g., bank managers or employees embezzling, check fraud, counterfeiting, credit card theft), antitrust cases, price fixing, money laundering, environmental degradation; and Internet fraud, to mention just a few.

Organized Crime. The criminal activity of groups of individuals who are organized to maximize efficiency and minimize the danger of apprehension and punishment is collectively called organized crime. Organized crime is in the business of satisfying human wants that are prohibited by the ideal norms of society and by the legal codes: members provide houses of prostitution and call-girl services, direct illegal gambling establishments, furnish drugs, manufacture and distribute pornographic materials, and make loans to high-risk borrowers at steep interest rates.

■ Crime Statistics: How Much Crime, and Who Commits It?

Crime statistics are compiled annually by the Federal Bureau of Investigation and published as the *Uniform Crime Reports* (UCR). However, the crimes reported by the FBI are limited to 29 categories and focus only on the eight index crimes. These numbers are compiled from crimes reported to police departments throughout the nation. It is thought that the actual crime rate is two to three times higher than what is reported because many crimes are never detected and the less serious crimes may even go unreported.

Another way of reporting crimes is the National Crime Victimization Survey (NCVS). The survey has been used since 1972 and was redesigned and reimplemented in 1993. It contains questions for crime victims; therefore, it does not count homicides but includes simple assaults and domestic violence as well as rapes, robberies, and aggravated assaults that have been reported to police.

In the spring of 2001, the FBI reported that the eight-year-long decline in serious crimes had ended and that, in 2000, crime had increased by 0.1 percent. By 2005, there was a dramatic rise in murder, robbery, and gun assaults, especially in the Midwest and in midsize cities. In a survey of 56 cities and sheriff's departments, it was found that homicides had increased overall by 10 percent and robberies by 12 percent between 2004 and 2005. In cities such as Boston, Cincinnati, Cleveland, Hartford, Memphis, and Orlando, homicides increased by 20 percent, while in Detroit, Fort Wayne, and Milwaukee, they increased by more than 30 percent. Aggravated assaults with guns, which rose by 10 percent, are particularly worrisome to police because they are considered a better measure of violence than murder. Even New York City and Chicago, two cities that had enjoyed a fairly long period of declines in crime, saw rising rates between 2004 and 2006: New York by 10 percent and Chicago by 4 percent.

Most of the crime is committed by young males in their late teens and early twenties. Some violence is random, other occurs among people who know each other, and some happens between gangs (Police Executive Research Forum, 2006). (See Table 6.2 and Figures 6.2 and 6.3.)

Although males are disproportionately represented as perpetrators of violent crime, the female crime rate has recently been inching upward. Partly, this may be an unfortunate side effect of a more egalitarian atmosphere in the society. A more dramatic reason for the increase, however, seems to be women's growing dependence on drugs, particularly crack. This dependence leads to involvement in criminal activities to provide for their needs. The rates for men and women, therefore, are getting closer. Noteworthy, too, is the fact that the victims of violent crimes committed by women are principally other women, whereas males victimize both males and females in almost equal numbers.

The Bureau of Justice Statistics, an agency of the U.S. Department of Justice, periodically publishes a variety of statistics on crime. Tables 6.2 and 6.3 and Figures 6.1 through 6.6 give a thorough overview of the status of crime in the United States.

■ The Criminal Justice System

Although deviance performs some useful functions in society, crime cannot be ignored. Every society has felt the need to protect itself from violent deviants, as well as to punish those who have committed deviant acts. Unfortunately, the judicial system, comprising the institutions that have arisen to deal with the dispensation of justice, is anything but ideal. These institutions consist of the police, the courts, and the prisons. In the United States, as in most societies, all three tend to be fraught with problems, so that only seldom is the intent of justice served.

The dilemma faced by a democratic society is how to protect the innocent, punish the guilty, and still respect each individual's rights. Preventing crime and effecting swift punishment of crime would be simpler if law enforcement could restrict people's movements, tap their phones, and search their homes at will. But in so doing, the freedom and privacy of many innocent people would be violated. To prevent such abuse, the writers of the U.S. Constitution provided a number of safeguards, such as allowing citizens the right to be presumed innocent until proved guilty, the right not to incriminate themselves, and other rights. Law enforcers are restricted in their ability to search homes and question suspects. Such procedures protect citizens, but they enfeeble the criminal justice system, which cannot act as decisively as it could in a repressive or totalitarian political system.

(Text continues on page 148)

TABLE 6.2 Uniform Crime Reports (Preliminary) Index Crimes—Where They Occur

Region	Violent crime	Murder	Forcible rape	Robbery	Aggravated assault	Property crime	Burglary	Larceny-theft	Motor vehicle theft	Arson
Total	+1.3	+0.3	−1.9	+6.0	−0.7	−2.9	+0.2	−3.5	−4.7	+1.8
Northeast	−0.1	+2.5	−5.6	+2.2	−1.2	−0.8	+1.5	−0.5	−6.9	−0.5
Midwest	+2.1	+0.2	+0.3	+5.1	+0.6	+0.1	+4.0	−0.4	−3.6	+4.6
South	+0.6	+1.1	−2.0	+4.6	−1.0	−3.2	−0.2	−4.4	−1.8	−1.8
West	+2.8	−2.0	−1.4	+11.6	−1.0	−5.6	−2.6	−6.3	−6.5	+4.4

Uniform Crime Reports Percentage of Change, 2002–2006

Years	Violent crime	Murder	Forcible rape	Robbery	Aggravated assault	Property crime	Burglary	Larceny-theft	Motor vehicle theft	Arson
2003/2002	−3.0	+1.7	−1.9	−1.8	−3.8	−0.2	+0.1	−0.5	+1.1	−6.3
2004/2003	−1.2	−2.4	+0.8	−3.1	−0.5	−1.1	−0.5	−1.1	−1.9	−6.4
2005/2004	+2.3	+3.4	−1.2	+3.9	+1.8	−1.5	+0.5	−2.3	−0.2	−2.7
2006/2005	+1.3	+0.3	−1.9	+6.0	−0.7	−2.9	+0.2	−3.5	−4.7	+1.8

Source: U.S. Department of Justice – Federal Bureau of Investigation, June 2007. Preliminary Annual Uniform Crime Report, January–December 2006. Washington, DC.

Box 6.3 Natural Born Killers?

In the past several years we have witnessed a spate of killings perpetrated by young people. Children and teenagers have been involved in killing other children and teenagers, college students have killed their peers as well as professors, and a number have killed their own parents and grandparents.

Is this a new phenomenon, or has it always taken place? There are no easy answers to such questions, of course, but a pattern seems to appear when parents, teachers, psychologists, and the adolescent perpetrators themselves are queried.

■ Most of the assailants appear to be of above-average intelligence but display serious problems of self-esteem. They feel unloved, picked on, and inferior to such an extent that they are angry and suicidal. They hope to end their lives but want to do it in a way that would gain them notoriety.

■ They have easy access to guns, particularly to those with rapid-fire capability. Many live in homes where guns are available, in which adults use them to hunt and are negligent about keeping them locked away. But even when they are not available in homes, they are easy to buy.

■ They seem obsessed by the more violent aspects of pop culture, including rap lyrics, violent television and movies, and violent Internet sites.

■ Most of the teenage killers give warning signs in their writings in school or in verbal threats about the violence to come.

In speculating about the causes of violent, callous, and remorseless juveniles, professionals blame a combination of factors: the availability of guns, the culture in which our children are immersed, the possibility that many are not aware of the finality of death. But some of the blame is also attributed to parents with broken marriages and stressful and hurried lives in which their children play a secondary role at best.

Although no single factor can be attributed as causal—after all, many children have difficult lives, listen to violent lyrics, and watch violent movies and yet do not kill—psychologists believe that deep depression and a desire to die are at the bottom of juvenile murder (Egan, 1998, 1 and 20). That should give us, as a society, pause.

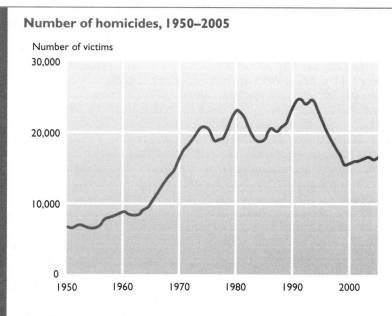

Number of homicides, 1950–2005

FIGURE 6.1 After falling rapidly in the mid to late 1990s, the number of homicides began increasing in 1999.
Source: FBI, 2007. Uniform Crime Reports, 1950–2005.

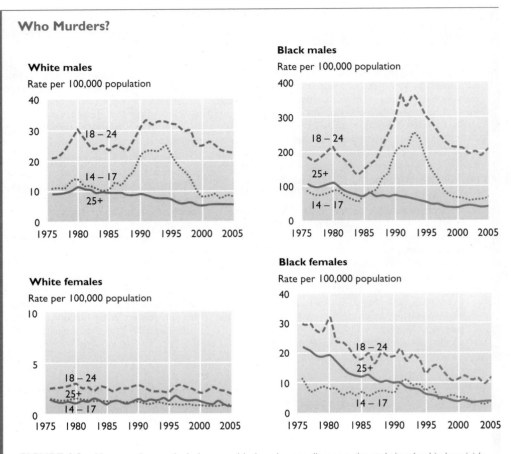

Who Murders?

FIGURE 6.2 Young males, particularly young black males, are disproportionately involved in homicide compared to their share of the population.
Source: Bureau of Justice Statistics, 2007. "Homicide Trends in the U.S.: Age, Gender, and Race."

As a result of its perceived ineffectiveness, the criminal justice system is universally criticized by victims, on the grounds that it coddles criminals, and by the perpetrators, on the grounds that police treat suspects brutally, courts convict unjustly, and prisons are barbaric places.

Is the criticism justified? It is true that a large percentage of serious offenders are never apprehended. Large numbers of criminals are never punished, and, of those arrested, better than half manage to get off free because busy dockets force many charges to be dropped. The vast majority of those who are convicted receive reduced penalties as a result of plea bargaining, a procedure in which defendants agree to plead guilty to lesser charges. The result is that only about 5 percent of all perpetrators of serious crimes ever serve time and, of those, nearly 80 percent are released early on parole (see Figure 6.4). White-collar criminals are seldom punished to the full extent of the law because their financial status allows them to hire the best legal advisers, who are able to manipulate the loopholes in the legal process to their advantage.

In the meantime, the cost of fighting crime is constantly increasing. In 2005, the latest year for which figures are available, the cost for police, prisons, and courts had risen to $185

Who Are the Victims?

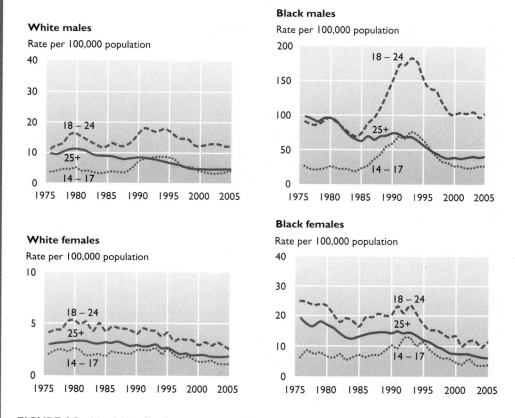

FIGURE 6.3   Homicide offending patterns are similar to victimization patterns.

billion, an increase by a large percentage from the previous decade. The increase is largely due to increases in prison inmate populations in state and federal prisons. The number of inmates jumped to 1.5 million in 2006, up from 488,000 in 1985. In addition, the number of inmates in local and county jails tripled (see Table 6.3). The rise in inmate population is the result, at least partly, of decisions by the public and politicians to become more punitive. More offenders have been sentenced to prison terms and for longer periods of time. The punitive legislation was passed mainly in the 1980s and 1990s, when state budgets were growing. Today, as states are facing deficits, it has become imperative to change punishment policies.

Imprisonment

Among democratic nations, the United States has emerged as the nation with the highest imprisonment rate. With more than 13.5 million people being incarcerated every year, 2 million people going to jail or prison every day, our rate of incarceration is 702 inmates per 100,000

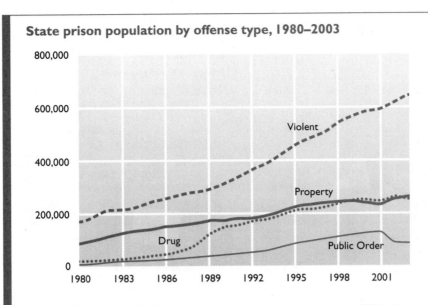

State prison population by offense type, 1980–2003

FIGURE 6.4 Over half of the increase in state prison population since 1995 is due to an increase in the prisoners convicted of violent offenses.
Source: U.S. Department of Justice, Bureau of Justice Statistics, 2006. "Correctional Populations in the United States, Annual" and "Prisoners in 2005."

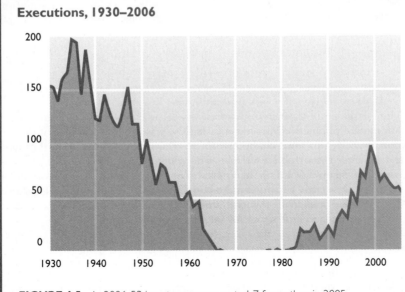

Executions, 1930–2006

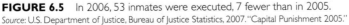

FIGURE 6.5 In 2006, 53 inmates were executed, 7 fewer than in 2005.
Source: U.S. Department of Justice, Bureau of Justice Statistics, 2007. "Capital Punishment 2005."

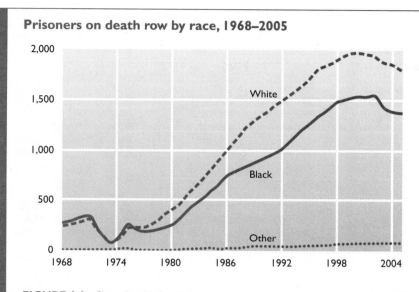

Prisoners on death row by race, 1968–2005

FIGURE 6.6 Since the death penalty was reinstated by the Supreme Court in 1976, more than half of those under sentence of death have been white.

Source: U.S. Department of Justice, 2007. Bureau of Justice Statistics. "Capital Punishment 2005."

population, as compared to Japan's rate of 53. With so many people behind bars, our prisons are bulging because we also jail more people for lesser crimes than do other Western industrial nations. If present incarceration rates remain unchanged, an estimated one of every 20 persons, or 5.1 percent, will serve time in a prison during his or her lifetime. Those chances are higher for men than for women. They are also higher for African Americans, who are jailed at a rate five times higher than whites, and Hispanics who are imprisoned at a rate three times as high as whites (Bureau of Justice Statistics, 2007). The length of sentence is also high compared to terms of imprisonment in other nations: murder in the United States may be punished by life imprisonment or execution; in Sweden, imprisonment is of much shorter duration, and the death penalty was abolished in the 1970s.

Recidivism

Neither the fact nor the length of imprisonment seems to deter crime. (Arrest seems to deter it, however. According to one study, arrested offenders are less likely to commit a crime at a future date than are offenders who are released by police without being arrested [Smith and Gartin 1989].) Prisons are termed "crime schools," where inmates learn how to be better criminals. Rates of recidivism—the repetition of criminal offenses—are high. Conversely, one of the reasons for a temporary decline in the crime rate has been attributed to an increase in incarceration.

A recent study, however, maintains that harsher prison conditions lead criminals to offend again. The study, which tracked almost a thousand inmates who had been released from federal prisons in 1987, found that those who were in a low-security lockup rather than in a minimum-security facility ended up back in prison twice as often as those in the easier form of imprisonment. Harsh prison conditions, in short, do not seem to deter offenders from breaking the law again (Chen, 2007).

TABLE 6.3   Number of Persons under Correctional Supervision

Year	Probation	Jail	Prison	Parole	Total
1980	1,118,097	183,988	319,598	220,438	1,842,100
1981	1,225,934	196,785	360,029	225,539	2,008,300
1982	1,357,264	209,582	402,914	224,604	2,194,400
1983	1,582,947	223,551	423,898	246,440	2,476,800
1984	1,740,948	234,500	448,264	266,992	2,690,700
1985	1,968,712	256,615	487,593	300,203	3,013,100
1986	2,114,621	274,444	526,436	325,638	3,241,100
1987	2,247,158	295,873	562,814	355,505	3,461,400
1988	2,356,483	343,569	607,766	407,977	3,715,800
1989	2,522,125	395,553	683,367	456,803	4,057,800
1990	2,670,234	405,320	743,382	531,407	4,350,300
1991	2,728,472	426,479	792,535	590,442	4,537,900
1992	2,811,611	444,584	850,566	658,601	4,765,400
1993	2,903,061	459,804	909,381	676,100	4,948,300
1994	2,981,022	486,474	990,147	690,371	5,148,000
1995	3,077,861	507,044	1,078,542	679,421	5,342,900
1996	3,164,996	518,492	1,127,528	679,733	5,490,700
1997	3,296,513	567,079	1,176,564	694,787	5,734,900
1998	3,670,441	592,462	1,224,469	696,385	6,134,200*
1999	3,779,922	605,943	1,287,172	714,457	6,340,800*
2000	3,826,209	621,149	1,316,333	723,898	6,445,100*
2001	3,931,731	631,240	1,330,007	732,333	6,581,700*
2002	4,024,067	665,475	1,367,547	750,934	6,758,800*
2003	4,120,012	691,301	1,390,279	769,925	6,924,500*
2004	4,143,466	713,990	1,421,911	771,852	6,995,200*
2005	4,162,536	747,529	1,446,269	784,408	7,056,000*

Note: The 2003 probation and parole counts are estimated and may differ from previously published numbers.
*Totals for 1998 through 2005 exclude probationers in jail or prison.

Source: Bureau of Justice Statistics, 2007. *Correctional Surveys (The Annual Probation Survey, National Prisoner Statistics, Survey of Jails, and The Annual Parole Survey).* Washington, DC.

What Price Punishment?

Critics of the American justice system maintain that we are spending too much money on a vast network of prisons, instead of spending it to solve the problems of the urban poor, which might prevent many from becoming criminals and consequently prisoners. Many states, for instance, spend $30,000 or more a year to house a prisoner, which does not include the cost of new prison construction. It seems logical to argue that if such amounts were spent on children from underprivileged backgrounds, many fewer homeless, parentless, and unsupervised children would drift into crime. In fact, the argument continues, prisons have become far better places for some individuals than the outside world is: prisons provide housing that is often far superior to the tenements or homeless shelters where some inmates grew up. Inmates receive three meals a day; decent medical care, especially for victims of AIDS; drug and alcohol detoxification programs; remedial education; and job training. In

Currently, 38 states allow capital punishment. The military establishment and the U.S. government allow the death penalty as well. The issue of whether such punishment is consonant with the values of a civilized society is ongoing in light of many instances in which inmates have been put to death and were later found to have been innocent.

addition, as inmates soon discover, many of their friends and relatives are in prison, too, so that they find themselves surrounded by a large social network on the inside.

Imprisonment is contemporary society's form of punishment. Punishment is thought to fulfill a number of functions in society: It is imposed for retribution, so that presumably the offender suffers as the victim has suffered ("an eye for an eye"). It is used as a deterrent, in the hope of instilling fear of punishment in the offender. It is done for rehabilitation, under the assumption that if offenders see the damage they have done, they will not repeat their crimes. Finally, it offers societal protection, because imprisoned offenders are unable to commit crimes.

Whether imprisonment does what it is supposed to do is a hotly debated issue. Every society has wrestled with it, but none have resolved the problem, even with the help of the social sciences. Although punishment of a criminal makes the noncriminals in a society feel better—in the sense that it reaffirms the norms by which the society lives—imprisonment has seldom worked, either as a deterrent or as a form of rehabilitation. Even the societal protection function is temporary. Societies will have to continue to search for a solution in their political and economic systems, whose inequalities and competitiveness may impel some individuals to crime. And individuals may have to search within themselves for the causes of the dark side of the personality that allow them to harm others as well as themselves.

The Death Penalty

The ultimate punishment, of course is death. Through much of human history, death—by crucifixion, hanging, axing, guillotine, or firearms—was the accepted punishment for whatever infraction those in power considered punishable. Most Western societies have abolished the death penalty, but the United States reinstated it in 1976. Currently, 38 states have capital punishment and 12 do not (see Figures 6.5 and 6.6). Whether to execute those accused of heinous crimes is a controversial subject, and the population at large is greatly divided. A Gallup poll in 2003 revealed that support for capital punishment was at its lowest level in 25 years; still, 64 percent supported it, and only 32 percent were against it. When respondents were given the sentencing option of life without parole, those in favor of the death penalty decreased to 53 percent, those who preferred life without parole totaled 44 percent, and 3 percent expressed no opinion. In 2006, the same poll found that two in three Americans favored the death penalty for convicted criminals: 67 percent were for it and 28 percent against it (Gallup poll, May and October 2003 and October 2006).

The rationalization for keeping the death penalty is that it acts as a deterrent to crimes so heinous that life imprisonment is insufficient. However, criminologists have found that this is not a valid rationale. A survey of 67 heads of professional criminological organizations determined that 83 percent did not believe the death penalty was a deterrent, while only 11.9 percent thought that it was (Radelet and Akers, 1996). The professionals differ from the general public: 51 percent of respondents in a Gallup Poll in 1991 thought the death penalty was a deterrent, and 41 percent thought that it was not. It is important to observe, however, that in the last 20 years, the homicide rate in death-penalty states has been 48 percent to 101 percent higher than in non–death-penalty states (Bonner and Fassenden, 2000, A1).

Regardless of whether capital punishment is or is not a deterrent, the problem with imposing it is that frequently the wrong person is accused, indicted, and prosecuted for a crime, and if such a person is executed, that represents the ultimate injustice: killing an innocent. As it is, between 1973 and 1995, two-thirds of death penalty cases were overturned on appeal, because of incompetent counsel or information withheld by prosecutors or police or for other reasons. In addition, improved DNA technology is able to prove the innocence of some inmates. Finally, it remains to be determined whether persons afflicted with mental illness or retardation or who are juveniles should be treated in the same way as those behaving in full consciousness of their actions.

The Chapter in Brief

Life in society requires a sufficient degree of order to allow peaceful coexistence. By performing the roles that go with their statuses and by obeying most of the norms of the society, individuals ensure that the social system works.

Norms and roles are learned through socialization, but the latter is never perfect, nor are informal controls adequate to maintain social order in large societies. Deviance refers to behavior or traits that conflict with significant social norms and expectations and are judged negatively by a large number of people. Deviance is relative to time and place, to who commits the deviant act, and even to who does the defining. Moreover, there are kinds and degrees of deviance.

Deviance performs some useful functions in society: it strengthens nondeviants' faith in the value of conforming to social norms; it contributes to social stability; and it often heralds positive social change. On the other hand, large-scale deviance is damaging to the social order, and when it goes unpunished, it tends to demoralize those who conform to social norms.

Explanations as to why some people conform and others deviate from social norms have been offered by theorists from the perspectives of biology, psychology, and sociology.

Biological theories attribute deviance to certain physical traits or body types. Psychological theories attribute it to mental or physical disorders, while Freudians blame it on the imperfect development of the superego. Mental disorders include brain disorders or mental retardation, which are physical (organic) in origin but may become emotional disturbances. In addition, mental disorders may be psychosomatic (unrelated to a physical cause) or may consist of neuroses such as phobias, amnesia, obsessive-compulsive reaction, and dissociative reaction. A more severe kind of personality disorder consists of maladaptive behavior such as that exemplified by the sociopath (who engages in antisocial behavior without anxiety or remorse) or the sexual deviant. Finally, the most severe forms of mental illness are psychoses: schizophrenia, paranoia, bipolar disorder, and hallucinations.

Treatment of personality disorders and mental illness includes psychotherapy, behavior therapy, psychopharmacology, electroshock therapy, and hypnotherapy.

Sociological theories include the anomie theory (when there is a lack of balance in the social system and values are insecure, the individual responds with such deviance as innovation, ritualism, retreatism, or rebellion); the differential association (cultural transmission) theory (all behavior is learned in interaction with others in small, intimate primary groups); and labeling theory (which stresses the process by which individuals are labeled as deviant and their treatment as a result of that label). Labeling theory has a conflict perspective in that deviants are seen as victims as well as perpetrators. None of the theories can be accepted uncritically; all contribute to the explanation of deviance, but they do not explain its existence in absolute terms.

One form of deviance that is extremely damaging to individuals and society is crime. A crime is an action that has been defined by law as wrong because of its destructive nature. As such, it is prohibited to members of society, and those who disregard the prohibition are punished. The chief categories of crime are juvenile delinquency, social-order (victimless) crime, white-collar crime, organized crime, and crimes against person and property—the most threatening and frightening category. Statistics on crime are compiled annually by the FBI and published as the *Uniform Crime Reports*. The stress is on the eight index crimes consisting of murder, rape, robbery, aggravated assault, arson, burglary, larceny, and auto theft. These statistics reveal that those who commit crimes are largely under 21, males, urban residents, and African Americans; but, because only the unsuccessful criminals are arrested and most crimes go unsolved, undetected, or unreported, these statistics cannot be considered totally valid.

The United States is one of the most punitive societies: the number of inmates in our prisons and jails is very high, and 38 states allow the death penalty. The crime rate has declined in recent years, but is inching upward again. The constantly increasing cost of maintaining prisons and jails, police, and courts may force legislators to pass more lenient imprisonment laws.

Terms to Remember

anomie Durkheim's term for a condition of normlessness. Merton used anomie to explain deviance, which he thought occurred when cultural goals cannot be achieved through legal institutional means.

bipolar disorder A psychosis characterized by extreme swings in emotion from deep depression to a high degree of excitement.

cultural transmission (or differential association) Theory of deviance (Sutherland, Miller) based on the proposition that all human behavior, including deviant behavior, is learned through symbolic interaction, especially in primary groups.

deviance Norm-violating behavior beyond the society's limits of tolerance.

differential association See *cultural transmission.*

ectomorph In Sheldon's typology (biological theory of deviance), a thin and delicate body type whose personality tends to be introspective, sensitive, nervous, and artistic.

electroconvulsive shock therapy A treatment of severe mental disorders (particularly depression) through the application of severe electric shock. It is a painful procedure and is sometimes abused.

endomorph In Sheldon's typology, a round and soft body type whose personality is social, easygoing, and self-indulgent.

index crimes The eight crimes whose rates are reported annually by the FBI: murder, rape, robbery, aggravated assault, burglary, arson, larceny, and auto theft.

labeling A sociological theory of deviance that explains deviant behavior as a reaction to the group's expectations of someone who has once been decreed as deviant.

mesomorph In Sheldon's typology, a muscular and agile body type with a restless, energetic, and insensitive personality.

neurosis A mild personality disorder; an inefficient, partly disruptive way of dealing with personal problems, but seldom troublesome enough to require institutionalization. Neuroses include amnesia, phobias, obsessive ideas or repetitive actions, and repression of thoughts or experiences.

paranoia A psychosis characterized by the feeling of being persecuted or of being an important personage (delusions of grandeur).

personality disorders Mental disorders that lie somewhere between the neuroses and the psychoses in severity. They include sociopathy, sexual deviance, and addiction.

psychosis A serious mental disorder in which there is loss of contact with reality. Requires institutionalization when individuals become incapable of functioning in society. Psychoses include schizophrenia, paranoia, and bipolar disorder.

psychosomatic disorders Physical ailments developed as a result of emotional tension or anxiety.

psychotherapy A treatment for psychoses and mental disturbances that includes analysis, group therapy, family therapy, and others, centering around verbal exchanges.

schizophrenia A label for a psychosis that varies in severity from inability to relate to others to total withdrawal from reality.

sociopath A person suffering from a personality disturbance in which antisocial behavior does not elicit remorse.

Suggested Readings

Adler, Freda, and William S. Laufer, eds. 1994. *The Legacy of Anomie: Advances in Criminological Theory.* Vol. 6. New Brunswick, NJ: Transaction Books. A collection of essays focusing on the anomie theory, with its roots in the thought of Emile Durkheim and its development by Robert Merton, noting its continued importance in our attempts to understand deviance.

Campbell, Anne. 1991. *The Girls in the Gang.* 2nd ed. Cambridge, MA: Basil Blackwell. What makes individuals, and especially females, join criminal gangs? This is the question pursued in this insightful account of young women in a New York street gang.

Cole, David. 1999. *No Equal Justice: Race and Class in the American Criminal Justice System.* New York: The New Press. A law professor writes about the role of race and social class in the arrest and conviction rates in the United States.

Currie, Elliott. 1998. *Crime and Punishment in America.* New York: Henry Holt. A sociologist discusses the increase in the prison population and offers policy alternatives for managing violence in the society.

Falk, Gerhard. 1990. *Murder: An Analysis of Its Forms, Conditions, and Causes.* Jefferson, NC: McFarland. An overview of violence in the United States, including discussions of public policy, social diversity, punishment, as well as the use of drugs, as these factors combine to result in our high murder rate.

Reiman, Jeffrey. 2002. *The Rich Get Richer and the Poor Get Prison?* 7th ed. Needham Heights, MA: Allyn and Bacon. A conflict perspective on the criminal justice system, focusing on the racial and class inequalities that, according to the author, lie at the bottom of the problems created by crime in the United States.

Web Sites of Interest

http://faculty.ncwc.edu/toconnor/data.htm
Crime data sources in Criminal Justice: how crime data are collected, analyzed, and put to use. A useful site by the Criminal Justice Department of North Carolina Wesleyan College.

http://www.lukol.com/top/society/crime/
Everything you ever wanted to know about crime, with links to specific types of crimes, national and international.

http://www.abacon.com/sociology/soclinks/deviance.html
Allyn & Bacon's own Web site on the sociology of deviance.

7

The Great Divide:
Ranking and Stratification

IN THIS CHAPTER, YOU WILL LEARN THAT

- *people are differentiated as to gender and age in all societies; they are differentiated as to the amount of wealth, prestige, and power they hold in societies that produce a surplus;*

- *the importance of such differentiation lies in the social meanings that are attached to it;*

- *ranking inherently results in inequality because it implies that some persons are superior to others because of the desirable attributes or commodities they possess;*

- *where scarce goods are distributed unequally, a stratified system results;*

- *the theoretical explanations for inequality follow a conservative or liberal tradition;*

- *social scientists have developed several models of stratification systems;*

- *there are various ways of determining social class;*

- *the consequences of social class and the factors involved in social mobility affect human lives;*

- *poverty seems to be a stubborn side effect of inequality.*

Governments proclaim that their citizens are all equal before the law. Religions stress that all people are "God's children." Scientists assert that all of humankind is descended from a common stock. Humanitarians lobby for legislation to equalize the lifestyles of all members of society, while communist governments maintained—before their almost universal collapse—that they had already attained such equality. Philanthropists donate money for the same purpose—or to lessen their guilt for having so much more than others. In short, the idea that all humans are, or should be, equal is a frequent theme, at least in the cultures of

Western societies. And yet, perhaps the very insistence on this theme reflects the reality that people are anything but equal.

As we saw in Chapter 5, the similar-looking babies in hospital nurseries are socialized into quite different adults. Not only appearance, but differences in gender, age, skin color, manner of dress and speech, and many other attributes characterize individuals. These differences are easily visible. More important are the differences that affect people's lives dramatically, among which are the amounts of wealth, status, and power that individuals possess.

Differences are characteristic of all life forms. In human societies, however, the way the differences are interpreted is immensely important. That is, what counts are the *social meanings* people give both to chance biological facts and to cultural traits. These are judged as being more or less desirable. Consequently, they are ranked, and ranking produces inequality. In other words, because some traits are valued more highly than others, people who lack the valued traits are not considered equal to those who have them. By the same token, because many resources are scarce and hard to obtain in most societies, those who have less of these scarce resources are considered unequal to those who have more of them.

■ Social Differentiation, Ranking, and Stratification

The physical world is full of examples of inequality. The fact that it is common knowledge that "the bigger fish eats the smaller fish" indicates that inequality is taken for granted in nature: some individuals in each group have an advantage in the task of survival. Social scientists are not concerned with that type of inequality.

Of concern is the fact that all human societies practice *social differentiation*. People everywhere are categorized according to some trait (sex, age, race, ethnic background, religion) and according to how much of the scarce resources (wealth, power, prestige) they possess. Further, as noted earlier, people are ranked on the basis of having or lacking some of the above attributes. Ranking involves a value judgment; in effect, the society establishes that it is better to be one thing than another, to have more of some things than less. Eventually, ranking results in stratification, a condition in which categories of people in a society are treated unequally.

All groups, human as well as animal, eventually develop a social hierarchy, or dominance order. The reason for such a hierarchy is to provide an orderly method of access to and distribution of resources. In a way, it is a method of preventing continuous fighting over scarce—and, therefore, especially desired—resources.

In simple societies, there is social differentiation based on sex and age. Sometimes, as a reward for special talents, some individuals or groups are given greater amounts of prestige, influence, and wealth. For example, nomadic hunting and gathering groups have very few possessions. At most, they have a few bows and arrows, primitive knives, and some utensils made of shells, animal skins, or animal organs. When the hunt is successful, every member of the tribe is given a fair share of the kill, and they all gorge themselves. When no animal has been killed, everyone goes hungry. Hoarding, especially of meat, is impossible, because without methods of preserving it, meat spoils. As a result, no individual or family has an opportunity to accumulate more food than another. From an economic point of view, all members of such groups are equal, though they are differentiated according to sex and age: men and women, young and old, have different statuses and perform different roles. In addition, the most talented hunters, those who exhibit special skills in magic, and the elderly, who have some knowledge resulting from experience, all have higher positions in the tribe. They are given more respect and honor; in effect, their words and decisions carry more weight than those of the lesser-endowed individuals. They may receive an extra ration of meat or drier shelter. Even in these simple societies, then, there is inequality in the sense that some individuals get more than others. However, the inequality is limited to single individuals, who are rewarded or punished for their own actions, and not to whole categories of people. This is an important distinction from the way inequality occurs in more complex societies.

■ Stratification

The more complex societies are, the more unequally they tend to distribute their scarce goods. The unequal distribution of scarce resources leads to **social stratification**, meaning that the society is divided into a number of strata, or layers. Stratified societies use a system of ranking according to:

1. *wealth*, or how much of the societal resources a person owns;
2. *prestige*, or the degree of honor a person's position in society evokes; and
3. *power*, or the degree to which a person can direct others as a result of the preceding factors.

Wealth, which includes *income* and *property*, is an element of *social class*, whereas *prestige* is an element of *status*. In turn, class, status, and power are the so-called *dimensions* of stratification. That is, stratification systems are analyzed by looking at each of these phenomena.

Stratification occurs in every society that has produced a surplus. A society that produces no surplus gives little opportunity to acquire wealth or prestige and the power based on them. Thus, stratification is intimately related to economics because the layering of people into social levels boils down to attempts to answer the question: Who gets what, and why? (That is, how shall the scarce resources in the society be distributed and for what reason?) Different societies answer these questions differently, according to these economic systems. Consequently, their stratification systems vary.

■ Theoretical Views on Stratification

Stratification systems essentially separate people into haves and have-nots. Attempting to analyze why stratification emerges, most social thinkers have concluded that some social inequality is inevitable. The *classical conservative* position is that inequality is part of the law of nature. It holds that people are basically selfish and greedy. Social institutions must curb this greed and selfishness or the society will not function smoothly. The curbing is done by institutions; however, institutions also promote inequality. Inequality is the price societies must pay to ensure peace and order. Later, the so-called social Darwinists proposed that because the resources of society were scarce and people had to compete for them, only the strongest, the most intelligent, or those most willing to work would acquire most of the good things in life. This situation would result in inequality, but at the same time it would ensure that only the worthiest people in a society rose to positions of power and privilege. Ultimately, this would benefit society, for such people would provide enlightened leadership.

In the *classical liberal* view, humans are considered as essentially good rather than selfish and greedy. It is society and its institutions that corrupt people, because each individual or group must struggle to get a share of the scarce goods and services that the society offers. The struggle becomes divisive and ends with the dominance of one group over others.

The dominant group is able to exploit the others and, once in a position of power, to impose its will on the remainder of society. Inequality and stratification are then unavoidable.

Structural-Functionalist Perspective

The intellectual descendants of the conservative viewpoint are represented by the *structural-functionalist* school of thought in sociology. Functionalists stress the needs of the society rather than those of the individual, reasoning that the needs of individuals can be satisfied only within the society. The existence of every society depends on the regular performance of specific tasks that are difficult and require special intelligence, talent, and training. Societies must institute systems of rewards with which to lure the most talented, the most intelligent, and the best-trained individuals to perform these tasks. The positions most essential to the welfare of a society, and positions for which there are few qualified personnel, must be the ones that are most highly rewarded (Davis & Moore, 1945). It may be argued that collecting garbage is almost as vital to the health of a society as practicing medicine, because uncollected garbage is a threat to public health, but collecting garbage requires little training or talent; therefore, many individuals are capable of performing this function. Practicing medicine, on the other hand, requires a long period of study and training. Not all individuals are capable of undergoing the discipline of such training; therefore, there are

Scenes like this were frequent in the major cities of the United States and Britain in the nineteenth and early twentieth centuries when capitalism reigned unobstructed. Moral repugnance at the extremes of wealth and poverty fueled the acceptance of more liberal ideas.

fewer potential doctors than potential garbage collectors, and consequently doctors should be much better rewarded.

In addition, functional theorists stress the need for order, stability, and balance in society. Even though it produces some social inequality, they maintain, a system of stratification has a stabilizing influence on society. It prevents conflicts from erupting and disrupting the orderly functioning of the society. (Structural-functionalism is also called the *equilibrium theory*, because of its emphasis on harmony and balance.) Finally, functionalists conclude that inequality is built into the social system because not all types of work are equally necessary for, and thus valued by, the society.

Criticism of structural-functionalism centers around the facts that (1) what is an essential function is subject to interpretation (is a professional football player or an entertainer essential?) and (2) stratification systems prevent some talented people from developing their talents, while some untalented people receive rewards in spite of their limitations.

Conflict Perspective

The intellectual descendants of the classical liberal view are today's conflict theorists. They argue that inequality is the product of the conflicts and dissensions that originate in people's desire for power. The possession of scarce resources gives the possessor power. Groups struggle with one another to obtain power, and the group that emerges victorious tries to impose a stratification system on the society by enrolling some institutions— religion, education, the political system—to legitimize it. Thus, stratification systems are mechanisms of coercion.

The best-known conflict theorist was Karl Marx. He stated that all of history was a record of class struggles caused by the unequal distribution of rewards in societies. All societies are stratified, according to Marx, because in every society one group tries to protect its economic interests at the expense of other groups. Further, the institution of private ownership of the means of production leads to the modern division of societies into social classes. These classes are in conflict with one another because the owners *(bourgeoisie)* have, and want to keep, a monopoly of power over the nonowners *(proletariat)*. The owners obtain and maintain power both by force and by instilling a value system and ideology in the masses that legitimize their power. Once they are in control and with a system of stratification in operation, the system is perpetuated through various institutions. The family transmits either wealth, opportunity for education, and prestige, or poverty and lack of opportunity, from one generation to another. Schools, too, prepare some individuals for leadership roles and others for menial occupations. Christianity helps people accept values that justify the status quo and encourages the poor to seek their reward in an afterlife, while other religions direct the faithful toward a spiritual quest or offer solace from pain.

A criticism of conflict theory, and of Marxism in particular, is that it neglects to address two important issues: first, that people are naturally unequal in the amount of talent and intelligence they have and the amount of work they are willing to do; and second, that to a great extent the existence of inequality is a motivating force for people. The more hard-working, talented, and intelligent people will tend to rise to the top in any economic system, and the existence of inequality will motivate people to try to get to the top.

The functionalist and the conflict theories of stratification are not mutually exclusive. There is evidence that societies exhibit stability and consensus as well as conflict and dissension. The two theories suggest two different ways of looking at stratification systems of societies, but they do not offer definitive answers as to the causes of stratification, nor do they provide methods for doing away with inequality.

■ Dimensions of Stratification: Class, Status, and Power

The basis of all stratification systems, as was noted, is ranking of people according to their possession of things that are scarce and, therefore, highly prized. These scarce resources are popularly categorized as wealth, prestige, and power, or, in more sociological terms, *class, status*, and *power*. It is according to these dimensions that people are assigned a rank in society and relegated to a stratum with others who are ranked similarly.

Class

Although discussions of social class figure prominently in the media and the term is commonly used in conversation, most people would have difficulty defining the term with accuracy. Americans, in fact, have an especially mistaken conception of social class: they volunteer the information that most of them belong to the middle class, and they appear only slightly aware of the vast differences in lifestyles of different groups of people.

Definitions of Class: Marx and Weber.   As noted earlier, Karl Marx viewed the division of society into classes as determined by the relationship of a group in society to the *means of production*. Groups that own a large proportion of the society's wealth—particularly the tools and capital necessary to produce that wealth—have control over groups that own little of either. The groups lacking capital must sell their labor to survive. Thus, Marx's approach to stratification and his concept of class are essentially *economic* in nature.

Arguing that the Marxist view was too simplistic and that class was only one dimension of stratification, the renowned sociologist Max Weber (1864–1920) proposed a threefold approach to the phenomenon and added the concept of life chances to his definition of class (Gerth & Mills, 1946). Weber defined class objectively as consisting of groups of people who had similar lifestyles dictated by their economic position in society, that is, by the goods they possessed and their opportunities for increasing their income. Modern social scientists refer to money, goods, and services as *property*.

Life Chances.   Property is not the only determinant of class, according to Weber: equally important are a person's life chances. **Life chances**, in Weber's view, are the opportunities that each individual has of fulfilling his or her potential in life. A person's life chances are determined by his or her position within the stratification system. The higher that position is, the more access there is to scarce resources and thus the more positive are the life chances of the individual. The lower the position, the less access there is to scarce resources and the more negative are the life chances.

Today, the Weberian concept of class tends to predominate. **Social class** is defined as "an aggregation of persons in a society who stand in a similar position with respect to some form of power, privilege, or prestige" (Lenski, 1966, 74–75). In other words, some people, because of a similarity in occupations, income, education, and lifestyles, set themselves apart from the rest of the population. In time, they become sufficiently differentiated from others and unified—sometimes unknowingly—among themselves to constitute a separate social level or stratum—a social class.

The notion of life chances is exemplified by students who attend private secondary schools. The structure, discipline, and the superior education they provide—as well as the network of friendships they encourage—lead almost universally to occupations that ensure entrance into the upper classes.

Status

Status is the degree of social esteem that an individual or group enjoys in society. In the Weberian sense, status means prestige rather than simply a position within the social system. The most important element of status is that it is a ranked position—high, middle, low—determined by how the role attached to the status is valued. For instance, because the role of physician, particularly that of a specialist in a difficult field, is highly valued in our society, that position has a high status in the United States.

There is frequently overlap between class and status, but the overlap does not always, or necessarily, occur. Some people may have high incomes and lack status; conversely, some may have high status and lack a substantial income. Status is very important to most people, and the desire to obtain high status is learned as part of socialization. The concern for status "influences almost every kind of decision, from the choice of a car to the choice of a spouse. Fear of the loss of status, or honor, is one of the few motives that can make men lay down their lives on the field of battle" (Lenski, 1966, 37–38).

Most people are quite adept at judging each other's status. In the United States, status tends to depend primarily on occupation (achieved status is more frequent than ascribed status). The reason is that occupations are good indicators of income and particularly of education. In all surveys where respondents have been asked to rank a variety of occupations, the occupations requiring graduate-school training have been ranked highest. Although high-ranking occupations generally carry with them high incomes, this is not always the case: it is true for specialized physicians, some attorneys, and many corporate executives, but it is not true for college professors and research scientists.

Additional determinants of status are being born into a highly respected family ("old money"), living in the "right" kind of neighborhood, attending private preparatory schools and Ivy League universities, belonging to exclusive country clubs, and being members of the "right" church denominations. The factors that influence social status, then, include occupation and source of income, race, education, sex, age, religion, and ethnic origin.

Box 7.1   Class, Status, and Power in America

If we compared the income of ordinary Americans to the income of some Americans, we would see great disparities. For instance, compare your net worth or salary or that of your family to that of some CEOs and celebrities, as reported by Forbes magazine for the year 2006 (http://www.forbes.com):

1. Bill Gates, CEO of Microsoft Corporation: net worth $53 billion
2. Warren Buffet, stock market investor: net worth $46 billion
3. Lawrence Ellison, CEO of Oracle Corporation: net worth $19.5 billion
4. Oprah Winfrey, television personality: net worth $1.5 billion
5. J. K. Rowling, author of the Harry Potter books: net worth $1 billion
6. Tiger Woods, golfer: estimated earnings between June 2005 and June 2006 $90 million
7. Tom Cruise, actor and producer: estimated earnings between June 2005 and June 2006 $67 million
8. Shaquille O'Neal, basketball player: earnings between June 2005 and June 2006 $30 million
9. 50 Cent, rapper and hip hop artist: earnings in 2005: $41 million
10. Derek Jeter, baseball player: earnings between 2005 and 2006 $27 million

In which social class would you place each of the above persons? Why? Are any of them status inconsistent? Do they possess power? social or political? Are the two connected? Moreover, it is self-evident that the income of the celebrities and of the heads of corporations is vastly greater than the income of the majority of Americans. Is this right? Do these celebrities deserve to earn so much more than you and your family? Do they improve society's quality of life? Do they affect your life personally? Would you be any worse off if they did not exist?

The functionalist theorists would answer that yes, these people deserve their high incomes because they have special talents, and we reward them because they entertain us or they provide us with products we need or want. The conflict theorists would assert that such an unequal distribution of resources is patently unjust and that the high-income celebrities and CEOs are a part of a social class in a stratification system that is dangerous because it gives immense power to those who possess such large resources. Such power allows them to manipulate policies to their advantage.

What course should a society follow to minimize such vast differences? Some societies have tried communist and socialist ideologies that purport to do away with social classes and to divide resources more equally. They have proved to be dismal failures. Is inequality inherent in the human condition, then?

Status Inconsistency.   One would be justified in assuming that characteristics directly opposed to those associated with high social status indicate low status. However, in studying industrial societies, sociologists have become aware of the phenomenon of *status inconsistency*. A person may have amassed immense wealth, but if it is derived from organized crime and the person lacks the education and most of the other traits of high status, that person is status inconsistent. Conversely, a person may lack any visible means of support because of having gambled away the family fortune but may retain a high status because of the past glory attached to the family name.

Findings that people are subject to status inconsistency have led to theories speculating that such people will tend to suffer more frustration and dissatisfaction than those whose status is consistent (Lenski, 1966). Persons who are ranked higher on one variable of status than another—women doctors, for instance, or minority baseball stars—try to stress the higher-ranked variable and deemphasize the lower-ranked. Unfortunately, others will judge them by their *master status*, which is the status that society considers the most important of several alternatives. The woman doctor will be seen as a woman first and may be mistaken for a nurse. The athlete who has made it to star status may be admired for his athletic prowess and his high income, but he may be ignored by some people as a guest or friend. People who suffer from status inconsistency, particularly those who are denied *high* status, take out their frustrations by turning away from upper-status groups, at least in terms of political action or philosophy (Cohn, 1958; G. Marx, 1967).

Power

The third important dimension of stratification—some consider it the most important dimension—is power. **Power** is defined as the ability to carry out one's wishes in spite of resistance. It is the ability to get other people to do what one wants them to do, with or without their consent. Stratification based on power is, in Weber's view, essentially political rather than economic. In fact, Weber used the term *political class* or *party* to mean an elite, a group that is more powerful than other groups in society. Power is exercised in all social systems, from the simplest to the most complex.

As applied to stratification, power can be divided into personal power and social power. *Personal power* is the freedom of individuals to direct their own lives in a way they themselves choose, without much interference. Such freedom often goes with great wealth. *Social power* is the ability to make decisions that affect entire communities or even the whole society. Social power may be exercised legitimately, with the consent of the members of society. In this case, it is called *authority*. Parents, teachers, and the government all represent different levels of authority. Social power may also be exercised illegitimately, that is, without the official approval of society. Organized crime, for instance, exercises power illegitimately.

Power is such an important dimension of stratification because it affects the manner in which society's goods and services are distributed. It is deeply interwoven with the other dimensions, class and status. High-status individuals have little trouble attaining positions of power, either in government, the professions, or corporate and banking circles. In turn, those in positions of power can control decision making in such a way that events are favorable to them. In traditional, nonindustrial societies, power is often held by a small elite, while the majority of people are relatively powerless. In industrial societies, however, power is spread among many people, largely as a result of universal suffrage and the generally better living standard of the majority of the population.

■ Systems of Stratification

Historically, societies have exhibited a variety of stratification systems. A **stratification system** is the overlapping manner in which societal members are ranked into classes, status groups, and hierarchies of power. To distinguish among them, social scientists use models, abstract conceptions that they place on an ideal continuum. At one extreme of the continuum is the closed, or caste, stratification system. The middle is represented by the estate system. At the other extreme is the open, or class, system. The stratification system of each society fits somewhere along this ideal continuum.

The Closed Society: Caste

Whether a society has an open or a closed stratification system is determined by the way its members obtain wealth, prestige, and privilege (the Weberian class, status, and power). In a **closed, or caste, stratification system**, class, status, and power are ascribed, that is, determined strictly on the basis of family inheritance rather than on individual effort or merit. In a closed society, the individual is born into a specific social stratum, called a *caste*, and has no opportunity to move in or out of it.

Classical India offers a good example of a closed society. The caste system that flourished in India for many centuries was distinguished by the fact that people were divided into a number of castes, representing areas of service to society and ranked in order of their importance to it. Some ranking also resulted from struggles for power or conquest by other groups. Religion and tradition forbade members of one caste to intermarry or interact in any way with members of other castes. Each caste was restricted in occupation and the status of each individual was ascribed, so that a person inherited a specific social position and was unable to change it regardless of effort or achievement. (Only a limited number of people,

The resident of the White House definitely possesses status and power, though not necessarily wealth. In a democratic society, however, these dimensions are only temporary.

particularly if they exhibited extraordinary military prowess, were able to attain a higher caste, although disobeying certain norms could plunge a person into a lower one.) The caste system has been legally abolished in modern India, which has been deeply influenced by Western democratic thought; but many Indians, particularly those living in rural areas, still follow some elements of the caste system that for so long had been justified by religion and traditional mores.

The Estate System

The estate system was the economic and social system of feudal Europe and, in different forms, has characterized a number of nations in Asia. As in the caste system, in the **estate system of stratification**, social positions were also ranked according to their functions; however, in theory, all the estates were considered to be equal in importance. The three main estates were the nobility, the church, and the peasants, and within each estate there was a stratified hierarchy of positions.

Supported by religion and tradition, the estate system permitted quite a bit more mobility among social strata than did the caste system. Because only eldest sons could inherit the title and possessions of a noble family, the remaining sons had to enter either the military or the clergy. Occasionally, serfs who had distinguished themselves were freed and given land, and some peasants were allowed to enter the lower ranks of the priesthood.

The remnants of the estate system are still visible in some modern societies that retain a landed gentry and inherited titles of nobility. Also, some elements of the system may be recognized as having existed on the plantations of the American South a century ago, although slavery falls more within the caste spectrum on the continuum.

The Open Society: Class System

Modern industrial and postindustrial societies such as the United States most nearly approximate the model of an open society. Open, or class, societies have these characteristics in common: (1) classes exist but are not institutionalized as in the caste and estate systems; (2) class lines are unclear, so people do not display excessive class consciousness, but inequality stemming from class divisions is apparent; (3) status is usually achieved, but there is evidence to indicate that status tends to be ascribed to the lowest and the highest social classes; (4) social mobility is possible and occurs frequently.

Open, or class, systems work best in industrial societies that have market economies, because these offer more opportunities for achieving wealth and status than do societies with centralized economies. In government-controlled economies, people may not have the opportunity to choose their jobs and maximize advantages.

Social mobility—essentially, changing class membership—is possible and encouraged in open systems; however, it is not evenly distributed in the society. Limitations based on racial, ethnic, regional, educational, and even religious factors restrict mobility. However, the individual is still permitted much more leeway for social as well as physical movement than in closed systems.

Class systems in all societies have certain characteristics in common. The rise of social classes is almost always accompanied by the development of central political institutions, foremost among which is the state. Even the so-called classless societies that espoused a communist or socialist ideology—all of which had strong states before their downfall—also had a class system. Moreover, the more surplus a society produces, the more stratified it is and the more complex its class system is. Even though in technologically advanced societies the large surplus that is produced filters down to all social classes and starvation-level poverty exists to only a very small extent, class inequalities remain flagrant. Finally, power and wealth appear to be the most important elements of class systems, with prestige playing a less important role.

In contemporary industrial societies, power and wealth are closely interconnected in both capitalist and socialist economies. In capitalist countries, the wealthy are more likely to come to power, and in socialist nations the powerful are likely to become wealthy. However, the stratification systems of both kinds of economies are strikingly similar. Societies that have a long tradition of feudal-like stratification, although they have become open in the industrial era, retain strong class boundaries.

■ Determining Social Class: Occupational Prestige and Socioeconomic Status

Social scientists disagree not only about the number of social classes in existence but also about the standards that determine who belongs in which class. The categories used by researchers to pigeonhole people into social classes are arbitrary and artificial.

Historically, a number of approaches have been used to determine social class. Today, however, most researchers use one of two. In the *occupational prestige* approach, researchers ask people which occupations and sources of income are the most prestigious. This approach depends on a large sample, usually on a national scale. The occupational prestige approach has proved to be the best index of social class in the United States because of its practicality. Occupation determines the amount of money that is earned, which in turn determines, in many cases, the amount of power wielded and the prestige held. But money alone does not determine social class. Some occupations are rated very high even though the monetary rewards are relatively low, and vice versa.

A more common methodological device is based on an index that combines a number of dimensions relevant to stratification. One such index measures socioeconomic status (SES). Such an index shows at a glance the position of individuals in the social and economic pecking order. The development of such an index is possible despite instances of status inconsistency because of the related nature of the dimensions of stratification in American society.

■ Social Classes in the United States

As noted earlier in the chapter, people are not generally aware of social classes in the United States. That is, they are not class conscious in the Marxian sense of working for the self-interest of their class, and they tend to characterize themselves as belonging to the "middle class." In fact, social classes are very fluid in our society, first, because we lack a traditional landed aristocracy, and second, because social mobility allows people to change social class. Still, there is no question that people live different lives according to their social class; and so, in spite of the difficulty of assigning people to specific classes according to a rigid system, some descriptive technique is necessary.

There are a large number of models of class structure, beginning with the Marxian model, which divided people into the bourgeoisie (owners of the means of production) and the proletariat (workers). Usually, however, the American class structure is divided into five

TABLE 7.1 Historical Income Tables—Families. Mean Income Received by Each Fifth and Top 5 Percent of Families, All Races, 1990 to 2005 (Families as of March of the following year. Income in current dollars.)

Year	Lowest fifth	Second fifth	Third fifth	Fourth fifth	Highest fifth	Top 5 percent
2005	$14,767	$35,137	$56,227	$84,095	$176,292	$308,636
2004	14,199	33,797	54,243	81,041	168,663	293,837
2003	13,871	32,896	53,016	79,713	163,322	281,467
2002	14,017	32,521	51,869	77,145	159,298	278,790
2001	14,021	32,466	51,538	76,646	159,644	280,312
2000	14,122	32,289	50,747	74,791	156,919	278,063
1999	13,308	30,934	48,827	72,067	147,702	254,665
1998	12,526	29,482	46,662	68,430	140,846	246,520
1997	12,057	28,252	44,575	65,363	134,285	235,021
1996	11,388	26,847	42,467	62,052	125,627	217,355
1995	11,265	25,955	40,637	59,457	119,453	204,863
1994	10,387	24,575	38,808	57,366	115,608	198,336
1993	9,739	23,390	37,066	54,946	111,017	191,612
1992	9,586	23,121	36,527	53,094	98,602	155,557
1991	9,734	23,105	35,851	51,997	95,530	147,817
1990	9,833	22,935	35,322	50,797	94,404	148,124

Source: U.S. Census Bureau, 2007. Historical Income Tables—Families. "Mean Income Received by Each Fifth and Top 5 Percent of Families, All Races: 1990 to 2005."

or six layers, consisting (more or less) of the following percentages: upper-upper, 1.4 percent; lower-upper, 1.6 percent; upper-middle, 10 percent; lower-middle, 28 percent; upper-lower, 34 percent; and lower-lower, 25 percent. The population may also be divided into quintiles, or fifths, as the Census Bureau does (Table 7.1).

The Upper Classes

The upper classes actually consist of two groups: the upper-upper, including only 1 percent of the population of the United States, and the lower-upper, counting approximately 2 or 3 percent of the population. The upper-upper class consists almost exclusively of people who belong to it as a result of ascribed status, that is, inherited, "old" wealth. Possessing vast fortunes accumulated through several generations, and added to through shrewd investments, this group lives an exclusive lifestyle few Americans even imagine. Members of this social class generally reside in elite neighborhoods, in mansions often filled with first-rate art, in addition to owning additional vacation homes here and abroad; they send their children to private preparatory schools (which they themselves also attended) and Ivy League universities, where they pursue liberal arts degrees rather than specifically vocational courses of study. Conscious of their privileged situation, most engage in philanthropic endeavors, volunteering time and donating money to hospitals, charitable and artistic organizations, and other "worthy" causes. In this way they establish themselves as the "elite" of the cities in which they live. Eventually they come to know members of the political establishment, from governors to members of Congress, from Supreme Court justices to the President of the United States. Needless to say, such acquaintances add not only prestige but also power.

The lower-uppers, often disposing of similar or even greater income, differ in that the income tends to have been earned. These are mostly "self-made" individuals, whether their current wealth comes from talents—sports, show business, television, movies or from shrewd business transactions. Some may have inherited some wealth or have received a fine education, while others may come from very modest backgrounds. A perfect example is Bill Gates, the son of professional and well-to-do parents, a self-described "technie nerd" who purveyed an interest in computers into the Microsoft Corporation, a company that has made its founder a multibillionaire.

These two groups receive a lion's share of the income produced in the United States. For instance, in 2004, of all American households (divided into fifths, or quintiles, meaning that each fifth is equivalent to 20 percent), the highest fifth received 47.9 percent of the aggregate income of the United States; the next fifth received 23.0 percent; the middle fifth received 15.4 percent; the second to the lowest fifth received 9.6 percent; and the lowest fifth received 4.0 percent. As for the top 5 percent, they received 20.9 percent (U.S. Bureau of the Census, 2007). (A distinction should be made between income, which is earned yearly, and wealth, which includes all of an individuals's accumulated possessions. Although there is considerable inequality in incomes, the inequality in wealth is still more dramatic: the richest fifth owns around 85 percent of the nation's wealth, while the poorest fifth has a negative net worth of around 0.7 percent because they are in debt. As for the top 1 percent of U.S. households, they own close to 35 percent of the nation's private wealth, which is more than the combined wealth of the bottom 90 percent.)

Although the income of the lower-uppers is often astronomical—some CEOs and TV and movie personalities earn as much in a day as the average American worker does in a year and sometimes in a lifetime—they are still disdained by the upper-uppers as the "new rich" who find it necessary to engage in conspicuous consumption to show the world they have "arrived." The upper-uppers, on the other hand, do not have to prove anything to anyone, having always lived in privilege. Therefore, they tend to be much more discreet and understated in their lifestyles. It is the lower-uppers, however, who are taken as role models by most Americans for just their kind of success stories make up the "American dream" and are a popular cultural goal.

The Middle Class

Between one-half and three-quarters of the American population fits into the middle class (and many more think they are middle class when they actually are not). This category, then, must also be subdivided into an upper-middle, middle-middle, and lower-middle classification. In addition, because it includes such a wide spectrum of Americans, it is difficult to specify boundaries between these subdivisions.

In general, it may be said that the upper-middle class consists of highly educated professionals—doctors, lawyers, stockbrokers, accountants, and so on—and owners of family businesses. Such persons tend to make comfortable incomes, live mostly in the suburbs, actively participate in community affairs, try to expose their children to enriching experiences, and attempt to give them a good education. The group also includes young urban professionals, so-called yuppies, who are better educated than their parents and, being single or recently married, prefer to live within the city limits to take advantage of cultural and recreational opportunities. Their yearly income varies from around

$150,000 and up (slightly lower in small cities and rural areas), while their assets are thought to be between $368,000 and $5 million. They represent approximately 17 percent of the population.

The middle-middle class (and the lower-middle, depending on income) consists of small shop owners; the lesser professionals, such as public school teachers; and a variety of white-collar employees, from sales clerks to bank tellers, from nurses to office workers, and so on. Their incomes are lower than those of the upper-middle class, and families usually depend on more than one paycheck.

Judging from polls, most people believe they are upper-middle or middle class: in 2000, 69 percent said so, whereas only 24 percent said they considered themselves working class, and only 6 percent put themselves in either the lower or the upper class (Gallup/CNN/USA Today Poll, 2000). If one chooses the mathematical middle of the population (that is, the middle quintile), their household earnings in 2006 were around $48,201 (Figure 7.1).

The middle class has been stereotyped, ever since it appeared following the Industrial Revolution in Europe, as consisting of people with a narrow range of ideas, who follow conforming lifestyles. In the United States, they were thought to inhabit the suburbs, where they lived in identical houses with two-car garages and the husband commuted to work while the wife chauffeured the children to a variety of activities. They were thought to be family-centered on the surface and conventionally religious. When sociologists began to investigate the

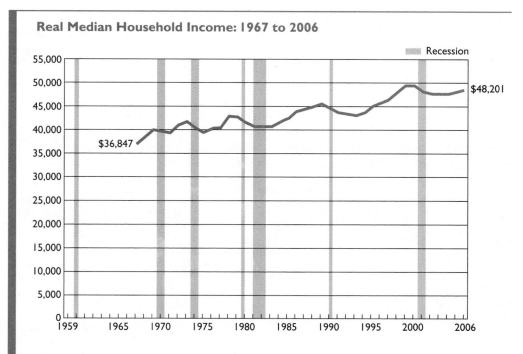

FIGURE 7.1

Note: The data points are placed at the midpoints of the respective years. Median household income data are not available before 1967.

Source: U.S. Census Bureau, *Current Population Survey, 1968 to 2007 Annual Social and Economic Supplements.*

suburbs with empirical studies, however, they found that they contained a wide variety of people with differing values and economic realities. In short, it is still difficult to define who, exactly, is "middle class," but we know that because this social class is so large and diverse, it is also very influential as a cultural symbol.

In the last decade, both in the United States and in other industrial nations, we have seen the emergence and coming to the fore of a professional middle class whose power derives from the members' high level of education, their reasonably high incomes, and their overlapping social and family ties to the high and middle levels of the business community. This class, sometimes termed the "New Class," is especially important because it tends to generate most of the ideas that eventually find their way into the cultural mainstream (Ehrenreich, 1989, 6). This professional middle class consists of journalists, academics, writers, media commentators—in other words, persons in possession of skills important in an information society.

The Working Class

The working class comprises approximately one-third of the population and may include members of the lower-middle class. It consists of people who work in skilled or semiskilled occupations, such as craftsmen, foremen, lower-level managers, nonretail sales representatives (representing around 30 percent of the population), or unskilled blue-collar occupations, such as retail sales, service workers, and low-paid manual workers (representing about 13 percent of the population). The incomes of such workers range between $25,000 and $35,000 a year (up to $50,000 in large cities) and generally fall below those of the middle classes. Some "pink collar" workers—secretaries, office workers, sales clerks, restaurant workers—who earn modest weekly wages can also be counted as members of the working class, although many of them prefer to think of themselves as middle class. Table 7.2 shows the distribution of incomes.

TABLE 7.2   Distribution of Income: Households by Total Money Income, Race, and Hispanic Origin of Householder, 2000 to 2006 (Income in 2006 adjusted dollars. Households as of March of the following year)

Race and Hispanic origin of householder and year	Number (thousands)	Total	Percent distribution								
			Under $5,000	$5,000 to $9,999	$10,000 to $14,999	$15,000 to $24,999	$25,000 to $34,999	$35,000 to $49,999	$50,000 to $74,999	$75,000 to $99,999	$100,000 and over
All Races											
2006	116,011	100.0	3.1	4.4	5.9	11.8	11.5	14.6	18.2	11.3	19.1
2005	114,384	100.0	3.2	4.7	6.3	12.1	11.1	14.8	18.3	11.4	18.2
2004	113,343	100.0	3.3	4.6	6.4	12.1	11.6	14.3	18.5	11.4	17.8
2003	112,000	100.0	3.2	4.8	6.4	12.0	11.3	14.7	17.8	11.8	18.1
2002	111,278	100.0	2.9	4.8	6.5	12.0	11.5	14.3	18.2	12.0	17.8
2001	109,297	100.0	2.8	4.6	6.3	11.7	11.5	14.7	18.3	12.1	18.1
2000	108,209	100.0	2.6	4.6	5.9	11.7	10.9	15.1	18.6	12.3	18.3

Source: U.S. Census Bureau, 2006. "Income, Poverty and Health Insurance in the United States: 2006."

The working class is undergoing dramatic changes in the United States as a result of globalization and the shift of manufacturing to countries where labor is cheaper. But even in more stable times, this social class has always been subject to layoffs and temporary employment, so that working people's financial situation has always been precarious. With a household income often derived from minimum wage jobs, two or more people must work. Despite a periodically booming economy, most young working-class families cannot afford to buy a house, even though their parents were able to buy one years ago in a modest neighborhood. In addition to economic problems, working-class people also tend to have jobs that are menial, repetitive, and unchallenging, so that they obtain little satisfaction in performing them. Most working-class children cannot afford college—although approximately one-third of this group do manage to obtain a college degree—and so are forced into jobs immediately after high school. Of course, lacking skills, the jobs that are available to them are few and low paying.

This social class is diverse in its ethnic and racial composition, but proximity has not resulted in solidarity. Rather, the various ethnic and racial groups see one another as competing for jobs, especially in transitional times when many manufacturing jobs are disappearing and heavy industry is using robots and computers instead of human brawn.

The Poor

The U.S. government defines *poverty* as the level of income at which a person is incapable of providing such basics as food, clothing, and shelter. The Census Bureau listed 12.3 percent of Americans, representing approximately 36.5 million people, as living below the poverty line in 2006 (Figure 7.2).

The measurement of poverty was instituted in 1964. It called for establishing a range of income levels according to factors such as family size, sex and age of the family head, number of children under 18, and urban or farm residence. Every year, revisions of price levels are based on changes in the consumer price index. Records show that the poverty rate varied between 11.1 percent and 14.2 percent from 1967 to 1981. It then peaked at 15.2 percent in 1983, declined to 12.8 percent in 1989, and rose each year after 1989 until the decline beginning in the mid-1990s. The recession that hit the United States in the first four years of the new century pushed the poverty rate upward again. Table 7.3 shows the numbers and percentages of people and families in poverty in 2006 according to various characteristics.

Poverty in this society is the condition of having less income than the average person; thus, we are not dealing with *absolute deprivation*, or not having enough income to provide the barest necessities for survival. We are dealing with *relative deprivation*, a condition in which people are deprived in comparison to others in their society at a particular time and place. From that point of view, some commentators have maintained that the poor in the United States have actually made progress in the last three decades, judging from their consumption spending and use of major modern household conveniences.

Poverty occurs more frequently among some groups than others. It is chronic, for instance, in families with a female householder in which no husband is present. This phenomenon is referred to as the *feminization of poverty*. As a result of the increase in illegitimate births and greater rates of dissolution of marital and nonmarital unions, single parenthood is no longer rare. Since the mid-1980s, the poverty growth rate for children under 6 years of age has been several percentage points higher than that of any other age group and much higher than the overall poverty rate. In 2004, for instance,

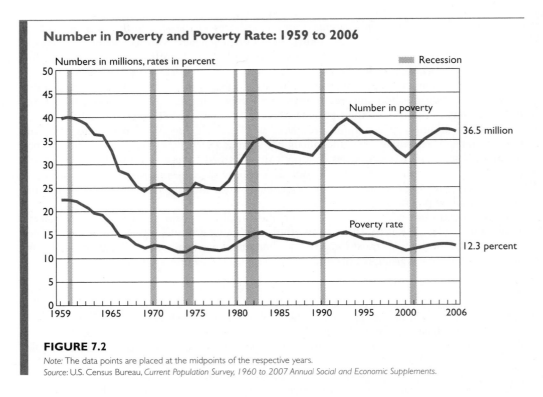

FIGURE 7.2

Note: The data points are placed at the midpoints of the respective years.
Source: U.S. Census Bureau, *Current Population Survey, 1960 to 2007 Annual Social and Economic Supplements.*

the poverty rate for related children under 6 was 19.9 percent. The number of children under 18 who lived in poverty was 12.3 million. This represents a poverty rate of 17.2 percent. A study by the National Center for Children in Poverty concluded that the United States has the highest rate of young-child poverty of any Western industrialized nation and that the economic boom of the late 1990s was not sufficient to overcome such poverty (Sengupta, 2001, WK3). This situation has been exacerbated by the growing income gap between the affluent and the poor in this country, as well as by the federal welfare law passed in 1996 requiring a proportion of those on public welfare rolls to find jobs. Of 18 industrialized nations studied, American poor children received the least help (Bradsher, 1995b, A7).

The elderly, people over 65, make up about 9.8 percent of those who live below the poverty level. As their numbers increase, however, fewer of them remain in poverty. The current percentage, for instance, is considerably lower than the 35.2 percent who lived in poverty in 1959. Finally, and contrary to the stereotype, not all the poor are concentrated in inner cities: only around 17 percent of them live in large central cities, while about 9 percent live outside central cities. In addition, approximately 15 percent live in nonmetropolitan, rural areas, where employment is difficult to obtain.

The Ghetto Poor

Sociologist William J. Wilson has written about the existence of the "truly disadvantaged," a class consisting of approximately 10 percent of those who are officially poor (some

TABLE 7.3 People and Families in Poverty by Selected Characteristics: 2006 (Numbers in thousands. People as of March of the following year)

Characteristic	Below poverty in 2006		Change in poverty (2006 less 2005)[1]	
	Number	Percentage	Number	Percentage
People				
Total	36,460	12.3	−490	*−0.3
Family Status				
In families	25,915	10.6	−153	−0.2
Householder	7,668	9.8	11	−0.1
Related children under 18	12,299	16.9	−37	−0.2
Related children under 6	4,830	20.0	46	−
In unrelated subfamilies	567	41.5	*111	4.1
Reference person	229	40.4	48	4.6
Children under 18	323	44.9	53	5.2
Unrelated individuals	9,977	20.0	*−448	*−1.1
Male	4,388	17.8	73	−0.1
Female	5,589	22.2	*−522	*−1.9
Race[2] and Hispanic Origin				
White	24,416	10.3	−456	*−0.3
White, not Hispanic	16,013	8.2	−214	−0.1
Black	9,048	24.3	−120	−0.7
Asian	1,353	10.3	−49	−0.9
Hispanic origin (any race)	9,243	20.6	−126	*−1.1
Age				
Under 18 years	12,827	17.4	−69	−0.2
18 to 64 years	20,239	10.8	−211	−0.3
65 years and older	3,394	9.4	*−210	*−0.7
Nativity				
Native	30,790	11.9	−290	−0.2
Foreign born	5,670	15.2	−200	*−1.3
Naturalized citizen	1,345	9.3	−96	−1.1
Not a citizen	4,324	19.0	−105	−1.3
Region				
Northeast	6,222	11.5	119	0.2
Midwest	7,324	11.2	−95	−0.2
South	14,882	13.8	28	−0.2
West	8,032	11.6	*−541	*−1.0
Metropolitan Status				
Inside metropolitan statistical areas	29,283	11.8	*−815	*−0.5
Inside principal cities	15,336	16.1	*−630	*−0.9
Outside principal cities	13,947	9.1	−185	−0.2
Outside metropolitan statistical areas[3]	7,177	15.2	325	0.6
Work Experience				
All workers (16 years and older)	9,181	5.8	−159	−0.2
Worked full-time, year-round	2,906	2.7	12	−0.1
Not full-time, year-round	6,275	12.6	−170	−0.2
Did not work at least 1 week	15,715	21.1	−327	−0.6

(Continued)

TABLE 7.3 (*Continued*)

Characteristic	Below poverty in 2006		Change in poverty (2006 less 2005)[1]	
	Number	Percentage	Number	Percentage
Families				
Total	7,668	9.8	11	−0.1
Type of Family				
Married-couple	2,910	4.9	−34	−0.1
Female householder, no husband present	4,087	28.3	43	−0.4
Male householder, no wife present	671	13.2	2	0.2

Source: U.S. Census Bureau, *Current Population Survey, 2006 and 2007 Annual Social and Economic Supplements.* "Income, Poverty, and Health Insurance Coverage in the United States: 2006."

– Represents or rounds to zero.

* Statistically different from zero at the 90-percent confidence level.

1 Details may not sum to totals because of rounding.

2 Federal surveys now give respondents the option of reporting more than one race. Therefore, two basic ways of defining a race group are possible. A group such as Asian may be defined as those who reported Asian and no other race (the race-alone or single-race concept) or as those who reported Asian regardless of whether they also reported another race (the race-alone-or-in-combination concept). This table shows data using the first approach (race alone). The use of the single-race population does not imply that it is the preferred method of presenting or analyzing data. The Census Bureau uses a variety of approaches. Information on people who reported more than one race, such as White **and** American Indian and Alaska Native or Asian **and** Black or African American, is available from Census 2000 through American FactFinder. About 2.6 percent of people reported more than one race in Census 2000. Data for American Indians and Alaska Natives, Native Hawaiians and Other Pacific Islanders, and those reporting two or more races are not shown separately.

3 The "Outside metropolitan statistical areas" category includes both micropolitan statistical areas and territory outside of metropolitan and micropolitan statistical areas. For more information, see "About Metropolitan and Micropolitan Statistical Areas" at **http://www.census.gov/www/estimates/aboutmetro.html**.

commentators have called this segment of the population an *underclass*, but this term has negative connotations). This social class lives a subsistence lifestyle with government help. Its members have severe health problems or are seriously lacking in any salable skills. Unemployment and single-parent homes are the two major problems faced by this group. Unemployment has resulted from the exodus of unskilled and semiskilled jobs from the central cities to the suburbs and partly from the disappearance of such jobs altogether in favor of jobs that require more education and technological know-how (the restructuring of the economy and of American capitalism). This structural change has given rise to a persistent and in some cases permanent type of poverty, from which individuals, cut off from the rest of society, are seldom able to escape.

The Homeless

Another segment of the poor that has become much more visible than in the past consists of the homeless. The phenomenon began in the 1970s, continued through a recessionary period

In the past decade, class distinctions in the United States have become very evident, as the growing number of moguls—entrepreneurs in technology and financial areas—have left the rest of the population in the dust, so to speak. Here, simply a symbol of affluence versus life on the streets.

in the early 1980s, and, contrary to those who considered it a temporary problem, goes on today. Homelessness is a deeply disturbing situation to most Americans because it raises a variety of questions, among them: What is an individual's responsibility to his or her fellow human being, and what has gone wrong with American economic and social institutions to allow this condition to exist?

It is difficult to estimate the number of homeless in the United States, because, of course, they live on the streets or in train stations or in shelters whose inhabitants change daily. Sociologist Christopher Jencks has estimated the homeless population to be around 400,000, quite an increase from about 125,000 in 1980 (1994).

A more recent approximation of their number comes from a study of the National Law Center on Homelessness and Poverty. According to this study, approximately 3.5 million people, of whom 1.35 million are children, experience homelessness each year (National Law Center on Homelessness and Poverty, 2004).

The characteristics of this group have also changed in recent years: where once there were elderly alcoholics or disturbed or eccentric "bag ladies," today there are many young mothers with children; where once there were wage earners out on their luck, today there are dropouts with few skills, no experience, and few prospects for the future. The problems these new homeless exhibit are of such a nature that they initiate a never-ending cycle: they include mental instability, drug and alcohol use, unemployment, lack of education and job skills, alienation from family and friends, behavior problems, personal neglect, and disregard for personal responsibility. Many had depended on public assistance and are homeless as a result of the erosion of federal subsidies; others became homeless when state mental hospitals began discharging inmates in the 1970s following a movement whose adherents argued that the mentally ill should not be locked up unless they broke specific

Box 7.2   The Growth of Inequality

In the decade of the 1980s, that is, during the tenure of the two Reagan administrations, enormous wealth became concentrated in the hands of the top 1 percent of Americans. Wealth shifted toward those already wealthy, reversing a liberal democratic style that had predominated from 1932 to 1968. Moreover, the extent of wealth reached unheard of proportions. Toward the end of the Reagan years, there were almost one hundred thousand persons worth over $10 million, whereas in 1960 there had not been that large a number of single-digit millionaires (Phillips 1990, 4).

This situation has persisted into the twenty-first century. In 1989 the United States had 66 *billionaires*; by 2006 their number had risen to 442. The 400 richest Americans are worth one and a quarter trillion dollars, which represents one-ninth of the total Gross Domestic Product (GDP) of the United States, the world's richest economy. Moreover, the gap between the small minority of the wealthy and the huge majority of others has grown so large that it worries many social commentators. For instance, the top 1 percent of households in 2001 owned 33.4 percent of all privately held wealth. The next 19 percent held 51 percent. This meant that the top 20 percent of Americans held 84 percent of the country's wealth. The bottom 80 percent, then, were left only 16 percent of the wealth (see Figure 7.3). (An excellent description of the distribution of wealth in the United States, with many graphs and tables, may be seen at http://www.sociology/ucsc/edu/whorulesamerica/power/wealth.html, a web site of G. William Domhoff, professor of sociology.)

As a result, a new class of wealthy people has come into being with inordinate amounts of money and the power that goes with it. At the same time, the social classes at the bottom of the stratification heap have either lost income or are swimming in place. Such gaps bespeak of increasing inequality among social classes, an inequality that has dramatic ramifications in the quality of life of people and which, therefore, presents issues of ethics and justice.

This reallocation of income has been accompanied by dramatic technological innovations that are affecting the entire spectrum of the society and that cannot easily be controlled or regulated by governmental policies. The most important innovation is the transition of the economy from a predominantly industrial system in which a multitude of products are manufactured, to a predominantly informational system in which services are rendered, research is carried on, and information is passed on to consumers. The new economic system requires totally different skills, which a large majority of Americans have not yet acquired. As a result, those whom the former industrial system favored with well-paying jobs have lost much ground. However, only about one-third of the increase in income inequality is the result of the faster-growing wages and salaries of the upper classes, according to the Brookings Institution. Additional reasons for the increasing gaps between rich and poor include: the well-off marry each other, increasing their household income; there are more divorces in the lower classes, which lowers household incomes; and there is more immigration, which increases the number of low-income households (Samuelson, 2001, 45).

Still, that it is now possible to become wealthy by earning salaries, rather than depending on accumulated or inherited wealth, is also a point leading to increased inequality. Twenty-five years ago it was impossible to become very affluent by working. Today, executives of corporations earn fabulous salaries and receive tremendous bonuses, in addition to being able to exercise stock options. Even some rank-and-file workers in technology companies have earned enough to enable them to join the affluent. By abolishing taxes on many stock dividends and capital gains, in addition to other benefits for the affluent such as eliminating the estate tax, the gap becomes larger still.

One would expect that the increasing inequality among social classes would lead to political instability and protest movements. This has not occurred, and according to one economics commentator, it will not occur because Americans care less about inequality than about opportunity. Obviously, there has been opportunity in the society, as the many newly minted multimillionaires can attest. To support this claim, the author reports on a study by Harvard University and the London School of Economics that measured personal happiness from the mid-1970s to the mid-1990s, a period of rising inequality in both the United States and Europe. The study revealed that Americans considered themselves "pretty happy" to "very happy" in much higher proportions than Europeans (economic inequality is higher in European countries to begin with, and increased even more in that period, but European governments have tried much harder to reduce it). The researchers concluded that the United States is a more mobile society than the Societies of Europe and there are more opportunities to move up or down the stratification ladder. Therefore, "Americans don't get so upset by rising inequality because they don't feel it dooms them," while Europeans are much more fatalistic about their place on the economic ladder (Samuelson, 2001, 45).

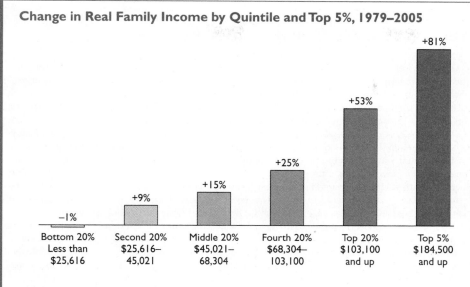

Change in Real Family Income by Quintile and Top 5%, 1979–2005

Bottom 20% Less than $25,616	Second 20% $25,616– 45,021	Middle 20% $45,021– 68,304	Fourth 20% $68,304– 103,100	Top 20% $103,100 and up	Top 5% $184,500 and up
−1%	+9%	+15%	+25%	+53%	+81%

FIGURE 7.3

Source: U.S. Census Bureau, *Historical Income Tables*, Table F-3, 2006

laws. Unemployment, decreasing demand for unskilled and day labor, the increase of women with children and no husband, and alcohol and drug abuse are additional factors leading toward homelessness.

A 2005 report on homelessness in America's cities found that requests for emergency shelter for individuals increased by 9 percent from the year before. Requests by homeless families also increased by 5 percent, but 29 percent of such requests by families and 23 percent by individuals had gone unmet. In 86 percent of cities, emergency shelters have had to turn away homeless families because of lack of resources. In 55 percent of cities, families are forced to break up in order to be sheltered. In addition, requests for emergency food assistance also increased by approximately 7 percent, of which 26 percent have gone unmet. Finally, in the cities studied, the average length of homelessness was eight months (U.S. Conference of Mayors, 2006).

The report cited a lack of affordable housing as the chief cause of homelessness. Additional causes include low-paying jobs, substance abuse and the lack of needed services, mental illness, domestic violence, poverty, and changes and cuts in public assistance. About 23 percent of homeless people in the cities are considered mentally ill, 30 percent are substance abusers, 17 percent are employed, and 10 percent are veterans.

The composition of the homeless, according to the report is as follows: single men make up 51 percent of the homeless population, families with children 30 percent, single women 17 percent, and unaccompanied minors 2 percent. The racial and ethnic composition is estimated at 42 percent African American, 39 percent white, 13 percent Hispanic, 4 percent Native American, and 2 percent Asian (U.S. Conference of Mayors, 2006).

Box 7.3 Welfare: Are We Our Brothers' Keepers?

Beginning with the Great Depression, the idea emerged that in a civilized society, the government had a responsibility to alleviate the misery in which a segment of the population lived. Social Security and a host of other programs were the result of this idea, and every president following Franklin D. Roosevelt wanted to add some ammunition to the "war on poverty" (President Lyndon Johnson's battle cry). Unfortunately, as is often the case, in trying to solve one problem, myriad new ones are created. With respect to entitlement programs, it has become apparent that generation after generation has remained in the same condition: living at or near the poverty level at the government's expense. A whole host of social problems has accompanied such a condition, from drug addiction to crime, from unemployment to lack of education, from fatherless homes to abused children. Perhaps the most acute problem is the fact that the work ethic and work habits came to be generally lacking in a portion of this population, forcing them deeper into this dead-end lifestyle.

While welfare reform had been a subject often debated and abandoned in Congress, it was not until 1996 that a bill was passed that was meant to end welfare as we know it forever. The bill was designed to convert welfare from an entitlement given to individuals, to a grant given by the federal government to the states, which would then distribute the fund as they saw fit. As the welfare rolls were high at that point, the grants were also high. The law also stipulated that cash payments to poor families be limited to five years, and that 25 percent of a state's welfare recipients be working or enrolled in training programs within the following year and 50 percent by the year 2002.

How has welfare reform worked out? The welfare rolls have decreased dramatically (by 2006, the number of people on federal welfare rolls had dropped more than 57

percent) but at a high cost to individuals. First, because now the states determine how federal money is distributed, it depends on where the poor live as to how much they receive, including what training, child care facilities, and other services are available to them. During the economic boom of the 1990s, and in a period of full employment, some states invested their swollen budgets on helpful programs but others did not. With the economy less buoyant much of the bounty on the part of the states has lessened. But more to the point, not all welfare recipients have been leaving welfare at the same rate. Surveys show that whites have been going off welfare at much greater rates than African Americans and Hispanics The reasons for the disparity are multiple: partly, they may be due to discrimination on the part of potential employers or landlords. Mostly, however, it seems that minority welfare recipients have less education, lower incomes, and more children. More of them have never married, ensuring lower rates of child support, and live in poor, central city neighborhoods far from the suburbs where many jobs are located. In addition to the difficulties encountered by lack of transportation and child care (especially in the case of welfare mothers) or of any saleable skills, many recent immigrants also do not speak English. Finally, as a number of studies have shown, having spent a lifetime not working and without a model of a life centered on work, many welfare recipients have a very difficult time keeping jobs, even when they get them. They lack the discipline of punctuality, they do not know how to present themselves to employers in terms of dress and speech, and they are often frustrated by the boredom and repetitiveness of low-skill jobs. Hence, to answer the question of how the reform bill is working, the way out of welfare appears to be a long and tortuous road (U.S. Department of Health and Human Services, ACF; last updated June 28, 2006).

■ Social Class and Its Consequences

The concept of life chances, particularly the fact that they differ according to social class, was noted in the earlier discussion of Weber's views on social class. Not only do life chances differ, however; there are marked differences in lifestyles, encompassing such characteristics as family life, child rearing, education, personal values, consumption, leisure activities, political outlook, religion, and health. The bottom line is, of course, that the consequences of different positions in the stratification system make for a great deal of inequality. These differences in lifestyle are described below in very general terms; they are not to be understood as fitting every individual in the social class described.

Family Life

Because people tend to marry partners of their own social class, clear patterns eventually emerge. From the point of view of marriage stability, there are fewer divorces among the upper classes. The higher divorce rate among the lower classes may be caused by the frustration and anxiety that economic problems and unemployment create. At the same time, upper-class people are preoccupied with maintaining a strong family, because that is the chief medium of transmission of property. In lower-class families, marriages are much more patriarchal with respect to sex roles. Women tend to interact to a greater extent with female relatives and men with male friends than in the higher social classes. The lower classes, finally, have a high percentage of female-headed families.

Child Rearing

Middle- and upper-class child-rearing practices stress independence of action and behavior, according to principles of right and wrong. Parents in these social classes tend to use temporary withdrawal of love rather than physical punishment for social control. As a result, although children in the middle and upper classes may be prone to guilt feelings, they tend to become more independent, self-directed, and achievement-oriented than individuals in the lower social classes. Parents in the latter tend to emphasize obedience to rules and staying out of trouble and tend to punish infringements more harshly. Each social class is preparing its offspring to follow in its occupational footsteps.

Education

The different socialization experiences lead middle- and upper-class children to be more successful academically, a fact reinforced by values that stress such achievement. This academic advantage tends to further upward social mobility, whereas children in the lower classes, lacking models and valuing higher education less, are hampered in upward mobility. In terms of income alone, the differences between those with only eight years of education and those with five or more years of college are striking.

Religion

The upper and upper-middle classes tend to be overwhelmingly Protestant, and there is a close correspondence between the various Protestant denominations and social class. The higher social classes identify more closely with denominations that offer subdued rituals, such as the Episcopalians, Congregationalists, Presbyterians, and Methodists. The lower social classes appear to be more comfortable with denominations that offer colorful rites, such as those found in the Baptist church and in fundamentalist and revivalist sects.

Politics

Although there are regional and, of course, individual differences, in general terms it appears that being a registered voter, voting regularly in elections, and taking an interest in civil and political affairs are activities engaged in more frequently the higher one's social class. Party affiliation is similarly correlated: the more privileged people tend to support the Republican Party, in part because the latter has symbolized a free-market, unregulated economy in which it is easier for the wealthy to protect their income. The less advantaged, on the other hand, particularly if they are also urban dwellers, favor the Democratic Party, which has historically fought for the rights of the working class. According to The Pew Research Center for the People and the Press, 38 percent of people in the upper quintile vote for Republicans and only 27 percent vote for Democrats. Conversely, 42 percent of the lower-income quintile votes Democratic, while only 20 percent votes Republican (August 2, 2005). The affluent are more liberal on social issues such as abortion, gay and lesbian rights, feminist issues, affirmative action, and so on. Those of lower social standing tend to be liberal on economic issues that favor them, such as job security, guarantees of full employment, and so on, but conservative on other social issues.

Health

Because health care is neither free nor cheap in the United States, as it is in many other industrial societies, it follows that those with a higher income can purchase more health and medical care than those with a lower income. Studies have shown that the incidence of disease among the higher social classes is smaller than among the lower classes for that reason. A substantial segment of the population is not covered by any form of health insurance because of the expense involved; yet, it is only such insurance that allows middle-income people to obtain adequate care. According to the Census Bureau, 47 million Americans were uninsured in 2006, which represents an all-time high (see Figure 7.4). Disease, neglect, accidents, and violence are causes of death for poor children in their first year of life to a much greater extent than for children in higher social classes. Finally, even life expectancy is higher at the higher social levels.

Research in the area of public health, moreover, indicates that status, in and of itself, determines to a great extent how healthy a person is. In other words, it is not just wealth, good nutrition, higher education, quality of medical care, and good genes that make a person healthier than others who lack those attributes, but simply the status of being in a high social class. "Your position in the hierarchy very much relates to how much control you have over your life and your opportunities for full social engagements" (Cohen, 2004, A17).

Both the incidence and treatment of mental illness are much higher for lower-class persons than for the upper classes. In particular, lower-class patients are much more likely to be treated with tranquilizing drugs and to be hospitalized in state institutions for longer periods. Upper-class patients tend to be treated by private therapists with various types of psychotherapy and spend only brief periods in private mental clinics. Some studies also indicate a high degree of mental impairment among persons in the poorest social classes.

Arrest and Conviction

The rates of arrest and conviction are higher for lower-class individuals, many of them minorities, than for members of the upper and middle classes. The harsher treatment by the criminal justice system is partially due to the types of crimes committed by lower-class persons—robbery, burglary, larceny, and auto theft—as opposed to those committed by

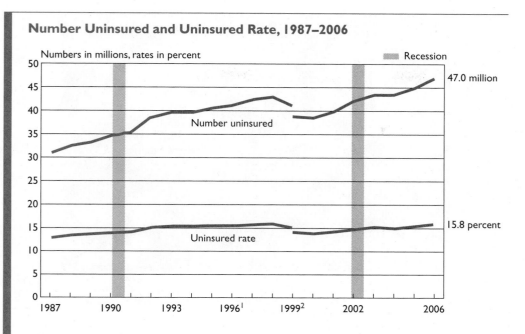

Number Uninsured and Uninsured Rate, 1987–2006

FIGURE 7.4

[1]The series starting in 1996 reflects an approximation of the impact of an editing error that was corrected in the 2005 ASEC (estimates of 2004 coverage).

[2]Implementation of Census 2000-based population controls occurred for the 2000 ASEC, which collected data for 1999. These estimates also reflect the results of follow-up verification questions that were asked of people who responded "no" to all questions about specific types of health insurance coverage in order to verify whether they were actually uninsured. This change increased the number and percentage of people covered by health insurance, bringing the CPS more in line with estimates from other national surveys.

Notes: Respondents were not asked detailed health insurance questions before the 1988 CPS.

The data points are placed at the midpoints of the respective years.

Source: U.S. Census Bureau, *Current Population Survey, 1988 to 2007 Annual Social and Economic Supplements.*

middle- and upper-class persons—forgery, tax evasion, fraud, and embezzlement. The latter crimes are not considered to be as "wrong" as the former because violence is seldom involved. Finally, persons of a higher social class can generally afford a better legal defense. The so-called "dream team" put together to defend O. J. Simpson could not possibly be afforded by anyone who was not super rich: it is estimated that the defendant in this case spent approximately $6 million by the end of the trial. Most (80 to 90 percent) of all felony defendants in the United States are too poor to hire their own lawyers and are represented by court-appointed attorneys (Gleick, 1995, 42). Such attorneys are remunerated on sliding scales depending on local jurisdictions. Payment can vary from $1,000 to defend a death-penalty case to $53,000. Obviously, the sort of defense a defendant obtains varies from location to location. In justice as in everything else, one tends to get what one pays for. Finally, the victims of crime tend also to be overwhelmingly poor or members of minority groups.

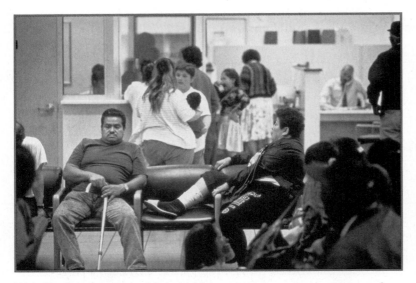

With 47 million Americans without health insurance, emergency departments of most hospitals are crowded and chaotic as they must deal with people who have nowhere else to go in a medical emergency.

Values

Research has shown that, in general, middle- and upper-class people have feelings of control over their lives, whereas persons in the lower class tend to be fatalistic, believing that luck and forces beyond their control govern their lives. The higher social classes engage in long-range planning and postpone present pleasures for future goals (deferred gratification) to a greater extent than do people from the lower social classes, probably because the latter have a much less bright future to look forward to. The higher social classes also display a more liberal attitude toward sexual behavior and religious beliefs than the lower classes. The working class, in particular, is intolerant of nonconformist behavior. The values and attitudes of the higher social classes tend to set the standard for the society.

■ Social Mobility

One of the principal differences between open and closed societies is that there is social mobility in open societies and none or very little in closed societies. The term *social mobility* refers to an individual's ability to change social class membership, status, life chances, and lifestyles by moving up (or down) the ladder represented by the stratification system of a society.

Social scientists also distinguish between *vertical mobility*, which occurs in an upward or downward direction, and *horizontal mobility*, which occurs when there is a change of status without a consequent change of class. For instance, vertical mobility may be exemplified by a high school teacher who is promoted to principal (upward mobility), or the principal who proves ineffective as an administrator and is demoted back into the classroom (downward mobility). A school superintendent who takes a job as an executive of an insurance company at approximately the same salary is horizontally mobile. Usually, a certain amount of horizontal mobility is necessary to maximize chances for vertical mobility.

The Upwardly Mobile: Who Are They?

Various factors are responsible for vertical mobility, some dependent on personality traits, others on social circumstances. From studies on upward mobility, a profile of the upwardly mobile individual has emerged. Such an individual is (1) an urban resident; (2) an only child or one of two children; (3) influenced by ambitious parents, particularly a mother; (4) likely to acquire more education than his or her parents; (5) one who marries later and tends to marry a partner of higher status; and (6) one who waits to establish a family and limits its size to no more than two children.

Individuals who are upwardly mobile in comparison to their parents, or to the preceding generation, are displaying *intergenerational mobility*. If they also do better than their peers of the same generation, they are exhibiting *intragenerational mobility*.

Social Mobility in the United States

The United States has long been known as the land of opportunity, and there is a persistent myth that any individual, no matter what his or her origin, can rise to become a leader of the country, or at least someone in possession of wealth and prestige. At the very least, people expect to get well-paying jobs, own their own homes, and be able to send their children to college. This is, in fact, what is meant by the "American Dream" and by such phrases as "from rags to riches" and "a Horatio Alger story." The notion that hard work, thrift, ambition, and willpower are sufficient to ensure a person's rise in the stratification system has been part of the American ethic from the very inception of the nation.

How much truth is there in this notion? How does mobility in the United States compare with mobility in other industrial nations? After gathering opinion-poll studies from a number of industrial nations, researchers found a great amount of social mobility in all the industrialized democracies, refuting the idea that the United States is unique in the openness of its stratification system (Lipset & Bendix, 1959; Grusky & Hauser, 1984, 35; Kerckhoff et al., 1985). All of the researchers concluded, first, that much of the mobility occurred because in technological societies a great value is put on efficiency. The inefficient offspring of even upper-class parents are replaced by more talented persons from lower social classes. Second, mobility is caused by industrialization itself, which has resulted in the creation of more high-status occupations to replace the largely blue-collar, lower-status occupations of a more agrarian system. This type of mobility is called *structural mobility*. Lipset and Bendix found that, although the United States did not have an unusual amount of mobility, it did display more of the kind of mobility in which people may rise, but also fall, through individual merit.

Studies measuring long-distance mobility, that is, the rise of individuals from the very bottom to the very top of the stratification system in one generation, found that Americans do have a high rate of this kind of mobility. In the 1960s, a well-known study showed that a large percentage (37 percent) of the men in white-collar jobs had fathers with a blue-collar job, but an individual's own level of education was more responsible for upward social mobility than was the father's occupation. At the time, the researchers concluded that an individual's chances of occupational upward mobility were greatly influenced by the amount of education, the nature of the person's first job, and the occupation of the father. Structural mobility, however, was the factor most responsible for upward mobility (Blau & Duncan, 1967, 152–161). A later study substantiated that among the American business elite, only 1 in 10 of the top executives came from a wealthy home, and more than one-third had made it from humble origins (Lipset, 1976).

A particularly telling finding regarding mobility and the subject of inequality in general was that there is almost as much economic inequality among brothers raised in the same homes as among the population in general (Jencks et al., 1972). Inequality seems to be newly created within each generation, even among people who begin life in similar circumstances.

On the whole, it may be said that there is more upward mobility than downward mobility in the United States, though it occurs in the middle segments of the population rather than from bottom to top (Hauser & Featherman, 1977). In spite of the changes in the occupational structure of the society, the total amount of social mobility has hardly been altered in the past decades. However, the global restructuring taking place currently may ultimately lead to different conclusions. Even though there are still possibilities of great jumps up the economic ladder, most Americans do not move a great many rungs either up or down in their lifetimes.

In trying to increase social equality, the government can intervene by passing anti-discrimination laws, affirmative-action legislation, training programs, and other government programs. Over and above the impact of life chances, however, individual factors also play a part in a person's mobility: ability, work habits, deferring gratification, and, finally, sheer luck.

The trend toward widening income inequality and the fact that social mobility has been stagnant and uneven since the 1970s are indications, to some social commentators, that the country is becoming increasingly stratified. Research that compared the personal finances of 5,000 households (based on a survey conducted every year since the late 1960s) has indicated that the poor are more likely to remain poor and the affluent to remain affluent (Bradsher, 1995a, 4). For instance, while the top 1 percent of households had seen an increase of 17 percent in the year between 2003 and 2004, for the remaining 99 percent, the average gain was less than 3 percent. Moreover, the gain affected principally the top 20 percent of households. Again, in 2004, the top 1 percent of households received 36 percent of all income, on top of the 30 percent they had gained the year before (Glaeser, 2005; Hertz, 2006; Piketty & Saez, 2006). Most disturbing, however, is that the lowest quintile has seen its meager earnings decrease. The chances of this segment attaining a middle-class income are declining. In short, although mobility, and especially upward mobility, is still a very real possibility for some in our society, a number of trends cast a shadow over the continuing existence of the American dream. First, although the median income of U.S. families has consistently risen between 1950 and 2002, for some workers earnings have stagnated, while the cost of housing, education, and medical care has gone up. As a result, a proportion of workers must work at two or more jobs. Seasonal unemployment and low-paying jobs result in a substantial number of earners bringing home less than a living wage. This means that many young people wait to marry and continue to live with their parents even after college. This downward structural mobility engenders pessimism in many that they may be sliding down from the middle class: the American dream turned upside down.

Global Inequality

The existence of inequality as a constant feature of human societies was once accepted as a given. While the world has gradually embraced an ideology that finds gross inequities unfair, it has not found a means of eliminating them. On the contrary, it would appear that inequality persists not only within societies but also especially among societies. On a global basis, for instance, the so-called Third World, which houses 80 percent of the world's 6.6 billion people and accounts for 60 percent of the planet's land area, faces poverty that is far more severe and more extensive than people in the First World can imagine. (The First World consists of industrial nations with predominantly capitalist economies; the Second World consists of industrial societies that are undergoing transformations from generally socialist economies; and the Third World consists of societies that are primarily agrarian.) In the

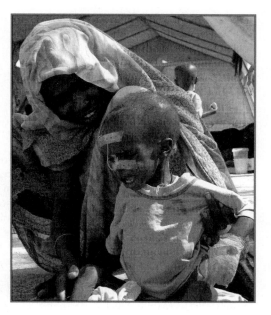

Global inequality has been made more visible by the constant conflicts in several African nations. Here, a refugee Sudanese mother comforts her malnourished child.

Third World, the majority of the people are poor, meaning that hunger, unsafe housing, and disease are everyday experiences for most. The definition of hunger refers to caloric intake below that necessary to prevent serious health risks and stunted growth in children. Around the world, deficient and inadequate diets, as well as unsafe water supplies, are the destiny of hundreds of millions of people. In sharp contrast, consumption of goods and services in industrial and developing nations is soaring.

The issue of global inequality will be dealt with in the context of international relations (Chapter 19); however, a few examples of inequality are helpful here. In 2001, private consumption in the United States was $24,436 per capita (meaning per person). In Canada, another industrial country, it was $16,727. In Azerbaijan, on the other hand, a developing country, private consumption expenditure per capita was $1,825, and in Ukraine it was $2,368. In 2000, 81.9 percent of the population of Ethiopia consumed less than $1 per day, as did 49.1 percent in Madagascar and 36 percent in Bangladesh, all Third-World countries. In the poor nations, the average household consumes 20 percent less than it did 25 years ago. The reason for this, in part, is that in many poor countries of South Asia and Africa populations are growing fast and living longer. Large families, in addition, deplete natural resources and household purchasing power. Richer nations are reducing population growth and have smaller families, so they can increase consumption. Here are some examples:

- Americans spend more on cosmetics (about $8 billion per year) than it is estimated it would cost to provide basic education ($6 billion) or water and sanitation ($9 billion) to the more than 2 billion people who are without them.
- Americans throw away 7 million cars a year and 2 million plastic bottles every hour.
- Total private consumption in high-income countries amounts to 81.5 percent, while in low-income countries it is 3.6 percent.

- The richest fifth of people consume 45 percent of all meat and fish, while the poorest fifth consume 5 percent.
- The richest fifth have nearly 74 percent more telephone lines; the poorest fifth have 1.5 percent
- The richest countries own 87 percent of the world's vehicles; the poorest own less than 1 percent
- The richest countries use 58 percent of total energy; the poorest countries use less than 4 percent.

Of course, asking the rich to consume less would not lead to the poor having more. Globally, some poor countries misuse public resources, spend disproportionately on military goods, or allow the wealthy to avoid paying taxes. Because 8 billion of the world's projected 9.5 billion people will be living in poor countries by 2050, it is imperative that a different pattern of consumption be found. The Human Development Report 2003, which compiled some of the aforementioned figures, suggests that poor countries adopt modern, efficient technologies, thus leapfrogging some of the mistakes that industrial nations have made. Ranking nations according to the life they provide for their people, the organization listed Canada, France, Norway, the United States, Iceland, Finland, the Netherlands, Japan, New Zealand, and Sweden as the top 10 of the 174 nations surveyed. The bottom 10 nations included Sierra Leone, Niger, Burkina Faso, Mali, Burundi, Ethiopia, Eritrea, Guinea, Mozambique, and Gambia. The report concluded that the world is facing an acute development

Box 7.4 World Hunger

The United States and most other industrial nations face an epidemic of obesity. People spend millions of dollars on diet books, diet foods, liposuction, tummy tucks, trying to avoid carbs or fat. The situation in developing or Third World countries is starkly and dramatically different. In those countries, just getting enough calories to live another day is a constant struggle.

In Malawi, for instance, children stand on the side of the road selling skewers of roasted mice. In Mozambique, people eat grasshoppers before the grasshoppers can eat their crops. In Liberia, during their civil war, every animal in the national zoo was eaten, with the exception of a one-eyed lion. No cats or dogs could be seen anywhere in the streets of the capital. But at least these foods provide some protein.

In the 1990s in Angola, World Food Program workers described how people would take old wood and leather furniture, boil the leather for many hours to soften it and remove the tanning toxins, and then boil it to make soup. Apparently, furniture or leather were eaten in many previous famines as well.

Another "coping mechanism" for hunger is strapping flat stones to one's stomach to avoid strong hunger pangs. In Somalia, people "eat" camel skin. In many African countries, people dig up anthills and termite mounds to recover the small grains that the insects have gathered. In Bangladesh, people who are hungry enough will eat a type of lentil that is known to destroy the nervous system. In Chad and West Africa, people eat plants that are known to be poisonous but are made edible by long pounding and soaking. Plants such as seaweed, tree bark, and grass, all of which have little nutritional value, are eaten in North Korea. The skins and bones of dead animals that even vultures won't touch anymore are boiled for "soup."

The final staple of the very poor around the world, and as close to the United States as Haiti, is dirt. In Zambia, street markets sell balls of edible clay. In Angola, "black salt" is sprinkled on cold food to make it more palatable. And in Haiti, biscuits called "argile," or clay, are a common snack to appease desperate hunger: they are made with clay and margarine or butter and are flavored with salt, pepper, and bouillon cubes. You can buy them for a penny apiece (McNeill, 2004, Section 4, 1, 12).

crisis, with many poor nations suffering severe and continuing socioeconomic reversals (Human Development Report, 2006. **http://www.undp.org/hdr2006;** see also **http://www.globalissues. org/traderelated/consumption.asp.**)

The Chapter in Brief

Stratification is a phenomenon present in all societies that have produced a surplus. It is the process by which members of a society rank themselves and one another in hierarchies (from low to high) with respect to the amount of desirable goods they possess and the prestige and power they enjoy.

All systems of ranking are based on differences among people. Differences based on age and sex are present in all human groups, but in more complex societies, people are differentiated as a category and ranked on the basis not only of biological but also of social characteristics.

Ranking has led to the existence of inequality. Inequality has been explained by a number of theories: functionalists maintain that inequality works to the advantage of societies because rewarding the performance of some tasks higher than others ensures that difficult tasks get done. Conflict theorists assert that inequality is the result of conflict among groups in society that struggle for power. The victors in the struggle impose their values on the rest of society. In a synthesis of the two theories, Lenski states that while inequality is inevitable, it tends to lessen as a society becomes more productive. However, government intervention is needed to break the advantage of some groups over others.

All stratification systems exhibit differentiation, ranking, and institutionalization. The most important dimensions of stratification systems are class, status, and power. A social class is an aggregation of persons in a society who stand in a similar position with respect to power, privilege, or prestige. Status is a ranked position of an individual in relation to other individuals in the social system. Power is the ability of one person or group to control the actions of other persons or groups, with or without the consent of the latter.

Stratification systems may be measured on an ideal continuum. On one end, the closed, or caste, system displays social inequalities that are institutionalized and rigid. In the middle, the estate system is less rigid, allowing some mobility. At the other end, the open system, typical of modern industrial societies, consists of a number of social classes and allows social mobility, although not to the same extent for all. Mobility is restricted by life chances—the opportunity to become a complete human being and reap the satisfactions of society—which differ according to social class.

Upward mobility in industrial societies is aided by urban residence, by coming from a small family, by having ambitious parents, by higher education, by late marriage, preferably to a mate from a higher social class, and by having no more than two children. Much of the mobility in the United States is structural mobility; that is, it is caused by industrial and technological change that upgrades jobs. Otherwise, there is more horizontal (across the job continuum) than vertical (up or down the job continuum) mobility, although talent, education, work habits, and luck sometimes lead to spectacular upward mobility.

Poverty is a tragic side effect of inequality. In the affluent societies, poverty is understood in terms of relative deprivation, of having less than one's peers. Women, children, minorities, and elderly tend to be poor in greater proportions than other segments of the population. In recent years, the gap between the rich and the poor has widened in the United States, causing fears that stratification may become more rigid.

Globally, too, the inequality between the First World and the Third World nations, where most people go hungry and live on about $1 a day, is becoming difficult to ignore. As these societies are also populous and politically unstable they may present a danger to the more affluent.

Terms to Remember

authority Social power exercised with the consent of others. Parents, teachers, and the government represent different levels of authority.

closed, or caste, stratification system A system in which class, status, and power are ascribed, mobility is highly restricted, and the social system is rigid.

conflict theory of stratification A theory of stratification according to which the natural conditions of society are constant change and conflict resulting from class struggles. Inequality is the product of such conflict, as one group is victorious over others and asserts itself over the rest of society.

estate system of stratification The prevailing system of feudal Europe, consisting of three estates of functional importance to the society. The estates were hierarchically arranged and permitted a limited amount of social mobility.

functionalist theory of stratification A theory in which social inequality is viewed as inevitable because society must use rewards to ensure that essential tasks are performed. The natural conditions of society are thought to be order and stability (equilibrium).

life chances The opportunity of each individual to fulfill his or her potential as a human being. Life chances differ according to social class.

open, or class, society A society in which the stratification system allows for social mobility and in which a person's status is achieved rather than being ascribed on the basis of birth. Open systems are characteristic of industrial societies.

power A dimension of stratification consisting of the ability of one person or group to control the actions of others with or without the latter's consent.

social class A dimension of stratification consisting of an aggregate of persons in a society who stand in a similar position with regard to some form of power, privilege, or prestige.

social mobility An individual's ability to change his or her social class membership by moving up (or down) the stratification system. Upward or downward mobility is vertical, whereas mobility that results in a change of status without a consequent change of class is horizontal.

social status A dimension of stratification consisting of an individual's ranked position within the social system, the rank being determined mainly by the individual's occupational role.

social stratification (ranking) A process existing in all but the simplest societies whereby members rank one another and themselves hierarchically with respect to the amount of desirables (wealth, prestige, power) they possess.

stratification system The overlapping manner in which members of society are ranked according to classes, status groups, and hierarchies of power. Analyzed on a continuum from closed to open.

structural mobility Upward mobility caused by industrial and technological change that pushes skilled workers into higher-status occupations.

Suggested Readings

Kushnick, Louis, and James Jennings, eds. 1999. *A New Introduction to Poverty: The Role of Race, Power, and Politics.* New York: New York University Press. A compendium of articles that examines the causes and characteristics of poverty in the United States and the reasons for its persistence.

Liebow, Elliot. 1995. *Tell Them Who I Am: The Lives of Homeless Women.* New York: Penguin Books. A participant observation study of women in a homeless shelter in Washington, DC. This study puts a human face on the anonymous "bag ladies" we see on the streets of our cities.

Riesman, David. 1993. *Abundance for What?* New Brunswick, NJ: Transaction Books. A question we seldom ask is discussed by a noted sociologist.

Schwarz, John E. 1997. *The American Dream in Question.* New York: W. W. Norton. As unskilled jobs disappear, the author maintains, the American Dream becomes more and more elusive.

Shipler, David K. 2004. *The Working Poor: Invisible in America*. New York: Alfred A. Knopf. A powerful new book that illustrates the plight of the 35 million Americans who live in poverty, although most of them work full time. The author examines the lives of these forgotten Americans who live in the shadow of prosperity and for whom the American dream is out of reach despite their willingness to work hard toward it.

Wilson, William Julius. 1997. *When Work Disappears: The World of the New Urban Poor*. New York: Knopf. This sociologist expands his views on the unfortunate consequences following the disappearance of unskilled jobs in inner cities: the flight of the middle class, the decline of inner-city businesses, and the plight of a working class left without work.

Web Sites of Interest

Several federal agencies maintain web sites with myriad statistics about the subjects of this chapter: income distribution, inequality, poverty, hunger, and so forth.

http://www.census.lgov/hhes/www.income.html
Income statistics in all varieties according to age, race, gender, in quintiles, and so on.

http://www.ssc.wisc.edu/irp
The focus is on the causes and impact of poverty and social inequality in the United States.

http://www.brook.edu/
A variety of opinion pieces, from a prestigious research institution, offering independent analyses of social policy.

http://www.bls.gov/
This is the web site of the Bureau of Labor Statistics, which provides much information on wages, employment, and the U.S. economy in general.

http://www.aspe.dhhs.gov/pic/
This is the web site of the U.S. Department of Health and Human Services, which also has a wealth of information on policies and statistics that have an impact on the population.

http://www.demos.org/inequality/
This site gathers materials about the growing inequality in the United States, which it considers a danger to democracy, community, culture, and economic health.

8

Minority Status: Race and Ethnicity

IN THIS CHAPTER, YOU WILL LEARN

- the definitions of minority based on race and ethnicity;
- how the majority has dealt with minorities in its midst;
- the causes and effects of prejudice and discrimination;
- some characteristics of the principal minorities in the United States;
- that the United States is likely to become a different, racially mixed, multicultural society in the future.

Humans have lived on this planet for many thousands, perhaps millions, of years and have developed sophisticated and technologically advanced civilizations, but in some respects they have remained very uncivilized. Perhaps they are still following a biological imperative, which makes them suspicious of strangers and inimical to others who are not part of their group. Whatever the reasons, it is clear that even in the twenty-first century, deep hatreds still divide us.

We speak of being interconnected in a global village. In fact, governments do interact with one another in terms of politics and economics: we are allies and trading partners, and the rapidity of communication possible today allows us to keep in touch with the far corners of the planet instantly. This interaction is also responsible for cultural diffusion, a process that has allowed every society to become acquainted with the products, if not the culture, of every other society. Interaction is not really such a new phenomenon: for thousands of years interbreeding has occurred on a large scale, so that no "pure" stock exists anywhere in the world (with the possible exception of small groups that may exist in inaccessible locations). On the whole, however, it seems that people have chosen to stress their differences rather than their similarities. As a result, much of human history has been primarily a record of struggles and conflicts, of conquests and oppression, even of genocide, with one group of people pitted against another.

Differentiating people according to specific variables is a universal cultural trait. In all societies, men are treated differently from women, children differently from adults, the elderly differently from the young. We have also seen in the preceding chapter that the poor are treated differently from the rich, the powerful differently from the powerless. As we all know, people of one skin color are also treated differently from people of another. With the rise of the nation-state, another reason for differentiation came into being: groups of people who differ in culture or religion are suddenly forced to owe allegiance to the same state, and to live side by side. As a result of immigration, colonization, or conquest, most nations have become plural societies consisting of a majority group and groups that differ from it because of culture, appearance, or religion—the so-called minorities. Occasionally, majority and minorities coexist in peace. More often, coexistence is marred by conflict. As examples, one need only mention Northern Ireland, the Middle East, South Africa, Rwanda, Darfur, or the Balkan countries of the former Yugoslavia. To a lesser extent, the United States also has problems of coexistence.

■ Majority-Minorities Relations: Defining the Terms

When two or more groups share the same territory but one of them has more power than the others, that group is considered the majority and the other groups are termed minorities. In other words, the terms *majority* and *minorities* do not imply any numerical value; that is, a majority is not necessarily larger in number than any of the minority groups. On the contrary, although this is not true in the United States, in many instances one or more minorities are superior in number to the dominant majority (South Africa was a glaring example before the end of apartheid).

As noted, minorities in the modern sense originated with the development of the nation-state. "Both the spread of dominance over formerly separate groups and the common desire to create a homogeneous nation (leading to attempts to repress cultural variation) have created the minority–majority situation" (Simpson & Yinger, 1972, 16). From the dawn of history and through many thousands of years, people lived in tribes, small groups consisting of several families. Tribalism is deeply embedded in the human psyche, and even today people view the world from a "tribal" perspective, expecting the society to which they belong to consist of their own physical and cultural type (Wagley & Harris, 1958, 241–242).

Because it does not depend on numbers, minority status refers to that category of people who "possess imperfect access to positions of equal power and to the corollary categories of prestige and privilege in the society" (Yetman & Steele, 1971, 4). Minority status, then, is conferred not on individuals but on whole categories of people who, on the basis of the ascribed statuses of race, ethnicity, and religion (and, to a different extent, on those of gender and sexual orientation, age, and disability) lack the kind of power that the majority group holds in a society.

By contrast, the majority, or dominant group, although it may be numerically smaller, controls the important sectors of social life, influencing the culture of the society in such vital areas as language, ideology, and even standards of beauty and worth. By definition, the majority controls access to positions of wealth, prestige, and power. Minorities find access more difficult the more they differ in looks and customs from the majority, and the fewer skills, talents, and the less education they have at their disposal. Mobility within the stratification system, then, has varied accordingly for the different minorities.

■ Common Characteristics of Minorities

People who are considered to belong to a minority group share some common features. First, they are recognizable by virtue of possessing visible ascribed traits: appearance, language, accent, or last name. Second, because they possess these traits, they are subject to differential treatment. Third, their self-image and identity are centered around their minority-group membership. And finally, they are aware that they share a common identity with others in the group (Wagley & Harris, 1958, 10).

Minority status is most commonly assigned to a group because of that group's ethnic origin, religion, or race (as noted earlier, there are additional reasons, but these three are the most frequent and basic). **Ethnicity** refers to a group's distinctiveness on social and cultural grounds that differ from those of the majority because of national background. Most immigrants who share with others a common language, culture, traditions, history, and ancestry, and are recognized as such by the rest of society, are ethnic minorities. Among those who have been in the United States for several generations, some retain and some have given up the language, customs, and sometimes even the surnames of their country of origin. However, as long as a majority of them feel bonds of solidarity with others who came from the same background, they are considered to be members of an ethnic group.

Religion is a set of beliefs and rituals dealing with the sacred. People of the same religion share their beliefs and rituals and derive a sense of identity from their religious membership. In the United States, Catholics and Jews, differing in religion from the Protestants who made up the original group of settlers and who eventually became the majority, have been subject to differential treatment in the past. Minority status based on religion has lessened in importance in the past half-century.

The most difficult factor to define is race. **Race** was a concept scientists used in the past to describe biological differences occurring in the human species. Contemporary scholars would like to do away with this term altogether, because it does not describe a scientific reality. The American Anthropological Association has issued a statement that although the term *race* was used to classify people into categories called races according to visible differences in appearance, the expansion of knowledge in this century has clearly shown that "human populations are not unambiguous, clearly demarcated, biologically distinct groups. . . . [DNA evidence] indicates that most physical variation, about 94%, lies *within* so-called racial groups" (Statement on "Race," American Anthropological Association, 1996, 569–570). There are no "pure" human groupings left anywhere because of the overlapping of genes in neighboring populations. "The continued sharing of genetic materials has maintained all of humankind as a single species." Therefore, the classification of people into races is artificial and does not correspond to clear and definite distinctions among humans. Neither does it correspond to national, religious, linguistic, cultural, and geographic boundaries, although isolation in the past may have been responsible for the existence of different gene pools. No social traits or behaviors of population groups have any connection with inherited racial traits. Finally, there is no scientific support for the idea that differences in personality, temperament, character, or intelligence are based on race. The Anthropological Association concludes: "Given what we know about the capacity of normal humans to achieve and function within any culture, we conclude that present-day inequalities between so-called 'racial' groups are not consequences of their biological inheritance but products of historical and contemporary social, economic, educational, and political circumstances" (see the complete statement on the Internet: **http://www.aaanet.org**).

■ The Making of Pluralist Society

One of the fundamental problems facing nations such as the United States has been how to make a functioning social unit, a society, out of the many disparate groups that have periodically come to its shores in search of a better future. A solution of sorts has, in fact, been achieved, for a majority of Americans do share sufficient common values and norms to maintain social stability. But the process has taken place by trial and error, and the results remain imperfect.

Ideologies Regarding the Treatment of Minorities

At different times in American history, different ideologies have prevailed regarding how minorities ought to be treated.

Anglo-Conformity.   The first of these, Anglo-conformity, represented an attempt to superimpose WASP (White Anglo-Saxon Protestant) values on all immigrants. Thus, it was expected that the language, institutions, and cultural patterns of the United States (which in turn were based on an English model) would be learned and absorbed by all newcomers.

The Melting Pot.   During the nineteenth century, the idea took hold that immigrants could make important contributions to the society. As a result, it was thought that the United States could mix, both biologically and culturally, all the various stocks within it, ultimately giving origin to an individual who would be the "New American."

While the educational system and the mass media have succeeded in molding second- and third-generation immigrants into Americans who accept most of the values and institutions of the society (they tend to be, in fact, some of the most ardent patriots), in other ways ethnic minorities have remained resistant to melting. Even when their ethnic background was no longer a focus of identity for second- and third-generation immigrants, their religion was. Sociologists found that marriage followed religious lines: British, German, and Scandinavian Protestants intermarried, creating a Protestant pool; Irish, Italian, and Polish Catholics intermarried, creating a Catholic pool; and Jews married other Jews of whatever

The immigration issue that bedevils current legislators is not new: our country is made up of immigrants from many parts of the world, looking to better their lives.

national origin, creating a Jewish pool (Kennedy, 1944; Archdeacon, 1983). Although there was a melting down of ethnicity, then, the United States was becoming a triple melting pot. This realization paved the way for the ideology of pluralism. As for the racial minorities, they hardly "melted down" at all.

Cultural Pluralism.   The ideology of cultural pluralism, the most widely accepted today, stresses the desirability of each ethnic group's retention of its cultural distinctiveness, but still within the boundaries of the wider American culture. In other words, the first commitment of every person is, ideally, to the good of the United States; but beyond that, in matters such as food, family, religious rituals, community associations, and so on, individuals retain, if they so desire, their ethnic ties. It is thought that people can, in this manner, contribute much more to the society, somewhat in the fashion of a dish that tastes much better than the variety of separate ingredients that make it up.

The decade of the 1960s saw a revival of ethnic feelings as it became apparent that success and upward mobility in the society were extremely difficult for some ethnic and most racial groups to achieve. African Americans, Hispanics, and Native Americans became active in protest movements to end their unequal access to opportunities and, in the process, seemed to rediscover their ancestry and use it as a springboard for political action. Activity in political organizations seems to have generated feelings of solidarity that were lacking before among many ethnic group members.

Multiculturalism.   The contemporary prevailing ideology is couched in the policy of multiculturalism. This policy began as an educational program that tried to focus attention on the cultural diversity existing in American society. It also made an attempt at promoting the equality of all cultural traditions. It differs from cultural pluralism in that it makes a concerted effort to take into consideration the point of view of minorities, rather than defining the society as

Many ethnic and religious minorities in the United States have assimilated and entered into mainstream society. Others, however, choose to accept the political values of American society but retain religious and traditional values of their countries of origin. This is the basis of cultural pluralism.

primarily a descendant of white Europeans. Its insistence on celebrating our diversity, rather than our unity as a nation, has caused much controversy and is not universally accepted.

■ Majority and Minorities: Processes of Coexistence

Cultural pluralism is not a goal in every society or in every historical era. Dominant majorities have treated the minorities in their midst in a number of ways, and minorities have reacted variously to their condition. Some of the processes with which societies attempt to deal with their minorities span the following continuum.

Segregation is an attempt to isolate a minority from the majority. South Africa, until quite recently, offered one example of segregation. In that society, the dominant group had forced minorities that were numerically superior into a condition of inferiority, restricting their freedom of movement and isolating them either on rural reservations or in urban enclaves. Segregation was also rampant in the United States, particularly in the South, prior to a number of Supreme Court decisions that made the segregation of public facilities illegal.

Accommodation is a situation in which a minority is conscious of the norms and values of the majority, accepts and adapts to them, but chooses to retain its own ethnic norms and values. Thus, it does not fully participate in the host culture but remains culturally, and sometimes linguistically, distinct. The Cuban community in Miami as well as some Muslim communities are good examples of minorities that have chosen accommodation.

Acculturation, or cultural assimilation, occurs when a minority group accepts and makes its own the norms and values of the host culture, often giving up a native language and traditions. In spite of this, such groups are often still refused consideration as equals.

Assimilation is a process by which minorities absorb completely the culture of the majority and enter into its mainstream. Generally, in the United States, the minorities that were most like the majority in looks and culture were assimilated most rapidly. Those most unlike the majority failed to be assimilated, and some no longer want to be.

Amalgamation takes place when all distinctions between majority and minorities are erased. In amalgamation, members of different ethnic and racial groups intermarry, so that eventually their offspring form a new and distinct ethnic, cultural, or racial group. Brazil is considered an example of a society that adopted amalgamation, although the process is far from perfect and does not reach throughout the entire society. In the United States, amalgamation has not taken place, but perhaps things are beginning to change. Interracial marriage, once taboo and against the law in some states, is now occurring at an increasingly rapid rate.

While pluralism and multiculturalism are the current ideals in democratic societies, the other policies—and worse kinds of treatment—are hardly unknown. Continued subjugation was for many years the policy of South Africa, one that only now is being slowly remedied. Expulsion has been practiced by Uganda, which expelled more than 40,000 Asians during Idi Amin's tenure, and Vietnam forced out close to a million ethnic Chinese. It has been practiced most recently in the former Yugoslavia, where several ethnic groups have cleansed their territories of each other. Extermination, too, in spite of murder being a taboo in all societies, has many antecedents. Europeans who settled the New World are guilty of exterminating, both directly and indirectly, the majority of the native populations in North and South America. In the twentieth century, in addition to the systematic destruction of European Jews, Gypsies, and Slavs by Nazi Germany, we have also witnessed the genocide of approximately 2 million Cambodians by the Pol Pot regime, as well as the massacre of Tutsis by Hutus, two ethnic groups residing in Rwanda. The twenty-first century is witnessing more ethnic cleansing in the Darfur region of Sudan.

Genocide, unfortunately, is not an uncommon method of eliminating groups with which one does not want to share a territory. Following the fall of Saddam Hussein's regime in Iraq, thousands of bodies have been dug out of various mass graves, presumably the victims of ethnic cleansing.

■ In the Way: Obstacles to Pluralism

Not all relations between groups that coexist in the same society are conflict producing, but many are. It is human nature to want to remain "top dog." Thus, majorities employ a variety of mechanisms to keep minorities from displacing them from their dominant positions in the social system. Most of these are no longer legal in contemporary societies, nor are they necessarily conscious efforts. Among them, the most destructive are prejudice, discrimination, and what is still referred to as racism.

Prejudice

Prejudice derives from the word *prejudgment*, which implies that a person makes up his or her mind about something without any real knowledge about it. Prejudgment is often a useful tool, even though it is based on stereotypes and hearsay, because it is sometimes necessary to depend on someone else's word or act on superficial impressions. But prejudice goes beyond prejudgment in the sense that a prejudiced person refuses to change even when confronted by unassailable evidence.

Prejudice leans heavily on stereotyping. In **stereotyping**, common, uniform characteristics are assigned to an entire category of people, without any allowance for individual differences. African Americans, for instance, have been stereotyped as athletically and musically superior to whites. In essence, a stereotype develops when the traits and behavior of some individuals are considered to be typical of the whole group, or a superficial aspect of a group's behavior is taken as that group's total behavior, without any attempt to explain its causes.

Box 8.1   Hate: Prejudice and Discrimination among
            Castes in India

The Indian Constitution, put in place in 1950, abolished the notion of untouchability, which had been a characteristic of the Indian caste system for centuries. The fact that some groups of people were considered too unclean to touch derives from ancient scriptures that describe how the gods created the world and its social system by sacrificing a primeval man. From the man's face they derived the high, priestly Brahman caste, his arms became the warrior caste, his thighs gave rise to the merchant caste, and his feet gave origin to the servant caste. Under these castes were those whom the gods declared to be unclean and untouchable to the higher castes. These groups were destined to do the filthy work of the society. There are still a large number of these subcastes. For instance, the Jatavs are scorned because their traditional work as cobblers necessitated the handling of dead flesh, and the Balmiki are the most vilified because of their work: carrying away the excrement that accumulates each night in the dry toilets of local homes.

Because they are so numerous, the subcastes have been granted some political rights by the Constitution, including a guaranteed 15 percent of seats in Parliament. In spite of this, their members are not unified. Political parties, however, do not ignore the votes they represent, since they number 150 million, more than one-sixth of India's population. Interesting them in political activism,

the parties have managed to secure some advantages for specific subcastes; but other subcastes have not reaped any benefits.

The interesting point in this scenario is that the hierarchical stratification of the society is so profoundly embedded in the culture, and so accepted, that the members of the subcastes themselves believe them to be right and just. Even though some of them complain that one caste has done better than another—and sometimes these complaints erupt into violence—feelings about each caste's place in the scheme of the society run deep. When two young people from different castes ran away together in a rural area of the state of Uttar Pradesh, the confrontation that followed resulted in the death of the girl's father at the hands of men from the subcaste of the young man. Members of the subcaste commented: "Balmikis are beneath us, and we cannot tolerate it when they run off with our girls." "Balmikis clear away the excrement. We are not going to do this job." When asked about discrimination they themselves experience from higher castes, and whether they did not want it to end, the answer was: "Discrimination against us may end. But discrimination against the Balmiki is right and must go on." Obviously, prejudice and discrimination are not rational attitudes but based on deep-seated feelings that are difficult to eradicate by law (Bearak, 1998, A3).

Scapegoating is another mechanism that fuels prejudice. *Scapegoating*, derived from the Biblical practice of offering a goat as sacrifice in exchange for God's forgiveness of one's sins, is a term that refers to the tendency of frustrated individuals to respond with aggression. If the source of frustration cannot be attacked directly, then a third party may become the object of aggression. In troubled times—high unemployment, high crime rates, inflation—some group can always be found to take the blame.

Why Are We Prejudiced?

Because prejudice is an obvious cause of hostilities among groups, it has been the subject of much research. Research by psychologists seems to point to feelings of anger rapidly seeking a target, particularly if that target happens to be of a different social group, sex, or ethnicity. This finding, added to previous research, suggests that prejudice may have evolutionary roots. It may have developed as a quick, crude way for early humans to protect themselves from danger. Anger is a signal that some level of threat or hostility exists in the environment, and logic indicates that the threat probably comes from someone not in one's same social group, because members of the same social group generally reinforce and protect each other (Wartik, 2004, D5).

Early sociological research seemed to indicate that prejudice was due to the isolation of groups from one another. However, the example of the South, where whites and blacks lived in close proximity and often on intimate terms (though always in a master-servant relationship), did not support this theory. In his book, *The Nature of Prejudice*, social psychologist Gordon Allport (1954) proposed a theory of contact. According to this theory, when two groups of equal status have contact with each other, prejudice decreases; however, if status inequality exists and one group is dominant over the other, prejudice remains the same or actually increases. In fact, in the South of today, a decrease in prejudice has been noted; at the same time, Southern blacks have risen in the stratification system, and with the elimination of the "separate but equal" public facilities, blacks and whites of the same social class are brought closer together. Allport, however, had to qualify his findings: it seems that even when status is equal between two groups, if there is also competition, prejudice becomes more intense. Conversely, if the groups cooperate to achieve some common goals, prejudice declines.

Another influential theory, focusing on prejudice as a personality trait, was based on a now classic study by T. W. Adorno (1950), in which a high correlation between the development of prejudice and a type of personality called *authoritarian* was found. People with that type of personality are oversocialized to accept only the norms and values of their own group, rejecting all others. They become very anxious when confronted with different norms and values and convince themselves that people who differ from them are somehow inferior, subhuman, or sinful. Other features of an authoritarian personality include submission to authority, admiration of power and toughness, conventionality, condescension toward inferiors, insensitivity to relationships with others, and a deep-rooted and partly subconscious sense of insecurity. In such persons, prejudice is merely part of a total outlook on life in which situations and problems are perceived in terms of absolutes—good or bad, right or wrong—and in which people are either heroes or villains.

Institutional discrimination was flagrant in South Africa during the period of apartheid, when a majority of black Africans were oppressed by a minority of white colonial rulers.

Discrimination

Whereas prejudice is an attitude or a feeling, discrimination consists of actions taken as a result of prejudicial feelings; for instance, the belief that all Puerto Ricans are violent is a prejudice, but the organization of a committee to prevent them from moving into a neighborhood is discrimination.

Prejudice and discrimination usually go hand in hand, but they can also occur independently of each other. A person may, as an example, continue to believe that Puerto Ricans are violent. If, nonetheless, that person, being a law-abiding citizen, allows Puerto Rican families to move into the neighborhood without harassment or interference of any sort, the person is exhibiting prejudice without discrimination. On the other hand, a person may not harbor prejudicial feelings about Puerto Ricans at all; but if, to retain the friendship of neighbors, the person signs a petition to keep a Puerto Rican family from buying property on their street, that person is discriminating without being prejudiced. In general, however, prejudice and discrimination are mutually reinforcing.

Discrimination is against the law in the United States. However, because it is so closely interrelated with prejudice, certain kinds of discrimination are still prevalent to a degree in the society. Discrimination is viewed as being of two types: attitudinal and institutional. **Attitudinal discrimination** refers to behavior that is prompted by the personal prejudice of a member of a majority or in response to the prejudice of others. **Institutional discrimination** refers to the system of inequalities existing within a society, apart from the prejudices of individuals. In *The Declining Significance of Race* (1978) and *The Truly Disadvantaged* (1987), William J. Wilson speculated that whereas in the past attitudinal discrimination was to blame for the unequal status of African Americans, today the fault is attributable largely to factors that have little to do with race and much to do with changes in the economy. Specifically, the shift from manufacturing to a service economy that has polarized the labor market into low-wage and high-wage sectors, technological innovations that require a highly skilled labor force, and the relocation of manufacturing industries out of the central cities are primarily responsible for blocking economic opportunities to African Americans. Even if all racial prejudice were eliminated, a good portion of African Americans would remain unemployed or underemployed and would fail to thrive.

Time after time, every group that has been at the bottom of the stratification system has encountered virulent prejudice and discrimination coupled with gloomy predictions that the group was too inferior ever to rise out of their low status. And yet, time after time, once such groups improved their occupational position and achieved an economic status comparable to that of the majority, prejudice against them diminished. As to the mechanisms of upward mobility, Stark (1985) suggests that they include geographic concentration, internal economic development and specialization, and finally, development of a middle class. Upward mobility is slowed for groups that lack a substantial middle class, and until a middle class develops, prejudice and discrimination tend to persist.

Racism

Prejudice and discrimination are the chief components of an attitude that is commonly called racism. Although racism is popularly understood as hatred of members of certain racial groups, in the language of the social sciences it used to have a more precise meaning. It referred to the ideology that some racial groups are superior to others based on a recognizable trait, such as skin color, and that this belief justified discrimination against the group deemed inferior. Related to this belief was the idea that both the physical and behavioral traits of racial groups are inherited biologically. Racism is, of course, related to the concept

Box 8.2   **An Ongoing Controversy: Affirmative Action**

To hasten the formation of a substantial middle class among minority groups that had been held back economically in the United States, the government instituted a policy that came to be known as *affirmative action*. According to this policy, preferences had to be granted in government contracts, employment, and college admissions to members of certain minority groups, particularly African Americans, women, and Hispanics. This policy, now better than 30 years old, has occasioned much controversy. On the one hand, there are those who argue that such a policy is blatantly wrongheaded because it goes against the principle of merit; in short, that contracts, employment, and college admissions should go to those who deserve them and not to those who simply belong to a specific minority group. These critics see the policy as reverse discrimination because it indeed discriminates against those who are deserving of a contract,

a job, or of being admitted to the college of their choice but who fail to attain these goals simply because they are not members of those minority groups. Even some minority members are against affirmative action, stating that they feel it is demeaning to their group: every group member who has achieved success feels tainted by the common belief that it was only the result of affirmative action.

On the other hand, the supporters of the policy argue that because of past discrimination it is necessary to set the merit principle aside and offer certain advantages based strictly on minority affiliation. The critics have been partly successful in weakening the policy in some states, where legislation has been enacted banning the use of race and sex in college admission, contracting, and public employment. Affirmative action, however, remains an issue of frequently hostile debate.

of race, which, as we saw earlier is no longer recognized as valid. Still, the concept as well as the term persists, and not just in the United States. All societies, throughout the ages, have practiced one form or another of racism, which is just another version of ethnocentrism (see Chapter 3). This ability of one group to feel superior to others has functioned historically to provide a rationale for a social order based on the domination of one group over another, that is, "to use beliefs in genetic superiority-inferiority as a means of justifying domination and exploitation of one racial group by another" (Yetman, 1985, 14).

As an ideology, racism originated in Darwin's theory of evolution, particularly its concept of the survival of the fittest (although Darwin himself never intended to give it this social meaning). This theory was applied to human groups (social Darwinism) and used to rationalize the colonization of a number of nations by Europeans. The latter were considered the most highly evolved and civilized of peoples; witness the development of self-rule and representative government among them.

Today, racism as an ideology has declined all over the world, and very few people in the United States would admit to subscribing to racist beliefs. The ideology, however, has been replaced by some stubborn forms of institutional racism and by a number of myths that each group believes about the other. The term remains in our vocabulary, although most people mistakenly attribute it to discriminatory actions or prejudicial feelings or simply as an expression of negative sentiments.

■ Racial Minorities

The four visible racial minority groups in the United States consist of Native Americans, African Americans, some Latinos, and Asian Americans (Table 8.1, note that the total population of the United States today has increased to over 300 million). With the exception of Asian Americans, racial minorities have had a different history than the more recently arrived ethnic minorities.

TABLE 8.1   Population by Race and Hispanic Origin: 2000 and 2004

(Numbers in thousands)

Race and Hispanic origin	April 1, 2000		July 1, 2004		Change 2000 to 2004	
	Total	Percent	Total	Percent	Number	Percent
Total population	**281,424.6**	**100.0**	**293,655.4**	**100.0**	**12,230.8**	**4.3**
One race	277,526.9	98.6	289,216.7	98.5	11,689.8	4.2
White	228,106.5	81.1	236,057.8	80.4	7,951.3	3.5
Black or African American	35,704.9	12.7	37,502.3	12.8	1,797.4	5.0
American Indian and Alaska Native	2,663.9	0.9	2,824.8	1.0	160.9	6.0
Asian	10,589.1	3.8	12,326.2	4.2	1,737.1	16.4
Native Hawaiian and Other Pacific Islander	462.5	0.2	505.6	0.2	43.1	9.3
Two or More Races	3,897.7	1.4	4,438.8	1.5	541.1	13.9
Race alone or in combination:*						
White	231,436.4	82.2	239,880.1	81.7	8,443.7	3.6
Black or African American	37,105.0	13.2	39,232.5	13.4	2,127.5	5.7
American Indian and Alaska Native	4,225.1	1.5	4,409.4	1.5	184.3	4.4
Asian	12,006.7	4.3	13,956.6	4.8	1,949.9	16.2
Native Hawaiian and Other Pacific Islander	906.8	0.3	976.4	0.3	69.6	7.7
Hispanic or Latino (any race)	35,306.3	12.5	41,322.1	14.1	6,015.8	17.0
White alone, not Hispanic or Latino	195,577.0	69.5	197,840.8	67.4	2,263.8	1.2

*The sum of the alone-or-in-combination populations is larger than the total because some people belong to more than one racial group.

Source: U.S. Census Bureau, *Population Estimates Program*, April 1, 2000, and July 1, 2004. Updated February 2007.

Native Americans

The original inhabitants of the North American continent had been living here for more than 20,000 years—though they themselves had been immigrants of sorts: they are thought to have crossed the Bering Strait when it was a land bridge connecting Alaska to Asia. They were displaced by the European settlers, who were more advanced technologically and who took advantage of the natives' lack of unity and tribal loyalties. The number of Native Americans was greatly reduced through diseases brought by the white settlers as well as through the constant warfare waged against them.

Because the settlers believed their culture was superior to that of the American Indians (so named because Columbus was searching for an alternate route to the Indies when he landed on Hispaniola), they were able to rationalize the seizure of land and to ignore any treaties or agreements between themselves and the native populations. After the United States became an independent nation, the government forcefully removed Indians from desirable land and pushed them onto reservations, where they remained isolated from mainstream society. The land on which reservations are located is managed in trust by the Bureau of Indian Affairs (BIA), an agency that has historically been more interested in conservation than economic development. Ranked as the most inefficient of 90 federal agencies, the BIA has a sorry record

Native Americans who remain on reservations suffer from a very low standard of living. These Navajos live in Navajo Country, the four corners where Utah, Arizona, Colorado, and New Mexico meet.

of waste, corruption, and red tape. Hence, conditions on reservations have been characterized by economic backwardness, inadequate education, substandard housing, and inferior health care. The number of Native Americans living below the poverty level in 2004 was 24.3 percent.

As of 2004 there were 4.4 million Native Americans in the United States including Alaska natives, most of them in the western states of California, Oklahoma, Arizona, and New Mexico and Alaska (see Figure 8.1). Many have now left the reservations and live in urban areas (although about 38 percent remain on reservations). However, they are the most disadvantaged of all minority groups: almost one-third live below the poverty level, and they have alarmingly high unemployment rates. High mortality rates from alcohol-related causes and high suicide rates are also indications of the substandard conditions in which many Native Americans still live. In many tribes, life expectancy is only 45 years, and they have the lowest per-capita income of any minority group in the United States. For instance, the Pine Ridge Reservation in South Dakota is home to the Oglala branch of the Sioux, the descendants of such famous war heroes as Crazy Horse and Red Cloud. Unfortunately, its 16,000 inhabitants are experiencing the most profound poverty in the United States. Fewer than 3 in 10 adults have jobs, nearly all of which are in government agencies. They are ravaged by isolation, disease, political infighting, and the inability to find jobs, leading to dependence on welfare and ultimately to depression and alcoholism. In a vicious circle that often plagues minorities, lack of skills and distance or isolation from jobs leads to unemployment, and the dependence on welfare develops habits not conducive to getting and keeping jobs.

The problems of Native Americans have been complicated by tribalism—many think of themselves as primarily Navajo or Cherokee, etc. because there is no uniform Native American culture or language. (Native Americans are divided into approximately 500 tribal groups, and around 50 of their original languages are still spoken.) Only in the past several

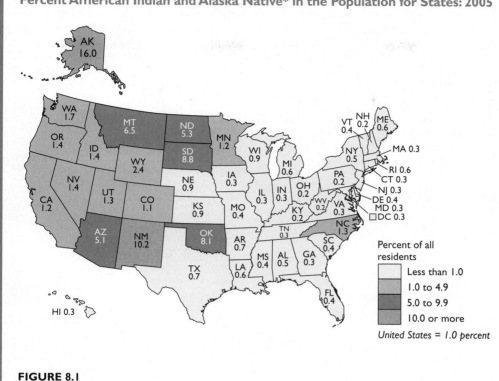

Percent American Indian and Alaska Native* in the Population for States: 2005

Percent of all residents

Less than 1.0
1.0 to 4.9
5.0 to 9.9
10.0 or more

United States = 1.0 percent

FIGURE 8.1

*Single race.

Source: U.S. Census Bureau, Population Estimates Program, July 1, 2005.

decades has a new militancy become evident, as witnessed by an increase in political activity through the American Indian Movement. This has resulted in the return of some lands as well as in an effort to develop economic self-sufficiency. Following the lessons of the civil rights movements, Native Americans are beginning to use the judicial system, so that more litigation on their behalf has been initiated in the past 20 years than in the previous 200. (See U.S. Census press releases on **http://www.census.gov.**)

Asian Americans

The two largest Asian minorities living in the United States used to be the Chinese and the Japanese, before the large-scale Asian immigration that began in the 1970s. Today, Asian Americans constitute a large, highly diverse, and overwhelmingly foreign-born population. Chinese and Filipinos make up the largest Asian contingents, followed by Japanese, Indians, Koreans, and Vietnamese (see Table 8.2). These groups are culturally, religiously, and linguistically different from each other as well as from the dominant majority, but are generally classified together in the public mind. The total number of Asians in the United States is over 13 million, or 4.8 percent of the U.S. population. This represents an increase from 1980, when they were 1.5 percent of the population. The new immigrants display a wide variety of cultural

TABLE 8.2   Asian Household Population by Detailed Group: 2004 (Data based on sample limited to the household population and exclude the population living in institutions, college dormitories, and other group quarters. For information on confidentiality protection, sampling error, nonsampling error, and definitions, see **http://factfinder.census.gov/home/en/datanotes/exp_acs2004.html**)

Detailed group	Population	Percent of Asian alone Population
Asian alone	**12,097,281**	**100.0**
Asian Indian	2,245,239	18.6
Bangladeshi	50,473	0.4
Cambodian	195,208	1.6
Chinese, except Taiwanese	2,829,627	23.4
Filipino	2,148,227	17.8
Hmong	163,733	1.4
Indonesian	52,267	0.4
Japanese	832,039	6.9
Korean	1,251,092	10.3
Laotian	226,661	1.9
Malaysian	11,458	0.1
Pakistani	208,852	1.7
Sri Lankan	22,339	0.2
Taiwanese	70,771	0.6
Thai	130,548	1.1
Vietnamese	1,267,510	10.5
Other Asian[1]	250,666	2.1
Other Asian, not specified[2]	140,571	1.2

[1]Includes Bhutanese, Burmese, Indochinese, Iwo Jiman, Madagascar, Maldivian, Nepalese, Okinawan, and Singaporean.

[2]Includes entries such as Asian American, Asian, and Asiatic.

Source: U.S. Census Bureau, *2004 American Community Survey, Selected Population Profiles, S0201, and Detailed Tables, B02006.*

forms, differing in social class and skills (Rodriguez, 1998, 21). However, they are becoming a group to be reckoned with in terms of their economic success and civic-mindedness.

In general, Asian Americans have been financially successful, exhibiting the highest median family income of any minority group ($56,161 in 2004), the lowest divorce rates (3 percent) and teenage pregnancy rates (6 percent), and the lowest unemployment rates (3.5 percent). Their poverty rate was 12 percent, although a percentage live on welfare, particularly those originating in Southeast Asia who immigrated after the Vietnam War. In California, which is the residence of almost 40 percent of the Asian population in America, Asians have a higher level of college degrees than whites, and they outperform them in both education and income within one generation. The proportion of Asians with a bachelor's degree or higher is 48.2 percent. Even more striking, 16 percent of Asian and Pacific Islanders 25 years old and over have advanced degrees (master's, Ph.D., M.D., or J.D.), while the corresponding rate for all adults in this age group is 9 percent (U.S. Bureau of the Census, **http://www.infoplease.com/spot/asiancensus1.html**) (Figure 8.2).

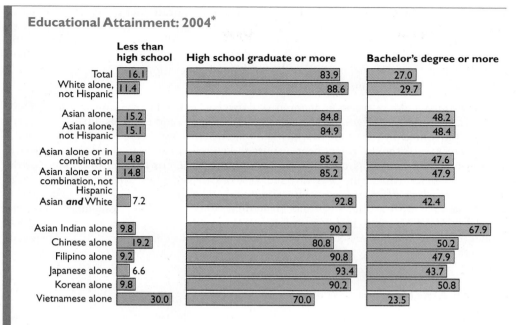

Educational Attainment: 2004*

	Less than high school	High school graduate or more	Bachelor's degree or more
Total	16.1	83.9	27.0
White alone, not Hispanic	11.4	88.6	29.7
Asian alone,	15.2	84.8	48.2
Asian alone, not Hispanic	15.1	84.9	48.4
Asian alone or in combination	14.8	85.2	47.6
Asian alone or in combination, not Hispanic	14.8	85.2	47.9
Asian *and* White	7.2	92.8	42.4
Asian Indian alone	9.8	90.2	67.9
Chinese alone	19.2	80.8	50.2
Filipino alone	9.2	90.8	47.9
Japanese alone	6.6	93.4	43.7
Korean alone	9.8	90.2	50.8
Vietnamese alone	30.0	70.0	23.5

FIGURE 8.2

*(Percent of population 25 and older. Data based on sample limited to the household population and exclude the population living in institutions, college dormitories, and other group quarters. For information on confidentiality protection, sampling error, nonsampling error, and definitions, see **http://factfinder.census.gov/home/en/datanotes/exp_ acs2004.html**)

Source: U.S. Census Bureau 2004 American Community Survey, Selected Population Profiles, S0201.

Chinese. Today there are approximately 2.8 million Americans of Chinese descent living in the United States, most of them in California and Hawaii. As a group, they have been upwardly mobile and are characterized by rising professionalization, being highly represented in medicine, engineering, and scientific research. Partly as a result of their high socioeconomic status, it has been easier for the Chinese to amalgamate, if they chose, as evidenced by their relatively high rates of intermarriage.

Japanese. The Japanese began to arrive at the beginning of the twentieth century and, like the Chinese before them, were subject to the same discriminatory practices, being considered part of the "yellow peril" that threatened to engulf white culture. Their real problems, however, peaked during World War II, when they were labeled as security risks and potential traitors. They were interned in detention camps, their property confiscated or sold.

At present, Japanese Americans make up 6.9 percent of all Asians in the United States. The generation born in the United States, known as the Nisei, were socialized to value education and conformity to the norms of the dominant majority. As a result, third-generation Japanese Americans rank highest among all nonwhite groups in education and income. They have experienced high rates of upward mobility, and a shift from jobs in small ethnic businesses to executive positions in the corporate hierarchy. This trend has also resulted in a great amount of amalgamation (40 percent have non-Japanese spouses), particularly among the best educated and most economically successful. Interracial and interethnic marriage increases with each generation. Whereas only 13 percent of foreign-born Asians marry non-Asians, 34 percent of second-generation and 54 percent of third-generation Asian Americans do (Rodriguez, 2003, 96).

Other Asians.   More recent immigrants of Asian background to the United States include Filipinos, Asian Indians, Koreans, Vietnamese, Cambodians, and Laotians, the last three as a result of the conflict in Indochina in which the United States became embroiled (see Table 8.2 and Figure 8.3). Although resentment against these groups has been sharp, particularly in areas where they are highly concentrated (during the 1992 Los Angeles riots, most of the hostility of black Americans was directed at Korean merchants whose businesses were located in black areas), many are economically upwardly mobile and appear to be entering the mainstream with greater ease than their predecessors. They are sometimes called the "model minority" because they are statistically more prosperous, more educated, and less prone to engage in criminal activities, succumb to drugs, or be unemployed than Americans in general.

African Americans

As of 2005 African Americans represent 13.4 percent of the total population of the nation and have been here longer than any other nonwhite group: by 1776, the year of American independence, nearly all African Americans were native-born. However, the entrance of blacks into the mainstream of American society has been complicated by their special problems and made more difficult by economic causes (Figure 8.4).

As is well known, African Americans originally did not come to this country voluntarily in search of a better future but rather were forced into slavery by greedy Africans and Europeans and sold to the colonists of North and South America as a form of cheap labor. As slaves in a foreign land, cut off from their native culture, they found themselves in a particularly vulnerable position. The culture that eventually emerged among the slaves incorporated some of the negative perceptions toward them exhibited by the dominant majority. And while other immigrants could always go back to their native land if things did not work out here, no such outlet was open to Africans.

Some historians have challenged the common view of slavery as a debilitating institution, responsible for splitting families or breeding slaves for the market. On the contrary, the fact that a social structure developed in spite of slavery could be considered a measure of black achievement. The black family that developed during slavery was a strong and enduring institution in a stable nuclear form and with a Victorian morality (Fogel & Engerman, 1974). Researchers have shown that black family life was vital during slavery, pointing out that the single-parent black household is primarily a phenomenon of recent decades and not a holdover from slave days (Gutman, 1976).

Because they have been until recently the largest minority group, African Americans represent the greatest threat to the majority in competing for jobs. This was especially true in the past, when restrictions on immigration left blacks as the only source of cheap labor and had them competing with a large pool of unskilled white workers. Size, of course, is also a powerful political tool; after barriers to voting were removed, African Americans took advantage of their strength, as witnessed by the increasing numbers who hold elected office around the country.

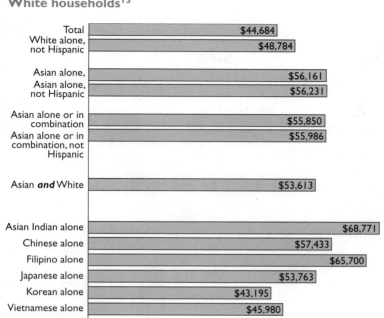

The median income of Asian households exceeded that of non-Hispanic White households[13]

Total	$44,684
White alone, not Hispanic	$48,784
Asian alone,	$56,161
Asian alone, not Hispanic	$56,231
Asian alone or in combination	$55,850
Asian alone or in combination, not Hispanic	$55,986
Asian *and* White	$53,613
Asian Indian alone	$68,771
Chinese alone	$57,433
Filipino alone	$65,700
Japanese alone	$53,763
Korean alone	$43,195
Vietnamese alone	$45,980

FIGURE 8.3   Median Household Income of Asian households: 2004 (Household income in the past 12 months in 2004 inflation-adjusted dollars. Housing units are classified by the race and Hispanic origin of the householder. Data based on sample limited to the household population and exclude the population living in institutions, college dormitories, and other group quarters. For information on confidentiality protection, sampling error, nonsampling error, and definitions. see **http://factfinder.census.gov/home/en/datanotes/exp_acs2004.html**)
Source: U.S. Census Bureau, *2004 American Community Survey,* Selected Population Profiles, S0201.
[13] Data reflect the median income of households in the 12 months prior to being surveyed. Income is expressed in 2004 inflation-adjusted dollars. It is based on the distribution of the total number of households and includes those with no income. Households are classified by the race and Hispanic origin of the householder.

Even though the deep prejudice and open discrimination against blacks made their upward mobility and integration into the society difficult, the principal obstacle seems to have been economic in nature. Until World War II, the great majority of African Americans lived in the rural South, a region that until recently suffered from backwardness and poverty. Education, housing, and health care were substandard in the rural South for both blacks and whites, because the Southern states could not tax their citizens sufficiently to support these services.

The advent of World War II brought a need for workers in the defense industries, which were located chiefly in the urban North. Trainloads of poor African Americans began leaving the South in search of the better pay that industrial work offered. However, these African Americans had been subsistence farmers or farm laborers. They lacked education and technical

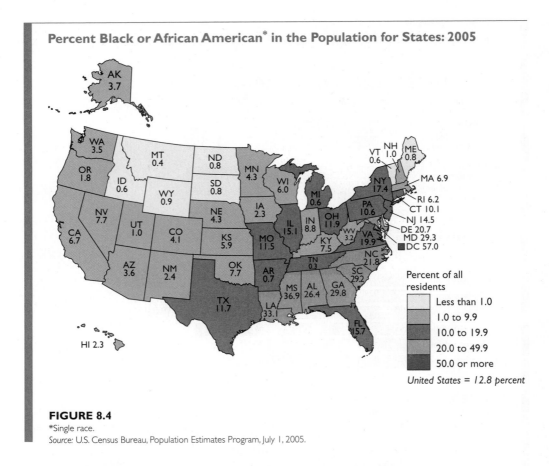

Percent Black or African American* in the Population for States: 2005

Percent of all residents

	Less than 1.0
	1.0 to 9.9
	10.0 to 19.9
	20.0 to 49.9
	50.0 or more

United States = 12.8 percent

FIGURE 8.4
*Single race.
Source: U.S. Census Bureau, Population Estimates Program, July 1, 2005.

skills and were not acquainted with the nature of urban life. According to Stark (1985), these traits made them comparable to immigrants from foreign cultures. From this perspective, they compare quite favorably with other ethnic and racial minorities, who improved their economic situation and thus began their entry into mainstream society in about two or three generations. Unfortunately, beginning with the 1970s, industrial and manufacturing jobs that had been an avenue of upward mobility for many previous generations of immigrants began to dry up in American cities, leaving a proportion of African Americans subject to unemployment and underemployment (Sowell, 1983).

In spite of this, conditions continued to improve for African Americans in the following years. First of all, while in the 1940s whites had favored the separation of the two races, by the mid-1990s a majority declared that blacks were their neighbors and that they had close friends among them. Blacks had begun to make substantial progress even before the civil rights movement and affirmative action were put into effect. By the mid-1990s, 40 percent of African Americans were squarely in the middle class (today, the tiny minority that had existed mainly within the boundaries of the black community has grown much larger); a third lived in suburbs, and a high proportion (59 percent of women and 32 percent of men) were in middle-class occupations. The past several decades have seen sharp increases in the

African Americans have made great strides in the past several decades, as evidenced by the popularity of presidential candidate Barack Obama.

number of black lawyers, doctors, and engineers, and the earnings of black government workers, pharmacists, mathematicians, designers, and engineers approximate, and on occasion surpass, those of their white counterparts. In fact, 26 percent of blacks age 16 and older work in management, professional, and related occupations.

Among other changes that occurred in the decade of the 1990s, the number of black office holders increased from 1,469 in 1970 to 8,406 in 1995; of the 435 representatives in the House, 39 are African American men and women; and black mayors were elected in a vast number of American cities. College attendance, which is closely related to economic achievement, increased from only 7.2 percent in 1960 to 37.5 percent by 1995 (however completion of four or more years of college in 1998 stood at 14.7 percent for African Americans, compared to 24.4 for the entire country). By 2005, 80 percent of African Americans aged 25 to 29 had a high school diploma; 17 percent had a bachelor's degree, and 1.1 million had an advanced degree (**www.infoplease.com/spot/bhmcensus.html**).

The income gap between whites and blacks has similarly narrowed; nonetheless, inequalities are still obvious. In 2002, ethnic and racial categories were redefined by the Census Bureau, allowing members to choose their own ethnic or racial makeup, so a single comparison of income and poverty is difficult to make. The annual median income of households that reported only black or black in combination with one or more other races in 2005 was $34,725, while the real median household income nationally was $46,242. The poverty rate was 24.3 percent and 24.1 percent, in contrast to the official national poverty rate of 13.5 percent. At the same time, as noted earlier, 26 percent of black men and 13.3 percent of black women worked in technical, sales, and administrative support jobs and managerial and professional specialty jobs. There were approximately 44,000 employed black physicians, 91,000 engineers, and 45,200 lawyers. Finally, 45.8 percent of all blacks owned their own homes (66.9 percent of whites did).

Another indication of the lessening of differences between the races is the dramatic change in the social and political attitudes about race. A survey by the Pew Research Center released in the fall of 2003 found that Americans of both races have become much more personally tolerant. For instance, the idea of blacks and whites dating is now widely accepted: in 1980, only half of the American public agreed that it was all right for blacks and whites to date each other; in 2003, 77 percent agreed. As for interracial marriage, 22 percent of all American adults state that they have a close relative who is married to someone of a different race. This is in contrast to 1970 when fewer than 1 percent of all married couples consisted of spouses of different races (Pew Research Center, 2005).

Another survey by the Gallup Organization showed similar conclusions. Most progress has been achieved in interracial relationships and the neighborhoods in which both races reside: 70 percent of whites, 80 percent of blacks, and 77 percent of Hispanics say they generally approve of interracial marriage. Compared to the 4 percent of whites who approved of such marriages in 1958, that represents gigantic progress. However, there are vast gulfs between the different races' perceptions of how minorities are treated. While only 38 percent of blacks agree that they are treated "very fairly" or "somewhat fairly" (and one-third say that members of their race are treated "very unfairly"), 76 percent of white respondents believe that they are treated fairly. Generational differences show up in this survey as well, although in a different light: young Americans (ages 18–29) are more likely than older respondents, especially the 65-plus segment, to favor the retention of distinctive cultures. Harvard sociologist William Julius Wilson suggests that such an attitude is a positive thing: it shows an acceptance of multiculturalism, an idea young people have acquired in school (Goodheart, 2004, 37–41, 75).

The year 2004 marked the fiftieth anniversary of *Brown v. Board of Education*, the Supreme Court ruling stating that segregated schools are unconstitutional. This was one of the most important decisions of the twentieth century and the origin of the entire civil rights movement. Unfortunately, integrated schools have not been the successes their supporters envisioned. Forced integration following the ruling began a movement of whites out of city neighborhoods into suburban areas and pushed many white students into private schools. Affirmative action, attempting to attain "diversity," has been quite successful in integrating higher education. Busing small children to public elementary and high schools, however, proved unsatisfactory to both whites and African Americans, and many cities began to ask the courts to overturn the Supreme Court decision. As the schools gave up the attempt to integrate, many schools became segregated again. Today, approximately 70 percent of black students attend schools in which racial minorities are a majority, and a third are in schools that are 90 to 100 percent minority. The ironic thing is that, in many instances, black families sue school districts that insist on keeping an integrated student body. For these families, the benefits of integration are not worth the burdens it imposes on them. (Further discussion of the impact of education on African Americans is in Chapter 13.)

While there is agreement that African Americans have progressed a great deal in attaining a status nearly equal to others in mainstream society, academic and demographic sources provide evidence for the existence of two African American communities. One is made up of middle-class and affluent blacks who have flourished as a result of the increased opportunities that came with the civil rights movement. The other consists of poor, mainly urban blacks, who remain socially and economically isolated from the American mainstream.

Hispanic Americans

The more than 42.7 million Hispanic Americans represent about 14.5 percent of the U.S. population and are growing five times faster as a group than the rest of the American population (Figure 8.5 and Table 8.3) (U.S. Bureau of the Census, 2005). Hispanics overlap the

Box 8.3   African American Males: An Endangered Species?

A number of new scholarly studies have issued pessimistic warnings about the future of African American males. In fact, despite the fact that African American women and other minorities are making strides into the middle class, the approximately five million African American males ages 20 to 39 who reside in our inner cities face a dire situation. They are said to feel disconnected from the mainstream society to a much greater degree than males of other racial or ethnic groups.

Focusing on this group, several researchers from top-notch universities have obtained truly alarming findings. They report that most males fail to finish high school, that they cannot get legitimate work, and that incarceration rates and prison life are endemic to this group. A summary of their most important findings includes the following:

1. More than half of all black men who live in inner cities fail to finish high school.
2. Incarceration rates have been steadily climbing for this group of men. While in 1995, 16 percent of black males in their twenties who did not attend school were in prison or jail, by 2004, 24 percent were incarcerated. Six of every 10 black men who had dropped out of high school had spent time in prison by their middle thirties.
3. The jobless rate of black male high school dropouts in their twenties is very high: it was 65 percent in 2000 and rose to 72 percent by 2004. This in comparison with 34 percent of white and 19 percent of Hispanic dropouts (Holzer, Edelman, and Offner, 2006).

The reasons for such a dire situation are numerous. Above all, the American economy has changed so that good-paying blue-collar and manufacturing jobs that had been available to men with high school diplomas or less are no longer available, or they pay minimum wage. Higher-paying jobs now require more education and more sophisticated skills. Moreover, many industries have left central cities and older suburbs, where most blacks still reside. Finally, being stuck in low-wage service jobs is not an appealing prospect for these young men.

Unfortunately, a majority of men respond to these hardships irresponsibly or self-destructively. Having no hope of obtaining good jobs after high school, they neglect school altogether, preferring to hang out on the street, where they are soon tempted to use and sell drugs. They derive self-respect by having many girlfriends, which often produces out-of-wedlock children whom they are unable to support.

Such behavior further limits their opportunities. Drug sales result in prison sentences, and criminal records prevent them from obtaining or keeping legitimate jobs, so that soon they find themselves behind bars again. And their fatherless children are almost always forced into similarly bleak lifestyles.

The authors of one such study recommend effective education and training programs to begin with prekindergarten. Adolescents and teens, in addition, should be given special intervention by means of mentoring programs, career-oriented education, employment in high school, and programs showing them that postsecondary education is available and possible. In addition, there is a need for raising the federal minimum wage and for establishing community backed services. Prisons should also attempt to offer programs to prepare the young men for life after prison.

Of course, such programs will be expensive. They will require an administration sympathetic to those who are left out of the mainstream. They will require people of good will to volunteer their services. The alternative, however, is a permanent class of outsiders that a wealthy society such as ours ought not allow to exist.

categories of racial and ethnic minorities inasmuch as some Hispanics are black, others are South American Indians, and still others are white. (Incidentally, Hispanic is a name used by U.S. agencies for bureaucratic convenience. Some Spanish-speaking individuals prefer to be called Latinos because the name refers to an indigenous culture, that of Latin America, rather than depending solely on the culture of Spain.) They have overtaken African Americans as this country's largest minority group. The majority of Hispanics live in New Mexico, California, and Texas. Other states containing Hispanic populations of one million or more are New York, Florida, Illinois, Arizona, and New Jersey.

Latino neighborhoods, even though statistically poor, seem to be thriving, with lots of small stores, markets, and motels, while poor neighborhoods in many central cities are

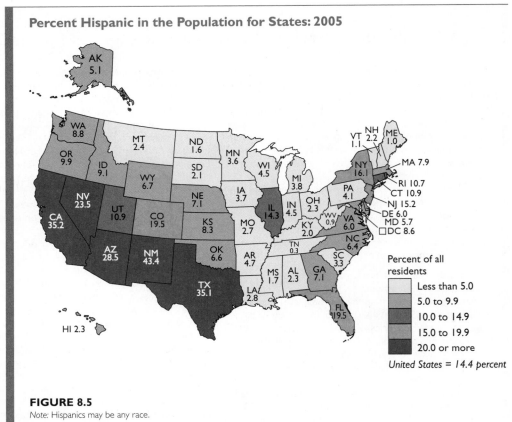

Percent Hispanic in the Population for States: 2005

Percent of all residents

- Less than 5.0
- 5.0 to 9.9
- 10.0 to 14.9
- 15.0 to 19.9
- 20.0 or more

United States = 14.4 percent

FIGURE 8.5
Note: Hispanics may be any race.
Source: U.S. Census Bureau, Population Estimates Program, July 1, 2005.

visibly declining. The reason is that Latinos have kept their communities intact, shopping at Latino stores, consulting Latino doctors, reading Latino newspapers, listening to Latino radio, and watching Latino TV stations. This strong sense of community will serve Latinos well in their quest for political representation and other rights in the face of hostility from other groups with whom they share their living space.

Latinos do not constitute a unified community, however, nor do they possess a common culture. This group is fragmented because members came at different times and from different places. In fact, Latinos range over a wide racial spectrum, as well, because they are the descendants of the original Spanish settlers of the New World and native populations of Central and South America, as well as the Caribbean. They are, however, bound together by their common Spanish language, by their Spanish surnames, and by their Roman Catholic religion. The three major subdivisions are Mexican Americans or Chicanos (approximately 26.7 million), Puerto Ricans (3.7 million), and Cubans (1.4 million). Other Spanish-speaking groups include natives of South American countries (Figure 8.6).

About 24 percent of Hispanics work in service occupations and 18 percent in managerial and professional occupations. The real median household income of Hispanics in 2005 was $35,967, and the poverty rate was 21.8 percent that same year. As for education, 58 percent of those 25 years old and over had at least a high school diploma, 12 percent in the

TABLE 8.3 Projected Population of the United States, by Race and Hispanic Origin: 2000 to 2050
(In thousands except as indicated. As of July 1. Resident population.)

Population or percent and race or Hispanic origin	2000	2010	2020	2030	2040	2050
Population						
Total	282,125	308,936	335,805	363,584	391,946	419,854
White alone	228,548	244,995	260,629	275,731	289,690	302,626
Black alone	35,818	40,454	45,365	50,442	55,876	61,361
Asian Alone	10,684	14,241	17,988	22,580	27,992	33,430
All other races[1]	7,075	9,246	11,822	14,831	18,388	22,437
Hispanic (of any race)	35,622	47,756	59,756	73,055	87,585	102,560
White alone, not Hispanic	195,729	201,112	205,936	209,176	210,331	210,283
Percent of Total Population						
Total	100.0	100.0	100.0	100.0	100.0	100.0
White alone	81.0	79.3	77.6	75.8	73.9	72.1
Black alone	12.7	13.1	13.5	13.9	14.3	14.6
Asian Alone	3.8	4.6	5.4	6.2	7.1	8.0
All other races[1]	2.5	3.0	3.5	4.1	4.7	5.3
Hispanic (of any race)	12.6	15.5	17.8	20.1	22.3	24.4
White alone, not Hispanic	69.4	65.1	61.3	57.5	53.7	50.1

[1]Includes American Indian and Alaska Native alone, Native Hawaiian, and Other Pacific Islander alone, and Two or More races.

Source: U.S. Census Bureau, 2004, "U.S. Interim Projections by Age, Sex, Race, and Hispanic Origin," **http://www.census.gov/ipc/www/usinterimproj/.** Internet release date: March 18, 2004.

same age group had a bachelor's degree, and about 714,000 persons 18 and over had an advanced degree in 2004. About 46 percent of Hispanics own their own home. Mexican Americans tend to have the largest families, and Cubans have the smallest.

Many Mexican Americans are actually native to the United States, having occupied the Southwest before the American colonization and annexation of Mexican land occurred. Others have continued to enter across the Mexican border in search of better jobs. Although the opportunities may be better for them in the United States than in Mexico, Mexicans have not been as upwardly mobile as some other immigrant groups. They are highly urbanized and are generally employed in low-wage service or manufacturing jobs in which employers are attempting to keep labor costs down and unions out. In southern California, they make up almost half the population when all the illegals are counted in. By the year 2050, it is estimated that Latinos will constitute 24 percent of the nation's total population.

Although Puerto Rico has had the status of an "associated free state" of the United States since 1898, when the territory was ceded to the United States by Spain, Puerto Ricans did not begin to arrive in large numbers until the 1950s. (Puerto Rico became a Commonwealth in 1952.) Today, almost 4 million Puerto Ricans reside in the United States, concentrated mainly in the cities of the eastern seaboard, particularly New York, and in the large cities of the Midwest.

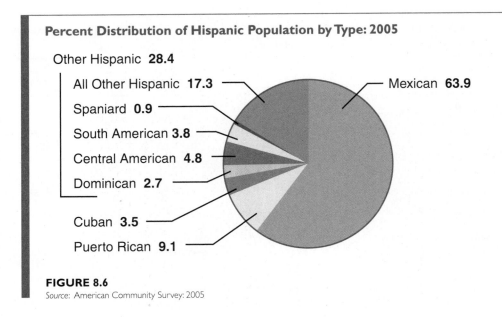

Percent Distribution of Hispanic Population by Type: 2005

Other Hispanic **28.4**

All Other Hispanic **17.3**

Spaniard **0.9**

South American **3.8**

Central American **4.8**

Dominican **2.7**

Cuban **3.5**

Puerto Rican **9.1**

Mexican **63.9**

FIGURE 8.6
Source: American Community Survey: 2005

As a group, Puerto Ricans are culturally and racially distinct from Mexicans, being a blend of predominantly black and Spanish cultures. Puerto Ricans are economically one of the most disadvantaged ethnic groups in the United States, with a median family income half the national average and a high percentage (23 percent) living in poverty. On every health indicator, Puerto Ricans fare worse than either Mexican Americans or Cubans; infant

The *Quinceañera*, a celebration of a girl's fifteenth birthday, is an important tradition among the Latino population.

Latinos are becoming increasingly politically active, as evidenced by the election of Antonio Villairaigosa as mayor of a major American city, Los Angeles.

mortality is 50 percent higher than among Mexican Americans and nearly three times that of Cubans. Moreover, the secondary effects of poverty—family breakups, single parenthood, apathy, unemployment—afflict Puerto Ricans to a greater degree than they do other Hispanics. Attempts are under way to channel the energy of the new generation into political activism to improve the group's welfare in this country. Currently, there are three members of Congress of Puerto Rican extraction.

Most Cubans came to the United States following Fidel Castro's rise to power. They differ substantially from other Spanish-speaking groups; overall they are much older and better educated. The reason is that the first wave to enter this country consisted of professionals running away from the communist regime in Cuba. They were able to use their skills, experience, and expertise in the economy almost immediately following their arrival. Their success is reflected in their income, which is higher than that of other Spanish-speaking groups. A later wave of immigrants, who arrived in 1980, do not appear to be equally skilled.

Most Cubans are concentrated in Miami, Florida (whose metropolitan population of nearly 5 million is approximately 60 percent Hispanic), where their financial success and high numbers have given them political clout sufficient to elect a number of Cuban-born officials. Unfortunately, this polyethnic city, rather than a model for a pluralistic society, is one of the country's most divided cities in terms of the endless complexities of racial and immigrant politics.

■ Ethnic and Religious Minorities

Looking a generation or two into the past, a majority of American families can find an ancestor who was born "in the old country." Therefore, the ethnic experience is familiar to a great number of Americans.

When one refers to "ethnics," the understanding is that one is speaking of the descendants of the waves of immigrants from southern and eastern Europe who arrived in the early years of the century. A number of sociological research projects have attempted to probe the depth of

Box 8.4 **Immigration and Its Discontents**

America is a land of immigrants—even its original inhabitants, the Native Americans that the English settlers encountered, had come from elsewhere thousands of years before. Nonetheless, the issue of immigration has never been resolved to the satisfaction of all Americans. Should our borders be open to all, at all times? Should only some people be allowed entry, at only some times? Should numbers be restricted by countries of origin? All of these questions have been asked and answered at different times in our history.

Today, immigration remains a divisive issue that the government is attempting to resolve. Because such a large number of people are trying to come here, a segment of the population believes that they take away jobs that should go to Americans. In addition, the complaint is that those who come in illegally are still benefiting from health care and schooling, paid for by tax dollars that American citizens must pay. On the other hand, to deny entry entirely seems unethical, since we have all been immigrants at one time or another.

The issue is essentially an economic one, but economists disagree about the effect of immigration. Some economists maintain that because the largest contingent of immigrants is poorly educated Mexicans, they tend to hurt the poorest Americans who depend on manual labor. This idea—that job seekers from abroad mean fewer opportunities and lower wages for native workers—is controversial in labor economics. The reason is that although the premise seems logical, there is another way of looking at it. In fact, supply-side economists maintain that a greater number of immigrants also increases the demand for goods and services, thus adding jobs and profits to the national economy.

Immigration policy, however, has never been based on economics, but more often had a racist or ethnocentric basis. The exclusionary acts directed at Chinese immigrants in the nineteenth and early twentieth centuries, as well as at immigrants from eastern and southern Europe, had some economic basis, but mostly they were a result of Americans' dislike for people who were different from them in culture or appearance.

In 1965, with the Immigration and Nationality Act, quotas were ended and substituted with a priority based on family reunification: that is, a person could enter this country if a relative was already here. Today, the proportion of foreign born is 12 percent of the population, and a large number enter the country illegally. It is the latter problem that makes it imperative to arrive at a logical and fair immigration policy, and therein lies the difficulty. Two bills are pending in Congress: the House bill would require employers to employ only legal workers and levy heavy penalties if they employed illegals. It also expects the government to build hundreds of miles of fencing on the U.S. southern border. The Senate bill would allow illegals who are already here to remain and provide them with the ability to attain legal status. It would also allow employers to bring in guest workers as long as they pay them as they would native workers. It remains to be seen what an immigration policy will ultimately look like.

Economists also believe that the country would be well served if we let in more immigrants with advanced degrees because we are already very dependent on foreigners to fill occupations in such areas as scientific research and nursing. These high earners would actually raise the national income. But they also maintain that unskilled immigrants do not take away jobs from unskilled Americans; the latter will not take jobs such as hotel chambermaids or lettuce pickers. Nonetheless, Americans who are unskilled do have to compete with unskilled immigrants. And this brings us to the ultimate problem: how to increase the skills and cognition of our youth so that they will not need to compete with unskilled immigrants. (An in-depth view of some of the issues discussed may be found in Roger Lowenstein, "The Immigration Equation," *The New York Times Magazine*, July 9, 2006, 36–71.)

Another way of looking at immigration is in how it affects the countries from which the immigrants originate. For instance, the largest number of immigrants to the United States come from Mexico. It is to our advantage that our neighbors to the south live comfortably and not in dire poverty, for it is the latter condition that sends them north in droves. According to one reporter, such immigration has left many Mexican towns almost empty, particularly of young men. However, California-style homes are going up in these communities, built by the money the immigrants send home and awaiting their eventual return. In the meantime, remittances to Mexico exceed $20 billion a year, and in 2003, they had become the country's second largest source of income, ahead of tourism and foreign investment.

While the money that enters Mexico from the paychecks of immigrants is a boon to the country and to its impoverished residents, it also creates problems. First, as most young men leave, the towns are populated by women and children, a condition that is not beneficial to the family unit. Second, this money reduces the incentive to work to the locals left behind and fuels inflation, making it harder for those who have no relatives in the United States to survive in dignity. Finally, although the men leave with the intention of returning, most do not. The crackdown on illegal immigration makes visits to Mexico and back dangerous, and the fewer the visits, the more familial ties weaken. In short, although the flow of labor across borders appears to benefit both economies, it is not without a more somber side (Quirk, 2007, 26).

feeling such ethnics have retained for their ancestors' countries of origin. The consensus is that, in the battle of the culture of the old country and the lifestyle of the new, the new has won hands down. A random sampling of ethnics found that only 2 percent of them ever had help in business from others who shared their ethnicity, only 4 percent experienced discrimination on the basis of their ethnic background, only 1 percent ate ethnic food on a daily basis, almost none were fluent in the language of their ancestors, only 2 percent belonged to ethnic lodges or social clubs, and only 11 percent lived in neighborhoods that had a significant concentration of similar ethnics. The great majority had intermarried, rarely participated in cultural events pertaining to their ethnic group, and considered themselves in actual behavior to be fully American (Alba, 1990). The conclusion reached by this researcher is that ethnicity is more of a symbol than a real identity for most Americans. In addition, whereas earlier ethnicity had an exclusive quality—you were either Jewish or Irish Catholic—today it is inclusive—you can be European-American regardless of where exactly you came from. The fundamental change here is that white Americans think of themselves in terms of sameness rather than difference, of universal rather than particular origins.

The United States continues to be a nation of immigrants. The Census Bureau estimates that better than 1 million immigrants have been granted legal permanent resident status since 2001, in addition to uncounted millions of illegal immigrants. In fact, immigration has been a chief instrument of growth for states that otherwise would have lost population—such as New York—or whose population growth would have been much smaller—such as California, or even Indiana. Many experts believe that the next decades will bring an equal or greater stream of immigrants, leading to a still different picture of American society.

White Ethnics: Catholics

Of the three factors affecting minority status, religion has been the least destructive in this society. The United States, founded as it was primarily by English and other western European settlers, remained a relatively homogeneous Protestant society until around 1820, when new waves of immigrants from Europe arrived. Even then, because most of the immigrants were also Protestants, they were fairly well absorbed into the WASP majority. Between 1860 and 1920, however, immigrants hailed from central, eastern, and southern Europe and differed not only in language but also in religion (see Figure 8.7).

The descendants of these immigrants have, since the 1970s, been dubbed as the "white ethnics." White ethnics, who prize both their American citizenship and their ethnic origins, are predominantly Catholics and represent about 25 percent of the American population. The Protestant majority viewed Catholics with great suspicion until a few decades ago, attributing their loyalty to the Pope as a form of betrayal of the democratic ideology. Nonetheless, individual Catholics and Catholic families have fared well, as exemplified by the election of a Catholic president, John F. Kennedy, in 1960.

A stratification hierarchy is visible among Catholics, with the Irish and other northern Europeans at the top, the eastern Europeans in the middle, and the Hispanic groups at the bottom. However, these internal divisions have been much lessened as the anti-Catholic feelings in the society have been reduced. Similarly, the differences between Catholics and Protestants in family size, income, education, and occupation are gradually disappearing. The current generation of Catholics are the most educated and prosperous in the history of the Church in the United States. The Church has also been absorbing large waves of non-European immigrants (Davidson, 2004).

At one time, white ethnics were distinguished by living in cultural enclaves (Little Italy, Slavic Village, etc.), in which it was easier to retain a native tongue and customs. Later

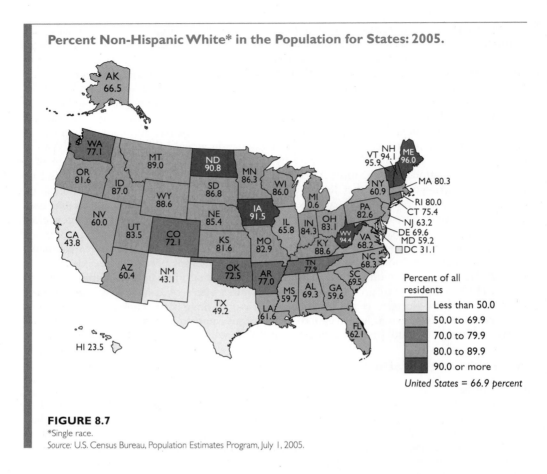

Percent Non-Hispanic White* in the Population for States: 2005.

Percent of all residents

Less than 50.0
50.0 to 69.9
70.0 to 79.9
80.0 to 89.9
90.0 or more

United States = 66.9 percent

FIGURE 8.7

*Single race.

Source: U.S. Census Bureau, Population Estimates Program, July 1, 2005.

generations have become dispersed in the suburbs, and with dispersion came a loss of ethnic traditions. Religion, however, tends to remain. As a result, Catholicism provides a means of attaining identity and of forming primary group relationships.

Jewish Americans

Jewish Americans—of whom there are some 5.3 million in the United States—are ethnic in the sense that they share cultural traits and religious beliefs that are distinct from the mainstream Christian society. However, although they may be affiliated with the Orthodox, Conservative, or Reform branch of Judaism, only 46 percent of American Jewish adults belong to a synagogue. Many adult Jews are not very active in religious affairs: Judaism represents mainly a source of identification for them.

The Jewish people are a classic example of a minority persecuted throughout the ages and throughout the world. In the United States, prejudice and discrimination against Jews were rampant in the first half of the twentieth century, as they were denied access to particular neighborhoods, schools, and social clubs. However, anti-Semitism never acquired the virulent proportions in the United States that it did in some other countries. In Germany, during

World War II, the destruction of the Jewish minority became a government priority, and by the end of the war 6 million Jews had been killed in Europe, an example of genocide that, it is hoped, will never be repeated.

In general, Jews have been very successful in the educational and economic spheres, being highly represented among college graduates (55 percent of adult Jewish Americans have a bachelors' degree, and 25 percent have a graduate degree). Many have attained high-earning positions—60 percent of all employed Jews are in one of the three highest status job categories: professional/technical, management, and executive. As a result of their high education levels and high-status jobs, their household income is also high. About 34 percent of Jewish households report incomes of over $75,000 (compared to 17 percent of all U.S. households), 24 percent have an income under $25,000, while the 2005 median household income is $46,242. Only 5 percent of Jewish households (and 9 percent of Jews 65 years old and over) report incomes that fall below the federal poverty line (**http://www.ujc.org**). Their economic success has made them targets of some Americans whose envy has blinded them to the true reason for Jewish success and who allow unscrupulous public figures to mislead them with ancient and spurious conspiracy theories. As a result, 68.5 percent of hate crimes were committed against Jews in 2005 (World Net Daily, 2006).

Intermarriage rates among Jews are quite high, a fact that worries many leaders inasmuch as it portends the end of ethnic solidarity. As late as 1965, 89 percent of Jews married other Jews, but since 1996, 54 percent of Jews who married have intermarried, and two-thirds of the children of all intermarried parents are not being raised Jewish. The current intermarriage rate stands at between 52 and 43 percent, depending on how intermarriage is measured. There remains strong opposition to out-marriage among Jewish people, and Orthodox and many Conservative congregations do not reach out to intermarried families, thus losing them. Moreover, because the children seldom grow up Jewish in a mixed marriage, the number of Jewish Americans is subject to attrition. It is probably because of

A Jewish wedding with the marrying couple standing under a rather contemporary *huppa*, a covering symbolizing the establishment of a new home.

the high rates of intermarriage, coupled with a fairly low birth rate, that the Jewish population in America has declined from nearly 4 percent following World War II to 1.8 percent today. Some commentators maintain that a kind of "reverse ethnic assimilation" is taking place, with a number of Yiddish expressions having entered everyday speech. As anti-Semitism becomes less sharp, group cohesion also tends to disappear. Nonetheless, as a reaction to the perceived loss of Jewish traditions and ethnic loyalty, a trend toward the Orthodox lifestyle is also being observed (Safire, 1995, A11).

■ The New Face of America

The makeup of the U.S. population is destined to change dramatically in the years ahead. Although the initial waves of immigrants stopped after the first two decades of this century, immigration resumed in 1965, and the more liberalized immigration laws, combined with favorable economic and political factors, have pushed immigration up (approximately 400,000 new immigrants have entered the country every year since 1986, not including illegal aliens, whose number is estimated at more than 7 million, and perhaps as many as 11 million). Moreover, the ethnic composition of the immigrants differs from that of earlier waves: only a small percentage are of European ancestry, while the majority are Mexican and Latin Americans, and almost half originate in various parts of Asia. As a consequence, demographers predict that by the year 2050, the white population will be about 72.1 percent of the total population of about 419,854 million. Blacks will make up about 14.6 percent, with about 61,361 million; Hispanics about 24.4 percent, with 102,560 million, and Asians about 8 percent with 33,430 million (U.S. Bureau of the Census, Population Projections Program, 2004).

With the passing of time, each generation has become more racially and ethnically mixed than the preceding one. This is one reason that the Census Bureau had to add such categories as "Race alone or in combination with one or more other races." A study by the Population Research Center, therefore, projects that the black intermarriage rate will increase so dramatically that by the year 2100, 37 percent of African Americans will claim mixed ancestry, more than 40 percent of Asian Americans will be similarly mixed, and the number of Latinos who will claim mixed ancestry will be more than twice the number claiming a single race or ethnicity (Rodriguez, 2003, 95). America, then, will have a new face.

The Chapter in Brief

Conflict seems to be an integral part of group life, especially when it involves a number of groups of dissimilar culture or appearance sharing the same territory. In such a situation, a majority–minorities relationship develops, in which minorities are denied equal access to the rewards of society. The status of minority is usually applied to groups that differ from the dominant group in appearance and/or culture, and sometimes also in religion, gender, age, and in being afflicted with disabilities.

The United States has minorities in its midst based on all these factors. Racial minorities have been the victims of the now discounted ideology of racism as well as of prejudice and discrimination. Racism is based on a faulty conception of the term *race*, whereby the cultural traits and the behavior of a group are thought to be genetically inherited. Actually, scientists used the word *race* to make very broad distinctions among populations that have inbred and interbred, and they no longer use the term.

In contrast to race, ethnicity refers to a group's distinctive social factors such as language, religion, values, beliefs, and food habits. Ethnic groups are subcultures within the larger society. Such groups are maintained by common national origin or history, by a strong in-group feeling, and by the belief in a shared destiny.

Most minorities have been subject to prejudice and discrimination. Prejudice is holding unproved beliefs about a group and retaining them even in the face of facts that prove the opposite. Discrimination is acting on such beliefs by denying members of a minority equal access to the sources of wealth, power, and privilege. Of the various kinds of discrimination, the institutional type is the most difficult to eliminate. However, it appears that as the socioeconomic status of each minority approaches equality with that of the dominant group, prejudice and discrimination against that minority disappear. The only situation in which conflict between groups is exacerbated is when the minority competes for scarce jobs. Equality of status tends to lead to cooperation among groups.

Dominant groups deal with their minorities in a variety of ways. The ideologies of Anglo-conformity—becoming like the original English Protestant settlers in language, values, and beliefs—and of the melting pot—becoming amalgamated into a new breed of American—have given way to the ideal of cultural pluralism. In a truly pluralistic society, various racial, religious, and ethnic groups retain their culture but coexist in harmony with the majority and enjoy equal access to the rewards of the society.

The United States, having long been a haven for immigrants from other nations, is aspiring to become a fully pluralistic society. For the time being, while some of its minorities have been absorbed into the mainstream, others remain distinct and still subject to prejudice and discrimination. Among the latter groups are African Americans, Hispanics, and Native Americans. The racially distinct Asian Americans (Chinese, Japanese) have achieved upward social mobility through education and professionalization.

The group described as white ethnics includes the descendants of nineteenth-century immigrants. These groups were sufficiently different from the WASPs making up the dominant group that they suffered considerable discrimination. Today, many no longer live in ethnic enclaves and the younger, college-educated generation has entered the mainstream. The older generation is represented in large numbers in the lower and working classes.

Among the religious minorities, Catholics and Jews were subject to prejudice and discrimination at the turn of the twentieth century and in its first several decades. The feelings of hostility may have been directed toward their ethnic origin—eastern and southern European—as much as toward their religions. In any event, both groups have done well socioeconomically, being represented among the highest earners and in the ranks of professionals.

Terms To Remember

accommodation A situation in which a minority is conscious of the norms and values of the majority, accepts and adapts to them, but chooses to retain its own, thus failing to participate in the host culture.

acculturation The process of adopting the culture, including the language and customs, of the host country.

amalgamation The result of intermarriage between distinct racial, ethnic, and cultural groups, resulting in the erasure of differences between majority and minority groups.

anglo-conformity The attitude, once held by the majority group, that the institutions, language, and cultural patterns of England should be maintained and that WASP values be superimposed on immigrants.

assimilation A process in which a minority group is absorbed into, or becomes part of, the dominant group in a society.

attitudinal discrimination Negative behavior against a particular group—or individual members of that group—prompted by personal prejudice.

cultural pluralism An ideal condition in which the cultural distinctiveness of each ethnic, racial, and religious minority group would be maintained, while individual members would still owe allegiance to the society in general.

discrimination Actions taken as a result of prejudicial feelings.

ethnicity A group's distinctive social, rather than biological, traits.

ethnic minority A group that differs culturally from the dominant group.

ethnocentrism Belief in the superiority of one's own group.

institutional discrimination A system of inequalities existing in a society apart from individual prejudice. Prejudice exists on a societal level; in effect, it is a norm of the society.

melting pot theory The belief that it is possible and desirable to culturally and biologically fuse all the various racial and ethnic groups in society.

minority group Any group in society that is kept from attaining the rewards of society on the basis of culture, race, religion, sex, or age. A category of people who possess imperfect access to positions of equal power, prestige, and privilege in the society.

prejudice Prejudgment of an individual or group based on stereotypes and hearsay rather than on fact or evidence, and the inability or unwillingness to change that judgment even when confronted with evidence to the contrary.

race An arbitrary manner of subdividing the species *Homo sapiens sapiens* based on differences in the frequency with which some genes occur among populations.

racial minority A group within a society that differs biologically from the dominant group in such features as skin color, hair texture, eye slant, and head shape and dimensions.

racism An ideology, prevalent in the past but now discounted, that some racial groups are inferior to others, that they display not only physical but also behavioral differences, and that both are inherited and undesirable.

segregation An attempt to isolate a minority from the majority.

Suggested Readings

Huntington, Samuel P. 2004. *Who Are We?* New York: Simon & Schuster. The author, a historian, paints a bleak picture of the future of American society, whose culture will be negatively affected by massive Latino immigration and consequent bilingualism. This is not a message most of us like to hear, but in a free society all points of view deserve a hearing.

Kotkin, Joel. 1993. *Tribes: How Race, Religion, and Identity Determine Success in the New Global Economy.* New York: Random House. The author speculates that certain ethnic affiliations—Jews, Japanese, British, Chinese, and Asian Indian—promote economic success because of the values of these ethnic cultures. Interesting, though subject to criticism.

McWhorter, John. 2003. *Authentically Black: Essays for the Black Silent Majority.* New York: Gotham Books. An African American linguistics professor whose ideas run counter to many assumptions maintained by the black establishment.

Pollard, Kevin M., and William P. O'Hare. 1999. *America's Racial and Ethnic Minorities: Population Bulletin 54.* A short compendium of contemporary racial and ethnic groups offers an excellent overview. It also discusses the changing definitions of race, namely the fact that the Census Bureau allows people to select more than one race, if they are bi- or multiracial.

Schaefer, Richard T. 2000. *Racial and Ethnic Groups.* 8th ed. New York: Prentice Hall. A global look at minority–majority relations. It also discusses women's subordinate role in many societies.

Scott, Daryl Michael. 1997. *Contempt and Pity: Social Policy and the Image of the Damaged Black Psyche, 1880–1996.* Chapel Hill, NC: University of North Carolina Press. An important book that tries to answer the question, "What are African Americans like?" Deals with questions of moral equality, racial conservatism, lack of self-esteem, and so on, as these are presented by the social sciences.

Waters, Mary C. 1990. *Ethnic Options: Choosing Identities in America.* Berkeley, CA: University of California Press. Irish, Polish, and Italian Catholics speak about the nature of their ethnic identity.

Young-Bruehl, Elisabeth. 1996. *The Anatomy of Prejudices.* Cambridge, MA: Harvard University Press. Although ethnocentrism is commonly considered the cause of prejudice and bigotry, this author offers an analysis based on psychological concepts linking racism, anti-Semitism, and sexism to an "hysterical," "obsessional," and "narcissistic" character, respectively.

Web Sites of Interest

http://www.infoplease.com/spot/bhmcensusl.html
Advertising itself as "All the knowledge you need," this site allows you to ask questions to which it offers answers. In this case, it reports in-depth on the subject of "African Americans by the Numbers." The information is of course available on the Census Bureau web site, but it is easier to find here.

http://www.census.gov/press-releases.html
This Census Bureau web site presents facts about Latinos, Asians, African Americans, and all other racial groups. Check out also: Statistical Abstract of the United States and American FactFinder for additional information about minority groups.

http://www.csmonitor.com/2006
The May 16, 2006, issue of the *Christian Science Monitor* deals with the subject of the number of illegal immigrants. "Illegal Immigrants in the U.S.: How Many Are There?"

http://www.pewhispanic.org/reports/report.php?report-52
The Pew Hispanic Center is a nonpartisan research organization concerned with Hispanic issues.

http://www.crf-usa.org/immigration/issues of immigration 2006.htm
The Constitutional Rights Foundation presents a number of lessons attempting to clarify the current controversy regarding illegal immigration.

http://aad.english.ucsb.edu
This web site presents a variety of opinions on the subject of affirmative action.

http://academic.udayton.edu/race
A university web site that presents under one roof, so to speak, a wealth of documents relating to race and racism.

9

Minority Status: Age, Gender, and Sexuality

IN THIS CHAPTER, YOU WILL LEARN

- that people are also treated unequally on the basis of such ascribed characteristics as age, gender, and sexuality;

- that the United States is becoming a society with an increasing proportion of elderly people;

- of the existence and meaning of ageism;

- that women are treated unequally;

- how we acquire gender roles;

- why sexism is an ideology that is detrimental to both men and women;

- that sexual orientation is also subject to differential treatment.

Societies differentiate among their members not only according to wealth, power, and status, not only according to race, ethnicity, and religion but also according to age, gender, and sexual orientation. In every society, each age group and each gender is assigned different duties, responsibilities, privileges, and roles. Some of this differentiation is a result of common sense. In the United States, young people cannot drive before they are 16, they cannot vote before they are 18, and they cannot run for the Senate before they are 30. These age restrictions have been set by law on the basis of the belief that people are too immature to engage in these activities at younger ages. On a more informal basis, a person in his seventies would hardly be expected to work on the construction of a 30-story office building, nor has it been thought fit, throughout human history, to have women in charge of protecting societies by going to war. Women's biological role in reproduction made them too precious to be allowed to be killed in war. Similarly, prohibitions against homosexuality can also be thought of as based on a societal fear that not enough new members will be produced if sex is not strictly heterosexual. In other words, to a certain degree, age, gender, and sexuality differentiation is based on what works best for individuals and society. Still, differentiation and the consequent stratification always imply inequality, and it is this factor that this chapter examines.

 # The Aging Society

The elderly—people aged 65 and older—constituted about 12.3 percent of the American population in the year 2003. This figure—35.9 million—is expected to rise to 72 million by 2030, when one in five people will be age 65 or older. The "old old" segment of the population—people 85 years and over—is growing at an even faster rate. In 2003, they accounted for 4.7 percent of all Americans, but projections show this percentage increasing rapidly by 2030 when the baby boomers begin to move into this age group. The Census Bureau projects that this population could grow to nearly 21 million by 2050 (Figure 9.1). Finally, in 2003 there were about 50,000 persons age 100 or older, and their number is also projected to grow quickly, provided that the dramatic gains in longevity continue. The problems of the elderly, then, are everyone's concern. On the other hand, because of advances in medicine, health care, and nutrition, the elderly are really becoming "younger" in the sense not only that they can expect to live much longer than previous generations but also that they can do so in reasonably good health.

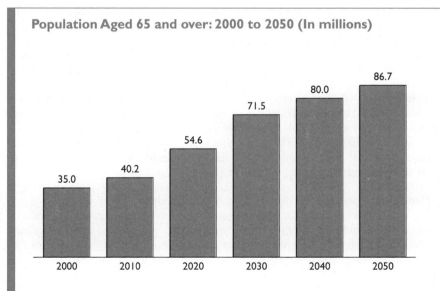

Population Aged 65 and over: 2000 to 2050 (In millions)

FIGURE 9.1

Note: The reference population for these data is the resident population.

Sources: 2000, U.S. Census Bureau, 2001, Table PCT 12; 2010 to 2050, U.S. Census Bureau, 2004.

Age is an ascribed characteristic according to which we are assigned a status. Unlike gender, however, which is a permanent status, age is transitional: we are constantly getting older, thus our chronological age and the consequent statuses change. At each stage of the transition, we must be socialized to age-appropriate behavior, and our relationship relative to the dimensions of stratification (how we fit into the stratification system) continually shifts.

We view aging and the elderly as problematic because our society is unable or unwilling to provide some of its members with satisfactory roles at certain ages. The reason is that industrial and postindustrial societies have tended to devalue the roles of the elderly, whereas the agrarian and other preindustrial societies assign honorable and prestigious roles to them. (Not all of them, however. The Tiwi of North Australia used to treat their old quite brutally, going so far as to bury alive—with only their heads uncovered—old women who could not care for themselves and leaving them to starve to death.)

Theoretical Framework

Social gerontologists—scientists who study the aging process as it affects the individual and society—examine aging from the perspective of a number of theoretical frameworks. Among the best known, **disengagement theory** posits that there is a reciprocal process of withdrawal occurring between an aging individual and society. An elderly person willingly withdraws from society because of awareness of his or her diminished capacities and impending death. And society withdraws from the aging person to allow a younger person to occupy his or her former statuses. The society's stability is thus maintained, and social roles are passed peacefully from one generation to the next. **Modernization theory** assumes that the status of older people declines as the society of which they are a part becomes more modern. Industrial and postindustrial societies like the United States stress youth and the importance of highly skilled occupations for which the elderly are not prepared. Hence, the elderly lose status.

Activity theory, the direct opposite of disengagement theory, maintains that the elderly person who remains active, replacing old roles with new ones that also require interaction with others, is best adjusted and most ready to accept the physical changes that lead eventually to death.

Disagreeing with both disengagement and activity theories, the **conflict perspective** focuses on the disadvantaged elderly and stresses political and economic factors that impinge on them and force them into a condition of dependence. An extension of the conflict view is **exchange theory**, in which the elderly are seen as being in a subservient position in American society. They lack the social and material resources that would make them valuable to others; therefore, they lose status (Dowd, 1980a, 1980b).

A Growing Minority.   Social scientists also look at the elderly as a minority group because they have unequal access to the rewards of society and experience prejudice and discrimination. Moreover, a definite ideology directed against them, ageism, is easily discerned in the society. Specialists in gerontology use all these elements to examine the conditions of the elderly in society.

Ageism

The ideology of **ageism**, whose existence can be readily picked up in even casual conversation, asserts, essentially, that the young are superior to the old. It provides the justification for prejudice and discrimination against the elderly in economic, political, and social areas.

One need not go far to uncover evidence of prejudice and discrimination against the elderly in society. First, the elderly are highly visible: they are wrinkled, their hair is white or they are bald, and many walk haltingly with canes or stooped over. Like most minorities, they are stereotyped: as senile, unproductive, poor, lonely, living in nursing homes and institutions, having no interest in or capacity for sex, being set in their ways and unable to change, and feeling miserable (Palmore, 1977). Although these stereotypes have some basis in fact, they can be proved to be mostly false.

Health.   *Senescence*, or the process of growing old, consists of *primary aging*, a biological process that starts early in life and affects all body systems, and *secondary aging*, which results not from natural aging alone but from disease, abuse, and/or disuse (Horn & Meer, 1987, 81). Primary aging affects all persons, and speed, strength, endurance, perception, and sensation eventually decline. However, these difficulties develop gradually and usually do not affect functioning until the eighties. In fact, in 2003 around 73 percent of older persons assessed their health as excellent or very good, compared to only 66.6 percent of persons aged 18 to 64. Nonetheless, most older persons have at least one chronic condition, and many have multiple conditions. Compared to the young, the elderly are less likely to suffer from acute or short-term diseases, such as the common cold and infectious diseases, but are more likely to suffer from chronic or long-term diseases, such as hypertension, heart disease, arthritis, cancer, or emphysema. The latter pose serious problems principally to those in their eighties. In addition, more than half of the older population report having at least one disability. Disabilities may be physical or nonphysical, and many are minor, but they increase in severity with age. About 80 percent of the elderly report at least one chronic health condition, and about one-half of people 80 and over have more than one disability and need assistance. Curiously, health care costs decrease as a person ages, because the oldest of old—those 85 and over—are fittest and tend to die rapidly of pneumonia or multiple-organ failure (Angier, 1995, B5).

Senility, involving serious memory loss, confusion, and loss of the ability to reason, is not a natural consequence of aging. In fact, such disorders occur in at most 20 percent of 80-year-olds, while only 10 percent of elderly Americans show mild loss of memory. The symptoms of senility may derive from other causes, including a reaction to drugs. However, about 2.5 million Americans do suffer from neurological diseases, particularly Alzheimer's, an incurable disease of the brain.

Few of the elderly are incapacitated to the point of being relegated to nursing homes. As of 2002, 53.6 percent of older persons lived with a spouse. Many more men than women live with their spouses: approximately 74 percent of older men and 54 percent of older women aged 65 to 74. Moreover, the proportion living with their spouse decreases with age, especially for women. Of women 75 and older, only about 29 percent lived with a spouse in a family setting in 2002. About 30 percent of the elderly, 7.9 million women and 2.6 million men, lived alone. With advanced age, the frequency of living alone increases: among women 75 and over, half lived alone in 2002. At the same time, almost 400,000 grandparents 65 years old and older had primary responsibility for their grandchildren (Department of Health and Human Services, Administration on Aging. A Profile of Older Americans: 2006).

As noted, only a minority of the elderly live in nursing homes: in 2000, only 1.56 million, representing 4.5 percent of the over 65-year-old population did. Again, however, this proportion increases with age: for those 85 and over the percentage rises to 18.2. An

TABLE 9.1   Labor Force Participation Rates (percent) of Men Age 55 and over, by Age Group, Annual Averages, 2004–2005

Year	Men			
	55–61	62–64	65–69	70 and over
2004	74.4	50.8	32.6	12.8
2005	74.7	52.5	33.6	13.5

additional 5 percent of the elderly live in some type of senior housing with supportive services available.

Work and Retirement.   Although in the past the elderly continued to be employed, sometimes until they died, in 2007 approximately 25,000 Americans 55 years and older were in the labor force (Table 9.1). Interestingly, although labor force participation of men 65 and older has decreased steadily, the participation rate for women of this age group has been rising slightly, to 11 percent since 1988. In addition, 21 percent of workers over 65 were self-employed in 1999, compared to only 7 percent of younger workers (Bureau of Labor Statistics web site, **http://stats.bls.gov/news/release/empsit.t06.htm**).

One reason for the decline in employment for men is that industrial and postindustrial economies need highly skilled and educated workers, which places the elderly at a disadvantage with respect to younger workers—their skills tend to be obsolete. Ageism also

The elderly do not have to stop being productive. This woman, helping children learn to read, feels much happier being useful, while the children are less likely to accept the stereotype of the elderly as useless.

promotes the idea that older workers are not as productive as younger ones. In reality, although the elderly experience a decline in perception and reaction speed, they perform as well as if not better than younger workers. The elderly tend to be consistent in their output, change jobs less frequently, have fewer accidents, and have a lower absenteeism rate than younger workers (Giniger, Dispenzieri, & Eisenberg, 1983). The Age Discrimination Act of 1967 protects elderly workers to a certain extent, especially the amendment prohibiting forced retirement before the age of 70. Individuals are not all alike in their readiness to retire. For some, retirement may indeed be welcome; for others, it may cause feelings of uselessness and of being dispensable, leading to depression, and in acute cases, to a wish for early death. The higher the social status of the worker, the higher the job satisfaction and the less likelihood of early retirement (Atchley, 1982). After retirement, the higher-status workers also tend to continue to be involved in their professions. The bottom line, however, is the amount of income during retirement: if that is adequate, most persons choose to retire.

Finances. Although many elderly people—particularly women and minorities—find themselves living in straitened circumstances, the majority do not live in poverty. In 2003, the median household income of persons 65 and over was $36,006. However, it was only $17,359 for male householders living alone and only $13,775 for female householders living alone. Of course, wealth is apportioned very unequally in this age group. For instance, for households containing families headed by persons 65 and over, the median income was $35,219 for whites, $26,599 for African Americans, and $22,512 for Hispanics (U.S. Bureau of the Census, *Current Population Reports* 2003). Still, some 3.5 million of the elderly 65 and over lived in poverty, with a poverty rate of 10.1 percent (Figures 9.2– 9.3).

Not only in the United States but also in other wealthy countries, the elderly live quite well, according to a study of pensioners that showed that their disposable income is 80 percent of the income of working people in their later years of work. In some countries, retirees have even more disposable income than younger working people: in Germany, for instance, the overall income of persons over 60 is 25 percent higher than that of younger Germans (*The Economist*, 2004, 6).

In 2002, the major sources of income reported by the Social Security Administration were Social Security (reported by 91 percent of the elderly); income from assets (reported by 58 percent), public and private pensions (reported by 40 percent), and earnings (reported by 22 percent), public assistance (reported by 5 percent), and veterans' benefits (reported by 4 percent). The elderly derived 38 percent of their aggregate income from Social Security, while between 18 and 23 percent came from pensions, assets, and earnings (U.S. Bureau of the Census, *Current Population Reports*, 2002, P60-221). But for those in the lowest fifth of the population, Social Security accounted for most of their total income, while for those in the highest income fifth, it accounted for only approximately 20 percent. For too many Americans, then, the "golden years" may be bleak (see Table 9.2 for 2004 numbers).

Interestingly, but not surprisingly, class divisions are most distinct in old age, in the sense that the wealthier elderly are so much better off than the poorer ones in length of life and enjoyment of good health and the good life. In most countries, people in the top social class live around five years longer than those in the bottom class (in Britain, the difference is 15 years). There are differences in life expectancy, especially in healthy life expectancy. For one thing, the poor elderly tend to live in neighborhoods that are crime-ridden and unfriendly, leading to their isolation and loneliness. For another, the elderly poor generally lack much education and did not spend their working life in the professions. This condition appears to

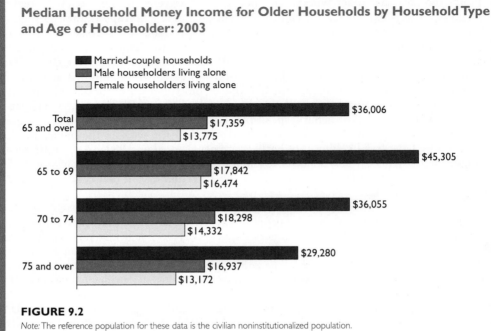

FIGURE 9.2
Note: The reference population for these data is the civilian noninstitutionalized population.
Source: U.S. Census Bureau, 2004, Table HINC-02.

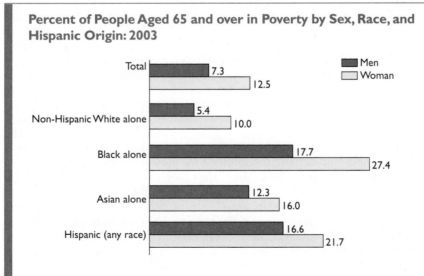

FIGURE 9.3
Note: The reference population for these data is the civilian noninstitutionalized population.
Source: U.S. Census Bureau, 2004, Table POV01.

TABLE 9.2   Aggregate Income for the Population Age 65 and over, by Source and Income Quintile (percent), 2004

Income Source	Lowest Fifth	Second Fifth	Third Fifth	Fourth Fifth	Highest Fifth
Total	100.0	100.0	100.0	100.0	100.0
Social security	82.6	83.4	66.6	47.5	18.9
Asset income	2.3	3.8	6.0	8.4	17.8
Pensions	3.5	7.0	16.6	25.7	21.2
Earnings	1.2	2.8	7.1	15.7	40.1
Public assistance	8.4	1.6	0.9	0.2	0.1
Other	2.0	1.5	2.7	2.6	1.9

Reference population: These data refer to the civilian noninstitutionalized population.

Source: U.S. Census Bureau, Current Population Survey, Annual Social and Economic Supplement.

lower their ability to remember things and solve puzzles: people with university degrees at 75 do better at those activities than people with little education in their 50s. Mortality rates for white American men with the highest levels of education were about 10 percent lower than for white men with the least education, and the difference in the period 1990–1997 rose to 70 percent (*The Economist*, 2004, 7). Those with little education also tend to live unhealthier lives: they smoke, are overweight, and do not exercise. Finally, the perception of where one is in the pecking order (the stratification system of the society) is also important. Those

TABLE 9.3   Living Arrangements of the Population Age 65 and over, by Sex and Race and Hispanic Origin (percent), 2004

Selected Characteristic	With Spouse	With Other Relatives	With Nonrelatives	Alone
Men				
Total	72.4	6.1	2.7	18.8
Non-Hispanic white alone	74.3	4.5	2.4	18.7
Black alone	55.6	13.0	4.9	26.6
Asian alone	77.0	12.0	1.1	9.9
Hispanic (of any race)	64.4	16.3	3.6	15.7
Women				
Total	41.6	16.8	1.9	39.7
Non-Hispanic white alone	43.7	13.3	1.9	41.1
Black alone	23.9	32.6	2.2	41.4
Asian alone	47.1	24.8	1.7	26.7
Hispanic (of any race)	37.1	36.0	2.1	24.8

Reference population: These data refer to the civilian noninstitutionalized population.

Source: U.S. Census Bureau, Current Population Survey, Annual Social and Economic Supplement.

who rank themselves as being low in status and not in control of their lives suffer worse health than those who rank themselves higher and in control of their lives.

Widowhood.   Loneliness and other negative consequences follow the death of a spouse, particularly of a husband, for it seems that men adjust to widowhood a little better than women (however, there are five times more widows than widowers; see Table 9.3 on page 233 for living arrangements). Men tend to remarry more often, are members of more organizations, know more people from their preretirement years, are more likely to own and drive a car, and have higher incomes than women. However, elderly widowers fare worse than women: they are much more likely to die from a number of causes, from heart attacks to suicide, than elderly women.

Box 9.1   The Silver Century

Within a year or two, and for the first time in history, there will be more people over 60 than toddlers under 5 in the world. Throughout recorded history, people aged 65 and over have made up, at most, 2 to 3 percent of most societies. Today, this age group makes up 15 percent of the inhabitants of wealthy nations. The defining demographic trend of this century, then, will be the increase in the proportion of the world's elderly persons.

What will this trend mean? Three situations are already visible. First, by the 2020s, there will be a bulge in retirement when the last baby boomers leave the work force. This will mean that a large number of elderly and very elderly (65+ and 85+) will need to be supported by a smaller and smaller proportion of the young still in the work force. The smaller proportion of young workers is a result of the widespread fall in fertility rates in industrial countries in which women are not having enough children to replace those who die. This is especially true in continental Europe and Japan, but even in the United States births only just equal deaths (in Japan, the number of persons 100 years and over doubled in five years, setting a record for the 33rd straight year as the world's longest-living nation). Therefore, when the baby boomers retire, the size of the labor force will plummet. Finally, with life expectancy rising, people are spending much more time in retirement (again, Japan's life expectancy as of 2002 is the longest in the world: 85.2 years for women and 78.3 for men). In the United States, 16 percent of men are still in the work force at 65, while in Europe only 4 percent are. Consequently, the large number of older people will have to be supported for a longer period of time by fewer younger workers. The welfare state system in Europe and America's Social Security system provide near-universal coverage for the retired, paid for by the current workers—who, as we saw, are a diminishing number.

Even some of the developing nations face similar problems. China, Iran, Brazil, and Turkey will be below replacement rate within 15 years. In China, thanks to the one-child policy, the fertility rate has decreased from six or seven children per woman in the 1960s, to below replacement rate. When the Red Guard generation reaches retirement age in around 2015, the working-age population will be too small to allow the continuous growth of China's economy.

Economists believe that there is a decade-long window of opportunity in which governments can forestall the collapse of systems that support the elderly. The negative impact of the retiring baby boomers will not be felt for another 10 years. At this time, governments will have to convince their citizens to postpone their retirements. This will not be easy. The idea of retirement is fairly recent—for most of history, people worked almost until they died—but it is a very popular idea. Workers began to retire as soon as they could afford to do so, even before social benefits were available, and they like retirement even more now that they live longer and more leisure activities are open to them. Governments will have to change the structure of pensions and benefits to make it more attractive to continue working longer. One thing is certain: a workplace revolution is coming. In the 1970s and 1980s, a large number of women entered the labor force. The next 25 years will bring in a large number of "older" workers, perhaps on a part-time basis. Such a future holds many positives: staying in the labor force can provide elderly workers with a more stimulating environment, companionship, and a bit of extra money (Cairncross, 2004, 3, 4)

Death and Dying.   Historically, death has been accepted as a normal part of human existence. Lack of knowledge regarding hygiene and disease prevention coupled with subsistence economies resulted in very high death rates in both hunting–gathering and agricultural societies. It was not until the industrial societies were well established that death rates plummeted. With the ability of societies to control death—to a certain extent, of course—came a change in attitude toward it. When death was common and was within the experience of everyone, it was considered an ordinary event. As it became rarer, it tended to become associated with old age, because, barring wars and accidents, it was mostly the old who died. Today, death is considered an out-of-the-ordinary event if it occurs at any time in the life cycle except in old age. As a result, it has acquired an aura of unnaturalness. And because religious beliefs that explained life and death as part of a divine plan have declined in importance in modern societies, the acceptance with which former generations greeted death has given way to the expectation that the miracles of modern medicine will bring us immortality. Death is no longer the natural capping of life; it is to be avoided at all costs and is considered separate, an antithesis to life.

This attitude toward death is reinforced by the fact that death has been removed from public life. People typically no longer die at home, in full view of family and friends; instead, they die in hospitals and nursing homes, and even there, dying patients are isolated from those expected to recuperate. Coupled with the fact that many elderly people are isolated from the rest of society to begin with, the result is that the population at large has seldom faced death, in the sense of seeing a person die.

In spite of this strong avoidance of death, the elderly seem less afraid of it than younger people, particularly if their health is such that they see little chance of a normal lifestyle in their future. The elderly are socialized into accepting death because they are more likely to see it in their spouses and peers. As an increasing number of Americans join the ranks of the elderly, the idea of death is likely to lose some of its sting. It is already more acceptable to speak about death, and many of the elderly make it clear that they do not want to have their lives prolonged artificially if it means suffering or isolation rather than improvement in

Not all the elderly are able to retire to play golf in fancy resorts, but for most elderly, the rocking chair on the porch is an idea from the past.

Box 9.2   The Eight Americas

Location, race, and income play such an important role in disparities in life spans that some scientists have said that there are really eight Americas, not just one. The healthiest Americans, and the longest lived, live about 30 years longer than the least healthy. Asian American women living in Bergen County, New Jersey, have an average life expectancy of 91 years. On the other hand, Native Americans in South Dakota have an average life expectancy of 58 years. Such a short life expectancy is comparable to that of some of the developing nations of Southeast Asia and sub-Saharan Africa. The gaps and disparities, moreover, have not closed over the last two decades in spite of the fact that about $5,000 a year per person is spent for health care in the United States.

These differences in mortality and longevity are not due solely to disparities in income, the availability of health insurance, violence, or the presence of AIDS, although these factors certainly contribute to them. According to a study conducted by Harvard University and partly funded by the National Institute on Aging, the principal contributors to increased mortality are smoking, alcohol, obesity, high blood pressure, high cholesterol, diet, and physical inactivity. In other words, much of the disparity is dependent on cultural patterns and lifestyles. As one researcher stated, "It's not just low income. It's what people eat, it's how they behave, or simply what's available in supermarkets" (Neergard, 2006). As an example, Native Americans who live in cities, away from the reservations in the West, have life expectancies similar to whites. Disparities were most pronounced in Americans aged 15 to 59 because according to the researchers, this age group is the most neglected by health policy initiatives,

which focus mainly on children and the elderly. Thus, a 15-year-old black urban male is 3.8 times as likely to die before the age of 60 as an Asian American.

The eight Americas consist of:

1. 10.4 million Asians, with a per capita income of $21,566 and life expectancy of 84.9 years
2. 3.6 million low-income whites, average income $17,758, life expectancy 79 years
3. 214 million middle Americans scattered across the country, average income $24,640, life expectancy 77.9 years
4. 16.6 million low-income whites in rural counties in Appalachia and the Mississippi Valley, average income $16,390, life expectancy 75 years
5. 1 million western Native Americans, average income $10,029, life expectancy 72.7 years
6. 23.4 million black middle Americans, average income $15,412, life expectancy 72.9 years
7. 5.8 million southern low-income blacks in rural counties, average income $10,463, life expectancy 71.2 years
8. 7.5 million high-risk urban blacks in thirteen urban counties, average income $14,800, life expectancy 71.1 years.

Finally, the healthiest state in which to live is Hawaii, with an average life span for both men and women of 80 years. The least healthy place to live is the District of Columbia, with a life expectancy of only 72 years. The researchers conclude that because socioeconomic inequalities are not being addressed in the United States, public health strategies must be established that would attempt to reduce risk factors for chronic diseases and injuries (Murray et al., 2006).

quality of life. During the past two decades, institutions called hospices—which do not attempt to cure but rather care for the dying—have sprung up to attempt to help the dying in the difficult period preceding death.

■ Women: Differentiation According to Gender

It is clear to all that the human race comes in two genders, male and female, and that both are needed if that race is to continue to exist. Yet it seems that a state of war is being waged between men and women all over the globe, producing neither winners nor losers, but much conflict. In developed countries, a high incidence of rape, various varieties of sexual harassment, domestic violence directed at women, and many other types of discrimination are the order of the day. In developing nations, especially where political conflicts are raging, women are the victims of virtual horror stories: they are denied education and the simplest human rights, rape on massive levels is used against them as a weapon of war, and they are still considered chattel or property of men. To what do we owe this enmity between the sexes?

As we saw in the previous two chapters, societies assign unequal statuses to various segments of their population. Women (and children) have usually had an inferior status in most societies of the world, and particularly where the family form has remained stubbornly patriarchal. One can understand why children should be somewhat subordinate to adults: they are physically weak and lack life experience and knowledge. But why women? What really differentiates men and women? Is it true that "Women are from Venus, Men are from Mars," as a best-selling book would have it? Why is rape so prevalent a crime even in our society when sexual mores are so relaxed that there is no stigma attached to having sex among consenting adults?

Biological Facts

One is born either male or female; maleness and femaleness, then, are *biological* terms, descriptive of biological facts. Masculine and feminine, on the other hand, are adjectives reflecting *social* conditions, that is, descriptive of how males and females are expected to behave in a given society, and how they come to feel about themselves and each other. The first is a **sex status**, ascribed and not subject to change except in extraordinary circumstances; the second is a **gender role**, achieved and, thus, subject to change according to place and time. The first lies within the realm of biology, the second within that of culture, but both are subject to social interpretations and influences and can be detached from one another only for the sake of analysis. In reality, biology and culture are deeply intertwined.

The biological differences between men and women may be roughly divided into those that are of an anatomical nature, those that are of a genetic nature, and those that are of a hormonal nature. **Anatomical differences** are the most obvious, for they consist of the physical structure and appearance of the two sexes. These differences include height, weight, distribution of body fat and hair, and musculature. Such traits are called the **secondary sex characteristics**, and they may be measured on a continuum: that is, not every woman is shorter, lighter, more rounded, less hairy, and less muscular than a man, just as not every man is taller, heavier, more angular, more hairy, and more muscular than a woman. In fact, the most important anatomical difference lies in the distinct reproductive systems of males and females. The reproductive system of women allows them to become pregnant and give birth. The reproductive system of men allows them to impregnate women.

Pregnancy and nursing force women to be unable periodically to perform certain economic and social functions, whereas the role of men in reproduction ends with impregnation. These facts have profound social consequences.

Genetic differences become apparent when analyzing the sex chromosomes, which contain the genes that determine heredity in all living creatures. All humans inherit two sex chromosomes, one from the mother and one from the father. Females inherit two X-chromosomes (XX), while males inherit one X chromosome and one Y chromosome (XY). A male is born when an ovum (egg) bearing the X-chromosome is fertilized by a sperm bearing a Y-chromosome (each month a female produces one ovum throughout her fertile years, which contains an X-chromosome; a male produces sperm, half of which is made up of X-chromosomes inherited from his mother and the other half of Y-chromosomes inherited from his father). Whether chromosomal differences influence the personalities, abilities, and behaviors of males and females has not yet been scientifically established.

Hormonal differences begin to be felt at about three months after fertilization and are responsible for the differentiation into the two genders. Up to this time, the fetus is sexually undifferentiated: it may become either a male or a female. Hormones are chemicals that are secreted into the bloodstream by glands located in the body. The function of hormones is to stimulate some chemical processes and inhibit others. The hormones involved in the development of sex characteristics are estrogen and progesterone, produced by the ovaries in females, and testosterone and androgens produced by the testes in males. Both males and females produce male and female sex hormones, but the proportion in which they are produced varies by gender. The fetus with the XY chromosomal formation begins to secrete testosterone, which has the function of inhibiting the development of female characteristics; hence, the fetus will be born a male. At puberty, it is again the sex hormones that determine the development of secondary sex characteristics—they induce the growth of beards in males and breasts in females. Hormones, then, are influential in physical development. They also affect human behavior. Animal experiments have shown that an increase of testosterone, even in females, produces an increase in aggressive behavior and sex drive. Research into the hormone oxytocin, present in humans and other mammals, shows that it is responsible for feelings of satisfaction and good will toward others. It also stimulates the sensations of sexual arousal and climax, ensures that new mothers nurture their young, and that the uterus contracts during childbirth. Researchers are going so far as to say that the hormone is an excellent candidate for involvement in the formation of social bonds, and they liken it to a bridge between anatomy and behavior (Angier, 1991).

Other researchers also attribute the differences between men and women to hormonal causes, especially to the infusion of hormones at the proper moment—before birth, and especially at puberty—which influences the brain to behave in a gender-specific way: males with more aggression, females with more nurturance. These conclusions are based on animal experiments that show that females injected with the equivalent of the hormone testosterone—or even female siblings who develop beside a male fetus in the womb—invariably exhibit more aggressiveness, acting more like males. Nonetheless, there is no conclusive evidence that hormonal differences explain differences in the behavior of the two sexes. Even where correlations between the level of testosterone and aggressive behavior exist, it is impossible to show a cause-and-effect relationship. At most, it may be said that there is an association between the two (Hoyenga & Hoyenga, 1979, 139).

Studies in medicine also point to evidence that male and female brains function differently. Researchers have discovered, for instance, that in women such functions as language are more evenly divided between the left and right halves of the brain, whereas in men they are much more localized in the left half.

Cultural Differences

The differences in behavior between the two sexes are obviously not due strictly to biological influences. Culture plays a significant part, although less so than was at first believed by social scientists and feminists. For instance, a well-known study by researchers Money and Erhardt (1972) involved a pair of identical twin males, one of whom, in a tragic accident, was totally castrated during circumcision. The parents of the twins were subsequently convinced to raise this twin as a female. Other than surgically constructing a vagina, nothing was done to the twin until puberty except that the parents treated "her" as a little girl: the mother let her hair grow long, adorned her with hair ribbons, and dressed her in frilly clothes. According to the researchers, soon the little girl was behaving as little girls are expected to behave in our society: she was neater than her brother, she was more willing to help with housework, and she requested dolls and a dollhouse as Christmas presents. Even though the twin was, biologically, a male, "she" acted as a female does in American society. However, it was observed that she tended to be a leader in games with peers and was rather a tomboy.

The story, however, does not end with ". . . and she lived happily ever after." In fact, a follow-up study paints a totally different picture. New research shows that, far from being satisfied with her assigned gender, the girl/boy rejected the female identity and at 14 years of age chose to live as a man, undergoing extensive reconstructive surgery to attempt to attain a semblance of the male genitals he had lost. "Despite everyone telling him constantly that he was a girl, and despite his being treated with female hormones, his brain knew he was a male. It refused to take on what it was being told" (Angier, 1997, A10). The recollections of the adult girl/boy (identified only as "John") and his parents were that he had never accepted a feminine identity. On the contrary, he had torn off the dresses in which his parents had dressed him, had refused dolls, had sought out male friends, had imitated his father shaving rather than his mother putting on makeup, and had even tried to urinate standing up. His -attempts to engage in feminine behavior were made only to obtain parental approval. He became especially unhappy when, at age 12, he was given female hormones and began growing breasts. At age 14 he threatened suicide, being friendless and thoroughly unhappy. When told by his father what had happened to him as an infant, "John" was relieved to hear it: "For the first time everything made sense, and I understood who and what I was" (Angier, 1997, A10). In short, what had been considered a classic case illustrating the importance of nurture and socialization on gender identification was turned on its head.

Nonetheless, the impact of culture cannot be discounted. If the behavior of the two sexes differed strictly on the basis of biology, then in all societies of the world, and in all instances, men and women would behave distinctly in the same ways. But they do not. Cross-cultural evidence indicates how deeply nurture can affect behavior. A classic study by anthropologist Margaret Mead (1935), who based her findings on an analysis of three preliterate tribes of New Guinea, revealed that men can act the way people think women do and vice versa. For instance, in one of the societies Mead studied, both men and women were gentle, emotionally responsive, noncompetitive, and lacking in aggression. In addition, both men and women were responsible for the care of children. In another tribe, however, both men and women had personality types that could be characterized as masculine; that is, both men and women were aggressive and violent. Women disliked anything connected with motherhood, such as pregnancy, nursing, and caring for their children. They were especially obnoxious to their daughters. Finally, in the third tribe, Mead found profound differences in the behavior of men and women. Contrary to expectations, however, each sex behaved in a manner that Americans would consider the opposite of how men and women "ought" to behave: women were domineering and aggressive and were the economic providers in the household. Men were passive, took care of the children, engaged in gossip, and liked to adorn themselves. Mead concluded from her analysis that sex roles vary in different societies; that is, a person born either a male or a female does not necessarily and always act in ways determined by his or her biological makeup. However, Mead never proclaimed the reversibility of sex roles and, in fact, tried to correct the mistaken assumptions—that females can be made to act exactly like males and vice versa—that a number of commentators made about her conclusions. She also

We are born male or female, but we are made men or women. It is culture that directs our behavior according to sex roles, some of which are anachronistic. These little girls are learning to play traditional gender roles in American society, but there are other gender scripts for women.

found, and reported in her book, *Male and Female* (1949), that the seven cultures she studied exhibited homicidal violence, headhunting, plotting, and fighting, all on the part of males. In short, to conclude that culture is solely responsible for gender roles is equally shortsighted.

Another cross-cultural comparison of six societies also showed that in all of them boys were more aggressive and violent than girls, and girls were more nurturing and emotionally responsive, especially to children (Whiting, 1963). Findings such as this substantiate long-standing conclusions that fighting and leadership are associated predominantly with males and that males are more prone to aggressiveness, sexual attack, promiscuity, homosexuality, voyeurism, and other forms of aggressive sexual activity (Ford & Beach, 1951; Murdock, 1957). The conclusions regarding the greater aggressiveness of males seem to be so over-whelming that a well-known anthropologist was moved to state categorically: "In every known society, homicidal violence, whether spontaneous and outlawed or organized and sanctioned for military purposes, is committed overwhelmingly by men" (Konner, 1988, 34). This view is supported by the work of sociologist Steven Goldberg in *The Inevitability of Patriarchy* (1977), in which he maintains that according to his research: (a) patriarchy is a universal characteristic of societies; (b) roles performed by males are given higher status than those performed by females; and (c) men are dominant in male–female relationships (Goldberg, 1989, 16–18).

What conclusions can be drawn from these conflicting facts? Do men and women behave differently because they are biologically different? Or is it rather that they are socialized to accept different roles? In short, what makes us men or women? Nature or nurture? As usual, the issue cannot be answered simplistically. Biological differences between the sexes surely exist, in some areas to a significant extent. The concern, however, is the social signifi-cance that these differences acquire in human societies.

Sex and Gender Differentiated

Although *sex* and *gender* are used interchangeably in common parlance, in the social sciences the two terms need to be differentiated. *Sex* refers to a person's biological identity, whereas *gender* refers to the socially learned behaviors and cultural expectations that attach to males and females. Sex merely marks us as male or female and determines whether we have a reproductive system that enables us to bear children or one that provides some of the material necessary to conceive them. As we have seen, this biological fact is not sufficient to ensure that we become men and women. Femininity—being a woman—and masculinity—being a man—are cultural concepts. Therefore, they differ from society to society, they are associated with specific historical eras and geographical settings, and they are learned and interpreted differently even by members of the same society. That is why some women and men, having acquired a sexual identity that does not correspond to their physical sex, attempt to change the latter by surgical and medical means.

■ The Cultural Construction of Gender

We saw earlier that culture provides us with a script according to which we essentially organize our lives. We learn this script so well that we—at least, most of us—become absolutely convinced that the way we do things in our society is the right and only way to do them. We accept a set of assumptions that we seldom bother to examine, and we come to believe that they are the "truth" that should guide and direct our lives. We, therefore, often cringe at the way things are done in other societies.

Traditional Gender Roles

We live out our lives by fulfilling a variety of roles. Among the most important of such roles are **gender roles**. The traditional gender roles assigned to males and females in our society, as well as in most others, are the **instrumental role** for males and the **expressive role** for females. The instrumental role stresses rationality, competitiveness, aggression, and goal-orientation. The expressive role emphasizes nurturing, emotion, and peace-making. Such traditional divisions of roles assume that there is a polarity between male and female roles, with behavior divided in two, as it were, and between opposite poles: emotion and nurturance at one end, reason and aggressiveness at the other. In reality, of course, there is a great deal of variety within each gender, and there are countless similarities in the roles of men and women (and the same roles may be filled by either men or women when the need arises or is perceived as arising).

Because they give birth to the young who depend for their survival on them, women have developed emotions and skills consonant with nurturing and care-giving. These have extended to other family members in need of care, such as the elderly or disabled. When societies were predominantly agricultural, women did a share of work outside the house alongside the men, in addition to tasks inside the house. But when economies began to depend on industry, men became the chief breadwinners outside the home. This occurred mostly in the middle classes, in which women were able to stay at home, expanding the expressive role. The notion then emerged that women were expected to sacrifice their personal goals and desires in favor of those of others. Working-class women incorporated all of these roles—they had to work outside the home, at menial or industrial jobs, and fulfill the caretaker functions at home. This traditional division of roles crystallized during the

Women have entered previously male-only fields, including such sports as boxing.

industrial age, when men began to perform their instrumental role through their work out-side the home.

In general terms, traditional roles, both masculine and feminine, have been upheld as the expected cultural models throughout the societies of the world, becoming stereotyped in the process. In our society, when people refer to the "typical" roles of men and women, they mean those that, in the past, were characteristic of a white, middle-class family. The stereotypes for other groups vary somewhat.

Gender Scripts

Gender roles, like all roles, are based on cultural scripts. The masculine script in our society has several variations. The traditional script includes distancing oneself from anything femi-nine ("sissy"), and being occupationally and financially successful. Those who cannot achieve success through legitimate means may embrace some subcultural ways, including violence and physical aggression, and/or adopting a "cool" pose consisting of a manner of dress and posture that bespeaks fearlessness and emotional detachment. This pose is used as a survival mechanism in a society perceived as hostile and discriminatory. Another masculine script is one in which the expectation is for the man to be self-reliant and confident to the point of being "tough" (a John Wayne type of person). A fairly popular script focuses on adventure, sometimes accompanied by violence and a need to humiliate an opponent. This script expects men to excel in contact sports, never to walk away from a fight, and to kill and maim the enemy (do what must be done) in war. Finally, an optional script that has been emerging of late is one in which the "new" male is emotionally sensitive and expressive and values an egalitarian relationship with women.

Feminine scripts are based on the expectation that a woman, in addition to being nur-turant, will be attractive in looks, not overly competitive, a listener rather than a talker, and one capable of adapting to various circumstances. The script provides that a woman not

---

Box 9.3   Women and Science

In spite of the pervasive scripts and the traditional roles women are expected to play in most societies of the world, many of them, today and throughout history, have overcome these obstacles. In addition to rulers known for their wisdom or shrewdness (Cleopatra, the female pharaoh Hatshepsut, Queen Elizabeth I, in addition to more modern prime ministers, such as Indira Gandhi and Golda Meir), many women have excelled in fields in which men predominate. Today, a substantial number of women are earning doctoral degrees in science and engineering and are working in such professions as architecture and construction, not to mention medical research. A number have even received Nobel prizes in science:

Marie S. Curie, Nobel Prize Winner in Physics, 1903, and in Chemistry, 1911
Irene Curie (Marie's daughter), Chemistry, 1935
Grety Radnitz Cori, Biochemistry, 1947
Maria Goeppert Mayer, Physics, 1963
Dorothy Crowfoot Hodgkin, Chemistry, 1964
Rosalyn Sussman Yalow, Medicine, 1977
Barbara McClintock, Medicine, 1983
Rita Levi-Montalcini, Medicine, 1986
Gertrude Elion, Medicine, 1988
Christiane Nüsslein-Volhard, Medicine, 1995
("Women Nobel Prize Winners," **http://www. factmonster.com/ipka/A0801697.html**. Accessed September 6, 2004).

---

show her intelligence but rather support, facilitate, and cheer on from the sidelines her husband's (or man's) accomplishments. She is considered lucky to have a man in her life, and his care as well as any needs of their children are to come before her own needs. Again, the script may differ somewhat for women in other ethnic groups, but it always includes primary responsibility for child care.

In recent years the traditional feminine script has been pushed to the back, while the script of "professional" or "working woman" has emerged (see Table 9.4). Often, women try to combine the traditional script with the working woman script, producing the "superwoman" script. This script is very difficult to achieve and maintain, and it causes much role strain. A lesser number of women appear to follow a "contented single" script, in which a working woman seems satisfied with a lifestyle that does not include a relationship with a man, although it may involve the creation of a family (perhaps in a lesbian relationship). Finally, we should mention a theme that is woven through all the cultural scripts for women, and that is the division of women into "good girl/slut." Even elementary school children are aware of this distinction attributed to females who are either sexually conservative or sexually active.

As is obvious, gender scripts are perceived as being opposite and mutually exclusive: women are one thing, men something else. In reality, as was already noted, men and women differ only slightly in the traits they display. A good portion of these traits overlap, and this is true of both physical traits (such as height, for instance) and behavioral traits (such as aggressiveness). Moreover, there are more differences within each gender group than between the two genders. The only exception to this pattern of overlapping traits seems to be dominance.

Male Dominance

Male dominance is a fact of life in the majority of the world's societies. In our own case, in spite of our belief that we are an egalitarian society, a group of little boys will invariably take over playground equipment in a situation of mixed-gender play, unless prohibited to do so by an adult (Franklin, 1988, 30). The many sexual harassment situations on jobs and in the military are another indication of such dominance. On an institutional level, a realistic look

TABLE 9.4   Women in the Labor Force in 2005

■ Women made up 46% of the labor force and are projected to account for 47% in 2014.

■ Women will likely account for 51% of the increase in total labor force growth between 2004 and 2014.

■ 66 million women were employed in the United States in 2005, more than ever before.

■ Half of all workers in high-paying management and professional jobs are women. They outnumber men in many occupations, including financial manager, human resource manager, accountant, budget analyst, teacher, and nurse.

■ The median weekly earnings of women working full-time are 81% of the median weekly earnings of men working full-time.

Unemployment rates

By Gender

Men	5.1%
Women	5.1%

By Race

Asian women	3.9%
White women	4.4%
Hispanic women	6.9%
Black women	9.5%

By Education (Women Only)

No high school diploma	9.7%
High school diploma	4.8%
Some college, no degree	4.5%
Bachelor's degree or higher	2.4%

is sufficient to illustrate the clear prevalence of men in the political, economic, social, and even religious arenas. There has never been a female President of the United States, and strong personality and interest in politics of a first lady have generally brought her nothing but criticism.

In the 110th Congress, there are 16 women in the Senate (out of 100 senators), and 71 women in the House of Representatives (out of 435 representatives). In administrative and managerial positions, women's share increased from 38 percent in the mid-1980s to 50 percent in 2005, the highest proportion in Western Europe and other developed nations (Women's Bureau, 2005). As for wage parity, it has never been achieved. In 2005, women earned approximately 81.0 percent as much as men. Median weekly earnings of female full-time wage and salary workers were $585 in 2005 compared to $722 for their male counterparts. (see Figure 9.4). African American and Hispanic women earned 63 cents and 53 cents, respectively, for every dollar that a white male earned. Women and men under 25 had fairly similar earnings, but women's earnings were much lower than men's in older age groups: women 25 and over made less than 80 percent of what men in the same age group earned (U.S. Department of Labor, Bureau of Labor Statistics, 2006).

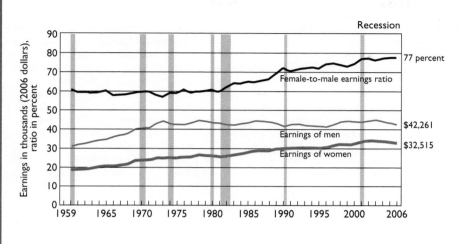

Female-to-Male Earnings Ratio and Median Earnings of Full-Time, Year-Round Workers 15 Years and Older by Sex: 1960 to 2006

FIGURE 9.4

Note: The data points are placed at the midpoints of the respective years. Data on earnings of full-time, year-round workers are not readily available before 1960.

Source: U.S. Census Bureau, *Current Population Survey,* 1961 to 2007 Annual Social and Economic Supplements.

In addition, many subtle gender expectations show male dominance expressed in the course of social interaction: men interrupt women more often than the other way around, women smile more often than men do, and men stare at women more often than the opposite (Mehrabian, 1971; Frieze & Ramsey, 1976; Frieze et al., 1978). And women seldom win arguments with men even though they may be good at reasoning things through and expressing themselves. This conclusion was reached by a 10-year study of the way in which men and women argue by British psychologist Elizabeth Mapstone (Kozma, 1997, 4E).

> What I expected to be able to show was that really there were no differences between men and women. What I discovered was that it mattered terribly who the other person was in the argument, and most especially it mattered what gender the other person was. . . .It's not true that all men are cool, rational beings and it's not true that all women are gentle, warm, nurturing creatures.

Theories of Gender Role Development

Why and how do gender roles emerge in a society? How do they become so deeply embedded in the culture that they are eventually incorporated into our very personalities and behavior? Such questions cannot be answered with any degree of certainty. We can only speculate by referring to a number of theories that have been used in an attempt to answer them.

Box 9.4 God Should Not Give Daughters to the Poor

Women in the United States have achieved an almost egalitarian status with men, certainly as pertains to their political and civil rights. We have seen, however, that there still are differences in wages between the sexes, and women certainly suffer other discriminatory conditions in the United States. One such condition relates to their sexuality. Many men divide women either into saints—their mothers or sisters—or women of easy virtue. Such an attitude is prevalent in many societies around the world. A number of societies keep women in conditions of subjugation that may as well be considered slavery. Women are often the targets of vicious assaults by warring factions—this was the case when the former Yugoslavia was in the process of breaking up and one ethnic group was attempting to cleanse its territory of another ethnic group. One of its methods was by brutal sexual attacks on women. Currently, the same actions are occurring in Darfur, a region of Sudan, in which women are continually raped and killed. In many developing countries, girls and women are sold by impoverished parents into brothels, or they are held like slaves by husbands and in-laws who abuse them and often kill them. They are also exploited and abused—and often killed—by feudal-like wealthy landowners who control the police and other government authorities, so that the women have no recourse and must suffer in silence. Poverty and being a woman are heavy burdens to carry in many places in the world. This condition prompted one mother to say that God should never give daughters to the poor.

Structural Functionalist Theory. This theory is one of the most dominant ones in sociology. It assumes that those elements are retained in a social system that aid in the survival of that system. The development of the instrumental and expressive roles in the family institution is a kind of specialization that occurs within all small groups. Such specialization is *functional* because it meets social needs as well as institutional needs. A strong family needs someone to make important decisions and someone to foster the emotional well-being of members. Because of the close bond between mother and child, the expressive role is more consonant with a woman's nature; the male acquires the instrumental role by default.

The critique that may be made of this theory is that it assumes that male dominance and female subordination are natural and inevitable, based on biological makeup. We have seen, however, that research does not prove the absolute truth of this assumption.

Conflict Theory. Conflict theory is the other of the two most popular sociological theories. This theory assumes that power and privilege are based on the resources that an individual possesses. In turn, power is the ability to influence or control the lives of others, and it also derives from the economic resources that an individual can muster. Frederick Engels, Karl Marx's co-author, maintained in his book, *The Origins of the Family, Private Property and the State* (1884), that male dominance in the family was the result of his control over the family's economic resources. He also insisted that the concept of patriarchy developed in tandem with that of property, because if property were to be inherited, it became important for a man to know that the children born to his wife were indeed his own. In this sense, simple societies were much more egalitarian because there was no need to worry about who was going to inherit what—there was precious little surplus to leave anyone. A more recent interpretation of the theory holds that those individuals who have a higher income, educational attainment, and occupational status have the greater power even in a relationship such as marriage. And because most men tend to marry women who are younger, less well educated, and who earn less money, they naturally become the more powerful partner.

Conflict theory has its shortcomings, also. There seems to be too much emphasis on economics, and too little concern over other facets of relationships, such as sex, love, and companionship, as well as traditional societal expectations that would force women into a more submissive stance vis-a-vis men. In particular, gender roles and stereotypes, which have a tremendous impact on behavior, are ignored.

Feminist Theory. Feminist theory has borrowed much of the framework of conflict theory, especially the fact that women are underrepresented in positions of power in the society at large, a reflection of the lack of power women have within the family. Feminists also point out the existence of the wage differential between men and women, of prevalent gender discrimination in hiring and promotion, of sexual harassment in the workplace, of the frequency of divorce and out-of-wedlock births, which have led to the phenomenon of the "feminization of poverty" and of violence as a means of controlling the behavior of family members.

As is true of conflict theory, feminist theory is also criticized for its emphasis on the negative side of male–female relationships, while paying scant attention to the positives of such relationships: companionship, affection and love, sexual satisfaction, and intimacy. Feminism as a social movement has also been accused of not doing enough for certain groups of women: minorities, the poor, those in traditional women's jobs, stay-at-home mothers, rural residents, and single welfare mothers. They are seen as representing mainly white, highly educated women, interested in such issues as abortion, gay rights, and political equality, while the average woman must contend with child care and economic survival.

Theories of Gender Socialization

Another group of theories focuses on the way cultural ideas about gender become part of an individual's personality and behavior patterns. Among the most influential theories are the social learning theory, the cognitive developmental theory, and the identification theory.

The Social Learning Theory. The social learning theory is based on the behaviorist notion that learning consists of observation, imitation, and reinforcement. In this view, children observe all kinds of behavior on the part of parents, peers, and others. They imitate some of this behavior: if they receive positive reinforcement for it—if parents seem delighted, or their friends approve, or teachers give them good grades—they continue this behavior. If the reinforcement is negative—parents scold them, friends laugh at them, teachers discipline them—they discontinue the behavior. Gender roles are learned in the same way. If a little girl puts on her mother's dress and primps in front of a mirror, and her mother smiles and says she looks pretty, the little girl assumes that females are supposed to dress up and look pretty. If a little boy does the same, and his father scowls and tells him that boys do not wear dresses unless they are sissies, then the boy realizes that his behavior is not proper for his gender.

Socialization into gender roles begins early. Parents respond to male and female infants differently, speaking more often to their daughters, whom they also touch more frequently and treat more delicately. The kinds of toys and games parents choose, the kinds of clothing they select for their children, the way they themselves behave and what they say directly about gender, even the jobs they hold—whether they are traditional for each gender or not, all offer subtle messages to their children regarding what is appropriate behavior for each gender.

Indeed, children observe and imitate the behavior of their parents, their siblings and peers, and characters encountered in the mass media. And they continue behavior that is rewarded. But not always, and not entirely. First, they do not imitate the same-sexed parent alone but both. Second, they are not merely passive entities but react to the messages they receive.

Cognitive Development Theory.   According to the cognitive development theory, children learn gender roles according to which stage of cognitive development they have reached at any point. Cognitive development, in turn, is the way information is processed by individuals at different stages of physical maturation (Piaget, 1950, 1954; Kohlberg, 1969). For instance, even though children at two years of age may have noticed that there are two genders, they are not sure to which one they belong, nor whether it is a permanent or a temporary condition (they may think that it depends on wearing dresses or having long hair). It is not until children are six or seven years old that they realize the reality of gender and its permanent nature. At this point, they proceed to select behavior befitting their gender, preferring to play with same-sexed playmates and sex-typed toys. They see gender as being rigidly defined; it is not until they are more mature that they perceive gender as more flexible, and gender roles as somewhat overlapping (Vogel et al., 1991, 605).

Children do not reach their ideas about gender roles without much input from the culture. With help from the numerous agents of socialization—parents, siblings, peers, teachers, the media—they construct what sociologists call *gender schema*, or a set of traits that are perceived as being central to a particular gender (Bem, 1981, 1983, 1985). These vary according to age: at first, they are quite concrete—only girls wear barrettes in their hair, only boys play hockey, for instance. With maturity, the schema grow more abstract: men do not display emotions, women do not make the important decisions. Whether these perceptions are correct or incorrect, they contribute to the individual's gender identity.

Identification Theory.   Building on Freudian ideas, sociologist Nancy Chodorow maintains that children of both genders initially identify and develop strong attachments to their primary caretaker, who is generally the mother (Chodorow, 1978). For girls, the problem later is the issue of separation from the mother, which may lead, during the teenage years, to hostility and feelings of competition with her. For boys, the issue is to make a dramatic identification shift from identification with the mother to identification with the father. This shift usually occurs by the age of six or seven. In fact, in both agricultural and traditional, craft-based societies, at this age boys begin to leave the mother, going out with the father to farm or learn a skill. To detach successfully from identifying with the mother, boys must reject activities associated with women. Hence, in traditional societies there are *rites of passage* designed specifically to mark a young man's passage from childhood to adulthood and from boyhood to manhood. These changes are then reinforced by membership in exclusively male organizations. In our own society, although the change in identification does not occur so dramatically, there is a general turning away from the feminine role on the part of young boys: they organize "boys-only clubs," as well as enjoying camping and fishing trips in male-only company. Moreover, in contemporary societies it is more difficult to make this switch in identity, because fathers are often absent for most of the day and do not offer a ready model. As a result, the young male often accepts a stereotypical gender role, one offered by peers and the media and often not corresponding to reality. This leads the young male to be anxious about whether he is fulfilling his role adequately and to overcompensate by trying to fill a rigid mold of the masculine role. This is one explanation for the "macho" image that some young males, particularly those whose status on the cultural totem pole is low, attempt to present to the world, as for instance, by joining gangs.

Agents of Gender Socialization

It should be clear that those most directly involved in creating gender identities for individuals are those closest to them. Therefore, parents, siblings, extended family members, peers, teachers, and, today especially, the mass media play the most significant roles in this activity. These are the same agents who socialize each new generation (see Chapter 5).

The Media.   The media have probably become more influential than any of the other socializing agents in maintaining gender stereotypes. In particular, it is television that has the impact, because children spend more time watching it than they do interacting with parents, siblings and other family members, teachers, and friends. In fact, the average child will have watched more hours of television by high school graduation than she will have spent in class! Television has tremendous educational value—children can be exposed to a great variety of skills, speech patterns and vocabulary, factual information, and emotions. At the same time, the medium is perceived as being authoritative, and children are not sophisticated enough to distinguish reality from fantasy. Fictional accounts of life, as represented in many of the situation comedies, are taken at face value by children, which is unfortunate because they hardly ever reflect reality. Women, especially, are almost universally presented in highly professional occupations—doctors, lawyers, newspaper reporters—although they are seldom shown actually working. Moreover, they are always beautiful and thin, seldom lose their tempers, and never lose their jobs, even when they are assertive with bosses. In spite of documentaries and news items focusing on gender inequality, family violence, and sexual assaults, most prime-time shows still show men more frequently than women and in more authoritative positions, thus persevering in the traditional gender role stereotype.

Even when factual news stories are reported, they tend to be more frequently about men, and when they deal with women they include such information as the woman's marital status, her age, her physical attributes, and often what she is wearing—information that would never appear with regard to a man.

In Sum.   Newspapers and magazines also repeat the gender stereotypes. In the past, every daily paper had a section dedicated to women, which dealt with issues thought to be important to women—new recipes for feeding the family thriftily and cosmetics to keep the wife and mother looking spiffy. Today, they no longer call the section "for women," but they present the same material in the guise of "food" or "fashion." Some magazines are clearly addressed to either men or women; *Playboy, Penthouse, Sports Illustrated, Gentlemen's Quarterly*, and others, are directed at men. *Vogue* and a myriad of other fashion magazines and *Good Housekeeping* and tens of other magazines dedicated to food preparation and other facets of housekeeping are intended strictly for female consumption.

We have been making the point that gender stereotypes are alive and well. Because we do acknowledge the very real differences between men and women, however, we might wonder whether it matters that gender roles are stereotyped. Unfortunately, there are consequences for individuals, families, and the society at large, a fact supported by polls showing that many people feel men in the United States enjoy a better quality of life than women. Although gender roles have undergone a dramatic change—from a hierarchical arrangement in which one sex was subordinated to the other to an androgynous arrangement in which both sexes fill both the instrumental and the expressive roles—gender expectations still limit a woman's lifestyle choices. Although about 60 percent of women of working age are in the workforce, it is still expected that a woman's most important role is that of wife and mother. Women who choose a single lifestyle, or who want to combine marriage, motherhood, and a career—or simply have a job—are subject to criticism as radicals who are undermining "family values."

Indeed, combining outside work and the care of children and family is a difficult enterprise. Even where spouses are willing to take on a fair share of tasks, it is hard to divide one's time in such a way that everything and everybody are satisfied. Although research shows that men are spending more time in child-care and nurturing activities, in most cases housework is still the woman's responsibility, with men taking on automobile maintenance and lawn-mowing duties. In short, in spite of a greater flexibility in gender roles, gender stereotypes continue to constrain both men and women. For women, the constraints—in addition to the sheer difficulty of managing several roles at once—take the form of low self-esteem and a high incidence of mental illness. One of every four women experiences clinical depression at some time during her life (McGrath et al., 1990), a ratio of about 2 to 1. The high ratio may be an indication that women are more likely to seek help for this condition than men, but it may also be an indication that the unequal power in marital relationships and inequalities in other areas of their life—as well as the subtle and obvious humiliations and harassment to which most women are subjected at some points in their lives—seriously impact on women's mental health.

Another example of women's feelings of inadequacy is the efforts a large majority of them expend to constantly improve their appearance. In spite of the advances women have made in aiming for and achieving careers, delaying marriage and motherhood, and having more egalitarian marriages, they seem to have internalized conformist cultural expectations of beauty and femininity. Every woman's magazine (including those written for teenage girls) has article after article about perfecting the size of her thighs, abs, and glutes, and beyond diet and exercise, when to undergo plastic surgery. Cosmetic surgery, once the province of the rich and the old, is now suggested to women at the appearance of their first wrinkle—that is, in their 30s. Some women have even been known to undergo toe-shortening or pinky-toe removal for the sake of fitting into high-heeled, pointy shoes. Collagen, botox, and implants into various parts of the anatomy are the order of the day, and the so-called reality TV shows are reinforcing women's preoccupation with looks, subjecting contestants to extensive surgery in a relentless pursuit of physical perfection. This attitude is hardly what the feminists of the 1960s meant when they complained about the narrow roles prescribed for women and decried in Betty Friedan's book *The Feminine Mystique*. Nor is it strictly the fault of men, although women undertake these procedures mainly to please or to appeal to men.

Women in our society are expected to look forever young, thin, and glamorous. This societal ideal has begun to worry health professionals who have declared that models who look like the one here are unacceptably thin.

In fact, men, too, experience difficulty with gender stereotyping. Not all men are comfortable fulfilling the instrumental role, especially where that role requires assertiveness or even aggressiveness. Moreover, the role of breadwinner is not easy, particularly in times of economic downturn or for individuals who lack marketable skills. Partly as a result of this difficulty, we see many men walking away from their families or being delinquent in supporting their children. Or they substitute the role of breadwinner for one of "macho man," fathering a number of children for whom they do not care and behaving in a deviant manner that eventually leads to prison.

How Can We Change?

Because of these reasons, it seems logical to attempt to change the stereotypes surrounding gender roles. Such changes, however, appear impossibly difficult to attain. Students of gender have suggested that *androgynous* roles, combining the expressive and instrumental roles in the same individual, would be ideal. An androgynous individual could pick and choose among feminine

---

Box 9.5   Adam's Curse

Perhaps we need not worry about changing stereotypical sex roles at all. A well-known and world-acclaimed geneticist, Dr. Bryan Sykes, has published a book based on his research of the Y chromosome, the chromosome that differentiates men from women. His research has led him to a startling conclusion: in about 5,000 generations, or in approximately 125,000 years, male fertility will be roughly 1 percent of what it is now. Eventually, then, males will be unable to breed, and reproduction will have to take place some other way. One of the ways in which it could take place has already been tried: Japanese researchers have created a mouse from the fusion of two eggs, that is, without the involvement of a male. As Dr. Sykes says: "I feel sure that humans will one day be able to reproduce by the fusion of two eggs. The children will always be girls . . . This is very feasible, and I think will happen in my lifetime. Importantly: This is not reproductive cloning because you are not making a genetic copy of a person. Here you are creating an entirely new individual with a mixture of genes from two parents, though both of them are female" (Dreifus, 2004, D2).

The name of the book is *Adam's Curse*, and it is based on the notion that the Y chromosome is flawed and doomed. The reason is that the chromosome is passed on from father to son without the ability to mix or exchange DNA with any other chromosomes. Thus, it cannot repair mutations through genetic recombination, even though it is subject to a higher mutation rate than other chromosomes. It is this process that will eventually lead to its total disappearance, according to Dr. Sykes.

Another interesting fact the author describes is the history of the Y chromosome. Dr. Sykes is one of the scholars who discovered ways to extract DNA from fossilized bones, and he has done so extensively. Tracing the distribution of the Y chromosome, he and other researchers have been able to discover a common ancestor of many contemporary people; for instance, people named Sykes or Macdonald. They also traced the extent of Viking settlement and intermarriage in the British Isles and northern Europe. Another finding was that the Y chromosome of Genghis Khan is now present in a million men in Central Asia. How did it happen that so many men carry the chromosome of one man who lived in the twelfth century? Apparently, when Genghis Khan conquered a territory, he killed all the men and impregnated as many of the women as possible, thus spreading his genes far and wide, and through time. Sykes's conclusion from this example and others is that there may be a genetic cause for male greed, aggression, and promiscuity. He maintains, in fact, that whenever geneticists look at evolutionary diagrams, they see some frequently occurring Y chromosomes that are not closely related to others. "These genetic 'explosions' are the legacy of a relatively few very successful men who have supplanted the Y chromosomes of their contemporaries, as Genghis Khan did. My guess is that the Y chromosome of every living man has spent at least one generation in the testis of a warlord" (Dreifus, 2004, D2). Research of this type shows that the social sciences and the exact sciences sometimes produce results that each type of scientific endeavor alone could not.

and masculine traits (or emotions or behaviors); he or she could be more flexible in a relationship; and could feel more "complete" and satisfied, in the sense of not being obligated to behave one way or another because of limitations superimposed by one's gender. Some researchers, however, have denied that androgyny leads to greater self-confidence and satisfaction. Rather, they believe that assuming the instrumental role on the part of both men and women leads to higher rates of self-esteem, flexibility, and mental health. Masculine-oriented persons appear to experience a lesser incidence of stress, anxiety, depression, neuroticism, conflicts in work and achievement, and general dissatisfaction with their lives than do feminine-oriented individuals (Basow, 1992). Obviously, the problem of changing stereotypes, or changing the gender roles based on them, will not be solved easily or rapidly, if indeed a solution exists.

■ Sexuality

While we agree that we are all sexual beings because of the biological imperative to reproduce the species, we are less in agreement with the statement that there are many ways of being sexual. These ways are elements of our cultural learning. In other words, it is our particular culture that tells us how, with whom, under what circumstances, and where it is proper to have sex. In most Western societies, a heterosexual, patriarchal pattern has been the most common cultural script.

Homosexual Behavior

Although homosexuality has been known to exist throughout history, it had been forced to live underground. Only recently has our society, and many others, accepted homosexuality as a right and prohibited discrimination against individuals who practice it. Homosexuals have transformed their status rapidly and dramatically. When World War II began, gay people in America had no legal rights, no organizations, a handful of private thinkers, and no public advocates. Today, the situation is much different. Homosexuals are out in the open and have a number of organizations that work to secure their rights and prevent discrimination. Before World War II, the societal attitude was that heterosexual sex (that between men and women) was the only "normal" form of sexual expression. Homosexual expression was stigmatized, and the majority of Americans practiced homophobia, meaning that they feared and dreaded being associated with homosexuality, and often acted on their hatred of homosexuals with violence. This attitude still exists, but homosexuals, who prefer to be referred to as "gays" when male and as "lesbians" when female, have become advocates for their rights as a minority group. As such, they have become not only visible but also politically active and have succeeded in convincing a large portion of Americans that heterosexuality need not be the only form of sexual expression (Kaiser, 1997).

There is no agreement among scholars as to why some people are heterosexual, others are homosexual, and still others are bisexual. The general consensus is that we are born with a sexual orientation that impels us to search out the opposite sex, the same sex, or both sexes. This orientation, however, may be culturally changed or suppressed. In the past, homosexuality was considered deviant behavior, even mental illness. In 1974, however, the American Psychiatric Association officially took it off the mental illness list.

What proportion of the population is homosexual has remained questionable. First, not everyone admits to it in surveys. Second, some homosexual behavior is only episodic in nature—perhaps in the form of teenage experimentation. Kinsey et al. (1948) had reported that about 10 percent of the population was homosexual, but a group of contemporary social scientists has

Gay weddings, once unheard of, are becoming fairly common, as an increasing number of states are allowing them.

developed more accurate samples, and they conclude that about 2.8 percent of men think of themselves as homosexual, and only 1.4 percent of women do (Laumann et al., 1994).

Although greater tolerance toward this lifestyle currently exists among the public at large, instances of "gay bashing" still occur and homophobia is a prevalent attitude among many Americans. In fact, in a book in which he interviewed in depth suburban residents of Tulsa, Atlanta, San Diego, and Boston, sociologist Alan Wolfe found that although middle-class Americans live by the precepts of nonjudgmentalism and are willing to accept almost anything, they are not prepared to accept homosexuality (Wolfe, 1998, 46–47). The majority still refers to homosexuality as abnormal, immoral, sinful, sick, and wrong. Nonetheless, as a result of the active engagement of gay and lesbian groups who invoked the civil rights legislation to maintain that they have the right to marry, a number of states have granted such couples some legal rights. Massachusetts is the only state that actually allows gays and lesbians to marry, but New Jersey, Vermont, Connecticut, and California offer a variety of civil unions or domestic partnerships that afford the same privileges as married couples have as far as taxes, health care, and inheritance are concerned.

Explanatory Theories of Homosexuality

No theory has successfully explained the causes of homosexuality. Psychoanalytic theories suggest that homosexuality is caused by a specific family configuration, namely, a dominating mother and a weak father or a rejecting mother and an absent father. However, these theories fail to explain why many in such families do not become homosexual and, vice versa, why children in some closely knit and loving families do.

Learning theories maintain that homosexuality, like other elements of socialization, is learned through such processes as imitation or rewards and punishments. These theories, too, do not take into account that homosexuals embrace this lifestyle in spite of punishment, and that heterosexual parents may produce homosexual children and homosexual parents may produce heterosexual children.

Biological theories attribute homosexuality either to inherited genes or to sex hormones. Geneticists have found higher rates of homosexuality among identical twins as compared to fraternal twins, thus leading them to believe that a shared recessive gene may be a causal factor. Scientists have also suggested that hormones affect future sexual orientation prenatally, inasmuch as they found that rates of homosexuality and bisexuality were "clumped" in specific families (Pillard & Weinrich, 1986). One neuroscientist examined the brain tissue of a number of homosexual men and heterosexual men and women. The tissue came from the hypothalamus—a zone in the center of the brain that regulates a number of essential body functions, including the sex drive. The finding emerged that, in heterosexual men, the specific area is three times as large as in homosexual men and heterosexual women. However, the scientist did not conclude that homosexuality depends on this cause, and his sample was very small (Suplee, 1991).

Nonetheless, it does appear that homosexuality is heritable, that is, that there is a genetic component to it, in spite of the difficulty of supplying cause and effect. In fact, because gay men have only one-fifth as many children as heterosexual men, a gene for homosexuality should soon disappear, according to evolutionary theory. Inasmuch as it has not disappeared, researchers have set forth a number of speculations. One is that homosexuality may be a by-product of a gene that persists because it enhances fertility in other family members. Studies have found that gay men have more relatives than heterosexual men, especially on their mother's side (Wade, 2007, D6). Another clue to the origin of homosexuality is birth order. According to another study, it appears that having older brothers increases the chances that a man will be gay. This theory is based on the speculation that some event in the womb produces some type of antibodies to successive male pregnancies. According to this study, approximately 15 percent of gay men can attribute their homosexuality to the birth order, and with each older brother, the odds of same-sex attraction increases by 33 percent (Wade, 2007, D6).

The conclusion of other researchers in this area suggests that sexual orientation is probably arrived at through a combination of factors. There may be biological causes—for instance, sex hormones that could be influencing the brain in the prenatal and early neonatal phases of development. There may also be cultural factors that strengthen hormonal predispositions. Some women, for example, may be attracted to a lesbian lifestyle because they are drawn to the more emotional and expressive way women love.

Bisexuality

Another form of sexual expression is bisexuality, or a person's attraction to both men and women (some researchers prefer the term *ambisexuality*). The percentages of people who define themselves as bisexuals have remained small; Kinsey's surveys (1953) indicated that 16 percent of single men and 9 percent of single women in their thirties could be termed bisexual. Later surveys (Knudson, 1990; Hite, 1981) both showed that approximately 6 percent of adults defined themselves as being bisexual, although Hite's survey concerned only male respondents.

Again, perspectives on bisexuality differ. On the one hand, some scientists maintain, as Kinsey did, that sexuality exists on a continuum and is not an either/or behavior. In this view, bisexuality represents a combination of heterosexuality and homosexuality. Other scientists have insisted that heterosexuals, homosexuals, and bisexuals form separate categories, basing their arguments on the facts that sex drive, production of testosterone, and certain psychological and social traits differ among the categories.

As to the causes of bisexuality, no specific or general theory has been proposed. In the largest study of bisexuality attempted, the findings were inconclusive: most men and women had no homosexual experiences before adulthood and seemed to drift into relationships with both men and women, almost casually. However, the reasons for entering into various

Box 9.6   Acquiring a Homosexual Identity

During the socialization process, children assume that they will play the roles consonant with their gender. By adolescence, however, some individuals begin to see that their fantasies and actual behavior do not agree with the heterosexual model. They note their disinterest in persons of the opposite sex or in activities that are perceived as characteristic of their biological gender. The result is that they experience feelings of confusion and turmoil.

At some point during or after late adolescence, most homosexuals accept their identity and begin to present themselves to others with that label. However, they are selective in their presentation. They may, for instance, be known to friends and relatives, or in the local homosexual community, but keep their sexual identity hidden on the job. This situation used to be almost universal but has changed in the past decade, as even persons in government and the church have "come out." One researcher summarized these stages in a model that includes sensitization (before puberty, when future homosexuals begin to be aware of feeling "different"); identity confusion (in adolescence); identity assumption (accepting and "coming out"); and commitment (the decision to accept homosexuality as a way of life) (Troiden, 1988).

Gays and lesbians appear to differ in their sexual behavior in the same way that men and women do. Differences appear to be due to gender more than to sexual orientation. Lesbians tend to have monogamous relationships just as heterosexual women do; they tend to equate love and sex; they are less sexually aroused by visual stimuli; they are not likely to objectify sex as a commodity; they are not very interested in sex with strangers or in public places; they look for long-term relationships; and they are less interested in sexual experimentation. All these characteristics are true of heterosexual women as well. Gays, on the other hand, are more promiscuous, just as heterosexual males are; they tend to separate love and emotional intimacy and sex; they are interested in pornography and are excited by visual stimuli; they are likely to objectify sex as a consumer product; they are not opposed to sex with strangers or in public places, often cruising for sexual partners in such locations; they like sexual variety and experimentation. Finally, such industries as prostitution, pornography, topless bars, escort services, and adult bookstores tend to be supported by both heterosexual and homosexual males, rather than by women of either sexual orientation (Goode, 1990).

relationships with either same-sexed or other-sexed individuals differed according to gender. Women who defined themselves as bisexual noted that their emotional needs are sometimes filled by men and at other times by women, while bisexual men sometimes rationalize their bisexuality as a need for variety in their sex lives (Blumstein & Schwartz, 1977).

Sexually Transmitted Diseases

An unfortunate consequence of all types of sex, but particularly of unprotected, promiscuous sex, is sexually transmitted diseases (STDs). STDs are defined as diseases transmitted from one person to another through sexual contact, including oral–genital contact, anal intercourse, and oral–anal contact. STDs include chlamydia, gonorrhea, syphilis, AIDS, and about 30 others. These communicable diseases are very common because the viruses and bacteria that cause them have become increasingly resistant to drugs and because looser sexual mores have led people to engage in sex at earlier ages and with multiple partners. STDs affect people of all ages and all social classes. Untreated, they are very dangerous, leading to infertility and, in the worst cases, death. However, most may be cured if caught early enough, and all are preventable when proper information is available and care and responsibility for one's actions is taken. Unfortunately, it seems that many people do not take such responsibility: the Centers for Disease Control (CDC) report that while approximately 700,000 cases of gonorrhea occur every year in the United States, the disease is becoming resistant to the antibiotics with which it has been traditionally treated. Should the bacterium become resistant to the new type of antibiotics as well, it would lead to a severe crisis.

Twenty years ago the nation became conscious of a scourge that afflicted homosexual males (and later drug addicts who shared needles): the emergence of the human immunodeficiency virus (HIV), the virus that causes autoimmunodeficiency syndrome (AIDS). Since then, AIDS has become a leading cause of death for some populations and is the fifth leading cause of death among all Americans between the ages of 25 and 44. More than 501,000 Americans with AIDS have died in the United States, including adolescents and children under 15, and the disease has become a major killer in many other societies, especially those in Africa. The number of people living with AIDS in the United States as of 2005 is estimated at more than 437,982, of whom 77 percent are males (**http://www.avert .org/statsum.htm**).

When it became clear how HIV was spread, the government and a number of health organizations initiated a strongly worded campaign among homosexuals and drug addicts with the aim of prevention and protection. For gays, it urged the absolute necessity of having safe sex, that is, sex protected by condoms.

For a while, the fear of becoming HIV infected had the desired effect: as horror stories emerged of young gay men dying horrible deaths as a result of AIDS, more and more of them abandoned unprotected sex with men they had in the past picked up in bars, in adult

TABLE 9.5 Estimated Numbers of Cases and Rates (per 100,000 population) of AIDS, by Race, Category, and Sex, 2005—50 States and the District of Columbia

| | Adults or Adolescents | | | | | | Children (<13 yrs) | |
| | Males | | Females | | Total[a] | | | |
Race/ethnicity	No.	Rate	No.	Rate	No.	Rate	No.	Rate
White, not Hispanic	10,852	13.1	1,830	2.1	12,681	7.5	8	0.0
Black, not Hispanic	14,216	103.6	7,776	49.9	21,992	75.0	39	0.5
Hispanic	6,558	39.7	1,865	12.2	8,423	26.4	9	0.1
Asian/Pacific Islander	444	8.2	104	1.8	547	4.9	1	0.1
American Indian/Alaska Native	152	15.9	44	4.4	196	10.0	0	0.0
Total[b]	**32,430**	**27.2**	**11,710**	**9.4**	**41,140**[c]	**18.1**	**58**	**0.1**

Note: These numbers do not represent reported case counts. Rather, these numbers are point estimates, which result from adjustments of reported case counts. The reported case counts have been adjusted for reporting delays, but not for incomplete reporting. Data exclude cases in persons whose state or area of residence is unknown, as well as cases from U.S. dependent areas, for which census information about race and age categories is lacking.

[a]Because row totals were calculated independently of values for the subpopulations, the values in each row may not sum to the row total.
[b]Includes person of unknown race or multiple races. Because column totals were calculated independently of the values for the subpopulations, the values in each column may not sum to the column total.
[c]Includes 302 persons of unknown race or multiple races.

Source: **http://www.cdc.gov/hiv/topics/surveillance/resources/reports/2005report/table5a.htm**.

TABLE 9.6 Cases by Exposure Category: the distribution of the estimated number of diagnoses of AIDS among adults and adolescents by exposure category. A breakdown by sex is provided where appropriate.

Exposure Category	Male	Female	Total
Male-to-male sexual contact	420,790	—	420,790
Injection Drug Use	172,351	67,917	240,268
Male-to-male sexual contact and injection drug use	59,719	—	59,719
Heterosexual contact	50,793	84,835	135,628
Other*	14,350	6,519	20,869

*Includes hemophilia, blood transfusion, perinatal, and risk not reported or not identified.

Source: CDC, Division of HIV/AIDS Prevention; **http://www.cdc.gov/hiv/stats.htm**.

bookstores, or in spas catering to gays. As a result, and because of new treatments and education efforts, AIDS-related deaths had declined in recent years, by 42 percent between 1996 and 1997 and by another 20 percent between 1997 and 1998. Unfortunately, while the trend was slowing for the gay male population, it was increasing among women whose partners were bisexuals or drug abusers and for minorities (See AIDS statistics in Tables 9.5 and 9.6).

New treatments can prolong the lives of AIDS victims and keep at bay the emergence of AIDS among the HIV infected. However, they have also had a negative effect. Some gay men, in fact, have acquired a false sense of security and are increasingly becoming careless, again engaging in high-risk sexual behavior. In particular, it is the generation of younger gays, who have not personally seen the devastation of disease and death that AIDS causes who are the most reckless.

Internationally, about 39.5 million people are estimated to be living with HIV/AIDS, of whom almost half are women and approximately 2.3 million are children (2003). In 2006, AIDS had caused the deaths of approximately 3 million people, including 2.6 million adults and 380,000 children. In some nations, the disease is leaving millions of children orphans and is causing major catastrophes for new generations (http://**www.avert** .org/worldstats.htm).

The Chapter in Brief

The elderly in the United States suffer from loss of status, income, and prestige, even though they are an ever-increasing proportion of the population. Because of the speed of technological change in modern industrial societies, many young persons are better informed and have more skills than the old, at least in certain areas. As a result, the old are devalued. In addition, the elderly suffer from declining health and vigor and so deviate from the ideal norms that prevail in a society that extols youth, beauty, and fitness.

Many of the elderly have financial difficulties in addition to health problems; this is especially true of elderly women and members of minority groups. Discrimination against the elderly has been obvious in the area of employment, where the cards are stacked against anyone over age 40. In addition, many employers enforce the retirement age of 70, which forces some employees to disengage before they are ready. Disengagement is supposed to be a mutual process by which the elderly give up social and occupational roles voluntarily so that these roles may be filled by younger persons. Other theoretical frameworks within which the elderly are studied include the modernization, interactionist, subculture, activity, exchange, and age stratification theories.

Many of the myths about the elderly are patently untrue. Not all are senile or miserable or lonely; only a minority have serious health problems; they are not all poor, nor do they all hate retirement. Most live independent lives. Many do face widowhood and the consequent loneliness of bereavement, and when their physical and mental health wane, they may face institutionalization. None of these are pleasant conclusions to life; however, inasmuch as the elderly are a growing segment of society, it is likely that the negative attitudes toward them will be somewhat reversed.

The fact that humanity exists in two sexes has brought it much conflict. In the war between the sexes, women appear to be the losers. From a biological point of view, the two sexes are needed for the species to reproduce: the function of males is to deposit sperm in the reproductive organs of females; the function of females is to carry the resulting embryo—and then the fetus—until it emerges as a fully formed human infant. Both parents can then nurture it until it can exist independently. Throughout history, these different biological functions have resulted in societies treating the two sexes differentially and unequally.

Differences between men and women are of an anatomical, genetic, and hormonal nature. These differences certainly have effects on the behavior of men and women. Some of these differences seem to indicate that females are more social, more suggestible, have lower self-esteem—at least beginning with adolescence—and are less achievement-oriented than males, who are judged to be more aggressive, assertive, and to have more analytical minds. There is also evidence that females are superior in verbal ability and seem inclined to nurture infants and children (the expressive role), while males excel in spatial and quantitative abilities, facilitating the instrumental role. What remains unclear is whether these traits are inborn or a result of differences in socialization experiences.

Even though we are born either male or female, we must become socialized into sex roles. Such socialization begins in the cradle: girl and boy babies are treated differently. Researchers theorize that socialization into sex roles occurs in the context of the functionalist and conflict theories through such processes as social learning, the cognitive developmental model, and identification. As to the agents of gender socialization, they are the family, the peer group, the school, and the mass media.

The fact that women have been treated unequally in most societies has had consequences on their lives. Traditional gender roles have been permeated by a sexist ideology that justifies the inequality between the sexes. The obvious effect of sexism is that many options have been closed to women, who have been relegated for centuries to the roles of wives and mothers and little else. Sociocultural changes in contemporary postindustrial societies have opened more avenues for women. However, the entrance of so many women into the workforce and the consequent displacement of marriage and family have left many women puzzled and confused. It remains difficult for many women to reconcile their aspirations for personal achievement with their desire for a traditional family life. As a result, both men's and women's gender roles still remain far from clear-cut.

In acquiring a sexual personality, not everyone is drawn to heterosexuality. Some individuals are drawn to members of their own gender, becoming homosexuals. Still others are attracted to both sexes, sometimes establishing a paired relationship with one gender after some experimentation, or otherwise remaining bisexual throughout their lives. Scientists have not established a definite cause for these behaviors.

A negative effect of unprotected or promiscuous sex is sexually transmitted diseases (STDs), the most dangerous of which is AIDS. This disease has killed many gay men and intravenous drug users and, increasingly, many women and children. It is also a scourge in developing nations, particularly in Africa.

Terms to Remember

activity theory In the study of the elderly, the theory that the key to successful aging is to replace former roles with new ones.

ageism An ideology that asserts the superiority of the young over the old. Used to justify discrimination against the elderly in political, economic, and social areas.

anatomical differences The differences in physical structure and appearance between the two sexes. The most important anatomical difference lies in the distinct reproductive systems of males and females.

cognitive development theory A theory that includes the idea that children learn gender roles according to which stage of cognitive development they have reached. Cognitive development is the way information is processed by individuals at different stages of physical maturation.

conflict theory A theory that assumes that power and privilege are based on the resources an individual possesses.

disengagement theory A theory of aging that posits that the elderly withdraw from their former social and occupational roles so that these may be filled by the young. This should occur by mutual consent.

exchange theory In the study of the elderly, the theory that the disadvantaged position of the elderly in American society is due to their lack of the social and material resources that would make them valuable in interactions with the young.

expressive role Emphasizes nurturing, emotion, and peacemaking.

feminist theory A theory that has borrowed much of the framework of conflict theory, especially the fact that women are underrepresented in positions of power in the society at large, a reflection of the lack of power women have within the family.

gender roles Traditionally, the **instrumental** role is assigned to males and the **expressive** role is assigned to females.

hormones Chemicals that are secreted into the bloodstream by glands located in the body, whose functions are to stimulate some chemical processes and inhibit others.

instrumental role Stresses rationality, competitiveness, aggression, and goal-orientation.

interactionist theory In the study of the elderly, a theory that focuses on the shared meanings that the elderly hold in common.

male or female Biological terms, descriptive of biological facts. They refer to a **sex status**, ascribed and not subject to change except in extraordinary circumstances.

masculine and feminine Reflect **social** conditions, describing how males and females are expected to behave in a given society and how they come to feel about themselves. They are **gender roles**, achieved and, thus, subject to change according to place and time.

modernization theory In the study of the elderly, the theory that the status of older people declines as the society in which they live becomes more modern and industrial.

secondary sex characteristics Include height, weight, distribution of body fat and hair, and musculature.

sex chromosomes Contain the genes that determine heredity in all living creatures.

social learning theory A theory based on the behaviorist notion that learning consists of observation, imitation, and reinforcement.

structural functionalist theory One of the most dominant theories in sociology, which assumes that those elements are retained in a social system that aid in the survival of that system.

Suggested Readings

Epstein, Cynthia Fuchs, Carroll Seron, Bonnie Oglensky, and Robert Saute. 1999. *The Part-Time Paradox: Time Norms, Professional Life, Family and Gender.* New York: Routledge. A discussion of the conflicts inherent in the lives of women who work, the tension between the demands of career and family, and suggestions as to how to solve some of these conflicts with part-time work.

Faludi, Susan. 1999. *Stiffed: The Betrayal of the American Man*. New York: William Morrow. A feminist author maintains that even though American men remain the dominant sex, they feel increasingly misunderstood and unappreciated.

Dychtwald, Ken. 1999. *Age Power: How the 21st Century Will Be Ruled by the New Old*. New York: Putnam. A gerontologist takes a look at the elderly and speculates about their future social patterns.

Quadagno, Jill. 1999. *Aging and the Life Course: An Introduction to Social Gerontology*. New York: McGraw-Hill. An overview of the aged and of the process of aging from the point of view of sociology.

Stoller, Eleanor Palo, and Rose Campbell Gibson. 2000. *Worlds of Difference: Inequality in the Aging Experience*. 2nd ed. Thousand Oaks, CA: Pine Forge Press. The experience of growing old according to a diverse number of people differing in race, class, and gender. An anthology written from a sociological perspective, showing a variety of norms and social structures on the road to aging.

Westheimer, Ruth K., and Sanford Lopater. 2002. *Human Sexuality*. Baltimore: Lippincott Williams & Wilkins. As the title suggests, this is a textbook on human sexuality and deals with the entire spectrum of this subject in clear and understandable language. The well-known Dr. Westheimer answers letters and queries on a variety of sexual issues.

Web Sites of Interest

http://www.nih.gov/nia
The site of the U.S. government agency the National Institute of Aging. It provides links to other sites related to the subject of aging, as well as information on research and funding.

http://www.iwpr.org
The site of a public policy research organization whose purpose is to inform women and families on issues important to them. Deals with issues of poverty, employment, and aspects of health care, among many others.

http://www.4women.gov/owh
Another agency, part of the U.S. Department of Health and Human Services, that also specializes in women's issues, particularly those related to health.

http://www.vix.com/men/index.html
This site is a source for statistics, studies, and publications relating to men's issues.

http://www.indiana.edu/~kinsey
Web site of the Kinsey Institute where research on human sexuality continues.

http://www.who.int/hiv/strategic/en
The World Health Organization, an agency of the United Nations, provides the latest facts and figures on HIV/AIDS.

10

From the Plow to the Computer: Change, Collective Behavior, and Social Movements

IN THIS CHAPTER, YOU WILL LEARN

- *that change is a constant feature of life, but the speed of change has become more rapid in the modern world;*
- *that change may be viewed from several perspectives;*
- *some of the sources of change;*
- *the processes of social and cultural change;*
- *the relationship of technology to change;*
- *the meaning of collective behavior, and where and why it occurs;*
- *the definition and kinds of crowds, panics, mobs, riots, and mass hysteria;*
- *the nature of publics and public opinion;*
- *about social movements, their traits and characteristics;*
- *about some of the causes of social movements.*

Anew century began a few years ago. More importantly, not only a century, but a millennium has come to an end, a dramatically large segment of time in human terms. What changes can we expect to experience in the new century? We can only conjecture about the future, though we know something of the past. Because generations that came before us left a written record, we have some insights as to what life was like. When the first thousand

It has been a long way from hieroglyphics (like the one above, from a tomb in the Valley of the Kings in Egypt) to computers. Social change increases rapidly once a way is invented of communicating with many people at once, rather than one at a time.

years of the Christian Era were ending in Europe (in 999, that is) life for the majority was a grim struggle. Men considered themselves lucky to survive past 30 years, and 50 was considered a ripe old age (although, of course, some lived into their eighties). Women, too, barely made it to their thirtieth birthday, and many died regularly at childbirth. The years we know as childhood were unknown: children in every social class had to grow up as fast as possible and become useful members of society. This meant that emperors were leading armies while still in their teens, and many popes began their tenure while still in their twenties. At the eve of that first millennium in Europe, transportation meant an oxcart, and rapid transportation consisted of a horse and rider. Housing was mud-and-thatch huts for the serfs and timber castles for the feudal lords. Disease was rampant: tuberculosis regularly decimated populations, and leper colonies flourished outside many city walls. Vitamin deficiencies produced blindness, goiter, paralysis, and bone malformations, and those so affected made up the hunchbacks and beggars living at the mercy of the healthy and wealthy. The social order was rigidly divided into clearly defined strata: the nobility, who spent their time battling enemies to preserve their privileged status; the clergy, whose chief task it was to pray for the salvation of souls (because the end of the world was thought to be imminent, this was an important function!); and the serfs, who did all the back-breaking work in the society to feed and clothe the others. The dark nights, illuminated only by burning logs and the occasional candle, held terror for all, and each passing season was much like the one before.

In the thousand years between 999 and 1999 the world has changed dramatically. Human lives have been extended, many diseases have been tamed, transportation is rapid and efficient, communication—which did not exist except in embryonic form a millennium ago—overwhelms us. In the developed world, food and housing have become sophisticated and plentiful—though not for all individuals. Electricity enables us to work at night, and the industrial system creates millions of objects to fulfill our needs, real and imagined. But what used to be called, optimistically, progress has not been fairly distributed around the globe nor in individual societies. Nor has it eradicated totally the ancient scourges of disease, famine, war, pain, and suffering.

With all our new capabilities, can we predict what the twenty-first century holds in store? We no longer fear the end of the world, but most of us look to the future with some trepidation. The increase in global temperature, predicted by scientific entities, will lead to changes that are still unknown. Experts in the social sciences tell us that the twenty-first century will be one in which economics will play a dominant role. In the centuries ahead, the world will contain more democracies, which will mean a more peaceful coexistence among nations. The imperialism of the past, in fact, was based on the need to acquire new territory to exploit its raw materials. Increasingly, raw materials will be less important to manufacturing, as even oil is replaced by alternative fuels, solar power, and controlled nuclear fusion. The end of the petroleum age will also lead to a rearrangement in the status of nations and will force them to collaborate more fully with the United Nations to solve overarching problems that face the entire world. Europe and the United States will probably remain in the forefront as superpowers as long as they can manage to solve some of their internal problems.

Today, change is dramatic and fast. It was not always so. Human societies remained practically unchanged for many thousands of years. What has happened to cause such profound transformations? What makes change occur so rapidly now? What is change, anyway? Where does it originate? Can it be stopped or bent to our wishes? Can it be slowed or accelerated? Do we control it, or does it control us?

■ Society and Change

For most of human history, as we said, people born in one generation lived very much like their parents and could count on their children living very much as they had. Whatever change occurred was almost imperceptible because it was so slow. For the past 250 years, and especially for the past 50 years, such vast changes have taken place from one generation to the next that people separated by 20 or 30 years may be said to live in an altogether different society and be strangers to one another. Futurologist Alvin Toffler has called this concept "future shock," a condition akin to the culture shock that would be experienced by a person confronting a totally alien culture for the first time.

At the same time that dramatic changes constantly take place, a thread of stability is also apparent. The factor of stability holds societies together and binds each generation to the next.

The subject of change holds special fascination for social scientists because if the sources of change could be determined scientifically, and the course of change predicted, then the possibility of guiding change in the direction of attaining the highest common good could become a reality. Unfortunately, the subject of change is not so easily harnessed. Change is constantly analyzed, however, because it is apparent that it is the pivot around which much of contemporary life revolves.

Although change represents flux, or motion, analysis requires that social phenomena be viewed as if they were frozen in time and space (static). But they must also be observed from the perspective of dynamics, or the study of the sources of change. *Statics* and *dynamics* are two dimensions of the same phenomenon. They are coexisting entities, and the need to employ both in the study of change makes the project so much more complex. Complexity also results from the fact that change affects every aspect of individual and social life. The issues to be analyzed concerning change, then, are endless and multiform.

Box 10.1 **The United States: A Century of Change**

Among the sociocultural changes that have occurred in the United States in the last century, which have radically transformed the society, the following can be gathered from the information collected by the Census Bureau.

	1900	2000
Total Population	76 million	293 million (2004) (300+million 2007)
Women	37 million	152 million (2006)
Men	39 million	148 million (2006)
Minorities	9 million	(approx 98 million 2006)
Black	8.8 million	(38 million 2006)
American Indian	267,000	2.8 million (2005)
Chinese	119,000	Asian; Chinese, Japanese, and others approx. 14.5 million (2005)
Hispanic or Latino		42.5 million (2005)
Largest Cities	New York (3.4 million)	New York (8+ million)
	Chicago (1.7 million)	Los Angeles (3.8 million)
	Philadelphia (1.3 million)	Chicago (2.9+ million)
	St. Louis (575,000)	Houston (2+ million)
	Boston (561,000)	Philadelphia (1.5 million)
Largest States	New York (7.3 million)	California (36+ million)
	Pennsylvania (6.3 million)	Texas (23+ million)
	Illinois (4.8 million)	New York (19+ million)
	Ohio (4.2 million)	Florida (17.5 million)
	Missouri (3.1 million)	Illinois (12.5 million)
Size of Average Household	4.76 persons	2.60 persons
Births per Woman	4	2.05
Infant Mortality Rate (Deaths in the first year per 1,000 births)	165	6.8 (2005)
Number of Divorced	Men: 84,000	Men: 8.3 million
	Women: 114,000	Women: 11.1 million
Life Expectancy	Men: 46 years	Men: 74.7 years (2001)
	Women: 48 years	Women: 80 years (2001)
Persons Living Alone	1%	25.5% (2000)
Persons Living in Households of 5 or More People	50%	10% (2000)
Households Headed by a Married Couple	80% (1910)	53% (2000)
Urban Residents	40%	80%
Average Yearly Income	$8.360 (adjusted for inflation)	46,242 (2005)
Percent of Income Spent on Food	43% (1901)	2.4% (2005)
Suburban Residents	12% (1910)	52%
Number of Automobiles	8,000	241 million (2005)
Percent of Housing Units with Electricity	2%	99% (1997)
High School Graduates	13% (1910)	85.2% (2005)
College Graduates	3%	27.6% (2005)
Married Women in Labor Force	6%	59% (2005)
Men Over 65 in Labor Force	63%	18.5% (2004)
Hourly Wage of Factory Workers (adjusted for inflation)	$3.80 (1909)	$13.90 (1999)
Percentage of Unionized Civilian Labor Force	3%	12% (2006)
Family Farms	5.7 million	1.9 million (1997)

Source: U.S. Bureau of the Census, 2006 "Statistics in Brief."

Levels of Change

Change may be experienced on a micro level, on a middle level, and on a macro level. On a *micro* level, change is felt through new patterns of individual and small group interaction. The family, for instance, is a much changed institution, as will become apparent in a later chapter. The chief result of these changes is that the individual is faced with a large number of options: new norms of behavior, new values, new manners. Choice, while opening some horizons, also creates anxiety and confusion. In turn, anxiety and confusion can lead to feelings of normlessness, or anomie, which are harmful to the individual and to society.

At the *middle* level of social life, change is experienced in communities as a result of alterations in the economy and in the political system. As industry became the underlying force of economies in Western societies, people began moving in large numbers to cities. Urbanization, which is what we call this trend, is perceived as having lessened communal ties. At the same time, the urban setting presents many more opportunities to individuals. Similarly, groups or classes of people that were formerly excluded from the political process or from upward mobility have been increasingly gaining inclusion as a result of trends toward greater democratization of the political system and the greater opportunities that a capitalistic economic system offers.

Finally, on the *macrosocial* level, change is generated by social forces that are large-scale and revolutionary, affecting entire societies and regions of the world. Individuals and communities, where these changes are experienced, seem to be swept away by these social forces in the sense that they must adapt to them or perish. Urbanization, industrialization, and the advent of the information society are some of these macro-level changes, and they have a domino effect, transforming the social structures and institutions of societies.

Box 10.2   Sweeping Changes in the Political Game

The widespread use of the Internet is changing the way American politics is conducted. Both Republicans and Democrats maintain that the use of e-mail, interactive web sites, candidate and party blogs, and text messaging is much superior and far less costly than the previous instruments, namely, knocking on doors and using banks of telephones manned by volunteers. The new tools politicians use in campaigning makes it possible for them to raise money, organize get-out-the-vote efforts, and assemble crowds for rallies. Even advertising on television is taking a step back and diminishing in influence because the new technology allows campaigns to address themselves personally to more specific audiences. For instance, podcasts may be used with a daily downloaded message from a candidate, e-mail chain messages with peer-to-peer distribution may be sent, and messages may be addressed to networks of persons with similar political views.

The Internet has already affected the music industry, newspapers, and retailing, so it is to be expected that it is going to impact politics. Already in the 2004 elections it was very successful in fundraising, particularly in the campaign of democratic presidential candidate Howard Dean, who was one of the early users of the Internet. In 2006,

about 50 million people in the United States got their news every day from the Internet, which is available to 70 percent of Americans. With such figures, it becomes clear that the Internet will become a major tool for candidates of every stripe. In fact, its success in campaigning prompted the national chairman of the Republican Party to say that "the effect of the Internet on politics will be every bit as transformational as television was" (Nagourney, 2006, 17).

Despite its transformative power and the manner in which the Internet will in all probability change the way politics, and not only campaigning, is run, there are shortcomings with this medium. For one thing, the message will reach only those people who are interested in politics: those who are not, will not even have to hear the "bites" audiences are subjected to on television. For another, Internet use declines among persons 65 and over, yet that age group is the most faithful of voters and followers of political events. As a means of persuasion for political campaigns, therefore, the Internet is still in its infancy. There is no doubt, however, that it will become a new way of interacting with our representatives in government. Whether it will be a better or worse way, only the future will tell (Nagourney, 2006, 1 and 17).

■ Processes of Social and Cultural Change

Change may be willed or planned, borrowed or imitated from other societies; or phenomena may be discovered and technologies invented. And we know the processes through which change occurs.

Change occurs on both a societal and a cultural level. When change happens in society, it does so in the guise of a change in the patterns of interaction. That is, as a result of change, some members of society assume new statuses and fill new roles. For instance, the abolition of slavery was a social change because it gave former slaves a new status—that of free persons—in which they could assume new roles as the equals of other free persons. This kind of change, *social change*, occurs through planning, reform, or revolution.

On the other hand, change in culture, or *cultural change*, occurs as a result of scientific discoveries, technological inventions, new achievements in the arts, shifts in religious doctrines, and so on. In Western civilization there have been dramatic cultural changes: the belief that slavery was justified has given way to the belief that it is reprehensible; the assumption that the earth is flat has given way to the discovery that it is round; the invention of the automobile has transformed the way of life, affecting sexual mores, family traditions, and people's perceptions of the world.

Of course, society and culture do not exist one without the other. Social and cultural changes do not occur separately and distinctly. Changes in society cause changes in culture and vice versa. Social and cultural changes overlap and are viewed separately only for purposes of analysis. Social scientists use the term *sociocultural change*, or simply change, to mean both social and cultural change.

Social Change: Planning, Reform, Revolution

Planning is a self-explanatory process in which people are constantly engaged. Planning by governments at all levels results in continuous, though often slow, social change.

Reform involves efforts by either citizens or governmental agencies to correct laws or institutions. During the Great Depression, laws were reformed to provide citizens with jobs, to furnish them with the wherewithal to survive when they were unemployed, to help them with health care, and so on. In 1954, the law that allowed segregation of the races was reformed. Abortion and divorce laws have also undergone reform.

The train was an invention that put together elements already present in the society—the steam engine and wheels—when it became apparent that speed and comfort would be superior to that provided by a horse and carriage. This was especially true in the United States, where the tremendous distances made travel by the old method long, uncomfortable, and dangerous.

Revolution is change obtained through violent means by the people of a nation when their government ceases to be responsive to them or when they are occupied by another country. Revolution is analyzed in the context of social movements later in the chapter.

Cultural Change: Innovation and Diffusion

Because people are creatures of habit, they are conservative and resist giving up beliefs, values, and customs—aspects of nonmaterial culture—in favor of new ones. Nonetheless, some cultural changes necessitate giving up, or exchanging, the old for the new. The processes of cultural change include innovation and diffusion.

Innovation.   Innovation produces new elements, or new combinations of old elements, for absorption into the culture. Innovation is also always cumulative. Whether we speak of music, painting, or the latest space technology, they are all built upon foundations erected earlier. Innovation can take the form of a *discovery* or of an *invention*.

A *discovery* is a new perception of an already existing fact or relationship. Principles of physics and chemistry, the organization of the solar system, the existence of viruses and bacteria, are examples of discoveries. These phenomena existed all along, but humans were not aware of them. For a discovery to effect change, it must be put to use. There must be other technological inventions to support it, and a need for the discovery must be present. The principle of the steam engine was known by the Greeks some 2000 years ago, but they saw no need for such a machine, nor did they have the necessary technology to build one.

An *invention* is a way of putting existing knowledge to new use. Ideas or objects already present in the culture are combined in a new way to produce something more important than the sum of their parts. When the steam engine was combined with a boat to produce the steamboat, the new product became a more effective mode of transportation than boats powered by rowing or sails had been previously.

Societies do not change at the same rate, and the process of diffusion works in such a way that some, but not all, products of one society are willingly accepted by another. This desert dweller still uses camels as his mode of transportation but communicates via a cell phone.

Inventions can also occur in nonmaterial culture. The Constitution of the United States may be thought of as a cultural invention resulting from the philosophical traditions of Western Europe and the experience of the colonists in the New World.

Diffusion. Diffusion is a process in which cultural traits are spread from one society to another, or from one group within society to another. Diffusion is an important factor in cultural change. For instance, spaghetti was brought to the United States by Italian immigrants. The Italians had adopted noodles that had been brought from China, and today pasta is considered as American as apple pie (and it has become popular in many other countries, as well). Anthropologists claim that most of the content of a complex culture is the product of diffusion.

Diffusion tends to be reciprocal; that is, each culture in contact with another gives something to the other, although not always in the same proportion. A simple culture, as a rule, borrows more elements from a complex culture than the other way around, and a borrowing culture is usually selective. Asian societies have generally accepted Western technology (and fashion and music and food) but are only slowly accepting the West's system of values. Americans borrowed the idea of representative government from England but did not give it a parliamentary form. The traits that a society borrows tend to be modified rather than accepted wholesale.

The Sources of Change

What triggers change? Tracing the sources of change has been problematic for social scientists who have developed a number of theories and models to explain it. There are also more obvious sources of change, however.

The Physical Environment. The physical environment, over which people have little control, directs the cultural development of a society and the erection of social structures. It also promotes some and limits other changes. Earthquakes, volcanic eruptions, repeated flooding, severe droughts, and similar phenomena may effectively change the lives of the people in the area, sometimes wiping them out altogether.

Geography. In the past, geography played a crucial role, because change occurred more rapidly and more consistently in societies that were geographically at the crossroads, where each society was exposed to the culture of another. Conversely, little change occurred in societies that were geographically isolated from others because there were so few opportunities for cultural diffusion.

Population. Population movements, as well as increases and decreases in population size, are also sources of change. The baby boom that followed World War II required the building of many schools and the development of youth-directed industries. This same generation is today making special demands on jobs and housing and in the future will make the society top-heavy with older people. This will have consequences for the entire society.

Ideas or Belief Systems. Another source of social change originates in ideas or belief systems, also called ideologies. The American Revolution was a triggering mechanism for social change: it was fought because the idea that Americans ought to be independent of England took hold, and the idea emerged because dependence on England was an economic hardship.

Social Movements. Ideologies and belief systems are often incorporated into social movements, a form of collective behavior. Social movements attract a number of people who join together to either bring about or resist specific social or cultural changes. They represent an attempt on the part of members of a society to affect the social order through direct action.

War and Conquest.   Throughout the history of the human race, much social change has occurred as a result of wars, which yielded either the conquest of territory or its loss. War casualties can have a deep impact on population. Considering that in World War II alone, about 17 million military personnel and some 34 million civilians died, it becomes clear that a society can suffer a decline in population that will unbalance it for generations. There are almost certain to be changes in the economic system, for fewer men in the labor force may mean labor shortages. In turn, shortages may bring women into the labor force, with a consequent realignment of traditions and values. Wars also necessitate the manufacture of specific products—arms, means of transportation, and so on, so that new plants tend to be built, again accelerating economic growth. The losers in war face other changes—the imposition of foreign rule and a foreign language, forced movement to other areas, economic subjugation imposed through taxation and slave labor, and in the worst but by no means unique event, death.

In addition to leaving a traumatic and sometimes indelible mark on the survivors, wars may change a nation's values and norms through the forced contacts with other cultures. The best example is provided by Japan, a formerly closed society that, initially because of its military occupation by American forces, began to absorb American norms.

Finally, war can have drastic consequences on a society's social structure, particularly institutions. The growth of large research universities in the United States followed the fact that the USSR—then our Cold War enemy—was the first nation to launch a space satellite. The growth of the central government at the expense of local governments is also related to the fact that providing for national defense and security requires a large bureaucracy and wide-ranging taxing powers.

Random Events.   Random events and the acts of individual human beings can also lead to change, although there is no way to subject such phenomena to scientific inquiry. The assassination of a president, causing a vice president to take over the helm of a nation, can have dramatic consequences, as can the judgment of a general who loses a significant battle. Individuals, too, can have profound influences on the course of events in a society, although it is difficult to evaluate the effect of a single individual on social change.

Technology

The most obvious and revolutionary source of change throughout history has been technology. *Technology* includes all the methods, devices, and artifacts made by humans that help people to manage and control their environment. For prehistoric humans, technology consisted of the use of sharpened sticks and stones. For contemporary people, it includes everything from a simple shovel to a sophisticated computer.

Some technological discoveries or inventions have been so significant in terms of the sociocultural changes they have produced that they have been called technological revolutions. One such revolution occurred during the Neolithic, or New Stone Age (between 5000 and 3000 B.C.). In this period, for the first time in history, people changed their condition from food gatherers to *food producers*. They domesticated some animals and put them to use. They invented the plow. They began using four-wheeled vehicles. Later, they added the solar calendar, writing, and numbers, and they began to use bronze. Finally, they added irrigation, sailboats, looms, the making of bricks, the process of glazing, and a great architectural invention, the arch.

Results of the First Technological Revolution

Tilling the soil and keeping flocks provided people with a fairly dependable food supply and even an occasional surplus. Because the rate of starvation was drastically reduced, populations boomed. No longer needing to move in constant search of food, people settled permanently in one spot. A settled existence promoted the development of institutions—customs and traditions solidified into the family, religion, education, government, and the economy. In time, these pivotal institutions all grew in complexity. Temporary settlements became permanent villages and towns. Work that had to be done in these villages and towns was divided for the sake of greater efficiency. Goods and services began to be exchanged between a number of villages and towns, and new ways to control the environment accumulated. Villages grew into towns and then cities and eventually became city-states and nation-states. Religions progressed from beliefs in magic to more sophisticated forms, including monotheism. The family also underwent a number of changes and took on different forms in different societies.

■ The Industrial Revolution

By about the middle of the eighteenth century, a new technological revolution began yet another cycle of change, although the Industrial Revolution actually had its roots in much earlier events.

Inventions and Discoveries of the Industrial Revolution

The Industrial Revolution may be said to have begun with (1) the invention of a small number of basic machines, (2) the invention and discovery of some new materials, and (3) the discovery of new sources of power. The wide-ranging effects of these discoveries and inventions included the mechanization of agriculture and manufacturing, the application of power to manufacturing, the development of a factory system, a tremendous increase in the speed of transportation and communication, and dramatic changes in economic systems.

The Industrial Revolution brought us images such as this and an increased production of goods and services that much improved our life style. Now, however, a new technological revolution threatens to make ghost towns of once prosperous industrial cities such as Pittsburgh, shown here.

Among the most important machines invented during the first phase of the Industrial Revolution were the pendulum clock, the spinning jenny, the power loom, the blast furnace, and the steam engine. During the second phase, which is thought to have begun about 1860, the most important invention was the combustion engine, which enabled steam power to be applied to transportation and factory machine production. Steel was substituted for iron as the basic material of industry, and coal was replaced by gas and oil as principal sources of power (we are currently attempting to harness atomic and solar energy as well as other alternatives as sources of power). Electricity became a major form of industrial energy. The spread of electricity enabled messages to be sent over wires, telegraph, and telephones; gave people more time to work by providing light during the night hours; and supplied power for turbines and elevators so that skyscrapers could be constructed. Chemistry also flourished in this period, allowing people to manufacture products that were not originally found in nature, such as petrochemicals, synthetics, and plastics. Automatic machinery was developed, and labor became highly specialized. A third phase—which according to some is actually the beginning of a new technological revolution—began with *automation*, which was developed around the 1930s. Basically, this is a process in which machines control other machines, as contrasted with *mechanization*, which is the substitution of machines for human and animal muscle power. Automation effectively began following World War II, when the first computers were produced. Computers have been responsible for an information explosion that has practically doubled the ability to store and access knowledge in the last 30 years.

The third technological revolution is in its infancy and should mature by about the middle of the twenty-first century. This revolution consists of the joining of computers and telecommunications (image television, voice telephone, data information, text facsimile) into a single system, which will transform us into a true world society.

Industrialism

The system of production that came to be called industrialism (or industry) represented a radical departure from previous methods of manufacturing goods. In the Middle Ages, artisans or craftsmen organized in guilds (types of unions) produced an entire article and sold it directly to a buyer. As commerce expanded, some craftsmen relied on merchants to dispose of their merchandise rather than waiting for customers to come to their shops. Eventually, craftsmen began to depend on merchants to supply the raw material and to sell the finished product. Needing more workers, merchants began to employ entire families to produce a finished object out of raw or unfinished material and paid them by the piece. This system was alternately called the piece, domestic, or putting-out system. The piece system became the foundation of the English woolen industry. Farm families supplemented their small earnings by spinning the wool that merchants brought to their cottages (hence the name "cottage industry"). Eventually, the piece system became increasingly specialized as more and more articles were produced. The production of an article was divided into several steps that different members of the family or apprentices could easily perform. Specialization and division of labor are especially efficient ways of organizing production.

The Factory. With the invention and growing use of machinery in manufacturing, it became more convenient to house both the workers and the bulky machinery under one roof. This step introduced the *factory system* as the basis of industrialism. The former merchants—now called entrepreneurs and employers—had much more control over their workers when all the stages of production were housed in one location. They could pace the work of their employees—decide how many pieces had to be finished per hour or per day. And they could use their capital much more effectively when everything needed for production was at their disposal.

The Industrial Revolution came to the United States from Britain in the early part of the nineteenth century. It spread to Western Europe in the middle of that century and to Japan at the end of the century. After the Russian Revolution in 1917, Russia began a serious effort at industrialization, and in succession, so did China, India, and South America.

Technology and Social Change

Technology may also be defined as the practical application of knowledge because it builds upon existing knowledge and previous technology. Therefore, the more technologically advanced a society is, the more rapid is its technological progress. Needless to say, technological progress leads to change, and the faster the progress, the faster the pace of change. Technology is what supports the economic system of a society. The more advanced the technology, the more efficient it is as a system for creating wealth. The industrial system created wealth by mass producing millions of identical products. This production method enabled manufacturers to produce articles cheaply and make a profit by selling them to the largest market possible. Today the so-called smokestack era is coming to a close. Computer-driven technologies are reversing the previous industrial system of production in that they are making it possible to produce small runs of more customized goods and services aimed at more specific markets. In addition, constant innovation shortens the life cycles of products immensely, especially those of the technologies themselves. The approximate life of an innovative feature in the computer industry is approximately six months. As fast and as powerful as today's computers are, we will shortly see the appearance of a super-computer that will be able to calculate more than a trillion mathematical operations each second. This phenomenal technology reached its present point very rapidly: the first mainframe computer, which took up a whole room, was built by the Univac division of Sperry Rand Corporation in 1951; by the late 1970s, the size of computers was drastically reduced so that the personal computer could make its appearance; and by 1989, a chip the size of a thumbnail, like the Intel 486, installed in desktop computers, which cost around $1,000, had the power of the million-dollar machines of the 1970s. Today, personal computers are everywhere, they are fairly inexpensive, and they have spawned a whole new lifestyle: doing research, reading news, and shopping on the Internet, listening to music on an iPod, communicating via e-mail and instant messaging, and joining employees in international networks.

■ Modernization

The revolutionary changes that have ushered in modern times in the West and that are continuing to push new nations and former colonial powers into a similar mold consist of a number of processes collectively called modernization. *Modernization*, an all-encompassing process of economic, social, and cultural change, originated in the technology that transformed Western societies from a preindustrial to an industrial mode of production, and went on to affect all areas of human life. Some social theorists see modernization as a movement in which all the nations of the world are converging and will eventually become modern industrialized societies. However, while the nations of the

West began to modernize some 250 years ago, many poorer nations are still in the process of doing so. Consequently, the uneven rates of modernization have produced the division between the have and the have-not nations, but diffusion will eventually enable the laggard nations to catch up.

Logic suggests that an increase in the rate of technological progress triggered the chain of events leading to modernization. Of course, as was noted earlier, change is never wholesale or total. It occurs against a backdrop of stability—people still live in families, profess religious beliefs, celebrate major events in their lives, and so on, just as they did before modernization took place.

Learning to Be Modern

The process of modernization is strewn with difficulties in all societies. In the passage from agriculture to industry, modernizing has meant superimposing a totally new system of production on a relatively isolated society whose members had lived at a subsistence level (by hunting and gathering, by horticulture or pastoralism, or by agriculture). While industrialism produced wealth for some and allowed all to live somewhat better, it also destroyed a number of traditions and an entrenched way of life. In short, the social organization of societies undergoing modernization was altered, and a new type of organization and structure superseded it.

In Britain, for instance, the earliest industrialized nation in Europe, farmers and serfs had to learn to become industrial workers. They moved to urban centers, where industrial work was located. They learned to work in exchange for wages. They learned to accept a secondary relationship with their employers. And they learned to exist without the moral support of an extended family behind them. None of these learning experiences were easy or occurred rapidly. In fact, because they happened rather slowly, the new patterns had an opportunity to crystallize. New values—for instance, the value of profit, the work ethic, the desire for achievement, the deferment of gratification—new political and economic systems, and even new types of personality resulting from different methods of socialization had an opportunity to become entrenched in the society. Individuals eventually adjusted to the new social order, even though such adjustment was never perfect in any society.

In societies where modernization occurred late, rapidly, and through diffusion instead of evolution, things have been going much less smoothly. The dislocations and strains have been evidencing themselves in feelings of rootlessness, anomie, and often violence. One modern example is provided by former colonies. After gaining independence, these nations have attempted to modernize their economies as rapidly as they could, frequently creating conflicts when the forces of tradition clashed with those of modernization (Iran is one illustration of such a society). In most of them, there is still great political instability, which some groups periodically try to remedy by coups d'etat and violent overthrow of present governments to install military dictatorships. In others, various social movements are common. Some aim at a return to a previous national greatness; others stress millenarian religions promising a future paradise; still others work toward revolutions with the goal of establishing new social and economic systems or use nationalism as a motif to unite the people.

As a result, there has been an increasingly strong feeling among social scientists that the modernization model does not work for all societies. Some, in fact, suggest that it is possible that the development of technologically advanced nations actually inhibits the progress of developing nations.

Box 10.3 One Cost of Modernization: Car Wrecks

For most of the twentieth century, China was a society wracked by war, oppression by a brutal totalitarian government, and through it all, pervasive poverty. The last couple of decades, however, have seen dramatic changes occurring in this populous country. Although the communist party is still the purported ruling entity, the economic principles characteristic of communism—namely, a planned economy—have gradually given way to a system resembling capitalism in everything but name. This system has resulted in a booming economy, as better than a billion people have suddenly become voracious consumers.

The rise in consumption is evident everywhere in the country, from the well-dressed pedestrians, so unlike those in the plain and drab uniform of communist times, to the numerous cranes signaling feverish construction in many of China's cities, and especially in the increase in the number of cars.

Previously a country in which bicycles (and horses and buggies in the countryside) were a dominant feature, today the booming economy has made China the world's fastest growing car market. In the capital, Beijing, alone, the number of cars has increased by 25 percent from 2002 to 2003. This fact has created millions of new drivers who, combined with old and ineffective traffic laws, manage to contribute to a horrendous increase in road deaths. In 2002, more than 104,000 people were killed in traffic accidents, which is about two and a half times more deaths than in the United States. Of course, in the United States, cars have been a way of life for many decades, so that not only laws but also customs and traditions have evolved surrounding driving. In China, on the other hand, "the one rule is: no one stops for anyone else. Pedestrians don't stop for cars, and cars don't stop for pedestrians" (Yardley, 2004, A4). With the paucity of good roads, especially in rural areas, it is easy to see the kind of anarchy that exists. The inadequate transportation infrastructure, combined with a culture unacquainted with the demands of driving in traffic, makes current driving conditions nightmarish. Changing the prevailing culture and especially enforcing sociocultural changes for a population of 1.3 billion will be a challenge facing Chinese authorities for a long time.

(Jim Yardley. 2004. "Chinese Take Recklessly to Cars [Just Count the Wrecks]." *New York Times.* March 12, A4).

■ Collective Behavior

Every day, scenes of mass behavior stare at us from television screens: men and women with upraised fists, carrying signs, chanting slogans. In the past few decades, we have seen Chinese students clamoring for democracy, Eastern Europeans unhappy with their new governments, Russians lamenting the plight of their economy, Palestinians throwing rocks from the rooftops or blowing themselves up in suicide bombings. In the United States, too, on more than one occasion, we have seen the streets of our major cities erupt in violence that took many lives and destroyed whole neighborhoods. Sometimes, when a sports team wins an important victory, opposing groups of fans clash, and fights break out that may end in some persons' deaths. Traditional holidays, such as Halloween, have become occasions for mob violence in some locations.

Such events are disruptive, instances of civil disorder, and destabilizing to society. Of course, not all group gatherings are of that kind. There are happy crowds at concerts or football games; there are responsive crowds at religious services; there are worried crowds when a bank is rumored to be in financial difficulties. Even when people are not gathered personally in groups, they can fall prey to a specific kind of behavior. This is the case when fashions in clothing change.

What all these actions and events—and many other kinds of similar occurrences—have in common is that large numbers of people participate in them, and they either cause change or change brings them on. Urban, industrial and postindustrial societies with strong tendencies toward the mass society model are much more likely to exhibit this type of behavior than are traditional preindustrial or agrarian societies. Social scientists call this type of behavior **collective behavior.**

Collective behavior covers a whole range of behaviors that may be termed nonroutine and in which a large number of people engage. In essence, collective behavior differs from the interactive behavior that normally goes on in social groups, even though it may involve numbers of people reacting to the same situation. As noted in Chapter 4, most human behavior follows quite a regular pattern, so that it is predictable to a great degree. When people interact in the context of their statuses and roles, and within the framework of a normative system that is more or less shared, the resulting regularity is what makes life in society possible. But when people are suddenly thrust into an unusual situation for which there is no precedent in their experience, they find themselves without societal norms or guidelines to follow, without a social structure on which to fall back. They are then likely to imitate others who find themselves in the same situation. For instance, if a person is shopping in a department store and suddenly hears another customer yelling "Fire!," that person will be unsure of what to do. Such a person will likely act spontaneously, perhaps somewhat illogically or irrationally, and follow the actions of others who happen to be nearby at the time. This is the type of behavior termed collective, and it tends to occur in crowds, in mobs (riots, lynchings), at certain kinds of sports events or musical concerts, and at religious revival meetings.

We also call their behavior collective when people follow fashions, fads, or give in to a craze, when they make up a public or an audience, when they act on public opinion, propaganda, and rumors, and when they work to attain certain goals through social movements.

In spite of its lack of pattern, rarely is there a complete lack of structure in people's behavior. Only when an individual's life is threatened is he or she likely to act with complete absence of awareness of others. In most situations, even when collective behavior prevails, that behavior is partly structured and partly unstructured. Some situations of collective behavior start out being fairly structured and end up being completely disorganized. Audiences at rock concerts have been known to surge forward, jump on the stage, and destroy musical instruments. Other situations may start out disorganized and end by being structured. Many social movements—the labor movement, for one—begin by being nothing more than disorganized protests. Later they develop definite goals and apply ranked roles to their members; they evolve norms and techniques for social control such as characterize any organized group.

Many social movements, a large number of religious denominations, and several governments have originated in some form of collective behavior. An example close to Americans is that of the United States, which originated when a large number of settlers became dissatisfied with British rule and sought to change it through revolution.

Crowds

As mentioned, collective behavior occurs most often in crowd situations. A crowd is a temporary collection of people who respond to the same stimulus. There are different kinds of crowds: **casual crowds** consist of people who come together by accident, such as those waiting at a red light to cross the street; **organized crowds** come together for specific events, such as concerts or football games; **expressive crowds** gather to express feelings, as in a protest rally or religious revival meeting; and **acting crowds** come together to act out feelings, usually of a hostile nature, as exemplified by mobs, riots, and violent protest meetings.

Any crowd, even a casual one, may evolve into a panic crowd, a mob, or a riot if the right stimulus is present. Organized crowds are more receptive to mob behavior. People in crowds tend to develop a common mood. Emotions reach a high pitch, and a shared conception of what constitutes proper behavior emerges. This behavior is often unpredictable and antisocial. The reason, as was noted, is that a crowd lacks definite norms and is removed temporarily from most kinds of social control; one individual in a crowd does not personally know his or her neighbor. Therefore, it is easy for people to shed their identities and act as members of the anonymous crowd. In this way, no person needs feel guilty for antisocial actions.

Even though a crowd is more than the sum of the individuals who make it up (which is why there is in every society a long history of crowd violence, lynchings, and massacres), there are limits on how far a crowd will go in antisocial behavior. A crowd seldom does anything that individual members do not want to do. Crowd violence is rarely random, but rather is directed against a person or institution that is perceived as unjust or oppressive. Even then, a destructive crowd only temporarily commits acts that are strongly forbidden by societal norms.

Box 10.4 Other Forms of Collective Behavior: Mobs and Riots, Rumors, Fashions and Crazes, Panics and Mass Hysteria

Acting crowds that get out of hand and erupt into violence are termed mobs. *Mobs* are highly emotional and are motivated by the goal of doing harm to someone or to perpetrate some form of destruction. They are usually of short duration, although their leaders can whip emotions to a frenzy. Mob behavior is best exemplified in the United States by lynching, the hanging or burning of an individual by a group not legally authorized to mete out punishment. Today lynching is seldom used, but mobs have been known to drag people who are tied to a vehicle or beating someone to death. The individuals selected for this type of punishment are perceived as representing a threat to the group making up the mob. It is a method of social control by which low-status individuals attempt to maintain their dominance over other groups.

When an out-of-control crowd has no particular goal in mind, it becomes a *riot*. Violence and destruction are the hallmarks of riots, but the high emotional pitch of the crowd has no immediate direction. Riots may be triggered by even minor events, however, when some underlying anger or grievance exists. This long-suppressed anger boils over in random violence against persons and property, and

the rioters come under control only when their anger has run its course (or when the police prevail). Consequently, riots have periodically occurred in our major cities where a segment of minority populations is confined without much hope of a brighter future. Riots have also occurred among prison populations when inmates believed they were receiving unfair treatment or were subjected to substandard living conditions. And sometimes, the actions are not the result of anger but a release from stress, as happens when a crowd of students, happy to be on a spring break and fueled by alcohol, engage in high-jinks of a kind that can escalate into destroying property and harming people.

Rumors

Rumors are unsupported reports of events or projected events that often begin riots, panics, or mobs. These reports are not backed up by facts but continue to spread by word of mouth or through the mass media. Rumors may be helpful in situations of stress, when accurate information is not readily available. They may also prove disastrous because they are usually at least partially false. In accepting a rumor, people tend to hear what they want to hear. It helps them rationalize their participation in some form of crowd behavior, or it may only clarify a confused situation.

Fashions, Fads, and Crazes

These kinds of collective behavior are different from the preceding ones in that they are not quite as temporary and action directed. *Fashions* refer to manners of dress, architecture, or house decor and reflect the interests, values, and motives of a society at a given point in time. They are social patterns that find favor among a large number of people for a short period of time. Fashions differ from the more established social norms in that they are transitory. But fashions have a profound hold on people in urban industrial societies in which, with the proliferation of the mass media, they are immediately transmitted to millions of people around the world, so that what is designed in New York, Paris, and Milan is sold a few weeks later in Tokyo. In traditional societies, on the other hand, fashions change very little over the years.

The intent of clothing has also changed. Clothing in the past was used to distinguish different categories of people: males from females, members of high social classes from lower social classes, and one occupational group from another (Lofland, 1973). In modern industrial societies, there is no concern with maintaining tradition because people are more future oriented and because a person from a lower social class can rise and become a member of a higher social class. It then becomes necessary to judge people according to what they can buy, not according to what they traditionally wear. New fashions, especially in clothes, tend to emerge at the top of the social scale, acquire mass popularity through the media, are copied until they can be found in discount stores, and are then abandoned. Fashion is one facet of conspicuous consumption or the practice of spending money, to display one's wealth (Veblen, 1953). However, in leisure societies ever on the lookout for novelties, fashions can also follow the opposite road; that is, they may emerge from the lower classes and be copied by the affluent. In the case of blue jeans, for instance, idealistic college students wanted to look like disadvantaged Americans and so donned the uniform of the farmer and factory worker. Soon, however, "designer jeans" costing hundreds of dollars became the rage among the wealthy, and now jeans are the uniform of the young throughout the world.

Fads, also transitory social patterns that a large number of people undertake for short periods of time, refer more to leisure-time activities or the objects one would use while engaging in leisure activities. Within the past several decades, for instance, we have had the Pet Rock, the Mood Ring, Beanie Babies, Pokémon, and activities such as streaking, or running naked in a public place. Fads tend to disappear without leaving a trace, unlike fashions, which are often recycled. Fads sometimes evolve into *crazes* and are often ploys of business for profit making. Both are minor fashions that are more irrational and short-lived than true fashions, but crazes have a slightly more obsessive character than fads.

Panics and Mass Hysteria

Panics and mass hysteria are two forms of collective behavior that are similar in that they may occur among people who are dispersed over a wide area and they are both characterized by a high emotional charge. In a *panic*, people react to a stimulus, most often a threat, with irrational, violent, and sometimes self-destructive behavior. As was mentioned, the shout of "Fire!" may provoke a panic in which people trample on each other and block off exits to the point of causing themselves harm or death. *Mass hysteria* is the ultimate kind of fad or craze, in that it is compulsive and irrational. It is also a form of dispersed collective behavior because people are not necessarily together in a crowd; in fact, more often they have no direct contact with one another. It also tends to be an exaggerated response to a perceived threat, real or imaginary.

Masses

Another form of collective behavior occurs among people who are not in close proximity, as in crowds, but who are connected to one another in more indirect ways. Contrasted to crowds, masses are more diffuse and do not necessarily find themselves in the same physical setting. Rather, masses are large numbers of people responding to the same set of shared symbols; for instance, the audience for a particular television program constitutes a mass (Lofland, 1981). Collective behavior can occur in masses, just as it does in crowds (or in both at the same time). Fear, hostility, and joy are the basic emotions that can motivate the behavior of both crowds and masses.

Publics and Public Opinion

Collective behavior is at work in publics and public opinion as well. A *public* is defined as a scattered collection of people who share a common interest or concern about an issue or who are affected by a common occurrence. The readers of the *New York Times*, for instance, university students, moviegoers, voters, and members of a fan club are all examples of publics.

The bond that holds a crowd together is emotion, whereas the bond that holds a public together is intellect. A crowd is gathered at one place, but a public is dispersed, and each member is able to communicate directly only with a small number of other members—or with none at all, as in the case of the television public. The mass media help to create and hold publics together. In fact, in industrial, technologically advanced societies, publics are really mass publics, meaning that they are large regional or national populations who can become potentially either spectators or participants in a variety of collective behaviors. Some

Box 10.5 The Theory of Mass Society

Social thinkers have long speculated about the causes of change. They have wanted to know the reasons why change occurs at different rates in different societies; whether change is a random, haphazard process or a recurrent, patterned one; why some civilizations rise and fall whereas others never rise at all; and whether a common destiny awaits all societies or each is fated to exist in its own individual pattern. To this end, they have offered a large number of theories. None of the theories, however, answers their questions completely. One of the more interesting ones is the theory of mass society.

As noted, the process of modernization has been problematic for most societies. The United States has not escaped this fate. According to Robert Bellah, the most rapid and profound transformation in the history of the United States occurred in the years between the Civil War and the entry of the United States into World War II (Bellah et al., 1985, 42). At that time, a new national society came into being with new technologies, particularly transportation, communication, and manufacturing. This transformation of old economic and social patterns caused political conflicts and complex cultural changes. It created the figure of the entrepreneur and the "self-made" person as models of individuals to be imitated. It strengthened the importance of individualism. It also introduced the division of life into a number of separate functional sectors such as "work" and "leisure," "white collar" and "blue collar," "public" and "private." This division was well suited to the needs of the corporate form of organization that had come into being, but was in total contrast to the patterns of the preceding century in which the individual had been closely integrated in the life of family and community. In short,

modernity has entailed a process of separation and individuation as opposed to the ties of kinship and community.

Modernity conditions our consciousness, and the sense of fragmentariness without any overall patterns begins to characterize the entire culture, which is thus named the "culture of separation." The fragmentary nature of culture, apparent in both intellectual pursuits and in popular culture, particularly in the mass media, has the effect of disconnecting the individual from feeling integrated into the society, a part of the whole. The danger in individuals who feel themselves to be only parts of a "mass of interchangeable fragments within an aggregate" (Bellah et al., 1985, 281) rather than members of a society in which they are well integrated, is the establishment of an authoritarian state to provide the coherence that the culture no longer provides.

The United States is not in imminent danger of such a situation, mainly because there still exist traditions, deriving from religion, from strong beliefs in republican and democratic ideals, and from families and schools, that provide the individual with the sense of "growing up in a morally and intellectually intelligible world" (Bellah et al., 1985, 282). So our culture is, despite perceptions to the contrary, still one of *cohesion*; but the danger of the erosion of meaning and coherence in our lives is ever present, and only the desire of the people, their yearning for what has been lost, keeps it at bay.

The description of the perils that face individuals who feel disconnected from their society is similar to the mass society model which social commentators developed in the 1950s. In essence, the *mass society* model described a society composed of masses of people who are widely distributed and anonymous rather than being well integrated into a social system. As a consequence, the social system is loosely organized and somewhat disorganized. The masses may react to the same stimuli—they may watch the same news on television, for instance—but they do so separately, without reference to one another. Masses, in contrast to individuals or groups, are not part of any broad social groupings, not even social classes. "The mass merely consists of individuals who are separate, detached, anonymous, and thus homogeneous as far as mass behavior is concerned" (Blumer, 1969, 86–87).

The theory of mass society helps explain why societies in which change is constant and in which people experience *anomie* (a state of normlessness) are often an easy prey for totalitarianism. The speculation is that in their confusion, anomic individuals are easily drawn into participation in mob hysteria, panics, or radical social movements. The latter, all forms of collective behavior, may indeed lead to an erosion of democratic institutions and the establishment of authoritarian institutions.

In spite of the trends pointing to an increase in the number of people who live alone, or who marry late, or who divorce, a more optimistic interpretation of mass theory was presented by social theorist Edward Shils (1961). While admitting that "a part of the population in mass society lives in a nearly vegetative torpor, reacting dully or aggressively to its environment" (Shils, 1961, 3), Shils pointed to the positive aspects of such a society, in which larger elements of the population are able to make choices more freely and have learned to value pleasures that were previously limited to a small elite. Shils concluded that even though all types of social movements tend to flourish in mass society, totalitarian regimes are bound to fail in the long run because of increasing demands for equality and political participation, also resulting from social change.

mass publics are temporary, their composition changing quickly: the public watching a television program at 7:30 on Saturday night will dissolve at 8:00 when the program ends. The definition of a mass public may be qualified as an unstructured collectivity in which some members are constantly losing interest in the event that made them members in the first place and are constantly being replaced by others.

Publics are more characteristic of complex societies than of simple ones. The reason is that complex societies are heterogeneous and members have innumerable and varying interests. They

An organized crowd may evolve into a panic crowd, a mob, or a riot if the right stimulus is present. Such a crowd may engage in unpredictable behavior because a common mood develops and emotions reach a high pitch.

Public opinion in contemporary societies is diffused through the mass media. In an election year, much of that opinion is shaped by candidates for office who are not bashful in using censorship and propaganda in their messages.

are constantly confronted with a large number of issues of both a local and a national nature. These issues may be at odds with one another. One group may want to preserve our national forests, whereas another may want to be able to hunt game or to log the timber in them. In a less complex society, such issues are not likely to arise: norms and values are shared to a greater extent by all, and very few individuals question the traditional way of doing things.

Publics exert an important influence on society, particularly because mass communication is so instantaneous and pervasive. At the same time, the lifestyles of mass publics have been greatly changed by the postindustrial society in which there is time and leisure to pursue sports and hobbies, in which automobiles have long been produced for the masses, and in which the media of communication are used not only to inform but also to induce consumerism. Mass publics have changed the outward appearance of the country: highways and freeways and roads of all sorts crisscross it, while stadiums and golf courses, shopping malls, and amusement parks stretch out from coast to coast. Mass publics have also created new industries: fast food, popular music, the movies, and so on.

Public Opinion

The large number of publics, each concerned with its own issue or activity, attitude, and beliefs, give rise to public opinion. Public opinion is a generic term that refers to the attitude or judgment of a large number of people on a specific issue. It may be thought of as the dominant opinion on that issue among a specific population. It is particularly important in the political sphere.

Public opinion has a special meaning in a society characterized by mass publics, because here public opinion is diffused through the mass media. In traditional societies, governments and economies are run according to the will of ruling authorities. The leaders do not care what individual societal members think about specific issues. In industrial societies, most of which are democratic and consumption-oriented, the leaders and industrialists must take into consideration what the public thinks about their style of leadership (or they will not be reelected) or their products (or they will not be bought).

Public Opinion and the Mass Media

It would seem logical that public opinion reflects the values and attitudes of a society, but values and attitudes internalized in childhood remain fairly continuous throughout an individual's lifetime, whereas public opinion fluctuates, sometimes very rapidly. Although there may be consensus in the society about certain values, public opinion is usually divided at any given time about a variety of issues. For instance, while there is a consensus on the value of world peace and democracy, public opinion was divided between those who saw the necessity of the United States invading Iraq and removing its dictator and those who believed peace should be maintained at any cost. How to conduct the war on terrorism is causing a similar division in public opinion, even though acts of terrorism are universally dreaded.

The strongest influence on public opinion is exerted by the mass media—newspapers, television, films, the Internet, etc. That is one reason why candidates for political office attempt to create an "image" that they can "sell" to the public. Some commentators even feel that the mass media create public opinion. Newspapers sometimes prompt public action by exposés of corruption in city government or some other local social problem. At the same time, newspapers often support certain issues or the election of specific candidates in vain. Motion pictures, but especially television, have often been accused of creating public opinion. There is little question that in fact movies and television influence the public in a variety of ways. Movies and situation comedies show how different classes of people, in different social settings, behave. Television, in addition, with its constant barrage of commercials, also influences the consumption habits of the viewing public. Advertising is not only a multibillion-dollar industry, it has become somewhat of a science, able to reduce a message to an image and a fraction-of-a-second "bite." Consumers, in this way, buy not only toothpaste or hamburgers but also political candidates, including candidates for the highest office in the land, the presidency. There are obvious dangers lurking in such methods, because such selling techniques can overcome the influences of primary, reference, occupational, and status groups (see Chapter 4).

Public opinion is also shaped by the constant repetition in the media. Both the pessimism following the Vietnam War and the optimism during the Reagan administration were equally promulgated by the media. Individuals and groups who have prestige and power in local communities or in the nation also affect public opinion. Many well-funded special-interest groups are able to alter public opinion: for instance, the American Medical Association, which represents only 2 percent of Americans, has an enormous influence on health care. Political leaders, labor leaders, religious organizations, and business all attempt to use public relations to affect public opinion. Members of a variety of groups reflect the views of the group to which they owe the highest allegiance. And people create public opinion through interaction and mold it according to their own social background and group memberships. When they are unsure of how to react with regard to a particular event, or what stance to take on a particular issue, people tend to debate, discuss, and exchange information with others.

Social movements exert one of the strongest effects on public opinion. For instance, the 1960s and 1970s saw the emergence of the civil rights and feminist movements, as well as the pro-abortion and gay rights movements. Public opinion swung from one extreme of the political pendulum—the conservatism of the 1950s—to the other. The 1980s and 1990s, as well as the first years of the twenty-first century, saw a return to political conservatism and a stress on "values."

Propaganda and Censorship

Being able to manipulate public opinion is of great benefit to some individuals and groups in society. Car manufacturers want the public to buy their products. Political candidates want to be elected. Teachers want their salaries increased. The administration in office wants to have the citizens' support. Religious organizations want their members to follow the precepts of their faith. All these groups, and countless more, exert influence on public opinion through propaganda and censorship.

Propaganda is a deliberate attempt to persuade a person to accept a particular belief uncritically or to make a certain choice rather than another. Advertising, sales promotions, public relations, political campaigns, fund-raising drives, billboards, and even Sunday school lessons use propaganda. Propaganda is a manipulative device that depends on emotional appeal, often playing on the fears and anxieties of people. Advertisements for cosmetics, deodorants, and tooth whiteners promise to make people attractive and young looking, which is what people want to be and are afraid they are not. Propaganda also relies on the "good old values" of the past (the "one-room schoolhouse," "Grandma's apple pie") and on the desire of people to belong or be popular ("Everybody's doing it").

Propaganda is quite successful when it does not attempt to change the opinion of people too drastically. However, in democratic societies, those involved in propaganda for a specific person or product have a lot of competition. The education and sophistication of the public further limit the effectiveness of propaganda. Finally, although strong trends may be temporarily thwarted by propaganda, ultimately they are not affected by it.

Because propaganda gives a one-sided interpretation of an issue or shows only the good side of a product, it distorts the information available to the public. **Censorship,** on the other hand, deletes all or parts of the information. Many of our important institutional organizations use censorship. Certain groups with their own agenda would have us pull specific books off library shelves because they do not approve of, or agree with, their contents (book censorship, as well as censorship in all forms of art, is extensive in totalitarian regimes). The government and the military institutions withhold information in the name of national security and defense. Families and religious organizations tend to censor some information regarding sex. Political candidates tell us only what they want us to know about themselves and their intentions once in office. Manufacturers choose not to tell us that the car or the refrigerator they are selling us is built so that it must be replaced every few years. The mass media report some and fail to report other news. In and of themselves, propaganda and censorship are neither good nor bad, but both may be put to uses that are either beneficial or detrimental to people.

■ Social Movements

Approximately 100 years ago, the autocratic empire of the all-powerful Czar Nicholas of Russia was swept away by a tide so strong that it was able to overcome an entrenched government that had wielded absolute power over the people for centuries. In the process, a backward, agricultural society was transformed into one of the two world super-powers. In the fall of 1991, a second quake shook the same society, and soon the world watched in wonder as crowds began to pull down the huge statues of the heroes of the preceding regime. As falling idols came crashing to the ground, one could not help but speculate about the forces that impelled such dramatic changes. What are these forces, how do they come into being, and why and how do they eventually decline?

One of the principal ways in which change is effected is by social movements. Social movements are a type of collective behavior that leaves the greatest impact on societies. **Social movements** are defined as "collective enterprises to establish a new order of life" (Blumer, 1951, 200), as well as collective efforts either to change the sociocultural order or to resist such change (Killian, 1964, 430). This type of collective action represents the personal involvement of individuals and their intervention in directing, redirecting, furthering, or resisting change.

A collective action may be considered a social movement when the following factors are present: (1) it has a specific ideology; (2) it awakens a strong sense of idealism and solidarity, involving dedication and loyalty in followers; (3) there is an orientation toward action; and (4) a significant number of people are involved.

Although some social movements are almost entirely unorganized, most are pursued in voluntary groups or associations. These are secondary groups (see Chapter 4) organized for attaining a definite goal. Both social movements and voluntary groups are characteristic of urban industrial societies that are experiencing rapid social change. In some nations, social movements develop into political parties, pursuing their goals by attaining political power. Marxism is an example of an ideology that has prompted social movements in a number of societies, and in some has attained—and lost—political power. In other nations—such as the United States—the goals of this ideology have been pursued in voluntary associations that never acquired political power. In still other countries—France, Italy, Portugal—it has become a political party represented in Parliament. Finally, in the former Soviet Union, as well as in the People's Republic of China, the movement had become the party in power (although with alterations of the ideology), whereas in Chile, it came to power but was subsequently overthrown.

Revolutionary social movements have a profound impact on societies. The Russian Revolution, which turned out one ruling class—a monarchy—and substituted it with another—the Communist Party—transformed a backward, agricultural nation into a world power. Unfortunately, the lives of its citizens were not much improved because the new government became a dictatorship. Here, one of the leaders of the revolution, Lenin (1879–1924), making a speech in Moscow in 1919.

Types of Social Movements

According to how one views social movements, they can be classified into four types: alternative, redemptive, reformist, and revolutionary. An example of an **alternative** social movement is an organization such as Planned Parenthood, whose concern is population growth and whose goal it is to influence people of child-bearing age to practice birth control and take responsibility for their sexual conduct. **Redemptive** movements also affect selected segments of the society and not the whole society, but here the attempt is at a radical transformation. Fundamentalist Christianity is such a movement, and converts perceive themselves as having been born again. Somewhat related to the redemptive type are **expressive** movements, which are directed at individuals who are expected to change in such a way that they will work toward changes in society or adapt better to society as it is. Expressive movements are often religious in nature, but they can also turn quite revolutionary, as in the case of the Islamic revolution in Iran. On the other hand, they may be secular, as exemplified by the numerous human potential movements that were popular in the 1970s. These movements were designed to achieve self-fulfillment for the individual.

Reformist Movements

The two social movements that have had the most influence on societies and their governments have been the **revolutionary** and the **reformist** or reformative movements. Reform movements attempt to change some feature of an existing social order without changing the entire order. They want to change the society, but in a limited way. Such movements are most successful in democratic societies, where there is relative freedom to criticize institutions and channels exist through which reforms can be put into effect. Reform movements may be progressive, in the sense of wanting to promote new social patterns, or they may be reactionary, in the sense of wanting to preserve the status quo or return to past patterns. Recent reform movements in the United States have included the women's movement, the civil rights movement, and the movement to remove the social stigma of homosexuality (see Table 10.1).

■ Revolutionary Movements

If we were to put all forms of collective behavior on a continuum that ranked them as to the extent of their effect on societies, revolutions would be at one extreme, and fads and crazes would be at the other. In the twentieth century, for instance, there were the Russian and Chinese revolutions, which have brought in communist regimes and radically altered the societies in which they occurred, and a fascist movement, which had revolutionary consequences in European societies. On the other hand, in spite of the fact that some people become deeply involved in a fad or craze, none of the latter can be said to have left an indelible mark on a society.

Revolutionary movements consider the present social order so inadequate, corrupt, unjust, and beyond salvation that they seek its total removal and substitution. In effecting such absolute change, revolutionary movements must often resort to violence. In **nationalistic** revolutionary movements, a predominantly foreign government is overthrown and replaced with a native one. **Class** revolutionary movements substitute one ruling class for another in the same society. The American revolution was nationalistic, whereas the French, Russian, Chinese, and Cuban were all class revolutions. Revolutionary movements should not be confused with revolts, or coups d'état, which merely replace individual members of the ruling class. Revolutions change the structure of the major social institutions.

TABLE 10.1   The Most Important American Social Movements

Name	Description
Abolitionist	In the northern states during the three decades preceding the Civil War; seeking the abolition of slavery in all of the states and territories.
Populist	Disaffected farmers in the South and the West in the 1880s and 1890s sought public control over railroads, banks, grain elevators, and the provision of cheap money.
Labor	The effort of workers to protect jobs, to ensure adequate wages and benefits, and to guarantee a healthy work environment. Union building was particularly prominent during the 1880s, 1890s, and 1930s.
Women's Suffrage	This movement emerged to win voting rights for women. Active in the late nineteenth and early twentieth centuries.
Civil Rights	The purpose of this movement was to win civil and political rights for African Americans. It was especially effective during the 1960s.
Anti–Vietnam War	During the late 1960s and early 1970s, this movement was directed against the continued involvement of the United States in the Vietnam War.
Women's Liberation or Feminist Movement	A movement attempting to gain equality for women in all aspects of American life during the 1970s and 1980s and currently.
Antinuclear	A world movement, periodically active during the 1970s and 1980s, to end the nuclear arms race (e.g., "The Freeze" campaign) and the construction of nuclear power plants.
Environmental	Came to prominence in the 1970s and is growing in momentum; its goals range from control of pollution to protection of wilderness areas, and especially to counter global warming.
Religious Fundamentalist	The latest of many examples of religious fundamentalism to take political form in American history; became part of the conservative platforms of the 1970s and 1980s, as well as 2000 and 2004, aiding the electoral victories of Ronald Reagan, George Bush, and George W. Bush who used campaign slogans promising to protect family and Christian morality values.

Factors Encouraging Revolutionary Movements

The predisposing factors to joining revolutionary movements are similar to those predisposing people to join less radical social movements, but the conditions that prompt a person to join a revolutionary movement may be perceived as being extreme. Revolutionary movements are more characteristic of totalitarian societies than they are of democratic ones, because in democracies, public opinion and reformist movements exert pressure on the government, so that eventually changes desired by a majority of the people occur. In totalitarian regimes, public opinion is often ignored and social movements are not tolerated. People feel the only way they can effect change is by overthrowing the government. In this attempt, success is never certain.

The most important condition for revolution is the widespread realization that the legitimate government has failed and it is necessary to bring about change at any cost. This condition is called a **crisis of legitimacy**. Sometimes revolution is aided by a breakdown of discipline and efficiency in the ruling body. Some members of this body, especially the intellectuals, become disillusioned and may even join the revolutionary movement. Others abandon the role of rulers. Therefore, in many cases, very little violence is actually needed to wrest the government from the hands of the rulers. Many revolutions have been relatively bloodless compared to wars and genocidal programs such as those carried out in Hitler's Germany.

As to the results of revolutions, they are seldom as drastic or as ideal as they promise to be. Customs and institutions, though certainly subject to change, are difficult to uproot. Sometimes precisely the unpleasant features of the old social order survive the revolution. Nonetheless, a number of revolutions—the American, the Russian, and the Chinese, to cite the most obvious examples—have brought about changes of tremendous importance for the people of their societies.

Revolutionary movements receive considerable notoriety because they reflect the discontent of people who believe that change is occurring too slowly. However, there are movements that reflect the belief of some groups that change occurs too rapidly. These movements are called **change-resistant,** and their purpose is to stop or eradicate certain changes in society. The Ku Klux Klan is an example of a change-resistant movement, and there are many others.

The effectiveness of social movements depends on the type of organization they are able to form and maintain and how deep their influence is on the society. Although each movement is unique, it seems that all move through four definite stages (Blumer, 1969; Mauss, 1975). In the first stage, **emergence**, dissatisfaction in a segment of the society with regard to a specific issue is pinpointed by a group or an individual who brings it to public attention. In the second stage, **coalescence**, leaders must plan a strategy, determine policies, make alliances with other groups, solicit new members—in other words, they must build interest and spread their vision to the society at large. In the third stage, **bureaucratization**, it becomes necessary to establish a formal organization so that the everyday work of the movement can proceed in an orderly fashion. While adding stability and longevity to a movement, bureaucratization sometimes holds it back, because building an organization does not require the same skills as keeping the enthusiasm of the members (Piven & Cloward, 1995). In the fourth and last stage, social movements **decline** (Figure 10.1). This can happen in a positive way for the movement, that is, through institutionalization. Or, if a movement reaches its goal, it has no further need to exist, and so it breaks apart (but this seldom happens, because most movements are not single-issue oriented). Sometimes poor leadership, repression by the government, loss of interest on the part of members, or fragmentation due to a multiplicity of unresolved views are the death toll of a movement. Finally, the leaders of a movement may

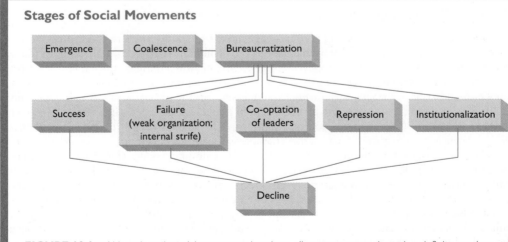

Stages of Social Movements

Emergence — Coalescence — Bureaucratization

Success | Failure (weak organization; internal strife) | Co-optation of leaders | Repression | Institutionalization

Decline

FIGURE 10.1 Although each social movement is unique, all appear to pass through a definite number of stages.

be diverted from their efforts by enticements offered by the established power structure. This process is called **co-optation**. And the movement itself may become a part of the power structure, as is true of the labor movement.

Social movements originate mainly as a result of **relative deprivation** and **rising expectations**. People feel relatively deprived when they compare themselves with others and find themselves to be suffering in the comparison. The failure of rising expectations is also related to dissatisfaction based on relative deprivation. **Rising expectations** are experienced when the standard of living goes up in a society, but not for all segments of the population. As life gets better, in other words, people begin to take all the improvements for granted and continue to expect more.

Social movements flourish in societies that are undergoing rapid social change, as people become subject to feelings of anomie and alienation. **Anomie** is a feeling of normlessness, of not knowing which behavioral guidelines to follow when several sets of norms coexist. **Alienation** is a feeling of separateness from society, of powerlessness and isolation, which convinces individuals that they are unable to influence their own fate. People who have feelings of anomie and alienation are attracted to social movements, as well as those who are dissatisfied on a variety of grounds, who are restless and confused, and who need some focus in their lives.

Contemporary social movements tend to have global concerns: the environment, the danger of nuclear proliferation, women's rights, gay rights, animal rights, and similar issues. Because power to legislate is centralized in the government, most of the new social movements are national and international in scope. Additionally, the new social movements have a tendency to focus on issues regarding the quality of life, rather than on issues of economic well-being, such as the labor movement of old did. As a result, these movements attract the interest and support of middle-class people instead of workers and the dispossessed.

Terrorism

One type of social movement that is difficult to define but that has become a threat to many countries is terrorism. According to United States law, "the term 'terrorism' means premeditated, politically motivated violence perpetrated against noncombatant targets by subnational groups or clandestine agents, usually intended to influence an audience." Terrorism is not new, but whereas in the past it had been limited to individual countries—the IRA in Northern Ireland, the ETA in Spain, the Tupac Amaru (Shining Path) in Peru, the Red Brigades in Italy—with definite ideologies and goals, today terrorism has become a transnational movement of ill-defined groups with ill-defined ideologies and ill-defined goals. The difficulty in defining terrorism lies in the fact that so many different groups engage in terrorist acts. Some of these groups may be thought of as attempting to begin nationalistic revolutions, efforts to bring in new forms of government, or to gain independence from governments perceived as colonial or occupying. Other groups may be considered reactionary social movements, in that they reject changes associated with modernization and try to bring back older forms of rule, mostly ancient theocracies. The latter seems to be the intent of the terrorist group that threatens the West and especially the United States, Al Quaeda, which perpetrated the horrific destruction of September 11, 2001, and continues to plot other events around the world. It has often been said that "one man's terrorist is another man's freedom fighter," meaning that, to those who agree with the terrorists' goals, their actions appear justified. However, those actions result in the death of innumerable numbers of innocent people who have nothing to do with whatever grievance the terrorists have. Such is the case of the many victims of suicide bombers who merely wait for a bus or are doing their shopping. No ethical system can find justification for such acts.

The Chapter in Brief

Change is an integral part of nature and of all living things, although a degree of stability is equally characteristic of individuals, societies, and cultures. The mechanisms of sociocultural change are easier to determine than its causes. The principal processes of cultural change are discovery, invention, and diffusion. On the other hand, change in the structure of society—or social change—occurs through planning, reform, and revolution. Sources of change include the physical environment, the size and structure of populations, ideology, events and individuals, social movements, and technology.

Sociocultural change has been triggered chiefly by technological progress. Technology includes all the methods and devices that help humans manage and control their environment. The first technological breakthrough was the invention of agriculture. A second was the advent of the machine era, or the Industrial Revolution. Although this movement accelerated in the middle of the eighteenth century in Great Britain, its roots go back several centuries. Its effects are still being felt by the world. The most significant changes brought about by the Industrial Revolution are a surge in the growth of population; industrialization, or the dependence of the economy on industry; and urbanization, or the growth of cities at the expense of rural life.

Modernization is the kind of change that occurred in modern industrial societies. It has meant the transition from an agricultural and preindustrial to an industrial mode of production and has been a difficult process in all societies. Where it occurred slowly, over a number of generations, it was eventually integrated into the existing social order. Where it occurred rapidly, there has been great political instability and other forms of dislocations. In modern industrial societies, technological progress has occurred at the most rapid rate in history.

Technology has radically altered people's lives both physically and in the area of cultural values. It has been so important, in fact, that some thinkers speculate that it determines a society's culture, structure, and history. There is always a cultural lag when the nonmaterial aspects try to catch up with the material ones. This lag also produces problems and disorganization.

Technologically advanced societies are more often subject to various forms of collective behavior than are traditional societies. Collective behavior occurs in situations that are highly charged with emotion and in which the usual norms do not apply. Such situations include crowds (riots, mobs, panics), rumors, fashions, fads, crazes, publics and audiences, public opinion, propaganda and censorship, and social movements. Collective behavior is relatively unpatterned and unstructured.

Crowds are assemblies of people who respond to a common stimulus. Crowds may be casual or organized, expressive or acting. People in them develop a common mood and a shared concept of how to behave at the moment. Crowds are temporary and their members remain anonymous and impersonal. Therefore, crowds can commit atrocities without their members feeling guilty.

Publics—scattered collections of people who temporarily share a common interest or concern about an issue—are also a form of collective behavior. The large number of publics in advanced societies generates public opinion, which is the attitude or judgment of a majority of people on a specific issue. Public opinion is especially important in democratic societies and is greatly influenced by the mass media. The latter sometimes use propaganda and/or censorship to manipulate public opinion. Propaganda is a deliberate attempt to persuade people to accept a belief uncritically or to make a specific choice. Censorship distorts information by suppressing or deleting parts or all of it.

Social movements are collective attempts to establish a new order of life—either to change the social order or to resist change. Important factors in social movements are changing perspectives and ideologies. Social movements are rooted in discontent and flourish when a society experiences anomie, alienation, relative deprivation, and rising expectations, but their goals are long-range solutions. The ultimate aim is to effect change to the point that it becomes institutionalized. Social movements may attempt reforms by trying to change only some features of an existing social order, or they may be revolutionary, seeking the removal of a present order and substitution with a new one. The stages in social movements include emergence, coalescence, bureaucratization, institutionalization, and/or decline.

A type of social movement that is very difficult to define is terrorism. It refers to premeditated, politically motivated violence perpetrated against noncombatant targets. It may be considered nationalistic and revolutionary, but also reactionary; whatever its goals, it is impossible to justify it because of the number of innocent victims it takes.

Terms to Remember

alienation A feeling of powerlessness and insecurity, of not belonging in society, producing boredom and meaninglessness. Alienation provides a fertile ground for social movements and is characteristic of people in mass society.

censorship A method of control used to limit the information available to the public.

change-resistant movement A social movement reflecting the discontent of people who believe that change is occurring too rapidly and want to stop it or reverse it.

class revolutionary movement A revolutionary social movement in which one ruling class is replaced with another in the same society.

collective behavior Type of behavior that tends to occur in crowds, mobs, fashions, fads, crazes, rumors, panics, and in publics, public opinion, and social movements. It is characteristic of a collectivity of people who are responding to a common stimulus under conditions that are usually temporary, unstable, unstructured, and unpredictable, so that existing norms do not apply.

crowd An aggregate of people gathered in the same place, at the same time, either casually or for a predetermined reason, responding to a common stimulus. Crowds may be expressive or acting. An acting crowd may develop into a panic, mob, or riot.

cultural change Change in values, beliefs, and norms that may be brought about by scientific discoveries, technological inventions, new achievements in the arts, or shifts in religious doctrine.

diffusion A process of cultural change in which cultural traits are spread from one society to another (or from one group to another).

discovery A process of cultural change in which an already existing fact or relationship is newly perceived.

fads and crazes Minor fashions, short-lived and often irrational.

fashions A kind of collective behavior that represents a transient social pattern followed for a time by a large segment of people. Fashions affect the entire spectrum of social life.

invention A process of cultural change in which old cultural ideas or existing objects are combined in new ways to produce ideas or objects more important than the previous ones had been separately.

mass communication The relatively simultaneous exposure of large heterogeneous audiences to symbols transmitted by impersonal means from organized sources to whom audience members are anonymous.

mass society The model (theoretical construct) of a society toward which societies are ultimately drifting. It consists of an undifferentiated mass of people and an elite capable of dominating and manipulating it. It is highly urbanized and industrialized and displays secondary relationships, lack of traditional values, alienation, anomie, pressure to conform, and subjection to manipulation through the mass media.

modernization A model of sociocultural change that describes the transformation of small preindustrial societies into large industrial ones.

nationalistic revolutionary movement A revolutionary social movement in which a predominantly foreign government is overthrown and replaced with a native one.

propaganda A deliberate attempt to persuade people to uncritically accept a particular belief or to make a certain choice.

public Persons in society who are geographically dispersed but who share a common interest, who express that interest, and who know that others are aware of their interest.

public opinion The totality of opinions, attitudes, and judgments expressed by publics.

rumor An unsupported report of an event or a projected event. Important in bringing about manifestations of more active types of collective behavior.

social change Change in the patterns of social interaction in which a substantial number of society's members assume new statuses and play new roles. Takes place through planning, reform, or revolution.

technology All the methods and devices that help humans manage and control their environment.

terrorism A kind of transnational social movement that uses premeditated, politically motivated violence against noncombatant targets.

Suggested Readings

Branch, Taylor. 1988. *Parting the Waters: America in the King Years, 1954–1963*. New York: Simon & Schuster. A detailed examination of the civil rights movement with an emphasis on its charismatic leader, Martin Luther King.

Etzioni, Amitai. 1991. *A Responsive Society: Collected Essays on Guiding Deliberate Social Change*. San Francisco: Jossey-Bass. As the title implies, the author, a respected sociologist, makes suggestions as to how change may be directed to yield specific goals.

Gates, Bill. 1995. *The Road Ahead*. New York: Viking. What the chairman of Microsoft sees down the Information Highway.

Rifkin, Jeremy. 1998. *The Biotech Century: Harnessing the Gene and Remaking the World*. New York: Jeremy P. Tarcher/Putnam. A new revolution is in the making in the area of biotechnology, and the author looks at some of the changes such a revolution will produce in our lives.

Turkle, Sherry. 1995. *Life on the Screen: Identity in the Age of the Internet*. New York: Simon and Schuster. The long-term implications of millions of people interacting on the Internet are analyzed from a sociological viewpoint.

Web Sites of Interest

http://www.wfs.org/index.htm
For people concerned with how social change will shape our future, the web site of the World Future Society, a nonprofit educational and scientific organization, provides interesting information.

http://gsociology.icaap.org/report/summary2.htm
A sociological analysis of the many theories and research relating to social change.

http://www.ropercenter.uconn.edu/pom/pom_list.html
A nonprofit, nonpartisan organization that provides polling data and public opinion research on a number of topics.

http://www.interweb-tech.com/nsmnet/resources/default.asp
This web site provides links to a number of activist organizations, some of which may be social movements in the making.

http://www.fashion.net/sites/onlinefashion/websites/index.html
Inasmuch as fashion is part of collective behavior, it may prove interesting to check out some of the sites relating to fashion.

http://www.hoaxbusters.ciac.org
The Internet has become a peculiarly efficient instrument of rumor mongering. This web site attempts to stop the spread of unsubstantiated rumors.

http://people-press.org
This is the web site of the Pew Research Center for the People and the Press. It is an excellent source of surveys, polls, articles of commentary about items in the news—in short, everything that relates to public opinion.

http://www.ict.org.il
This is the web site of the International Policy Institute for Counterterrorism. It deals with all issues of terrorism and offers a wealth of resources about the subject.

Population, Urbanization, and Environment

IN THIS CHAPTER, YOU WILL LEARN

■ *about the importance of the discipline of demography and its various concepts;*

■ *about the types of changes that occur within populations and their effects on societies;*

■ *of the dangers of overpopulation;*

■ *the meaning and effects of urbanization;*

■ *about the characteristics of American cities;*

■ *the difference between the process called urbanization and the attitude of urbanism, which has become predominant globally;*

■ *about the emergence of suburbanization and metropolitanization;*

■ *the nature of the urban crisis;*

■ *about the discipline of ecology;*

■ *that humans have damaging effects on the various ecosystems, including on the global ecosystem.*

As we saw in the previous chapter, the principal sociocultural change following each technological revolution was a dramatic increase in population. After the Industrial Revolution, in addition, population growth was accompanied by a rise in the number of cities and ultimately an urban way of life that now pervades all industrial societies. In turn, large populations, the industrial system, and an urbanized lifestyle have wreaked havoc on the planet's environment. They have pushed the human species into acting in ways that are contrary to the ways in which they behaved when small groups of them roamed the vastness of the earth.

The triple trends that follow the process of modernization in societies around the world include a dramatic increase in population, a rush by rural residents to the cities, and the consequent damage that urban overcrowding, as well as the industrial system, do to the natural environment. China, for instance already has more than a billion people, many of whom are crowding into environmentally damaged cities.

All living things follow an instinctive urge to reproduce themselves. This urge is given the weight of a divine commandment in Western societies by the Biblical injunction to be fruitful and multiply. Non-Western societies are similarly affected by the need to procreate, judging from the seriously overpopulated world for which gloom and doom are periodically prophesied. In reality, if people were distributed evenly over the surface of the earth, there would only be about 55 people per square mile. The real problem, then, is population density, which varies from zero in some uninhabited regions of Antarctica to an average of 77,000 people per square mile on the island of Manhattan. In the United States, there are counties in the Great Plains region with fewer than 6 persons per square mile.

The distribution of people is a very vital issue because the welfare of a society often depends on such characteristics of its people as birthrates, death rates, sex ratios, age groups, marriage incidence, divorce frequency, and mobility. The gathering and interpretation of statistics in these areas are done by the discipline of **demography,** which is the scientific study of how births, deaths, and migration affect the composition, size, and distribution of populations.

Population density can be measured in a variety of ways. Looking at continents, 76 percent of the human population lives in Eurasia, 9 percent in North America, 10 percent in Africa, and 5 percent in South America and the Pacific islands. Looking at political units, 22 percent of all humans reside in the People's Republic of China, 15 percent live in India, 6.5 percent in the former Soviet Union, 5.5 percent in the United States, and the rest of humanity is distributed in much smaller percentages throughout the remaining countries of the world.

■ Demographic Processes: Dynamics of Population Change

The chief source of information for demographers is the census, a sort of head count describing the composition and distribution of people according to their origins, skills, and activities, in addition to their location. In the United States, an elaborate census is conducted every 10 years (as prescribed by Article I of the Constitution). The accuracy of the census is important because not only are the seats in the House of Representatives apportioned according to the population of each state but also a number of federal entitlement programs are similarly allocated on the basis of census results. An example of the kinds of data the Bureau of the Census collects is provided by a rapid perusal of its "USA Statistics in Brief" in Table 11.1. These figures change every year as a result of three factors: the number of births, the number of deaths, and the number of people who move into a location or move out of it. Demographers refer to these factors as the birthrate, the death rate, and migration.

Birthrates

The crude **birthrate** is defined as the number of live births per 1,000 people during one year. (The actual formula that demographers use to obtain the crude birthrate is the number of live births in a given year, divided by the total population of a country and multiplied by 1,000.) A more accurate concept is **fertility** rate, which is "the number of births that 1,000 women would have in their lifetime if, at each year of age, they experienced the birth rates occurring in the specified year" (Table 11.1). **Fecundity** rates represent the biological potential for reproduction (how many births per 1,000 women of that age group could occur). At the height of the baby boom years, 1947, the crude birthrate in the United States was about 27 per 1,000. In 2005, the crude birthrate was 14, conspicuously lower than the post–World War II high and very low compared to a nation such as Afghanistan, with a birthrate of 53.4 per 1,000, or Uganda, with a rate of 51.1, but higher than the rate of Japan (8.7), Greece (9.5), or Italy (9.7).

Birthrates do not generally correspond to population density. In fact, densely populated areas such as Western Europe and Japan have low birthrates, as we saw, whereas sparsely settled regions such as Arabia and interior Africa have very high birthrates. From the perspective of economics, high birthrates occur in the less industrialized and less urbanized countries of the world, the so-called underdeveloped nations. Conversely, highly industrialized and urbanized nations tend to have the lowest birthrates. Therefore, birthrates are recognized as the best single socioeconomic variable differentiating developed from underdeveloped nations. This distribution of birthrates is comparatively new: between 1840 and 1930, the population of Europe grew from 194 million to 463 million, approximately double the rate for the world as a whole.

Death Rates

The crude death rate, also called mortality rate, is the number of deaths per 1000 people of a given population per year. On a worldwide basis, death rates are highest in tropical Africa, whereas urban, industrial nations have low death rates in addition to low birthrates. However, some less urban and industrial nations, such as Thailand, Turkey, and Ecuador, also exhibit low death rates even though their birthrates are moderate or high. The reason for this disparity is that the percentage of young people is higher in developing countries than it is in developed countries. Still, in 2004 the death rate in the United States was 8.2 per 1000, whereas in Sierra Leone it was 20.62 per 1000 (United Nations, 2007).

TABLE 11.1 USA Statistics in Brief—Population by Sex, Age, Region, Vital Statistics, and Health

Population	2000	2005	2007
Resident population (1,000)	281,425	296,410	302,952
Male (1,000)	138,056	146,000	
Female (1,000)	143,368	150,411	
Under 5 years old (1,000)	19,176	20,304	
5 to 17 years old (1,000)	53,119	53,166	
18 to 44 years old (1,000)	112,184	113,313	
45 to 64 years old (1,000)	61,954	72,838	
65 years old and over (1,000)	34,992	36,790	
Northeast (1,000)	53,595	54,642	
Midwest (1,000)	64,395	65,972	
South (1,000)	100,236	107,505	
West (1,000)	63,199	68,291	

Percent of population	2000	2005
Male	49.1	49.3
Female	50.9	50.7
Under 5 years old	6.8	6.8
5 to 17 years old	18.9	17.9
18 to 44 years old	39.9	38.2
45 to 64 years old	22.0	24.6
65 years old and over	12.4	12.4
Northeast	19.0	18.4
Midwest	22.9	22.3
South	35.6	36.3
West	22.5	23.0

Vital Statistics	2000	2004
Birth rate per 1,000 people	14.4	14.0
Total fertility rate[1]	2,056	2,046
Death rate per 1,000 people	8.5	8.2
Heart disease	2.5	2.2
Cancer	2.0	1.9
Infant death rate[2]	6.9	6.8

Health	2000	2004
National health expenditures (billion dollars)	1,359	1,878
Medicare (billion dollars)	225	309
Public assistance medical payments (billion dollars)	208	304
Persons without health insurance (percent)	14.2	15.7

NA = Not available.

[1]The number of births that 1,000 women would have in their lifetime if, at each year of age, they experienced the birth rates occurring in the specified year.

[2]Death of infants under 1 year, excluding fetal deaths; rates per 1,000 registered live births.

Death can result from a number of causes: traffic accidents, suicide, disease, or starvation. The great leveler of death rates has been Western medical technology, which in this century has reached almost every corner of the world. It has dramatically decreased death rates everywhere, even in locations where they had remained stubbornly high. Decreasing death rates, in fact, are a major cause of excessive population growth in third world nations.

A truer measure of the quality of life in a society, or in a segment of a society, is the infant mortality rate. The infant mortality rate reflects the number of deaths among infants under one year of age for every 1000 live births. In developing countries, that rate tends to be over 30, whereas in developed nations it tends to be under 20. In 2001, the infant mortality rate in the United States was 6.8 per 1000, and 18 nations reported even lower infant mortality rates. By contrast, the infant mortality rate in Sierra Leone in 2004 was 145.24, in Angola it was 192.50, and in Niger 122.66. In the United States, the rate varies greatly according to social class and race: infant mortality among the poor and minorities has been twice as high as that among the well-to-do in the last several decades. In fact, as of 2005 the infant mortality rate in Mississippi rose to 11.4, and among African Americans in that state it increased to 17 per thousand births. This means that 65 more babies died in 2005 than in 2004 (Eckholm, 2007, p.1).

Infant mortality has some impact on life expectancy, which is the average number of years a person of a certain age can expect to live. In developing nations the average life expectancy is 64.4 years, but it may be much lower: it is 42.18 in Niger, 36.79 in Angola, and 40.88 in Ethiopia. In the United States, life expectancy has gone from 40 years at the turn of the preceding century to 77.43 for persons born between 1995 and 2000. Even Americans currently 65 to 75 years old can expect to live about 20 years longer. But again, not all categories of Americans have such prospects: at birth, life expectancy was about 6 years higher for white persons than for black persons. At age 65, white persons still were expected to live 2 years longer than black persons (Table 11.2). However, for persons who lived to age 85, life expectancy is slightly higher among black persons than among white persons (CDC, 2006, Table 27). The differences between genders are most likely genetic in nature; the differences between races are probably caused by variations in lifestyles resulting from social class, or perhaps black persons who live till 85 are healthier than white persons. (Most of the gains in the last 150 years in life expectancy have come from reductions in the deaths of infants and women in childbirth.)

Migration

Between 1880 and 1910, more than 28 million Europeans moved from that continent to the United States. Their movement is defined as international migration—movement of people from one country to another. In migration, **push factors** encourage people to leave one geographic area for another and **pull factors** attract people to a new area. For instance, in 1840 the potato famine was the push that made people leave Ireland, and the employment opportunities in the United States were the pull that attracted the Irish to come here. Today, similar push-and-pull factors are acting on Mexicans and Southeast Asians in their efforts to immigrate into the United States.

Immigration

We are a nation of immigrants. Immigration peaked in the first two decades of the twentieth century and did not begin to climb again until 1965, with legislation that eliminated ethnic bias and loosened quotas. Since 1980, an average of 570,000 people a year have come to these shores, not including the approximately 3 million illegal aliens who are in the country. The Immigration Reform and Control Act of 1986 was supposed to lessen the flood of

TABLE 11.2 Life expectancy in years at birth, at 65 years of age, and at 75 years of age, by race and sex: United States, 2004

[Data are based on death certificates]

| | Updated February 2007 | | | | | | | | |
| | All Races | | | White | | | Black or African American | | |
Specified Age	Both Sexes	Male	Female	Both Sexes	Male	Female	Both Sexes	Male	Female
At birth									
2004[1]	77.8	75.2	80.4	78.3	75.7	80.8	73.1	69.5	76.3
At 65 years									
2004	18.7	17.1	20.0	18.7	17.2	20.0	17.1	15.2	18.6
At 75 years									
2004	11.9	10.7	12.8	11.9	10.7	12.8	11.4	9.9	12.2

[1] For all races, both sexes in 2005, life expectancy is 77.97

Sources: Centers for Disease Control and Prevention, National Center for Health Statistics, National Vital Statistics System; Grove RD, Hetzel AM. Vital statistics rates in the United States, 1940–1960. Washington, DC: U.S. Government Printing Office, 1968; Arias, E. United States life tables, 2004. National vital statistics reports; Hyattsville, MD: National Center for Health Statistics. 2006, forthcoming.

undocumented aliens across U.S. borders because it prescribed high fines for employers who hired them. In reality, the illegal border crossings increased (Parrillo, 1990, 536). The Census Bureau calculates that legal and illegal aliens accounted for one-fourth to one-third of the country's population growth in the 1980s. In addition, the origins of the immigrant differs from that of previous waves (see Chapter 8).

Internal Migration

Between 1910 and 1955, millions of poor whites and blacks left the economically ailing South of the United States for the industrial jobs in the North. They were engaging in internal migration. Today, it is the South and the West that are growing in population, whereas the Midwest and Northeast are losing population. Internal migration does not affect the size of a nation's population; it affects the populations of regions and local communities. Internal migration has been very important in the history of the United States. We are a mobile country whose citizens willingly follow the siren song of better opportunity, whether it leads west, north, south, or east. Reversals, then, are common. Since 1980, nearly 100,000 more African Americans have moved into the South than have moved out, reversing an 80-year tide of migration. Most of them are moving to the South for new jobs, for a better quality of life, or to renew family ties. Although most migration is driven by economic opportunity, the South has become more hospitable to African Americans in the sense that laws on civil rights, voter registration, and school desegregation and laws against discrimination on the job have created a much more tolerable atmosphere for black families (Weiss, 1989, Y29).

The Midwest, too, is experiencing something of a rebound, although Americans continue to favor the West and the South as places to live: as of 2006, the 50 fastest-growing metropolitan areas were distributed between two regions—23 in the West and 25 in the South (U.S. Bureau of the Census, Current Population Reports, 2006). The population of the United States is concentrated as follows: 36 percent live in the South, 23 percent in the West, 22 percent in the Midwest, and 18 percent in the Northeast. The most populous states in the nation are California (35.5 million people), Texas (22.1 million), and New York (19.2 million). (U.S. Bureau of the Census, Economics and Statistics Administration, 2003. U.S. Census Press Release, December 18. Accessed 6/22/04.) Sociologists and demographers had predicted that the coastal states would come to hold a greater proportion of the nation's population. The reason for this situation is economic: the coastal states account for the largest percentage of the real growth in wages and partnership income. The industrial heartland of the United States traditionally had been in the region around the Great Lakes because industry needed the transportation provided by the waterways and the region was also rich in coal and iron ore. However, the rise of the information economy has moved population following jobs to the rim states of Massachussetts and New Jersey in the East and the Silicon Valley (from San Francisco to San Jose) in the West (see Figures 11.1 and 11.2).

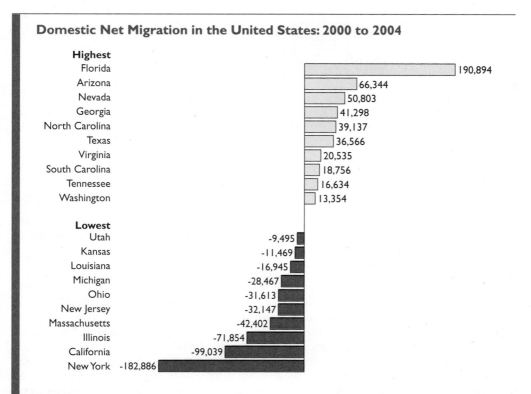

Domestic Net Migration in the United States: 2000 to 2004

Highest
Florida	190,894
Arizona	66,344
Nevada	50,803
Georgia	41,298
North Carolina	39,137
Texas	36,566
Virginia	20,535
South Carolina	18,756
Tennessee	16,634
Washington	13,354

Lowest
Utah	-9,495
Kansas	-11,469
Louisiana	-16,945
Michigan	-28,467
Ohio	-31,613
New Jersey	-32,147
Massachusetts	-42,402
Illinois	-71,854
California	-99,039
New York	-182,886

FIGURE 11.1 Highest and Lowest Average Annual *Levels* of Net Domestic Migration for States: 2000–2004

Sources: U.S. Census Bureau, Population Estimates Program, 2004; U.S. Census Bureau (Current Population Reports) Issued April 2006.

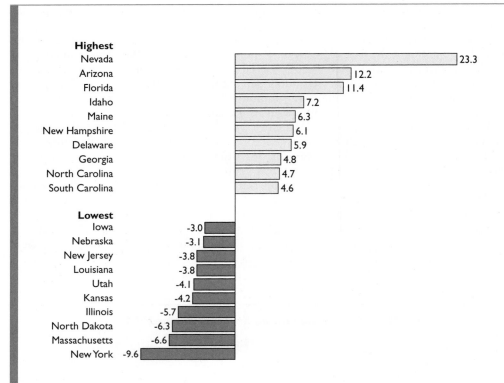

FIGURE 11.2 Highest and Lowest Average Annual *Rates* of Net Domestic Migration for States: 2000–2004
(Rates per 1,000 average population based on population estimates for July 1, 2000, and July 1, 2004)
Source: U.S. Census Bureau, Population Estimates Program, 2004.

■ Characteristics and Composition of a Population

Demographers calculate not only a population's size—which is affected by birthrates, death rates, and migration rates—but also a number of other characteristics, the most important of which are the sex ratio, the marriage rate, and the age structure.

Sex Ratio

The sex ratio indicates how many males there are in a population in any single year per 100 females. More boys than girls are conceived and born (124 are conceived, 105 are born), but the ratio of males to females in the United States is 96.7 males for 100 females. The reasons for the greater number of females are to be found in the higher rates of miscarriage of male fetuses, and males' susceptibility to disease, accidents, and violence. This is particularly true in wartime, but even in normal times women outnumber men beginning at about age 25 through old age. In relatively advanced countries, there are about 105 females for every 100 males. In third-world countries, however, the opposite is true: although 5 or 6 percent more boys than girls are born, in India there are only 92.9 females for every 100 males, in China there are 93.8 females for every 100 males, and in Afghanistan there are 94.5 females for every 100 males. These conditions are due to high rates of female infanticide and the general negligence—if not outright murder—of female children, whom the cultures of these nations do not value to the same extent as males. It is reported that at least 60 million females in Asia are missing and feared dead, while around the world more than 100 million females are missing, victims only of their gender.

Because the sex ratio is fairly even in the United States, the marriage rate is high (because each individual has the possibility of obtaining a mate). In addition, the marriage rate is positively related to the birthrate: the baby boom occurred after World War II, when soldiers came home, married, and had families. Beginning in the 1960s, late marriages, divorces, and increasing numbers of unmarried adults decreased our birthrates to their present low.

Age Structure

The age structure of a society influences it in a variety of ways. A society whose members are concentrated in the age group 20–65 has a large labor force and few nonproductive dependents. On the other hand, if members are concentrated in the under-20, or the over-65 age group, the society has a large number of nonproductive individuals, which the government has to help support. A population with a large number of young people will also tend to have high birthrates, a situation occurring at present in developing countries. Naturally, a population with a high number of elderly people has a high death rate.

The age and sex composition of a population can be shown graphically by what is called a *population pyramid*. Each bar in such a graph represents a **birth cohort**, or all the people born in a specific time period. In a developing country, the pyramid has a truly pyramidal shape because its bottom is constituted by the largest birth cohort—the population consisting of those under 20. The top consists of a small proportion of those over 65. In a developed country, the declines in both the birthrate and the death rate make for a structure with a wide middle and a rather narrow base and top (Figure 11.3).

The population pyramid is a useful tool for social planning. Obviously, in a society in which the majority of the population is under 20, there will be a need for maternity wards in hospitals, schools, and child care services. One whose members are predominantly old will need additional nursing homes, health care geared to the aged, provisions for pensions and Social Security, and so on.

Some demographers maintain that the widening gap between the age cohorts in different parts of the world is a time bomb (Bell, 1987, 15–16). The proportion of young people under 15 years in all of Africa is between 40 and 50 percent of the population; in almost all of Latin America it is about 40 percent of the population; in most of Asia, it is between 30 and 40 percent; while in the United States and Canada it is about 22 percent. What this means is that in the next 20 years there will be more than a doubling of the rates of entry into the labor forces of the nations with large percentages of young people. This will create conditions of unemployment and underemployment, which will add to the political instability of those nations. In addition, because of the huge increases in the number of women of child-bearing age in the next several decades—caused, in turn, by the young age structure of the population at the world level—a population momentum will result in a doubling of world population by 2050 to about 9.1 billion people, an increase of better than 50 percent over 1999.

One of the values of demography as a scientific discipline is its predictive function, for it is to the advantage of society to be aware of future trends and prepare for them. In the

Population Pyramid Summary for United States

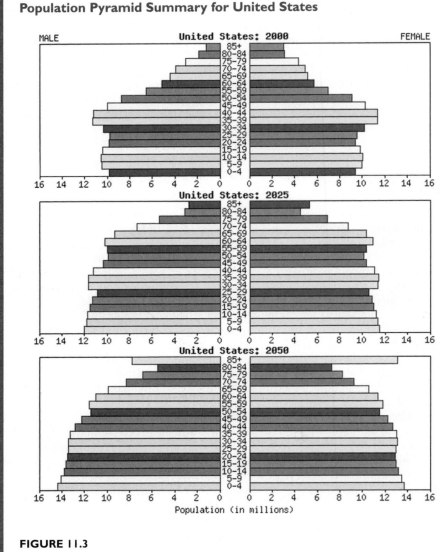

FIGURE 11.3
Source: U.S. Census Bureau, International Data Base

United States, the Census Bureau not only collects data reflecting the present but also attempts to make projections about the future. The Census Bureau has been projecting that the population of the United States by 2050 would stand at a high of 419.854 million. The United Nations has also predicted that the United States will continue to increase in population during the first half of the twenty-first century. The reasons are twofold: one, the large number of immigrants who continue to arrive; and two, the higher fertility rate we display, which is unique among the developed nations. This will put the United States in a position of

Population Pyramid Summary for Mexico

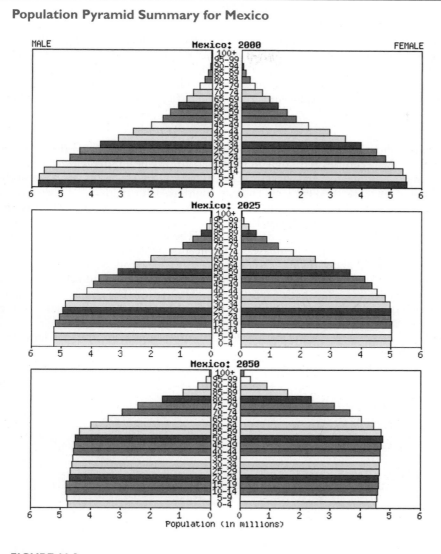

FIGURE 11.3 *(continued)*
Source: U.S. Census Bureau, International Data Base

being the only developed country among the world's most populous nations with a tremendous impact on the world (Crossette, 2001, A5). In fact, because of their habits of high consumption, Americans use up more than one-third of the world's energy and material resources, even though they are less than 6 percent of the world's population. However, China is fast approaching a high level of development and consumption and so it may usurp U.S. dominance.

■ Population around the World

The media often refer to a "crisis" of population, by which they mean that the number of people in the world has been increasing *geometrically* (that is, it has been doubling: 2, 4, 8, 16, 32, etc.) at ever shorter intervals of time. At present, world population is doubling every 35 years, so that every year there are about 74 million more births than deaths (Figure 11.4). In contrast, from 1 A.D. to the middle of the eighteenth century, the birthrate doubled only every 500 years.

Malthus and Marx

The increasingly shorter intervals at which population doubles have created the problem of overpopulation. Two centuries ago, some thinkers had already begun to realize that the earth would become overpopulated and lack sufficient resources unless birthrates were curbed. The best known of these thinkers was Thomas Malthus, who published his treatise, *An Essay on the Principles of Population*, in 1798. In it, Malthus asserted that, whereas under favorable circumstances populations grow by geometric progression, the food supply increases by arithmetic progression—1, 2, 3, 4, 5, and so on. Therefore, eventually the food supply would become exhausted, causing increases in the death rate through starvation. Although he was quite pessimistic about the possibility of reversing this trend, Malthus suggested the use of preventive checks to control fertility. Later marriage and enforced celibacy were the checks he favored, neither one a particularly realistic alternative. The gloom of the Malthusian prophecy has been tempered by great advances in technology, agriculture, and methods of birth control. Nonetheless, the prophecy still has relevance, particularly for the developing nations in which, largely as a result of lower death rates, population growth does indeed outpace food production.

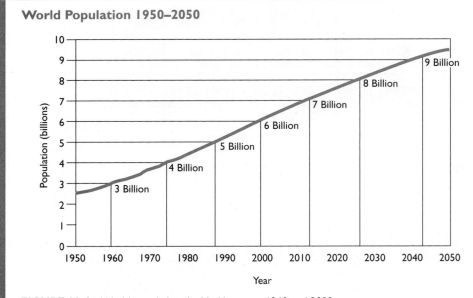

World Population 1950–2050

FIGURE 11.4 World population doubled between 1960 and 2000.
Source: U.S. Census Bureau, *International Data Base,* August 2006 version.

Karl Marx disagreed with Malthus about the causes of overpopulation. Inasmuch as he tended to attribute all the evils of society to the unequal distribution of resources, he maintained that the real issue was underproduction and limited employment opportunities, all failures of the capitalist system. If the society were well ordered, an increase in population would mean an increase in production and, thus, in wealth. But because of the way in which property was held in capitalist societies, workers remained poor and competed for the few jobs available. As a solution, Marx proposed a radical restructuring of society, particularly a more equitable distribution of food, housing, and the other necessities of life.

Demographic Transition

Demographers have calculated that if the current rate of population growth continues unabated, in a few centuries the population of the world will reach such a level that each person will have only one square foot of land area at his or her disposal. Of course, no one could live in such a minuscule space, but the calculations give dramatic evidence of the nightmarish possibilities. So do the following figures: the world gains 141 new human beings each minute, 10,000 each hour, 203,000 each day, and approximately 74 million each year! Every three years, the new additions to world population equal the total population of the United States. A world population of 6.1 billion people was reached by mid-2000 (the 5 billion mark was passed in 1987), and by 2150 the world population is expected to top 9 billion. Finally, nearly 50 percent of the world's population was born in the last 25 years (see Figure 11.5).

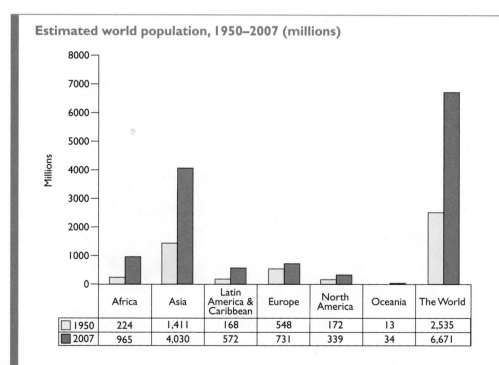

Estimated world population, 1950–2007 (millions)

	Africa	Asia	Latin America & Caribbean	Europe	North America	Oceania	The World
1950	224	1,411	168	548	172	13	2,535
2007	965	4,030	572	731	339	34	6,671

FIGURE 11.5

Source: World Population Prospects: The 2006 Revision, New York: United Nations, 2007, table 1.1.

However, most population experts expect that the growth rate will remain constant but will level out at some point between 8 billion and 15 billion people. This leveling off will take place if people attain zero population growth (a situation in which people only replace themselves) worldwide or if the demographic transition theory continues to function (see below).

As noted, for most of human history the rates of population growth were barely sufficient for people to replace themselves. A high birthrate was necessary to compensate for the extremely high death rate. In addition, famine, disease, and wars periodically decimated many of the world's populations.

The Industrial Revolution, with its many technological innovations, changed all that. In the West, populations began to explode around the middle of the eighteenth century, but despite Malthus's warnings the uncontrolled growth failed to frighten people, who thought that technology would keep progressing and, thus, always ensure an adequate food supply. Population growth this time around was also accompanied by an increase in the standard of living. This correlation was interpreted as meaning that rapid growth was actually needed for economic expansion. After all, if there are more people, more products are consumed and more people are needed in the workforce to produce still more articles for consumption. In reality, rapid population growth erases any gains derived from improvements in agricultural and industrial technology.

In the past 200 years, the Western world has undergone what demographers call a **demographic transition**. Essentially, this means that Western societies have gone from high mortality and fertility rates to low mortality and fertility rates. Population grew rapidly for a time, and death rates dropped before birthrates did. Soon, however, birthrates were also falling off, and the population growth rate began to stabilize at a relatively low level.

In the belief that this transition represents a general pattern, demographers have pieced together a conceptual model of population growth. According to the model, societies pass

The highest rates of population growth occur in the poorest regions of the world. In many societies of Asia, Africa, and Arabia, women typically have between five and eight children. Here is an extended three-generation family with seven children.

through three basic stages of population growth. In the first stage, birthrates and death rates are both high, leading to a balance achieved through cycles of growth and decline. In the second stage, death rates decline but birthrates remain high, leading to unchecked population growth. In the third stage, birthrates decline, leading to stabilization of population. The model allows for shifts in population growth following unusual events, such as wars and depressions.

In applying the model, it may be seen that tropical Africa, tropical South America, and the eastern and middle sections of Asia are currently in the first stage. Parts of North Africa, the temperate part of South America, India, the People's Republic of China, and several other Third-World nations are in the second stage. The United States, Australia, New Zealand, Japan, Canada, the United Kingdom, and northern and western Europe are all in the third stage.

Zero Population Growth

As of the 1970s, the industrial world (the United States, Europe, Japan, Australia) began to display extremely low population growth rates. In the United States, the fertility rate had declined for the first time below the replacement level or between 2.08 and 2.04. In the year 2000, the fertility rate in the United States stood at 2.07. (The replacement level is 2.1, the 2 representing the rate if each person merely reproduced himself or herself, and the 0.1 representing the people who remain childless.) Demographers refer to this phenomenon as **zero population growth.** This lower rate can be best appreciated by recalling that as recently as 1961 the American rate was well over 3.6 children per family. However, while the United States is a zero-population-growth (ZPG) society, the actual number of births has increased since 1970. The reason for this is that women born during the baby boom years following World War II have been in their child-bearing years from approximately 1970 into the 1990s. But although the absolute number of births may be higher, the number of births per woman is no higher than the ZPG.

In almost achieving ZPG, the United States is following the lead set by other urban, industrial nations. Conditions in cities, where most people are concentrated in these nations, do not lend themselves to large families. Housing is scarce, industrial jobs are not open to children, and it is expensive to educate and provide health protection for many children. Thus, urban families, regardless of religion and culture, tend to curb their fertility. Ireland, France, and Italy, for instance, are all Roman Catholic nations whose religion forbids birth control, yet the birthrate in these nations is among the lowest in the world and is declining. The average fertility rate in Western Europe is 1.6, while in Japan and South Korea it is 1.5 (see Figures 11.6 and 11.7).

In spite of the optimism that may be engendered by the demographic transition model and the fact that a number of societies have attained zero population growth, the danger of overpopulation cannot be ignored. The human race is multiplying very rapidly, which has prompted the United Nations and the Population Reference Bureau to point out that the most rapid expansion is occurring in poor, underdeveloped nations, where food, housing, sanitation, and economic opportunities are already in short supply. If present trends continue, zero growth worldwide can be expected to occur no sooner than by the year 2040.

Population Policies

As mentioned, the rich nations of the world are experiencing slow rates of population growth, while many of the developing nations have a very low standard of living

Global Fertility Levels Relative to Replacement Level: 2002-2050

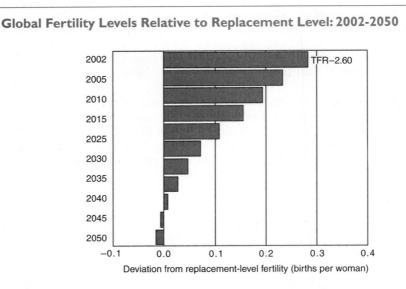

FIGURE 11.6 The level of global fertility is projected to drop below replacement by midcentury.
Note: Global total fertility rates were derived by calculating weighted age-specific fertility rates from country-and-age-specific births and numbers of women.
Source: U.S. Census Bureau, International Programs Center, International Data Base, and unpublished tables.

Fertility Rates Have Fallen in Every Major World Region, but Are Still Highest in Sub-Saharan Africa

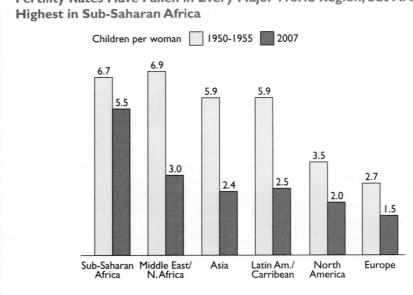

FIGURE 11.7
Source: United Nations, *World Population Prospects: The 2006 Revision* (2007); and C. Haub, *2007 World Population Data Sheet.*

(including abject poverty and periodic famines) and rapidly increasing population growth. To counteract these factors, a number of nations have had to implement policies to try to control either growth or lack of growth of their populations. In the West, the low birthrates have prompted pro-natalists (those in favor of an increase in birthrates) to maintain that there is a danger that Western values, chiefly political democracy, may not survive. Others fear that economic prosperity may be undermined. Vital, productive, and creative societies may become passive and conservative. This would slow technological innovation, while a small workforce would have difficulty paying for the Social Security and health benefits for an older, retired population (Wattenberg & Zinsmeister, 1986; Cherlin, 1987).

On the other side of this spectrum have been nations such as China, India, Bangladesh, and Singapore, whose governments have imposed various methods of population control on their citizens. Some states in India, with the encouragement of the central government, forced men to be sterilized after having fathered their second child. Fines and imprisonment were the punishment for refusal. The program met with so much opposition that it effectively toppled the government of Prime Minister Indira Gandhi in 1977. Currently, even though it has a fertility rate of 4.7 children per woman and will become the most populous nation in the world by approximately 2045, India is back to a voluntary population control program. Bangladesh was similarly unsuccessful with its forced sterilization program, and though it offers economic incentives to encourage sterilization, its fertility rate is a very high 6.3 children per woman. Singapore, which used both rewards and punishment in its goal to establish a two-child family, was so successful that it has had to reverse itself and is encouraging people to have three or more children if they can afford to. China, which tried to use the reward-and-punishment combination, has initially had less success. The Chinese government launched a one-child-per-family campaign, offering substantial rewards to couples who produce only one child: salary bonuses, free schooling, priority medical care, admission to the best schools, and preference in employment. Conversely, those who have more than one child must pay all costs for each additional child, are taxed 10 percent of their income, and are denied promotion. From 1979 to 1986, this method worked so well that China's birthrate was cut in half. But since 1986, the rate has begun to increase again, partly because some Chinese are willing to pay the fines to have more children and partly because the Chinese government was being criticized for encouraging abortions even late in pregnancy (some parents even engaged in female infanticide in their quest for their one male child). The result is that, having entered the 1990s with more than 1 billion people, China's population will double by approximately 2025. India, however, will overtake China in total population by 2037. A population of more than 2 billion people strains the economy of any society, and particularly one that has made gains only of late and with great difficulty (Table 11.3).

Findings published by the independent Population Crisis Committee indicate that population policies in Asia have been unsuccessful in slowing growth and continued population growth is contributing to an intensifying crisis in ecological and human resources. They add that it is unlikely that China and India will be able to stabilize growth until well into this century, by which time they may have added more than 1.5 billion people to the world (Crossette, 1992). Almost 98 percent of the world's population growth occurs in the poorest and less developed regions of the world that can least afford to support a large population. In many of these societies, where women have an average of 3.4 children, fertility rates are the highest (about 6.5), contraception use is the lowest (15 percent of married women), infant mortality rates are among the highest, life expectancy is among the lowest, as is the yearly gross domestic product (GDP) per capita—$1,130 (Population Reference Bureau,

TABLE 11.3 The Top Ten Most Populous Countries: 1950, 2002, and 2050.* Less developed countries dominate the list of the world's ten most populous countries.

1950**	2002	2050
1. China	1. China	1. India
2. India	2. India	2. China
3. United States	3. United States	3. United States
4. Russia	4. Indonesia	4. Indonesia
5. Japan	5. Brazil	5. Nigeria
6. Indonesia	6. Pakistan	6. Bangladesh
7. Germany	7. Russia	7. Pakistan
8. Brazil	8. Bangladesh	8. Brazil
9. United Kingdom	9. Nigeria	9. Congo (Kinshasa)
10. Italy	10. Japan	10. Mexico

Rankings of future or past top-ten countries

11. Bangladesh	11. Mexico	14. Russia
13. Pakistan	13. Germany	16. Japan
15. Nigeria	21. United Kingdom	24. Germany
16. Mexico	22. Italy	29. United Kingdom
32. Congo (Kinshasa)	23. Congo (Kinshasa)	35. Italy

*More developed countries/less developed countries.
**Current boundaries.

Source: U.S. Census Bureau, International Programs, Center, International Data Base, and unpublished tables.

2001). However, in 2007 the average number of children per woman worldwide declined from 5.0 (1950) to 2.7, although in sub-Saharan Africa the average remained at 5.5 (PRB, 2007). Worldwide contraception use also increased to 62 percent from less than 10 percent in the 1960s.

Why do birthrates remain high in the less developed countries? First, because of diffusion, advances in medicine and technology have filtered into industrializing nations, reducing the death rate while the birthrate remains high. Because industrialization has been superimposed on the society, there has been no time to develop the value of small families, as happened in the industrial nations. Consequently, there is a cultural lag between material and nonmaterial culture. As they have been for thousands of years, children are valuable in agrarian societies: they offer hands to work the earth and constitute a kind of old-age insurance for parents who cannot count on pensions or Social Security. Moreover, gender inequality is prevalent in such societies, and a man's ability to have many children is a symbol of his manliness. In many countries of Latin America, even though women may want to curb their fertility and do understand how to use contraceptives, their men will not allow them to do so. In rural Africa, on the other hand, lack of education and ignorance of how conception takes place or of effective forms of birth control contributes to the high birthrate, as do high infant mortality rates and death rates of children (parents have many children in the hope that at least some will survive).

Box 11.1   Americans as the Census Bureau Sees Us

Every decade the Census Bureau counts the heads of Americans, just so we know how many we are. However, counting heads is the least of what the Bureau does: its surveys also tell us, probably in more detail than we care to know, everything about us. How tall we are, how fat we are, how many pounds of sugar we eat yearly, how much television we watch, how many times we marry, how much education we have . . . and on and on to infinity.

Well, then, what do we look like? We are the fattest inhabitants of the planet, spending about eight-and-a-half hours a day watching TV, using computers, listening to the radio, or reading. Adolescents and adults spend more than 64 days a year watching TV, and a little more than a week using the Internet. In 2005, the Internet was used by 97 million people for news, by 92 million to buy a product, by 91 million to make travel reservations, by 16 million to find a professional networking site, and by 13 million to create a blog.

We are taller than preceding generations: while 24 percent of Americans in their seventies are shorter than 5 foot 6, only 10 percent of persons in their twenties are no taller than that. We are losing manufacturing jobs: they decreased in every job category except for pharmaceuticals. Jobs in textile mills fell by 42 percent, and the fastest growing job is that of home health aide. We do produce one element in huge quantities: solid waste is produced at a rate of 4.4 pounds per person per day, up from 3.7 pounds a decade ago.

We are wealthier than past generations: in 2005, more than half of American households owned stocks and mutual funds. Those people had a median household income of $65,000. The younger generation wants to copy this lifestyle: 75 percent of college freshmen state that their primary objective in attending college is to be financially very well off, whereas in the 1970s, 79 percent said their goal was to develop a meaningful philosophy of life. Nonetheless, we are producing more women doctors: 27 percent of doctors were women in 2005, whereas in 1980 only 12 percent were. And 42,000 men and 41,000 women earned professional degrees in 2004, whereas in 1970 only 2,000 women and 33,000 men earned such degrees.

Some facts about us are negative. A high number of us have no health insurance, and with medical costs rising, they can only pray that their health remains good. Technology has made it possible for our leisure time to be private, and this trend will continue: we will read less and watch less broadcast television, but will spend more time using the Internet and watching cable and satellite television. This privatization of entertainment—you don't have to go to the theater or to the movies but can get it all while remaining alone in your living room—may lead to a lack of social contact, and social isolation is not good for humans, the social animals.

On the other hand, our national divorce rate that had made us the most divorcing people on earth for several decades has decreased as of 2005: the rate, 3.7 per 1,000 people, was the lowest since 1970 (with the exception of Nevada, which still claims a rate of 6.4 per 1,000—but this is a decline from 11.4 in 1990).

These and many more facts may be learned from the Census Bureau, and now we need not wait for the decennial count. The bureau will issue demographic and social data for areas with populations of over 65,000 every year in the American Community Survey (ACS) of the U.S. Census Bureau, Public Information Office.

■ The Urban Society

Around the globe, the movement toward the cities continues unabated. In developing countries, every day brings thousands of rural residents to the large urban centers in search of jobs in an effort to avoid a life of backbreaking work with few rewards. Many never find the promised land and are condemned to live in makeshift shacks, eking out a livelihood by their wits. In the developed nations, some cities have remained vital, but not without exhibiting certain phenomena—a high crime rate, for instance, makes life in them less than ideal. In the United States, which is already a preeminently urban society, many cities are, or have been, in some form of crisis situation. Cities that were once centers of industry and commerce have lost population and business to the suburbs. With the consequent lower tax revenues, these cities cannot offer the services that middle-class residents demand. Consequently, they tend to become home to the poor and the recently arrived. The transition to an information society has deprived some cities of their essential role, as jobs have been lost and not recuperated. Many job holders are suburbanites who do not remain in the city outside of work hours. City streets become deserted after six o'clock. In short, although cities have been meccas to people all over the world, in some situations they reach a point at which they decline and die.

Urbanization

As was mentioned earlier, one of the most significant effects of the sociocultural changes leading to modernization has been the extensive urbanization of societies. **Urbanization** is the population trend in which cities and their suburbs grow at the expense of rural areas. Industrial nations become urbanized because factories and plants are established in the center of populated areas so that a ready labor pool will be available. In turn, industry attracts labor from surrounding areas, resulting in the growth of cities. A larger population requires additional services; hence, it acts as a magnet to more commercial enterprises. An industrial economy can support densely populated areas, whereas in rural areas the land must be used for agriculture rather than to accommodate people and commerce.

Urbanization, however, does not account for all city growth. As a result of increased birthrates, decreased death rates, or immigration from abroad, cities may grow without a parallel decrease in rural population. Or they may grow because of overall population increase in both rural and urban areas. This has been the case in developing nations, where the death rates have been cut by improved hygiene and medical findings but values regarding the control of births have not caught up.

■ The Industrial Revolution and the Growth of Cities

The shift from rural to urban living began with the Industrial Revolution in Great Britain. Factories located in cities attracted a large number of people who could no longer make a living on the land. Science and technology had improved agricultural methods. New iron and steel plows, reapers, threshers, harvesters, tractors, and combines did much of the work once done by humans. Crop rotation, chemical fertilizers, irrigation, and insect and disease control increased yields per acre without necessitating additional human labor.

The continued improvements in agricultural methods, then, led directly to a decline in the rural population. In the United States, for instance, the average farm worker in 1820 produced enough food to feed four people. By 1950, one worker produced enough for 15½ people; by 1969, enough for 47 people; and today enough for 50 people. Such superefficiency in food production has resulted in the disappearance of the small farmer, forcing many young farmers to abandon the rural way of life in favor of city life. At the same time, commercial agriculture creates a demand for agricultural machinery, which is produced in urban centers, adding still more to the trend toward urbanization. Urbanization, then, has been the hallmark of all industrial and industrializing nations.

In 2005, approximately 49 percent of people worldwide lived in urban areas, a percentage that is estimated to grow to 60 percent by 2030 (United Nations, 2007). This represents quite a difference from 1900, when 86.4 percent were rural dwellers and only 13.6 percent lived in cities (Palen, 2006). Urbanization as a population movement is continuing: in the United States, approximately 80 percent of people live in urban areas. The fastest rate of

TABLE 11.4   **Ten Megacities** (Population of Urban Agglomerations with 10 Million Inhabitants or More in 2005 and Their Average Annual Rates of Growth, 1975–2005 and 2005–2015)

	Urban agglomeration	Population (Millions)				Average Annual Rate of Change (Percentage)	
		1975	2000	2005	2015	1975–2005	2005–2015
1	Tokyo	26.6	34.4	35.2	35.5	0.93	0.08
2	Ciudad de México (Mexico City)	10.7	18.1	19.4	21.6	1.99	1.05
3	New York-Newark	15.9	17.8	18.7	19.9	0.55	0.60
4	São Paulo	9.6	17.1	18.3	20.5	2.15	1.13
5	Mumbai (Bombay)	7.1	16.1	18.2	21.9	3.15	1.84
6	Delhi	4.4	12.4	15.0	18.6	4.08	2.12
7	Shanghai	7.3	13.2	14.5	17.2	2.28	1.72
8	Kolkata (Calcutta)	7.9	13.1	14.3	17.0	1.98	1.73
9	Jakarta	4.8	11.1	13.2	16.8	3.37	2.41
10	Buenos Aires	8.7	11.8	12.6	13.4	1.20	0.65

Note: Urban agglomerations are ordered according to their population size in 2005.

Source: United Nations, Department of Economic and Social Affairs, Population Division (2006). *World Urbanization Prospects: The 2005 Revision.* Working Paper No. ESA/P/WP/200.

urbanization is claimed by Africa, but 70 percent of the population of Latin America will also live in urban areas in the twenty-first century. Moreover, these areas are becoming larger and larger: while at the beginning of the twentieth century there were only four cities with a population of over 2 million, there were 87 such cities by 1990, and today cities and their surrounding areas have grown to tremendous sizes (Table 11.4).

Urbanism

Industrial societies have been undergoing an urban transition whose ultimate effect is urbanism as a way of life. In contrast to urbanization, which is an ongoing process, **urbanism** is a condition, a set of attitudes, a quality, or a way of life distinct from the rural. It refers to the fact that the traditional rural values of predominantly agricultural societies have been replaced by urban values. Moreover, these urban values are spread through the mass media globally, so that all industrial nations are beginning to look and think alike.

The transition from rural to urban residence has forced people to make adjustments that have had profound effects on personality and on social organization. The nuclear form of the family, the lack of a support network represented by the extended family and friends and neighbors, separation from the ties of the primary group, all led to an increase in individual freedom of action. But freedom of action in anonymous circumstances can result in behavior that is considered deviant or antisocial. The individual becomes a victim of anomie and alienation. In practical terms, a decrease in informal controls by the primary group necessitates an increase in formal controls by secondary groups such as government agencies, the police, and the courts. So the urban resident pays the price for freedom from primary group interference by increasing bureaucratization and an impersonal lifestyle. In the early decades of the century, social scientists felt that life in the big city was conducive to social disorganization and led to a decline of community, because in the city there is no agreement on a multiplicity of norms.

American Cities

The extent of urbanization in the United States is clear when a few statistics are considered. When the first census was taken in 1790, 95 percent of the people lived in rural areas and only 5 percent lived in cites. By 1987, only 2 percent of the population lived on farms, and by 2000, 21 percent were described as rural residents and 77 percent as urban residents. In short, the urban trend introduced by the Industrial Revolution imported from Britain had caused an astonishingly large number of people to be brought together in cities, effecting tremendous social, economic, and political changes.

The growth and dominance of the industrial metropolis continued into the 1950s. Since then, a countermovement, sometimes referred to as urban decentralization, has been taking place (Edmonston & Guterbock, 1984). This movement includes suburbanization, the growth of megalopolis or regional cities, and the loss of population from central cities in the Northeast and Midwest in favor of the Sunbelt.

Suburbia

As stated, from the middle of the nineteenth century until well into the 1950s, the population trend was toward urban areas. Since then, the trend has been toward suburbanization and metropolitanization, movements out and away from the central city but not back toward the rural areas. The most significant growth occurred in the suburbs, small communities on the outskirts of the central city and somewhat dependent on it. Residents of suburbs now outnumber residents of the central city.

The movement to the suburbs has had a variety of causes. First, cities expanded so rapidly that industry and business encroached on residential areas, forcing people to move ever farther from the city center. Second, a general increase in the standard of living permitted people to build larger and more comfortable homes on land that was cheaper than land in the city. People also began to want to escape the dirt, crime, and noise of the city. Finally, the widespread use of the automobile for transportation made it possible for people to reach jobs that were far from home.

The Impact of the Consumer Culture on the Growth of Suburbia

Following World War II, a combination of factors had brought in a consumer culture, which has since come to dominate American culture. The essence of the consumer culture is a focus on acquisition of material objects made possible by affluence, mobility, and leisure. For instance, the automobile, mass produced and, thus, cheap enough to be available to a majority of people, led to the growth of the highway system on which the automobile could move freely and rapidly. In turn, highways were especially responsible for the spread of suburbanization to the extent that it became a pervasive national phenomenon. At the same time, other facets of social change became apparent and were reinforced by suburbanization.

As the cities had done before them, the suburbs spawned their own lifestyle, revolving around the absence of the father for long portions of the day, the necessity for a private vehicle, and the chauffeuring of children to various activities. In addition, trips to the shopping center or suburban mall had become the focus of recreation for suburbanites. The booming

Box 11.2 Urban Theories

The processes of urbanization and urbanism have provided a fertile field to sociologists, economists, and urban specialists, because the rapid growth of cities brought with it enormous social problems that these social scientists were called upon to solve. But even preindustrial cities were subject to negative stereotypes: suffice it to mention the cities of Sodom and Gomorrah, which are described in the Bible as representing the most evil impulses inherent in human nature. In American literature and history, the same stereotype of the rural as good and the urban as evil has predominated and has even had an effect on American politics. Many states failed to revise legislative and congressional districts in accordance with new population shifts toward the city, giving rural residents larger representation in state and federal legislatures than their numbers warranted. The situation was finally corrected by the Supreme Court decision in *Baker v. Carr*, but the fairness of having two senators represent both densely populated and sparsely populated states is still subject to question.

The discipline of urban sociology, which emerged at the beginning of the century, offered a number of urban theories. Robert Ezra Park of the Chicago school (1864–1944), saw the city as an ordered conglomerate of distinctive regions—ethnic communities, red-light districts, industrial districts—which worked as a complex social organism and changed in relation one to the other. He saw the city in a positive light, as being attractive to people because it offered each individual something to enjoy or a niche in which to feel comfortable (Park, 1967, 41). Louis Wirth, another Chicago school sociologist, defined a city as "a relatively large, dense, and permanent settlement of socially heterogeneous individuals," and thought that these characteristics of cities produced psychological stress and social disorganization (Wirth, 1938, 28).

The theory of urban ecology, which was the basis of urban analysis for many years, assumed that cities do not consist of a haphazard collection of residential, commercial, and industrial buildings. Rather, both buildings and people are distributed according to interdependent patterns within a geographic area. Three major models were developed by the urban sociologists of the Chicago school to explain the way people and facilities were distributed in American cities. The **concentric-zone** model stressed the relationship between social status and distance from the center of the city: the higher the social class of residents, the farther they lived from the central business district. The **sector model** focused on the tendency of cities to grow outward from the center in wedge-shaped areas extending from the center to the outskirts, or along river valleys, water

courses, and railroad lines. The **multiple-nuclei** model placed less importance on a central business area, suggesting instead that cities consisted of a number of nuclei, each of which was at the center of a specialized area.

Modern urban social scientists are less pessimistic about urbanism, seeing much more organization in the city than disorganization, and a creative and productive atmosphere. The notion that community declines as a result of urbanization has been challenged by a number of observers of the urban scene. Herbert Gans argues that the city is a mosaic of "urban villages" within which the individual can spend most of his or her life (Gans, 1962, 1982). Suttles (1970) reports on research in slum neighborhoods that exhibit feelings of solidarity among residents who identify and are acutely aware of the boundaries of their communities. Claude Fisher (1984) adds that the city actually promotes feelings of belonging because individuals can find a variety of subcultures (ethnic, religious, artistic, intellectual, homosexual) within which they may feel comfortable, something that cannot be done in rural areas. City life is viewed as providing an enriching, creative experience that actually enhances intimacy. Community is not eroded, but rather than being based on a common place of residence, it comes to depend on the ability to meet with other like-minded people (Kornblum & Williams, 1978). David Harvey notes that urbanism is just one aspect of the created environment brought in by the pervasiveness of industrial capitalism (Harvey, 1973, 1984, 1985). Whereas in preindustrial societies the social and economic life of city and countryside were clearly distinct—and the walls around the city were the tangible proof of this separation—in industrial societies such distinctions are blurred as space is continually "restructured" by large firms and investors who make decisions as to where to locate. Even the layout and architectural features of cities and neighborhoods in them are the results of struggles and conflicts between groups in society. The city represents broader social forces at work in society; in particular, they reflect the power of government and market forces, which dictate who can live where or where specific buildings will be located. At the same time, there is resistance to the wealthy and powerful; thus, the city is the originator of a range of social movements, as well as representing the most important aspect of capitalism, collective consumption. Finally, cities are seen as artificial environments constructed by the people who inhabit them. However, even rural areas are similarly affected by human intervention: those living in isolated rural areas are also politically, culturally, and economically bound to the wider urban society.

This Tokyo shopping mall is the latest and most modern of such institutions. Shopping malls are a consequence of suburbanization and the decline of city centers. They offer a place to gather, chat, eat, visit a doctor, and sometimes attend religious services, in addition to shopping.

economy permitted one family member—usually the husband and father—to be the sole breadwinner, leaving the wife and mother to do the chauffering and shopping chores.

Originally, the suburbs attracted young married couples who were planning fairly large families—the baby boom parents of the years following World War II. The postwar economy increased individual incomes and made mortgage money available, so that for the first time home ownership became a dream almost all could fulfill. Most of the early suburbanites were between 25 and 45 years old, with children ranging in age from infancy to the teens. They were predominantly white, middle-income, high school graduates, politically conservative, and morally "proper." From these beginnings there developed the stereotype of the suburbs as "bedroom" communities of almost identical homes.

Suburbia and Social Class

Today, the heterogeneity of the city is also found in the suburbs. With increasing rates of divorce, single-parent homes are to be found in the suburbs as frequently as in the city. Thus, the generalizations that urban residents used to make about the suburbs have been largely proved wrong. In addition, whereas originally suburbanization was a movement of white persons of middle-class or upper-middle-class background, leading to a high degree of racial segregation, minorities have also flocked to the suburbs since the 1970s. It appears that suburbanization is solely a function of social class: middle-class blacks are moving from cities to suburbs much as their white counterparts did a decade or two earlier. In fact, so many of the more affluent minorities are leaving urban centers that some sociologists fear that urban deterioration cannot help but increase because those who are leaving are predominantly the middle and solid working class (DeWitt, 1994, A12). Suburbanization has become a movement defined by social class primarily because of the problems that are perceived to exist in central cities: crime, poor schools, unsafe neighborhoods, and so on.

Social class has repercussions on suburbs in other ways, too. For a variety of reasons, including a downturn in the economy, more suburban households saw real declines in median household income from 1979 to 1989 rather than income growth. The net result has been that working-class suburbs have suffered, much as central cities have, while affluent suburbs have grown and prospered. This income gap between suburbs adds to a situation in which people of different incomes live isolated from one another (Minerbrook, 1992).

At first, suburbs depended on the central city for shopping and for commercial, cultural, and recreational activities. Later, city and suburbs became interdependent, with the suburbs providing the labor force for business and industry that were still housed in the city. Increasingly, however, the suburbs are becoming independent of the city. Business and industry have relocated in the suburbs and are housed in large shopping malls and professional complexes. Both jobs and facilities are now locally available to the suburban resident. Suburbs have mushroomed at the expense of the central city, which lost an important tax base when people, commerce, and industry moved away. Without tax money, the city cannot provide important facilities, forcing more people, commerce, and industry to move out. The central city is then left with a run-down transportation system, outmoded physical facilities, inadequate police protection, and poor schools. Only those who cannot afford to move out remain.

■ Metropolitanization and Megalopolis

Some suburbs have grown so large that they have become towns and cities in their own right. These small cities, smaller suburbs, and the central city around which they are clustered make up the ecological city, or the metropolitan area. The U.S. Bureau of the Census uses "metropolitan areas," a collective term, as the basis for measuring units of population. The Standard Metropolitan Statistical Area (SMSA) consists of one or more counties containing at least one city of over 50,000 people or two cities totaling that number. Metropolitan areas with populations of 1 million or more are designated as Consolidated Metropolitan Statistical Areas (CMSAs). The Micropolitan Statistical Area comprises one urban cluster of 10,000 but less than 50,000 people. The term *Core Based Statistical Area* (CBSA), coined in 2000, refers collectively to metropolitan and micropolitan statistical areas. As of 2001, there were 17 CMSAs in the United States, 362 metropolitan statistical areas, and 560 micropolitan statistical areas, the largest ones being New York, Long Island, and northern New Jersey, with a population of 21 million and Los Angeles, Riverside, and Anaheim with over 16 million. So thoroughly urban are these areas that it is easier to refer to them as regions of the country rather than cities.

The principal criterion for a definition of metropolitan area is that it has a "contained" economy. This means that it is an area where a majority of people live, work, earn, and spend. As of the first decade of the twenty-first century, there were 362 metropolitan statistical areas in the United States and 560 micropolitan statistical areas (U.S. Census Bureau, Population Division, 2005) and they constituted about 80 percent of the nation's population, or almost all of the nonrural portion of the country. This pattern represents a return to the dominance of metropolitan areas, which began in the second decade of the past century.

The growth of metropolitan areas has meant a large concentration of people in comparatively small areas. This trend damages central cities and creates problems in local governments because each municipality, county, township, city, and village within the metropolitan area maintains its own government. In this bureaucratic maze, agencies and officials of neighboring governments are often at odds with one another, resulting in a waste of money and resources. Urban specialists have long favored some form of metropolitan government, but federal studies have concluded that nothing short of a broad regional government will relieve the chaotic situation of metropolitan areas.

Megalopolis

The large number of metropolitan areas is leading to a new phenomenon in the United States as well as in other industrial nations, that of urban sprawl known by the term *megalopolis*. In a **megalopolis**, one metropolitan area is joined to another without interruption. One such complex is the Great Lakes chain, beginning in Buffalo and continuing solidly to Milwaukee and farther west. By the year 2000, an estimated 40 million people were housed in this complex alone. Another megalopolis, the Boston-Washington complex, contains around 80 million people, while a third rapidly growing megalopolis is the one extending from San Diego to the San Francisco Bay area. On a global level, there are megalopolises in Japan, Great Britain, northwestern Europe, northern Italy, Brazil, and even in China (Table 11.4). Urban sociologists point out that a megalopolis is not just an overgrown metropolitan area but rather a system of cities distributed along "a major axis of traffic and communication" (Gottman, 1978, 56). Megalopolises are interdependent because they share not only the physical infrastructure—highways, railways, waterways, telephone lines, pipelines, water supply, and sewage systems—but also the flow of traffic, the movement of people and goods, and the flow of telephone calls and mail. At the same time, the megalopolis may remain exceedingly varied, containing cities, towns, villages, suburbs, with their diverse populations also differentiated as to social class and ethnicity, so that the regions resemble a mosaic.

■ The Urban Crisis

It has been well-publicized by the media that American cities are in trouble. The crisis of the cities has two components. First, suburbanization left the cities struggling to provide all the necessary services, and the departure of many upper-middle-class families, in addition to businesses and industries, resulted in a loss of more tax revenues. Second, there has been a shift in the regions of the country that are experiencing growth. The older, larger cities in the northeastern and north-central areas of the country are losing population as industrial jobs are becoming more scarce, while southern and southwestern cities, many of them new, are growing faster than the national average. Because cities have tended to grow rapidly, very little planning has gone into their physical shape, and their social structure has also given rise to problems. The large concentration of people in cities requires buildings that are close together and many stories high. Without proper planning, this necessity can lead to ugliness, to lack of green and open spaces, to an "asphalt jungle" look. Modern city planners are much more aware of the need to pay special attention to a pleasing appearance, so that the cities of the future will probably be much more attractive than those of the past.

Slums and Ghettos

One consequence of the flight to suburbia has been an enlargement of areas called slums and ghettos. A slum is an area that has changed from what it was before but has not yet attained a new form. Residents of slums tend to be new immigrants, either from abroad or from rural areas of the country. They stay in the old, often decaying areas of the city because they are unskilled and can work only at menial jobs. Many exist on welfare, are victims of discrimination and segregation, and are unfamiliar with the cultural and physical aspects of the rest of the city.

Following the influx of African Americans from the rural South during and after World War II, most central areas of cities became ghettos. Ghettos are similar to slums in their origins, conditions, and problems, but they tend to contain a particular racial or ethnic group. Often, residents are members of the working poor (people who are chronically unemployed or underemployed), mothers with dependent children, the elderly, and the disabled.

Population Drain

The problematic aspects of cities cause a constant movement of population out of cities, but generally, when one segment moves out, another moves in. At least, that had been the pattern up to the late 1950s, when people began leaving cities for the suburbs. The decline in the heavy industry that had been a mainstay of the Great Lakes region's economy also contributed to the exodus away from the large cities of that region. Population loss leaves cities with a budget deficit and the unhappy need to raise taxes on housing and commercial property, which risks alienating more homeowners and driving out more businesses and jobs, or to cut spending and reduce services and risk making the city even less desirable (Levine, 1991, A9).

■ Attempts to Reclaim the City

Many cities have been fighting back vigorously to regain their former status. For one thing, cities still offer many desirable activities and jobs and so attract a substantial number of people. Many young professionals prefer to live in the central districts, near jobs and entertainment. Even married couples with children find real estate in cities to be more within their means than in the suburbs. Many instances of "gentrification," or the reclaiming of decaying neighborhoods by middle-class, professional families, are being noted. Gentrification, however, has also encountered criticism because the former residents of the gentrified neighborhoods are moved from housing they could afford into even worse areas.

Urban Renewal

The same criticism was raised when the government tried to resolve the plight of the cities through programs of urban renewal. Urban slums had been a reality in industrial societies ever since the Industrial Revolution brought rural people into the cities. There was always at least one group of people who, for a variety of reasons, could not find work and, thus, were condemned to live on the fringes of society, with government help. Following World War II, however, the government, in addition to simply helping the urban poor, began to provide loans to cities for building low-cost housing and later for slum clearance and public housing.

Unfortunately, these programs never worked. Slum clearance resulted in moving the urban poor from one neighborhood to another, with no benefit to the residents, only to those involved in the clearance and construction businesses. Public housing had equally little success. There is some stigma attached to living in public housing, and residents have no reason to display any pride of ownership. Therefore, the property, already shoddily built without consideration of people's wants and needs, is soon subject to acts of vandalism and wanton destruction.

The government has also tried to offer subsidies to people with insufficient incomes so that they may compete in the private housing market. These attempts have met with little success. Owners of rental property discriminate against families with many children or those with women as heads of households or in which the father is disabled. There is the fear of neighborhoods being overrun by an "undesirable" element. Suburbs and small towns have effectively kept out public housing or federally subsidized low-rent housing for the same reasons.

Urban renewal is an ineffective remedy for the crisis of the cities. If the same people continue to live in renovated buildings, the benefits accrue to them but not to the city because they continue to be unable to pay higher taxes. On the other hand, if slum areas are cleared in favor of new, expensive housing, commercial buildings, or shopping centers, benefits accrue to the city because these structures provide a good tax base but not to the former residents, who are displaced. However, the city is then able to attract middle- and upper-class residents and even shoppers from the suburbs. People come to the newly refurbished theaters and restaurants, and jobs can be created for city residents.

The Future of Cities

The fate of cities in the twenty-first century is uncertain. In the United States, cities contain the worst social problems that face society: crime, poverty, racial conflicts, pollution. At the same time, the larger the metropolitan area, the better are the opportunities for employment, recreation, and education. Some urban thinkers are convinced that cities can be revitalized because they serve the most important human function: they offer a place for coming together (Whyte, 1989). Others are less optimistic, particularly in view of the fact that urbanization is an ongoing process and the sheer numbers of people who will be urban residents in the twenty-first century are staggering. In addition to all the problems that plague American cities, the environmental pollution in some of these cities is beginning to affect the residents' health. It seems imperative that governments plan a survival strategy for cities, but the road is strewn with obstacles and high costs.

■ The Natural Environment

Populations and the physical and social structures they erect exist within the framework of a natural environment. This natural environment has been progressively damaged precisely because of the growth of population and the disregard in which people have held their habitat. In Asia, overpopulation has led to land degradation by overuse, water supplies are constantly under strain, and agriculture is handicapped by soil and water depletion. On a global scale, unabated expansion of population would soak up the world's capital and prevent the poorer nations from investing in technological development that might limit continued population growth. Environmentalists, therefore, paint apocalyptic pictures of the future. If the worst occurs, countless millions would become environmental refugees, swamping the nations that tried to conserve their soil, water and forests. The great-grandchildren of today's young people would have to share the planet with only a ragged cohort of adaptable species dominated by rats, cockroaches, weeds, and microbes. The world in which they survived would consist largely of deserts, patches of tropical forests, eroded mountains, dead coral reefs and barren oceans, all buffeted by extremes of weather (Linden, 1992, 64). This list of catastrophes does not even include the additional danger represented by global warming.

What a world to live in and to leave to our descendants as their inheritance! And the ways to prevent this scenario from becoming reality, in the experts' opinion, is to "cut human propagation in half, so the world's numbers do not exceed 8 billion by midcentury"

(Linden, 1992, 64), and to prevent the kinds of human activity that promote the rise in global temperature.

The World We Live In

The natural environment is the total complex of natural conditions and resources that occur in specific areas. It consists of such elements as landforms, climate, natural vegetation, soils, native animal life, underground and surface waters, and mineral resources. These elements do not remain static but vary from time to time and are different in different areas of the world.

There is a reciprocal relationship between the environment and people and their cultures. The environment affects almost every facet of people's lives, shaping their traditions and institutions; in turn, it is affected by people, often negatively. However, this relationship is not simple and direct. People can live differently in similar environments and even differently at different times in the same environment. And the same type of physical environment may be used in different ways by people who perceive land use differently.

The Ecosystem

The very technology that allowed people to limit the death rate, prompted spurts in population, and crowded large numbers into cities where there were industrial jobs is now endangering human life on earth by ignoring or despoiling the natural environment. Neglect of the environment is not new; however, the early humans saw themselves as insignificant inhabitants of a natural world to which they were related and on which they were dependent. Even though some of their actions damaged the environment, they acted out of ignorance. The complex technology that produces myriad articles for easing human life today has inspired in contemporary humans the notion that they are in control of the world and perhaps of the universe. Thus, the humble attitudes of our primitive ancestors, who tried to appease the spirits of plants and animals they thought responsible for their existence and welfare, have been replaced by confidence that nothing is impossible to humans. This arrogant attitude is a threat to the ecosystem.

The *ecosystem* is the way living things interact and interrelate among each other and their environment. The interaction maintains a balance that permits life to continue. People, land, animals, vegetation, atmosphere, and social processes are so interdependent that even slight alterations in one affect the others. The photosynthetic activity of green plants (that is, the fact that they take in carbon dioxide and give off oxygen) allows human life and produces the oxygen needed for the machinery of the industrial system. Without plants and animals and the microorganisms that live in them, there would be no pure water in lakes and rivers. Without certain processes that take place within the earth, there would be no food crops, oil, or coal. The ecosystem is, in short, the biological capital of humans: human productivity depends on it, and the most advanced technology will be useless if it is destroyed.

Ecology

The ecosystem, that delicately balanced, interdependent system consisting of living beings, nature, and the earth they inhabit, has been the focus of attention in recent years as more people have begun to show concern about the environment. The discipline of ecology, which studies the interrelationships in nature, has been in the forefront in the effort to make people aware of what is happening to where they live.

In ecological terms, there are various levels of ecosystems. A particular swamp or river is a local ecosystem; an ocean is a regional ecosystem; the planet Earth is a global ecosystem. An ecosystem is easily made unstable: unforeseen events often disturb its balance. Floods and droughts change the soil, as do gradual climatic changes, population explosions, and the disappearance of particular species. However, the tendency of any ecosystem is to return to a balance. Each species of life has its niche in the physical environment, somewhat in the same way that each individual occupies a status in the social environment. The niche occupied by humans in the various ecosystems is different from that of other species because humans can affect and alter their environment, rather than waiting to adapt to it through evolution. Because humans have developed culture and social structure, they can act in a variety of ways toward the physical environment: they can cultivate trees or cut them down, clean rivers or pollute them, build roads and houses or leave the land alone. Other species must wait for nature to take its course, for they are limited in their behavior. Thus, humans have not only a great advantage over other living species but also a responsibility to organize themselves in such a way as to remain in harmony with their environment. In this they have not been very successful.

We should note here that the idea of equilibrium is not universally accepted. A number of ecologists are revising the long-held balance theory following an accumulation of evidence to the effect that the real constant in nature is eternal turmoil: "Change and turmoil, more than constancy and balance, is the rule" (Stevens, 1990, B5–B6). While the change in thinking has not yet produced a current new theory to replace the old one, the developing conviction that nature is ruled more by flux and disturbance is becoming the dominant idea. Those scientists who are not quite ready to abandon the notion of equilibrium in ecosystems agree that although there may be great disturbances and fluctuations in small populations within small ecosystems, these fluctuations may not appear as important if the larger picture is considered. Thus, they bring in the importance of scales of time and space. However, the consensus seems to favor an ecology of constant change and disruption, particularly following studies of naturally occurring external factors—such as climate and weather—that dislocate ecosystems.

Disruption of Ecosystems

The harmony of the global ecosystem is disturbed by overpopulation, environmental pollution, and environmental depletion. Overpopulation puts stress on the ecosystem because of an increase in birthrates without a consequent increase in death rates. Environmental pollution refers to the degradation of air, land, and water, as well as the physical aspects of the environment (eye and noise pollution). *Environmental depletion* is the term used to mean that natural resources are decreasing in proportion to increased demand for them (as in the case of energy).

Environmental Pollution

Pollution is the result of human actions, that is, human tampering with the environment that has harmful consequences. Pollutants are sometimes unforeseen and unwanted by-products of human activities or the residue of products made by humans, used and thrown away. The central point is that as a society we want to consume more, which means we must produce more, and which ultimately means we create more waste.

Pollution may be of the air, water, or land and may also involve our senses such as seeing and hearing. Every year, about 140 million tons of pollutants are released into the air as by-products of burning fossil fuels (oil, natural gas, coal). The automobile is the heaviest

Every day, tons of garbage are deposited in landfills of the wealthy nations whose conspicuous consumption is creating problems of disposal.

polluter, accounting for about 80 percent of air pollution. Among the worst effects of pollution are acid rain, caused by sulfur dioxide emissions from coal-burning plants, and depletion of ozone, a form of oxygen normally found in the upper atmosphere, where it absorbs the ultraviolet radiation of the sun. Acid rain has been killing fish in lakes, reducing crop yields, and damaging buildings. The decrease of ozone does harm to human eyes, throats, and lungs. A reduced ozone layer may result in a vastly changed climate on earth, the destruction of some animal and plant life, a greater incidence of skin cancers, and possibly damage of a genetic nature to both plants and animals, including humans.

In addition, carbon dioxide emissions resulting from the burning of fossil fuels (oil and coal) have grown dramatically in the past century. These emissions are contributing factors to climate change, specifically to rising temperatures that are thought to result in extreme weather patterns, and in turn to the spread of infectious diseases. Unfortunately, the United States is the largest contributor to total carbon dioxide emissions in the world, though China may soon surpass us (United Nations, 2007 World Population Data Sheet).

Through the cleaning of the bilges of tankers alone, an estimated 22 million barrels of oil are dumped annually into the oceans. Other kinds of water pollution are due to organic sewage, overfertilization of water by excess nutrients, water-borne bacteria or viruses, and organic chemicals such as insecticides, pesticides, and detergents that are toxic to aquatic life. Chemicals of all sorts can change the ecosystem of a body of water, killing fish and creating unpleasant tastes in the water supply.

The earth's soil is being polluted in a number of locations by pesticides, herbicides, chemical wastes, radioactive fallout, and garbage. Some of these pollutants are also harmful to humans, yet increasing amounts of them must be used to control certain pests as these become resistant to the chemicals; residues of the chemicals tend to remain in the soil for a long time—sometimes years after the chemicals have been banned.

Prolonged exposure to intense noise not only damages human hearing but can also increase irritability and prevent sleep. A noise level of 80 decibels is annoying to most people, yet the noise level in a third-floor apartment adjacent to a freeway is about 87 decibels. Decaying property, smog, noxious odors, and inhibited visibility all take away from people's enjoyment of the environment.

Environmental Depletion. The air, water, and land can be cleaned up, but once a resource is depleted, it is gone forever. Then an alternative source must be found. No nation in the world is completely self-sufficient in terms of its natural resources. Even the United States has to import large amounts of mica, bauxite, tin, and iron ore that are used annually in this country. Of course, the resource of most concern is oil, because our consumption of energy has been rising rapidly since the turn of the century. The United States uses more energy than other countries. Americans spend more on automobiles than on food. Demand for electrical power has also constantly increased, tripling between the 1940s and the 1970s. Some experts maintain that nuclear sources are our only hope for the future, but others point out that these sources have severe limitations. Their safety is dubious, and they pose potential hazards.

The Greenhouse Effect. Finally, the so-called greenhouse effect is causing concern. Essentially, the greenhouse effect refers to the heating of the earth's atmosphere by burning coal, wood, and oil, which produces carbon dioxide, nitrous oxides, chlorofluorocarbons, and methane. These gases accumulate in the atmosphere and act as an insulating barrier, retaining heat from the earth that should be returning to space. Thus, the earth becomes hotter because the insulating barrier traps heat as do the glass panels in a greenhouse. The effects of such a warming trend could be catastrophic, but it is still possible to counteract these damaging effects if governments become serious about legislating changes in consumption and conservation of resources, reducing the combustion of fuels and finding alternative sources of power.

Although talk of "global warming" had been heard for decades, it was not until early 2007 that scientists presented the world with a detailed portrait of the effects of climate change driven by human activity. The greenhouse gases that have been building up in the atmosphere have already produced changes from the poles to the tropics, from the melting of the polar ice caps to the desertification of former temperate climates. Scientists are predicting that the earth's climate and ecosystems face inevitable and profound changes: increasing droughts in southern Europe and the Middle East, in sub-Saharan Africa, and in the American Southwest and Mexico. On the other hand, flooding will endanger low-lying islands and river deltas of southern Asia. In fact, a rise of only three to five degrees Fahrenheit could lead to the inundation of coasts and islands inhabited by hundreds of millions of people. The worst effect of these climate changes is that the poorest countries would bear the brunt of them. While some regions would receive more rainfall and a longer growing season, regions that are already suffering from inclement weather, a scarcity of resources, and coastal hazards would be affected very negatively. Such nations, and even the poor in wealthier nations, are least equipped to adjust to climate change (see the United Nations' Intergovernmental Panel on Climate Change, **http//www.ipcc.ch/**).

Doomsayers have never been very popular, and in the past humanity seems to have always found escape from its own destruction in the emergence of new sources of food and energy. In fact, economists have argued that an accepted tenet of economic theory, limits to growth, may be misguided because whenever prices rise in reaction to scarcity, they stimulate human ingenuity to improve, invent, and find alternatives. However, the example of cultures that have disappeared is instructive: an island in the Pacific, Easter Island, shows indications of having once harbored a flourishing culture. By the time the Europeans landed there in the early eighteenth century, however, the few thousand inhabitants lived in extremely primitive conditions. It seems that a swelling population led to stripping trees on the island, so that eventually there were no building materials for housing or fishing boats. The people were forced to live in caves, and clans made war on each other to acquire the dwindling resources. In time, the victorious clans enslaved and finally cannibalized the vanquished, and a once-proud culture was reduced to a barbaric struggle for survival (Linden, 1992, 65).

The current report makes very clear that unless governments and individuals make a concerted effort to rein in greenhouse gas emissions, the earth will be three to seven degrees warmer by the next century. We have already seen that warmer oceans make for more intense hurricanes, that precipitation has decreased over the subtropics and tropics and increased in other parts of the Northern and Southern hemispheres, and that heavy precipitation has become more frequent in areas where it was not characteristic. These phenomena will continue and, if unchecked, will produce an earth different, but not better, than the one we know now.

To summarize, the human species is faced with a threat to its physical and mental well-being, with an ecological imbalance and the consequent disappearance of entire species of animals and plants, and with a hazard to world peace because of the imbalance in the standard of living between the developed and the developing nations. Environmental problems, however, have a low priority for political leaders and the public in general. Yet, because of the complexities involved, any solution to these problems must involve governmental action. It is probable that some cultural values must be changed before people learn to appreciate their environment to a greater extent than is true at present.

The Chapter in Brief

Population density varies dramatically, with two-thirds of humanity concentrated in the area that runs through the southern half of Japan, the plains and hills of eastern China, the coasts and Ganges River plain of India, and the industrial districts of Europe as well as those of the United States. Birthrates and death rates are calculated on the basis of how many births and deaths occur in a given year per 1,000 people. High birthrates are characteristic of the less industrialized and less urbanized nations. This fact has engendered the demographic transition model, which holds that societies pass through three basic stages of population growth. Stabilization occurs in the third stage, in which birthrates decline. Lowering a population's birthrate is a cultural, and not a technical, matter.

The United States reached zero population growth in 1972, but the birthrate could go up again at any time. However, urban industrial nations curb and stabilize their populations because it is so difficult to have large families in such societies. The rapid growth of population, or population explosion, was predicted 200 years ago by Thomas Robert Malthus, who warned that overpopulation would become a threat to humanity because populations grow by geometric progression while food production increases arithmetically, at a much slower rate. The Malthusian prophecy has little relevance for the developed nations, but it may be applied to the developing nations, where population increase does pose serious problems.

The mechanization of agriculture and the factory system have led many people to move from the land to the city, where the jobs are. The movement of people from rural areas to cities is called urbanization. Of course, cities predate the rise of industry, but even the cities of antiquity tended to rise around rivers where the soil was fertile and where transportation was possible, leading to trade and commerce. Urbanization in the industrial era is different, however, in that it is a universal trend that is forever stamping entire societies as urban in nature. Life in cities has given rise to a lifestyle and tradition that, spread through the mass media, are becoming dominant in the national culture. Secondary relationships, formal organizations, and the institutions of the economy, government, and education have been strengthened, at the expense of primary relationships and the institutions of the family and religion.

In the United States, a further development in urbanization has been the trend toward suburbanization. Suburbs grew when people began to escape urban problems and as a result of the popularity of the automobile and the consumer culture, but today suburbs resemble cities. However, cities have suffered from the movement because they lack a sufficient tax base and cannot provide services to the remaining residents. Metropolitanization, or cities and suburbs that have grown large and in certain locations follow each other without interruption for great distances, is another current problem. Large metropolitan areas, also called megalopolises, have unique problems such as the need for an expanded governmental bureaucracy. Although such programs as urban renewal and gentrification have attempted to remedy the plight of the inner cities, these areas are still plagued with problems, basically because they remain the home of those who cannot afford to move out of them.

Overpopulation, together with urban and industrial lifestyles, has engendered problems that threaten the environment. First, natural resources are finite and cannot support the dramatic increases in population. Second, our careless disregard for the environment threatens to destroy it because of the way it is being polluted. In particular, it is the accumulation of greenhouse gases in the atmosphere, a side effect of automobile emissions and other industrial processes, that are endangering the planet by creating global warming. We are already seeing these effects, from the melting of the polar ice caps to the creation of deserts, from extreme droughts to tragic floods, from severe hurricanes to disappearing ecosystems. Moreover, the people who are most at risk from these phenomena are the ones least likely to be able to prevent them or adjust to them: they are the poor of the world. Humans are only one element in the global ecosystem; however, their arrogance is such that they believe themselves to be at the center of creation. A change in cultural values and government action will probably be necessary before the pollution of the air, land, and water, as well as the wasting of natural resources, will be reversed.

Terms to Remember

biosphere A thin film of air, water, and soil surrounding the earth.

birthrate The number of births per 1,000 persons in a specific population per year.

death rate The number of deaths per 1,000 persons in a specific population per year. Same as mortality rate.

demography The study of the growth or decline of populations, their distribution throughout the world, and their composition.

ecology The study of the relationship between living organisms and their environments.

ecosystem A contained system of living and nonliving entities, and the manner in which they interact and maintain a balance that permits life to continue.

fecundity The biological potential for producing offspring.

fertility rate The average number of births per 1,000 women between the ages of 15 and 44, or during women's reproductive years.

infant mortality The rate that reflects the number of deaths among infants under one year of age for every 1,000 live births.

life expectancy The average number of years that a person at a given age can expect to live.

megalopolis A complex in which one metropolitan area follows another without interruption. Also called urban sprawl.

metropolitanization The tendency of suburbs, small cities, and surrounding rural areas to cluster around a central city and be considered as a single unit.

mortality rate The number of deaths in a population per year.

pollution The degradation of air, land, and water as well as the esthetic aspects of the environment.

population density The ratio of people to a land area.

population pyramid A graphic expression of the age and sex distribution of a given population.

sex ratio Ratio of the number of males in a population in any single year per 100 females.

Standard Metropolitan Statistical Area (SMSA) Term used by the U.S. Bureau of the Census to designate units of population consisting of a county or counties that include a city of 50,000 or more people. Metropolitan

areas containing one million or more people are called Consolidated Metropolitan Statistical Areas (CMSAs).

suburbs Smaller communities on the outskirts of central cities and somewhat dependent on them.

urbanism A condition, a set of attitudes, a quality, or a way of life distinct from the rural.

urbanization A population trend in which cities grow at the expense of rural areas.

zero population growth A condition in which each person replaces himself or herself only (replacement level of 2.1); thus, the birthrate and the death rate are the same.

Suggested Readings

Anderson, Elijah. 1992. *StreetWise: Race, Class, and Change in an Urban Community*. Chicago: University of Chicago Press. A participant observation study that follows residents who are being displaced by gentrification, as well as those who come into the newly gentrified neighborhood.

Brown, Lester R. 2000. *State of the World: A Worldwatch Institute Report on Progress Toward a Sustainable Society*. New York: W. W. Norton. A collection of essays dealing with environmental issues on a global level.

Commoner, Barry. 1990. *Making Peace with the Planet*. New York: Pantheon. An early activist in the pro-earth movement speaks about the necessity of reconciling our needs for technological progress with protection of the environment.

Eade, John. 1996. *Living the Global City: Globalization as Local Process*. New York: Routledge. An examination

of the way the new global economies, and all they portend, affect the everyday lives of ordinary people.

Feagin, Joe R. and Robert Parker. 1990. *Building American Cities: The Urban Real Estate Game*. Englewood Cliffs, NJ: Prentice Hall. A paperback whose theme is the effect of wealth and power and the development and decline of American cities.

Phillips, E. Barbara. 1996. *City Lights: Urban-Suburban Life in a Global Society*, 2nd ed. New York: Oxford University Press. An analysis of the major challenges facing American cities as they await the arrival of the global society.

Weeks, John R. 1998. *Population: An Introduction to Concepts and Issues*, 7th ed. Belmont, CA. Wadsworth. A textbook in population studies, including examinations of issues in the United States and in the world.

Web Sites of Interest

http://www.epa/gov
This is the web site of the Environmental Protection Agency, the federal agency responsible for ensuring that the environment is protected.

http://www.greenpeace.org/
The web site of an activist, voluntary organization whose purpose is oversight of the government agencies in charge of protecting the environment.

http://www.census.gov/ftp/pub/ipc/www/idsbsum.html
Everything one could possibly want to know about national and global population, as well as issues relating

to urbanism, metropolitanization, and megalopolis, may be found on the census bureau web site.

http://www.prb.org
Another voluntary organization, the Population Reference Bureau, provides additional information on international and domestic population issues.

http://www.un.org/esa/population/publications/littmig2002/htm
This United Nations web site contains reports on the world's migrant population and information on immigration policies.

12

Pivotal Institutions: Marriage and the Family

IN THIS CHAPTER, YOU WILL LEARN

■ *about the important cultural functions that institutions perform;*

■ *of the importance of the family as the primary institution;*

■ *about the components of the family institution and its historical forms;*

■ *of the changes in the form of the American family;*

■ *about the problematic aspects of divorce;*

■ *of the effects of the changes in the American family.*

The media constantly remind us that our institutions are failing us. Newspapers, news magazines, and television programs trumpet such sad truths as "The Family Is Falling Apart," "American Education Is a Shambles," "People Have Little Faith in Government," "Religion Has Declined in Significance," "Income Gap Increasing," and so on. What exactly are institutions, and why do we perceive them as failing us?

We have stressed a number of times that the most important product of the social way of life—which is the only way in which humans can sustain life—is culture (see Chapter 3). Culture has been called the cement that holds the social bond together. It is the thing that makes people human and distinguishes them from other living creatures. In particular, it is the normative ("rules for living") component of culture that is central to human life because it provides a design for living. Culture may be considered the first "how to do it" guide people ever had, and it is a best-seller still. The most vital parts of the normative system, in turn, are institutions, which were described previously as ingrained patterns of behavior representing societal solutions to universal human needs. (Review pivotal institutions in Chapter 3.)

■ The Basic Institution: The Family

The family is the most basic and oldest social unit, and traces of it can be found in all societies, past and present. In spite of the many controversies that have flared around it in technologically advanced societies, it is still going strong. It is generally believed that the family began the cycle of institution building. In the course of human history, in all known societies, it has been the family that provided the individual with an identity, with a social status, and with physical as well as moral support. Other pivotal institutions, as well as less important ones, have gradually emerged, usurping some of its functions, yet the family has remained a pervasive force in human lives, the most relevant of primary groups, and the most important element in the socialization process.

To attest to the universality of the institution, anthropologist George Murdock (1949) studied 250 societies and found evidence of a nuclear family in all of them. Murdock speculated that the family is universal because it is functional, that is, because it performs the four functions fundamental to social life: sexual, economic, reproductive, and educational. These functions are vital to society.

Family Forms

Although the institution of the family is universal, its forms vary from society to society. All families, however, share the following features: they are social groups that originate in marriage; they consist of husband, wife, and children born of their union (although in some family forms other relatives are included); they bind members with legal, economic, and religious bonds as well as duties and privileges; and they provide a network of sexual privileges and prohibitions, and varying degrees of love, respect, and affection (Levi-Strauss, 1971, 56).

Historically, the family has existed in two chief forms. One is the **extended,** or **consanguine,** family (consanguine means "of the same blood"). The extended family includes not only husband, wife, and their offspring but also a number of blood relatives (with their mates and children), who live together and are considered a family unit. The extended form is typical of traditional, agricultural societies, for in these societies it is advantageous to cooperate in order to secure a better livelihood. Psychologically, too, an extended family provides benefits: child rearing is a communal responsibility, and the child forms affectionate relationships with many persons. Parents are thus relieved of being the sole providers of socialization. Consequently, physical neglect or mistreatment (child abuse) is almost unheard of in extended families. On the other hand, the individual must stifle personal goals and desires, because the welfare of the family unit has priority over the welfare of the individual. Finally, extended families have a well-defined hierarchy of authority to which the individual is subservient.

The other family form is the **nuclear,** also called the **conjugal,** form (conjugal means "joined" or "united" in the sense of "married"). A nuclear family includes the nucleus (center) of father, mother, and their children. To the children, the family into which they are born is consanguine because they are related to their parents by blood ties; it is also their family of **orientation** because they obtain their socialization within it—they are oriented toward life in society. To the parents, theirs is a family of **procreation** because their relationship depends on having produced children.

The nuclear family is typical of urban industrial societies in which there is significant geographic and social mobility. Where such mobility exists, individuals are attracted to urban centers, where they can find better jobs. There, they form new family units, leaving behind their families of origin. In industrial societies, moreover, many functions originally performed by primary groups have been transferred to secondary ones. Protection, education, health care, money lending, nursing, and so on, have been taken over by separate institutions. Thus, the large extended family unit, which is almost totally self-sufficient in agrarian societies, is no longer necessary in urban, industrial societies; on the contrary, it is counterproductive in an urban environment, where housing is scarce and education expensive. Finally, in an industrial society, achieved status is more important than ascribed status. Therefore, what a person does through his or her own effort is more important than the family's social position (Goode, 1963). This makes it even easier to leave the extended family behind. In short, the lifestyle of the nuclear family is compatible with the values of industrial societies and their more open stratification systems. As a result, the nuclear family has become the norm in the so-called developed nations of the world and will eventually become prevalent in many of the developing societies as well.

Kinship Systems

A number of people who are related by common descent, by marriage, or through adoption form a kinship system. Kinship systems vary from society to society: the number of marriage partners, who may marry whom, where newlyweds live, and authority patterns all vary tremendously across cultures.

Family Functions

As noted earlier, many of the former functions of the family have been taken over by newer institutions. Still, in whatever form it appears, including the newest "alternatives" to the traditional family, the family continues to fulfill these important functions: it regulates sex, it controls reproduction, it is the principal agent of socialization, and it provides affection and companionship.

Regulation of Sex. No known society leaves the regulation of sex to chance. That is, all societies attempt to channel the sex drive in such a way that sexual relations take place between persons who have legitimate access to each other—who are married or otherwise legally united in a paired bond.

Most societies encourage marriage and give high status to married people. They also make a distinction between marriage—a union sanctioned by the society and its legal system—and unions entered into by consenting partners without such sanction. Most societies discourage the single state.

Reproduction. Ensuring that reproduction takes place so that there is always a new generation growing up has been one of the fundamental functions of the family since the beginning of human group life. In many societies, an individual is not considered an adult until he fathers a child or she gives birth to one. Some societies attach no stigma to children born out of wedlock; rather, provisions are made for the children's incorporation into the family structure. However, reproduction outside the family has not been sanctioned in any society.

In the United States, social change in the family institution has had the effect of increasing the number of single mothers. Some unmarried working women make a deliberate choice to have a child even though they remain unmarried, but most single mothers are teenagers whose children are unplanned. The large increase in out-of-wedlock pregnancies is the result of liberalized sex norms without a consequent adjustment in values.

Socialization.   As discussed in Chapter 5, most societies depend on the family to socialize their young. Societies that have attempted to transfer this function to other agencies have had mixed results at best. Although the function of socialization has remained basically within the family, schools and the peer group have taken over a large portion of the process. The family, however, retains the function of agent in establishing an individual's identity and readying him or her to exist in the wider society.

Affection and Companionship.   The human need for affection and companionship appears to be fundamental. Numerous studies have indicated that lack of affection in an individual's developmental years may lead to an antisocial personality and even physical illness. Children who receive faultless physical care but no affection often become ill or even die (Spitz, 1945, 53–57, is the classic study on the subject; many others have since replicated these findings). Although groups other than the family may provide companionship, affection is more likely to be found only within the family and, increasingly, within the nuclear family.

■ Marriage

At the basis of almost every kinship system is marriage, a legal concept defining the union of a man and a woman, or various combinations thereof, living together in a sexual relationship with the expectation of producing offspring (today this definition needs to be amended, as men and women do not necessarily include having children as one of the purposes of marriage and as same-sex partners contemplate marriage). This relationship is defined and sanctioned by tradition and law. It should be stressed that marriage is an invention of the legal system; that is, it came into being because people thought there should be a binding contract between a man and a woman regarding their mutual privileges and obligations. The family, on the other hand, is a social invention that emerged out of people's needs.

The definition of the marriage relationship includes guidelines for behavior in matters of sex, obligations to offspring and in-laws, division of labor within the household, and other duties and privileges of marital life. The origin of the institution is shrouded in mystery. In Western societies, marriage has been influenced by the religious ideas of Judaism and Christianity, but it has also retained many of the facets of the secular philosophies of Greece and Rome. In all of these cultures, legal marriage was seen as a way to help societies regulate sexual activity, encourage procreation, and develop accountability, as well as provide for parental care, mutual help, and affection. Today, modern societies are faced with a new controversy—whether to extend legal marriage to same-sex couples. Most religions, of course, prohibit homosexual acts on the basis that they preclude procreation; nonetheless, homosexuality has been a part of the human condition as far back as history allows us to see (see Chapter 9). As the ideals of human rights have evolved, so too has the idea among a segment of the population that same-sex couples should have the ability to marry. Legal marriage would enable such couples to enjoy the same financial privileges of heterosexual married couples in matters of insurance, inheritance, and adoption of children. However, the taboo against such a form of marriage is still very strong, and governments, cities, and states have only now begun to deal with this issue. Although the city of San Francisco issued marriage licenses for a while, it was eventually prevented from doing so. Massachusetts is the only state that allows same-sex marriage, although several other states allow civil unions. A number of fundamentalist Christians who are opposed to such marriages have tried to amend the Constitution to forbid such unions, so far without success.

Although every society encourages marriage, as opposed to unregulated sex, the forms marriage takes vary in different societies. The two broad subdivisions in forms of marriage are monogamy and polygamy. **Monogamy** describes the union of one man with one woman. **Polygamy** is the term for plural marriage, which can in turn be subdivided into *polyandry*, or the union of one woman with several men; *polygyny*, or the union of one man with several women; and *group marriage*, involving several men living with several women.

Around the world, monogamy is the most common form of marriage, probably because an approximately equal number of males and females reach maturity and are available for mating. Polygyny is the most common form of polygamy. It was once widely practiced, particularly in Muslim societies, as well as in certain subcultural groups (the Mormons in the United States, for instance). Today, the custom is more limited, both because of the diffusion of Western values and because it is expensive to maintain a number of wives and all the children they produce. Polyandry is an uncommon form of marriage, practiced chiefly in areas in which physical existence is difficult and seminomadic, so that more than one husband is required to support a wife and her children. Though it exists, group marriage has never been practiced consistently or extensively in any known society.

Limitations on Marriage

Every society regulates its members' choice of mates by specifying whom they may marry and whom they may not marry. All societies, for instance, require that marriage occur outside a particular group, whether it be family, clan, tribe, or village (*exogamy*). A universal example of exogamy is the *incest taboo*, or prohibition of sexual relations between mother and son, father and daughter, sister and brother, grandparents and grandchildren, and so on. This taboo, although it has occasionally been broken for

In every society, marriage is celebrated with a ceremony to emphasize the importance of the institution that is the foundation of the family.

particular reasons in some societies and is broken today in more families than is generally thought, has existed in every known society. Anthropologists tend to think that the incest taboo originated because incest is not functional for society. It tends to damage family structure, while marrying outside the family builds bonds of dependence among families, establishing a cohesive society and ensuring the creation of new families (Lévi-Strauss, 1971, 55). Traditional societies also required that their members marry within other specified groups—for instance, within a person's own race, religion, and social class (*endogamy*). However, in industrial and postindustrial societies this requirement is being gradually disregarded.

Love and Marriage in America

Our society is one in which romantic love and marriage are presented in idealistic terms. We view "falling in love" as a high point in our lives, and we expect to "live happily ever after" when we marry—and we marry in large numbers, and often, though not as often as we used to. The Census Bureau reports that between 1975 and 2002, the share of Americans who had never married increased from about 24 percent to 29 percent. The decline has been most dramatic for African Americans: the percentage of blacks who had never married in the same period increased from 32 percent to 43 percent, a percentage that persists today. Since the mid-1990s, however, trends in marriage have stabilized for both whites and African Americans, but the percentage of Hispanics who have never married has increased. (See Table 12.1 for percentages of marriage and divorce in the United States.)

Today's marriage scene is very different from the past. As of 2005, 51 percent of women live without a spouse, as opposed to only 35 percent in 1950 and 49 percent in 2000. More men than women are married and live with their spouses: 53 percent. Marriage rates among African American women are very low, as noted, so that only 30 percent of them live with a spouse (this compares with 49 percent of Hispanic women, 55 percent of non-Hispanic white women, and more than 60 percent of Asian women). In fact, married couples represent a minority of households, for the first time.

What are some of the reasons for this change? First of all, the loss of stigma and the frequency of divorce, discussed later. In addition, women have entered the work force in droves and so are less dependent on men in the institution of marriage. They also marry later, and many live with unmarried partners for a while before, or even instead of, marrying. Divorced women often do not remarry, relishing their new-found freedom, whereas men remarry more quickly. Finally, women live longer than men, and so there is a large contingent of widows. Younger women seem to understand that they will spend longer parts of their lives unmarried and so are preparing for this eventuality. Some scholars maintain that the trend represents a tipping point from which there is no going back: Americans will spend half of their lives outside marriage (Roberts, 2007). Others point out that the total number of married couples is still high and that eventually many Americans marry. However, the fact that so many adults spend much of their lives single or with partners but unmarried has a number of social and economic implications: it affects the work force, it changes how and to whom manufacturers advertise, and it impacts on sales of housing and rental procedures.

Romantic love as a prerequisite for marriage is a modern invention. In preindustrial societies, marriage was an economic arrangement between families. Love between the partners had nothing to do with it, although the partners were expected eventually to come to love one another. With modernization, particularly the fact that young adults of

TABLE 12.1 United States Marital Status, 2005 American Community Survey

Subject	Total	Now Married (Except Separated)	Widowed	Divorced	Separated	Never Married
Population 15 years and over	227,798,491	53.4%	6.0%	10.2%	2.2%	28.1%
Age and Sex						
Males 15 years and over	110,298,693	55.9%	2.4%	8.9%	1.8%	31.0%
Females 15 years and over	117,499,798	51.0%	9.4%	11.5%	2.6%	25.5%
Race and Hispanic or Latino Origin						
One race	224,632,785	53.6%	6.1%	10.2%	2.2%	27.9%
White	174,053,411	56.4%	6.3%	10.5%	1.7%	25.0%
Black or African American	26,016,835	34.0%	6.5%	11.6%	5.0%	43.0%
American Indian and Alaska Native	1,784,919	42.5%	5.6%	13.2%	3.3%	35.3%
Asian	10,098,735	61.7%	4.3%	4.7%	1.3%	28.0%
Native Hawaiian and Other Pacific Islander	306,385	50.9%	3.6%	8.1%	2.6%	34.8%
Some other race	12,372,500	49.9%	2.9%	7.1%	4.1%	36.0%
Two or more races	3,165,706	39.3%	3.7%	11.6%	2.8%	42.6%
Hispanic or Latino origin (of any race)	29,569,863	50.6%	3.4%	7.6%	3.9%	34.6%
White alone, not Hispanic or Latino	157,897,990	56.9%	6.6%	10.8%	1.5%	24.2%

Source: U.S. Census Bureau, 2005. American Community Survey Office. Page last modified: September 12, 2007.

both sexes could find wage-paying work, came the ability to make one's own marital choices. And, of course, if one can choose one's own mate, one chooses a person who is appealing, attractive, and with whom one feels at ease and shares a number of interests—at least, at first. Hence the introduction of romance as a preamble to courting and inspiration for marriage.

Even though there is free choice in American society, that choice is much more socially determined than is at first obvious. Not only are endogamy and exogamy at work—spouses are chosen within certain groups and outside other groups—but also people overwhelmingly marry mates who are very much like themselves. This tendency is called *homogamy*, while its opposite, marrying a person with different traits, is referred to as *heterogamy*. Homogamy persists in such features as age, proximity, social characteristics, individual characteristics, and even degree of attractiveness.

The Stages of Marriage: Satisfaction and Dissatisfaction

Because of the American preoccupation with romantic love, most couples enter marriage with a number of highly romantic and idealistic notions of what married life will be like. Everyday life, however, has a way of destroying such illusions. The early years of marriage are often reported to be the most difficult because they require the most amount of adjustment to be made. At the same time, when questioned as to the *marital quality*, or satisfaction with married life, most couples admit that at no time is it higher than in the first few years of marriage.

Box 12.1 Arranged Marriages

Can an arranged marriage be a happy marriage? To Americans, to marry someone chosen by one's parents, often without hardly seeing the person, seems a horrible way to enter into such an important relationship. And yet, odd as it may seem to us, women in other cultures swear by this method. For instance, an Indian living in the United States revealed in an article how successful her arranged marriage has turned out to be. She mentions the method used by her parents to select her husband-to-be: first, the family and economic background, religion, caste, and values of the groom must be similar to those of the bride. On the other hand, his personality and physical traits should differ or complement those of the bride so that instead of adding merely stability and comfort to the relationship, differences would generate energy, good health in the offspring, and a bit of spice. The bride in this case thought she wanted a man with specific traits. Her parents, however, searched for a different list of attributes, as do most parents in a culture where arranged marriages are the norm. She was looking for the artistic type, but her parents chose a corporate type. A month after the two met, and after daily telephone conversations between the United States, where the groom worked, and India, where the bride resided, he proposed and she accepted. As she notes.

The first two years of our marriage were difficult. I discovered differences between us that had not been apparent during our courtship. I loved going out dancing, trying different wines, hiking and camping, experimenting with various ethnic cuisines. Ram loved Indian food, Indian music, visiting with family. I automatically branded him old-fashioned and hide-bound, not my type. . . . But Ram was very Western in his thinking. . . . It was the realization that I could learn from Ram that began my process of falling in love. . . . As I grew to respect his mind, his positive attitude toward life, his success, I forgot that muscular men weren't my type. Instead, I began noticing the sensual, upward curve of his lips, his generous laugh, and how hugging him felt like coming home. By our second anniversary, I could look at my marriage and honestly say that I was a happy and fulfilled woman. (Shoba Narayan, 1998. "Lessons from an Arranged Marriage." New Woman, January, 79–100)

Indians are not the only group among whom arranged marriages are common. In the United States, some Muslim and Jewish communities also practice such marriages. Muslim immigrant families arrange marriages even for their American-born children. Similarly, religious Jews such as the Hasidim choose partners for their children who will share the traditional Jewish values of their parents. Of course, not all children are agreeable to this arrangement, nor are all arranged marriages successful. But it is interesting to note that many of them are.

Box 12.2 The Scientific Study of Marriage?

Can an institution such as marriage, based so deeply on emotion, be studied scientifically? Apparently, it can. At least, researchers in a number of universities are attempting to explore the forces that strengthen or strain marital ties. They are doing it by evaluating facial expressions and gestures, by monitoring body functions such as heart rate, blood pressure, and the release of stress hormones, and by using cameras to observe couples in a number of different interactions. Such research has enabled researchers to predict in more than 90 percent of the cases who will stay together and who will part. It has also contradicted many conventional notions of what it is that makes for a happy or an unhappy marriage.

The physiological findings demonstrate that husbands and wives are very sensitive to every aspect of each other's presence. Just being in the same room together, even without speaking, alters a number of bodily rhythms, and spouses are able to read each other without even being conscious of it.

In one study, psychologists studied newlyweds over the first decade of marriage. They found that the most important difference between those who would stay together and those who would split began at the very start of the relationship. When the couples who would stay together made comments about each other, only 5 of every 100 comments were putdowns. Among couples who would separate, 10 of every 100 comments were insults. Multiplied over a span of 10 years, it meant that couples destined for divorce were flinging five times as many insulting comments at each other as couples who would remain together. The first conclusion reached in this study, then, is the fact that no matter what the spouses' socioeconomic level or their backgrounds, all satisfied couples regulate their relationships by balancing out positive to negative events at an approximate ratio of five to one.

Another finding is that couples who stay together find ways of cooling off to lower their bodily arousal. This can be simply a matter of saying, "It's not all your fault." Couples who are unable to deescalate hostility this way find that their bodies react violently. Their hearts beat to the bursting point, blood pressure rises, the stomach constricts, palms sweat, and stress hormones flow through

the body, in a process called "flooding." Nonscientists call it anger. When this happens, the brain cannot process any new information, so communication becomes impossible or harmful. Men are especially subject to flooding and remain in this condition for longer periods of time. The inability to recover from flooding is linked to spousal violence. Some men try to avoid violence by withdrawing from an argument. This would seem a wise move, but in reality, withdrawal causes flooding in the wife, so it begins a vicious circle that disrupts relations and leaves both partners emotionally and physically debilitated. Even worse, the nervous system seems to keep track of flooding, making individuals hypersensitive to it, often precipitating it, and leading to the perception that conflicts cannot be resolved. Finally, chronic flooding causes the nervous system to reorganize its memories, in a sort of defense mechanism, so that eventually spouses have trouble remembering any pleasant or even neutral details about their early relationship.

The greatest stresses in a marriage are represented by parenthood and by extramarital affairs. In one study, 92 percent of new parents reported lower satisfaction and more conflict after the birth of a child. In another study, only 19 percent of parents said that their marriages improved after the birth of a child. Taking on the role of parents tends to make spouses vulnerable to an affair. Even partners in a loving marriage often give in to an affair because of an excessive need for admiration or thrills, or the desire to forge a new image of oneself in someone else's eyes. Although an affair represents the most damaging blow to a marriage, two thirds of the couples in one study decided to stay together and reported finding a new closeness by virtue of having overcome the ordeal together.

What holds a marriage together through strain and stress, then? In a study of couples who have remained together for 40 years or more, it appears that what these couples do is soothe one another and try to prevent each other's distress during conflict. They also seem to be more mellow in their attitudes toward marital differences, which prevents much conflict from arising. Finally, years of living together seem to erase many gender differences and establish a more unified view of their marriage and of life in general (Schrof, 1994, 66–69).

This seeming contradiction may be attributed to the differences in *marital scripts* with which couples enter marriage. Marital scripts (Broderick, 1993) are the expectations as to how husbands and wives ought to behave. Unfortunately, because people are socialized in different families, these scripts are often mismatched. Even unimportant matters that could easily be solved if they were brought out in the open may cause misunderstanding and arguments and, if left unsolved, may lead to a breakup of the relationship. At any rate, 43 percent of first marriages end in separation or divorce within 15 years. One in three first marriages ends within 10 years, and one in five ends within 5 years.

Another critical time in a marriage occurs when a couple become parents. A baby puts a lot of strain, particularly on its mother, in the first months of its life in terms of the sheer amount of time and work it demands. This leaves the couple very little time to spend together in activities, including sex, that bound them together previously. Couples who have children at a very young age and a short time after marriage experience feelings of dissatisfaction; a number of studies have consistently shown that children make the marital relationship less satisfying. In fact, children and money are what most couples argue about most commonly.

Marital satisfaction declines even further when children reach school age. In fact, there seems to be a direct correlation between marital satisfaction and parental relationships with children: parents who have few difficulties with their children report more satisfaction with their marriage than parents who are experiencing difficulties with their eldest children (Steinberg & Silverberg, 1987).

Marital quality is somewhat higher among older married couples than among those in their middle years. This may be a reflection of the fact that the worst marriages have already broken up by this time, or that problems in a marital relationship improve after the children leave home. Some studies seem to point to the fact that the strains associated with having and raising children continue to have negative effects on the quality of marriage even into the later years. Other studies that followed couples who had remained married for a long time showed that marital problems have a tendency to decrease in such marriages, while love and affection increase (Weishaus & Field, 1988).

A report prepared by the Centers for Disease Control's (CDC) National Center for Health Statistics focusing on conditions associated with long-term marriages, divorce, and separation found that marriages tend to last longer under certain conditions: if a woman is not too young; if a woman was raised throughout childhood in an intact two-parent family; if religion was important; and if she came from a family with a high income, or lived in a community with a high median family income, low male unemployment, and low poverty (**http://www.cdc.gov/nchs/pressroom/01news/firstmarr.htm.** Accessed 4-28-07.).

The Role of Power in Marriage

The traditional role of women placed them in a subordinate position to men, especially in the marriage relationship. In today's marriages, the individuals involved generally subscribe to an egalitarian view, with each partner holding an equal amount of power to make decisions for the marital unit. In reality, however, egalitarianism is difficult to attain, and when marital relationships are studied objectively, it appears that either one or the other partner wields greater power. According to the **resource theory**, the distribution of power depends on the resources each spouse brings to the marriage (Blood & Wolfe, 1960). These resources may be of an economic nature, such as the ability to earn income, education, and occupational prestige, or of a noneconomic nature, such as companionship, emotional support, and social skills (Safilios-Rothschild, 1970). Of course, in a society such as ours, in which economic success is of great importance, the spouse who occupies the higher status because of earning ability occupies the higher status in the marriage in general. Thus, in spite of the increasing numbers of women who are in the labor force, because they generally earn less than men, they also tend to have less power in the marriage (Szinovacz, 1987). Their lesser power not only means they do not make the most important decisions, but also that they do most of the menial but necessary work around the house.

Changing Marital Patterns

Modernization and the general affluence it brought in industrial societies greatly changed the structure and substance of family life. An almost equally dramatic change has occurred in this century, particularly in the past few decades. Because of improved birth control methods, liberalized sex norms, and the entrance of women into the work force, the birthrate has greatly declined (see Chapter 11), voluntary childlessness has increased, and the divorce rate, which skyrocketed all through the last half of the twentieth century, is just beginning to stabilize. Marriage rates have been declining: in 1960, for instance, 69 percent of men and 66 percent of women were married. In 2006, only 55 percent of men and 51.5 percent of women were married (U.S. Bureau of the Census, *Current Population Surveys*, June 2006). Some of this decline may be the result of delaying the age of first marriage. Again in 1960, age at first marriage was 20 for women and 23 for men. Recently, age at first marriage has been 25 for women and 27 for men. Other factors in the decline of the marriage rate may be the increase in numbers of unmarried persons living together, or cohabitation, and a slight decrease in the number of divorced people who remarry. Finally, there has been a visible increase in the incidence of persons remaining single. Nonetheless, when viewed over a 60-year period, the marriage rate has remained fairly constant. Over this period, the average rate has been 10.1 marriages per 1,000 people. In 2006, the rate was 7.3 per 1,000 people (Table 12.2).

TABLE 12.2 Births, Marriages, Divorces, and Deaths: Provisional Data for 2006

| | 12 Months Ending with October | | | | |
| | Number | | Rate | | |
Item	2006	2005	2006	2005	2004
Live births	4,242,000	4,139,000	14.2	14.0	14.0
Fertility rate	—	—	68.3	66.6	66.2
Deaths	2,412,000	2,424,000	8.1	8.2	8.2
Infant deaths	27,800	27,800	6.5	6.7	6.7
Natural increase	1,830,000	1,715,000	6.1	5.8	5.8
Marriages[1]	2,146,000	2,255,000	7.3	7.6	7.8
Divorces[2]	*	*	3.6	3.7	3.7
Population base (in millions)	—	—	298.6	296.0	293.1

*Category not applicable.
—Data not available.
[1]Marriage figures exclude data for Louisiana in 2006. Populations for marriage rates also exclude Louisiana.
[2]Divorce figures exclude data for California, Georgia, Hawaii, Indiana, Louisiana, and Minnesota in 2006 and 2005; and California, Georgia, Hawaii, Indiana, and Louisiana in 2004. Populations for divorce rates also exclude these states.

Source: National Vital Statistics Reports (NVSR), National Center for Health Statistics, Vol. 55, Number 20.

Another change in marriage patterns is that there is a "marriage gap" between those who marry and those who do not, and that gap is between the well-off and the less well-off. According to statistics, more college-educated women marry and are less likely to divorce. Fifty-nine percent of college-educated women aged 25 to 34, in fact, are married, compared to 51 percent of women that age who are not college graduates. In the 35 to 44 age group, 75 percent of college graduates are married, compared to 62 percent who are not. This situation holds true even for those 65 years old and older: 50 percent are married versus 41 percent who are not (U.S. Census Bureau, Current Population Survey, June 2006). The gap holds true for men as well, although to a lesser extent. The gap is one of social class, because whereas in the past many women "married up"—that is, they married a man higher up in the stratification hierarchy—today the prevailing norm is that an educated woman marries an educated man, both having high earning power. Such a couple forgoes many of the problems of a financial nature that threaten marriages of persons from lower social classes. As many jobs in manufacturing have been lost, working-class males have had a more difficult time maintaining a family and so are less eager to marry.

On a more philosophical level, Robert Bellah, in *Habits of the Heart*, argues that Americans' pursuit of individualism and their preoccupation with the self are incompatible with relationships that demand commitment, such as marriage and the establishment of a family. Most Americans, he points out, believe that the meaning of one's life is to become one's own person, achieve self-fulfillment, and find oneself. Such a process involves breaking free from family, community, and tradition (Bellah et al., 1985, 82). If love and marriage are viewed as sources of psychological gratification, judged according to whether they make the individual feel good, it is possible to conclude that the expectations and obligations inherent in the role of husband and wife, and especially those of parents, are antithetical. That is, our conceptions of love and marriage conflict with the older social functions of the family that formerly acted as a tie to the larger society. Those roles imply unselfishness and concern for others and are in conflict with a preoccupation with the self and self-fulfillment. The conclusion is that

> . . . in the twentieth century, marriage has to some extent become separated from the encompassing context of family in that it does not necessarily imply having children in significant sectors of the middle class. . . . Social pressure to marry is not absent, but it is probably weaker than ever before in American history. . . . Finally, one can leave a marriage one doesn't like. Divorce as a solution to an unhappy marriage, even a marriage with young children, is far more acceptable today than ever before (Bellah et al., 1985, 89–90).

■ Divorce

The most notorious change in the marital pattern is that divorce has become a frequent and accepted part of it. The high rates of divorce in urban industrial societies reflect (1) the separation of marriage from religion, (2) the emancipation of women, and (3) the change in values to a new emphasis on individuality and personal happiness.

Industrialization has had the effect of increasing divorce rates wherever it has appeared. In the United States, marriage rates have remained more or less stable since the turn of the twentieth century, but divorce rates increased from 0.9 divorces per 1000 people in 1910 to 5.3 in 1981 and finally stabilized at 3.6 per 1000 in 2006. The annual divorce rate nearly doubled in the decade of 1965 to 1975. The American rate is the highest in the world: about 4 out of 10 marriages end in divorce.

In the past, the majority of divorces were granted to people between 20 and 35 years old who had been married a short time or who married when either spouse was a teenager. Today, the age group exhibiting most divorces is the 45- to 49-year olds. The median age at divorce is 35.6 for males and 33.2 for females. Over one-third of divorces take place by the fourth year of marriage, and the median duration of marriages that end in divorce is about seven years. Location also seems to play a part in the number of divorces. The state with the lowest divorce rate is Massachusetts (2.4), while the highest rate is held by Nevada (9.0).

Leading causes of divorce are personality differences and incompatibility; more specific individual problems, such as drug and alcohol abuse, infidelity, physical or psychological abuse, and financial difficulties, are more seldom cited as causes. Poor communication skills, a lack of commitment to the marriage, and a dramatic change in priorities are also frequently mentioned as springboards for divorce. Women appear to be more unhappy in marriages and are more likely to initiate separation leading to divorce. Marital instability that often leads to divorce can also include (1) marrying on the rebound, (2) hostility toward the family of orientation of one of the spouses by the other, resulting in pressure to move far away, (3) dramatic differences in the spouses' family backgrounds in terms of religion, ethnicity, race, education, or social class, resulting in differences in values, (4) dependence on one of the families of orientation for income, shelter, or emotional support, (5) unstable marriages in the families of either spouse, (6) marriage after being acquainted for less than six months or after an engagement period of more than three years, and (7) pregnancy before marriage or very shortly after marriage (McGoldrick & Carter, 1988). Of course, this is not to say that marriages in which one or more of these circumstances exist will necessarily break up. It is only an indication that such marriages have a good statistical probability of ending in divorce.

In spite of the widespread belief that half of all marriages are fated to end in divorce, many marriages remain stable. A research study under the auspices of the National Center for Health Statistics has calculated percentage-point decreases in the risk of divorce or separation during the first 10 years of marriage. The factors responsible for a decrease in the risk of divorce include: an annual income over $50,000 (as against under $25,000), having a baby seven months or more after marriage (as against having one before marriage), marrying at over 25 years of age (as against under 18), coming from an intact family of origin (as against having divorced parents), having a religious affiliation (as against having none), and having some college (as against being a high school dropout) (Bramlett & Mosher, 2002, 23).

It seems that the likelihood of a woman divorcing within 10 years of her first marriage rose, regardless of her education, until the mid 1970s. Since then, however, divorce rates have been different for women of varying educational attainment. For instance, for women with a four-year college degree who married between 1990 and 1994, the divorce rate was 16.5 percent (whereas it had been 29 percent for similarly educated women who had married between 1975 and 1979). However, for women with only a high-school diploma, the divorce rate remained constantly high, and it increased among women who did not finish high school. Such differences in divorce rates may be a result of economic factors; the more educated women dispose of a higher income, and financial difficulties make divorce much more likely (Martin, 2006. **http://www.demographic-research.org**).

Remarriage

In 80 percent of the cases, both partners remarry, although divorce occurs more frequently among couples who have been married more than once. In fact, the likelihood of a new marriage ending in divorce is 43 percent, while the actual percentage of remarriages ending in divorce is 60 percent (Americans for Divorce Reform, 2001). There are more divorced women than divorced men principally because men are more likely to remarry and they do it sooner than women. About 6 percent of married couples have been married three or more times. The frequency of divorce and remarriage has led analysts to call these marriages *serial* or *throwaway*.

In the last two decades, the rate of divorce has increased most rapidly among middle-aged Americans. About 15 percent of the 40–54 age group are divorced. In addition, people in this age group are not remarrying as much as they used to. The explanation that has been offered by demographers and sociologists contradicts the time-worn myths of women desperate to find husbands. In fact, according to experts, it is women who are skeptical of marriage nowadays. Women are becoming self-sufficient, and they are increasingly loath to lose their independence. And, of course, it is difficult for men to marry if women are not interested. One sociologist calls women's lack of interest in marriage "the real revolution" of the last 20 years.

Another finding of the research into this phenomenon is that while unmarried women, as long as they have a stable financial situation, cope very well with the unmarried status, men do less well. Women have social and bonding skills that allow them to create a social network to sustain them, but men often lack such skills. Unmarried men, even when they have enough money, have more difficulty than women in fitting into a social group. As one grows older, it becomes more important to be a part of a social network than to be successful occupationally. Creating such a network has usually been the work of women. As we saw earlier, women appear to instigate most divorces, and men, faced with divorce, tend to question their worth and competence. Women, by contrast, are more pragmatic: they are more concerned with finances, making unfamiliar decisions, and relocating. As long as these immediate problems are resolved successfully, they adjust well to their new status, citing a new "sense of freedom" to boot. The only women who report feeling unhappy after a divorce are young mothers who experience financial difficulties and who are overwhelmed with their responsibilities.

Divorce as the New Norm

The prevalence of divorce has made it much more acceptable. A growing number of people realize that divorce is a natural product of social change, and a majority are beginning to consider the divorced status "normal." Polls show that people believe divorce to be an acceptable solution to an unacceptable marriage. The women's movement has popularized the notion that it is all right for women to be independent and assertive and that men are not necessary to women's happiness. All these factors have made it easier for both partners, but for women especially, to seek a divorce instead of remaining in an unhappy marriage. In fact, an overwhelming majority of divorced people feel they made the right choice in divorcing and deny that they would have been better off staying married (of course, those who weathered a period of discord in a marriage but decided to stick it out also believe that they made the right decision!).

In addition, divorce laws have become much simpler in recent years. Almost half of all states have adopted forms of "no-fault" divorce in which neither party has to prove that the other is to blame. Finally, support systems have sprung up to help couples with their emotional, financial, and legal problems as they go through a divorce. Books about how to handle divorce abound on library shelves, colleges offer courses on the same subject, and free counseling is also widely available to those in need.

The no-fault divorce was hailed as progressive because it was designed to eliminate the humiliations and bitterness of accusatory confrontations between the divorcing spouses. However, its effect on women and children was not as expected. The consequences of no-fault divorce are a steep decline in the standard of living, little hope of receiving alimony, far too little money for child support—in short, "an economic disaster" for wives and children (Weitzman, 1985). The courts tend to award a modest amount in alimony for a short period of time, and then the expectation is that the woman will learn to stand on her own economic feet. Although this expectation is realistic for a woman in her twenties, particularly if she is childless, it is utterly unrealistic for older women or women with several children, who have spent the best years of their lives being housekeepers and, thus, have few marketable skills. Child support payments are also generally low, but the principal problem with them is that the noncustodial parent, most often the father, tends not to make them at all or to make them only sporadically. In fact, so many fathers are delinquent in their support payments that federal legislation now mandates that payments be automatically deducted from paychecks. "Dead-beat dads," however, continue to avoid their responsibilities.

Consequences of Divorce: Wounds That Do Not Heal

In spite of its frequency and "normality," divorce is not easy for the divorcing couple and is even less easy for their children, if there are any. From the numerous studies that have been made on the subject, it has been possible to learn that women suffer more stress and trauma from divorce than do men (Albrecht, 1980, 59–68). The reason may well be that men are generally in a better economic position and so their postdivorce adjustment is facilitated. In fact, a majority of divorced women report that their income following divorce decreased considerably. A group called Americans for Divorce Reform reports that women after a divorce experience a 45 percent drop in standard of living.

A child going over to dad's for the weekend has become a norm in our divorce-prone age.

Although from this perspective divorce is much easier for the male, the psychological adjustment may be harder for men: four times more divorced men than married men kill themselves (Moffet & Scherer, 1976), and men who are not remarried within six years following divorce have higher rates of car accidents, alcoholism, drug abuse, depression, and anxiety (Brody, 1983, C1).

A much better adjustment to divorce is made by couples who are childless and who divorce after a few years of marriage: they join the ranks of single people with very little trace of their former status. Not so for those who have been married a long time or those who have children: they remain forever "the formerly married" (Hunt & Hunt, 1980, 340–354).

The effects of divorce on children are more difficult to evaluate, although a large number of children are fated to go through the experience of their parents' divorce. All children whose parents divorce report being traumatized, but the consensus of the research seems to be that the earlier the divorce occurs, the better for the children. Preschoolers may react more emotionally in the short term, but they also recover much more quickly than older children. It is the 9- and 10-year-olds who are especially shaken by divorce, because their self-concept depends on having parents physically present in the household. In one such study, children expressed feelings of sadness and powerlessness even years later, with boys especially vulnerable. And teenagers manifest the damaging effects of divorce even more overtly (Wallerstein & Kelly, 1983, 438–452). Wallerstein and Kelly note that 68 percent of those who were teenagers at the time of parental divorce had behavior problems, with boys tending to commit crimes such as drug peddling and theft and girls involved in alcohol and drug abuse (Conant & Wingert, 1987, 58).

Most children maintain that the conflict preceding divorce is much worse than the divorce itself. Thus, the difficulties associated with "children of divorce" are probably more correctly the result of years of parental fighting (Luepnitz, 1979, 79–85). In particular, children show improvement after a separation or divorce in cases where one of the parents is alcoholic or abusive. In some instances, the parents actually become more effective after the divorce, because much of the tension is removed.

A second study by psychologist Wallerstein, which followed the original families five years after divorce, seems to indicate that the wounds of divorce heal very slowly, if at all. Some of the findings of that study include the fact that, although the adults involved in the divorce were doing reasonably well five years later, the children were not. About "37 percent of the sample were depressed, could not concentrate in school, had trouble making friends and suffered a wide range of other behavior problems" (Wallerstein, 1989, 20; see also Wallerstein & Blakeslee, 1989). In the 10-year follow-up study, 45 percent of the children, who were now adults, were doing fairly well, but 41 percent were doing poorly. "They were entering adulthood as worried, underachieving, self-deprecating and sometimes angry young men and women" (Wallerstein, 1989, 20). The researchers conclude that divorce is not perceived as a single event but as a chain of events, relocations, and radically shifting relationships, "a process that forever changes the lives of the people involved" (Wallerstein, 1989, 20).

Although the Wallerstein study has been criticized, mainly because it fails to present a control group with which the findings can be compared, it is clear that although divorce may on occasion be a solution to an impossible marriage, it is at no time an easy or desirable solution. The researchers found much anger in the divorced partners even 10 years after divorce, and only a small minority had remarried happily for the second or third time. The real tragedy of divorce, however, appears to be the effect on children, particularly, as was noted earlier, in view of estimates that 38 percent of all children born in the mid-1980s will see their parents divorce before they turn 18.

A new critique of Wallerstein's study—and of family-health specialists in general— has come from a study published in 2002. In this study, *For Better Or For Worse: Divorce*

Reconsidered, the psychologist E. Mavis Hetherington maintains that the vast majority of children begin to function reasonably well two years after their parents' divorce. In addition, a certain proportion of women and girls actually do better after the divorce than if they had stayed in an unhappy family situation, and 70 percent of divorced parents are living happier lives than they would have otherwise (Hetherington & Kelly, 2002). The researcher concludes that although 25 percent of children of divorce do have serious social, emotional, or psychological problems—as opposed to 10 percent of children from intact homes—nonetheless 75 percent of such children recover and function within a normal range. The difference between the two researchers, Wallerstein and Hetherington, lies in their methodology. Wallerstein interviewed a small number of children, but in depth, following them for a long period of time into their adult years. Hetherington amassed statistical data on 1,400 families and 2,500 children, but never interviewed any, although some have been followed for about three decades. Hetherington admits that divorce can devastate and ruin lives, but she believes that the negative effects of divorce have been exaggerated, while its positive effects—the fact that women and girls are given the opportunity for "life-transforming personal growth"—have been neglected.

Still another researcher who spent three years interviewing 1,500 young adults, half of whom came from divorced parents and half from a control group of children from intact families, maintains that even if a divorce is amicable, it induces suffering in children and leaves indelible marks on them. In *Between Two Worlds: The Inner Lives of Children of Divorce*, Elizabeth Marquandt states that divorce fundamentally restructures childhood. When parents marry, they combine their beliefs, values, and lifestyles and construct a common "world." When they divorce, each parent returns to his and her previous world. The children are then forced to make sense of the world by answering certain questions relating to their identity when they are young and alone, questions that all children face on the way to adulthood and that parents usually help them answer. As a result, children of a divorced family say they felt like a different person with each of the parents. They considered their parents to be polar opposites even if they did not fight. The children kept secrets for their parents and felt they had to take care of them instead of the other way around. They also felt alone as children, they were angry and had feelings of loss, and finally, they felt like outsiders in their home or homes (Marquandt, 2006).

In the last decade of the twentieth century, the frequency of divorce experienced a slowing. Some commentators attribute the slowing to the aging of the baby boomers, who were beginning to move into their senior years, typically a time when divorce rates are low. And marriage specialists maintain that they are seeing a countertrend in attitudes toward both marriage and divorce. It seems that divorce does not look as attractive as it did a decade ago. People have come to recognize that although divorce can bring freedom and independence, it also brings with it economic hardships, and remarriage brings with it the same problems as first marriages. There is also a growing realization that the cause of a person's unhappiness may not necessarily be a spouse, as well as the conviction that the wounds of divorce can be severe and permanent (Hall, 1991, B4). Whatever the reasons, polls and marriage counselors agree that there is an increased effort to keep marriages from falling apart.

■ The New American Family

It is safe to say that the American family, like other contemporary institutions, is still undergoing the aftereffects of modernization. Much attention has been focused on it by social scientists because the changes in it have been more visible than elsewhere, particularly from mid-century on. Infected by the ideological ferment of the 1960s, many young people began to see the family as a repressive institution and a breeding ground of conflicts under the surface. It became fashionable at that time to consider "alternative lifestyles," and many drifted away to try communal living arrangements. Most of these dissolved after a few years: it is apparently not a functional family life.

Forms of the New American Family

The stereotype of the nuclear family consisting of Daddy, Mommy, two kids, and a dog or a cat no longer corresponds to reality. With the high incidence of divorce and subsequent remarriage, American families look quite different than they did 20 years ago.

The Single Lifestyle.   An alternative to the traditional family that seems to have taken hold is simply remaining single. This alternative has always been available to people, but in the past it carried a much greater social stigma. The bachelor uncle or the maiden aunt was looked on as a misfit who lived at the margin of a relative's family. Of course, in extended families there was always room and a function for them, whereas in nuclear families there was not. Today, single Americans represent 41 percent of all U.S. residents age 18 and older. They tend to be homeowners in the suburbs, resembling in their lifestyle their married-with-children neighbors (**http://www.census.gov/press-release/006840.html**).

Living Together.   The custom of unmarried couples living together—cohabitation, in the language of the social sciences—has emerged in the past 20 years as an expected stage of premarital life for many. According to the U.S. Census Bureau, the number of unmarried couple households in 2005 was 5.5 million (4.9 million heterosexual couples and around 700,000 homosexual couples), an increase from 3.2 million couples who were living together without being married in 1990. This means that over half of all first marriages are preceded by living together. Cohabiting is most popular for the 24–35 age group, while the next highest number of couples are found in the under-25 age group. Even though approximately 30 to 40 percent of college students are cohabiting at any given time, cohabitation is not limited to them. Working couples are almost twice as likely to cohabit as college students. In fact, couples who cohabit tend to come from lower-income, lower-educational backgrounds. Among women 19 to 44, 60 percent of high school dropouts have cohabited, as compared to 37 percent of college graduates (Qian 1998; Bumpass & Lu 2000). Opposite-sex unmarried couples were more likely to be in households with incomes at or below the poverty level (23.4 percent), while married couples were least likely to be in such households (4.8 percent). In addition, married couples are more likely to be homeowners (82 percent), while opposite-sex unmarried partners are least likely to be homeowners (44.3 percent). Same-sex unmarried couples, on the other hand, are more likely to own a home—76 percent for males, 71 percent for females (U.S. Census Bureau, American Community Survey, 2003). A positive relationship appears to exist between higher levels of education and higher income and marriage; in other words, persons with more education and higher social and economic status tend to marry rather than cohabit.

Cohabitation is not a movement limited to the United States. In many Western countries such as England, Canada, Sweden, Denmark, and Australia, persons in the 18–25 age group, and even some in their forties and fifties, either currently cohabit or have done so in the past. In Sweden, there are slightly more than two married couples for every cohabiting couple, and half of all babies born in Sweden are born to unmarried mothers. This situation may be a result of the lack of privileges the government gives to married couples: in fact, married couples cannot file income taxes jointly, nor can they claim other deductions for raising children.

Cohabiting unions are not generally successful. The rituals and ceremonies with which marriages are celebrated in every society serve to involve the family and community, and in a sense the whole society, since marriage is a legal contract recognized by the state. Their involvement, in turn, has the result of keeping couples together. When the involvement is lacking and couples are left to their own devices, their relationship tends to be more brittle and a breakup becomes more common. In fact, one study showed that 10 years after the wedding, 38 percent of those who had lived together had divorced, as compared to 27 percent of those who married without having lived together before. An analysis based on a federal government survey of over 13,000 individuals indicated to sociologists that couples that cohabit before marriage are more willing to accept divorce as a solution to marital problems and are not subjected to pressures from their families to remain in an unsatisfactory marriage (Bumpass & Sweet, 1995).

The Single-Parent Family.   One of the fastest-growing types of family is made up of one divorced parent and a child or children. In the past, that parent was almost exclusively the mother. Increasingly, fathers have requested and received custody of children. Divorce is not the only cause of single-parent families. Death, ill health, and institutionalization contribute to the numbers of such families. However, divorce is now a predominant cause, in addition to the fact that unmarried women are much more likely to keep illegitimate children rather than give them up for adoption, as in the past.

Single parent families tend to be temporary, ending either when the child reaches majority age and moves out of the house or when the parent remarries (if widowed or divorced) or marries for the first time. However, the number of single-parent households has increased dramatically. In 1970, for example, 40 percent of all households consisted of married-couple families with children, but in 2000 they made up only 24 percent of all households.

In 2002, 16.5 million children (23 percent) were living with a single mother, and 1.8 million lived in a household with their mother and her unmarried partner. Moreover, 3.3 million children under 18 lived with their father, and 1.1 million of them lived in a household that included the father's unmarried partner. The proportion of children with single mothers varied greatly by race and Hispanic origin: almost half (48 percent) of black children, 25 percent of Hispanic children, and 13 percent of Asian children lived with single mothers. Nine percent of black children also lived in their grandparents' household, compared with 6 percent of Hispanic children and 4 percent of white children.

The Census Bureau also reports that children living with single mothers or apart from both parents are most likely to be in households receiving public assistance. The lower income of such households compounds the problems of caring for children single-handedly. Not only do women earn less than men, but also there is only one income in single-parent households. Women with small children may have to work only on a part-time basis, and women who head families tend to have less education than the average American woman (40 percent of women who head households did not graduate from high school). Additional difficulties encountered by such households revolve around lack of time and that the one parent present must play the roles of two parents in the face of fatigue and worry over money matters. This fact is particularly regrettable in the light of research which suggests that poor parenting, no matter what the structure of the family, is primarily responsible for deviant behavior among children (Patterson, 1980).

The Blended or Reconstituted Family.   Another common form that is created as a result of remarriage is the blended or reconstituted family. This type of household consists of

Box 12.3 **The Census Bureau Looks at Unmarried and Single Americans**

Single Life

89.8 million
Number of unmarried and single Americans in 2005. This group comprised 41 percent of all U.S. residents age 18 and older.

54%
Percentage of unmarried and single Americans who are women.

60%
Percentage of unmarried and single Americans who have never been married. Another 25 percent are divorced and 15 percent are widowed.

14.9 million
Number of unmarried and single Americans age 65 and older. These older Americans comprise 14 percent of all unmarried and single people.

86
Number of unmarried men age 18 and older for every 100 unmarried women in the United States.

55 million
Number of households maintained by unmarried men or women. These households comprise 49 percent of households nationwide.

29.9 million
Number of people who live alone. These persons comprise 26 percent of all households, up from 17 percent in 1970.

Parenting

32%
Percentage of births in 2004 to unmarried women.

12.9 million
Number of single parents living with their children in 2005. Of these, 10.4 million are single mothers.

40%
Percentage of opposite-sex, unmarried-partner households that include children.

672,000
Number of unmarried grandparents who were caregivers for their grandchildren in 2004. They comprised nearly 3-in-10 grandparents who were responsible for their grandchildren. (Source: American FactFinder)

Unmarried Couples

4.9 million
Number of unmarried-partner households in 2005. These households consist of a householder living with someone of the opposite sex who was identified as their unmarried partner.

Education

82%
Percentage of unmarried people age 25 or older in 2004 who were high school graduates.

23%
Percentage of unmarried people age 25 or older with a bachelor's degree or more education.

Editor's note: The preceding data were collected from a variety of sources and may be subject to sampling variability and other sources of error.

Source: U.S. Census Bureau, Public Information Office, Last Revised: August 09, 2007.

the two remarried partners, children of either previous marriage, and sometimes children of the current marriage.

Blended families have been described as representing the wave of the future, especially if the high divorce rate continues. Such families have their own sets of problems. Relationships are multiplied under the circumstances of several remarriages—one has several sets of siblings, grandparents, and other relatives. Occasions for jealousy and rivalry are similarly increased. Because women tend to get custody of children, a remarried man will often have children who do not live with him, while he lives with children who are not biologically his. Some research also seems to indicate that girls who reside in a household with a stepfather tend to have a higher incidence of sexual activity, drug involvement, and school-related problems than girls who live with both natural parents or with just their mother (Cherlin,

1981). These findings, however, are not meant to be interpreted as establishing a cause-and-effect relationship; that is, the fact that a girl lives in a household with her mother and her mother's new husband does not mean that she will engage in undesirable behavior. The findings do point to a potential for problems in a household where conflict and tension are present or where a child is filled with hostility and resentment.

The Small, Childless, or One-Child Family. Families in the Western world have been growing smaller since the Industrial Revolution. In 1930, the average family in the United States consisted of 4.11 persons; in the 1980s, it consisted of 3.21 persons, and in 2000 of 2.59 persons. Family size depends on the fertility rate. Between 1960 and 1989, fertility in the United States declined by almost 50 percent, from 3.7 children per woman to 1.9 (Popenoe, 1995, 50). Today, the rate is an even 2.0. But the trend toward childless marriages, or marriages in which only one child is produced, is something fairly new in American society.

Some of the reasons for the decline in the number of children per family are economic in nature. Because more women are working to maintain comfortable standards of living, extended leaves of absence are hardships on the family. Women who want careers also feel that they are more likely to be promoted if they are not frequently absent to care for ill children. And, of course, the availability of contraceptives, abortion, and sterilization make it relatively easy to remain childless or to have only one child. Finally, because the media have publicized the opinion of some behavioral scientists that parents largely determine how their children turn out, many married couples fear to undertake parental roles. At the same time, a countertrend is also discernible in that increasing numbers of women in their thirties and forties, having pursued successful careers and feeling that their biological clocks are running out, are deciding to have children while they still can. This trend has become so apparent that the media have labeled it an impending "baby boomlet." This new trend may keep the birthrate from slumping too far.

Partnerships of Single People. Finally, a new type of family form consists of people who do not marry legally but who cohabit. Sometimes such cohabitation is a preamble to

Some families are becoming extended as a result of being blended or reconstituted, that is, because of several remarriages and various sets of children and relatives.

marriage, as discussed previously. In the case of homosexual couples, however, cohabitation is the equivalent of marriage. To legalize the situation of homosexual and heterosexual cohabiting couples, some states have attempted to pass legislation to facilitate their obtaining the same rights to hospitalization and bereavement leave as married couples enjoy. These attempts have been only partially successful, as they give origin to deep controversies. Many see them as steps in the direction of an expanded view of what constitutes a family.

■ Some Unintended Effects of the Changing American Family

There is little doubt that we are seeing a changed family institution. Just as the nuclear form followed the dramatic changes in society due to industrialization and urbanization, so a new form will eventually take shape in adaptation to the postindustrial information society that is currently in the making. In the meantime, a number of problems assail this institution resulting from the sociocultural changes in progress.

Child Care

A severe problem for couples with children in which both partners must work or want to work is the difficulty of obtaining proper care for the children. With 60 percent of mothers with children under 14 in the labor force, child care is a serious problem. There are increasing pressures for the government to help, for now it is no longer only the poor who are in a bind, but middle-class parents as well. Throughout the country, the picture is the same: day care is hard to find, difficult to afford, and frequently distressingly bad. The few good facilities have such long waiting lists that one must apply even before children are born. Even those who can afford to pay nannies and in-home baby-sitters complain that many are

---

Box 12.4 Daddy Is Donor Number 200

One result of the increasing number of single-sex unions has been the proliferation of a form of "assisted reproductive technology." What is meant by this terminology is that a substantial number of women, some homosexual, some unmarried, some with infertile husbands, choose to use sperm from anonymous donors to become pregnant and give birth to their biological children. Only now the donors are not necessarily anonymous: with the advent of the Internet, it became possible for children of sperm donors to connect with their biological fathers and even with half-siblings—the children of the same donor but different mothers. The web site that offers this service is the Donor Sibling Registry, which encourages anonymous donors to abandon their anonymity, so that probable offspring could get in touch with them. However, it appears that most matches are between half-siblings, and most fathers are known only by the number that sperm banks use for identification purposes.

Several observations may be made in regard to this phenomenon. First, most of the children who seek information about their biological fathers do so because they consider biological identity very important. They believe that their bond to their unknown father is stronger than if they had been adopted. Second, both the children and, in many cases, their mothers have been anxious to create a kind of family network with their half-siblings and the mothers who used the same donor. When they find each other, they communicate via e-mail or instant messaging, they arrange meetings and outings, and they attempt to contact the sperm donor—their father. These efforts could be interpreted as the truth in the old saying, common in all societies, that blood is thicker than water.

irresponsible and tend to move on. Those who must take their children to so-called professional baby-sitters complain that conditions are unacceptable: either there are too many children for one caretaker, or the caretakers are untrained and tend to plop the children—and themselves—in front of the TV set. To add insult to injury, it seems that some corporations are making an effort to help some families, particularly those at the higher end of the salary scale. One survey indicated that flextime was available to 62 percent of families with family incomes greater than $71,600 but to only 31 percent of workers with children under 6 and family incomes under $28,000 (Lewin, 2001, A20).

What is even more perplexing is that we do not know what effect child rearing by strangers has on the children. Initially, it was thought that it was preferable to have children cared for by strangers than to have mothers forced to stay at home when they would rather be at work. It was assumed that mothers, kept from expressing themselves in creative endeavors, or even in menial work that would give them a degree of independence or self-esteem, would take their hostility out on their children. This may very well be true, but a current survey of research suggests that extensive day care in the first year of life raises the risk of emotional problems in later life. Psychologist Jay Belsky, who had coauthored a report concluding that day care can be perfectly fine for young children, reversed himself later when he stated in an article that babies who spend more than 20 hours a week in nonmaternal care during the first year of life risk having an "insecure attachment" to their mothers. These children are more likely to become uncooperative and aggressive in early school years (Wallis, 1987, 63). This work has been criticized in turn. The bottom line is that we still do not know which method of child care is best, but we can speculate that a well-trained and well-paid mother substitute will do as well as a biological mother in caring for children.

Whether maternal care is a prerequisite for the development of psychologically sound individuals is not the issue. The point is that what a child needs is interested, affectionate,

With over 60 percent of American women in the workforce, provision for child care is essential. Unfortunately, day care work is labor intensive, expensive for parents, and low paying for workers. It, therefore, seldom offers what a child most needs: interested, affectionate, stable care. This center is one of the good ones because it provides three workers for five babies.

stable care. One child psychologist maintains that an infant should be showered with irrational love, and in view of the way in which personality is formed, this seems like a sensible idea. Unfortunately, day care is labor intensive, meaning that it hurts in two ways: it is expensive for parents and low paying for workers. Day-care workers rank in the lowest 10 percent of American wage earners, a fact that contributes to an average turnover rate of 36 percent a year. At the same time, parents pay anywhere from $40 a week for home-based groups to more than $300 a week for live-in nannies, with no guarantee that either will focus on the child or reflect the parents' own values. In the meantime, government efforts at subsidizing day care have come to naught, partly because of the traditional attitude that motherhood—together with the flag and apple pie—are prototypical American ideals. In short, day care is seen as a threat to family values because it encourages—or enables—mothers to work outside the home. During the Reagan era, state and federal spending earmarked for day care was actually cut, despite the fact that having dependable care for children is the first step out of poverty for women as heads of households. Private business, although slow to act, has begun to jump on the bandwagon, recognizing that providing child care for employees reduces turnover and absenteeism, engenders company loyalty, and lessens stress.

Family Violence

Incidents of family violence probably are not limited to the present. Whenever a number of persons live under one roof, the scene is set for disagreements and, under some conditions, for the flare-up of violence. In addition, definitions of what constitutes violence and cruelty differ. For instance, when women were considered the personal property of a father or a husband—as was the case in many societies—it did not seem strange that even the law permitted the proprietor to use violence against them. And certain parental attitudes are also considered cruel and violent today, whereas in the past they were not. Children were regularly abandoned as late as the eighteenth century in Europe. According to one historian, in southern Italy the number of abandoned children was as high as 50 percent. Parents abandoned their offspring when they were unable to support them, were unwilling to keep them because

Family violence is not a pretty picture. Women and children are the most frequent victims.

of some physical defect, and when they did not want to be bothered with them. Societies did not have severe sanctions against abandonment (Boswell, 1989).

In today's societies, violence is universally condemned, but it is certainly an ever-present factor in our lives, including our family lives. The statistics on family violence are not encouraging: domestic violence is the leading cause of death among women, according to the Surgeon General. About 2 million women are battered every year, making battering the largest single cause of injury to women nationally, occurring more often than auto accidents, muggings, and rapes combined; some form of violence occurs in 28 percent of all marriages; 22 to 35 percent of women seeking emergency procedures are victims of domestic violence; 33.5 percent of all female homicide victims in 2000 were killed by their husbands or boyfriends; and at least 40 percent of all abuse cases involve alcohol or drugs (Gelles & Straus, 1988; Domestic Violence Stats & Facts, 2006). As of 2002, 22 percent of murders were of family members—9 percent were murders of a spouse, 6 percent were murders of sons or daughters by a parent, and 7 percent were murders by other family members. Fifty-eight percent of the victims of family murder were female, while 8 in 10 murderers who killed a family member were male (see Tables 12.3 and 12.4). Moreover, of the types of family violence that are reported, sexual abuse is the fastest-growing category. Sociologists Gelles and Straus maintain that Americans are far too tolerant of violence between family members because there is a feeling that what goes on behind the closed doors of a home is nobody's business. In addition, the growing use of crack has worsened the problems of abuse, and children of alcoholic and drug-addicted parents are more vulnerable to other adults who may want to victimize them. Although family violence cuts across all economic classes, child abuse is more frequent in households where the parents are poor, urban, single, young, and live under chaotic circumstances.

Child Abuse.   Child abuse refers to a wide range of maltreatment. In addition to sexual abuse and physical harm, serious neglect of a child's emotional and physical needs and incessant berating of a child are also included. Findings indicate that the long-lasting effects of all these kinds of abuse have much in common. In 2005, the number of American children subject to abuse of some kind was 899,000, which is a rate of victimization of 12.3 per 1,000 children. Of those, 62.8 percent suffered neglect, almost 16.6 percent suffered physical abuse, 9.3 percent were sexually abused, and 7.1 percent were emotionally maltreated. The National Child Abuse and Neglect Data System reported an estimated 1,400 child fatalities in 2002 (a "child fatality" is the death of a child caused by an injury resulting from abuse or neglect) (National Clearinghouse on Child Abuse and Neglect, April 2004 and Administration for Children and Families. **http://www.acf.dhhs.gov/programs/cb/pubs/cmos/index.htm**. Last updated 04/09/2007).

The highest victimization rates occur in the 0–3 years age group as these children are the most vulnerable—they are small and dependent and cannot defend themselves. Sexual abuse rates are higher for female children than for male children. Children younger than one year old accounted for 41 percent of the fatalities, while 76 percent were younger than 4 years old. However, many researchers and practitioners believe child fatalities are underreported, especially because states vary in their definitions of the causes of such fatalities.

Numerous studies have found that those who were victims of child abuse are more troubled as adults than those who were not; they make up an overwhelming number of prostitutes, violent criminals, alcoholics, drug abusers, and patients in psychiatric hospitals. Moreover, the more severe the abuse, the more extreme are the later psychiatric symptoms. A study of 15 adolescent condemned murderers in the United States found that 13 had been victims of extreme physical or sexual abuse, some of it characterized as "murderous" by the researchers (Goleman 1989, A1, A22).

TABLE 12.3 Demographic Characteristics of Family Murder Victims Compared to Nonfamily Murder Victims in 2002, by Relationship

| | | Percent of Murders in Which the Victim was the Offender's— | | | | | | | |
| | | Family Member | | | | Nonfamily Member | | | |
Victim Characteristic	All Murders	Total	Spouse	Son or Daughter	Other Family	Total	Boyfriend or Girlfriend	Friend or Acquaintance	Stranger
All murders	100%	100%	100%	100%	100%	100%	100%	100%	100%
Gender									
Male	71.3%	42.5%	19.0%	50.8%	63.8%	79.2%	29.0%	83.4%	86.1%
Female	28.7	57.5	81.0	49.2	36.2	20.8	71.0	16.6	13.9
Race									
White	56.6%	65.9%	70.3%	61.2%	63.9%	54.1%	52.0%	53.1%	56.3%
Black	39.9	29.7	23.9	34.7	33.1	42.7	44.6	43.8	40.2
Other	3.5	4.4	5.8	4.1	3.0	3.3	3.3	3.1	3.5
American Indian/ Alaskan Native	1.1	0.8	0.1	0.6	1.7	1.2	0.8	1.3	1.1
Asian/Pacific Islander	2.4	3.6	5.6	3.5	1.4	2.1	2.6	1.8	2.4
Age									
Under 18	12.8%	26.2%	1.0%	85.4%	11.1%	9.1%	3.9%	10.2%	8.7%
Under 13	7.6	23.4	0.0	80.2	8.0	3.3	0.4	4.4	2.3
13–17	5.1	2.8	1.0	5.2	3.2	5.8	3.4	5.8	6.4
18–24	23.5	8.1	7.9	4.4	11.1	27.7	21.4	27.4	29.9
25–34	24.3	15.4	27.5	4.2	9.9	26.7	30.2	26.3	26.4
35–54	29.8	32.5	47.5	5.2	35.6	29.0	38.5	28.6	27.1
55 or older	9.7	17.7	16.0	0.8	32.2	7.5	6.0	7.5	7.9
Total murders	9,102	1,958	787	500	671	7,144	668	4,113	2,362
Percent of all murders	100%	21.5%	8.6%	5.5%	7.4%	78.5%	7.3%	45.2%	26.0%

Note: Murder includes nonnegligent manslaughter. Data identifying the victim's relationship to the offender were reported for 56.2% of 16,204 murders. Of these 9,102 murders with recorded relationships, victim gender was reported for virtually 100%; race for 98.8%; and age for 97.6%. Detail may not add to total because of rounding.

Source: FBI, 2002 Supplementary Homicide Reports.

TABLE 12.4 Demographic Characteristics of Family Murderers Compared to Nonfamily Murderers in 2002, by Relationship

		Percent of Murders in which the Victim was the Offender's—							
		Family Member				Nonfamily Member			
Offender Characteristic	All Murders	Total	Spouse	Son or Daughter	Other Family	Total	Boyfriend or Girlfriend	Friend or Acquaintance	Stranger
All murders	100%	100%	100%	100%	100%	100%	100%	100%	100%
Gender									
Male	89.8%	79.2%	83.1%	61.9%	87.5%	92.7%	74.6%	93.4%	96.7%
Female	10.2	20.8	16.9	38.1	12.5	7.3	25.4	6.6	3.3
Race									
White	52.7%	65.3%	69.4%	62.4%	62.9%	49.2%	48.9%	50.3%	47.2%
Black	44.3	30.7	25.7	34.2	34.1	48.0	48.8	46.3	50.8
Other	3.1	3.9	4.9	3.5	3.0	2.8	2.3	3.4	2.0
American Indian/ Alaska Native	1.2	1.0	0.1	0.8	2.0	1.3	0.6	1.7	0.7
Asian/Pacific Islander	1.9	3.0	4.8	2.7	1.1	1.6	1.7	1.7	1.4
Age									
Under 18	6.5%	5.5%	0%	5.1%	12.0%	6.8%	1.2%	6.7%	8.8%
Under 13	0.2	0.8	0	0.2	2.0	0.1	0	0.1	0
13–17	6.3	4.7	0	4.9	10.0	6.8	1.2	6.6	8.8
18–24	34.4	17.3	4.1	30.3	23.2	39.4	21.4	38.0	47.6
25–34	27.5	26.9	24.0	33.9	25.2	27.7	32.2	27.5	26.7
35–54	26.6	38.9	53.5	25.0	32.0	23.0	41.1	23.8	15.7
55 or older	5.0	11.4	18.3	5.7	7.6	3.1	4.1	4.0	1.2
Total murders	9,102	1,958	787	500	671	7,144	668	4,113	2,362
Percent of all murders	100%	21.5%	8.6%	5.5%	7.4%	78.5%	7.3%	45.2%	26.0%

Note: Murder includes nonnegligent manslaughter. Data identifying the victim's relationship to the offender were reported for 56.2% of 16,204 murders. Of these 9,102 murders with recorded relationships, offender gender was reported for 98.9%; race for 97.6%; and age for 94%. Detail may not add to total because of rounding.

Source: FBI, 2002 Supplementary Homicide Reports.

Not all abused children go on to abuse their own children. The strongest predicting factor from childhood of becoming an abusive parent was not having been abused as such but rather having felt unloved and unwanted by one's parents, an attitude also found in families in which there is no overt abuse. One of the differences between the abused children who go on to become abusers and those who do not is whether they realize that their parents were wrong to abuse them. Children who come to believe that their parents should not have abused them, that they were not so bad that they deserved the abuse, can still love their parents and decide not to repeat the parents' behavior. But children who believe that the abuse was justified, that they indeed were bad and, thus, deserving of abuse, are likely to repeat the abuse with their own children.

The perpetrators of fatal child abuse do not fit any single profile. Many studies have noted, however, certain common characteristics: perpetrators tend to be young male high school dropouts who live at or below the poverty level, suffer from depression, have difficulty coping with stressful situations, and have experienced violence firsthand. Most instances of physical abuse seem to be caused by fathers and male caretakers; mothers tend to be responsible for deaths resulting from child neglect (**http://www.childwelfare.gov/can/index.cfm**, accessed 05/02/2007).

Teenage Pregnancy

A phenomenon that is hardly new, but that attained tremendous proportions in the last several decades, is that of out-of-wedlock, and particularly teenage, pregnancies. The teen pregnancy rate had risen steadily from the mid-1980s, reaching a peak in 1991. The rate was accompanied by a large increase in sexual activity among teenagers, who admitted to being very lax in the use of contraception, a situation that worried parents and social workers. Of course, the dangers of sex for young people are not limited to pregnancy. According to research, unprotected sex has led to increasing rates of infection with herpes 2, a sexually transmitted virus. Finally, the specter of AIDS looms ominously in instances of unprotected sex.

Teen pregnancy is problematic for two generations, that of the parent and that of the child. Teen mothers are as likely as other single women with young children to live below the poverty level (only half of those who give birth before age 18 complete high school). They are also more likely to be dependent on welfare: 60 percent of females under 30 who receive Aid to Families with Dependent Children (AFDC) had their first child when they were teenagers. Moreover, never-married mothers go on welfare in greater numbers than divorced women, and they stay on longer, becoming trapped in long-term welfare dependency. While 40 percent of never-married mothers stay on welfare for 10 years or more, only 14 percent of divorced mothers do. Thus, marital status, more than any other single factor, determines whether a woman will become a long-term AFDC recipient (Besharov & Germonis, 2001). Finally, the offspring of never-married mothers tend to experience high rates of illness and mortality and later in life are heirs to educational and emotional problems. Children of teenage parents are more likely to be abused by immature parents and unfortunately tend to repeat their parents' experience: a high percentage of girls who give birth in their early teens are daughters of teenage mothers.

Fortunately, beginning in 1997, the teen pregnancy rate began to decline, reaching a record low of 94.3 pregnancies per 1,000 women aged 15 to 19 years old. The rate has continued to slide, falling by 1 percent in 2004 to 70.0 per 1,000 women aged 15 through 19 (National Center of Health Statistics, 2006). The decline was noted in all racial and ethnic groups, but the greatest dip was for non-Hispanic black teenagers. For this group, the rate has plummeted by more than half, from 119.2 per 1,000 aged 15 to 19 years in 1991, to 63.1 in 2004. The birth rate for unmarried women increased 3 percent in 2004 to 46.1 births per 1,000 unmarried women aged 15–44 years (see Table 12.5). The reasons for the decline

TABLE 12.5 Birth Rates for Women Aged 10–19 Years, by Age and Race and Hispanic Origin of Mother: United States, 1991, 2002, 2003, and 2004, and Percentage Change in Rates, 1991–2004 and 2003–04 [Rates per 1,000 women in specified group]

Age and Race and Hispanic Origin of Mother	2004	2003	2002	1991	Percent Change, 2003–04	Percent Change, 1991–2004
10–14 years						
All races and origins[1]	0.7	0.6	0.7	1.4	17	−50
Non-Hispanic white	0.2	0.2	0.2	0.5	0	−60
Non-Hispanic black	1.6	1.6	1.9	4.9	0	−67
American Indian total[2,3]	0.9	1.0	0.9	1.6	−10	−44
Asian or Pacific Islander total[3]	0.2	0.2	0.3	0.8	0	−75
Hispanic[4]	1.3	1.3	1.4	2.4	0	−46
15–19 years						
All races and origins[1]	41.1	41.6	43.0	61.8	−1	−33
Non-Hispanic white	26.7	27.4	28.5	43.4	−3	−38
Non-Hispanic black	63.1	64.7	68.3	118.2	−2	−47
American Indian total[2,3]	52.5	53.1	53.8	84.1	−1	−38
Asian or Pacific Islander total[3]	17.3	17.4	18.3	27.3	−1	−37
Hispanic[4]	82.6	82.3	83.4	104.6	0	−21
15–17 years						
All races and origins[1]	22.1	22.4	23.2	38.6	−1	−43
Non-Hispanic white	12.0	12.4	13.1	23.6	−3	−49
Non-Hispanic black	37.1	38.7	41.0	86.1	−4	−57
American Indian total[2,3]	30.0	30.6	30.7	51.9	−2	−42
Asian or Pacific Islander total[3]	8.9	8.8	9.0	16.3	1	−45
Hispanic[4]	49.7	49.7	50.7	69.2	0	−28
18–19 years						
All races and origins[1]	70.0	70.7	72.8	94.0	−1	−26
Non-Hispanic white	48.7	50.0	51.9	70.6	−3	−31
Non-Hispanic black	103.9	105.3	110.3	162.2	−1	−36
American Indian total[2,3]	87.0	87.3	89.2	134.2	0	−35
Asian or Pacific Islander total[3]	29.6	29.8	31.5	42.2	−1	−30
Hispanic[4]	133.5	132.0	133.0	155.5	1	−14

[1] Includes origin not stated.
[2] Includes births to Aleuts and Eskimos.
[3] Data for persons of Hispanic origin are included in the data for each race group according to the mother's reported race; see "Technical Notes."
[4] Includes all persons of Hispanic origin of any race; see "Technical Notes."
Note: Race and Hispanic origin are reported separately on birth certificates. Persons of Hispanic origin may be of any race. Race categories are consistent with the 1977 Office of Management and Budget (OMB) standards. Fifteen states reported multiple-race data for 2004. The multiple-race data for these states were bridged to the single-race categories of the 1977 OMB standards for comparability with other states.

Source: National Vital Statistics Reports, Vol. 55, No. 1, September 29, 2006.

are attributed to young people delaying sex until a later time, having sex less frequently, and using birth control more responsibly.

In the 1960s, it was fashionable to speak of the "death of the family" as critics assailed the institution for being hopelessly outmoded and dysfunctional. Today, although only one in four is "traditional," it is difficult to conceive of the family as ceasing to exist entirely. The family continues to be the emotional center in people's lives. The fact that it is in constant flux speaks for its vitality. For instance, in addition to the variety of lifestyles discussed above, it is being reported that the family seems to be growing more extended as elderly parents, divorced offspring, and unmarried teenagers all return to or remain in the parental nest. The demographic shifts and advances in medicine are increasing the number of three- and even four-generation families who often live in a single home. The experiences of living in such a home may not necessarily be joyous, but it brings out what poet Robert Frost said about the family: it is the one place where they have to take you in when you have nowhere else to go. In spite of all its faults, the family is still the most efficient and satisfactory transmitter of culture, socializer of children, and nurturer of old and young that has ever been devised.

The Chapter in Brief

The culture that each society produces becomes a blue-print for the behavior of each new generation. Among the most important elements of culture are institutions, which are the habits, or traditional ways of doing things, that eventually crystallize into patterns of behavior. Institutions develop around human needs that are essential to the individual. The most pivotal human institutions are the family, religion, education, economy, and government.

The family is the oldest of all societal institutions. Most of the functions of the family in modern industrial societies have been reduced to control of sex and reproduction, socialization of the young, and provision of affection and companionship.

The family has undergone changes in form as a result of modernization. It has become nuclear and more egalitarian, with the preferred form of marriage being monogamy. Although marriage partners are not chosen by parents, as they are in traditional societies, even in urban industrial societies mate selection is not random. It is influenced by endogamy, or marriage within one's group, and homogamy, or marriage to partners with similar traits. In most marriages, the partners are of the same race, religion, and social class, as well as similar in age and physical appearance, education, and residence. Interracial marriages are infrequent not so much because of prejudice and discrimination—although these factors are of course present—but because endogamy and homogamy are so strongly embedded in our institutional framework.

The nuclear form of family is better adapted to life in an urban industrial society than is the extended family because it allows members more freedom to pursue upward social mobility. Its isolation from the support system of an extended family and the intensity of the emotions within it, however, make it particularly susceptible to conflict. Divorce and desertion are two prominent results of conflict, as are child abuse and mate abuse. Divorce is also a corollary of liberalized sexual norms and of changing attitudes toward marriage. As the necessity for having many children declines, the focus of marriage shifts away from the idea that it is the duty of everyone to marry to replenish society. Increasingly, marriage is entered into for affection and companionship.

New forms of the family keep appearing. For example, some homosexual couples choose to live in a marital union that sometimes includes children, biological (of one of the partners) or adopted. A number of states have introduced legislation to make such unions as legal as heterosexual marriages, but this notion still elicits much controversy.

Among alternatives to traditional family life, one finds the single-parent family, the blended or reconstituted family, the small, childless, or one-child family, and, increasingly, the multiple-generations family. The problematic issues deriving from the changes in the family include difficulties in adjustment for children of divorced parents, an increase in family violence, including child and spouse abuse, the inadequacy of child care for families in which both spouses must work, and the high incidence of out-of-wedlock, especially teenage, pregnancies. But changes and transformations only testify that the family institution endures.

Terms To Remember

consanguine Another term for the extended family. Also, the way parents are related to their children, that is, by blood ties.

extended family A form of the family consisting of the nucleus—two spouses and their children—and other blood relatives together with their marriage partners and children. Common in preindustrial societies.

incest taboo An almost universal prohibition of sexual relations between mother and son, father and daughter, sister and brother, and other relatives as specified by the society.

institution A pattern of behavior (culture complex) that has developed around a central human need. A blueprint for living in society.

monogamy The most common form of marriage, consisting of the union of one man with one woman.

nuclear or conjugal family A form of the family consisting of two spouses and their children living together as a unit.

polygamy A form of marriage in which multiple spouses—either wives or husbands—cohabit as family units.

Suggested Readings

Fisher, Helen. 2004. *Why We Love: The Nature and Chemistry of Romantic Love*. New York: Henry Holt. When you fall in love, it's your brain directing your behavior, under the pressure of chemistry. An anthropologist delves into an area most scientists seldom pursue —romantic love.

Furstenberg, Frank F., Jr., and Andrew Cherlin. 1991. *Divided Families: What Happens to Children When Parents Part*. Cambridge, MA: Harvard University Press. A troubling account of what happens to children after their parents' divorce, especially in terms of the psychological consequences.

Hays, Sharon. 1996. *The Cultural Contradictions of Motherhood*. New Haven, CN: Yale University Press. The author maintains that the new ideology of "intensive mothering" makes too great demands on mothers.

Hochschild, Arlie Russell. 1997. *The Time Bind*. New York: Metropolitan Books. The author claims that, possibly, many family members escape to the outside world of work rather than spending "quality time" with the family.

Strasser, Mark. 1997. *Legally Wed: Same-Sex Marriage and the Constitution*. Ithaca, NY: Cornell University Press. A subject we will probably hear much more about, same-sex marriage, discussed from a legal and constitutional point of view.

Wallerstein, Judith S., and Sandra Blakeslee. 1989. *Second Chances: Men, Women, and Children a Decade after Divorce*. New York: Ticknor & Fields. A longitudinal study of children of divorce. This is the 10-year report, and its conclusions about the adjustment of children of divorce are pessimistic.

Web Sites of Interest

http://www.ncfr.com/about_us/index.asp
The web site of the National Council of Family Relations (NCFR) is a good source for research and dissemination of knowledge about issues relative to the family.

http://www.divorcereform.org/
Americans for Divorce Reform is an organization that was developed as a result of this common experience. It brings together much information about the practice, as well as links to news, pub`lications, opinions, and legislation about divorce.

http://www.fam.org/
This site is run by the Stepfamily Association of America, an organization that develops and tries to disseminate information about stepfamilies, as well as advocating for social changes that would help stepfamilies.

http://www.contemporaryfamilies.org
A nonprofit organization, the Council on Contemporary Families provides information on issues relating to families, including offers of educational materials and sponsoring conferences on needs of families.

http://www.fvp.org
The Family Violence Prevention Fund is a nonprofit organization that focuses on research, information, policy, and education related to family violence.

Pivotal Institutions: Religion and Education

IN THIS CHAPTER, YOU WILL LEARN

■ *the reasons for the emergence of the institution of religion;*

■ *how religion is viewed from the perspective of the social sciences;*

■ *the functions of religion in society;*

■ *the characteristics of religion in America;*

■ *the trends in contemporary religion;*

■ *the ultimate place of religion in contemporary societies;*

■ *the definition and characteristics of education;*

■ *about the role of education relative to social class, race, and ethnicity;*

■ *the nature of the crisis of American education;*

■ *about the status of higher education.*

After the family, religion probably ranks as the second oldest institution, a universal institution that has been present in all societies we know about. In different cultures, people light candles to have their prayers heard or perform ritual dances. Some kneel in front of a statue or a painting; others touch the floor with their foreheads in the direction of Mecca. Some cover their heads as a sign of respect; others keep their heads uncovered for the same reason. Some chant and sway while worshipping; others sit and kneel occasionally. Some attempt to ensure their continued survival and prosperity by a moral life and good deeds; others by sacrificing the lives of captured enemies (although this is no longer true anywhere) or of animals. As differently as the rituals may be performed, at bottom they are the expression of the same human yearning and need, namely, to determine the source of life, its purpose and meaning, and the ultimate nature of mortality. "The evidence of mortality is all around us, and we are driven to determine if transcendent reality is malicious, benign, or simply neutral" (McCready & Greeley, 1976, 23). **Transcendent reality** is the reality that lies beyond human perception. Thus, one definition of religion is that it is an activity that relates to the "beyond" of human life. In short, religion attempts to transcend the routine of every-day life through the creation of sacredness.

The reason for the emergence of religion is obvious: life everywhere is uncertain, there is much suffering and death, and people do not know how they came to inhabit the earth or what happens to them after death. This uncertainty has stimulated not only curiosity but also attempts to gain an understanding of human circumstances, a desire to know whether human life has a purpose, and the resignation to accept conditions and events that seem un-just. People everywhere have attempted to transcend reality by devising rites and rituals to act as ways of communicating with forces outside everyday experience.

Because of its universality and its durability, religion has been the object of much inter-est on the part of social scientists and other philosophers before them. It is one of the oldest subjects of inquiry. On the other hand, people distrust scientists when they speak out on reli-gion, preferring the interpretation of the sacred offered by theologians and preachers. This is understandable in view of the fact that religion is widely believed to be a matter of divine revelation in which it is only necessary to have faith. However, social scientists do not at-tempt to assess the validity of religion or of any particular religion. They merely study the clear and definite influences of religion on individuals, groups, and societies. It is as a part of culture and, therefore, as a social product, that social scientists analyze religion.

■ The Great Religions of the World

The universality of religion testifies to the human quest for a spiritual facet that seems to be lacking in everyday life. Societies, however, express the need to transcend reality differently. In particular, each society emphasizes the aspects of its culture that it deems important. Reli-gion reflects those important elements. A society that is strongly patriarchal tends to worship male deities; agricultural societies worship gods of fertility, frequently female; warlike soci-eties revere vengeful gods. In addition, in societies of the distant past in which livelihood de-pended on hunting and gathering and primitive agriculture, each family took care of religious worship and rituals, without any intermediaries such as priests. In many societies, each family had its own deities whose purpose was to protect and benefit it. The relationship between deity and worshipper mirrored the relationship of the individual to family or tribe (the deity was seen as the protective father or, in a herding society, as the good shepherd).

A vast variety of religions developed throughout the world. Today, the world's religions may be categorized into (1) monotheistic, (2) polytheistic, (3) ethical, and (4) ancestral. Monotheism, or belief in one god, includes Christianity, Judaism, Islam, and Zoroastrianism. Of these, Christianity has the largest number of adherents, more than 2 billion, or one-third of the world's people. In turn, Christianity is divided into three principal groups, Roman Catholic, Protestant, and Eastern Orthodox, who share a belief in God as the creator of the world and in Jesus Christ as the world's savior. In terms of number of followers, Islam is the second largest religion in the world. The more than 1 billion Muslims accept the teachings of the Prophet Muhammad, who established the religion in the seventh century A.D. The religion stresses the total surrender of the faithful to the will of Allah (God), who is the creator, sus-tainer, and restorer of the world. Judaism, from which Christianity evolved, has almost 15 million followers. Judaism is the oldest monotheistic religion and centers on Yahweh, the Old

Islam is the second largest religion in the world. It has lately grown in prominence because large numbers of Muslims have immigrated to Western societies and want to practice their religion in previously predominantly Christian nations. In addition, a fanatical minority of Muslims wants to wage a holy war against what they call the "infidels" or non-Muslims.

Testament God, who is said to have chosen the people of Israel to testify to His existence. Zoroastrianism is also a pre-Christian religion and is followed by approximately a quarter of a million faithful (but according to other sources by 2.7 million), mainly in India, who worship an all-powerful God engaged temporarily in a continuing battle with evil.

Polytheism, or a belief in many gods, is most prominently represented by Hinduism. Most Hindus—there are approximately 900 million of them—live in India and Pakistan, but also in southern Africa and Indonesia, believe in a hierarchy of gods, from regional deities to those representing caste groupings. An altogether different emphasis is found in the ethical religions, which include Buddhism, Confucianism, Shintoism, and Taoism. Not concerned with a personalized god, these religions revolve around a set of principles that define the order of the universe. Followers who lead an ethical life as prescribed by these principles seek to achieve harmony in both their personal lives and the commonly shared social life. Shintoism also includes the worship of one's ancestors and has a strongly nationalistic aspect, which the Japanese, who are the main adherents of this religion, have tried to minimize since World War II. Together, these religions have more than 1 billion adherents, residing mainly in China (Confucianism, Taoism), India (Buddhism), and Japan (Shintoism) (Figure 13.1 and Tables 13.1 and 13.2).

Although they are practiced by only a scattered few, remnants of what may be called primitive religions still remain. Among these is **animism**, a belief in spirits or animate beings (souls) who exist and are active on people's behalf. These spirits can attach themselves to, or acquire the form of, people, or animals, or inanimate objects (mostly rivers, trees, or mountains). Spirits are not worshipped in the same way as gods are. They must sometimes be appeased through special rituals, influenced to act favorably to human destiny by magic, or called on for help in times of distress. A type of animism called shamanism is common

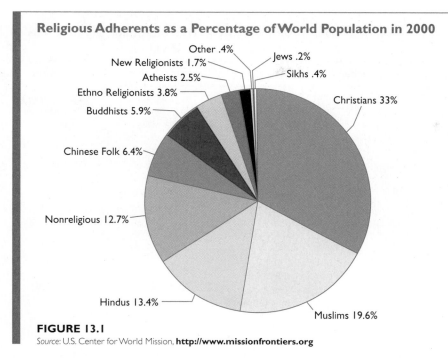

Religious Adherents as a Percentage of World Population in 2000

Other .4%
Jews .2%
New Religionists 1.7%
Sikhs .4%
Atheists 2.5%
Ethno Religionists 3.8%
Christians 33%
Buddhists 5.9%
Chinese Folk 6.4%
Nonreligious 12.7%
Hindus 13.4%
Muslims 19.6%

FIGURE 13.1
Source: U.S. Center for World Mission, **http://www.missionfrontiers.org**

among tribal people in North and South America. Another form of animism, **totemism**, is popular among native peoples of Australia and some Pacific islands. Totemism is the belief that supernatural forces, represented by objects in the immediate environment (such as plants or animals), direct human existence. These objects are worshipped and venerated through established rituals. One example of totemism is found in the Melanesian belief in **mana** as a sacred power that is attributed to people or things and that can be used for good or bad purposes. Echoes of totemism may be found among those of us who have touched a "lucky" charm—such as a rabbit's foot—before an important event.

■ Religion in the Social Sciences

When social scientists first focused their attention on religion, the common opinion was that religion was an attempt by primitive people to explain reality. Eventually, these social scientists maintained, religion would be replaced by science. Other social thinkers sought to explain religion in terms of a universal concern with the idea of soul, which originated among primitive people from a mistaken interpretation of dreams and death. Religion, in short, was viewed as a relic of times when humans lived in a state of ignorance about their world.

Religion as Social Integration

An alternative view of religion saw it as dealing with the sacred as opposed to the profane (Durkheim [1912], 1947, 209). The **sacred** is separate from everyday experience; it is the unusual, unexplainable, mysterious, and powerful facet of life, and it, therefore, deserves

TABLE 13.1 Religions of the World; Number of Adherents; Basic Information on Various Religions from http://www.religioustolerance.org/worldrel.htm

Religion	Date Founded	Sacred Texts	Membership	% of World
Christianity	30 CE	The Bible	2,039 million	32% (dropping)
Islam	622 CE	Qur'an & Hadith	1,226 million	19% (growing)
Hinduism	1,500 BCE with truly ancient roots	Bhagavad-Gita, Upanishads, & Rig Veda	828 million	13% (stable)
No religion (Note 1)	–	None	775 million	12% (dropping)
Chinese folk rel.	270 BCE	None	390 million	6%
Buddhism	523 BCE	The Tripitaka & Sutras	364 million	6% (stable)
Tribal Religions, Shamanism, Animism	Prehistory	Oral tradition	232 million	4%
Atheists	No date	None	150 million	2%
New religions	Various	Various	103 million	2%
Sikhism	1500 CE	Guru Granth Sahib	23.8 million	<1%
Judaism	(Note 3)	Torah, Tanach, & Talmud	14.5 million	<1%
Spiritism			12.6 million	<1%
Baha'i Faith	1863 CE	Alkitab Alaqdas	7.4 million	<1%
Confucianism	520 BCE	Lun Yu	6.3 million	<1%
Jainism	570 BCE	Siddhanta, Pakrit	4.3 million	<1%
Zoroastrianism	600 to 6000 BCE	Avesta	2.7 million	<1%
Shinto	500 CE	Kojiki, Nohon Shoki	2.7 million	<1%
Taoism	550 BCE	Tao-te-Ching	2.7 million	<1%
Other	Various	Various	1.1 million	<1%
Wicca (Note 2)	800 BCE, 1940 CE	None	0.5 million?	<1%

Notes:

■ **Note 1:** Persons with no formal, organized religion include agnostics, freethinkers, humanists, secularists, etc.

■ **Note 2:** We have included Wicca even though their numbers are small because such a large percentage of our site's visitors are of that faith. There is no reliable measure of their numbers. Some Wiccans believe that their faith can be traced back to the origins of the Celtic people; others suggest it is a recently created religion.

■ **Note 3:** There is no consensus on the data of founding of Judaism. Some claim that Adam and Eve were the first Jews, and lived circa 4000 BCE; others suggest that they never existed. Some would place the date at the time of Abraham, circa 1900 BCE; others consider Abraham to be a mythical character. Some date it to the Exodus from Egypt circa 1490 BCE; others say that no Exodus happened, and the ancient Hebrews were originally a group that gradually separated from the main body of Canaanites and developed a different culture.

reverence and respect. The **profane,** on the other hand, includes the objects and events of everyday life that are usual, explainable, and repetitive. Primitive people were aware of a force greater than themselves, a force that had to be obeyed and on which they depended for survival—but they did not know what that force was or where it came from. Therefore, they invented the concept of deities (gods), who have supernatural power and control over

TABLE 13.2   Names of the Places of Worship and English Titles by Which Local Leaders Are Called

Religion	Place of Worship	Title of Local Leader
Christianity	Church, Cathedral, Temple, Mission	Pastor, priest, minister
Islam	Mosque	Imam
No religion	None	None
Hinduism	Mandir, Mandira, Temple, and other names	Priest
Buddhism	Pagoda, Stupa, Temple	Monk
Atheists	None	None
New Asian religion	Various	Various
Tribal Religions, Animism	In nature	Shaman
Judaism	Synagogue	Rabbi
Sikhism	Gurdwaras	Granthi (professional reader)
Shamanists	In nature	Shaman
Confucianism	Temple, Shrine, Seowon	Unknown
Baha'i Faith	House of worship	Usually a lay leader
Jainism	Temple	Priest, Pandit
Shinto	Temple	Priest
Wicca	Circle, Grove	Priestess, Priest, Wiccan
Zoroastrianism	Atash Behram, Agiyari, Prayer rooms	Mobed, Dastur

Source: **http://www.religioustolerance.org/worldrel.htm**

humans. And they also invented rituals that they hoped would appease these deities and make them well-disposed toward humans. Thus, in this view, religious beliefs and practices deal with a very real object—human society. Again in this view, religion is an expression of human solidarity, the recognition that the individual is aware of the social system and the web of relationships occurring within it and, finally, the individual's dependence on it despite its sometimes dictatorial nature. The theory also speculates that religious concepts, and particularly religious rituals, evolved in a situation of collective behavior, and finally, that a clan's god, or totem, represented the clan itself. Thus, in worshipping the totem, the members of the clan recognized that the power of the clan was superior to their power as individuals. The laws of the totem then became the most important laws of the clan. In this manner, religion became the cement that held together different elements of a society by establishing an order for doing things and ultimate reasons for doing them. This function of religion is called the **function of social integration**, in that religion unites distinct individuals into a unified moral community.

A Functionalist View of Religion

The above insights provided a framework for contemporary social scientists who conjecture that religion has existed in all societies because of the important functions it performs for individuals. In the functionalist interpretation, the individual in society has two fundamental needs. One is the need to adapt, master, and control the physical environment to survive. The other is the need to express one's feelings, to respond to objects and to the feelings of others, and finally, to enter into relationships with others. This last need, called the **expressive** need, has been found to be of crucial importance to humans. Religion has the capacity of fulfilling these important needs. It does so because it transcends the common

Every religion develops rituals that are methods of dealing with the sacred. In the Jewish religion, when a boy or girl reaches the age of 13 they undergo a bar or bat mitzvah, a rite of passage that indicates that they have reached manhood or womanhood.

experience of human beings in their natural environment, and the need to transcend everyday experience exists and makes itself felt because of certain characteristics of the human condition, such as **contingency, powerlessness,** and **scarcity** (O'Dea, 1966). In the functionalist view, religion acts as a mechanism that helps people adjust to these frustrating but inevitable facts of existence by reaching beyond ordinary experience and establishing a link with the sacred through the ritual of worship.

In addition to the function of social integration discussed above, religion performs the following functions:

1. It helps individuals ease doubts about security and identity. This function is particularly important in times of rapid social change, in which problems of identity are common.
2. It clarifies the physical world, making it understandable, familiar, and meaningful. In teaching beliefs and values, it offers individuals a point of reference to the society's normative system: it reinforces what is considered good and what is considered evil in the society.
3. It supports societal norms and values by transforming them into divine laws. Because socialization is never perfect, deviance from societal norms is frequent. But whereas people may break societal rules, if they are believers they break divine rules less easily. In this sense, religion reinforces the society's system of social control.
4. It helps individuals face life at critical stages—entering adulthood, marriage, the birth of children, and so on. Religion helps people accept the new roles forced on them through **rites of passage,** or the rituals that have been established around certain critical times: birth, puberty, marriage, and death. These rites (funerals, weddings, communion, confirmation, bar and bat mitzvah, etc.) help to dissolve some of the tensions surrounding the approach to a new stage of life.

5. It helps people deal with guilt for their transgressions, offering a way back to a constructive life. Religion, by virtue of the special feeling of power that members of a religious group derive from their relationship with a superior being, has the capacity to relieve people's guilt, enabling them to start over again on a new course.

A Conflict View of Religion

The news media have been full, in recent years, of conflicts between Protestants and Catholics in Northern Ireland, Muslims and Jews in Israel, Muslims and Hindus or Christians in India, Pakistan and other Asian and African nations, and Muslims and Orthodox Christians in the Balkans. In addition, the so-called Jihadists, or fundamentalist Muslims, seem intent on committing terrorist acts against the West and its religions. These conflicts keep many nations from achieving peace and many young people from achieving adulthood. Conflict theorists, among whom the most noted was Karl Marx, have explained this negative aspect of religion.

Marx perceived religion to be an ideology that merely masked the real interests of the ruling classes and served as a tool to keep the lower classes oppressed (Marx & Engles, 1964). Marx arrived at this conclusion from the ideas of theologian Ludwig Feuerbach. Feuerbach speculated that God was a figment of human imagination and creativity. People invested this creation with all the noblest and most excellent traits so that it might serve as an ideal to which they could aspire. However, eventually people forgot that they had created God and began to stand in awe of Him, worshipping Him to ensure His good will. Living in fear of something they themselves created, Marx insisted, was a profoundly alienating experience. He meant that people felt "alien" or strange in a world they perceive as hostile because they have lost control over it. Religion, in Marx's view, became alienating both on a personal and on a social level. It not only creates conflicts between the clergy and the lay population, and between people of different religions, it also is used by the economically and politically dominant classes to justify the existence of injustice and inequality. It maintains the status quo because it represses the anger of the exploited lower classes and offers future rewards in an afterlife. That is why religion, in Marx's view, is the "opiate" of the people: it makes them passive and satisfied with their miserable lot on earth by promises of immortality after death, instead of a rightful share in the present life.

Marx was right on some points regarding religion. If religion supports the norms and values of society, then it also supports the status quo. It is, therefore, a conservative force opposed to change. There is no shortage of examples of conflict caused by religious differences. However, religion also brings about positive social change, which Marx failed to recognize. There are numerous examples of how the sacrifice of some of the faithful improves the lot of the oppressed. One example in the fairly recent past was that of **liberation theology**, which developed out of the idealism prevalent in the 1960s. This was a fusion of Christian principles and political activism of a Marxist nature, which the Catholic Church had adopted in Latin America. (Although its adherents maintain that the tragic suffering of the world's poor is antithetical to Christian morality, Pope John Paul II had condemned liberation theology, claiming that political activism detracts from the otherworldly concerns of Christianity and that political controversy is detrimental to Catholicism.) As for the United States, there is no doubt that religious values have played an important part in abolishing slavery and in the passage of civil rights legislation. In short, while religion tends to be a reflection of the class system of a society, and a conservative force in it, it can also be the impetus for radical social change.

■ Religion and Social Control

Social scientists have noted other functions of religion. For instance, Max Weber pointed out that the religious worldview often becomes the secular principle on which social orders are based. The democratic principle that all people are created equal is a reflection of the religious belief that all people are God's creatures. In *The Protestant Ethic and the Spirit of Capitalism*, Weber (1904 [1958]) refuted Marx's theory of economic determinism by speculating that sometimes religious ideas caused social change. Using a comparative methodology, Weber concluded that the reason for the emergence of Western capitalism seemed to have been the Protestant Reformation, with its new values of hard work, discipline, and industriousness that acted as avenues to worldly prosperity. These values came to be known as the **Protestant work ethic,** an attitude that maintains a strong hold on our thinking even today. According to this ethic, the drive to accumulate wealth was based on a genuine religious impulse, not on greed. Eventually, these originally religious ideas influenced all of people's activities, including the economic ones. Weber added that these same religious ideas affected social control as well. Protestant ideology, by justifying the power that the wealthy exercised in society, aided and abetted the system of stratification, which of course is based on inequality. Even before the rise of Protestantism, ruling dynasties described themselves as being of divine origin and monarchies alleged that they reigned by virtue of divine right.

Weber's work is significant in its implications that a worldview, created by religion according to the attitudes of each culture, has far-reaching social consequences. Thus Protestantism, and especially Calvinism, defined reality in such a way that it unintentionally stimulated and radically altered existing economic structures. Not only are religious ideas sometimes responsible for social change, then, but they are powerful features of social control.

The Institutional Context

Many religions originate in the personal experiences of a charismatic leader who claims to be the spokesperson of the deity. The death of even the most charismatic of leaders, however, makes it necessary to institutionalize the religious experiences of the early participants. Such institutionalization involves turning a relatively spontaneous and subjective experience into patterns and behavior that all can routinely follow. Some of the patterns of the institutionalizing process include: cult activities, behavior involving worship or ritual; a pattern of ideas collectively called beliefs; and the social organization or social structure of a religious group (O'Dea & O'Dea Aviad, 1983).

Common Features of Religions

Once they are institutionalized, all religions consist of beliefs, rituals, and organization.

Beliefs.   Religious belief systems include myths and theology. **Myths** are narratives that recount how certain events have been invested with the quality of sacredness. They are stories—often in the form of parables—that communicate in plain but emotionally charged terms a basic idea about either activities or moral prescriptions of the divine being. The power of a myth lies in its ability to bind believers into a community of faithful. For example, the stories told about the first Christmas—the birth of Christ in the barn of the inn at Bethlehem, the three Kings who come to worship guided by a star and the gifts they bring, the humble shepherds who stop in and shyly salute the newborn—have as a goal the unifying of the Christian community at Christmas time.

Theology is the rational system of ideas that explains a belief system. It usually develops when a priestly class comes to be differentiated from the lay members of a religious group and is often spelled out in doctrines or articles of faith. Jewish and Christian beliefs are contained in the Bible, Muslim beliefs in the Koran. The function of these holy books is to explain and justify the sacred and the need for the particular ritual in a form easily understood by people.

Rituals.   Ritual is a very important practice because it represents the correct form of behavior of people toward the sacred. It is a mechanism for maintaining sacredness. Any kind of behavior may become ritualized: dancing, gathering in a specific spot, drinking from a special container, or eating particular foods. At a Jewish Passover Seder, symbolic foods are served accompanied by the reading of the historic events—the escape from slavery in Egypt. This annual commemoration has the function of uniting the Jewish people into a community with a common past. The Christian Mass is a similar representation of the original experience and a way for the worshippers to express their relationship to the sacred (O'Dea & O'Dea Aviad, 1983, 42). Because ritual represents the correct form of behavior toward the sacred, it eases some of the dread connected with it.

Ritual practices have been incredibly rich and imaginative. They have ranged from the offering of human sacrifices to the consumption of peyote, a hallucinogen; to forms of physical activity like dancing, to fasting and the mortification of the flesh by pain or the denial of sleep. All these methods are designed to achieve a spiritual state in which one is thought to be more receptive to the sacred. Sociologists who have analyzed ritual think that it helps people attain the feeling of self-transcendence (of being beyond and outside oneself). Such an emotion is part of the revivalist ritual associated with the fundamentalist sects of Christianity. In modern times, the role of beliefs is more important than that of ritual, which is perhaps why so many young people are attracted to more colorful religious expressions.

The most common form of religious behavior, found in almost every religion, is prayer. However, the notions of mana and taboo are also part of religious ritual behavior. **Mana** is a reference to the power that adherents of a religion believe inheres in an object, power that is transmitted to any individual who touches the object. Many Christians believe they will be cured if they visit shrines commemorating some miraculous act; and to many Jews, touching the Western Wall, the only remaining wall of the Temple in Jerusalem destroyed 2,000 years ago, is also of great significance. The opposite of mana is a **taboo**, or a prohibition against having physical contact with certain objects. In some religions a strong taboo concerns contact between persons of different status; in others, the taboo involves mainly foods. The Mormons forbid the use of tobacco, alcohol, and beverages containing caffeine, while the laws of Kashrut forbid Jews the consumption of pork and shellfish, as well as the combination of dairy and meat dishes at the same meal.

Finally, ritual also includes the use of symbols meant not only to identify the particular religion but also to represent the sacred. Christians use the symbol of the cross, Jews the star of David, and so on. The use of symbols is popular even in the secular world, where flags have a similar role.

Religious Organization.   Western societies are particularly rich in the diversity of their religious groups. For example, even though Christianity is the predominant faith of the West, it contains a large number of various religious expressions. Moreover, although religion is an enduring institution, it is also dynamic in nature. It has undergone numerous changes of an organizational character. Christianity began as a splinter group of Judaism; Protestants similarly broke away from Catholicism; and Baptists, Presbyterians, Methodists, Lutherans, and many others offer varying interpretations of Protestantism. Religious organization follows the classification into church, sect, and cult.

Church. A church is a religious organization that is thoroughly institutionalized, well accepted, and well integrated into the social order of society. The Roman Catholic church; such Protestant churches as the United Methodist, the National and the Southern Baptist; the Church of Jesus Christ of Latter-Day Saints; the Greek Orthodox church; and the Jewish congregations are all churches in the United States (*church* here does not refer to a house of worship, only to a method of organization). Churches are differentiated into the **ecclesia** and the **denomination**. The ecclesia is an official state religion to which most citizens of a society belong. Sometimes the ecclesia has a monopoly on religious belief. In such cases, it is called a **universal church**. In most Arab countries Islam is the universal church. The Catholic Church of medieval Europe was also a universal church. The denomination, on the other hand, is not officially linked to any state or national government. In the United States, for instance, the separation of church and state is an important constitutional principle. In many modern societies, there may be an ecclesia but not a universal church: the Anglican Church in England and the Catholic Church in most of Latin America are examples of contemporary ecclesiae in Western societies. In these societies, the beliefs and values of the secular, or worldly social system, and those of the religious system are closely related. The ecclesia has great influence in nonreligious areas of life and vice versa.

As noted, the United States has no ecclesia; instead, a large variety of denominations coexists. Denominations, more simply called churches, are especially characteristic of pluralistic societies with a longer history of industrialization. They coexist more harmoniously when there is separation of church and state; they are tolerant of other religious organizations; and membership in them is mostly hereditary, although they accept converts. They do not make great demands on their members for religious commitment, being content with occasional church attendance and financial support.

Sect. A sect is usually a breakaway movement, denoting rebellion against the conservatism of the established church. At first, it consists of a small group of people who come together voluntarily (as opposed to what happens in a church, into which most people are born). Successful sects in turn become denominations of the established church.

Sects generally reject an official priesthood, preferring to divide religious responsibilities among the lay members. Often, a charismatic leader makes up for lack of professional training with emotional commitment. Commitment and participation by members are high, and valued. Sects emphasize religious emotions and expression to a far greater degree than do denominations. They are also less concerned with the formal and traditional aspects of religion. Church and sect are frequently in conflict. The sect stresses the need for the purity of religious thought and uncompromising faithfulness to the spirit of religion. The church emphasizes the necessity of maintaining a stable institution and faithfulness to the letter of religion.

As noted, in time some sects gain a large enough membership to become institutionalized. Because this has occurred on many occasions, sociologists regard sects as denominations in the making. Most sectarian organizations last for one generation only or become transformed by the second or third generation. The Anabaptists, Huguenots, Mennonites, Presbyterians, and Baptists, among others, were once sects, but all have become denominations since the Reformation. Today, Jehovah's Witnesses, the Assembly of God, and the various Pentecostal groups are examples of Christian sects, while Hasidic Jews exemplify a sect of Judaism.

Cult. Finally, **cults** are the least conventional and the least institutionalized forms of religious organizations. They are temporary and tend to revolve around the figure of a charismatic leader. Cults share with sects the fact that they tend to reject the status quo, and that they are small, voluntary, and exclusive religious groups attempting to establish a new religious system. But while sects break away from an existing religious organization, cults attempt to found a new religious tradition that has no ties to an existing religious group. Cults are usually temporary groups of followers clustered around a leader whose teachings differ substantially from the doctrines of either any ecclesia or denomination. They may consist of religious innovations—when leaders maintain to have received new revelations or insights—or be based on ideas imported from other societies.

Again, cults that persist often develop into sects and even churches. The Unification Church and Christian Science are illustrations of cults that have become sects or churches (McGuire, 1987). The early Christians were Jews who began a cult that considered Jesus of Nazareth the Messiah the Jews were expecting. Cults have a strong appeal to the alienated of a society. They had a particularly large flowering in the decades of the 1960s and 1970s, an era of political and social unrest when a rash of new cults attracted large numbers of young adults.

■ Religion in America

Religion in the United States has characteristics that distinguish it from religion in many other societies. For one thing, the United States has never had a state religion to which citizens were expected to belong. On the contrary, the idea of the separation of church and state has been firmly ingrained in the society. Most of the early settlers were themselves religious dissenters, who then attempted to maintain religious homogeneity in the new society. These attempts did not succeed for long. The denominational pluralism of American religion is one of its characteristics.

Moreover, the coexistence of many denominations makes it necessary for religious organizations to compete for attention and to attract as many faithful as possible. Religion, therefore, has had to borrow many practices from the economic marketplace. In the United States, religion is practiced in the context of voluntary organizations and often appears to be rather secular, or worldly, rather than spiritual. Church buildings are used for recreational purposes, to play cards and bingo, and to discuss problems of politics and sex. American religion, then, is relatively secular, highly bureaucratized, specialized, and efficient. Moreover, it is characterized by more optimism and less emphasis on self-sacrifice and punishment than in many other societies. As a society we are more likely to choose a religion that promises peace of mind and the freedom to enjoy the fruits of our labor than one that promises eternal damnation and the need to repress our desire for pleasure.

Finally, this institution may be described as both stable and changing. That is, new religions are constantly appearing, participants and members of various religious organization change, and even religious ideas differ from one generation to the next. Yet the basic patterns of commitment and participation remain much as they were in the past, and the three most prominent religious groups continue to be the Protestants, Catholics, and Jews, although, mainly as a result of increases in immigration, Islam is rapidly catching up.

Religiosity in America

Religiosity refers to a person's depth of feeling regarding issues pertaining to belief in God, life after death, heaven and hell, and how religious beliefs translate into behavior. From the

The rise of fundamentalist sects whose preachers often become television and radio celebrities has also brought into existence the so-called megachurches that attract hundreds and thousands of worshippers for services.

point of view of religiosity, the United States is among the most religious countries in the Christian world (Lipset 1963, 150). Newer research also indicates that Americans are the most religious people in the world and certainly among the industrial nations. A 44-nation survey indicated that in 2002, 59 percent of Americans said that religion played a very important role in their lives, as opposed to about 33 percent in Great Britain, 30 percent in Canada, 11 percent in France, and about 27 percent in Italy (Pew Global Attitudes Project, 2002). Views on religion seemed to correlate with annual per capita income: the wealthier the nation, the less importance it places on religion—with the exception of the United States.

The vast majority (some 85 to 90 percent) of Americans say they believe in God, and 66 percent are convinced of this belief without reservations (Baylor Institute for Studies of Religion, 2006; Harris Interactive Poll, 2003) High percentages express a belief in an afterlife, specifically in heaven (54 percent) and hell (31 percent) (Barna Research Group, 2004). Other surveys on religion confirm some myths and shatter others. Religiosity, defined as a belief in God, is higher in the Midwest and South than in the East and West of the United States. Women and African Americans are more likely to believe in God than are men, Hispanics, and whites. Persons with no college education are more likely to believe in God than those with postgraduate degrees: 82 percent versus 73 percent. Older persons express a belief in God in higher numbers than younger people: 83 percent of those 65 and over versus 71 percent of those aged 25 to 29. Finally, more Republicans than Democrats believe in God: 87 percent versus 78 percent (only 75 percent of Independents say they believe in God) (Harris Interactive Poll, 2003).

When church affiliation is analyzed, new research indicates an increase in the percentage of the population that reports no religious affiliation. For instance, in 1988 it was reported that 8 percent of the population subscribed to no religion. This percentage had risen to 14.3 percent in 2004. A more precise way of asking respondents about their religious affiliation, however, shows a current percentage of 10.8, or one in ten Americans. In spite of being unaffiliated and almost never attending church, 44.5 percent believe in a higher power, and 11.6 percent have no doubt in the existence of God, 31.6 percent pray at least occasionally, and 10.1 percent pray daily.

Among those affiliated with organized religion, 33.6 percent are evangelical Protestants, 22.1 percent are mainline Protestants, 21.2 percent are Catholics, 5.0 percent are African American Protestants, 2.5 percent are Jews, and 4.9 percent are affiliated with other denominations (Figure 13.2). According to these figures, less than 5 percent of the United States population claim a faith outside of the Judeo-Christian mainstream, and the highest and most consistent levels of belief and practice are found within black Protestant and evangelical Protestant religious groups.

Church attendance had declined during the post–World War II period, especially among Roman Catholics during a period when they disagreed about matters of birth control. According to the General Social Survey, 24.2 percent of people attend church every week or nearly every week, 21.2 percent attend once a year or less, 13.2 percent attend several times a year, and 8.6 attend several times a week (GSS, 2004). Women attend more frequently than men, Protestants are more likely than Catholics to attend church once a month or more, and

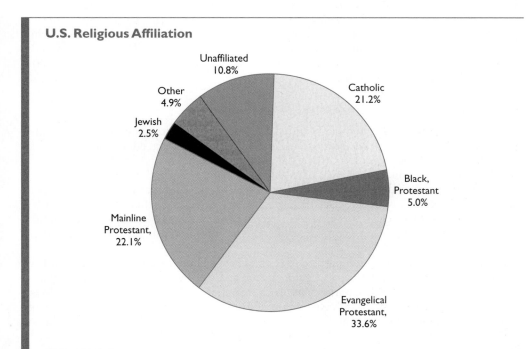

U.S. Religious Affiliation

Unaffiliated 10.8%

Other 4.9%

Jewish 2.5%

Catholic 21.2%

Black, Protestant 5.0%

Mainline Protestant, 22.1%

Evangelical Protestant, 33.6%

FIGURE 13.2

■ Barely one in ten Americans (10.8%) is NOT affiliated with a congregation, denomination, or other religious group.

■ Fewer than five percent of the U.S. population claim a faith outside of the Judeo-Christian mainstream.

■ Fully a third of Americans (33.6%), roughly 100 million people, are Evangelical Protestant by affiliation.

Source: Baylor Institute for Studies of Religion 2006. *American Piety in the 21st Century*. Baylor University, Waco, TX.

TABLE 13.3 Religious Service Attendance	
Never	16.8%
Once a year or less	21.2%
Several times a year	13.2%
Once a month	6.8%
2–3 times a month	9.1%
Every week or nearly every week	24.2%
Several times a week	8.6%

Source: National Opinion Research Center, 2004. General Social Survey, 2004.

Jews have the lowest attendance—16 percent attend a synagogue once a month or more often (Harris Interactive Poll, 2003) (Table 13.3).

According to the Pew Forum on Religion and World Affairs, the impact of religion has increased around the world, a fact that has policy and security implications for the United States. Religions appear to exert considerable influence on transitions toward democracy, and religious political parties and movements have been achieving popular support in a number of nations. At the same time, grievances based on religion have been factors in civil wars, conflicts among states, and international terrorism. Demographic changes are also apparent in religions: the global south is experiencing a rapid growth of Christianity, while Western nations are undergoing increased immigration of Muslims. These factors will be important in shaping public attitudes and government policies (Pew Forum Resources, 2006; **http://pewforum.org/world-affairs**).

Religious Affiliation and Social Correlates

Religion has an impact on a number of social factors. A person's religion may be correlated with social class, political views, professional and economic standing, education levels, social mobility, and attitudes toward controversial social issues such as gay marriage, abortion, school prayer, and so on. The relationships should not be understood as being ones of cause and effect; of course, individuals in a variety of social classes embrace a variety of religious expressions. Nonetheless, social class membership has influenced religion and religion has had an impact on social class. For instance, degrees of religiosity, as well as some denominations, are related to either conservatism or liberalism, and both in turn to political attitudes and affiliation.

Measured in terms of church participation rather than church membership, those at both extremes of the stratification system (the upper class and the lower class) engage in very little church activity. The most active participants in church affairs are chiefly from the upper-lower and the lower-middle social classes. Among these strata, church activism and doctrinal belief are the most intense. The upper-middle class shows a high degree of participation, but it is a participation motivated more by the desire for social recognition, or for "doing the right thing," than by moral conviction (Glock & Stark 1965, 20–21).

The relationship between religion and stratification can be seen most clearly in the religious affiliation of different social classes. Higher-status individuals—status being measured by income, occupation, and education—are Episcopalians, Presbyterians, and Jews. Somewhat lower in rank are the remaining Protestant denominations, such as

Congregationalists, Methodists, and Lutherans. Working-class Protestants are more apt to gravitate to the colorful rituals of radical sects. In fact, the two largest Protestant groups, the Baptists and the Methodists, grew dramatically in the nineteenth century precisely because they were the churches of the disinherited: they required neither an ordained, educated clergy, nor an intellectual theology, nor did they stress ritual. Thus, they tended to appeal to the largely uneducated immigrants and natives on the Western frontier and in the cities and rural areas of the East. Immigration from Germany and Scandinavia further enriched Protestantism by adding different strains of Lutheranism. Today, however, the mainline Protestant churches are losing ground to evangelical churches. Catholics have maintained their numbers mainly as a result of immigration from Latin American nations. Meanwhile, the Southern Baptists, the Mormons, the Jehovah's Witnesses, the Assemblies of God, and the Churches of God in Christ have increased membership, some by substantial percentages (Shorto, 1997, 60).

In the past, both Republicans and Democrats shared almost equally many religious attitudes, such as belief in God, the importance of prayer, and so on. Within the last 15 years, however, religious commitment has increased among Republicans, but not among Democrats. White Evangelical Protestants, who were once evenly divided between Republicans and Democrats, are today two-to-one in the conservative, Republican camp. Catholics, on the other hand, having been once strongly liberal and Democratic, are today much more politically divided (Pew Research Center, 2004; Baylor, 2006).

Religion, Race, and Ethnicity

On a global level, religion is associated with ethnicity. Thus, Islam predominates throughout the Arab cultures of the Middle East, Hinduism is identified with India, and Confucianism is linked to the culture of China. Christianity and Judaism, however, are spread throughout a disparate variety of nations and cultures.

In the United States, of course, each ethnic group brought its own religion; there is a fusion of nationality and religion. Religion has played a particularly important role for African Americans, most of whom became Christians when they were brought to the Western Hemisphere. As a result of their experiences during slavery, African Americans developed a ritual richer in emotion and spontaneity than their white counterparts. The black sociologist Franklin Frazier noted that religion played an important role in the social organization of blacks ever since their arrival (Frazier, 1966). Following the period of slavery, blacks formed their own churches, out of which other forms of black organization emerged: economic cooperation in the black community and the establishment of educational institutions. The black church also became the center of black political life.

With the massive urbanization of African Americans, the black church became more secular, addressing crucial problems of the here and now: dislocation, prejudice, and poverty. As African Americans have become more fully integrated into the mainstream of society, a portion of the middle-class African Americans has joined Episcopalian, Presbyterian, and Congregational churches, many located in suburban areas and racially integrated. Thus, the black church has ceased being the central institution it once was for African Americans with results that many think have been detrimental to the black community, particularly its young males. Still, many African American leaders have come up through the ranks of the black church, and today a similar role is played by the black Muslims and other Islamic sects.

Another aspect of the relationship between religion and ethnicity is the unpleasant one of prejudice (discussed in Chapter 8). Religion plays a divisive and conflict-producing role in the interaction of diverse groups. In the latter part of the nineteenth century, when immigration was largely from predominantly Catholic nations, prejudice was virulent against the Irish, the Poles, and the Italians. They were accused of loyalty to the Pope rather than to the United States, and it was not until the 1960s that a Catholic president was elected. Anti-Semitism has been a millennial expression of bigotry against the Jewish people, originating with the early Christians and often used for political, economic, and other selfish reasons. It uses stereotypes and conspiracy theories to scapegoat a group that has been a minority in most societies. Thus, some people believe that all Jews are wealthy, that they control the media and the higher-paying professions, as well as banking and corporate affairs; in reality, these segments of the economy are generally in the hands of white, Anglo-Saxon Protestants. In recent years, there has been a revival of anti-Semitism in Europe, and in the United States, as some blame the presence of Israel in the Middle East and its actions against the Palestinians for the chaos and instability of that region and the terrorism it has unleashed.

Terrorism, especially that experienced by the United States in September, 2001, has also provoked a backlash against Muslims in the United States. In addition to individuals committing a variety of acts of violence against them, even the government has made life difficult for some Muslims, denying them entry for purposes of study, subjecting them to intensive interrogation and searches, and even detaining some for lengthy periods without access to the judicial process.

The Sanctification of the American Way of Life

Have the functions of religion diminished in contemporary societies? Statistics seem to indicate that, at least in the United States, they have not. As noted above, although church attendance has dropped somewhat in the past 20 years, it is still among the highest in the industrial world; a vast majority of Americans profess some religious faith and belief in God, or at least in some universal force or spirit. On the surface, then, Americans seem to be a very religious people. In the classic work, *Protestant, Catholic, Jew* (1960), sociologist Will Herberg noted that although Americans were increasing their membership in churches and synagogues, they were less committed to their religious beliefs and ethics than they were to the idea of belonging to specific religious communities. In other words, establishing places for themselves in society as members of a particular church was the important factor to Americans. Because they were using religion for social purposes, religious beliefs themselves came to have less meaning. In fact, Americans have tended to adopt the secular principles of democracy, the so-called American way of life, as a kind of religion.

Sociologist Robert Bellah has expanded this view of the American use of religion by suggesting that what really exists in the United States is a "civil religion" that sanctifies the American political system, past and present leaders, and the American mission in the world, as well as the ultimate place the nation will assume in history (Bellah, 1970). With such statements as "One Nation under God," and "In God We Trust," religious legitimacy is being lent to ideals of democracy. But the traditional churches do not see civil religion as a threat because it makes no claims as to its doctrinal merits, nor does it attempt to become organized. Civil religion is the kind of religion that is all things to all people. Bellah maintains that the emergence of civil religion is one more indication of the positive function of religion as an integrating element of society. Without it, societies lose direction and may become prey to social disintegration.

Box 13.1 Science and Religion

In Western societies, science and religion have often been at loggerheads. Both science and religion are concerned with some of the same questions: Who are we? Who put us here? Are we alone in the universe? Why are we here? What is the purpose of life? The answers were first offered by religions, and were based on prescientific observations, which were accepted on faith. Nature and the universe, in the ancient world, were seen as the creatures of a divine power. Nonetheless, as time went on, people continued to engage in careful observations of the heavens and increasingly sophisticated mathematical calculations. These activities yielded dramatic results. By 1400 B.C., Chinese scholars had established a solar year consisting of 365 days. Indian scholars formulated the decimal system. Geometry, astronomy, and a classification of all living organisms were contributions of ancient Greece. None of these discoveries hampered religious thought.

The advent of Christianity and its acceptance of the Biblical explanation of creation, however, put some scholars on a collision course with the church. They reasoned that if the universe was created by a rational God out of nothing, the results had to be only one of an infinite number of possibilities. Therefore, the laws that governed this universe could be discovered only through empirical experimentation. The results of such experimentation conflicted with religion. First Copernicus, a Polish astronomer, then Galileo, an Italian one (who was able to use one of the first telescopes) proved that the earth and other planets circled the sun. This discovery ran counter to the neat Aristotelian position, embraced by Christianity, that the earth was the center of the universe, with nature serving humans and humans serving God. Consequently, Copernicus was denounced by Martin Luther and Galileo was tried and condemned to house arrest by the Inquisition. Many others were treated even more severely—burned at the stake, for instance, for daring to contradict biblical teachings.

During the period known as the "Enlightenment" in the eighteenth century, science took giant steps forward, forcing a further estrangement between religion and science. It became clear at this point that most living things had undergone profound changes in their attempt to fit into given environments—they had evolved. Evolution contradicts the teachings of the church, according to which God created all living things at one time, and they have remained immutable. When Darwin published *On the Origin of Species*, he was derided and strongly attacked. In this work, he posited that species evolved and changed as a result of variations in offspring that were either eliminated or maintained in the struggle for survival. His theories were distorted by his enemies, and he was vilified as the mentor of the idea that humans derived from apes.

The conflict continued into the twentieth century, as scientists became able to date rocks and fossils and found them to be millions of years old, rather than the thousands of years proclaimed by the Bible. As late as 1925, a Tennessee school teacher, John Scopes, was indicted, put on trial, and convicted for teaching evolutionary theory. A number of school districts continue to demand, even today, that "creationism," that is, a Biblical interpretation of creation, be included together with the teaching of evolution. This, in spite of the fact that Pope John Paul II apologized, in 1992, for the Roman Catholic Church's condemnation of Galileo and endorsed evolution as part of God's master plan.

Will science and religion continue forever their uneasy coexistence? From one point of view, they must. Science, in fact, is based on perpetual skepticism and doubt; religion is based on unshakable faith. Hypothesis and experimentation yield tentative truths, always subject to revisions; faith yields convictions, whose truths cannot be proved by either experimentation or calculation.

■ Contemporary Trends

Social scientists have generally assumed that the dominant trend in contemporary religions is toward **secularization**. By secularization is meant a trend away from the stress on the supernatural, spiritual, traditional version of a faith and toward a more worldly, practical, rational version of it. The implication is also that religion ceases to have the influence it had on society and culture, as well as on the individual, as the authority of the religious institution wanes. For instance, education and social welfare were once the province of religious institutions, whereas today they are the responsibility of government. The reason for secularization is, of course, people's greater dependence on science as scientific knowledge has multiplied in the past 200 years. It is a shift away from an understanding of the world in religious terms, that is, based on faith, to an understanding of it on scientific terms, based on empirical evidence.

On the surface, it appears that such secularization would lead to the end of religion. In fact, it is true that the most established denominations are losing members and attendance is declining. However, this trend is not one-dimensional. The religious bodies that have not given in to secularization—that, on the contrary, may have originated as a reaction to secularization—are also thriving.

Sociologists Stark and Bainbridge (1985) point out that the need for the supernatural has not diminished in contemporary societies, despite their rationalistic bases. Not only are many people convinced of the relevance of astrology or Zen, but also most Americans who are raised in a home where religion played a minor role (or was nonexistent) eventually join a denomination. Finally, evangelical and fundamentalist sects and denominations are flourishing. As a result, Stark and Bainbridge conclude that when religious bodies become too secularized, sects break away and attempt to revive the old religious traditions. Secularization, in their opinion, is a self-limiting process prompting religious revival and innovation. Just as, centuries ago, Christianity, Judaism, Islam, and Buddhism originated as cults to counteract the weaknesses in the dominant religions of their day, so today new cults are acquiring power where dominant religions are losing it.

Another sociologist, Peter L. Berger, has admitted to having made an error in his early thinking when he said that modernity necessarily leads to a decline in religion. He now says that, with the exception of a few places such as Western Europe, and a few groups such as humanistically educated intellectuals, most of the world is as religious as ever. However, the fact that contemporary societies are mainly pluralistic (contain a variety of different peoples) affects the way in which people believe. Namely, people now believe with much less certainty, a fact they find disconcerting because it fails to provide answers to some of life's most basic questions. This, Berger says, is what attracts people to religions or cults that do offer some certainties. The liberal denominations are more likely to tolerate the uncertainties deriving from scientific findings and are, therefore, stagnating (Steinfels, 1998, A11).

Secularization may not have diminished the importance of religion in contemporary society, but the failure of the dominant religions to change, and the evidence of deviant behavior on the part of some members of the clergy, are proving problematic. For instance, in recent years, a number of Catholic priests have been accused of pedophilia. Not only were these priests abusers and sexual predators of children and teenagers, but their actions were, in many instances, overlooked by the church hierarchy, and they were shuffled from parish to parish rather than being defrocked and criminally prosecuted. This scandal has aroused many American Catholics, who add other complaints to the main complaint that the church hierarchy is not aware of, or responsive to, the concerns of the majority of Catholics. They cite such matters as the church's attitude toward birth control, divorce, celibacy, and the ordination of women—or at least their lack of relevance—as matters that need to be discussed. So far, the church hierarchy has failed to address them.

Finally, a number of religious groups have appeared in the United States in the past two decades that are outside the Judeo-Christian tradition altogether. Groups based on Eastern religions such as Islam, Buddhism, and Hinduism have attracted large numbers of devotees. Some 4 percent of the population identified with a faith other than Protestantism, Catholicism, or Judaism. Islam is catching up to Judaism as the largest American non-Christian religious group (between 1.3 and 2 percent of the population or around 6 million is Jewish and 0.5 percent or 1.1 million is Muslim) (Kosmin et al., 2001). Many Muslims in the United States are not American citizens, but their numbers have been augmented by the influx of African Americans, who represent 25 percent of Muslims in this country. The fastest-growing Eastern religion is Buddhism, which has attracted a number of celebrities. These groups stress personal religious experience and commitment and de-emphasize rational, bureaucratic religious organization. Some of the reasons for the flourishing of such groups include the fact that a complex and diversified society spawns complex and diversified belief systems; that these groups represent a search for meaning, or identity; that they are a reaction against the materialism and militancy of the society; or that they attempt to inject some concreteness into what is perceived as a climate of moral ambiguity.

Fundamentalism and Politics

The trend running counter to a secular and bureaucratized religion, represented by the mainline churches, coupled with a desire to retain or return to a way of life more characteristic of the past, has produced a revival of fundamentalist sects. These sects advocate the literal interpretation of the Bible and the personal intervention of God in human affairs. Their ministry is greatly and successfully amplified by the electronic mass media. A parallel movement is that of the evangelicals, with a stress on salvation and on the acceptance of Jesus as a motivating force behind a dramatic change in one's life (the "born again" concept). Both of these movements share common characteristics. For one thing, they interpret the Bible literally, particularly the Gospels or the first four books of the New Testament. This literalness provides them with certainty in an uncertain world. Further, fundamentalists and evangelicals tend to be less tolerant of religious diversity, because they are passionately convinced of belonging to the only "true" religion. Moreover, fundamentalists insist on a personal experience of religion. Thus, they foster rituals that bring out the individual's personal relationship with Jesus and belief in His intervention in the individual's everyday life. Finally, fundamentalists are repulsed by the contemporary world, which they feel is too secular, and, therefore, antagonistic to religion. Although fundamentalism is mainly a Christian, and especially a Protestant, phenomenon, there are fundamentalist groups among Catholics, Muslims, and Jews also.

The fundamentalist revival goes hand in hand with political conservatism. Fundamentalist religion appeals to those who feel threatened by certain facts of contemporary life and would prefer to return to an earlier, simpler time and the more stable values that seem to have prevailed then. To that effect, they exert pressure on the political system in favor of such issues as censorship of school textbooks, school prayer, withholding information on sexual matters, denying contraception to adolescents, and the choice of abortion to women. They also are in favor of limiting the civil rights of gays and lesbians, particularly marriage. This political pressure is possible because fundamentalist organizations are able to attract large amounts of money. Although the power of fundamentalist religion came to be recognized during the presidential candidacy of Ronald Reagan, in reality the movement had been growing throughout the twentieth century. Critics maintain that fundamentalism plays on the naiveté of people who are still resisting some of the changes that came in the wake of the industrial revolution. Primarily, fundamentalists resent the trend toward scientific explanations of phenomena and favor following divine precepts as guides to life. However, what evolved into the so-called Christian Right is not monolithic.

In the early years of the century, evangelicalism was thought to be the religion of the disinherited. Today, evangelicals have risen in income and education closer to mainline Protestants. They are increasingly likely to have college degrees and important, well-paying positions in various segments of business and industry. This growing wealth and education have allowed them to participate in the political process: they can make large donations to candidates who support their interests. Although they exhibit interest in issues that concern other Americans, such as global warming and terrorism, the Iraq war and education, they are still predominantly focused on the "moral breakdown" of the society and remain strongly politically conservative and Republican.

Fundamentalism is bolstered by a type of religious activity that came into being with the advent of television, the electronic church. This term refers to radio and television audiences who participate in services—mainly preaching—by religious leaders. The latter have become celebrities who wield power and influence derived from the fact that an estimated 5 percent of the national television audience are regular viewers of religious programs. As much as 16 percent of all television programming is of a religious nature (Shorto, 1997, 61). In the mid-1990s, there were 257 religious TV stations in the country. More important than the fact that their message reaches these vast audiences is the fact that the electronic preachers are able to solicit contributions, which add up to hundreds of millions of dollars annually. Of course, the reasons for soliciting contributions is to allow the continuation of the programs, in addition to charitable work, but often much of the offerings end up in the pockets of the electronic preacher. After a number of scandals involving misuse of funds and sexual escapades on the part of a few of these preachers, support for the electronic church has declined.

The Role of Women in Religion

The traditional role of women in all religions was totally passive. They were encouraged to pray and follow all the precepts of the religion; however, they were not allowed to participate in any important religious functions or rituals. Women could not become priests, whose function is to be intermediaries between God and people, nor could they become rabbis, whose function is to teach. This attitude is reflected in the statement of St. Paul that the man is the head and the woman just an appendage to him and by the Orthodox Jewish male's prayer thanking God for not having been born a woman.

The impact of the feminist movement forced some denominations to change their attitudes. Accordingly, Protestant seminaries have seen a dramatic increase in the enrollment of women. The number of female clergy almost doubled between 1977 and 1986. Ironically, the admittance of women into the clergy has occurred largely among the more fundamentalist organizations as well as in the theologically liberal denominations (Jacquet & Jones, 1991). In the early 1990s, the Church of England joined a number of other Protestant denominations in permitting the ordination of women, a step that had already been taken by the Anglican churches of Canada, New Zealand, and the United States. This act divided the 70 million Anglicans worldwide. It also put an end to an attempt to reunite the Anglican and Catholic churches, which had separated in the time of King Henry VIII, some 465 years ago. The Vatican, in fact, has vowed that Catholicism would never accept women for ordination. The hierarchy in Rome steadfastly refuses to give women any voice in church affairs except as nuns. Among the denominations of Judaism, the Reform have accepted the ordination of women as rabbis; the Orthodox refuse to do so; and the Conservatives are divided on it.

The traditional role of women in almost all religions was a passive one—they were encouraged to pray, and that was all. As a result of the feminist movement, a number of churches have begun to ordain women, but not without creating much controversy. Here, a newly ordained Episcopal bishop in a California diocese.

■ Education

Education was institutionalized much later than the other pivotal institutions. Because humans lack highly developed instincts, the knowledge they accumulate about survival in groups, as well as all the technology necessary to make life easier, must be transmitted to each new generation. However, in traditional, preindustrial societies, the transmission of culture occurs within the family. It consists mainly of the teaching of skills necessary for survival in the society, as well as knowledge of ritual and religious myths. This knowledge is easily absorbed as children go about the business of living, following their parents and trying to imitate them. Most of this learning takes place during the process of informal socialization. In other words, education is embedded in the family institution.

As societies grow more complex, many more specialists are needed to act as administrators and executives of the increasingly formal organizations that take care of the business of the society. The informal socialization system is no longer adequate. Children cannot follow their parents into the workplace. At this point, a more formal kind of learning must be instituted, in which specially trained individuals instill skills, values, and a concrete body of knowledge in the young. The habits and traditions that evolve around this formalized type of socialization—otherwise known as schooling—have become the institution we call education.

Education in America

American education has a number of characteristics not found in other societies. As may be easily surmised, for most of human existence formal education was the privilege of the few rather than the right of many. In both Eastern and Western societies, only the rulers and high-position administrators, together with a few scholars, were even literate, let alone educated. But from the very inception of this country, the ideals, if not the reality, of democracy

A typical American kindergarten classroom.

A typical developing world classroom.

presupposed universal political participation, which, in turn, required a well-informed citizenry. Even 100 years before the American Revolution, before democratic ideas had taken hold, religious considerations caused the Massachusetts Bay Colony to establish a mandatory school system that focused on the four Rs: reading, 'riting, 'rithmetic, and religion. The Protestant colonists wanted everyone to be able to read the Bible personally, rather than depending on the interpretation of ministers.

Compulsory mass education was not instituted until the second half of the nineteenth century, when large waves of immigrants began pouring into American cities. Many of them spoke no English and could neither read nor write. It was necessary to "Americanize" them so as to make them fit to become citizens of the nation. The idea of rendering the immigrants literate in English was reinforced by industry, which was beginning to require more skilled laborers to handle its increasingly complex technology. A certain degree of education, at first represented by an eighth-grade diploma and later by a high school diploma, became a prerequisite for all but the most menial jobs. In this period, the function of schooling was to provide the means for each person to become self-supporting. Obviously, school systems reflect the needs of the society, and as the needs change, so do the systems of schooling.

The traditional view of American education is that, as a society, the United States has been deeply committed to the principle of educating all. The framers of the Constitution, as noted previously, were convinced that democracy required a literate and well-informed electorate. Economic policies (capitalism) reinforced the ideals of democracy, because they required that all persons have the opportunity to compete equally in the marketplace. There is a widespread assumption, then, that the value of education is an asset to the entire society, not to the individual alone. As a result, education in the United States is supported by taxation on everyone, and all parents are legally bound to send their children to school at least until the age of 16.

Critics of education disagree with the traditional view. These critics, who espouse a revisionist view, maintain that the elite—those in positions of power in the economy and government—develop an educational system that corresponds to their particular needs, and not to the needs of the masses. Thus, in the nineteenth century, working-class and immigrant children had to be socialized in such a way as to provide better workers for the nation's factories and businesses. The fundamental goal, then, was to instill proper work habits and to make immigrants fit into American society. The needs of individual students were at best secondary or accidental. The model for the school systems appearing around the country was the so-called Lancaster system. It emphasized rote memorization of facts and strict discipline in the classroom and in every aspect of student behavior. Every detail of the day was thoroughly regulated. In short, the system imitated an assembly line in a factory, producing students who were ready to perform factory jobs. Of course, the Lancaster system did not become universal: it prevailed primarily in urban, industrial centers. But the revisionists use the example of this system to point out that the elites are able to exert their control even in the type of education offered the people of a society.

The Functionalist View of Education

The traditional and revisionist views of education are reflected in the functionalist and conflict approaches that social scientists employ in analyzing the institution. In the functionalist perspective, education does certain things for society. Clearly, some of education's functions are **manifest** (that is, intended), and some are **latent** (that is, unintended). Among the most important manifest functions is that of supplementing the socialization process begun in the family. Specifically, schools teach students how to read, write, and compute; such basic facts as the history of their country and of other countries of the world; and the essential laws governing physical phenomena. In this way, schools help preserve the cultural heritage of the nation. They also point out and reinforce the values, beliefs, norms, and attitudes of the majority of people in the society, thus stressing values students acquire from family socialization. During the influx of large masses of immigrants, the idea was that children from different backgrounds could learn to become Americans by reciting the pledge of allegiance, learning to play baseball, finding out why one celebrates Thanksgiving, and so on. The purpose of such experiences was to give students a common ground, to foster a sense of national unity and solidarity. This may be called the **moral function** of education, and schools still

Education has always been more important in American society than in many other societies, perhaps because the Founders insisted that an informed citizenry was a prerequisite for a democratic form of government. Consequently, the tradition of the local schoolhouse is deeply etched on the American psyche.

subscribe to it. Additionally, American history and government are presented in their ideal, rather than in their real, form. It is not until students reach the university level that they are asked to assess the culture and institutions of their society critically.

Today, schools also function to help select, guide, and prepare students for the social and occupational roles they will eventually fill in society. The learning of social roles includes socialization that results in shaping the kind of personalities needed for the society. American schoolchildren learn to be competitive, to value success, to be hardworking, and to conform to group norms. They also learn what they might grow up to *do* in the society. This last item is an especially important function in industrial societies.

Finally, in addition to preserving and disseminating past and present cultural knowledge and teaching skills, schools also function to **generate new knowledge**. This function is especially true of higher education. It consists of searching for new ideas, techniques, or inventions to facilitate human life. Genetic engineering, cures for cancer and other diseases, new technologies in all areas of industry, as well as many unknown factors of human behavior are all pursued in university laboratories.

Latent Functions. Among the latent functions of education is the custodial function that schools perform. When children are in school, both parents are able to work. The general acceptance of this function and the growing demand for child-care centers to accommodate younger children after school are indications that people feel that the state should contribute toward the care of its future citizens.

The fact that students are brought together for long periods of time, some of them for more than 20 years, contributes to the formation of youth subcultures. Occasionally, some of these subcultures become deviant or countercultural. All are very influential on the young and can create generational conflicts. At the same time, interaction between young adults facilitates the initiation of relationships that often lead to romance and marriage.

Finally, education affects attitudes. Studies indicate that high school graduates are more tolerant of political and social nonconformity than those who did not complete high school. College graduates are more tolerant than high school graduates. Education has a positive effect on such values as egalitarianism, democratic principles, and tolerance of minority and opposition views. We do not know, however, whether these effects are permanent.

The Conflict View of Education

Based on an essentially Marxist perception that economic interest lies at the base of most human behavior, conflict theorists focus on the fact that a conflict of interests exists among a variety of categories of people, and further, that those with power will turn any situation to their advantage. Conflict theorists point out that schools reinforce the stratification system of the society both by legitimizing it and by preparing students for different statuses. Schools teach the values of achievement and competition as techniques for upward social mobility; the assumption is that those who are in high-status positions that they won through competition and achievement merit their positions. Schools also sort students into different categories, in theory according to ability and talent, so that each may fulfill his or her potential as a productive and creative person. The unintended effect of this selection process is that middle- and upper-class students are assigned to academic, college preparatory courses, whereas lower-class and minority students are frequently assigned to general and vocational study programs. Of course, the issue is not that simple: there are a number of reasons why middle-class students are better prepared to attend college and then go on to professions. But the schools appear to do their part in perpetuating this reality.

Conflict theorists consider the functions of education to be, in the main, negative. They assert that the educational system is used by the elite to manipulate the masses and maintain their power in the society (Bowles & Gintis, 1976; Collins, 1979). In particular, they claim that the real aim of education is to allocate, or place, people in a given social status. For that purpose, a hidden curriculum exists alongside the visible one. This curriculum teaches students to be competitive, obedient, and patriotic, values that elites need to imbue in people who are going to fill certain jobs. The end result is that the values of the group in power are taught uncritically in schools.

Teachers are generally drawn from the ranks of the middle class, so they favor students who have been socialized to value the same things, and they use examples and teaching methods that are understandable to middle-class students but may be lost on lower-class, ethnic, or minority students.

The upshot of these real functions of the educational system, according to critics, is that all the credentials, diplomas, and degrees conferred by schools on students who have done well in their systems are not really necessary for performing most jobs. Even **credentialism**, or the practice of requiring degrees for certain specialized occupations, which was instituted to ensure that professionals would have to study a specific body of knowledge, is criticized by conflict theorists. They maintain that credentialed occupations also happen to be high-paying and prestigious, and obtaining credentials is just a way of ensuring that only those whose family already has a high social position remain in that same social stratum. It is true that education actually creates new occupations and places selected people in them, increasing the number of specialized and elite positions in society. For example, there were no economists, sociologists, geneticists, or football coaches before universities set up these specialized bodies of knowledge or forms of athletics. These actions by the universities have helped create more positions at the top of the occupational ladder and have restricted those at the bottom. However, it is also true that such positions have been accessible to students in the lower social classes who had the discipline to pursue successfully a course of study.

■ Characteristics of American Education

In addition to an early recognition of the need for universal, mass education, another characteristic of American education is the fact that schools are subject to **community control**. Local school districts are created in each community, and the schools within the district are attended by children residing in that community. The district's board, elected by local residents, makes decisions for the schools. This zealously guarded tradition results in a variety of standards in the nation's schools and in inequality in the way schools are funded (wealthier states fund more generously than poorer states, and wealthier districts are more generous to their students than poorer districts). This inequality is avoided in most other nations, where school funding is determined by a central government.

Upward Mobility as a Cure-All for Social Problems

One trait especially characteristic of American education is the fact that people consider it to be a first and necessary step toward economic and, therefore, social upward mobility. That is one reason why American schools stress training, in the sense of transmitting skills and information that can be used in the performance of a job, at the expense of education, in the sense of developing creative and critical abilities. Repeatedly, American parents have said they wanted their children schooled to obtain better jobs and not particularly to stimulate their mental powers or develop any potential creative talents. Most parents think that schools should teach students to respect law and authority and should shy away from subjects that prompt controversy.

Because of the strong belief that one must be educated to be a good American citizen, education is frequently viewed as a cure-all for all manner of social problems. If there are too many traffic deaths, the schools institute driving education programs; if alcohol and drugs are abused in the society, the schools provide for drug education programs; if there are too many unwanted teenage pregnancies, the schools attempt to solve the problem by establishing sex education programs. While the intentions are noble, there is little proof that such programs significantly affect the solution to social problems.

Education, Class, and Race

As noted, the United States set out on a course of educating every individual, and in some aspects it has succeeded in this enterprise. As of 2006, 86.1 percent of persons aged 25 and over held high school diplomas. Viewed in terms of race, 91 percent of whites, 81 percent of African Americans, 59 percent of Hispanics, and 87 percent of Asians were high school graduates. (U.S. Bureau of the Census, Press Release March 15, 2007.) As of that same year, 28 percent in that age group also had a bachelor's degree. Mass education, however, does not necessarily mean equal education nor does the large number of people graduating from high school and attending college necessarily signify a high degree of intellectual achievement.

Census Bureau surveys have shown that educational inequality has decreased slowly over the past 50 years as white graduation rates leveled off in the 1970s, while blacks made major gains in high school graduation rates. Some inequalities are still apparent, however. After years of progress, for instance, in which the gap between test scores of black and white students had narrowed, the gap began to widen again between 1990 and 1999. The Department of Education reported in 2000 that the average black 17-year-old was reading only as well as the average white 13-year-old (Zernike, 2000, A14). Moreover, the gap was widest among the children of the best-educated parents, suggesting that what was considered to be the result of urban poverty and disadvantage could no longer be attributed to those characteristics. In 1971, there was a 44-point difference in reading scores between white and black students whose parents had attained higher than a high school education. In 1990, that gap had narrowed to 27 points but grew again to 36 points in 1999.

The result of the education gap is that it is producing an income gap and consequently a social class gap. The information economy requires a degree of education that was less important in agricultural and industrial societies. In those types of economies, even people without much education could obtain jobs—in fields or in factories—that would provide a decent livelihood. In the information economy, other skills, of a more academic nature, are paramount. Increasingly, a college education is the gate into the middle and upper classes. Possessing a professional degree translates into earning a much higher income: In 2006 adults with professional degrees earned an average of $79,946 whereas those with less than a high school diploma earned $19,915 (U.S. Census Bureau, March 15, 2007; see also Table 13.4.).

In short, the dilemma that American schools face is that entrance to the professions and many other kinds of high-paying jobs require the credentials that schools confer on the individual who successfully completes a course of study. On the other hand, the course of study is not equally attainable by all students. First, there are differences in intellectual abilities among people, which of course affect the outcome of their educational careers. Perhaps of greater impact are factors related to social class and race that tend to impede the progress of some students.

Schools seem unable to work to the advantage of all students for a variety of reasons. One reason is the extremely bureaucratized structure of American schools, which tends to alienate students from lower-class and minority homes. The stress on order and regularity, on silence and lesson plans, and on staying in line is further sharpened by the attitude of teachers, who manage to communicate to lower-class students that they will not achieve academically as well as students from higher social classes. This self-fulfilling prophecy usually comes true.

The extensive testing that students continually undergo, although attempts are made for it to be objective and fair, also discriminates against lower-class children whose culture and experiences do not prepare them for competitive test taking. The tests are given in standard English and deal with subject matter that is more familiar to middle-class students. At the same time,

Table 13.4   Education Pays in Higher Earnings and Lower Unemployment Rates

Unemployment rate in 2006 (Percent)	Education attained	Median weekly earnings in 2006 (Dollars)
1.4	Doctoral degree	$1,441
1.1	Professional degree	1,474
1.7	Master's degree	1,140
2.3	Bachelor's degree	962
3.0	Associate degree	721
3.9	Some college, no degree	674
4.3	High-school graduate	595
6.8	Less than a high school diploma	419

Note: Data are 2006 annual averages for persons age 25 and over. Earnings are for full-time wage and salary workers.

Source: Bureau of Labor Statistics.

test scores are given much weight when it comes to channeling students into either college preparatory or vocational programs, so ultimately a student's future is affected. Finally, students who consistently test low acquire a low self-image, coming to believe that they are not smart and cannot achieve academically. Again, this self-fulfilling prophecy tends to prove them right. Conflict theorists see in this process an attempt at "cooling out" the poor, that is, destroying in disadvantaged students any aspirations they may have to better their social situation.

It must be emphasized that neither administrators nor teachers purposely or consciously discriminate against certain students. It is simply the nature of the system to be self-perpetuating. Teachers are successful products of the schools. It is difficult for them to know how to reach students who come from backgrounds in which education is not a foremost value, where books, magazines, or newspapers are unknown, in which parents are perennially frustrated and worried about money problems, in whose homes there are no quiet corners in which to study, and, most important, in which there is neither hope nor expectation that a successful school career will lead to a better life.

The Role of the Family

The most important determinant of scholastic success is the family. The values, attitudes, and behavior of a family have a direct relationship to future academic success of the individual for several reasons. First, middle- and upper-class families foster the viewpoint that occupational success is desirable and that it is attained through educational achievement. Parental and peer pressure to do well in school is strong on upper- and middle-class students. Teachers, too, may unconsciously express their higher expectations of these students' success. The family backgrounds of students from the higher social classes generally include parents who are college educated, whose homes are filled with books and magazines, and whose activities include trips to theaters and museums, riding lessons, and music or dance lessons—in short, what is generally considered an enriched environment. Not the least consideration is the fact that middle- and upper-class families can afford the high tuitions and room and board at prestigious universities.

Box 13.2   Attempts at Making Education Work

With the exception of Asian Americans and Jewish Americans, who have taken full advantage of the upward mobility made possible by becoming credentialed professionals, most current minorities have not been well-served by American schools, as noted in the text. Educators and the government have made a variety of attempts to find an educational system more in touch with the needs of minorities, but so far not much has borne fruit.

Initially, schools were segregated because children went to neighborhood schools. Many blacks and Hispanics who lived in inner-city neighborhoods and attended inner-city schools finished fewer years of school and obtained lower grades and lower achievement and IQ test scores than white students. To find out why, sociologist James Coleman and a group of his associates undertook an exhaustive research project with the aim of comparing the facilities of schools in white and black neighborhoods (1966). They found that the schools differed little in physical facilities: they were approximately the same in age, had the same library and laboratory equipment, and spent the same amount of money per pupil. In addition, teacher qualifications and class sizes were similar. Coleman and associates concluded that the variation in achievement between white students and black and Hispanic students was due primarily to family background and to the fact that minority students have little sense of control of their environment. Coleman also found that when black students attended school with whites in a harmonious desegregated situation, their school performance improved. He speculated that the reason was that the schools were permeated by a middle-class atmosphere that had a positive influence on minority students without lowering the performance of white students.

Chiefly as a result of this research, busing to achieve racial integration was instituted in a number of large urban school districts. In some, busing has been successful. In others, it was greeted with hostility. A later study by Coleman (1981) reached the conclusion that private schools do a better job of educating students and, in particular, that Roman Catholic schools come closest to the American ideal of educating all alike. The reason students learn more in private than in public schools—regardless of background factors such as family income, parents' education, race, number of siblings, and whether the mother worked while the child was in elementary school—is that private schools provide a safer, more disciplined, and well-ordered environment and are, therefore, conducive to learning.

It appears then that education, which had been hailed as the foremost step to upward mobility both by the public at large and by social scientists, is no longer able to play this role. For one thing, factors other than education have just as powerful an influence on the jobs people take. For instance, family background is responsible for more persons entering the same category of occupation as their fathers than is the amount of education obtained (Jencks, 1979). In short, although highly educated people indeed earn more than those with little education, there are many other factors that distinguish the rich from the poor. Even though the schools represent a way out of poverty for some, they also reflect social inequality and in many ways reinforce it. Such were the conclusions of sociologist Christopher Jencks and seven of his colleagues in their book *Inequality* (1972). The authors concluded that "equalizing educational opportunity would do very little to make adults more equal," that "the character of a school's output depends largely on a single input, namely the characteristics of the entering children," and "everything else, the school budget, its policies, the characteristics of the teachers—is either secondary or completely irrelevant" (255–256).

In spite of these pessimistic findings, educators and the federal government have not given up in their attempt to raise the achievement level for all students. In 2002, the president signed a law, titled No Child Left Behind, designed to close the test-score gap between minority and white students by 2014. This law holds schools responsible for making sufficient progress each year, regardless of social, economic, physical, or intellectual differences. The law requires states, school districts, and individual schools to report test results for every ethnic and racial group every year, with the expectation that these results will show improvement until equality is reached among all groups. Essentially then, it is based on the belief that schools can make a difference.

As of 2007, unfortunately, no significant improvements have been seen in narrowing achievement gaps. Slight gains have occurred at some grade levels and in some locations, but on the whole, test-score gaps are still very deep. African American and Hispanic high school students' performance in reading and arithmetic is at levels that white and Asian students reach in junior high school: in short they are two to three years behind.

Changes are envisioned for the future, including pouring more resources into education. However, it is becoming increasingly clear that schools alone cannot achieve miracles and that changes in students' backgrounds are the missing link in equality of achievement. Orlando Patterson, a black Harvard sociologist maintains that it is the "cool-pose culture" that many black youths subscribe to that is at fault in preventing them from taking school seriously. By *cool-pose culture* he means "hanging out on the street after school, shopping and dressing sharply, sexual conquests, party drugs, hip-hop music and culture, the fact that almost all the superstar athletes and a great many of the nation's best entertainers are black" (Patterson, 2006, 13). This culture is so satisfying and brings young blacks, especially males, so much respect, even from whites, that they prefer it to the mainstream culture. In fact, the cool-pose culture is supported by the mainstream culture, especially by the corporations that profit from hip-hop music, professional basketball, and homeboy fashions. The difference between minority students and white and Asian students is that the latter are more selective: as the author says "they know when it is time to turn off 50 Cent and get out the SAT prep book" (Patterson, 2006, 13).

While that is one social scientist's opinion, most research does seem to support the premise that the home and the family have much to do with academic success. Because academic deficiencies lead to stratification problems, resulting in a class of people kept out of the mainstream, it seems imperative to find a way to narrow the gaps in student achievement as soon as possible.

Students from disadvantaged backgrounds, on the other hand, often have little idea of what college is all about. Teachers and guidance counselors sometimes do not bother to supply them with the necessary information for college admission because they assume that these students will not continue their education. The values and expectations of lower-class families and peer groups do not tend to be conducive to academic success.

Many studies have suggested that private schools do better than public schools in educating all alike. The main reason is that they provide a safer, more disciplined, and well-ordered environment that is more conducive to learning.

Lower-class families, for instance, aware of their lack of opportunities, value education less as an avenue toward upward mobility. They pressure their children into conformity and value obedience to rules, in preparation for blue-collar jobs in which orders must be taken from a variety of superiors. At the lower socioeconomic end, families also tend to be larger. Both parents and older siblings are likely to be at work most of the day. And the verbal skills of the parents are probably limited, because they are likely to have interrupted their educations sometime in their teens. Most of the trappings of the enriched environment are lacking because they are expensive. None of these features promotes success in the academic portion of schooling.

The importance of the family in determining scholastic success is supported by the Educational Testing Service report mentioned previously. The report also concludes that the key to better performance in school is a better environment at home. Expectations at home must be high, and academic achievements valued. Among the main reasons for the success of Japanese schools, in fact, are the psychological payoffs offered to Japanese children for school performance. Very often, however, the reality in the United States is that schoolchildren are latchkey children who must be responsible for taking care of themselves.

Higher Education

If universal, mass education is a comparative newcomer, higher education is even more so. For most of recorded history, higher education consisted of a master surrounded by pupils who may have come from great distances to learn from him. In addition, most of the learning revolved around religion, the law, and medicine and was designed to train theologians, philosophers, lawyers, and physicians. The university evolved with the development of science and the resulting need for constant research. However, today the university in the United States is quite different from its forerunners in the various countries of Europe.

Although professional schools that combined training with research were an American innovation, only a small minority of Americans in the past aspired to university degrees. The prevailing attitude was that an eighth-grade education was sufficient preparation to share in the "American dream." As a result, only those with great abilities and motivation, as well as those with wealth and leisure, even considered a university education.

Following World War II, however, several factors reversed the situation. First, industry was expanding, and there was a greater need for technologically more sophisticated and better-trained workers. The economic boom also increased social mobility, and more people began to see the importance of a college education for attaining a higher standard of living. These factors led to a gradual change of attitude, so that a college education came to be considered a right reserved for many, or even for all, not just a privilege for the few. This new attitude was reflected in government legislation enabling veterans to receive a free college education under the GI Bill.

The foremost result of the changes mentioned was a spectacular growth in the number of colleges, their size, and the numbers of students attending them. Whereas in 1870 only 1.7 percent of persons aged 18 to 21 were attending colleges and universities, in 2003 the college completion level of persons 25 to 29 was 28 percent (U.S. Bureau of the Census, 2004).

That rate, however, has not been going up. In fact, the proportion of students who earn a degree has been stable for the last 30 years. Overall, 63 percent of four-year college students earn a degree after six years, but a breakdown along ethnic and racial lines shows that many fewer African Americans and Latinos have degrees within six years (Pope, 2004, A6). In 2006, a study from the National Center for Public Policy and Higher Education found that the United States ranks quite low on rates of college completion compared with other developed nations. The highest proportion of college degrees belong to 35- to 64-year-olds. This means that the younger generation is not completing college to the same extent as the older generations did. Failing to attain a college degree is relevant to a person's future wage-earning potential, which is significantly greater for college graduates than for high school graduates, as we have seen.

One of the reasons for this poor completion rate is the cost of a college education today. A year at a public four-year university costs an average of 31 percent of a family's income. For families in the lowest quintile of income, however, it represents 73 percent of annual income, while for families in the top 20 percent it represents only 9 percent (Lewin, 2006, A24). As a result, many more students from the richest stratum of the society attend college than those from the lowest, even though universities offer scholarships and grants to students from low-income families.

Another marked change in the universities is concentration on the development of scientific research, technical skills and methods, and such forms of professional knowledge as law, medicine, public health, social welfare, and the management sciences. As a result, a radical alteration of the purpose of the university occurred: from education in its broadest sense to the pursuit and imparting of knowledge in a narrow field of specialization. It was at this point, when the acquisition of knowledge for its own sake and to broaden one's horizons was being replaced by technical knowledge acquired for the purpose of obtaining better positions in the stratification system, that college began to appeal to the vast majority of the population—the masses.

With the dramatic increases in enrollment, institutions of higher learning have become more specialized and differentiated. The largest schools have acquired the name of **multiversities** because of their size (they usually consist of a number of campuses dispersed through a state) and because of the many functions they perform, not only for their community but often for the nation. The finest medical and research centers are parts of such multiversities. Large state universities and colleges are other popular forms of public institutions—the universities containing professional or graduate schools, and the colleges offering a basic four-year course of study. Finally, there has been a mushrooming of community (also called junior) colleges, generally funded locally by cities or counties, and aided by state and federal funds. These offer a two-year degree at minimal tuition rates in a vocational area, or they serve a preparatory function for transfer to a four-year school. Even though some of the public multiversities and state universities have excellent reputations, the highest status is accorded to a number of private schools that still practice selective admission procedures, charge very high tuition rates, and that until very recently clung to a classical liberal arts tradition.

As of 1997, women have also been surpassing men in educational achievement. This is particularly true of black women. The Census Bureau reports that over the past decade, the number of women with a bachelor's degree or higher increased by nearly 7 percentage points, from 19 percent to 26 percent. Men had only a 4 percentage point increase, from 25 percent to 29 percent, during the same period (U.S. Census Bureau, Press Release, 2004) The number of African Americans in college has grown by 43 percent since the 1970s. But from 1977 to 1997, the number of bachelor's degrees, which had increased by 30 percent for black men, increased by 77 percent for black women. These facts could have very negative implications for African American males: the fewer college-educated males, the fewer corporate board members and professionals in positions of power. It could also have a deleterious influence on the African American family, as black women will have a difficult time finding black men to marry who could equal them in earning power and, thus, share equally in household expenses.

Some Contemporary Issues in Higher Education

During the decades of the 1960s and 1970s, universities witnessed a great deal of student unrest. There were a number of reasons for this unrest, mostly mirroring issues prevalent in the society at large. Students protested the unpopular war in Vietnam and particularly the military draft. Students also voiced their dissatisfaction with the way the society was dealing with minorities, including racial minorities, women, homosexuals, and the physically disabled. Many were attracted to the political left, pointing out the unhealthy relationship of some universities with the government, corporate, and business communities. Finally, they agitated against what they perceived as an overwhelming bureaucratization of higher education, against what they saw as infringements of academic freedom, and for a greater voice in the life of the university.

According to many critics, the ultimate result of the protests has been a lowering of standards across the spectrum of universities and a loss of confidence in the functions and goals of higher education. Schools that prided themselves on their academic freedom—where faculty and students could discuss controversial subjects—have been muzzled. Today, faculty and students are often accused either of being racist, sexist, and homophobic or of pushing "politically correct" ideas down the throats of unwilling students. The fragmentation of the society at large, the inability of a substantial number of people to agree on basic values, is reflected in the controversies on most American campuses today.

Additionally, a number of factors have combined to make college education more difficult to achieve. Tuitions have skyrocketed, as was pointed out, so that bright middle-class and lower-middle-class students cannot hope to attend the nation's top schools, which are the ones that open the most doors to success. Restrictions on financial aid to middle-class students have further fueled the downward migration in higher education. Affirmative action legislation, according to which a certain number of slots must be kept open for minority students even if their grade-point averages and other entrance requirements are lower than those of other students, has also proved to be a sticking point. Finally, many universities find themselves in a situation similar to that of the University of Chicago. This school, founded in 1892 and heavy with top-flight scholars (Seventy Nobel Prizes) and known for the excellence of its core curriculum and for maintaining the importance of the life of the mind, appears to be giving up:

> . . . with colleges today increasingly viewed as employment credentialing stations, students as customers and learning for its own sake as a quaint idea whose time has passed, the University of Chicago finds itself a victim of its own high-mindedness and in a painful identity crisis (Bronner, 1998, 1, 18).

Recognizing such a crisis, the federal government has decreed that colleges and universities should be much more accountable and responsive to students than before. A commission convened by the U.S. Secretary of Education in 2006 found that American higher education has failed to adapt to the changing needs of the information economy and that it is self-satisfied, risk-averse, and expensive. The commission pointed out that in the decade from 1993 to 2003, average tuition and fees at four-year colleges and universities climbed by 38 percent. Between 1990 and 2004, aid packages for the top income quartile increased by more than 300 percent, while financial need among the lowest-income families increased by 80 percent. According to a national test, over the last decade, the percentage of college graduates considered literate has decreased by 40 percent. Finally, the commission claims that there is no coherent way to measure the performance of colleges in educating students. Suggestions for changes in higher education include the need to establish closer coordination between the K–12 systems, as is the case in most other industrialized nations; demands for more accountability on the part of colleges in the kinds of students they admit and on the part of high schools for the kinds of students they graduate. In addition, the commission proposes that assistance be given to students on the basis of family need; that a way be found to limit tuition increases; and that schools be required to demonstrate student achievement by means of national examinations, with results available to the public. It remains to be seen whether Congress, busy with an unpopular war and fear of terrorist acts against the homeland, will find the determination to act on these suggestions (U.S. Department of Education, 2006).

The Chapter in Brief

Religion has been found in every society because, as thinking animals, humans are curious about the meaning and purpose of life. However, sociologists study religion only as a manifestation of culture and to uncover relationships, effects, and behavior.

The major religions of the world may be categorized into monotheistic, polytheistic, ethical, and ancestral. The monotheistic religions include Christianity, with the largest membership, followed by Islam and Judaism. Hinduism is the largest polytheistic religion; Buddhism, Confucianism, and Taoism are ethical religions. Shintoism, practiced by the Japanese, is an ancestral religion.

Religion, when first studied by the social scientists, was considered to be the result of people's attempts to explain a reality they did not understand. It was suggested that religion dealt with the sacred and that the object of religious beliefs and practices was society itself. This viewpoint has been incorporated into the theory of functionalism, whose theorists assume that the functions of religion include relief of feelings of frustration, explanations of the physical world, the support of norms and values of society, provision of a means for repentance, and help during the difficult stages of life.

The ideas of Karl Marx were forerunners of the conflict position with regard to religion. Marx believed that religion and the idea of God were human creations, but that people forgot they invented God and began to fear Him. Fear produced alienation, and Marx considered religion as the most alienating of institutions, especially because it allowed the dominant classes in society to exploit the masses and keep them in subordinate positions by defending the status quo. However, Marx did not consider that religion also functions to promote social change, often to the benefit of the downtrodden. Religion also functions as a creator of meaning and thus is a reflection of each culture. A famous study, *The Protestant Ethic and the Spirit of Capitalism*, traced the rise of capitalism as an effect of the religious ideas of Protestantism, especially of Calvinism. Religious ideas contributed to change in society in addition to enforcing the norms of society, legitimizing the political power of leaders and the behavioral demands of institutions.

Religions continue to have functions in society. One of these functions is to provide an identity and a feeling of community to people through membership in religious groups. However, we have also developed a kind of "civil religion" by making holy some of our political ideals, national heroes, and our common destiny.

All religions display beliefs, rituals, and organization. Religious organizations are divided into churches, sects, and cults. Religion in America is denominational, and the methods of the marketplace are used to recruit and hold members.

Modern trends in religion include secularization and bureaucratization. Religious organizations resemble other kinds of voluntary associations that deal with mental health, family togetherness, and social welfare. A reaction to this lack of spirituality may be seen in the emergence of a number of sectarian movements of a pentecostal and evangelical nature.

The transmission of knowledge from one generation to the next is the primary function of education. Education also functions to recruit and prepare students for social and occupational roles in the outside world, to integrate into the wider culture the various subcultures that are part of it, and finally, to generate new knowledge through research. Schools also perform custodial functions, contribute to the formation of a youth subculture, and sometimes effectively change attitudes.

The best predictor of academic success is socioeconomic status, which is a function of the family. This is not a direct economic relationship but rather takes into account differences in family lifestyles, in styles of communication, in values and expectations of parents, and so on. Middle-class families prepare their children for a successful experience in school, where they are taught by middle-class teachers with similar cultural goals and expectations. Life in the lower-class family does not adequately prepare a child for a successful school experience, and because a large number of minorities are still positioned in the lower and working classes, they have been generally the least successful in academic pursuits (exceptions are the new immigrants, prevailingly Asian, who value education as an avenue for upward mobility and who have high rates of success in academia).

Although education has been considered the gateway to upward mobility—and for many people it has been—the increase in the number of high school and college graduates has begun to change this relationship. Many other factors seem to be responsible for the kinds of jobs people get. Thus, a rethinking of what our educational goals should be is in order.

Higher education is also in disarray nowadays. First of all, the goal of higher education is much changed—rather than leading to a well-rounded personality, it now leads to a narrow specialization and professionalization. Universities experienced a boom after World War II and again in the 1960s as a result of the GI Bill and demographic factors. Now, however, enrollments are flat, and few Americans are receiving postgraduate degrees, particularly in the hard sciences. Moreover, many campuses are seats of controversy as the establishment of a new curriculum often pits traditionalists against minorities, women, and homosexuals. Finally, ethnic and racial groups are increasingly segregating themselves, a reflection of the fragmentation of the wider society.

A variety of reforms have been tried in the past three decades in an effort to improve American education. Unfortunately, to date nothing seems to have worked, possibly because of the anti-intellectual values prevalent in the society and the apathy of parents, products of the same educational system.

Terms to Remember

animism Belief that many objects in the world are inhabited by spirits.

church A religious organization that is institutionalized and well integrated into the socioeconomic life of a society and in which participation is routine.

cult The least conventional and least institutionalized of religious organizations. It consists of groups of followers clustered around a leader whose teachings differ substantially from the doctrines of the church or denomination.

denomination A subdivision of the church that is considered equally as valid as the church.

ecclesia A church to which a substantial majority of the population belongs.

education The formal aspect of socialization in which a specific body of knowledge and skills is deliberately transmitted by specialists.

ethical religions Those that stress the need to live an ethical life so as to attain harmony in personal life and in society (Buddhism, Confucianism, Taoism).

latent functions Those functions that are the unintended consequences of the process of education.

mana A concept according to which there exists a supernatural force that can attach to any person, object, or event.

manifest functions The desired, expected, and agreed-upon functions of education.

monotheism Belief in the existence of one God (Judaism, Christianity, Islam).

multiversity A large university, consisting of a number of campuses dispersed around a state.

polytheism Belief in the existence of many gods (Hinduism).

profane The objects and events of everyday life that are common, usual, explainable, and repetitive.

rites of passage Rituals established around critical times of growth and maturation: birth, puberty, marriage, and death.

ritual Behavior that follows the creation of sacredness and provides a mechanism for maintaining the sacred.

sacred Objects, events, or persons distinct from the profane, that is, that are uncommon, unusual, unexplained, mysterious, powerful, and, therefore, deserving of reverence and respect. Religion deals with the sacred.

sect A religious organization that is a revolutionary movement breaking away from the church or denomination. It stresses the spirit, rather than the letter, of religion.

self-fulfilling prophecy The research-supported idea that if teachers treat students as if they were bright and capable, students will perform up to the teachers' expectations, and vice versa.

tracking The grouping of students according to their ability.

universal church An ecclesia that has a monopoly on religious belief. A state religion.

Suggested Readings

Darling-Hammond, Linda. 1995. *The Right to Learn: A Blueprint for Creating Schools That Work*. San Francisco: Jossey-Bass. An advocate of progressive education and a liberal of the old school, the author describes a number of schools around the country that are achieving results by teaching for understanding rather than for test taking. The problem with most schools, however, is that teaching is geared to an anachronistic factory model that leaves little opportunity for learning in depth or personal contact.

Feagin, Joe, Herna Vera, and Imani Nikitah. 1996. *The Agony of Education*. New York: Routledge. This book deals with the experiences of African-American students on predominantly white campuses and includes suggestions for improving these experiences.

Hitchens, Christopher. 2007. God Is Not Great: How Religion Poisons Everything. New York: Twelve/Warner Books. An irreverent but entertaining look at religion by an irreverent and well-educated author.

Jencks, Christopher, and Meredith Phillips, eds. 1998. *The Black-White Test Score Gap*. Washington, DC: Brookings Institution Press. An anthology of a number of readings focusing on tests, bias, socioeconomic backgrounds and parenting, stereotypes, and other causes of the gaps in SAT test scores.

McGuire, Meredith B. 1992. *Religion: The Social Context*, 3rd ed. Belmont, CA: Wadsworth. A textbook in the sociology of religion, focusing on the connection of religion and social change.

Noonan, John T., Jr. 1998. *The Lustre of Our Country: The American Experience of Religious Freedom*. The unique concept of freedom of religion stems from the genius of our Founding Fathers, especially James Madison. They battled to overturn the old Christian practice of coercing belief.

Ravitch, Diane, and Joseph P. Viteritti, eds. 1995. *New Schools for a New Century*. New Haven, CT: Yale University Press. This is a collection of ten essays resulting from a seminar led by the editors, who are scholars of education.

The essays conclude that schools must be challenged from outside before they can change in any significant way.

Rose, Michael. 1995. *Possible Lives: The Promise of Public Education in America*. New York: Houghton Mifflin. The author believes that upgrading the skills and knowledge of America's children is linked to their economic prospects—education has become a more critical component of people's economic success than it ever was in the past.

Stark, Rodney, and William Sims Bainbridge. 1997. *Religion, Deviance, and Social Control*. New York: Routledge. The authors, sociologists who often write about issues in religion, take on questions revolving around the common-sense notion that religion prevents a certain degree of deviance and contributes to social control in society.

Web Sites of Interest

http://www.ed.gov/nces/index.html
The National Center for Education Statistics is an agency of the U.S. government that collects and publishes reports on the status of education in all its aspects.

http://www.census.gov
The Census Bureau is one of the best sources of information on education attainment, income, race, sex, age, and family status.

http://www.aauw.org
This is the site of the American Association of University Women, an organization promoting equality for women in education.

http://www.academicinfo.net/religindex.html
This site provides links to a number of resources available on the subject of religion.

http://www.igc.apc.org/culturewatch
This web site of CultureWatch Online offers information about the religious right.

http://www.pluralism.org
Developed by a professor at Harvard University, this interesting web site provides studies and documentation of the growing religious diversity in the United States as a result of its immigrants.

http://religiousmovements.liv.virginia.edu
A helpful web site of the University of Virginia showing how religious groups develop, grow, stagnate, and /or die, etc.

14

Government: The Institution and the Theories and Ideologies That Underlie It

IN THIS CHAPTER, YOU WILL LEARN

- *the reason for the emergence of the institution of government;*
- *the purpose and functions of government;*
- *the importance of legitimacy and authority in the exercise of political power, as well as the types of authority;*
- *the differences between the state and government;*
- *the definition of a nation-state;*
- *that social movements, governments, and economic behavior are based on ideologies;*
- *the differences between autocratic and democratic ideologies;*
- *about the dominant totalitarian ideology of the right and the social movement it spawned;*
- *about the dominant totalitarian ideology of the left and the social movements that followed;*
- *the principles of the democratic ideology and of its subideologies of capitalism and democratic socialism.*

Government is never very far from our thoughts. How could it be otherwise? We cannot drive a car, vote, or have a drink if we are underage without a government agency's okay. We cannot decide that we will not attend school if we are under 16: a government agency will send truant officers to find us and bring us into the classroom. We cannot play our stereo full blast, because if a neighbor complains, an agency of government will make us turn it down or haul us off to jail for disturbing the peace. We cannot build any kind of house we want, even on our own lot: a government agency will first ensure that certain zoning regulations are satisfied. And these are just minor examples of government interference. Government decides who is a citizen, who can vote or work in the country, who is to obtain unemployment compensation or disability pensions. Government wants to know if a child is born, and who dies, as well as where, and how death takes place. In short, government is everywhere; it touches our lives in a million ways, reaching into our very kitchens and bedrooms. Why do we let it? Why do we need it? What is government, anyway?

■ The Institution of Government

Remember that pivotal institutions revolve around important human needs. One fundamental prerequisite of humans as biological organisms is a daily supply of water and food and some covering and shelter from the elements. Just as important and urgent is the need to be able to live in a sufficiently orderly environment, protected from outside enemies. In small groups, these needs are satisfied simply and without much conflict. When small groups of individuals become hundreds, matters become more complex. That is, when food is grown and not simply gathered, when objects are manufactured not simply found—in short, when clans or tribes settle into a permanent life style—then a process must be instituted for making important decisions for the benefit of the group. This process consists of organizational patterns of behavior that eventually crystallize into the institutions of the economy and government. In turn, these patterns and their organization are shaped and buttressed by the ideologies prevalent in each society.

The U.S. Capitol is one of the symbols of our government.

■ Government and Politics

The decision as to who gets what of a society's rewards, and why they get it, is inherent in the institution of the economy. The implementation of the economic decisions and of all decisions that affect the society is left up to the institution of government. The two institutions are deeply intertwined. They consist of a number of patterns and traditions for getting things done. They also include people, a body of representatives with the authority and sufficient power to see to it that decisions made for the society are carried out, respected, and obeyed.

In most modern societies, the source of ultimate power is the **state,** because it has a monopoly on the use of force within its borders. The state, however, is an abstract concept; the real day-to-day exercise of power is done by the **government,** which consists of a number of individuals who hold power in the name of the state. The process by which some people or groups acquire and maintain power is called **politics.**

Government, the institution, may be defined as the pattern of statuses and roles that a society develops to fulfill the need for order within and the need for defense against threats from without. It includes a system of norms, values, laws, and general patterns of behavior that legitimize the acquisition and exercise of power. The institution also determines the relationship of the government to the members of society. It is important to remember that, in essence, to govern means to control, and government can also be defined as the legitimate use of force to control human behavior within specific territorial boundaries.

The Purpose of Government

Societies need government because a group way of life requires a certain degree of social order. There are some things people must do and others they must refrain from doing to prevent chaos and maintain relative peace. In small societies, the family institution is sufficient to maintain social control over its members by exercising moral control. **Moral control,** which is essentially cultural learning, lies within the individual, having been internalized through socialization.

When societies grow large and complex, other institutions—religion, education, and government—must take over some of the functions of maintaining social order by exercising social control. **Social control** is the process by which a group induces or forces the individual to behave in a designated way by enforcing taboos, mores, and folkways. In large, complex societies, moral control and social control must be supplemented by political control. **Political control** is social control exerted by forces outside the individual, such as laws and agencies in charge of punishing those who violate laws.

The Functions of Government

The most important function of government is to **implement political control.** This involves maintaining order, settling disputes, and coordinating the activities of members of society. In addition, government must protect citizens from external threats. It does this by creating and maintaining armies, by providing such armies with weapons, and by securing strategic military installations. In some societies, the military institution itself acts as the government. In most, however, civilians are in charge of the government and the military is subordinate to it.

The government is also in charge of planning and maintaining those facilities and activities that involve large portions of the population. Government agencies regulate the economy, build highways, are in charge of traffic regulation, fund schools, maintain national parks and museums, help run some hospitals, provide some health care, and so on. Government also subsidizes activities that are valued by the society but the private sector does not pursue, such as the arts. The above functions are **manifest**, or deliberate.

The unintended, or **latent**, functions of government have often included a great deal of repression. In the United States, however, governmental repression has been minimal. Latent functions here have included the formation of party machines, which were common in the past, as well as the alleged existence of power elites that act to maintain the status quo, including a system of social stratification. Even in nations that consider themselves classless, administrative and managerial elites have come into existence. The relationship between political power and socioeconomic status is entrenched everywhere.

■ Political Power: Legitimacy and Authority

Power is central to the political process because whoever exerts political control in a society must have power to do so. Power is a difficult concept to define. The early sociologist Max Weber defined it as "the probability that one actor within a social relationship will be in a position to carry out his own will despite resistance" (Weber, 1957, 152). Power is a significant factor in all kinds of social interaction. Parents have power over their children, professors have a certain degree of power over students, employers have power over employees, and so on. People have greater or lesser amounts of power according to the statuses they occupy in society and the roles they fill.

In today's contemporary societies, moral control is insufficient. Only political control, here represented by a traffic officer, forces individuals into behavior patterns—stopping on red, proceeding on green—that are consistent with the needs of the society.

Power relationships are always somewhat reciprocal. That is, the child has some power over the parent: he or she can throw a temper tantrum or refuse to eat until the parent gives in. An employee can "take home" office supplies, or products, or pad expense accounts. A student can flatter the instructor to improve chances of a passing or above-average grade. In short, there are ways of sabotaging the power-holding individual in most interactions.

Power can be asserted in a number of ways. One way is to promise a **reward** in return for compliance. Another is to **coerce**, or threaten with punishment, the individual who does not comply. Finally, power can be asserted through **influence**, by being able to manipulate information or to have an effect on values, attitudes, and feelings. Television commentators and popular authors have power over many people because their statements are accepted as authoritative by a large public. Political leaders have a similar effect.

Legitimacy

Political power is power exercised by the state through its government. The reason the state can wield power is that people accept its authority. When power is held by an individual or group that is not acceptable to the members of society, that power is considered illegal and illegitimate. This kind of power is coercion, as when an armed thug demands the wallet of an unarmed victim.

Authority

For power to be legitimate, it must have authority. Authority is power over, or control of, individuals that is socially accepted as right and proper. A police officer who holds a gun to a suspect while trying to make an arrest is not displaying coercive power because it is the right of the officer to do so, inherent in the authority vested in his or her status. A private citizen engaged in the same activity, on the other hand, is committing a crime, because the citizen has no authority to hold a gun to anyone (except in self-defense). In other words, *authority is the legitimate possession of power*.

A government must have legitimate authority to be accepted. That is, citizens must believe "that the existing political institutions are the most appropriate ones for the society" (Lipset, 1963, 64). No political system, not even one born of violence and functioning through force, can survive for very long without legitimacy. When people question the legitimacy of their government, the situation is called a *crisis of legitimacy* and is usually resolved with the overthrow of the government. The 1989 democracy movement in China exemplified a crisis of legitimacy, but the Chinese government was able to crush it.

Types of Legitimate Authority

How does an individual or group or a government acquire authority? In other words, how does power become legitimized? In a classic thesis, German sociologist Max Weber maintained that the sources of authority lie in tradition, the law, and charisma (Weber, 1957, 324–369).

Traditional Authority. The oldest type of power that people know is authority that depends on tradition. The legitimization of power in this type of authority depends on the past. The authority of a person or group is accepted because "it has always been so." The religious authority of churches and the political authority of the government rest heavily on traditional sources.

Traditional authority tends to prevail in relatively homogeneous, nontechnological societies because citizens have similar group identification, sharing most of the same values, beliefs, and attitudes. However, even in heterogeneous and highly technological societies there are traditional sources of authority. The Constitution of the United States, as an example, is accepted by most Americans as an almost sacred document that forms the basis of the governmental system. Legislation that runs counter to the letter of the Constitution is considered illegitimate.

Legal-Rational Authority.   Legal-rational authority is based on rules that are arrived at in a rational manner. Systems based on legal-rational authority are organized in a bureaucratic fashion because this pattern of social organization limits the exercise of power. In a bureaucracy, power resides in a social position and role rather than in a specific individual. In addition, this pattern of organization defines and specifies the exact amount of power that each role entails. Authority is based on obedience to the "rule of law" rather than on loyalty to any given individual or group.

Legal-rational authority appears in complex, multigroup societies. In such societies, members are heterogeneous and belong to many subcultures. These societies usually experience rapid social change, resulting in a lack of uniformity in values, attitudes, and beliefs. Legal-rational authority is accepted because societal members are convinced that those who hold authority are using rational methods for the benefit of all. Social change, moreover, is reflected in frequent modifications to the law.

Charismatic Authority.   One type of authority does not rest on tradition, reason, or the law. Rather, charismatic authority derives from the person of an exceptional leader. Such authority may appear in a society that has a traditional base or in one that has a legal-rational base. Charismatic leaders seem to possess special characteristics that are described as magnetic,

Nazism was a totalitarian ideology of the right that owed much of its appeal to the charismatic personality of Adolf Hitler, who promised the German people a return to a former greatness at a time when they were suffering economic difficulties and humiliations due to their defeat in World War I.

fascinating, and extraordinary by their followers. Such leaders as Mao Zedong, Adolf Hitler, Martin Luther King, Fidel Castro, and John F. Kennedy have been described as charismatic.

Charismatic authority does not encourage stable social organization nor a stable political system. It has no system of rules, either traditional or rational, with which to guide behavior. In fact, it resists attempts at routinization or bureaucratization. Stability can be established only if the system based on the charismatic authority of a leader evolves into one of the other two systems of authority.

■ The State

Most societies today are nation states. The term *state* is frequently misunderstood and confused with the term *government*. Government, as the preceding discussion has shown, is the *institution* that develops as a consequence of the need to maintain social order in a society. Government, however, is a *process* that also includes the people who exercise political power in a society. The state is the abstract embodiment, or the *symbol*, of the political institution. Government provides political control through its political processes, through the laws it establishes and implements, and through the work of its agencies. The state is the formal representation of government. The functions of the state are carried out by the government. Government is the working, active arm of the state. Individuals and groups that make up the government, together with the laws they pass and the procedures they establish, change with time and with each administration; but the state goes on.

In some societies, it is easy to differentiate between the state and its government because the offices of the head of state and the head of government are held by two different persons. For instance, in Great Britain the queen is the head of state, whereas the prime minister is the head of government. Many other parliamentary democracies have a president as head of state and a prime minister as head of the government. In the United States, however, both offices are inherent in the position of president.

The state differs from all other institutions in two essential ways. First, membership in the state is compulsory for all living within its territorial limits, with the exception of those who are designated as aliens or temporary visitors. Second, the state differs from all other aspects of social organization in that its political control is complete. The state, and the state alone, can seize a citizen's property, can deprive a person of freedom by imprisonment, or, as a last resort, can take a citizen's life as punishment for a capital crime.

In a parliamentary system such as that of Britain, the head of state and the head of the government are embodied in two separate persons. The Queen is the head of state and the Prime Minister is the head of government.

These two conditions of the state are necessary if the state is to exercise effective, organized political control. If individuals could resign from the state, they would be relieved of all obligation to obey its laws. Moreover, because the state has the duty of enforcing certain patterns of behavior on all persons within its boundaries, the state's government must have the authority to use whatever sanctions are necessary to achieve this purpose. The state must possess **sovereignty**, or the supreme political power, which derives from its capacity to monopolize the use of force within its borders. A state's sovereignty is recognized both by its own citizens and by other states.

The basic components of the state are territory, population, government, and sovereignty. Within its territory, through its government, on the basis of its sovereignty, and for the benefit of its people, the state performs certain functions and deals with other states.

The state, in other words, is defined in terms of the size and complexity of the society in which it is found. It emerges in societies with large populations containing high numbers of composite groups, social classes, and associations. It is a means of governing such societies in that the state brings together under common rule many kinds of people. State societies are seldom ethnically homogeneous, and they usually display inequalities in the distribution of wealth and of economic functions. The existence of a state is a mark of a society's complexity of organization.

The state emerged or was established in many places, in many historic eras, and under many conditions. Throughout history there have existed city-states (some still exist today), empire states, theocratic states, tribal states, nation-states, centralized states, and decentralized states, autocratic, oligarchic, and democratic states, as well as states stratified by social class or by social estate. In spite of its various forms and diverse origins, their common feature has been their emergence as an institutional solution to the problem of governing large and complex groups of people. And the historical trend has been to reduce the number of

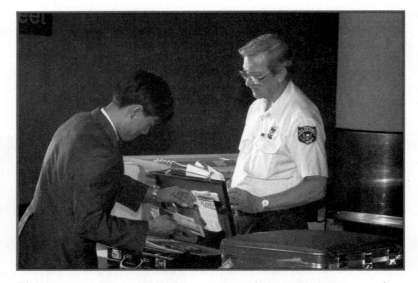

One can enter a country only with permission, and a sovereign country may deny entrance to whomever it chooses. Here, a customs official checks a traveler's passport.

state forms to one predominant one, namely, the nation-state. This has occurred chiefly by means of cultural diffusion from Europe to other parts of the world, where the form was drafted on and combined with native systems of political rule.

Theoretical Views of the State

The fundamental reason for the emergence of government and its symbol, the state, as has been noted repeatedly, is the maintenance of social order. Theorists who see life from a functionalist perspective naturally accept the idea that the institution originated to perform this specific function. One of the older expressions of this idea may be found in the writings of Thomas Hobbes (1588–1679), an English philosopher, who speculated that the state emerged as a result of a "social contract" made by the people to end their existence in a "state of nature" in which life was "solitary, poor, nasty, brutish, and short." Modern social thinkers of the functionalist school perceive the state as an institution that is working quite well in maintaining law and order.

In addition, the state acts as an arbitrator in conflicts among individuals, as planner with the official goal of providing the greatest good for the greatest number, and to maintain relations with other states. Thus the state allocates scarce resources, regulates the economy, funds new research, protects those unable to work, looks out for the environment, and generally provides for the needs of the members of society. It also makes trade agreements, political alliances, or war with other states. All of these functions require a centralized source of authority.

Theorists who view life from a conflict perspective maintain that the state emerged to protect the rights of a privileged few. The conflict view derives from the works of Jean-Jacques Rousseau (1712–1778), who disagreed with Hobbes, believing instead that before the emergence of the state people lived as "noble savages" in peace and harmony. It was when the idea of private property developed that people began to fight among themselves and then had to resort to a central authority—the state—to restore peace. This central authority was not impartial but rather served the interests of the upper classes and kept the majority poor and oppressed.

These ideas were taken up by Karl Marx, who thought that all but the most primitive societies consisted of at least two classes. Of these, one dominated and exploited the others by means of social institutions. The state came to be an instrument in the service of the ruling classes. Marx concluded that the state would cease to exist only when the last stage of the evolution of societies was reached. In the classless societies that would follow communism, the state would "wither away," because in such societies there would no longer be any need to safeguard the interests of any one group.

As always, both the functionalist and the conflict perspectives show only one version of reality. It may be argued that the state maintains the status quo and with it some instances of social inequality. It may be equally argued that large, complex, heterogeneous societies cannot function without a central body with the authority to make certain vital decisions for the society.

■ The Nation-State

The continuous growth in size and complexity of societies led people to seek political organization first in clans based on kinship, later in tribes that were collections of clans, and finally in city-states. Around the fifteenth century, city-states gradually began to emerge as nation-states.

The nation is a culture group residing within the territory of the political state. A group of people are considered a nation if (1) they are permanent residents of a defined territory, (2) they exhibit some form of government, (3) they have a common culture, and (4) they declare themselves to be, and are considered by others to be, sovereign. When a group becomes a nation, older loyalties to family or tribe must be subordinated to the new political order, and a common literature, history, and a sense of a common future develop. A nation comes to have a "we" as against "them" feeling; that is, it develops a sense of unity so strong that, in spite of a lack of cultural uniformity, people consider themselves as separate from all others (who are then designated as "foreigners"). Historically, nationhood seems to have come first to the English, who, taking advantage of the dissolution of the medieval order, were able to achieve a sense of themselves as a separate and self-conscious people, although they retained a number of the institutions from the preceding social order. Few other nations were able to achieve this consciousness of themselves as a nation. While the United States originally had a self-concept of nationhood based on its English characteristics, today its preoccupation with ethnicity has given rise to doubts regarding its identity (Greenfield, 1992). A number of other nation-states have problems in this area: Canada with its French-speaking minority, which does not want to give up its language or culture; Israel with its Arab minority, which does not want to give up its territory; and China with Tibet, which does not want to give up its sovereignty. Yugoslavia, which has emerged from a civil war in which several ethnic groups were pitted against one another, has been divided into several nations. The former country represents the dark side of nationhood in the sense that older tribal loyalties have never really been abandoned. They were merely hidden during the communist period, when nationhood was superimposed on peoples who considered themselves distinct.

The development of national states has been of vital importance in the modern world. Principally, the loyalties and beliefs of nationalism have been motivating forces in the organization of complex, technological societies in the urban-industrial period. They have also been important forces in establishing and maintaining international antagonisms as a result of the ideology behind the nation-state, which is nationalism.

Nationalism

Nationalism may be defined as a set of beliefs about the superiority and difference of one's own nation and a defense of its interests above all others. It implies that the individual identifies with the nation, its culture, its interests, and its goals. Nationalism is ethnocentrism that cuts across all other loyalties to stress loyalty to the national group.

Historically, nationalism is a new movement. It first appeared in the second half of the eighteenth century. Before then, in the aftermath of the feudal era, all of the Western world was relatively unified in culture and religion. The rulers of most Western nations constituted an international society of governing classes because of frequent intermarriages and kinship relations. The events following World War I, particularly the appearance of a number of communist and fascist regimes, effectively destroyed this unity. The new regimes stressed nationalism because they felt that a drive for national supremacy would strengthen them internally. Their goal was to create a monolithic state whose people had only one allegiance to the government and one overwhelming feeling of patriotism.

The classical liberals of that time, moreover, believed that the nation-state was the natural unit of self-government in human society. They thought that once the vast empires that had dominated the Western world disappeared, people, no longer oppressed by them, would live in harmony with one another, without need for wars or conflict. Marxists were even confident that modernization and the spread of socialism would eventually get rid of nationalism, and that it ultimately would have the same role as ethnic cooking: a quaint reminder of a past cultural tradition. But they were all wrong, as nationalism and the feelings of nationhood proved to be powerful forces all through the twentieth century, giving rise to wars and atrocities even into the new century.

In the United States, a strong sense of national identity emerged, at first as a result of a common ethnicity in terms of language and culture. Later, it was reinforced by a sense of "specialness," as people came to believe that the nation had a historical mission to be the model for other nations of the globe. In other words, the idea of nationhood was combined in the United States with some of the ideals of the Enlightenment period regarding the aim of universal civilization. However, the United States has not become the first universal nation; on the contrary, we have been for the past several decades experiencing a sharpening of more narrowly ethnic feelings that sometimes result in our questioning our national identity. Many of us have become hyphenated Americans, a fact that has some commentators stating that a national allegiance that depends on subscribing to abstract principles is insufficient to maintain nationhood.

■ The Ideologies Behind the Nation-State

The former Yugoslavia, now divided into its many component parts, had been in the news throughout the 1990s. The news reports told incessantly of war and starvation, of atrocities and refugees, of war criminal trials, of people thrown out of their ancestral homes and people taking over the ancestral homes of others. And yet, a few years ago, Yugoslavia was a unified country, a nation, whose people lived in reasonable harmony with one another. It is true that they were made up of a number of different ethnic and religious groups, but this did not seem to stop them from trading, interacting, and marrying each other.

What happened to break up their cohesion, to turn former friends into bitter enemies, to split families, pitting brother against brother? In a word, it all started with an ideology. For nearly 50 years following the end of World War II, the ideology had been one of unity. Those same people who today proclaim themselves to be proud Slovenians, Serbs, Muslims, Croatians, Bosnians, and Montenegrins, with deep wounds and profound hatreds for one another, were compelled by a communist dictator, General Tito, to bury the past and consider themselves one nation. That ideology was forced on them, but it worked. When communism unraveled all around them, however, a new ideology was needed to cement the nation. Such an ideology was found by revisiting the past; but, rather than uniting, it led to the breakup of the nation.

Ideology is a system of beliefs, or doctrines, that provide a basis for collective action (Mannheim, 1936). Ideologies tend to develop around a central value, such as equality or racial purity. Those espousing a particular ideology claim to speak for major social groups in society: Marxists for the working class, feminists for all women. Some ideologies defend or rationalize the status quo, others criticize it and exhort people to change it. All followers of an ideology maintain that only they give the true picture of what the world is really like. As a result, ideologies are the underpinnings of all social movements and eventually of governments.

The Role of Ideology

First, ideologies explain why things are the way they are. Second, they reinforce the feelings of participants, clarifying them and making them a part of a program for action. Third, they direct members to behave in such a way that the desired change will be obtained. And finally, they educate people, justifying their actions.

The dispossessed, those who cannot count on legitimate political processes, are especially vulnerable to ideologies that promise a rapid solution to their desperate condition. Islamic fundamentalism has been a movement in a number of Muslim lands in which a majority of people suffer from high unemployment, political corruption, and declining living standards. These factors lead some individuals and groups to use terrorist tactics, having accepted the ideology that Muslim regions should be free of non-Muslims.

In spite of their important functions, ideologies often distort the truth. They also have a tendency to make of their followers "true believers," that is, supporters who are blindly loyal to them. In turn, the kind of fanaticism blind loyalty evokes does not respect the truth.

Ideologies tend to arise during periods of crisis and among those segments of society to whom the dominant world view has become unacceptable (Shils, 1968, 66–76). When groups of people begin to feel exploited or neglected, or if their status is being threatened by social change, or if their needs and desires are being thwarted in an existing order, they turn to a new or newly rediscovered ideology in which they see hope for a better future. In fact, ideologies are embodiments of ideas in action. Thus, they are meaningless outside social movements, some of which eventually become governments. Ideologies need to be organized and disseminated, and this is done by harnessing people into action.

Political Ideology

Ideologies vary in scope from comprehensive to partial. Totalitarian ideologies, for instance, insist that public authority control all the meaningful areas of life, while democratic ideologies limit themselves to a more restricted sphere.

Ideologies are abstract. That is, they do not necessarily reflect reality but are a model derived from the author's perceptions of reality.

Ideologies are reductionist, in that they set forth general and simple explanations and goals that are easily understandable. Although ideologies are meant to result in action, they do not always precede action. Sometimes, actions come first and then an ideology is formed to justify them.

Finally, although a number of ideologies guide human lives, it is the political ideology with its economic repercussions that affects the social life of people most directly. Political scientist Robert Lane describes the nature and functions of political ideology in the following terms: Political ideology refers to concepts that: (1) deal with the questions: Who will be the rulers? How will the rulers be selected? By what principles will they govern? (2) constitute an argument; that is, they are intended to persuade and to counter opposing views; (3) integrally affect some of the major values of life; (4) embrace a program for the defense or reform or abolition of important social institutions; (5) are, in part, rationalization of group interest but not necessarily the interest of all groups espousing them; (6) are normative, ethical, moral in tone and content; (7) are (inevitably) torn from their context in a broader belief system and share the structural and stylistic properties of that system (Lane, 1962, 14–15).

One of the most important functions of ideology is to make the governors acceptable to the governed. In his book on the nature of government, Robert MacIver asserts that it is not force but the myth complex of society that makes people accept others as their rulers (MacIver, 1947, 17). This myth complex, which is the author's term for ideology, lends government a justification without which no prince or parliament, no tyrant or dictator could ever rule. Any government needs legitimate authority to continue to exist. And the underlying fabric of authority is ideology.

In pluralistic, heterogeneous societies, people tend to hold conflicting ideologies. In theory, the individual can pick and choose from among a number of such ideologies. In reality, most people are socialized into accepting the prevailing ideology, so that only a few even realize that a multiplicity of ideologies are available. In societies in which only one official ideology is allowed to exist, those who hold conflicting ideologies are persecuted as enemies of the state.

The foremost contemporary political ideologies that govern the lives of societies are divided into the autocratic (totalitarian, or dictatorial and authoritarian) and the democratic. The first group includes fascism, Nazism, and Soviet and other variants of communism; the second group includes democratic capitalism and democratic socialism.

■ Autocratic Ideologies

The basis of all autocratic ideologies is the belief that government should be in the hands of one individual—or group of individuals—with supreme power over the people of the society. Throughout history there have existed many forms of autocratic governments: primitive kingships, despotism, tyranny, and absolutist monarchies such as those of czarist Russia. Military dictatorships and other forms of temporary or emergency rule are also autocratic in nature. The distinguishing feature of autocratic regimes is that the ruler does not have to account to anyone for any actions. The ruler makes all decisions without being subject to any law. In effect, the ruler *is* the law, while the people are subjects in the true sense of the word: they have no political rights at all.

Authoritarianism

In modern times, traditional autocracy has been replaced by ideologies of the right and of the left that we call either authoritarian or totalitarian. Authoritarian systems are autocratic in the political arena but leave a measure of choice up to the individual as long as the latter does not interfere with the rule of the leader or the party elite. Many nations throughout the world, though they define themselves as democratic or socialist, are really authoritarian regimes.

Totalitarianism

Totalitarian regimes differ in major ways both from the modern authoritarian systems and from the autocracies of the past. For one thing, they control the individual in all aspects of life, social and religious as well as political. For another, they are based on modern technology and mass legitimation (Friedrich & Brzezinski, 1966, 4). The word *totalitarian* came into existence when what were thought to be short-lived dictatorships of the left and right became permanent regimes. Totalitarian regimes have many aspects in common: (1) Their official ideology expresses a revolt against present society and idealistic hopes for a future society of perfect men and women; (2) they maintain a single party that functions as the organization through which the ideology is fostered and kept alive; (3) the state has an all-pervasive secret police and totally controls the mass media; (4) the state has a monopolistic control of arms, which means that force is concentrated in its hands; and (5) the economy is centrally planned and controlled. These features of totalitarian ideology have enabled many totalitarian states to exert total control over the lives of individuals. Such an attempt was never made by the older autocracies, nor is it made by the contemporary authoritarian regimes that are not totalitarian (Friedrich et al., 1969, 126; Gregor, 1968, 20–21).

The destinies of political systems that have evolved from totalitarian ideologies—fascism, national socialism (Nazism), communism (Soviet, Chinese, Cuban, North Korean)—have all been different. World War II put an end to fascism and Nazism, which have reappeared only sporadically in various nations. Communism continued to prosper for much of the twentieth century but has in the last few years dramatically collapsed in its major stronghold, the Soviet Union and its satellites. It is still hanging on in Cuba, North Korea, and much more tenuously in China and a few other nations. (Even in China communism is losing its hold, as market economies have proved more capable of producing the consumer goods all people seem to crave.) Communist movements, in the form of guerrilla warfare, have appeared in Central and South America (i.e., the Shining Path movement in Peru) and in various nations of Africa.

Totalitarianism of the Right: Fascism and Nazism

Fascism and Nazism, which no contemporary society admits to following, exemplified totalitarian regimes of the right that flourished in the first half of the twentieth century. Fascism emerged in Italy under the leadership of Benito Mussolini after World War I (a fascist government came to power in 1922). In 1933, a similar movement appeared in Germany, where it acquired the name of national socialism or Nazism. Eventually, the movement crossed over into Asia, where it was embraced by Japan. It also took hold in the Western Hemisphere: Argentina established a fascist dictatorship under General Juan Peron in 1943 that lasted until the middle 1950s. In addition, fascism, in its various national transformations, appeared in Spain as the Falange party and in France, Romania, Hungary, and other nations under a variety of names.

Although there are differences between fascism and Nazism, the two movements have enough similarities that the latter can be considered merely a subtype of the former. Principally, they are identified by two different leaders: Benito Mussolini with fascism and Adolf Hitler with Nazism.

The principal elements of fascism included a distrust of reason, the denial of basic human equality, a code of behavior based on violence and distortion of truth, government by the elite, totalitarianism, racism, imperialism, and opposition to international law and order (Ebenstein, 1973). The ideology had fanatical and dogmatic overtones and presented issues that could not be discussed critically but must be accepted on faith. For instance, race was an issue for the Germans, and the infallibility of a leader was one for the Italians. Fascists also rejected the Judeo-Christian-Greek concept of equality. The fascist ideal is the concept of inequality, in the sense that some persons were considered superior to others: men to women, soldiers to civilians, party members to nonparty members, one's own nation to other nations, the strong to the weak, and the victors in war to the vanquished. Fascists considered it a fallacy that people were capable of self-government; rather, they preferred to believe that only a small minority of the population, qualified by birth, education, or social standing, were able to understand and do what was best for the whole society. It followed that in a fascist system, the government consisted of a self-appointed elite and was not dependent on popular consent, free elections, a free press, or an opposition.

Fascism was totalitarian in all social relations; in its objective, which was to control all phases of human life from birth to death; and in its means, because fascists were willing to use any form of coercion, from verbal threats to mass murder, to attain their goals. With the defeat of the Axis powers during World War II, the most virulent forms of fascism and Nazism were wiped out. Nonetheless, the ideology crops up sporadically in a number of social movements.

Totalitarianism of the Left: Communism

Communism, an economic and political system whose goals are total government control of the economy and total income redistribution with the ultimate aim of a classless society, is based on one of the most misunderstood and feared ideologies. And yet its avowed goal—the establishment of an egalitarian society—has been the ideal of some of the world's best minds and hearts through the centuries. Communism as it is known today originated in the conditions following the social changes brought about by the Industrial Revolution. The ideology sprang up as a reaction to the hunger, disease, poverty, and lack of medical care that were the daily realities of urban industrial masses in the nineteenth century. These conditions had been observed and lamented by many social thinkers and critics. Karl Marx proposed his own version of utopia, communism, which soon fired the imagination of vast numbers of followers.

The Marxist Foundation: Materialism. The basis of Marx's thought, as already noted, was the idea that people's conditions—in fact, all relationships in life—rested on an economic base. Culture, law, government, religion, esthetics, philosophy, and so on, were actually superstructures erected on economic foundations in every society. The economic base was so strong that it determined not only the superstructure but also the way people thought and behaved. As an example, in all societies, those who own property (or the means of production in industrial societies) determine the course of events in that society. Those who lack property are subject to, or at least directed by, others. This state of affairs, said Marx, began when the right to private property was asserted and will not stop until property is possessed by all.

Marx also stressed that change in societies (as in all facets of life) was constant and that it proceeded through struggle. In societies that were at the capitalist stage of development (as most Western societies were at the time of his writing), the struggle was between the bourgeoisie—the entrepreneurs who owned the means of production—and the proletariat—the industrial workers. There was little doubt in Marx's mind that the struggle would eventually be won by the proletariat.

Box 14.1 Communism and the USSR

The initial thrust toward revolution and the establishment of a communist regime came from a Russian disciple of Marx, Vladimir Ilyich Ulyanov, better known as Lenin (1870–1924). Lenin proceeded to rationalize the reasons for the continuing existence of capitalism (imperialism provided additional markets, as well as raw materials and cheap labor) and concentrated on ensuring that revolution would occur. He organized a small group of revolutionaries dedicated to the goal of overthrowing the post-czarist provisional government in Russia (the czarist regime had been previously overthrown). They finally succeeded in 1917, and a Europe that was exhausted from World War I allowed the revolutionary regime to become entrenched. Lenin became obsessed with maintaining the revolution and for this reason felt that revolution elsewhere had to be postponed. He urged workers around the world to consider Russia their own country, representing their hopes and defending their interests. This internationalism, while ostensibly remaining constant, gave way during World War II, when nationalism was reawakened in people who once more came to the defense of their own countries. (For that matter, the Soviet Union itself was an amalgam of about 150 different nationality groups who obviously did not feel allegiance to the values and traditions of Great Russia in spite of the attempts of the Communist Party to impose a uniform culture on the people. In fact, as soon as communism lost its hold, the various nationalities began to clamor for independence.)

Although Lenin, and subsequently his successor Stalin, tried to turn the Marxist ideology into political practice, the latter differed quite dramatically from the former. There was only one political party—the Communist Party—and one leader of that party, so that decision making became virtually unilateral and dictatorial. One of

Stalin's decisions was to industrialize the country rapidly, and for that purpose forced agricultural collectivization was instituted. Consumer goods had to give way to heavy industry. Farmers and workers were expected to work as hard as they could and produce as much as they could, but the state paid them as little as possible so that more could be accumulated for capital investment. Needless to say, people do not respond positively to hardships when no rewards are in sight, particularly when failure or disobedience is punished severely.

The economic system shaped by Marxist-Leninist thought is characterized by rigidly centralized planning. Such a scheme is in total contrast to the capitalist pattern, in which each entrepreneur decides what to produce and where to invest. Central planning, designed to be more efficient than the capitalist model, in reality proved to be inefficient. It lent itself to abuse and corruption and to the development of a vast bureaucracy that contributed to making life miserable for the average citizen. Nonetheless, in spite of the disruption caused by purges and the severe losses of life and property in World War II, the Soviet Union, before its breakup, had become the second largest producing nation in the world, with a higher coal and steel production than that of the United States. That may be one reason why some of the developing nations had elected for a time to follow Marxist-Leninist economic models.

At its most repressive, communism remained dogmatic in its intent to abolish private property and nationalize the means of production everywhere. It continued to preach the necessity of class warfare, the dictatorship of the proletariat, and the concentration of power in a tightly structured party. Where it survives, it still maintains that it is reaching for that ultimate goal, the classless society.

Historical Prediction: The Dialectic. Marx arrived at this prediction through a basic tool of analysis called the dialectic (hence, the Marxist position is sometimes referred to as dialectical materialism). The dialectic as a method of inquiry is of Greek origin. It is basically a method of question and answer in which a position is stated (thesis) and then criticized until the opposite position is arrived at (antithesis). Finally, a middle position between the two opposites is attained (synthesis), and the process begins anew.

Marx used the dialectic method to interpret history. He maintained that because change in the economic system is reflected in the entire superstructure of society, it is possible to predict the course of history by noting economic changes and the course of the economy by

Today's Moscow is a far cry from what it was during the communist era. Having embraced a Western-style market economy, many Russians are able to enjoy luxury goods that they were denied during communism, when all efforts were directed at creating a powerful industrial nation.

noting historical patterns. The latter include a struggle between the old and the new in which the new always wins. Thus, feudalism overcame slavery, capitalism overcame feudalism, and socialism—and eventually communism—would inevitably overcome capitalism. Ultimately, Marx went on, the bourgeoisie would be destroyed, and its place taken by the proletariat. This condition would occur in a stage called communism, which, however, would not be attained without violent revolution. The struggle was already apparent to Marx; he said he could see in capitalism the seed of its own destruction. Marx was quite specific about where the revolution would occur. He predicted that the most likely place would be Germany, from which it would spread to other highly industrialized nations, gradually reaching the less industrial ones. This prediction of Marx, as well as many others, was wrong; the revolution occurred in Russia, at the time one of the least industrialized nations of Europe.

Another prognostication that did not materialize was the predicted deterioration of the working class in capitalist economies. Trade unions and the welfare state combined to secure the well-being of workers, who consequently did not overthrow the bourgeoisie. Capitalism demonstrated that it could change to meet certain challenges, refuting Marx's certainty that it would never change and was, therefore, doomed to fail.

Finally, Marx underestimated the power of nationalism. He addressed the workers of the world, urging them to throw off their chains. But the workers of the world felt themselves to be primarily German, Russian, French, or Italian and only secondarily members of the proletariat. When World War I broke out, the workers of each nation flocked to the defense of their country against the advice of communist ideologues, who repeated Marx's

Box 14.2 Communism in China

Chinese communism has also undergone a traumatic experience. When Mao Zedong, the communist leader, triumphed over the corrupt rightist Nationalist Chinese government, he inherited a vast, populous country, whose people for the most part were dirt-poor survival farmers. The Communist Party instituted a number of campaigns of ideological brainwashing in which intellectuals, artists, property and manufacturing plant owners, and middle-class persons generally, were described as "capitalist-roaders." They were either executed, imprisoned, or sent to far-off rural areas to be "re-educated." In spite of these cruel methods intended to rid the society of the bourgeoisie, the Chinese communists succeeded in feeding, clothing, providing health care, and educating the formerly starving masses of Chinese. In addition, the communists virtually stamped out graft, prostitution, and drug addiction, problems that had been endemic during the period preceding the communist takeover, partly as a result of foreign (including American) exploitation. The communists redistributed property, giving people hope and confidence that their lives would hold a better future. At the same time, abuses occurred, especially during the Cultural Revolution, as people existed in an atmosphere of rigid dogmatism, acquiescing in the personality cult of Mao and living in the fear that saying something politically suspect might send them to jail.

After the death of Mao and with the coming to power of Deng Xiaoping, the bleak egalitarian poverty of the Maoist period seemed to have drawn to a close. The new leader, in fact, abolished communes, encouraged trade with the West and a Western style of entrepreneurship, and opened the door to Western ideas, enabling the Chinese people to taste the joys of consumerism. Washing machines, television sets, and disco dancing became realities for some and seemed to become attainable for many as the average income more than doubled during the last 10 years.

The economic reforms have engendered success after success. Visitors to China are amazed at the improvements in living standards and the growing optimism of the people, as well as the construction boom and the apparent high standard of living. Political reform, however, has not followed economic reform, and decisions continue to be made by the ruling elite with no accountability to the people. Nonetheless, the changes in present-day China are astounding. The gross domestic product (GDP) representing the real growth rate of the economy, was 10.5 percent in 2006. This is a tremendous figure, compared to the American growth rate which hovers around 3 percent. It has allowed the Chinese economy to be the largest after the United States. The Chinese unemployment rate is only 4.3 percent, and only 10 percent of the population lives below the poverty rate (CIA, The World Factbook, accessed 5/16/2007).

In spite of the Communist ideology subscribed to by the government, China has developed a stratum of wealthy individuals beyond the wildest dreams of the Maoist generation. According to *Forbes Magazine*'s lists of the world's wealthiest people, China has close to twenty billionaires, the 400 richest Chinese are worth a combined total of $38 billion, and the children of this elite group are sent not to study Communist ideology but such skills and experiences as golf, ballet, private music lessons, horseback riding, ice-skating, skiing, and so on. Even their attitudes toward sex have changed: whereas even five years ago books and magazines with sexual content were heavily censored and banned, today soft-core pornography is being published and popular web sites publish erotic photos and materials. These changes are being attributed to urbanization, greater mobility permitted by the market economy, and the popularity of the World Wide Web. It is a small wonder that a number of commentators are beginning to proclaim that the twenty-first century will be the Chinese century.

warnings that national sentiment was only part of the superstructure by which the bourgeoisie reinforced their dominance over the proletariat.

In spite of the failure of many of his predictions, Marx's ideology has taken root in a large number of nations. For most of the twentieth century, almost half of the world lived under regimes that considered themselves Marxist and were anticipating the imminent fall of capitalism. Surprisingly, most of these nations, contrary to being the industrial monsters prophesied by Marx, were economically underdeveloped.

Mao Zedong would be very surprised to find a Ferrari dealership in today's China, ostensibly still a communist country.

■ Democratic Ideologies: Democracy

Although many nations refer to themselves as "people's democracies," it takes more than a self-imposed name to be a democracy. Democracy is an ideology, a philosophy, a theory, and a political system. In the Western view, democracy is a way of life containing elements that define the relations of the individual to society and government. These elements may be summarized as follows: (1) rational empiricism, (2) emphasis on the individual, (3) instrumental nature of the state, (4) voluntarism, (5) the law behind the law, (6) emphasis on means, (7) discussion and consent in human relations, and (8) basic equality of all human beings (Ebenstein, 1973).

In more familiar terms, the democratic ideology stresses the value of the individual. The individual is the basic unit of a democratic society, and both the values and processes of the political system revolve around him or her. Moreover, the individual is considered to be a person with a separate identity and worth, whereas autocratic systems value individuals only as members of a larger social whole.

Another central tenet of democracy is the principle that all persons are born free, that they are not subject to the rule of others, and that consequently the only legitimate basis for rule is people's consent to be ruled. This principle is founded on the ideas of John Locke and Jean-Jacques Rousseau regarding the social contract. According to these philosophers, the social contract was a mutual agreement entered into by people who empowered an entity, later called the state, to protect them by enacting and enforcing a number of laws. The state and its government are dependent on consent and contract; essentially, it is the trustee of the people and its power derives from their consent. It exists at the pleasure of the people and has no authority or purpose except as assigned by the people.

Citizen participation and an environment in which diversity and opposition are allowed to flourish are also elements of democracy. The first is facilitated by an educated citizenry, and the second is important because free and unique individuals will necessarily exhibit ideas and interests that clash. The important point is that in a democracy conflicts are resolved through the political process.

The above principles are to be found in what is called the "classic" democratic ideology. Of course, democracy as a political system suffers in the translation from the ideology on which it is based (the American political system will be discussed in the following chapter). Many modern societies, particularly those in the Western tradition, have embraced some of the democratic ideals and combined them with specific economic ideologies. Two of the best known are democratic capitalism and democratic socialism.

Democratic Capitalism

Capitalism developed as an explanation of and a rationalization for the industrial system and some of the new attitudes that system required. Nevertheless, capitalism is more than an economic system and is inextricably bound up with democracy, particularly in the United States. Some political scientists refer to capitalism as a subideology, a blend of political and economic ideas that are mutually reinforcing (Ebenstein, 1973, 219).

The ideas of classical capitalism were expressed by Scottish philosopher Adam Smith in his famous treatise, *The Wealth of Nations* (1776), whose central features included a belief in private ownership of property with no limitation on its accumulation, the existence of a profit motive, the dynamics of a free market, and the presence of competition. These conditions had to operate in an atmosphere of freedom from government interference: individual entrepreneurs must be free to innovate, workers must be free to seek higher wages, and investors must be free to look for the highest returns. Government was to keep its hands off the economy (laissez-faire), tending instead to its basic functions of keeping peace and defending the nation.

The private ownership of property (or the means of production in an industrial economy) was considered beneficial in two ways. First, ownership of many assets means having power over individuals who have fewer assets, so it is preferable that such power be diffused among individual property owners rather than being concentrated in the state, where it may lead to abuse. Second, it was believed that progress, in the sense of economic growth for the benefit of the entire society, would be attained more easily if each individual used personal incentive to get ahead, including the incentive to make a profit.

Smith maintained, further, that the free market system worked smoothly, as if an "invisible hand" were directing it. In more recent times, the market system has been called planning by inducement, to differentiate it from planning by direction, a method used in the centralized economies of both fascist and communist systems. In the latter, the government tells people what and how much to produce. In the market system, no one tells producers what and how much to produce; they decide on their own according to factors of supply and demand. Ultimately, then, the free market results in consumer sovereignty: consumers create demand, and producers satisfy this demand by supplying the required products.

Classical capitalism also stressed the importance of competition. It was thought that entrepreneurs would offer the best merchandise at the cheapest price to make more sales (and so more profit). In modern capitalism, competition has been diluted because of the existence of private or state monopolies.

The profit motive, another central point in classical capitalism, was certainly not a new invention. However, more opportunity for profit exists in a capitalist economy because capitalism guarantees freedom of trade and occupation, freedom to own property, and freedom to make contracts. At the same time that it offers all these opportunities, capitalism also allows for loss. Bankruptcies and failure are part of the system, and every year some enterprises have huge losses (typically, 4 out of 10 corporations report net losses yearly, and of 10 businesses begun in any one year, 6 fail that same year).

Classical capitalism has undergone many transformations, and today's capitalist economies are called mixed economies, particularly because a certain amount of government intervention has become mandatory. Although most property is still held privately, the government regulates the economy through taxation and legislation and even controls a certain amount of manufacturing and distribution. Primarily, the government ensures that the economic game is played fairly and the losers are not totally destroyed.

■ Socialism

Socialism, which like democracy is a philosophy and a political system in addition to being an ideology, is capable of coexisting with capitalism. Socialism is also subject to a vast variety of definitions, has throughout history reflected a large number of visions, and has assumed a multiplicity of roles. In general, socialism refers to an economic concept, but democratic socialism is an ideology that rests on both economic and political assumptions.

Democratic Socialism

A socialist economy within a democratic political system is called democratic socialism. Great Britain and the Scandinavian countries are the most prominent examples of democratic socialism, although they have departed in degrees from a socialistic ideology in the last decade. These societies, also called welfare states, did not use revolutionary means to come to power. Rather, they prefer to work within a democratic system, generally parliamentary in nature, which uses the electoral system to obtain representation in the government. Economic policies in these societies are carried out by those who are elected to public office.

The most fundamental assumption underlying democratic socialism is that "participation in political decision making should be extended to economic decision making" (Sargent, 1969, 97). This assumption is what makes the system democratic, because it states that voters should be able to control their economic condition, as they do their political condition, through the government they elect. In all other respects, democratic socialism accepts and supports the democratic ideology, both in theory and in practice.

Democratic socialism assumes that the state and its government are the necessary instruments through which people can achieve and maintain their objectives. The state must lead the society in the following objectives: holding most property in the name of the people (i.e., publicly), especially all major industries, utilities, and transportation; limiting the accumulation of private property; and regulating the economy.

Socialists also believe that direct planning of the economy can prevent depressions; that wealth should be distributed in such a way that there is only a small income differential among people; that a comprehensive welfare state would eradicate special privileges and create more equal opportunities for all; and that the working class is the backbone of the society.

One of the greatest appeals of democratic socialism is its concern with humanitarian issues. Socialists accuse capitalists of failing to solve fundamental problems in society—poverty, disease, inequality—primarily because they are too preoccupied with profits. They maintain that only when the economic system is controlled by the people will solutions be found. Unfortunately, the means of solving the problems are sometimes as bad as the problems themselves. In socialist countries, the individual is provided with a considerable amount of economic security. There is a comprehensive health care program, and food and housing are available to those too old or too sick to work. At the same time, the system spawns a large, complicated bureaucracy that is not directly answerable to the people and is often not responsive to them. In this sense, democratic socialism faces the same challenges as capitalism.

Democratic socialists argue that by ensuring everyone of economic security, they are making liberty possible for everyone. Democratic capitalists argue that only when property is held privately are people free to compete for rewards. In spite of its commendable goals, socialism has been suffering a long period of ideological stagnation and electoral defeat.

Many societies that had in the past embraced communism and socialism as their socioeconomic ideologies are today straying from them. Having found a strictly centralized, planned economy difficult to manipulate, these societies have adopted, although some still to a limited degree, the profit motive and price setting through the instrument of a market system. In fact, both communism and socialism seem to be drawing toward capitalism in many respects, while the latter, because of growing government regulation, is beginning to acquire some aspects of socialism.

The Chapter in Brief

The institution of government arises out of humanity's need for social order. When social control can no longer be administered within the family because of the size and complexity of a society, some kind of body with the authority to make decisions binding on the society becomes essential.

To be acceptable to members of society, government must have authority. Authority may have a basis in tradition, in reason and the law, or in the charisma of a leader. Authority may be defined as legitimate power. Power is the ability of one person or group to influence the behavior of another person or group in a desired direction. Force or the threat of force underlies power.

While government is process, the state is the formal abstract structure representing government. Its elements are territory, population, government, and sovereignty. The state's chief aim is to impose organized political control over its citizens, and it can do so because it has a monopoly over the legitimate use of force within its territory.

The organization of societies into nation-states is a comparatively recent event in history. A central government that oversees a particular territory in which people have similar characteristics develops a sense of unity and nationhood. Nationalism is the ideology behind the nation-state; it may be defined as a set of beliefs about the superiority of one's own nation and a defense of its interests above all others.

Ideologies—which underlie social movements and forms of government—are systems of ideas that are rational, intelligible, and organized into a logical pattern of thought. The political systems of societies are all built on ideological structures, and the most important function of ideologies is to make the governors acceptable to the governed.

Political ideologies fall into either the autocratic or the democratic camp. The basis of autocratic ideologies is the belief that government should be in the hands of one or more individuals who have supreme power and are above the law. In modern times, traditional autocracies have been replaced by totalitarian regimes that offer prescriptions for a lifestyle with implications in all facets of life. Fascism and Nazism are two such totalitarian ideologies of the right.

A totalitarian ideology of the left that enjoyed wide popularity in the twentieth century, but now seems to be on the wane, is communism. Its main thrust is the establishment of an egalitarian society. Its founder was Karl Marx, who based the ideology on materialism, or the notion that people's conditions and beliefs were determined by economic relationships. Although Marx was accurate and perspicacious on many points, he was also wrong on a number of them: where the revolution would occur, how nationalistic workers would be, and the course of capitalism.

Democracy is the ideology most directly opposed to autocracy. Its primary concerns are the individual and his or her rights. It postulates that individuals are by nature rational, moral, equal, free, and endowed with certain rights. As a result, in its political system, the state and its government are considered mere instruments and act as trustees of delegated power. Capitalism is a subideology in the area of the economy. Its central features include the private ownership of property, the existence of a profit motive, the dynamics of a free market, and the presence of competition. Today's capitalistic economies are usually called mixed economies because of the government controls and regulations that have become mandatory.

Democratic socialism assumes that participation in political decision making should be extended to economic decision making. Additional assumptions are that major national industries should be publicly held, the profit motive and excessive competition are against the public good, higher priority should be given to public needs than to private wants, extensive national planning would avoid the production of frivolous goods and services in favor of necessities, only a small income differential should exist, and a comprehensive welfare state should eradicate special privileges.

Terms to Remember

authoritarianism A type of autocracy (see below) in which power is held by an absolute monarch, dictator, or small elite. Power is limited to the political sphere.

autocracy An ideology directly opposed to democracy, in which government rests in the hands of one individual or group who holds supreme power over the people.

charismatic authority According to Max Weber, a type of authority based on the leadership of a person with charisma. A charismatic leader is thought to possess special gifts of a magnetic, fascinating, and extraordinary nature.

communism A political and economic ideology whose ultimate goal is total government control of the economy and total income redistribution, leading to the creation of a classless society.

democracy An ideology, philosophy, theory, and political system assuming the basic value of the individual, as well as his or her rationality, morality, equality, and possession of specific rights.

democratic capitalism A blend of political and economic ideology whose tenets include the private ownership of property, the profit motive, a free market economy, and competition. The function of government in this system is to ensure that the economic game is played fairly.

democratic socialism A blend of political and economic ideology whose chief assumption is that participation in political decision making should be extended to economic decision making. The function of the government in this system is to control and guide the economy for the benefit of the voters who elected it.

fascism A totalitarian ideology of the right that became prominent in various nations beginning in Italy under Benito Mussolini.

government A pivotal institution arising out of the need to maintain order, control, organize, protect, and defend the people of a society. Government is the acting arm of the state; it includes a political process in which a body of representatives is endowed with authority and power to make and carry out decisions for the society and see to it that order is maintained and laws are obeyed.

ideology A system of ideas, values, beliefs, and attitudes that a society or groups within a society share and accept as true.

legal-rational authority According to Weber, a type of authority accepted by members of society because it is based on rational methods and laws and is exerted for their benefit.

nation A culture group residing within the territory of a political state.

nationalism The ideology behind the nation-state. A set of beliefs about the superiority of one's own nation and a defense of its interest above all others.

Nazism The German version of fascism that flourished under the leadership of Adolf Hitler.

politics The people and processes that make up and direct the government of the state, its policies, and its actions.

power The probability that one individual in a social relationship will carry out his or her own will despite resistance. The ability of one person or group to direct the behavior of another person or group in a desired direction, under the ultimate, though not always obvious, threat of force.

rule of law A constitutional principle holding that those in public authority derive, maintain, and exercise their powers on the basis of specific laws, and not on the basis of their personal power.

state The abstract embodiment, or the symbol, of the political institution or government.

totalitarianism A type of autocracy of the left or of the right, characterized by a totalist ideology, a single party, a government-controlled secret police, and a monopoly over mass communications, weapons, and the economy by the ruling elite.

traditional authority According to Weber, authority that is based on reverence for tradition.

Suggested Readings

Busky, Donald F. 2000. *Democratic Socialism: A Global Survey*. New York: Praeger Publishers. An in-depth, well-referenced, and up-to-date analysis of the history of social democratic parties and governments worldwide from their beginnings in the nineteenth century to the present.

deTocqueville, Alexis. 1969 [orig. 1834–1840]. *Democracy in America*. Garden City, NY: Doubleday/Anchor. A classic examination of the new political system and the new society of the United States as viewed by an aristocratic Frenchman on a journey in the 1830s. His insights are as sharp now as when he wrote them.

Kershaw, Ian and Moshe Lewin, eds. 2004. *Stalinism and Nazism: Dictatorships in Comparison*. Cambridge University Press. Two historians who specialize in Nazism and Stalinism summarize the research on those political movements. In addition, they provide new perspectives on these two dictatorships of the modern era: the cult of personality, the war machine, and the changed attitudes in postwar Germany and Russia.

Lieberthal, Kenneth. 1995. *Governing China: From Revolution through Reform*. New York: W. W. Norton. An overview of the changes undergone by this ancient nation, with a focus on the continuity from imperial times through the communist revolution and beyond.

Lind, Michael. 1995. *The Next American Nation*. New York: The Free Press. Subtitled "The New Nationalism and the Fourth American Revolution," this book proclaims to be the manifesto of American liberal nationalism, which the author defines as a prescription for prosperity and justice based on a "cultural fusion and genetic amalgamation . . . for Americans of all races."

Malia, Martin. 1994. *The Soviet Tragedy: A History of Socialism in Russia, 1917–1991*. New York: The Free Press. See also: Pipes, Richard. 1994. *Russia under the Bolshevik Regime*. New York: Knopf.

These two books offer analyses and interpretations of the ideology of communism as it was lived in Soviet Russia, that is, from the Russian Revolution to the dismantling of the Soviet system.

Service, Robert. 2007. *Comrades! A History of World Communism*. Cambridge, MA: Harvard University Press. A survey of the varieties of Communist ideologies and regimes, illustrating the patterns that make up totalitarianism. A controversial, but engaging introduction to this important modern movement.

Taha, Abir. 2005. *Nietzsche, Prophet of Nazism: The Cult of the Superman*. New York: AuthorHouse. A philosophical look at the roots of Nazism with discussions relative to the belief in Aryanism, a doctrine of racial superiority.

Web Sites of Interest

http://polisci.nelson.com/ideologies.html
This web site offers links to works of a wide range of political philosophers whose ideas have shaped modern political systems.

http://www.historyguide.org/intellect/lecture24a.html
A site that provides lectures on modern European intellectual history, Lecture 24 deals with the age of ideologies with reflections on Karl Marx, while Lecture 23 offers a general introduction to nineteenth-century ideologies.

http://www.fordham.edu/halsall/mod/modsbook33.html
A Fordham University web site that offers the Internet Modern History Sourcebook, which contains thousands of sources relating to historical subjects.

http://xroads.virginia.edu/~hyper/detoc/home.html
Titled "Democracy in America," this web site focuses on deTocqueville's view of nineteenth-century America and the continued development of its democratic political system.

http://www.ned.org
This is the web site of the National Endowment for Democracy, a nonprofit organization with the purpose of supporting freedom and developing democratic institutions throughout the world.

In addition to these sites, search engines can supply the names of numerous others that deal with such ideologies as socialism, capitalism, communism, autocracy, totalitarianism, and so forth.

The Government of the United States of America

IN THIS CHAPTER, YOU WILL LEARN

■ *the historical sequence in the establishment of American political institutions;*

■ *about the implications of the executive branch;*

■ *the weaknesses of the legislative branch;*

■ *the functions of the judicial branch;*

■ *the importance of limited government.*

> We hold these truths to be self-evident, that all men are created equal, that they are endowed by their Creator with certain inalienable Rights, that among these are Life, Liberty and the pursuit of Happiness.
>
> We the People of the United States, in Order to form a more perfect Union, establish Justice, insure domestic Tranquility, provide for the common Defence, promote the general Welfare, and secure the Blessings of Liberty to ourselves and our Posterity, do ordain and establish this Constitution for the United States of America.

Every American schoolchild is familiar with at least some of these words. They have become the myths with which we clothe parts of our history. Their sound evokes an emotional response, just like the American flag waving on the Fourth of July. The words, of course, are part of the documents we hold sacred, the Declaration of Independence and the Constitution of the United States. As familiar as they are to us, the posterity mentioned in the preamble to the Constitution, few of us are likely to have thought much about what such documents mean, and especially what they meant then, when they were written. For indeed they were spectacular for their times, and the political system that was spawned by the ideology behind them, cumbersome and inefficient as it may be, has served American society quite well for more than 200 years. That is a record few societies have been able to equal.

The emergence of the United States as a nation goes back to 1776, at the time of the Declaration of Independence. Until that time, as is well known, the settled territories of the New World had been merely colonies of Great Britain. Claiming a "long train of abuses and usurpations," and accusing the King of Great Britain of absolute despotism, the representatives of the colonists resolved to "dissolve the bonds which have connected them with another, and to assume, among the powers of the earth, the separate and equal station to which the Laws of Nature and of Nature's God entitle them." In other words, the decision was made to establish a separate, sovereign nation-state. This did not happen until the 13 independent states were joined into a union, when the Articles of Confederation were ratified by all the states in 1781. The U.S. government itself began to function only when the Constitution was ratified by a sufficient number of states in 1788 and George Washington was inaugurated as the first president the following year (see Figure 15.1 for the differences between government under the Articles of Confederation and government under the U.S. Constitution).

A Comparison Between Federalism and Confederation

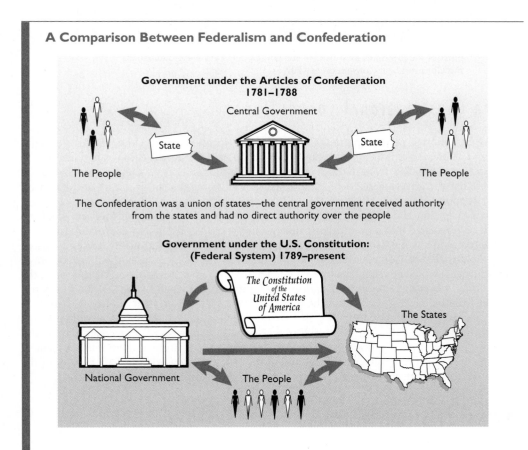

Government under the Articles of Confederation
1781–1788

Central Government

The People   The People

State   State

The Confederation was a union of states—the central government received authority from the states and had no direct authority over the people

Government under the U.S. Constitution:
(Federal System) 1789–present

The Constitution of the United States of America

The States

National Government   The People

FIGURE 15.1 The federal union is a union of *people,* that is, both the national government and state governments receive authority from the people (through their vote) and exercise direct authority over them through legislation.

Most of the principles by which we still govern ourselves were outlined at the Constitutional Convention of 1787.

■ The Constitutional Convention

With the exception of political parties, all the political institutions of the United States were conceived and delineated at the Constitutional Convention of 1787. As the colonies had just fought a war to free themselves from dependence on a British monarch, it was understood by all the delegates that the government to be established would be republican in nature and based on popular support. However, although these ideas struck a positive chord in many people, there was much suspicion and cynicism among the delegates about the validity of this new ideology. Could it be translated into a political instrument that would not disintegrate into mob rule?

The delegates were also dissatisfied with the weak central government that had existed under the Articles of Confederation—the first document drawn up after the Declaration of Independence—which envisioned a loose confederation of independent states. At that time, the colonists had no vision of a unified nation. They thought that each of the 13 states was too different from its neighbors and that the huge continent still to be settled did not lend itself to unity. They were fearful that a republic that covered such a vast geographic area could not survive. During the Revolutionary War, each state assumed the powers of a sovereign nation and jealously guarded its independence. The Articles of Confederation did establish a central government, but it was a very weak one, and in the long run, unworkable. The failures of the Articles of Confederation led many citizens to insist that a new constitution was needed.

■ What Is a Constitution?

The object of every revolution is to institute a new political order. After the American Revolution, it became apparent that a new agreement was needed between the governors and the governed that would reflect the new values, interests, and beliefs of the community.

Box 15.1   **The Constitutional Convention**

In writing the Declaration of Independence, Thomas Jefferson was influenced by the English philosopher John Locke. Locke, in his *Second Treatise on Government*, maintained that it was absurd for people to continue being ruled by the "divine right" of kings, or hereditary aristocracies that were not subject to control by the people. He suggested that legitimate government could be established only by the people themselves, and that such government could exist only by their consent.

In their resolution to develop a system of government that would represent the common good of each person and the interest of each state, the representatives of the thirteen states may be considered true revolutionaries. The signers of the Constitution have been accused of plotting to preserve the interests of their (high) social class. They were, after all, wealthy landowners and professionals, as well as merchants and budding industrialists, and their privileged status in society was beginning to be challenged by the new economic system imported from Britain, industrialism. Some of them may have felt that a strong central government would stop the grumbling of the small farmers and the new industrial workers flocking to the cities. And certainly not all were convinced of the desirability of a government based on the consent of the governed (democracy) rather than one based on the rule of a landed, wealthy elite (aristocracy).

Some historians have claimed that merchants and businessmen, who constituted an ascending social class in the colonies at that time (in the 1780s), wanted a strong national government so that industry and trade would be promoted, private property would be protected, and the public debt—of which they were the creditors—would be paid off (Current et al., 1983, 170). Other historians have maintained that the motives of the framers were much less mercenary; but even if their motives were not monolithic, it is indeed true that, as a class, the framers were the wealthiest and would have had a greater concern for maintaining the status quo than the general population.

Although greater equality and popular participation in government, the main principles of democracy, were not what the leaders of the American Revolution had in mind, the winds of change were in the air, the Revolution having set loose some egalitarian and democratizing tendencies that it was too late to inhibit. Whether or not the convention was called primarily to preserve power or the status quo, the need for a written constitution that would lay the foundation for a new, workable type of government was soon established. This Constitution was rapidly approved by almost all of the states, and suffrage on the issue was widely held. It appears that constitutional principles were accepted by the general population, including small farmers and artisans, and the minutes of the convention do not point to any maneuverings for maintaining the status quo. Again, there is no doubt that some representatives were committed to protecting the rights of a wealthy minority, but the chief concern of the large number of those present was for a government that would survive and be functional while serving the interests of all groups in the society.

To most people, the word *constitution* suggests a specific written document drawn up in the past to guide political procedures. However, a constitution need not exist in a written form. The term, and especially its adjective, *constitutional*, has a particular meaning and a strict connotation. The term is reserved to describe a government that is subject to **limitations** and that operates in accordance with general rules rather than arbitrarily. In other words, the existence of a constitution places a system of effective restraints on political power.

The idea of a written constitution became popular during the revolutionary struggles that accompanied the formation of many nation-states. Today, most of the so-called developed nations have written constitutions. Ironically, Great Britain, where many of the ideas of constitutional government originated, does not have a written constitution. The principles and concepts of its constitution are contained in ordinary laws and statutes, as well as in the Magna Carta, the great charter outlining certain liberties due British subjects.

The constitution that underlies the American political system has acquired an iconic image, so that the document itself is treated with the respect of a religious object.

Constitutions establish a framework for government. They limit the power of the government by stating the bounds of its authority. They provide specific procedures for governmental action—and, by implication, forbid other actions. The governed are guaranteed protection against possibly arbitrary actions of the governors. The ultimate authority is vested in the law: the law is supreme over governors and governed alike.

The so-called *rule of law* is an important principle of constitutionality. (It is in direct opposition to the "rule of men" that prevails in most autocratic regimes.) This principle holds that those in public authority derive, maintain, and exercise their powers on the basis of laws specifically drawn up and not on the basis of a leader's will. Consequently, every act of an elected or appointed official is carried out under the authority of the law and is subject to the judgment of appropriate legal authorities.

■ The Constitution of the United States

The Constitution that underlies the American political system similarly imposes restraints on the government. The four major constitutional principles of American government, for instance, are (1) federalism, (2) separation of power and checks and balances, (3) judicial supremacy, and (4) limited government. Federalism ensures a dispersal of power, because it is a system in which state governments retain supremacy in certain constitutionally specified areas (states' rights) and the national government retains supremacy in others. Political power is also dispersed by its separation into three branches: the legislative, the executive, and the judicial. The Constitution establishes a judiciary system that is topped by the U.S. Supreme Court. The latter constitutes a further restraint on political power because it functions as the final authority in interpreting the meaning of the Constitution. Finally, political power is limited by the fact that the Constitution grants individuals some rights and liberties that are outside the control of the government.

Federalism

One of the most important contributions of the Constitution to American government—as well as a peculiarly American invention—has been the system we call federalism. This system is contrasted with a **unitary** form, in which political power is centralized in a national government, and with the **confederate** form, in which political power belongs ultimately to the governments of the individual states. **Federalism** may be defined as a system of distributing political power between a central national government and the governments of the geographic regions into which the nation is divided: in the case of the United States, individual states. The power of each is supreme in its own area. The allocation of power is outlined in the Constitution and may be altered only by a constitutional amendment, a process in which both the national government and the individual states are equally involved (see the constitutional limits and obligations outlined in Box 15.2).

Box 15.2 Constitutional Limits and Obligations

Both the national government and the state governments are subject to certain restraints mandated by the Constitution. These limits are necessary for federalism to work. For instance, states are prohibited from:

■ making treaties with foreign governments;
■ coining money, issuing bills of credit, or making anything but gold and silver coin a tender in payment of debts;
■ authorizing a private person to interfere with the shipping and commerce of other nations.

Without the consent of Congress, states cannot:

■ tax imports or exports;
■ tax foreign ships;
■ keep troops or ships in time of peace (except for the National Guard);
■ enter into alliances or compacts with other states or foreign nations that would increase the political power in the states, which might interfere with the supremacy of the national government;
■ engage in war, unless invaded or in such danger as to make any delay perilous (and, the invasion of one state is equivalent to an invasion of the whole United States).

The national government, on the other hand, guarantees to each state:

■ a republican form of government;
■ protection against domestic insurrection;
■ that it will refrain from exercising its powers in such a way as to interfere with the state's ability to perform its responsibilities (today, such protection derives from the political process; that is, from the fact that representatives elected from the states participate in the decisions of Congress, thus protecting states' rights and interests).

States also have certain obligations to one another that the Constitution spells out:

■ *Full Faith and Credit:* Article IV of the Constitution requires that each state recognize (give full faith and credit) the public records, public acts, and civil judicial proceedings of every other state. This means that if you marry in one state, you are considered married in every state, and if you have a driver's license in one state you can drive in every other state (although if you decide to reside in a different state, eventually you will have to obtain a license in the state of your residence).
■ *Extradition:* Because most criminal law is state law, most crimes perpetrated are committed against the state, not the national government. Nonetheless, states are charged by the Constitution to return a person who has committed a crime in another state to that state for trial or imprisonment. This provision prevents criminals from simply escaping to neighboring states to avoid prosecution.
■ *Privileges and Immunities:* The Constitution requires each state to provide all privileges and immunities offered to its own residents to all citizens who happen to be in that state. This provision was meant to prevent states from discriminating against persons from other states: If you travel to New York State and you are from Nevada, you still pay the same sales tax as New York State residents, and the police are obliged to offer protection to you. (But there are exceptions: Only residents of a particular state can vote in that state's elections, and students attending schools in a state in which they do not permanently reside pay higher tuition at that state's universities.)

In theory, at least, the state governments in a federal system are not subordinate to the central government. They are sovereign in certain areas of jurisdiction and share sovereignty, power, and responsibility for decision making with the central government in many other areas. The Tenth Amendment to the Constitution delineates the powers allocated to the national government and to the states. It specifies that those powers not delegated specifically to the U.S. government by the Constitution, and not prohibited by it, are reserved for the states or the people.

The United States, in reality, has a great many governments. Not only is there a national (central) government, there are governments in each of the 50 states and, in addition, thousands of smaller governmental units within the states, such as counties, cities, towns and townships, special districts, and school districts. All these governments have a special relationship to each other. State governments can create, change, or abolish the smaller governments of counties, cities, towns, and special districts. State governments, then, are more independent and more powerful than the smaller governments and together with the national government form the basis of the federal system.

How Federalism Has Worked

The federal system has worked particularly well in countries of a large size, with considerable regional differences, and with a number of different racial and ethnic groups. The heterogeneity of such a country makes a unitary form of government impractical. And the federal system has a number of advantages. Under a federal system, government is closer to the people. It is possible for many to become personally involved in the numerous agencies of local governments. Also, administrative functions are decentralized, because the national government shares with the state governments the responsibility for the implementation and direction of many programs (the Interstate Highway System is one example). In addition, the states act as proving grounds where both legislation and legislators may be tried for effectiveness without involving the entire nation.

Of course, federalism also has its disadvantages. Chief among these is the existence of a complex bureaucracy with numerous agencies quibbling and squabbling about the extent of their authority and their share of resources. A further problem is the inequality with which some programs that have been made the responsibility of the states are administered by the different states. Not only does each state place different values on various programs and carry them out accordingly, but often how well a program is carried out depends on the resources of the state. Education and welfare programs are particularly dependent on the resources of the individual states. A predominantly rural, sparsely populated state allocates fewer funds to welfare and education than a large industrial state.

The nature of federalism and the way power has been allocated between the national government and the individual states has undergone a variety of changes during our history. In addition, because this allocation is not very clearly outlined in the Constitution, the Supreme Court has had to intervene on a number of occasions and so has had a hand in defining the federal system.

Trend toward Centralization

Partially to repair such inequities, the tendency has been for the national government to assume more and more of the responsibilities previously assigned to the states. To many, this tendency represents a usurpation of power, and they clamor for the restoration of states' rights. To others, the tendency is unavoidable and represents a welcome helping hand. Problems emerging from the urbanization and industrialization of the nation, such as overcrowding, unemployment, crime, pollution—to mention just the most visible ones—simply cannot be solved by state governments. Not only have most state governments until recently been dominated by rural elements opposed to city interests, they also lack the financial resources and the professional expertise to solve such gigantic problems.

The federal government, on the other hand, has both huge resources and many departments whose staffs are trained in specific areas of health, education, policing, transportation, social welfare, and housing. And the president and Congress cannot turn deaf ears to the states' needs, because citizens of the states are the ones who vote them into office.

In many instances, the federal government has had to impose federal controls because of the inefficiency with which the states were meeting their obligations. An example is civil rights legislation. This legislation was imposed by the federal government on the states, through several acts of Congress, to compel the states to accept the Supreme Court's 1954 decision that racial segregation in the schools was unconstitutional. Another area in which the states lagged was consumer protection. This lag prompted the federal government to pass legislation making its own agencies responsible for maintaining standards of meat inspection, automobile safety, truth in packaging and lending, and many other areas, including water and air quality.

The Impact of the Federal Government

The federal government has its greatest impact on state and local governments in the funds it makes available through numerous **grant-in-aid** programs. These grants originally consisted of public land, but now they are in the form of cash. Today, federal grants help build and maintain highways, airports, hospitals, libraries, health programs, the Social Security system, public education, vocational education, public housing, crime control, and welfare. The purpose of these grants is to equalize the services that rich and poor states are able to provide for their residents. These grants have also revitalized some state programs, especially where funds are shared in some proportion between state and federal governments.

The system of grants, however, has been criticized. In granting aid, the federal government has the right to specify in detail how and for what purpose local governments can use federal funds. It has been proposed that a better way of sharing revenues would be for the

One of the areas in which federalism has been successful is the interstate highway system: the federal government provides funding for its construction and maintenance, as do the governments of individual states.

federal government to return a given percentage of the revenues it collects in taxes to the states. Revenue sharing on a small scale was started in the early 1970s. This system also has problems, however, particularly in allocation and control. These problems may damage some segments of a state's population, most probably the urban poor.

In spite of the trend toward centralization, there is cooperation among all levels of government. Local, state, and federal agencies cooperate in an almost endless number of activities. Examples of such cooperation may be found in the Social Security system, the Selective Service, the National Guard, and so on. The federal government has also experimented with trying to solve problems on a regional level. One such experiment, and a successful one, is the Tennessee Valley Authority (TVA), which develops the resources in the area of the Tennessee River basin. Because it seems to be the most workable system for a large, heterogeneous nation faced with many problems, such cooperative federalism is likely to continue to exist.

A turn toward conservatism in the U.S. political arena began in the 1990s. This trend included exhortations by a number of political leaders to return more power to the states. Of course, power carries with it the responsibility for the economic well-being of the states, which would revert to their citizens. Republican legislators resumed arguing the "states' rights" position, citing the Tenth Amendment to the Constitution as the instrument that limits the national government to its appropriate role in American society.

■ Separation of Powers

The principle of separation of powers is prescribed by the Constitution and provides for the legislative, executive, and judicial functions to be divided among three separate branches of government. That is, one branch formulates and enacts laws, another sees that the laws are carried out, and a third determines whether the laws are in agreement with the Constitution.

The principle of separation of powers was not new to the writers of the Constitution. It had been expressed by a number of thinkers of the time, particularly John Locke and Charles Montesquieu. These thinkers maintained that it was too tempting for frail human nature to allow too much power to accumulate in one body of government. In particular, persons entrusted to make laws should not also be allowed to execute them.

The three branches cannot be absolutely separate. Legislators are not the only ones who make laws, the president is not the only one who executes them, and the courts are not the only ones who pass judgment. If this were not the case, the government could not act at all: the president might refuse to enforce a law passed by Congress, Congress might refuse to accept the pronouncement of the Court, and the system would be deadlocked. Consequently, another principle, that of **checks and balances,** was incorporated to ensure that the three governmental branches can check on and balance one another. A degree of independence for each is assured by some processes, while a great deal of interdependence is assured by others. For example, the president's powers relating to Congress are limited, in that the president cannot remove any members of Congress or shorten or lengthen their terms of office. In turn, the powers of Congress are limited in relation to the executive branch, in that Congress cannot remove a president from office except by impeachment, a difficult and unpleasant process. The judicial branch is independent of the other two in that appointment to the Supreme Court is for life. Also, Supreme Court pronouncements on constitutional principles are binding on both the president and Congress. However, the Court is dependent on the other two branches in that appointments to it are made by the president with the advice and consent of the Senate.

In short, the principle of separation of powers does not really separate powers so much as it provides that they be shared, for each branch is involved directly with the workings of the other two. In such a situation, responsibility for public policy is difficult to pinpoint. For a comparison of the American system of separation of powers and the British parliamentary system, in which responsibility is concentrated, see Figure 15.2.

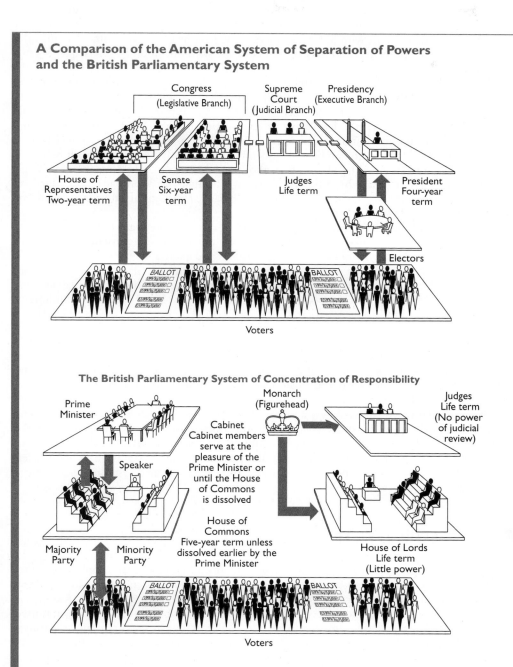

A Comparison of the American System of Separation of Powers and the British Parliamentary System

The British Parliamentary System of Concentration of Responsibility

FIGURE 15.2

How Checks and Balances Work

Each decision-making body of the government is brought to office by a different constituency. The president is elected by all the citizens of the nation who meet certain requirements. House members are elected by the voters of congressional districts. Senate members are elected by the voters of individual states. And members of the Supreme Court are appointed by the president with Senate approval. The lengths of terms of office are also different for the three branches, and they do not coincide with one another. Consequently, it is impossible to renew the entire government at any one time.

Each of the three bodies has the ability to check on the decisions of the others. Congress is divided into two houses (a condition called bicameralism), each of which has absolute veto power over the other. Bills cannot become law without the approval of both the House and the Senate. Congress is granted legislative or law-making powers, but the president is supposed to recommend and initiate legislation. Although the president has the power to veto proposed legislation, this veto can be overridden by a two-thirds majority of both houses of Congress. It is congressional legislation that allocates power to the executive branch. While the president is given power in military and foreign affairs, the approval of two-thirds of the Senate is necessary for the signing of treaties. Finally, presidential programs depend on Congress for funds.

Once they are installed on the bench, Supreme Court members are quite independent. Appointment, however, is made by the president with the advice and consent of the Senate. Congress, in addition, may vary the number of justices and exert a degree of control over the cases heard by the Court. The justices are also subject to impeachment. In turn, the Court can invalidate both presidential actions and congressional legislation that are deemed contrary to the Constitution. This last power, called judicial review, is not specifically authorized by the Constitution but is now interpreted as being implied by it.

Criticism of the Separation of Powers

Criticisms of the system of separation of powers range from the fact that it is cumbersome, unwieldy, and slow to the fact that diffusion and fragmentation of authority make it easy to "pass the buck." These characteristics, moreover, lead to a tendency to maintain the status quo, because changes occur so slowly and painfully. There is also a certain degree of governmental powerlessness in instances when legislation is opposed by important private-interest groups. Sometimes the system seems to be confused and lack purpose. On the other hand, the system does provide more stability than many parliamentary systems, in which the legislative branch is the most important and a government crisis can cause the parliament to call for new elections.

■ The Presidency: The Executive Branch

The office of the presidency emerged from the Constitutional Convention only after much discussion. At that time, there existed no models on which to pattern the presidency. Most contemporary governments were unacceptable to the recently independent Americans. The old Greek and Roman republics offered models of multiple leadership in committee-like organizations. But these, too, were feared by the representatives as tending to paralyze action. What finally took shape as the office of the chief executive included the following features: (1) there was to be only one chief executive; (2) the executive was ensured a four-year term that could be terminated only by death or impeachment; (3) the electoral base for the presidency would be independent of Congress; and (4) the executive was to be provided with certain constitutional powers independent of Congress, the electors, the people, and the states.

The Nature of the Presidency

Many points were left unanswered and undefined by the delegates at the Constitutional Convention. Consequently, the office has continued to evolve and take shape with each individual president. Although it has been said that the power of the office depends more on the president's capacities as a persuader than on real authority, presidential impact on the population of the United States is considerable. It is also generally felt that the office has grown in strength and prestige to a greater extent than the other two branches of government. As a result of involvement in Vietnam, which began as a presidential action without the consent of Congress, and other actions that have been interpreted as excesses of presidential privilege, a movement to curb presidential power emerges occasionally.

Traditionally, much has depended on the personality of the president. Individual presidents seem to mold the office to fit their perception of it. There have been presidents who believed that they had no authority outside that specifically granted them by the Constitution. There have been others who believed that the president could do anything to fulfill the needs of the nation, unless it was specifically forbidden by the Constitution or by the laws of the country. Others still have taken what is commonly called a caretaker's role: they have considered their job to be a purely administrative one. As a rule, history has tended to honor the active, dynamic presidents who have become actual political leaders of the nation. (See the list of all the American presidents and their party affiliations).

In his roles as head of state and chief diplomat, a U.S. president must present a powerful as well as a glamorous image to the world. President Reagan and his wife Nancy played those roles very well.

American President, 1789–2008

Name	Party	Birth/Death	Term
1. George Washington	Federalist	1732–1799	1789–1797
2. John Adams	Federalist	1735–1826	1797–1801
3. Thomas Jefferson	Democratic-Republican	1743–1826	1801–1809
4. James Madison	Democratic-Republican	1741–1836	1809–1817
5. James Monroe	Democratic-Republican	1748–1831	1817–1825
6. John Quincy Adams	Democratic-Republican	1767–1848	1825–1829
7. Andrew Jackson	Democrat	1767–1845	1829–1837
8. Martin Van Buren	Democrat	1782–1862	1837–1841
9. William Henry Harrison	Whig	1773–1841	1841
10. John Tyler	Whig	1790–1862	1841–1845
11. James K. Polk	Democrat	1795–1849	1845–1849
12. Zachary Taylor	Whig	1784–1850	1849–1850
13. Millard Fillmore	Whig	1800–1874	1850–1853
14. Franklin Pierce	Democrat	1804–1869	1853–1857
15. James Buchanan	Democrat	1791–1868	1857–1861
16. Abraham Lincoln	Republican	1809–1865	1861–1865
17. Andrew Johnson	Democrat	1808–1875	1865–1869
18. Ulysses S. Grant	Republican	1822–1885	1869–1877
19. Rutherford B. Hayes	Republican	1822–1893	1877–1881
20. James A. Garfield	Republican	1831–1881	1881
21. Chester A. Arthur	Republican	1829–1886	1881–1885
22. Grover Cleveland	Democrat	1837–1908	1885–1889
23. Benjamin Harrison	Republican	1833–1901	1889–1893
24. Grover Cleveland	Democrat	1837–1908	1893–1897
25. William McKinley	Republican	1843–1901	1897–1901
26. Theodore Roosevelt	Republican	1858–1919	1901–1909
27. William H. Taft	Republican	1857–1930	1909–1913
28. Woodrow Wilson	Democrat	1856–1924	1913–1921
29. Warren G. Harding	Republican	1865–1923	1921–1923
30. Calvin Coolidge	Republican	1872–1933	1923–1929
31. Herbert Hoover	Republican	1874–1964	1929–1933
32. Franklin D. Roosevelt	Democrat	1882–1945	1933–1945
33. Harry S Truman	Democrat	1884–1972	1945–1953
34. Dwight D. Eisenhower	Republican	1890–1969	1953–1961
35. John F. Kennedy	Democrat	1917–1963	1961–1963
36. Lyndon B. Johnson	Democrat	1908–1973	1963–1969
37. Richard M. Nixon	Republican	1913–1994	1969–1974
38. Gerald R. Ford	Republican	1913–2007	1974–1977
39. James Earl (Jimmy) Carter	Democrat	1924–	1977–1981
40. Ronald Reagan	Republican	1911–2004	1981–1989
41. George Bush	Republican	1924–	1989–1993
42. William Jefferson (Bill) Clinton	Democrat	1946–	1993–2001
43. George W. Bush	Republican	1946–	2001–2008

The Roles of the President

The presidency is a multifaceted institution. Some of the countless roles the president plays follow:

1. **Chief of State.** This is a ceremonial role that involves greeting foreign dignitaries or being present at the launching of important projects.
2. **Chief Legislator.** The president may initiate legislation, but the support of Congress is still needed to carry it through. Much of the effectiveness of a president's leadership, therefore, depends on an ability to persuade, threaten, cajole, or intimidate Congress into cooperating. The role has been forced on the president by default, because the cumbersome nature of Congress makes its legislative leadership less than effective at times.
3. **Chief Administrator.** In this capacity, the president heads the complex federal bureaucracy. Control over federal agencies is shared with Congress, which creates them, defines their function, and appropriates funds. The president and Congress share the power of drafting the budget, reorganizing administrative agencies, and appointing and removing officials.
4. **Chief Diplomat or Foreign Policy Maker.** This is probably the president's most important role. The president is the official channel of communication between the United States and foreign nations, even though appointments to diplomatic posts and the signing of treaties require congressional approval. The president is also Commander in Chief of the Armed Forces, although the Constitution grants Congress the power to raise armies and declare war. Thus, a president can react to a war situation speedily and without the prior approval of Congress. In the eyes of some critics, certain presidents have abused this power (by initiating or escalating conflicts in North Korea, Vietnam, Cambodia, Libya, Kosovo, Afghanistan, and Iraq. This role has been a major point of contention, which Congress attempted to solve in 1973 by passing the War Powers Resolution. Under this resolution, the president must consult with Congress in every possible instance before involving U.S. troops in hostilities; must notify Congress within 48 hours of having committed troops; and cannot hold troops in any foreign intervention for more than 60 days without congressional approval.
5. **Party Leader.** Upon being nominated a candidate for the presidency, the nominee assumes the title of leader of the party, even though involvement in party politics may have been minimal up to this point. This title is retained by the president, whose statements on party policy become authoritative. The president is instrumental in carrying out the party platform, and the national party organization is under close presidential supervision. However, state and local party organizations remain largely outside presidential control.

The numerous roles of the president force the chief executive to be a kind of jack-of-all-trades. As for the presidential role envisioned by the writers of the Constitution, it is obvious that their intent has been reversed. Whereas they had conceived the office as a device for minimizing personal power, in effect, the office tends to maximize it. One reason for this is simple: in time of crisis, when swift and effective leadership is called for, the cumbersome apparatus of Congress tends to be anything but dynamic.

■ Congress: The Legislative Branch

The major function of the legislative branch is to **enact legislation** binding on the entire nation. Because of its two-chamber structure, the interests of the members' states and districts, and legislation proposed by the executive branch, enacting legislation is a slow and painful process involving compromise and negotiation. For this process to be fair, input from a variety of interests must be taken into account. Thus, the second function of the legislative branch is to ensure a system of **representation**. The third function of the legislative branch is **oversight**, which means that it must supervise and investigate the manner in which the legislative bureaucracy is carrying out and implementing the laws Congress mandated.

The delegates to the Constitutional Convention wanted to make sure that the new system of government would include some sort of popular representative assembly. The difficulty lay in reaching an agreement on how best to protect the interests of the wealthy minority against the impulsiveness and excesses of the common people who constituted the majority. Further, the delegates needed to reconcile equitably the interests of the heavily populated states with those of the sparsely populated ones. A compromise was finally struck in which the House of Representatives was to be the forum for the people of the entire nation and the Senate the forum of the states and of minorities.

As to how the people would actually be represented, two alternatives were open to the delegates. They could devise a system of representation based on geography, in which each legislator represented a group of persons living in the same area. Or they could follow the parliamentary system, in which the population was divided politically and each legislator represented a group of persons sharing the same political orientation and living in the same geographic area. The first alternative, which the delegates ultimately chose, is called the single-member constituency system. The second is called the proportional representation system.

Again, reality today is not what was envisioned by the founders. Conflicts between large and small states have not occurred, but a situation did arise in the Senate in which the more populated states were underrepresented while the sparsely populated states were widely overrepresented. Whether the Senate truly represents minorities and whether the House of Representatives really represents the people on a national scale are also debatable issues.

The Issue of Representation

The Constitution leaves the manner of election of representatives to the individual states. The state legislatures chose to divide the states into congressional districts for elections. Because in the course of time these districts became populated by different numbers of people, rural districts tended to be overrepresented and urban and suburban districts tended to be underrepresented in the House. Beginning in 1962, however, reapportionment has been correcting this situation. Districts must now be reapportioned every 10 years, after the Census. However, the manner in which members of Congress are chosen prompts some scholars to contend that Congress represents not "the people" but "some people," namely local elites who tend to exert influence on national decision making. And as a general rule, members of Congress tend to be concerned not with the general public welfare but only with the welfare of those in their districts.

The issue of representation is further clouded by the apathy of congressional constituents, less than half of whom even know their congressional representative's name or how he or she votes on any given legislation. In the past, studies have shown that members of Congress did not seem to represent the feelings of most of their constituents, especially in the sphere of foreign relations and social welfare. The conclusion may be drawn that, except on the subject of civil rights, members of Congress are unaware of their constituents' preferences and constituents are unaware of their representatives' voting behavior, even on major issues. It may be inferred, then, that only a politically active, interested minority of constituents is usually influential.

Because Congress is the body charged with making laws, it is only natural that its main function is to debate public issues. In the Senate, the relatively small number of members (100) permits a semblance of free debate, but the large number of representatives in the House does not. Thus, the House Rules Committee determines the specific time allotted for the debate of important legislation, and time is then divided equally between the two parties. Because of this function, the Rules Committee is very powerful. It determines whether motions and amendments may be made, and this power is sometimes extended to include decisions about the merits of certain legislation. Bargains may be struck between proponents of a bill and chairpersons of legislative committees to have certain objectionable items deleted from a bill before a rule is granted as to the procedure to be followed in the debate of proposed legislation. This situation, so accommodating to brokerage politics, has been somewhat improved with the adoption of a fixed set of procedural rules. Another improvement is that the membership of the committee has been enlarged to break its former control by Southern conservatives.

Congressional Committees

Debate is only one step in enacting legislation. Most of the tedious deliberations regarding the purpose of the legislation and how best to have it passed, the language in which to frame it, and other points of this nature are delegated to committees, which are, in effect, subgroups of Congress, or legislatures in miniature. They have the responsibility for controlling the flow of legislation. Also, they deal with proposals according to their subject matter, and each committee is eventually expected to develop expertise in its subject.

Seniority Rule. The most controversial characteristic of congressional organization, and one that particularly affects the allocation of members to committees, is **seniority rule.** According to this hallowed rule, the chair of each committee goes without question to the member of the majority party who has served longest on the committee. The only way to attain a chair, then, is to outlast one's colleagues on the committee, hope that one is reelected several times, and pray that one's party is the majority party. Criticism of seniority rule has been voiced, particularly by the liberal segment of Congress, because its members have been, in the past, consistently overlooked for committee chairs in favor of Southern Democrats or Midwest Republicans. These used to be reelected term after term because of effective partisan machines in their congressional districts, but the hold of the Southern Democrats was broken by the election in 1994 of many Republicans, making the Republican Party the majority party in Congress. The Democrats regained a number of seats in the 2006 elections, and are currently in the majority in both the House and the Senate.

Another function of congressional committees is to serve as sounding boards for the interest groups or lobbies, agencies, and occasionally private individuals who attempt to influence committee members. In this role, congressional committees become brokers among different interest and power groups. They sift the tremendous amount of information that comes in and stem some of the pressures for or against a given legislative proposal.

A committee chairperson can manipulate hearings in such a way that certain opinions are never given a forum at all. This procedure, together with filibustering and certain decisions of the Rules Committee, was used for years by the Southern conservatives in command of key committees to thwart civil rights legislation.

The organization of Congress leads to a certain degree of ineffectiveness. The older members cling to old traditions and demand deference from the younger members, and various committees exert a powerful influence and can often make or break proposed legislation. Soon after their election, the new members of Congress come to think of themselves as members of an elite group, which tends to interfere with their relationship with the constituents who elected them but strengthens the bonds with their fellow Congress members. Indeed, members of Congress do form quite an exclusive club, legislating for more than 300 million people. (See a profile of the membership of the 110th Congress in Box 15.3 and an organizational chart of

FIGURE 15.3 Senate Organization Chart for the 110th Congress.
Source: http://www.senate.gov/pagelayout/reference/e_one_section_on_teasers/org_chart.htm. Accessed 5/18/2007.

the Senate in the 110th Congress in Figure 15.3). Incoming members soon realize that if they do not abide by the rituals and traditions, their attempts at legislation will get nowhere. Thus, what emerges is brokerage politics, in which new members accommodate certain older key members and in exchange are nominated to important committees or are granted other favors.

Box 15.3 **Membership of the 110th Congress: A Profile**

Congress is composed of 540 individuals from the 50 states, as well as the District of Columbia, Puerto Rico, Guam, the U.S. Virgin Islands, and American Samoa.[1] This count assumes that no seat is temporarily vacant. The following is a profile of the 110th Congress.

Currently, in the House of Representatives, there are 237 Democrats (including four Delegates), 203 Republicans (including the Resident Commissioner). The Senate has 49 Democrats, including two Independents, who have aligned themselves with the Democrats, and 49 Republicans.

The average age of members of both houses, at the convening of the 110th Congress, is 57 years; of Representatives, 55.93 years; and of Senators, 61.73 years. The U.S. Constitution requires Representatives to be at least 25 years old when they take office. The youngest Representative, as well as youngest Member of Congress, is Patrick McHenry (R-NC), 31. The oldest Representative is Ralph Hall (R-TX), 83.

Senators must be at least 30 years old when they take office. The youngest Senator is Senator John Sununu (R-NH), who is 42 and a former Member of the House. The oldest Senator, as well as the oldest current Member of Congress, is Robert C. Byrd (D-WV), 89. The overwhelming majority of members has a college education. The dominant professions of members are public service/politics, business, and law. Protestants collectively constitute the majority religious affiliation of Members. Roman Catholics account for the largest single religious denomination, and numerous other affiliations are represented.

The average length of service in the House, at the beginning of the Congress, is about 10 years (5.07 terms); in the Senate, 12.82 years (slightly over two terms).

A record number of 90 women serve in the 110th Congress: 74 in the House, 16 in the Senate. There are 42 black or African-American members in the House, including 2 Delegates, and 1 black Senator. There are 30 Hispanic or Latino Members serving: 26 in the House, including the Resident Commissioner, and 3 in the Senate. Nine members (6 Representatives, 1 Delegate, and 2 Senators) are Asian, Indian American (Asian), or Native Hawaiian/other Pacific Islander. There is 1 American Indian (Native American), who serves in the House.

Female and Minority Members

Female Members. More women, 90, serve in the 110th Congress than have in any prior Congress. Seventy-four serve in the House and 16 in the Senate. Of the 74 women in the House, 53 are Democrats, including 3 Delegates, and 21 are Republicans. Of women serving in the Senate, 11 are Democrats and 5 are Republicans.

Black Members. There are 43 black or African-American members in the 110th Congress, 42 in the House, 1 in the Senate. All are Democrats, including 2 Delegates. This number equals that of black members serving in the 109th Congress, which was a record. Fourteen black or African American women, including 2 Delegates, serve in the House. Senator Barack Obama (D-IL) is the first black male Democrat to serve in the Senate.

Hispanic Members. There are 30 Hispanic or Latino members of the 110th Congress, the same number as in the 109th Congress, which had the largest number of Hispanic Members in a single Congress.[2] Twenty-seven serve in the House and three in the Senate. Of the Members of the House, 22 are Democrats, 5 are Republicans (including the Resident Commissioner), and 7 are women. The Hispanic Senators include 2 Democrats and 1 Republican. All are male.

Two sets of Hispanic members are brothers, and one set are sisters. Mario and Lincoln Diaz-Balart, Republicans from Florida, serve in the House. Ken Salazar (D-CO) serves in the Senate, and his brother, John Salazar (D-CO), serves in the House. Linda and Loretta Sanchez, Democrats from California, serve in the House.[3]

[1]This figure includes 100 Senators, 435 Representatives, four delegates (from the District of Columbia, Guam, American Samoa, and the U.S. Virgin Islands), and one Resident Commissioner (from Puerto Rico). Since 1789, 11,815 individuals (not including Delegates and Resident Commissioners) have served in Congress: 9,920 only in the House, 1,250 only in the Senate, and 645 in both houses.

[2]This number includes three Members of the House who are of Portuguese descent and belong to the Congressional Hispanic Caucus. Note, that until November 2006, a record number of 29 Hispanic Members (26 in the House; three in the Senate) served in the 109th Congress. On Nov. 13, 2006, Rep. Albio Sires (D-NJ) was sworn in to fill the vacancy caused when Rep. Robert Menendez (D-NJ) resigned from the House in Jan. 2006 after he was appointed to the Senate. Rep. Sires was also elected to the 110th Congress.

[3]Note that brothers Sen. Carl Levin (D-MI) and Rep. Sander Levin (D-MI) also serve in the 110th Congress as well as Sen. Edward Kennedy (D-MA) and his son Rep. Patrick Kennedy (D-RI).

Box 15.3 Membership of the 110th Congress: A Profile (*Continued*)

Asian Pacific Americans. Nine members are of Asian or Native Hawaiian/other Pacific Islander heritage. Seven serve in the House, six Democrats (including a Delegate) and one Republican. Two, both Democrats, serve in the Senate. Of those serving in the House, one is a Delegate, one is a black member with Filipino heritage, and one is Indian American (Asian).

American Indians. There is one American Indian (Native American) member of the 110th Congress, who is a Republican member of the House.

Foreign Born[4]

Eleven Representatives and one Senator were born outside the United States. Their places of birth include Cuba, Hungary, Mexico, Taiwan, Japan, Pakistan, Canada, and the Netherlands.

Military Service

According to the Military Officers Association of America, 131 members of the 110th Congress have had some form of military service.[5] The House has 102; the Senate 29. They have served in World War II, the Korean War, Vietnam, the Persian Gulf (1990–1991), Iraq (2003–present), and Kosovo, as well as during times of peace. Some have served in the Reserves and the National Guard. Several members are still serving as Reservists. Two Senators are former Secretaries of the Navy.

The number of veterans in the 110th Congress reflects part of the trend of a steady decline in the number of members who have served in the military. For example, 390 veterans served in the 93rd Congress (1973–1975); and 236 served in the 103rd (1993–1995). This may be attributed in part to the end of the Selective Service System draft in 1973.

[4]"Born Abroad," *CQ Today*, July 1, 2005, 10, supplemented by CRS.
[5]Military Officers Association of America, unpublished data supplemented by CRS.

The Subordinate Role of Congress

Critics have long said that the House responds 20 or 30 years after social problems arise, if at all. Younger members of Congress have been making renewed efforts to break away from outdated customs and irrelevant traditions and to restore initiative and a progressive outlook to the legislative body.

Although the Constitution gave Congress the potential for power, the role of Congress, especially in the fields of foreign relations and military affairs, has been a subordinate one. Most policy proposals tend to originate in the executive branch and from military and industrial pressure groups. As a result, the function of Congress has been one of acting on these proposals, deliberating on their advantages and disadvantages, and finally accepting, rejecting, or modifying the proposed legislation. Figure 15.4 on page 439 illustrates how a bill becomes a law.

The very structure of Congress does not lend itself to effectiveness and efficiency. Swift action is constantly impeded and thwarted by the committee system and by pressures from opposing interest groups and different constituencies. Inertia in the legislative process is further encouraged by lack of adequate staffs that could help members of Congress make intelligent decisions on the issues that come before them. Another obstacle to effective action is the fact that Congress cannot be, at the same time, responsive to the national interest and to the diverse interests of its constituents. Finally, because congressional members who displease their constituents or their seniors either fail to be reelected or have their projects defeated, the tendency against rocking the boat is strong. All these factors have in the course of time allowed Congress to be accused of no longer initiating laws but being content merely to approve or veto laws originating mainly in the White House.

How a Bill Becomes Law

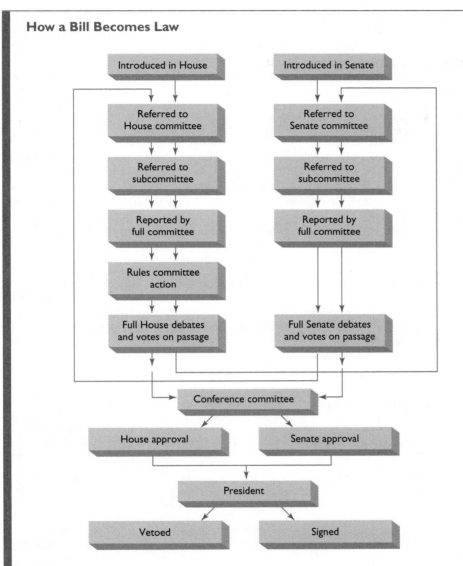

FIGURE 15.4

■ The Supreme Court: The Judicial Branch

The Supreme Court was designed to represent a final bulwark against majority tyranny. It was also intended as a check on the representational aspect of Congress and on the independent aspect of the presidency. To that purpose, the Constitution has been interpreted as granting the Supreme Court the power of judicial review.

Judicial review is the ability to judge whether a specific presidential or congressional act or a given piece of state legislation conforms to the spirit and letter of the Constitution. In essence, it is the power to declare laws unconstitutional. This power, which is not explicit in the Constitution, has been criticized on the ground that it is inconsistent with democratic principles. It has been said that it gives undue power to the Supreme Court, whose members are not popularly elected and whose terms are for life (Table 15.1).

The specifics of judicial review were not made clear by the framers of the Constitution. The current interpretation of the principle stems from the classic decision in Marbury v. Madison, in which Chief Justice John Marshall set forth the following guidelines:

1. The Constitution is the supreme law of the land, binding on all three branches of government.
2. It is the deliberate intent of the Constitution to create a government with limited powers.
3. Therefore, any act of the legislature, either national or state, that is in violation of the Constitution is void.
4. It is definitely within the province of the judicial branch to interpret the law.
5. If a law is repugnant to the Constitution, and the matter comes before a court, its judges are bound to declare the law void in deference to the supremacy of the Constitution.

Although the principle of judicial review is a feature lacking in most other democracies, it has become a very important factor in American political life. In essence, it may be said that some of the nation's most relevant policy decisions have been made not by Congress or the executive branch but by the Court. And indeed, many of the Court's decisions were made to protect certain minorities, just as the framers of the Constitution had intended. Other

Table 15.1   Chief Justices of the Supreme Court of the United States, 1789–2007

NAME	State App't From	Appointed by President	Judical Oath Taken	Date Service Terminated
Jay, John	New York	Washington	October 19, 1789	June 29, 1795
Rutledge, John	South Carolina	Washington	August 12, 1795	December 15, 1795
Ellsworth, Oliver	Connecticut	Washington	March 8, 1796	December 15, 1800
Marshall, John	Virginia	Adams, John	February 4, 1801	July 6, 1835
Taney, Roger Brooke	Maryland	Jackson	March 28, 1836	October 12, 1864
Chase, Salmon Portland	Ohio	Lincoln	December 15, 1864	May 7, 1873
Waite, Morrison Remick	Ohio	Grant	March 4, 1874	March 23, 1888
Fuller, Melville Weston	Illinois	Cleveland	October 8, 1888	July 4, 1910
White, Edward Douglass	Louisiana	Taft	December 19, 1910	May 19, 1921
Taft, William Howard	Connecticut	Harding	July 11, 1921	February 3, 1930
Hughes, Charles Evans	New York	Hoover	February 24, 1930	June 30, 1941
Stone, Harlan Fiske	New York	Roosevelt, F.	July 3, 1941	April 22, 1946
Vinson, Fred Moore	Kentucky	Truman	June 24, 1946	September 8, 1953
Warren, Earl	California	Eisenhower	October 5, 1953	June 23, 1969
Burger, Warren Earl	Virginia	Nixon	June 23, 1969	September 26, 1986
Rehnquist, William H.	Virginia	Reagan	September 26, 1986	September 3, 2005
Roberts, John G., Jr.	Maryland	Bush, G.W.	September 29, 2005	

Source: **http://www.supremecourtus.gov/about/members.pdf.** Accessed 5/18/07.

Table 15.2 The Most Influential Supreme Court Cases

Marbury v. Madison (1803)	Established the principle of judicial review
McCullough v. Maryland (1819)	Strengthened the power of the federal government over state governments
Dred Scott v. Sanford (1857)	Held that slaves were property and could never become citizens
Plessy v. Ferguson (1896)	Set forth the "separate but equal" doctrine
Brown v. Topeka Board of Education (1954)	Abolished the "separate but equal" doctrine, banning segregation in public schools
Miranda v. Arizona (1966)	Held that arresting officers must inform suspects of their rights
Roe v. Wade (1973)	Decided that women, under the right of privacy, had the freedom to choose abortion during the first three months of pregnancy

decisions according to critics, have had a much more political agenda. Table 15.2 lists other influential cases decided by the Supreme Court.

The Court System

The Constitution provides only for the inclusion of a Supreme Court as part of the national government. Congress establishes "inferior" or lower courts as they become necessary. Because of the federal form of government, the judicial system that has developed in the United States is complex. It includes a set of judicial hierarchies for each state in addition to the federal judicial hierarchy. In effect, each citizen is subject to two court systems, although the nature of each specific case determines whether the state or federal courts have jurisdiction. The federal courts are used in cases arising from any controversy involving the Constitution, the statutes and treaties of the United States, and admiralty and maritime law. Federal courts also have jurisdiction in cases involving ambassadors and members of the diplomatic corps, conflicts between states, and any controversy in which the United States is a party.

State courts, while not inferior to federal courts, have jurisdiction in cases arising out of state constitutions and state statutes, as well as out of the common law of their state. As noted, both federal and state courts are arranged hierarchically and parallel one another. In the federal system, the lowest level is composed of 94 District Courts, each with a bench of up to 24 judges. It is at this level that prosecution brought by the Department of Justice usually begins, because District Courts have jurisdiction over all cases tried under the laws and Constitution of the United States. The next level up is represented by 12 Courts of Appeal, each having three to nine judges. At the top is the Supreme Court. At one time, the Supreme Court was the forum for airing conflicts among sovereigns. Today, however, most cases it hears are appeals from rulings of lower courts. Cases may be appealed—or the Supreme Court may exercise its power to review the ruling of another court—through a writ of certiorari. This is basically an order by the Supreme Court to review the decision of a lower court. It can be issued at the discretion of the Court and requires the agreement of any four justices.

Functions of the Judicial System

One of the primary functions of the judicial system is to resolve conflict. Courts and judges hear and rule on disputes that are brought before them; they do not initiate these proceedings on the decision of a judge that a wrong has been committed. In other words, they decide

The justices who sit on the U.S. Supreme Court (here, in December 2003) represent a very important part of the American form of government. Their power lies mainly in the process of judicial review, which is essentially the power to declare any act passed by Congress, the president, or state legislatures as unconstitutional.

only actual cases or controversies between parties, and they do so in adversary proceedings. The adversary system puts certain constraints on judges and courts. While the latter have considerable power, they cannot use that power unless they are called to declare themselves. That is, while they have the ultimate ability to rule on what exactly is the law, they must wait passively until one party sues another, or the prosecution files a complaint, or the police arrest a criminal, before they can take any action.

Courts and judges guard and protect the legal system and the political structure. In this function, they administer the law, thus ensuring through such procedures as punishment, awarding damages, issuing orders, and overseeing the machinery of the law that the various constitutions, legislative acts, treaties, and judicial decisions are respected in the society.

They guarantee the political structure in three ways: by interpreting state or federal constitutions through judicial review, by making decisions limiting legislative and executive excesses, and by maintaining themselves above and independent of political and interest group pressures. They are expected to act as neutral referees.

Finally, judges and courts on occasion mold policy because their decisions may influence and control future legislation (Table 15.3). Because many laws are general, much of a judge's work at any level of the judicial structure lies in interpreting and applying the law to specific cases. For example, what does automotive negligence mean, exactly? Do defective brakes on one Ford Motor Company car constitute negligence? In exercising the judicial power to interpret and apply statutes to specific cases, a judge does, in a certain way, assert law-making power. Thus, judges possess a degree of choice that may be as great as that of other legislative bodies. This element of choice is sometimes criticized as being a violation of the separation of powers. Some even believe that it may pull the judicial institution into the political arena. That would be unfortunate, because the judges' neutrality and impartiality have long given the legal system the reputation of being a "system of laws, not of men."

Another criticism of the Supreme Court is that its decisions correspond quite closely with the dominant philosophy prevailing among the governing elite at any time. During the 1930s, when the philosophy of rugged individualism was popular, the Court reflected this conservative tone by handing down many decisions against President Roosevelt's attempts at social reforms. In the 1960s and 1970s, when the political climate was more liberal, Court decisions reflected this liberalism, as exemplified by legislation regarding civil rights, women's rights, and legislation protecting Americans with disabilities. Reflecting a more conservative time, in the 2000 presidential election the Supreme Court played a determining role in the election of President George W. Bush. The problem is that there is frequently a time lag between changes in philosophy and the decisions illustrating the changes. Often, this is a result of the justices' insulation from the facts of political life, which follows from their life terms on the bench. At other times, it is due to their relative independence of congressional and executive jurisdiction.

The nine justices who sit on the U.S. Supreme Court reflect further ties to the governing elites by their social backgrounds. Until the 1967 appointment of Justice Thurgood Marshall, no African American had ever served on the bench. There also were no women appointees until the 1981 appointment of Justice Sandra Day O'Connor. A quick biographical rundown, moreover, reveals that the majority have come from socially prominent, economically comfortable, and politically active families. Hence, the further criticism that some of the decisions handed down by the Court reflect the philosophical and moral sentiments of the American upper-middle class rather than of the majority of Americans.

■ The Importance of Limited Government

It was noted at the beginning of the chapter that one of the chief preoccupations of the framers of the Constitution was to establish a government whose power was limited. This principle of limited government was important to them because the history of the world was full of instances of powerful governments that oppressed the people they ruled. The principle continues to be fundamental to the American political system and bears stressing. Limited government is basic to constitutionalism because, in the democratic tradition, the purpose of a constitution is precisely to limit the power of government. The principle of limited government is expressed in the Constitution through the instruments discussed above: federalism, separation of powers, and judicial review.

Further limitations on government are embodied in the Bill of Rights and particularly in the First Amendment. This amendment guarantees the freedoms of speech, of the press, of assembly, and of religion against the exercise of arbitrary power. The Fourteenth Amendment forbids the states to deprive any individual of life, liberty, or property without due process of law. It also forbids them to deny equal protection of the law to anyone.

The purpose of limits on governmental power is not to weaken the government. A government must be able to deal effectively with threats from outside and challenges from within. At the same time, the founders of this nation and most people today recognize the importance of a national government that respects the rights of both states and individuals.

The rights guaranteed by the Bill of Rights have not been completely fulfilled. Perhaps they never will be. Whether or not the struggle for the fulfillment of these rights will continue depends on an informed and alert citizenry, eager to point out and correct any abuses.

The Chapter in Brief

The political system that developed in the United States following the Revolution was based on democratic ideology. One of the most important principles that resulted when the attempt was made to translate ideology into practice was the principle of limited government. This principle is carried out by several typically American institutions. The first and foremost of those is the Constitution, which prescribes that American government is a government subject to limitations and operating in accordance with general rules. The existence of a constitution imposes restraints on the power of government and allows the rule of law to prevail over individuals or groups with power. Essentially, the Constitution holds that those in public authority derive, exercise, and maintain their powers on the basis of laws.

The American Constitution imposes restraints on the power of government through the principles of federalism, the separation of powers, the system of checks and balances, and judicial supremacy. Federalism is a system that provides for the division of power between state governments and the national government. The separation of powers, establishing legislative, executive, and judicial branches, and the system of checks and balances are aimed at ensuring that power is not concentrated in any one area of the government. The judi-

cial system and the principle of judicial review establish the final authority for interpretation of the Constitution. The Bill of Rights sets limits on political power by granting individuals certain rights and liberties.

Not all of these political provisions have worked as the framers of the Constitution intended. Federalism, for instance, has shifted toward centralization, because in today's society many of the complex activities required of government cannot be performed by state and local governments. The executive branch has gained in power over the legislative branch, a fault perhaps of the ambiguity with which the Constitution describes the executive office. In addition, because the legislative branch is slow and cumbersome, presidents have found it expedient to arrogate to themselves powers that may not be properly theirs. This occurs particularly in times of crisis. The Supreme Court has a powerful tool at its disposal, namely, judicial review. Judicial review is the ability to rule on the constitutionality of laws originating either in the executive or in the legislative branch. The decisions of the Supreme Court have tended to reflect the current thinking of the government elite and of political activists. Nevertheless, the Constitution is flexible enough to permit change in any direction deemed favorable by the people.

Terms to Remember

checks and balances The method resulting from the principle of separation of powers in which each branch of government is directly and indirectly involved in the workings of the other branches.

concurrent powers Powers shared by the central government and the state governments, according

to the specifications of the Constitution of the United States.

constitutional government A government that is subject to limitations and operates in accordance with general rules rather than arbitrarily. The existence of a constitution places a system of effective restraints on political power.

federalism A form of government in which power is distributed between the central and regional units, each retaining sovereignty in specified spheres.

House Rules Committee The group with the power to determine the specific time allotted for the debate of important legislation. This is one of the most important committees in the House of Representatives.

implied powers Powers that are assumed by inference from the delegated powers granted to the central government, according to the Constitution of the United States.

judicial review The power exercised by the Supreme Court to invalidate presidential, congressional, and state legislative action that it deems contrary to the Constitution of the United States.

residual or reserved powers Powers reserved for the states or the people according to the Constitution of the United States.

seniority rule A principle strictly adhered to in Congress by which committee chairs and memberships are determined by years of service in Congress and on the particular committee.

separation of powers An arrangement prescribed by the Constitution in which three separate branches of government are entrusted with the legislative, executive, and judicial functions.

Suggested Readings

Barber, James David. 1992. The Presidential Character. 4th ed. Englewood Cliffs, NJ: Prentice Hall. An interesting work that attempts to predict presidential performance.

Galderisi, Peter, Marni Ezra, and Michael Lyons, eds. 2001. Congressional Primaries and the Politics of Representation. Latham, MD: Rowman and Littlefield. A selection of readings on the subject of congressional primary elections.

O'Brien, David M. 1990. Storm Center, 2nd ed. New York: Norton. The role of the Supreme Court in American politics.

Neustadt, Richard E. 1990. Presidential Power and the Modern President. New York: Free Press. An influential book whose theme is that what constitutes presidential power is the power of persuasion.

Sinclair, Barbara. 1997. Unorthodox Lawmaking: New Legislative Processes in the U.S. Congress. Washington, DC: Congressional Quarterly Press. An analysis, presented in great detail, of the American legislative process.

Walker, David B. 1995. The Rebirth of Federalism. Chatham, NJ: Chatham House. A historical review of American federalism and an analysis of its present-day condition.

Web Sites of Interest

http://www.rollcall.com
The online version of the Capitol Hill newspaper Roll Call, providing insights into what is going on in Congress.

http://thomas.loc.gov
Named after Thomas Jefferson, this Library of Congress web site provides information about the congressional process.

http://www.house.gov
The web page of the U.S. House of Representatives. Furnishes information on pending legislation, committee hearings, and party leaders and offers links to individual House members' offices and web sites.

http://www.senate.gov
The web page of the U.S. Senate providing similar information about this chamber as the House web site does about itself.

http://www.uscourts.gov/
Everything you need to know about the federal judiciary can be found on this site.

http://supct.law.cornell.edu/supct/
This is the web site of the Legal Information Institute at Cornell University. You can read current and past Supreme Court decisions here.

http://ap.grolier.com/
Much information and news about the presidency from Scholastic Classroom Magazines.

http://www.whitehouse.gov/
The White House home page with a wealth of information on issues, speeches, news, etc.

We The People: Democracy in Action

IN THIS CHAPTER, YOU WILL LEARN

- *how the ideology of democracy is interpreted and how it translates into practical terms when applied to a political system;*

- *which model of the location of political power—pluralism or elitism—best fits the United States;*

- *the nature, functions, negative and positive facets of interest groups (including lobbies and political action committees);*

- *the nature, functions, purpose, weaknesses, or strengths of political parties;*

- *that voting is the chief form of political expression;*

- *who does and does not vote in the United States;*

- *the meaning of public opinion;*

- *the importance of the mass media in the political process*

Every four years, the American people become witness to political hysteria. For months before the actual presidential election, we are inundated by newspapers, magazines, television programs and commercials, party conventions, and innumerable speeches in which candidates try to convince us why they, and the party sponsoring them, are indispensable to our lives. Individual candidates—and their families—are subjected to microscopic examinations of their appearance and character and to grueling campaigns in which their every action and declaration are subject to public scrutiny and criticism. Why do candidates submit to it and promise us the moon? Why do we believe them and vote them into office? Most of the arguments and promises are forgotten—or are impossible to deliver—a few months into the new administration; and we know it. The candidates undergo this trial by fire because they want the power and perquisites that go with political office. And we voters put them into office because somebody has to lead the ship of state. But in spite of the malfunctions of the system and the frailty of individual politicians, the political system under which Americans live has allowed for a peaceful transfer of power from one administration to the next, something that many other political systems have not been able to achieve. One need only point out the frequent coups and near-revolutions in Africa, or the tragic histories of countries such as Haiti and the former Yugoslavia, or note the instability even in parliamentary democracies such as Italy, where the government collapses every few months, to be forced to admit that, badly or not, the system at least works. How, exactly, does it work?

■ American Democracy

One of the chief tenets of democracy as an ideology is that government derives its power from the consent of the governed. This was the central idea in the Declaration of Independence and is termed *popular consent*. It follows that the individual has a major voice in determining the public decisions that affect his or her life. This so-called popular participation in the decisions of government is based on the democratic premise of individual dignity, extracted in turn from the natural law that guarantees each person life, liberty, and the pursuit of happiness.

Popular participation must be representative, because the size of the nation, even at its inception, did not permit total personal participation. From the point of view of the founders, popular participation was to be achieved through majority rule with respect for the rights of minorities. The right of the majority to govern itself is called *popular sovereignty*. Conflicts over public policy were to be resolved through decisions made by a body representing the majority. It was the right of entities representing the minority view to attempt to influence these decisions, and, in the final analysis, change them. In the process, those representing the minority view would try to become the majority. In essence, this describes the political process.

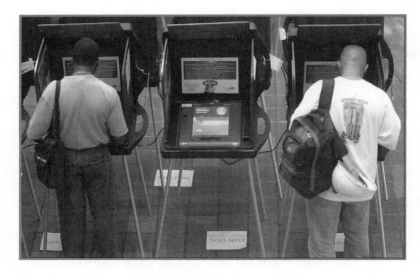

The consent of the governed, the essential principle in a democracy, is attained for the most part through voting because, first, the United States is too large for town-hall–style decision making, and, second, most people do not participate in political activities.

In a representative democracy, however, the fundamental issue concerns the functioning of that political process. Specifically, it concerns the amount and kind of influence that people exercise over the decisions of government. How representative of people's wishes are public officials? And, even more basically, who governs?

Although we are concerned here with the political process, we should not forget that a fundamental trait of American democracy is personal liberty. This concept has changed over the years: at first, it meant freedom *from* governmental interference in such matters as religion, speech, unreasonable search and seizure, and so on. Eventually, it came to include demands for *freedom to be* (for instance, to be free of discrimination based on race, gender, religion, or sexual preference).

■ How Is America Governed?

What does it mean to govern? In the simplest terms, to govern is to have the power to make decisions binding on the society. Viewed in these terms, who has power in the United States? Is it "the people," as the ideology expresses it? Or is it "some people," as reality indicates? The intent of the founders was to have some people govern as representatives for all people. Have they succeeded in their intent?

The classical, textbook model of democracy as conceived by the founders is referred to as the **majoritarian model**. It interprets the statement that government is to be by the people as meaning that government decisions are to be made by the majority of the people. In this model, several mechanisms are open to people to enable them to participate directly in the political process. The popular election of government officials is the foremost mechanism for direct participation, but this mechanism requires a well-informed and politically active citizenry that takes responsibility for choosing representatives wisely and defeating public officials whose behavior in office does not truly represent them. Public officials, in turn, are motivated to behave well and be responsive to the electorate because of the threat of defeat at the polls.

Not only are candidates chosen through elections, government policies may be decided through **referendum** as well. This mechanism is seldom used nationally but is used quite frequently on the state level. Citizens are also expected to learn about the issues, discuss politics, and propose legislation through a process called **initiative**. In this process, citizens circulate petitions, gather the required number of signatures, and, thus, place specific issues before the legislature. In sum, the majoritarian model of participatory democracy assumes that people can control their government if they take advantage of the mechanisms available to them (and computer technology could offer additional mechanisms), but they must be knowledgeable about government and politics, must want to participate, and must make rational decisions.

Obviously, these requirements do not describe the American electorate. As will be pointed out later in the chapter, only about half of eligible voters vote in national elections, and very small minorities are interested in or follow the political process. This fact has prompted commentators to speculate that the democratic model works in other ways, although there actually is no agreement on how closely the ideology functions when translated in practice. What most people do agree on is that there is quite a gap between the ideal and the real. This agreement is shared by the two most prevalent opposing schools of thought on how the political process really works in the United States (there are many others). One is the theory of elitism. The other is the theory of political pluralism, or broker rule (rule by compromise).

Elitism

Elitism, also called **class theory,** is a school of thought whose premise is that power in a society belongs to a limited number of individuals or groups, referred to as elites. Elitist theorists do not maintain that this is the way it ought to be; they merely report what they see as facts. Karl Marx was an elitist, because he claimed that capitalist societies were divided into the bourgeoisie (those who owned the means of production) and the proletariat (the industrial workers). He added that the bourgeoisie used the government as a tool to manipulate the proletariat. Closer to home and in this century, the late sociologist C. Wright Mills wrote that the most significant decisions, including those concerning war and peace, are made by a handful of people who represent the corporate rich, the military upper echelons, and the political directorate (Mills, 1956). Even President Dwight Eisenhower, who was a five-star general, upon leaving office warned of the danger of the influence of the "military-industrial complex" on government policy. Elitists also maintain that the consensus that supposedly exists in the society is, in reality, established by elites who are able to manipulate the masses through the mass communication media. Competition occurs only when issues are minor. There is indeed a multitude of interest groups, but their interaction does not result in the diffusion of power. In the view of elitists, the United States is a kind of **oligarchy** (rule by a few).

Although Mills's views are considered too extreme to reflect reality accurately, the elitist theory continues to have much influence among political scientists. The reason for its popularity is that it is difficult to see how democracy functions when such a large proportion of the electorate fails to participate in the political process. A number of political scientists have made statements to the effect that the "division into elite and mass is universal" (Lasswell & Kaplan, 1950, 219) and that "elites, not masses, govern all nations" (Dye & Zeigler, 1984, 414). In a later edition, this statement was amended to read "All societies are governed by elites, even democratic societies" (Dye & Zeigler, 1993, 19). It should be recalled here that the theory of mass society posits that society consists of the few who have power (the elite) and the many who do not (the masses). Moreover, the ultimate fate of all organizations is to be run by a small minority or plural elites, a situation described as the "iron law of oligarchy." The elite differ from the masses because they derive their values from their upper socioeconomic class origin. Members of the elite share a common lifestyle and identify with others of the same background even if, in their leadership role, they represent other groups and lower social classes.

Because of their high status, the men and women who make up the elite control the resources of the society. The largest institutions in the United States are the government and a number of large corporations. The leaders of these entities hold the power to govern in their hands, according to elitist theorists. In addition, these leaders, in formulating public policy, mold and uphold the values of the society as they see them. Public policy reflects not the will of the people (or the demands of the masses) but the values of the elite. Change does take place, but only because the elite influence the masses, not the other way around.

Elitist theorists admit that, in spite of the adversary nature of the situation, there is little conflict between the elite and the masses. The elite do not work against the public interest. In fact, they disagree among themselves and do not represent a monolithic power structure with exclusive control of the economic and political resources. Elitist power is relative: some elites may be monolithic, others may be more or less competitive. Some may control economic resources, organizations, communication, and/or information; others may have only a small amount of control. The elite may even be influenced by the masses, but it is much more likely that the elite will influence the masses.

Although a case can be made for the elitist model, the pluralist model discussed below is generally thought to be more reflective of reality. The foremost reason is that no one identifiable elite can be pointed to, nor does one identifiable elite always win when conflict over an issue appears. The few powerful corporations in such industries as oil, chemicals, steel, and communications would, for instance, constitute part of the ruling elite. Yet their interests do not always triumph: environmental groups have often forced these corporate giants to take steps to protect the environment that have run counter to their desire for higher profits. Smaller communication companies forced the breakup of AT&T, one of the nation's largest corporations, to destroy its monopoly over the telephone system. It seems, then, that even extremely wealthy and powerful entities yield to the demands of others. Nonetheless, elitist theorists are on the mark when they point to certain periods in American history when elites did have a definite advantage.

Pluralism

According to the pluralist view, decision-making power is diffused among numerous interest groups rather than being concentrated in any single person or group. Although interest groups continually compete with one another, they unite in coalitions when it is to their benefit to do so. They attempt to reach compromise solutions to the problems of decision making.

Political scientists maintain that a model of political pluralism includes the following assumptions and arguments. First, the basis of politics is the struggle for power. The parties to this struggle are organized interest groups. Second, the stability of the political system is promoted by the great number and diversity of these organized interest groups. Stability is ensured by an underlying consensus (agreement) on basic issues that acts to restrain group conflicts. Stability is further enhanced by the role of politicians as brokers, by overlapping memberships in interest groups, and by the possibility of the continuous formation of new interest groups. Although group bargaining is performed by what could be called elites, these are responsive and accountable to the people through elections.

In short, the pluralist position is expressed by political scientist Robert A. Dahl when he says that power in the United States is distributed according to a pluralistic model in which neither a majority nor a minority is responsible for governmental decision making. Rather, such policy making results from the "steady appeasement of relatively small groups" (Dahl, 1956, 146). The process through which appeasement occurs is continual bargaining or broker rule. The fundamental axiom of pluralist democracy, according to Dahl, is that "instead of a single center of sovereign power there must be multiple centers of power, none of which is or can be wholly sovereign" (Dahl, 1967, 24). The focus in the pluralist model is not the individual citizen but interest groups. The individual citizen is relieved of his or her duty to have knowledge of and interest in the political process. This duty is passed on to specialized groups and, specifically, to the leaders of such groups. The strength of interest groups contributes to a decentralized government structure, making it possible for minorities to exert decision-making power over the majority.

Conflict and Consensus

Elitists and pluralists also display opposing views regarding the importance of either conflict or consensus in the society. Admittedly, both conflict and consensus exist in every society. In addition, because politics revolves around the question of who will have power, conflict among individuals and groups is unavoidable in the political process. At the same time, if there were not at least a general consensus on the way conflict is to be mediated—in other words, on the rules of the game—the political system could not continue to exist.

Which predominates in the United States, conflict or consensus? Pluralists, as one would guess, maintain that there is a basic consensus in the society that allows some conflict to exist within its overarching framework. For instance, they point out that all the participants in political conflict (such as who will be elected President in any given four-year period) are fundamentally in agreement with the principles of liberal democratic capitalism, sharing the ideology of free enterprise, self-help, competition, and beneficent greed (Hofstadter, 1954, vii).

Elitists, on the other hand, believe that ultimately it is force that holds any society together. Force is seldom displayed by the elite, particularly in the United States. Instead, it is disguised as ideology supporting the status quo. The ideology is forced on the masses by a manipulative elite until it becomes an apparent—though not a real—consensus. In other words, the masses—we, the people—are brainwashed by the elite to believe that democracy is the best political system, and that what we have is a democratic system. In reality, the system works to the advantage of the elite.

A Realistic Democracy

Who, then, wields power in the United States? Some maintain that the reality falls somewhere between the concept of the ruling elite and that of pluralism. In fact, a synthesis of the two theories, called *realist democracy*, holds that democracy exists when the following conditions are met (Keller, 1963, 273–274; Dahl & Lindblom, 1976, xxxvii; Wolin, 1980, ix).

1. Competition among the elites allows the voters a choice.
2. New social groups can gain access to elite positions.
3. The elites benefit from constantly shifting coalitions, so that no one alliance of interest becomes dominant.
4. The elites present a united moral front (consensus) on basic democratic beliefs and ideals.

Both pluralists and elitists agree that the electorate is too apathetic, ill-informed, and self-interested to participate in the kind of system that democracy calls for. However, even though those who exercise power may constitute a ruling elite, they are still responsive to the people. The elite, whether they are government professionals or leaders in the private sector of the economy, is actually approved by the people; thus, it remains accountable to it because it needs the people to vote for it or buy its products. In the end, the people do not make the decisions, but they choose the individuals who do.

■ Interest Groups

As the preceding chapters amply illustrated, people are group creatures. In all societies, people belong to numerous groups, for numerous reasons. When a group acquires a distinct organizational structure to promote a particular shared interest of its members, such a group becomes an interest group.

The existence of a large number of interest groups is a distinctive feature of the American political system. **Interest groups** (sometimes called **pressure groups** or **lobbies**) are coalitions of individuals with similar attitudes and interests who attempt to influence public policy. **Public policy** is what government does or fails to do; more specifically, it is a plan of

Protesting legislation perceived as inimical is a right ensured by the U.S. Constitution. Here, demonstrators are protesting same-sex marriage after the state of Massachusetts legalized it. Protests, however, are short lived. Longer-term issues are taken up by interest groups and lobbies.

action that the government adopts to either solve a social problem, counter a threat, or pursue a goal. Because interest groups try to influence public policy, they resemble political parties. They differ from political parties, however, in the manner in which they pursue their goals. Interest groups do not have candidates who officially represent their interests, and they do not aim for complete control of government. Interest groups do not try to run in elections, nor do their names appear on ballots for people to vote on.

Americans, more than other people in the world, are ready to join—or even form—an interest group to pursue an interest or redress a perceived injustice. The large number of interest groups and their growth in recent years are attributed to the fact that Americans are not a homogeneous people, and each subcultural group forms associations to further its cause or protect its interests. In addition, change in society and in the economy has been rapid and dramatic, causing people to seek protection in unionization, the women's movement, the civil rights movement, and so on. When government expands and creates social programs, it benefits some individuals but hurts others; both the beneficiaries and the targets of government programs organize to protect themselves. Finally, political party organization has been progressively weakening, and interest groups have taken up the slack.

Functions of Interest Groups

The framers of the Constitution were afraid of what they called "factions" and what we call special interests. That is why they designed a government system in which power was fragmented between the state and federal levels and, on the federal level, among the executive, legislative, and judicial branches. However, interest groups have proved to have positive functions in a democratic society.

For one thing, they serve as links between the people and those who determine public policy, enabling the government to identify opinions to which it must respond. They act as channels of communication between their members and public officials. Each interest group is the best-informed source on the interest it is trying to further; therefore, it can be of genuine help to legislators when they are debating legislation on the subject.

For another, interest groups can clarify opinions and stimulate discussions of political issues. Interest groups sift, study, and debate various aspects of a particular issue so that the issue becomes understandable and consequently easier to resolve. Discussions, with the help of the mass media, help to educate the public.

Interest groups act as checks on other interest groups and on individual public officials. If the activities of one interest group become unreasonable or improper, another group brings this to public attention. If public officials become lax in the performance of their duties, their irresponsibility is frequently exposed by an interest group.

Interest groups provide representation based on something other than geography. They can supplement official representation by bringing to the fore issues and interests that reach beyond strict state or district lines. And, of course, according to the theory of pluralism, interest groups are what make democracy work. Conflict is resolved and policy is made as a result of competition and compromises among interest groups.

Formation and Growth of Interest Groups

Pluralists, who look with favor on interest groups, believe that such groups are formed in response to an issue or problem by those who are somehow touched by it. In reality, people do not automatically organize in such circumstances. The ingredients that must be present for an interest group to form are awareness, leadership, and the ability to overcome the so-called free-rider problem. Of these, **leadership** may be the most important. Most Americans are aware of the danger of pollution from automobile exhaust fumes, but few are willing to do anything about it. Most women are conscious of being treated unequally in terms of pay, but only a minority institute legal suits against employers.

According to political scientist Robert Salisbury, the crucial factor in turning the awareness of an issue into an organized movement to confront or challenge it is the quality of leadership (Salisbury, 1969, 1–32). Salisbury maintains that an interest-group leader plays a role similar to that of an entrepreneur in the business arena in the sense that he or she must market or sell the idea of organizing. Such a leader must also know how to take advantage of social trends and political opportunities, taking deliberate action to translate vague grievances into political strategy. Most successful interest groups also develop procedures for succession so that the group does not collapse when the leader retires.

The **free-rider problem** refers to the fact that many potential members interested in an issue decide to forgo the expense and effort of membership. Their thinking is that if the interest group succeeds they will reap the benefits anyway, and if it fails they will have lost neither time nor money. This logic makes much sense to people, particularly on issues that touch a large number of them, such as consumerism; and it is the reason why it is so difficult to recruit women, consumers, or poor people into organizations strong enough to have an impact. To overcome this problem, interest groups must make use of selective benefits, that is, perquisites available to members only. Thus, the American Association of Retired People offers cheaper rates on insurance policies, travel and related expenses, pharmaceuticals, and so on. Of course, some groups, such as unions, can force members to join so that they will be eligible to obtain a job. In most cases, however, strong incentives are definite pluses toward membership.

Lobbyists

Lobbyists are the people who do the main job for interest groups; that is, they represent the organization before the government. In this function, they make sure that the organization is visible in the government's eyes and that, in turn, government activity on relevant issues is known to the group's members. Some lobbyists work full time for an organization; others are retained from public relations or law firms. Organizations look for people who have experience in and knowledge about the workings of government, so people who have actually worked in government are prime choices for lobbyists. Lobbying is a lucrative profession; consequently, many former members of Congress remain in Washington to pursue it.

How do lobbyists influence lawmakers? One example is provided by the work of Price Waterhouse Coopers, an accounting firm that hired a former congressional staffer to lobby on tax issues for its clients. These clients included some of the biggest names in corporate America, including the General Electric Company, which wanted the government to allow them to retain a lucrative tax break. The tax break would cost the government (that is, the people of the United States), approximately $1.8 billion in federal revenue over 10 years. The former staffer, heading a team of other lobbyists, met many times with top Treasury officials, pushing hard with the argument that the provision was not really a loophole, and would not result in a revenue loss. It also helped that the former staffer was very knowledgeable about tax law, having written much of the tax bill passed while he was the top aide at the Joint Tax Committee. Apparently, he and his team were convincing, because the Treasury Department decided not to ask for any changes to this particular legislation (Abramson, 1998, 1–22, 23).

In a more recent example, as Congress is finally beginning to face the problem of global warming and the necessity of reducing the consumption of gasoline, the *New York Times* reports: ". . . the Senate on Monday began debating a sprawling energy bill that has already kicked off an epic lobbying war by huge industries, some of them in conflict with one another: car companies, oil companies, electric utilities, coal producers and corn farmers, to name a few. Industry groups have raced to sign up influential lawmakers and are nervously calculating how much regulation they might have to accept from the Democratic majority in Congress" (Andrews, 2007, A14).

As a result of such activities, lobbyists do not enjoy the best of reputations. Lobbying should involve passing on information to those who are responsible for policy making and making a compelling case for the goals of the organization. In reality, however, many lobbyists depend on personal ties to the centers of power to obtain results. A number of highly placed government officials have also received payments as consultants to private businesses that benefited from specific government actions. This constitutes dubious ethics.

Political Action Committees

The job of lobbying has been greatly facilitated by the creation of **political action committees** (PACs). These PACs are created by corporations, unions, and other interest groups who want to channel some of their money into political campaigns to support candidates who espouse their ideas. A PAC can collect money from stockholders or members and can donate the money (at the rate of $5,000 per candidate, per campaign; that is, $5,000 in the primary and $5,000 in the general election campaign, and whatever it likes in an independent campaign) to any campaign it chooses, as long as all expenditures are reported to the Federal Election Commission. (Table 16.1 illustrates who contributes and the limits to contributions.)

TABLE 16.1   Contribution Limits 2007–2008

	To each candidate or candidate committee per election	To national party committee per calendar year	To state, district & local party committee per calendar year	To any other political committee per calendar year[1]	Special Limits
Individual may give	$2,300*	$28,500*	$10,000 (combined limit)	$5,000	$108,200* overall biennial limit: • $42,700* to all candidates • $65,500* to all PACs and parties[2]
National Party Committee may give	$5,000	No limit	No limit	$5,000	$39,900* to Senate candidate per campaign[3]
State, District & Local Party Committee may give	$5,000 (combined limit)	No limit	No limit	$5,000 (combined limit)	No limit
PAC (multicandidate)[4] may give	$5,000	$15,000	$5,000 (combined limit)	$5,000	No limit
PAC (not multicandidate) may give	$2,300*	$28,500*	$10,000 (combined limit)	$5,000	No limit
Authorized Campaign Committee may give	$2,000[5]	No limit	No limit	$5,000	No limit

*These contribution limits are increased for inflation in odd-numbered years.

[1] A contribution earmarked for a candidate through a political committee counts against the original contributor's limit for that candidate. In certain circumstances, the contribution may also count against the contributor's limit to the PAC. 11 CFR 110.6. See also 11 CFR 110.1(h).

[2] No more than $42,700 of this amount may be contributed to state and local party committees and PACs.

[3] This limit is shared by the national committee and the Senate campaign committee.

[4] A multicandidate committee is a political committee with more than 50 contributors which has been registered for at least 6 months and, with the exception of state party committees, has made contributions to 5 or more candidates for federal office. 11 CFR 100.5(e)(3).

[5] A federal candidate's authorized committee(s) may contribute no more than $2,000 per election to another federal candidate's authorized committee(s). 2. U.S.C. 432(e)(3)(B).

Source: **http://www.fec.gov/pages/brochures/contriblimits.shtml**. Accessed 5/22/2007.

PACs have multiplied in recent years to more than 4,000, up from 608 in 1974. Their contributions to congressional campaigns have likewise increased exponentially, to many hundreds of millions of dollars every year. Candidates maintain that they can use the money from PACs without compromising their integrity, and PACs claim that they are not buying votes but only access to officeholders. However, most PACs have a conservative orientation, being sponsored by business and industrial corporations, trade associations, and so on, and because expensive media coverage is what to a great degree wins elections, PAC money is considered suspect by many critics.

Shortcomings of Interest Groups

The positive functions of interest groups, described earlier, must be judged against their shortcomings. Interest groups ignore the good of the whole nation, because they focus on the needs of a minority. The information they provide to the public is biased in the sense that they tell only their side of the issue—and there is always another side. Then, too, their power to influence is unequal because their effectiveness depends on their resources, which are also unequal. Finally, interest groups may pose a threat to democracy because they are not subject to the control of the electorate.

Pluralist scholars, writing in the 1950s and 1960s, seemed convinced that interest groups would offer a balanced kind of representation. Instead, in the past two decades, although there has been an increase in the number of interest groups, some interests have been better represented than others.

The proliferation of interest groups has also worked against the party system. Parties, as we shall see in the next section, often dilute issues because they must appeal to a broad segment of the electorate. Interest groups, on the other hand, focus intensely on a few issues. As a consequence, they are able to attract people who are passionate about one issue or another and will lobby the government to influence its policies on their behalf. This detracts from the effectiveness of the parties. Parties, however, are true instruments of majoritarian democracy because they can gather broad coalitions of people who, in making their concerns known, can effect large-scale social and economic change. Parties also represent those who are not represented by interest groups or are not well represented: they can generate collective power on the part of those who are individually powerless and against those who are individually or organizationally powerful.

While more than 60 percent of Americans say they are members of an organization, only about 40 percent are active in groups with a political focus. An even smaller percentage belong to political clubs or political action groups such as voters' leagues. Moreover, those who are active tend to be the better-educated segment of the population, which usually also means the more affluent segment. So, in the end, only a minority is represented by interest groups, while a majority is not represented at all.

Another criticism is that, as in all organizations, in interest groups too a small clique of leaders conducts the affairs of the group and makes all the important decisions. This situation is true both in groups that lobby to protect their own interests and in those that function in the name of the public, such as Common Cause or the various consumer protection organizations. Because the leaders generally have more liberal views than the rank and file, quite often interest groups do not even represent their own members.

Interest groups are not accountable to anyone but themselves, unlike elected officials, who are responsible to the public, at least at election time. Finally, although the multiplicity of interest groups is considered to be a healthy effect of the democratic system, not everyone agrees that their existence leads to good government. Some insist that their constant clamoring results in inaction, and an inactive government cannot plan or achieve justice (Lowi, 1979, xvi).

In spite of all the shortcomings of interest groups, it does not appear likely that Americans will abrogate their right to freedom of expression by ceasing to join or support such groups. Interest groups will continue to be an important characteristic of the American political system. In fact, it seems that interest groups have acquired all the technological trappings of campaigns, depending not only on lobbyists but also on consultants, pollsters, political strategists, marketers, and academics to energize the public on their issues (Mitchell, 1998, A1, A14).

■ Political Parties

Political parties are very important to a democratic system because they form the principal link between the citizenry and government through the mechanism of elections. They also link groups of people in society into coalitions, which makes the creation of majorities possible. Political parties as we know them today developed in the United States approximately 200 years ago (the Democratic Party dates back to 1792; the Republican Party was established in 1854, although it had existed in another form earlier). They represent the third base of democracy, the other two bases being a system of representation and the right to participate in the government by voting. This third element is the right to organize to gain access to power in the process of decision making.

The framers of the Constitution made no provision for political parties. They thought that popular elections would give the people a direct voice in matters of government without the need for intermediaries. It soon became apparent, however, that no group could operate effectively without some sort of organization to give it unity. Political parties came into being to offer leadership and to speak both for those who supported the government in power and for those who opposed it.

Purpose of Political Parties

Modern democracy would be unthinkable without political parties. This is because the unanimity and consequent one-party system characteristic of authoritarian politics is often forced on the people. It is, therefore, repugnant to democratic principles. The only unanimity required by a democratic system is on the issue of the desirability of the democratic system itself. In all other areas, democratic theorists recognize that conflict is inevitable, and they propose to mediate such conflict through the institution of a government of temporary coalitions (Schattschneider, 1942, 1). The job of placing a particular coalition in power is left to political parties.

The fundamental purpose of political parties, then, is to gain control of government and to take on the responsibility for conducting its affairs—in other words, to seize and exercise political power by legal means. Another way of putting this is that the job of political parties is to win elections. This is done in the name of the electorate, whose interests the parties loosely represent.

Functions of Political Parties

One of the most vital functions performed by political parties is determining and defining the ideals and interests of the people and clarifying them as issues and ideologies. These issues are then organized into a platform and presented to the electorate, which either approves or disapproves of them. The party with the most approved issues wins the election; now that it is the governing majority, it attempts to carry out the policies of its platform by making them the policies of the government.

The chief function of political parties in the United States is to win elections. In fact, the party that wins the presidency seizes control of the government and conducts its affairs for as long as the president remains in office. Every four years, therefore, political parties engage in a frenzy of nominating candidates and campaigning to get them elected.

A second function of political parties is to provide the personnel necessary to run the government. This is done by nominating, electing, and recruiting public officials. Selecting candidates for public office and rallying the support of voters behind these candidates becomes the everyday task of political parties. In fulfilling this function, political parties make the transfer of power a more stable process.

Parties also structure the choices open to voters by limiting the number of candidates to those who can realistically hope to win. In presidential elections, parties hold caucuses, present candidates at primaries, and organize national conventions, at which the final candidates who will run for office are chosen. (See Table 16.2 for lists of party activities in a presidential year.) Parties that have won in the past acquire a certain following of loyal voters, guaranteeing their candidates a steady base of votes.

Besides crystallizing issues, modifying through compromise the innumerable wishes of specific groups within the population, and acting as brokers when there are conflicts of interest, political parties also perform an educational function. Political parties share the task of socializing the individual in political matters. For some individuals, the party becomes a point of reference from which to make judgments on a confusing array of candidates and issues.

American political parties are generally viewed as uniting forces rather than divisive ones. Because there are only two major parties, a broad spectrum of interests must be encompassed by each. To win the support of the largest number of voters, the parties cannot afford to embrace extremist positions. Consequently, they adopt rather moderate, middle-of-the-road positions and are able to draw together very heterogeneous groups.

Features of the American Party System

The American party system is a two-party system. This means that the competition for control of the government takes place between only two parties. Although third parties

TABLE 16.2   Presidential Primary and Caucus Dates, 2008

2008

January
   3: Iowa caucus*
   5: Wyoming caucuses
   8: New Hampshire
15: Michigan
19: Nevada caucuses, South Carolina
29: Florida

February
   1: Maine caucus
   5: Alabama, Alaska caucuses, Arizona, Arkansas,
      California, Colorado caucuses, Connecticut,
      Delaware, Georgia, Idaho caucus, Illinois, Minnesota
      caucuses, Missouri, New Jersey, New Mexico caucus,
      New York, North Dakota caucuses, Oklahoma,
      Tennessee, Utah, West Virginia
   9: Louisiana, Nebraska caucus, Washington caucuses
10: Maine caucus
12: Maryland, Virginia
19: Hawaii caucus, Washington, Wisconsin

March
   4: Massachusetts, Ohio, Rhode Island, Texas, Vermont
   8: Wyoming caucus
11: Mississippi

April
22: Pennsylvania (considering Feb. 12, March 4)

May
   6: Indiana, North Carolina
13: Nebraska, West Virginia
20: Kentucky, Oregon
27: Idaho

May: Hawaii caucus***

June
3: Montana, New Mexico, South Dakota

Democratic National Convention
Aug. 25–28: Denver, Colo.

Republican National Convention
Sept. 1–4: Minneapolis-St. Paul, Minn.

*New Hampshire and Iowa laws dictate their elections will be held before all other similar contests. The dates listed are the original, tentative dates set by election administrators.
**Kansas Legislature voted not to fund or hold a presidential primary in 2008
***Hawaii Republican Party will select convention delegates during its May state convention, but the delegates will not be committed to any candidate

Sources: The Federal Election Commission, The National Association of Secretaries of State and **Stateline.org** reporting

occasionally come into existence and nominate their own candidates, they have never posed a threat to the Democrats and the Republicans, though that may change in the future. The two-party system contrasts with the systems of other nations, of both democratic and nondemocratic persuasion. In most other nations, in fact, either one party or a multitude of parties exists. We justify the two-party system in the United States by assuming that most Americans agree on essential matters of domestic policy. For instance, we agree almost unanimously on the validity of the principle of the separation of church and state. Consequently, there is no need for the existence of Catholic or Protestant parties or of Muslim and Christian parties. In other nations, where there is no such consensus, the multiplicity of parties represents the multiplicity of beliefs.

American parties differ from parties in other democracies in the following respects:

1. They are decentralized and weak organizations rather than strong and centralized ones.
2. They are likely to have fuzzy positions on issues rather than clearly defined ideologies and programs. Many issue positions of the two parties are very similar.
3. Each party receives support from a variety of social groups rather than from a specific, clearly defined group.
4. Last, the winning party does not necessarily dominate the whole government once it is elected (Prewitt et al., 1987, 299).

Winner Take All. The mechanics of the electoral process favor the two-party system. Congressional and presidential elections in the United States operate on the "winner-take-all" principle. The party that wins the majority of votes in a given district or state carries the entire district or state. This is in contrast to a system of proportional representation and multimember districts in which seats are distributed in proportion to the number of votes a party receives. Such a system has been advocated by many people in the United States as a more equitable means of providing minorities with representation. The forces of habit and tradition also help maintain the two-party system. Party loyalty tends to be instilled early and transmitted from generation to generation.

An interesting characteristic of American parties, and one that distinguishes them from many other contemporary political parties, is the fact that they are not based on a particular doctrine or ideology. Nor are party leaders and members in complete agreement on any principles. Within each party there is a vast spectrum of opinion on specific issues—as the congressional voting record shows. Members of Congress do not necessarily vote as their party dictates or desires. Finally, programs of both parties are phrased in very general terms and avoid issues that might produce conflict—again, to appeal to as many diverse interests as possible.

Party Organization. Because only two elective offices are nationwide and fewer than 500 are statewide, around 95 percent of party activists labor in local party organizations. They are more highly organized and tend to be strongest in the Northeast and Midwest and in urban areas, where they are active in campaigns for mayor, city council, the state legislature, county offices, and so on.

The next level of organization is the state level. At the state level, each party is headed by a central committee consisting of members of local party organizations, as well as by local and state officeholders. The chairperson, who is a fulltime employee, directs day-to-day operations, but the members do not meet regularly except when a campaign is imminent. Then, their activities include polling, research, and campaign management.

At the national level, the two parties are organized much like those at the state level, that is, there is a national committee, a national party chairperson, and a support staff. These are permanent positions, but the national party cannot decide nominations, nor can it determine candidates' policy. Its chief function is to provide assistance in presidential and congressional campaigns. Even more to the point, its role is to raise and spend money.

Third Parties. Whenever a third party becomes significant, its platform is simply incorporated into the platform of one of the two chief parties. Something like this occurred in the presidential election of 1992, when Ross Perot, a very wealthy Texas businessman, ran as the candidate of a third, independent party. In general, third parties come into existence when a large proportion of the electorate is dissatisfied with the candidates proposed by the two major parties. Third parties appear either to promote a specific cause—prohibition of alcohol, for instance—or an ideological position outside the spectrum of party politics; or they are splinter movements, offshoots of a major party whose followers believe they cannot obtain a fair hearing from either Democrats or Republicans; or they originate as a result of a popular individual with presidential aspirations, who hopes to gain a sufficient number of supporters to win election without the support of either major political party. Third parties serve as safety valves for popular discontent and to send a message to Washington that certain issues are not being addressed.

Dealignment or Realignment?

American history is characterized by successive periods in which either one or the other of the parties dominates. The transition from one party system to another is termed a *realignment*. The Republican Party held sway until the election of 1932, in the midst of the Great Depression (until then, it had controlled both houses of Congress in 15 of 18 elections, and the presidency in 7 of 9 elections (1896–1932). With the 1932 election, there occurred a realignment to Democratic dominance coupled with a fundamental change in how the role of government was conceived (between 1932 and 1972, the Democrats won 7 of 11 presidential elections and controlled both houses for all but 4 years). Beginning with 1980, the Republicans regained the presidency (though not Congress until 1994), but it is unclear that a realignment took place. White ethnics and the white South defected from the Democratic Party on the issue of race, and the New Deal coalition has been slowly disintegrating, but there has been no definitive substitution of the Democratic agenda with a Republican one. In fact, the ascendance of the so-called moral majority is thought to have helped elect a Republican president in 2000, and the events of 9/11 extended further the power of the Republicans who are perceived as being tough on terrorists and more ready to engage in war when it comes to homeland defense. The Republicans had a hold on both houses of Congress until 2006. The poor results of the war in Iraq, with a high number of American casualties and no resolution nor an end of the American presence in sight, as well as a number of scandals touching the administration, caused the voters to turn to the Democrats again. Today, the House of Representatives has a wide Democratic majority, although the Senate has a majority of only one.

The hold of the evangelicals over the Republican Party may be coming to an end as well. The evangelicals were focused on social issues such as abortion, gay rights, school prayer, "family values," and so on. One political commentator maintains that the reason such issues no longer dominate Republican politics is demographic: the older leaders of the Christian Right are being replaced by a generation for whom the sexual revolution of the 1960s is relegated to history, rather than to memory. As a result, the younger leaders are less concerned with a type of conservatism that focuses on issues of sexuality and reproductive rights and are much more concerned with economic issues. Most of all, they are interested in "winning" in Iraq and in the war on terror (Edsall, 2007, 26–32).

Finally, political observers have noted that Americans seem to care less for parties altogether (Wattenberg, 1994). As a result of the uncertainty surrounding the issue of what is going to happen to the parties, the term *dealignment* has been suggested (Flanigan and Zingale, 1998, 58–63). In short, rather than engaging in a realignment strongly favorable to one party, voters now tend to shy away from partisan loyalties, and the electorate wavers in its support for one party or the other. The result is the increased incidence of **split-ticket** voting, in which voters choose candidates from both parties for different offices. In the past, the majority of voters used **straight-ticket** voting, in which candidates from only one party were selected.

The Party System in Decline

Realignment or dealignment aside, the American party system has been subjected to criticism in recent years. The parties have been accused of being unresponsive to minorities and of not being representative of the majority. Critics say that the parties have stopped functioning as the basic mechanisms of popular control: not only have they failed to set up the programs desired by the electorate, but also they lack cohesion to turn these programs into legislative action, and they often misread the feelings of the majority. In addition, members of Congress tend to be more responsive to the interest groups within their districts—those that can help reelect them—than they are to party dictates. This tradition is defended by those who interpret responsible government as meaning that an elected official should be able to decide alone on the pros and cons of a particular piece of legislation. It is criticized by those who interpret responsible government as meaning that the official must vote according to the desires of the majority regardless of personal considerations.

Some of the reasons for the decline of the parties are rooted in changes in American society. The former ethnic communities have been largely disbanded in the wake of greater assimilation into mainstream society. Americans are geographically far more mobile than before, often traveling across the country in search of better jobs or opportunities. The family is no longer the cohesive unit of the past, so traditional forms of voting for a particular party no longer count as much as before. Direct and personal contact between parties and the electorate is no longer possible, and partisan appeals have to be made through the impersonal mass media, which makes them much less effective. At the same time, even though over 90 percent of Americans say they vote for the person, not the party, the proportion of Republicans and Democrats combined exceeds by far the proportion of independents, the proportion of Democrats exceeds that of Republicans, and the proportion of Democrats has decreased in favor of both Republicans and independents. Still, people and organizations continue to support political parties, particularly when important elections are approaching.

Whether a reform of American political parties would provide the citizens with more distinct choices is a subject of heated debate among political scientists today. Some favor dividing the parties along ideological lines, centralizing their organization, tightening their discipline to present a unified front, and rendering them a truer instrument of the public. Others defend the status quo, arguing that it is precisely the parties' ability to encompass a broad range of interests with their platforms and to act as brokers in conflicting situations that has contributed to their durability and enhanced their functionality. A thorough realignment along ideological lines would definitely lead to a multiparty system and to greater polarization of the American public. The American political system itself works against party reform because of such characteristics as federalism, the separate elections of the president and Congress, and the tradition of political localism.

America: Red and Blue?

Even though the parties do not espouse particularly diverse ideologies, the way Americans vote seems to indicate that some fault lines divide the electorate. For instance, there is a deep gap between urban and rural voters. In the past several elections, voters in metropolitan areas overwhelmingly voted the Democratic ticket, while those residing in the open spaces of the country's interior voted the Republican ticket. Nationally, a higher percentage of whites, but only a very small percentage of blacks, voted for the Republican candidate, whereas a very high percentage of blacks voted for the Democratic candidate.

Traditionally, the Democrats have been the party of manual workers and those on the lower rungs of the income ladder. Married persons vote Republican, while single persons vote Democratic. Those who did not finish high school vote Democratic, while college graduates vote Republican. Persons who believe abortion should be legal vote Democratic, and those who believe it should be illegal vote Republican. Households with guns vote Republican, and 36 percent of those who are against gun ownership vote Democratic.

Finally, the 2000 election has become something of a phenomenon in American politics, with the "red–blue" divide making a dramatic appearance. The division of the country into red and blue states—the red states having voted for the Republican candidate and the blue for the Democratic candidate—indicates to many observers of the American political scene that the American electorate has acquired a split personality. The United States appears to be a 50–50 nation, in which geography translates into differences in culture, values, and partisan allegiance (the red states include the South, the Great Plains, and most of the Rocky Mountain West, and the blue states include almost all of New England, the Mid-Atlantic area, and the West Coast.)

This division into red and blue states is obviously an oversimplification that has become a much-repeated cliché. In reality, if all factors in the 2000 election were taken into account, the country would appear to be several shades of purple—with the red and blue overlapping. While activists in both parties disagree with one another on a number of issues, most voters tend to be centrists. The current administration has been accused of being extremely partisan. It will be interesting to see whether future administrations will be able to work in tandem for the good of all the citizens of the nation.

■ The High Cost of Campaigning

One area of political structure that all agree needs reform is campaign expenditures. The United States has long campaign periods compared with the six-week limit on campaigns in Italy or the three-week limit in England. Campaigning is extremely expensive, forcing candidates to work very hard at fundraising. This system of raising money from private sources brings to the fore the question of whether money buys political influence. The funds for electoral campaigns are provided partly by party activists at all levels, who spend considerable time and energy raising money, and partly by the government.

Seeking funds is an arduous job. Not only are campaigns expensive, but their cost keeps increasing: in 1980, around $250 million was spent on all Senate and House campaigns. This figure had increased to $424 million by 1990 and to $800 million in 1998. By 2008, each candidate will need to raise $400 million, much more than the $274 million and the $253 million collected by George W. Bush and John Kerry, respectively, in 2004.

Legally, each party is allowed to give $10,000 directly to a House candidate and $17,500 to a Senate candidate. This is termed **hard money**, as are contributions from individual contributors (an individual can give up to $1,000 per election to each candidate and no more than $25,000 to all candidates in any one year) and interest groups.

Parties can also legally accept unlimited contributions from individuals as long as they are used in state and local campaigns for party activities—registration drives or advertising campaigns. This is referred to as **soft money**. Soft money is a result of a loophole in the law and has been the object of much controversy. In spite of what the money is allocated for, in fact, it is easy for a party to use it to the benefit of a particular candidate. Senator John McCain made banning of soft money the focus of his strong bid for the 2000 Republican presidential nomination. His efforts have finally paid off, as President Bush signed into law a bill that bans soft money contributions to political parties, while raising the legal limit on donations to candidates from $1,000 to $2,300.

Raising funds from individuals is difficult because the great majority of people do not dispose of enough income to make significant contributions to electoral campaigns. Consequently, candidates have to curry favor with the minority of individuals and business organizations who do have the ability to contribute. Generally, however, contributions are not entirely without cost. That is, the candidate is beholden to the contributor, and that can lead to abuses.

To forestall such flagrant currying of favor, Congress had already tried to strengthen earlier legislation by passing new laws in 1974 and 1976. This legislation limits contributions and expenditures in federal campaigns, requires candidates for federal office to disclose all the financial aspects of their campaigns, and provides a public funding system for presidential campaigns. The government offers matching funds to presidential candidates who qualify by showing widespread support as reflected by their ability to raise $5,000 in small contributions in each of 20 states. The law also imposes a spending ceiling on each of the candidates before he or she can accept public funding, resulting in a cutback in activities organized by political parties and an increase in activities organized by other groups, including unions and PACs. While public financing helps little-known candidates gain national attention by enabling them to purchase media exposure, it also helps incumbents remain undefeated: they have a head start because of their recognized names, and yet they receive the same amount of money as their challengers.

Although the finance laws have reduced the role of individual large contributors, all varieties of PACs are allowed to raise money and allocate at least $5,000 per candidate per race. Individuals and organizations can contribute money to a candidate as long as they do it directly and by their own initiative; rather than donating money to the candidate, one can purchase air time on a radio station in support of the candidate. Obviously, the wealthier a candidate's supporters, the more support they can offer. The danger is that Congress may be more responsive to the economic interests of those who fund election campaigns than to the interests of ordinary citizens.

■ Voting

In an ideal democracy, the political system is based on an informed, politically active body of citizens who agree on essential democratic values but may disagree on matters of policy. Differences are resolved by these well-informed citizens in a tolerant, rational manner through orderly discussions of the issues involved. Unfortunately, reality is quite different. Social scientists studying voter behavior and the climate of American public opinion have uncovered some disillusioning tendencies among the electorate.

First, the researchers found a rather cynical lack of faith in democratic processes and in the right to self-government on the part of some people. Second, democratic principles and values evoke a wide consensus when referred to in general terms, but when these principles are applied to specific issues, consensus is displaced by some form of conflict. Third, there is a greater commitment to democratic principles among the leaders, the politically active, and the well-educated minority than there is among the majority of the people. Finally, general cynicism about government and its ability to respond to the people's needs seems to be endemic.

Although suffrage—the ability to vote—is considered a precious right for which citizens in some countries are still fighting, in the United States only about 50 percent of the electorate votes in presidential elections (in the 2004 election, however, 59.1 percent voted). Nonpresidential elections during off years, when all congressional representatives, one-third of the Senators, and almost half of the governors are chosen, produce a turnout of about 37 to 39 percent of registered voters. And local elections draw only about 10 percent of the electorate, despite the efforts of volunteers and interest groups to encourage voting (see Table 16.3 for a comparison of voting behavior internationally).

Factors in Voter Turnout

Why such a poor record when voting is a direct channel for political participation, leading to the popular control of government and its leaders? The answers span a range from the practical to the ideological. On the practical side, there are barriers to voting. In most states, a person must register before being allowed to vote. Then, election day is not a national holiday, so people must go before or after work. Many people have no transportation to the polls. Absentee ballots, which can be used when one has to be away from one's city on election day, are available but are not easy to obtain and return. And, as noted, Americans have to vote many times—on local levels, on state levels, and on the federal level. Finally, when there is little ideological difference among candidates, or the outcome is a foregone conclusion, or the television networks announce a projected winner on the basis of exit polls before the polls close, many voters decide that it is unnecessary to cast their ballots.

Far more important are the reasons for not voting that are not the result of such practical considerations. Among these reasons are apathy, political alienation, or lack of political

TABLE 16.3   International Foundation for Elections.

Country	Date	Election	Registered Voters	Votes Cast	% of Registered Voters
France	April 22, 2007	Presidential First Round	44,472,834	37,254,242	83.77%
Mali	April 29, 2007	Presidential	6,884,352	2,494,846	36.24%
Bahamas	May 2, 2007	Parliamentary	150,743	137,475	91.20%
France	May 6, 2007	Presidential Second Round	44,472,733	37,342,004	83.97%
Algeria	May 17, 2007	Parliamentary	18,760,400	6,687,838	35.65%
Romania	May 19, 2007	Referendum	18,301,309	8,135,272	44.45%
France	June 10, 2007	Legislative First Round	43,888,483	26,525,147	60.44%
France	June 17, 2007	Legislative Second Round	35,223,911	21,130,346	59.99%
Turkey	July 22, 2007	Parliamentary	42,571,284	N/A	N/A
Sierra Leone	August 11, 2007	Presidential	2,600,000	1,984,106	76.31%
Sierra Leone	August 11, 2007	Legislative	2,600,000	1,783,851	68.61%
Kazakhstan	August 18, 2007	Parliamentary	8,419,283	N/A	N/A
Thailand	August 19, 2007	Referendum	45,092,955	25,978,954	57.61%
Jamaica	September 3, 2007	Parliamentary	1,293,373	808,240	60.40%
Sierra Leone	September 8, 2007	Presidential Second Round	2,600,000	1,783,851	68.61%
Guatemala	September 9, 2007	Legislative	5,990,031	3,621,852	60.46%
Greece	September 16, 2007	Parliamentary	9,921,545	N/A	74.14%

Source: **http://www.electionguide.org/voter-turnout.php**

Box 16.1 Peculiarities of American Voting: The Electoral College

Americans are called on to vote many times, for many offices, at many levels: for school boards, county officials, state legislators, judges, and so on. However, the most important vote they are asked to contribute occurs every four years, when the president is elected.

Voting for the president is not as clear-cut as it would appear. In fact, the American president is not elected on the basis of the popular vote, that is, according to how many people vote for a certain candidate. The president is elected by the Electoral College. Each state is assigned electoral votes based on the number of senators and representatives that state has in Congress. As we know, each state is represented by two senators, while the number of representatives varies according to the population of the state; thus, no state has fewer than three electoral votes. The candidate who wins a majority of popular votes in a state gets all of that state's electoral votes: In short, it is a winner-take-all system. Maine and Nebraska, however, split their electoral votes; they each give two votes to the winner of the state and allocate the rest of the electoral votes according to who won each congressional district.

Initially, the reason for the electoral college system was that the Founders feared that an uneducated citizenry could be easily manipulated and convinced to vote for the wrong individual. The Electoral College needs to meet only once, and so is not subject to undue persuasion. Mainly, however, the Electoral College was part of a compromise made at the Constitutional Convention to satisfy the small states. This compromise has had unfair results over the years. For instance, in the 2000 election, the State of Wyoming cast about 210,000 popular votes.

Since it has only three representatives in Congress, each elector represented 70,000 votes. California cast approximately 9,700,000 votes and has 54 representatives in Congress. Each elector there represented 179,000 votes.

In spite of this discrepancy, most of the time the candidate who receives a majority of the popular vote also gets the majority of the electoral vote. Up to the year 2000, only two candidates had won the presidency after losing the popular vote: Rutherford B. Hayes in 1876 and Benjamin Harrison in 1888. In 2000, the same thing happened to George W. Bush.

Another peculiarity of the American system in presidential elections is the primaries, mentioned earlier in the discussion of parties. Primaries are held in a number of states in the early stages of campaigning. Their function is to choose the most popular candidate, who will then have a greater opportunity at each party's national convention to be nominated as its representative in the race for the presidency. State laws in Iowa and New Hampshire have dictated that primaries take place there before any other state. Of late, however, other states have decided to hold primaries early as well, a situation that has caused controversy and arguments between the local and the national parties. The primaries are held early in the campaign, while the actual presidential election is held in late fall.

The long campaign season that begins in some years soon after the election of the president, as well as the electoral college and the primaries are some of the peculiarities of the American election system. They are often criticized, and attempts are made to change them, but to date they remain in place.

efficacy. All these reasons may be summarized in the statement one hears frequently from people who do not vote: "It wouldn't make any difference."

Apathetic voters feel that there is so little difference on the issues between the two parties that it really is a matter of indifference whether a Democratic or a Republican candidate wins. The feeling among the politically alienated is that conventional political participation is meaningless. Nothing the individual does will alter the course of political events.

The Nonvoters

Statistics show that the nonvoters in the United States are young and are of lower socioeconomic status than the rest of the population. Those least likely to vote are between the ages of 18 and 29. Persons over 65, on the other hand, are three times as likely to vote. According to some authorities, one reason for a low turnout for that age group may have been the lowering

The "consent of the governed" in a democracy is attained through voting, as most people do not engage in other political activities. However, because elections are held in November, standing in line to vote is not always pleasant.

of the voting age to 18. Young people move around more frequently than older people, and they have weaker ties to a political party because it takes time to forge such ties (Table 16.4).

Statistics also clearly show the relation of failure to vote and low socioeconomic status: the lower a person's income, the less likely is that person to vote. The lowest economic segment of the electorate is about one-third less likely to vote in presidential elections than the top segment (Verba, Schlozman, and Brady, 1995). They vote even less frequently in primaries and nonpresidential elections. Of the unemployed, only one-third bothers to vote. On the other hand, the higher a person's education, the more likely that person is to vote. In fact, some political scientists interpret statistics as showing that of all social and economic variables, education is the strongest single factor in explaining most types of political participation. Because education is correlated to occupation and the latter to income, it also follows that the higher a person's income, the more probable it is that person votes and participates in other ways in the political process. That income overrides the effects of race and ethnicity is demonstrated by the fact that, although a lower percentage of blacks than of whites votes, the difference disappears when one compares voting by black and white people in the same income group. In addition, more blacks have been voting in recent years, probably also a result of increased income—and higher levels of education—among segments of the black population.

The Pew Research Center takes frequent surveys on a number of social and political issues. Their summary of findings issued in the fall of 2006 supports the findings of social scientists: that among regular voters are whites, the affluent, the older, the college educated, the married, and the churchgoers. The nonvoters include the young (18- to 29-year-olds), those with a high school education or less, those with incomes of less than $20,000, blacks and Hispanics, and those who rarely or never attend church. The nonvoters are politically estranged, are uninterested in local politics, are more socially isolated from other people, and say they are too busy to vote. The Research Center divides voters into regular, intermittent, registered but rare voters, and unregistered adults. Each of these categories vote in diminishing numbers (The Pew Research Center, 2006, page ID 1084).

TABLE 16.4 Reported Voting and Registration, by Race, Hispanic Origin, Sex, and Age, for the United States: November 2004
(In thousands)

Race, Hispanic origin, sex, and age	Total	Total population								U.S. citizen		
		Reported registered		Not registered		Reported voted		Did not vote		Reported registered	Not registered	Not a citizen
		Number	Percent	Number	Percent	Number	Percent	Number	Percent	Number	Number	Number
All Races												
Both Sexes												
Total 18 years and over	215,694	142,070	65.9	73,624	34.1	125,736	58.3	89,958	41.7	142,070	54,936	18,688
18 to 24 years	27,808	14,334	51.5	13,474	48.5	11,639	41.9	16,169	58.1	14,334	10,564	2,910
25 to 44 years	82,133	49,371	60.1	32,763	39.9	42,845	52.2	39,288	47.8	49,371	21,860	10,902
45 to 64 years	71,014	51,659	72.7	19,355	27.3	47,327	66.6	23,688	33.4	51,659	15,524	3,831
65 to 74 years	18,363	14,125	76.9	4,239	23.1	13,010	70.8	5,354	29.2	14,125	3,635	604
75 years and over	16,375	12,581	76.8	3,794	23.2	10,915	66.7	5,459	33.3	12,581	3,352	442
Male												
Total 18 years and over	103,812	66,406	64.0	37,406	36.0	58,455	56.3	45,357	43.7	66,406	27,741	9,665
18 to 24 years	13,960	6,731	48.2	7,229	51.8	5,415	38.8	8,545	61.2	6,731	5,642	1,587
25 to 44 years	40,618	23,403	57.6	17,215	42.4	19,913	49.0	20,705	51.0	23,403	11,435	5,780
45 to 64 years	34,471	24,676	71.6	9,795	28.4	22,520	65.3	11,951	34.7	24,676	7,922	1,873
65 to 74 years	8,438	6,534	77.4	1,904	22.6	6,119	72.5	2,319	27.5	6,534	1,635	269
75 years and over	6,325	5,062	80.0	1,263	20.0	4,489	71.0	1,836	29.0	5,062	1,107	156
Female												
Total 18 years and over	111,882	75,663	67.6	36,219	32.4	67,281	60.1	44,601	39.9	75,663	27,195	9,024
18 to 24 years	13,848	7,603	54.9	6,245	45.1	6,224	44.9	7,624	55.1	7,603	4,922	1,323
25 to 44 years	41,515	25,967	62.5	15,548	37.5	22,932	55.2	18,583	44.8	25,967	10,425	5,123
45 to 64 years	36,544	26,984	73.8	9,560	26.2	24,807	67.9	11,737	32.1	26,984	7,603	1,957
65 to 74 years	9,926	7,591	76.5	2,335	23.5	6,891	69.4	3,034	30.6	7,591	2,000	335
75 years and over	10,049	7,519	74.8	2,531	25.2	6,426	63.9	3,623	36.1	7,519	2,245	286

Note: "Not registered" includes "did not register to vote," "do not know," and "not reported." "Did not vote" includes "did not vote," "do not know," and "not reported."

Source: U.S. Census Bureau, Current Population Survey, November 2004. Internet Release date: May 25, 2005

■ Political Opinion Making

Voting is acting on a political opinion. Both voting and expressing an opinion are guaranteed by the First Amendment to the Constitution. Voting, joining political parties, belonging to interest groups, and running for office are active ways of participating in the political process. Before such activities can be pursued, however, some political opinions must be formed. Socialization, the process through which people learn how to behave as humans and as members of a particular society, is also responsible for a person's political behavior. People acquire attitudes and interests and form opinions on the basis of specific circumstances and interactions. Attitudes are tendencies or predispositions that are acquired but that remain essentially unexpressed. They may lead a person to respond in particular ways to certain issues. For instance, because of something in one's background, a person may favor labor unions. Such a person would probably join and be active in a labor union or might vote for

Box 16.2 **Why Americans Are Uninterested in the Political Process**

As is well known, Americans do not take advantage of the fought-for and hard-earned privilege of participating in the political process. Especially in the past 40 years, there has been a precipitous decline in electoral participation. To many scholars, this downturn portends a bleak future for democracy. The author of *The Vanishing Voter*, a professor at Harvard's School of Government, maintains that people feel helplessly disconnected from the election process. This leaves a small number of unrepresentative voters who wield a disproportionate amount of power in deciding who should govern the nation. As an example of how cynical or unconcerned people are, the author cites the example of the 2000 election, in which there was little interest until after Election Day, when the 36-day Florida stalemate put the election of either candidate in doubt. In other words, what interested people was not whether the best candidate would win, but how a complex question would be resolved. The event became a kind of gamble, a form of entertainment.

The Vanishing Voter is the result of the author's work in the Vanishing Voter Project at Harvard, whose aim was to conduct weekly interviews with samples of Americans. In all, more than 80,000 persons were interviewed to ascertain how much attention they were paying to the 2000 campaign and election. The findings of these interviews should prove quite disappointing to both candidates: in spite of the millions of dollars both spent in an effort to sway the public to vote for them, the majority of people did not pay much attention. Months of campaigning and debates left very few memories: only 1 in 20 adults interviewed remembered even talking about the presidential

campaign by Thanksgiving of 1999. People also remembered very little about what the candidates stood for: they knew about Gore's position on prescription drug legislation and about Bush's on tax cuts. In short, the candidates did not get their points across, one reason being that for every minute the candidates spoke on national news programs, the reporters who covered them spoke six minutes.

The reasons the author gives for voter apathy are not new: the declining influence of the political parties, the negative attitude of the media, the length of the campaigns, the difficulty of registering to vote. He offers some remedies: primarily shortening the presidential nominating process and conducting a national primary instead of the staggered primaries in different states at different times. However, it seems that not even the September 11, 2001, attacks have changed people's attitudes toward the political process as evidenced by the rather low turnout during the primaries in 2004. Evidently, people are captivated either by compelling issues—such as Vietnam—or poignant ones, such as the custody fight for the Cuban boy whose relatives wanted him to remain in the United States, while his father wanted him back in Cuba. During this event, more airtime was dedicated to it on evening newscasts than to either presidential candidate. Ultimately, the author suggests, people are not interested in politics because they do not respect politicians. Attempting to engage people in the political process, then, may be impossible, unless better-quality candidates enter the fray.

(Thomas E. Patterson, 2004, *The Vanishing Voter*. New York: Knopf) legislation favoring labor unions. The attitude predisposes that individual toward a specific political frame of reference.

Actions based on attitudes have political ramifications. A person with a specific set of attitudes will generally care whether a Democrat or a Republican is elected President, and, therefore, will vote accordingly, believing that one candidate will serve his or her interests better. Expressing preferences in terms of attitudes and interests signifies that the individual has formed an opinion. Opinions, however, are easier to change than attitudes, especially if an opinion is not held strongly, if there are groups exerting contrary influences, or if evidence contradicting the opinion is readily available.

Public and Political Opinion

The terms *public opinion* and *political opinion* are often interchanged, but they should be differentiated. **Public opinion** is the totality of opinions expressed by members of a community on any general issue that touches the community. **Political opinion** is the totality of opinions expressed by people on political issues alone. Although both terms are used in the singular, we should be aware that there are as many public and political opinions as there are sides to any issue. Such statements as "public opinion condemns this act" are simply generalities. At best, they express the opinion of a majority.

The Mass Media

It is inevitable that in a nation where television sets are on for an average of seven hours each day, the mass media play an important role in opinion formation. It has been reported that children in industrial nations cite television as their primary source of information. In less industrial nations, parents retain that role. Despite the popularity and ubiquity of the Internet, most Americans obtain most of their news on television. As of 2007, 71 percent of people watched local TV news, 46 percent watched network evening news, 43 percent watched the Fox News Channel, 39 percent watched CNN, and 34 percent watched network morning shows. Twenty-five percent got their news from Google, Yahoo, etc., 22 percent from other TV news web sites, 54 percent still read their local daily newspaper, and 23 percent read news magazines. Lower percentages perused major newspaper web sites and online news discussion blogs (Pew Research Center for People and the Press, 2007, page ID 1137).

The danger of overreliance on the mass media is that, in the process of communicating information, interpretation becomes necessary. The news is relayed to the public by a third party, who usually has not witnessed the event first-hand. Although the intent of reporters may be objectivity, in reality, some bias always creeps in. For one thing, of necessity, only selected events are brought to the public's attention. Choosing which events to report is the function of individuals who use certain guidelines—report the events that are most interesting, for instance, or that have human appeal. This in itself ensures that objectivity is not total. It leaves the door open to propaganda and to selected emphases and biases.

A former presidential aide made the comment that politicians live and sometimes die by the press, and the press lives by politicians. This remark can be extended to all the media. In fact, the media and politicians enjoy both a symbiotic and an adversarial relationship. A *symbiotic* relationship is one in which the parties use each other to their mutual advantage. Politicians need the media both to get their messages across to the public and to see how those messages are being accepted. And the media need politicians because they are the purveyors of information and need a constant source of news. An *adversarial* relationship means that they are in conflict with each other. This kind of relationship stems from basic differences of perspective regarding the role of the media. Politicians generally expect the media to act as a channel through which their plans are passed on to the public exactly as they express them. In this role, the media would be merely a mouthpiece for the politicians' point of view. This is the role that the media do assume in totalitarian states, but in the United States, the media refuse to assume such a role. Instead, they maintain that their role is that of servants to the public. Therefore, they probe and question politicians, retaining the skeptical pose of watchdogs. Their aim is to make politicians accountable to the public, which, of course, they should be according to the democratic ideology. However, the pose occasionally makes life uncomfortable for individual politicians, and they lash out. In this sense, the media act as a check on government.

As noted, the media are not entirely free of bias either, although they are not as biased as some people think. Journalists are disproportionately college-educated, upper-middle-class individuals. In this, they are not representative of the majority of the population. They also disproportionately identify themselves as secular, liberal, and leaning toward the views of Democrats or independents. Still, they are not a monolithic group, and their personal leanings do not generally color what they report. The reason is that, with the exception of the public radio and television networks, most American media are private businesses established for the purpose of making a profit. Therefore, they attempt to attract as wide an audience as possible—the larger the audience, the higher the profits. To attract the widest audience, in turn, they must give the public what it wants, and what the public wants, it seems, is entertainment. News-as-entertainment is biased news because it emphasizes drama, human interest, conflict, and events with visual interest. But because we are a capitalist, heterogeneous society, for those who want information as education, public radio and public television, as well as specialized newspapers and magazines, provide it.

Unfortunately, it appears that young people do not focus on any kind of news programs—which probably accounts for their poor voting record. Apparently, young Americans under 30 care very little about politics; fewer of them read newspapers than any other generation of the last 50 years, and even though they obtain most of their information from television, they do not care about news. Of course, this does not bode well for their political socialization, nor does it contribute to the development of political opinion. Eventually, such lack of interest may lead to manipulation by those in power, something the founders of our nation tried desperately to avoid.

Sound Bites

Particularly during presidential election years, candidates try very hard to get on news programs. Consequently, they and their speechwriters attempt to come up with short and catchy statements that lend themselves to the seconds-per-image manner in which television news is presented. These snippets have come to be called "sound bites" and have come in for heavy criticism because they often distort rather than inform. Of course, it is possible to make concrete and substantial statements in a few seconds, but most campaign sound bites do not appear to do so. On the other hand, many candidates are not good public speakers, and others love the sound of their own voices, to the utter boredom of their audiences. The sound bite evolved because television and radio are media that survive only when they keep the public's interest. However, in something as important to the people as the election of political leaders, the public deserves more than being engaged momentarily.

The Chapter in Brief

According to the democratic ideology, individuals participate in the decisions of government. Because total participation is impossible, the function of governing has been taken over by competing interest groups, or by an elite, depending on which theory one accepts. Pluralists maintain that power is diffused among many interest groups. Elitists believe that the most significant decisions of government are made by a handful of persons. In reality, political power probably falls somewhere in between these two extremes.

Similarly, societies display both conflict and consensus, because people agree on some issues and disagree on others. The pluralists state that a basic consensus exists in the United States, and conflict takes place within the context of this broad consensus. Elitists, on the other hand, say that ultimately it is force that holds society together. Force need not be displayed openly. It is often concealed in the form of an ideology that the masses are forced to accept. This ideology becomes an apparent, but not a real, consensus. Social scientists have found that consensus exists more frequently on abstract principles but not on concrete issues.

Participation in the decision-making process is sought through membership in interest groups. Interest groups are coalitions of individuals with similar attitudes and interests who attempt to influence public policy—that is, what the government does or does not do. Interest groups resemble political parties but do not present candidates for election or aim for complete control of government. There are many interest groups in the United States.

Interest groups act principally through lobbying but sometimes through different forms of protest. They are most effective if they are united internally and if their members are of high status. Many of the activities of interest groups are performed in conjunction with the political parties.

Political parties have the principal function of placing particular groups in power. The purpose of political parties is to gain control of government and to take on the responsibility for conducting its affairs. The parties also define and clarify issues and organize them into a platform, provide personnel to run the government, act as the source of opposition and political socialization, and unify forces in the society. The American system is characterized by two parties with few ideological differences between them. They are organized according to a federal model, and there are more similarities between the leaders of the two parties than between the leaders and members of the same party.

The ordinary citizen participates in decision making principally by voting. Unfortunately, not many people take advantage of this privilege. The well-educated, high-income minority engages most consistently in political activity, including voting. The large mass of less-educated, lower-income people who really need the government fail to vote because they are either apathetic, ill-informed, or convinced that their vote will have no impact.

Though only a minority of people are politically active, almost all hold political opinions. Political opinions are formed in the process of political socialization. The mass media are also important to opinion formation. The danger is that people may be receiving propaganda instead of education, because the media select the news they report, in spite of their attempt to be unbiased.

Terms to Remember

democratic pluralism An interpretation of how the American political system works. This interpretation assumes that there are multiple centers of power, creating a situation in which political power is fragmented and diffused.

interest groups Coalitions of individuals with similar interests who compete with one another for a share of political power, attempting to influence legislation in their favor.

lobbying The principal activity of interest groups, consisting of attempts to influence public officials to pass legislation that will be beneficial to the group or the people it represents.

majoritarian model of democracy The classical model of democracy, in which the statement "government by the people" is interpreted as meaning that the majority of the people make all government decisions directly.

party platform A general statement of party positions and policies.

plural elites Groups with diffused power and leadership roles; the representatives of different segments of the population, to whom they are responsible through elections, interest groups, and partisan competition.

political opinion The totality of opinions expressed by members of a community on political issues.

politics The forces that make up and direct the government of the state, its policies, and its actions. Also, the institution that makes the decisions about "who gets what, when, and how" in society.

protest groups   Pressure groups characterized by protesting certain governmental actions or inactions and calling attention to their grievances by such means as marches, sit-ins, demonstrations, and acts of civil disobedience.

public policy   That which government does or does not do.

ruling elite   A group composed of representatives of corporate, financial, military, and governmental interests who—according to some social scientists—make all the relevant decisions in the nation, regardless of the wishes of the population at large.

Suggested Readings

Bagdikian, Ben H. 2000. *The Media Monopoly*, 6th ed. Boston: Beacon Press. An analysis of the increasing power of the press, especially the tendency of newspapers and news production companies toward monopolies of ownership.

Dahl, Robert A. 1999. *On Democracy*. New Haven, CT: Yale University Press. An influential political scientist, who has written much on the subject of democracy and pluralism, brings us up to date on what contemporary democracy really means.

Domhoff, G. William. 1998. *Who Rules America? Power and Politics in the Year 2000*. 3rd ed. New York: Mayfield. The foremost exponent of elitist theory (his first book was published in 1967) still maintains that "The owners and top-level managers in large income-producing properties are far and away the dominant power figures in the United States."

Downie, Leonard, Jr., and Robert G. Kaiser. 2002. *The News About the News: American Journalism in Peril*. New York: Knopf. Two *Washington Post* journalists attempt a critical assessment of the contemporary news media.

Entman, Robert. 1989. *Democracy Without Citizens: Media and the Decay of American Politics*. New York: Oxford University Press. An analysis of citizen participation and involvement in politics and public affairs in the context of news.

Kryzanek, Michael J. 1999. *Angry, Bored, Confused*. Boulder, CO: Westview Press. As the title suggests, this is an overview of contemporary citizens' attitude toward politics.

Nie, Norman H., Jane Junn, and Kenneth Stehlik-Barry. 1996. *Education and Democratic Citizenship in America*. Chicago: University of Chicago Press. A study attempting to analyze the relationship between education and political participation.

Phillips, Kevin. 2006. *American Theocracy: The Peril and Politics of Radical Religion, Oil, and Borrowed Money in the 21st Century*. New York: Viking. A well-known political analyst examines the coalition of forces that threatens our nation in this new century, forces similar to those that destroyed many empires of the past.

Patterson, Thomas E. 2002. *The Vanishing Voter*. New York: Knopf. An attempt to offer an explanation of the reasons for the decline in electoral participation, and what can be done to reverse this trend.

Taylor, Paul. 1990. *See How They Run: Electing the President in an Age of Mediaocracy*. New York: Knopf. This book is a case study of the 1988 election campaign. The author maintains that campaigns have become long, nasty, and trivial processes, while political discourse has come down to the level of demagogic emotional appeals rebroadcast by the media in the form of sound bites, photo opportunities, and "hot" issues.

Web Sites of Interest

http://www.rockthevote.org
An organization attempting to help young people realize the importance of the political process and the power they have to affect the political process in their communities and farther afield.

http://www.umich.edu/-nes
The National Election Studies (NES) is a site that provides survey data on voting, political participation, and public opinion.

http://vote-smart.org
This site provides information on candidates of both parties for a number of offices and general election news.

http://www.cmpa.com
CMPA, or the Center for Media and Public Affairs, is a nonpartisan organization whose purpose is the analysis of political news coverage.

http://www.newslink.org
This site provides access to a large number of news organizations.

17

The Economy: Concepts and History

IN THIS CHAPTER, YOU WILL LEARN

- the purpose and functions of the economy as an institution;
- the concepts that economists use in describing economies;
- the historical development of Western economies;
- the nature and features of the American economy in its historical framework;
- the characteristics of the corporate hierarchy;
- about the development of a global economic system.

At one time, not so long ago, to mention GM, or RCA, or US Steel, was to use symbols of vast economic wealth and power. These were the "giant corporations" that had made the United States the most affluent country in the world, as well as a leader in political and cultural values, the country whom all others respected or envied, loved or hated, but at any rate wanted to emulate. Today, some of these giants have been dwarfed and others, with such names as Microsoft, AOL, Yahoo, Google, and Apple, have taken their place. What happened in such a short span of time is, quite simply, that one economic era was passing and another was dawning. In the preceding era, the manufacture of a vast array of products was what made the country—and its citizens—rich. The United States was very good at this: we made machines that turned out so many things so quickly that their cost came down and almost everyone could buy them. But while we were basking in our success, and before we realized what was happening, others were learning to produce just as efficiently and more cheaply. Moreover, manufacturing itself is no longer as wealth-producing as it had once been. We have entered a period characterized by the use and manipulation of data, or information, to create new products. The emerging economy has been described as one of fashion, that is, as fickle and changeable in the products it creates and sells as the latest skirt length or tie width. To understand the changes we are facing and to which we must adapt, it is imperative to know exactly what an economy is, what it does, and how it has developed historically.

Work in today's postindustrial society differs dramatically from the past. The sectors of the economy have shifted so that we are now a predominantly service economy with professionals and less skilled workers.

■ The Economic Institution

Some elements essential to human survival are freely available: the air we breathe, for instance, or the water we drink (though even those two resources may be difficult to obtain in their unpolluted form in some areas). On the other hand, food, shelter, and protective coverings have been scarce resources in most societies. In some geographic locations, these resources are more abundant than in others, but everywhere an effort must be made to accumulate an adequate supply for survival. We have seen in the discussion of institutions that a primary responsibility of each society is to bring needs and resources together, that is, to solve a universal need in the best possible way. The patterns of behavior that have emerged in the course of time to help people obtain the scarce resources needed for survival make up the institution of the economy, one of the five pivotal human institutions (the other four being: the family, religion, education, and government). The economy, then, is in essence a blueprint for a system of behavior through which people adapt to their environment by making decisions and choices aimed at satisfying their needs and combating the problem of scarcity.

The first decision people in a society must make concerns the need for **production**. Production may mean hunting an animal and bringing it back to camp, sowing and harvesting a field, turning a bolt on an assembly line, or entering data into a computer. The point is that societies must motivate their members to perform those tasks so that they may eat, cover themselves, and have a safe place in which to be protected from the elements.

The next decision concerns the necessity of distributing what has been produced. **Distribution** is easy in a society that has no surplus: whatever is produced is immediately distributed and consumed. If there is a surplus, however, the question "Who gets what, and how?" becomes more difficult. Some individuals always accumulate more of the surplus than others. This gives them an extra edge—it makes them stronger, healthier, or wealthier—than others, and this advantage is multiplied when the excess is passed on to their children. Eventually, the result is a stratified society in which the methods of distribution include barter, gifts, dowries, monetary systems, wages, investments, and so on.

The final issue in the economy is **consumption**. Consumption, again, presents no problems in simple societies. In more complex societies, however, people develop desires for things that are not needed strictly for survival. They want more variety in food, more colorful clothing, more comfortable or luxurious housing. In industrial societies, moreover, consumption is encouraged because it makes the economy grow; however, on occasion, consumption must be limited because a certain resource is temporarily scarce (as when gasoline had to be rationed in the United States in the 1970s).

The study of the structure, functions, and general working of the economy belongs to the social science discipline of economics. Economists, as well as sociologists and psychologists, analyze the economy because the institution consists of the interactions of people in pursuit of a livelihood and because it is interdependent with other institutions. In particular, social scientists examine the various types of economic systems; the size, functions, and power of the formal organizations in which economic activities go on; occupations, work, and leisure, as these affect people; and similar issues.

Economic Decision Making

The basic questions that every economic system must decide may be summarized as follows:

1. Which commodities should be produced, and in what quantities?
2. How should these commodities be produced with greatest efficiency?
3. For whom should these commodities be produced (how should they be distributed)?

Different societies solve these economic questions in different ways. In some, the questions are solved by relying entirely on **custom and tradition**. Specific crops are grown or articles manufactured because it has always been done this way. In others, decisions are made by **command**. A ruler or body of representatives orders that such and such crops will be grown or such and such articles will be made. These rulings may also be based on tradition, or they may be made for reasons of personal aggrandizement or even because they are perceived to be (or alleged to be) beneficial to the people. Finally, in some societies, answers to the above questions are decided according to the working of a **market** that depends on supply and demand, on prices, profits, and losses.

Very few economies today are based entirely on only one of the systems described above. Most are a mixture of two or even all three of them. In the American economy, for instance, both private and public (governmental) organizations exercise economic control. Moreover, supply and demand never function in a clear-cut way. There are ways of creating demand and limiting supply to keep prices artificially high. Both the market and the command system are used to make economic decisions in Western industrial societies.

Basic Elements of the Economy

The goods and services that are produced in each society derive from the resources that are found naturally in that society. (Of course, when barter and trade come into being, resources may be imported from and exchanged with other societies.) **Resources** are defined as

We call our economy a *market system*, a term derived from a real marketplace where people still buy and sell despite the availability of supermarkets and shopping malls.

everything that is needed for the production of goods and services. Resources include material objects as well as the human energy used in producing goods and services. Material objects may be found in nature or may be made by people. The human energy expended in making products is called **labor,** while natural resources, such as land, minerals, and water, are called **land** by economists. Finally, material objects made by humans, such as machinery, factories, shoes, and computers, are known as **capital.**

Factors of Production

Labor, land, and capital, in addition to **entrepreneurship,** are the basic elements that must be combined in the production of goods and services. They are referred to as the **factors of production.** For example, when building a house, people are driven by the spirit of entrepreneurship to use human energy (labor) to put a structure on a lot (land) using both natural material objects (wood, stone) and human-made material objects (nails, hammers, bricks, etc.). In economic terms, the result is a good that one can use or that one can sell or trade for another good.

In addition to these basic factors of production, **technology, time,** and **efficiency** play important parts in production. The more skill and knowledge (technology) a society has, the more effective is its production of goods and services. Time is an economic resource that is scarce and precious: if production is to be effective, in fact, it must occur within reasonable time limits. Efficiency is also an important factor in production because it is a way of obtaining the highest output from a given combination of resources in the least amount of time.

Resources are versatile. They can be put to many different uses. Land can be used to grow crops or for building factories, apartments, or shopping centers. Labor can be used to harvest crops or to develop complex data systems or to teach. But resources are finite. They can be used up or destroyed and cannot always be replaced. Societies must, therefore, conserve their resources and try to replace those used up in production.

Economic Choices and Opportunity Costs

Because resources are scarce, versatile, and finite, people in each society find that they must make certain choices. The classic economic choice has been the one commonly referred to as between guns and butter, meaning that a society must choose between producing weapons for defense and growing food to feed its people. Almost every action illustrates this type of choice: even the fact that a student is reading this chapter rather than jogging or talking on the telephone demonstrates that, to obtain a good grade in social science, the student is willing to sacrifice doing other, presumably more pleasant, things. This sacrifice is called the **opportunity cost.**

Of course, in analyzing the economy we are not interested in personal opportunity costs. We are interested in the concept because we can then put a value on the resources needed to produce something, and so make rational choices. In some respects, economics can be defined as the study of how to allocate scarce resources so as to attain the greatest satisfaction for the greatest number of people. A society must decide whether to use land, labor, and capital in a specific amount of dollars to build a nuclear attack submarine (and so be able to defend the country from hostile enemies) or to build housing, or railroads, or highways, or any of a thousand other alternatives. Even an affluent society that can do many things at the same time has to make these choices at some point. Everything we do as individuals, and everything a society does, involves an opportunity cost.

Limits to Output: The Production Possibilities Frontier

Economic systems are geared toward increasing output, but output has limits. Resources and technology are the variables that affect the absolute production possibilities of a society. A society that has more factors of production can produce more goods and services. A society that has more technology (the knowledge of how to use resources) can achieve the same goal. Both resources and technology are fixed, however, so production possibilities are ultimately limited: there is just so much that can be produced at any given time. This is just as well, because people want a great variety of goods and services, so it makes little sense to concentrate on producing a large amount of one product. It is only important for people to realize that the more resources and technology are used in producing one product, the less resources and technology will be available for producing another. Economists maintain, therefore, that every society is faced with a **production-possibility frontier,** and they chart production possibilities on a graph as production-possibility schedules. These schedules illustrate how much of each commodity can be produced when available resources are split among the number of commodities desired.

Specialization of Labor

The economic conditions that we experience today are the results of conditions that arose around 10,000 years ago, when the first agricultural revolution transformed groups of hunters and gatherers into settled food producers. When people began to tend crops that had been planted and to care for animals that had been domesticated, they discovered that they could create surpluses. That is, they could produce more than they required for their immediate survival. This meant that not everyone was needed to work the land. The end result was **specialization of labor.**

Specialization is effective and efficient. It means that some people can devote themselves to tasks other than food production and that some become strictly consumers of products that others make. Because people have different talents, specialization gives each the opportunity to do what he or she does best.

Not only is work specialized in contemporary industrial societies, it proceeds according to a division of labor. This means that each worker repeats a single action, without necessarily knowing what the finished product will look like. Again, division of labor adds to the efficiency and rapidity with which a product can be manufactured. However, the method decreases workers' sense of control over their jobs, their independence, and the feeling of accomplishment that usually accompanies a job well done. In industrial systems, workers no longer make things; rather, they sell their labor to factory owners and become part of an anonymous "labor force." In the new economic era that is emerging, specialization may lose some of its importance, as the new processes require a less regimented, more creative worker.

Trade, Barter, and Money

If one specializes in making a particular product, it makes sense to trade it for a product that someone else makes and that one needs. In the past, trading was literally done in marketplaces. Today, the term is also used figuratively, especially in the context of the economy. In fact, the American economy is called a "market system" because groups of people specialize in producing specific objects and voluntarily exchange them according to contracts agreeable to both parties.

At one time, all economic systems depended on barter or on the direct exchange of goods. Barter, however, is cumbersome and awkward. This is where the concept of money comes in. **Money** is a medium of exchange. It makes it possible for one individual to sell a product to another individual who wants it, obtain money for it, and use the money to buy another product from a third individual who has it for sale.

■ Contemporary Economic Systems: How Choices Are Made

Economic institutions are both cultural and social systems. They are social systems because people hold specific statuses and play the roles corresponding to those statuses. They are cultural systems because patterns of behavior, values, and expectations emerge around a system of production. These patterns are then made legitimate by a philosophy or ideology that the people accept as valid. In the modern industrial societies of the world, the three economic patterns of behavior and the legitimizing ideologies that underlie them are capitalism, socialism, and communism, discussed in Chapter 14. (Of the three, only capitalism seems to hold its own, as communism has been largely abandoned, and socialism has acquired a more capitalistic face.)

The economic system of a society is determined largely by that society's concept of property. **Property** is defined as the rights that an owner has to an object, as compared with the rights of those who are not owners of that object. The concept of property arises because resources are scarce and it is profitable to own some of them. In most societies, ownership of property takes one of three forms: communal, private, or public. In the **communal** form of ownership, property belongs to a community. Any member of the community may use it but may not own it. In the **private** form of ownership, property belongs to individuals. Unless an individual gives permission, his or her property may not be used by others. In the **public** form of ownership, the state or an officially recognized political authority owns property in the name of the people. Generally, schools, highways, parks, and public transportation systems are publicly owned.

Although the manner in which property is owned determines the economic system of a society, none is limited strictly to one form. All societies recognize some private ownership, and some public ownership is essential to all. It is the extent to which one or the other form is recognized that differentiates one system from another.

All three economic systems—communism, socialism, and capitalism—lie at different points on an ideal continuum. What accounts for their differences is the extent to which the government intervenes in the economy. In modified capitalism, government interferes least, although intervention is increasing. In democratic socialism, government interferes in essential industries. In communism, government determines all economic action. The economies of modern societies are matters of degree rather than kind.

■ Western Economies in Historical Perspective

The economies of the Western world are mostly modified capitalist, mixed-market economies. Their roots go back to a momentous transformation that occurred in Western Europe as it was emerging from the Middle Ages. The transformation revolved around the transition from a chiefly agricultural to a chiefly industrial mode of production (see Chapter 10). This transformation was marked by conflict because fundamental changes had to occur in the class structure and in the values and beliefs of societies. In agrarian societies, for instance, wealth, power, and status had belonged to landowners. In feudal Europe, this class was the landed aristocracy; in pre–Civil War America, it was the plantation owners and other large landholders. When industry became the chief mode of production, the status and power shifted to those who controlled industrial and financial capital.

The Birth of Capitalism

Industrialization brought in its wake a middle class (or bourgeoisie) whose values and beliefs facilitated the accumulation of capital and its continued reinvestment. In particular, the idea of the value of the individual human being and of personal fulfillment had to take hold. These ideas were in opposition to those prevalent in the preceding feudal era, in which the importance of the individual was downplayed and happiness was not even an issue: at best, it was thought that people might attain it after death rather than in this life. In the new industrial system, the individual had to learn that it was okay to aspire to a better social status, wealth, and prestige, and that these could be acquired through hard work. Thus, the profit motive and the work ethic were given positive social value.

This transformation of values and beliefs was occurring at the same time that certain religious ideas, put in motion by the Protestant Reformation, were also circulating in Europe. The new religious doctrines extolled hard work, thrift, and denial of sensual pleasures and, thus, seemed to go hand in hand with some of the notions of capitalism. (As noted in Chapter 13, the relationship between the new religious ideas and the emergence of capitalism was analyzed by Max Weber in his classic work, *The Protestant Ethic and the Spirit of Capitalism* (1904, 1905, 1958). The doctrines appealed especially to the emerging merchant classes in England and Holland who came to be called Puritans. The Puritans were convinced that their way of life was particularly pleasing to God; thus, they became especially receptive to the new economic system, capitalism, and eventually brought it with them to the New World.

As industrialism required a reorganization of values, so capitalism at first required a rearrangement of concepts about the function of an economy. Instead of gold and silver, which landowners used as an exchange medium, the basis of wealth became ownership of

In the early years of capitalism, families such as the Rockefellers, the Swifts, the Vanderbilts, and the Armours amassed vast fortunes which they spent in much conspicuous consumption. Today's tycoons seem to imitate the "robber barons" by building "McMansions," such as these on the shore of Rhode Island.

the factors of production: land, labor, and capital, as well as the spirit of entrepreneurship. In addition, the factors of production were abstracted, dehumanized, treated as objects, and bought and sold in the marketplace. In particular, labor, which once was given to a landowner in exchange for food, shelter, and protection, could now be sold in exchange for wages to the highest bidder. Wealth shifted from landowners to those who owned or controlled the means of production—those who had machines, tools, and materials. These new owners were the merchant middle classes. And the latter were employing free citizens, rather than serfs or vassals, to do the labor needed for production.

The new economic system greatly increased the production of goods and services, putting them within reach of many more societal members. The once poor and powerless, but sheltered and protected, serfs and apprentices became a working class (in Marxian terms, the proletariat). In exchange for wages, they gave up individual responsibility for their work, which became the responsibility of the employer.

During the nineteenth century, capitalism in Western societies was organized as a factory production system in which factories were owned by a few powerful individuals and families. Toward the end of the century, however, this system began to decline and to be replaced by **finance** and **industrial capitalism.**

■ Aspects of Industrial Capitalism

Up to the middle of the nineteenth century, the predominant form of business organization had been the company, owned and managed by a single owner or a partnership. Although some of these companies operated on a large scale, a great proportion of their profits had

Building railroads was a form of industrial capitalism that not only enriched the owners, but also expanded the country, allowing people to move into places that had been isolated previously.

to be reinvested in the company, keeping the amount of cash disposable for growth at a minimum. These business organizations prevalent during the early part of industrialism were concerned mainly with manufacturing, mining, and transportation, all forms of industrial capitalism.

Today, of the millions of businesses in the United States, two-thirds are still sole proprietorships. A sole proprietorship is the simplest form of business organization, having the advantage that the owner is in sole and total control of the enterprise. However, this form of business organization has a number of disadvantages: the owner has unlimited liability for any debts the business incurs; it is difficult to raise sufficient money to make the business a big success; and when the owner dies or retires, the enterprise goes out of business. It is symptomatic of these disadvantages that three of every five new businesses go bankrupt before their third year of operation.

Partnerships, a slightly more complex form of business organization, involve two or more individuals, who agree to contribute some of their own resources to an enterprise in return for a share of the profits or losses. The advantage is that more money can be raised, but decision making is usually more difficult and each partner is liable for all the debts and claims against the partnership. This form of business organization is the least common in the United States, making up less than 10 percent of all firms and accounting for less than 5 percent of all firm sales.

The Corporate Form of Industrial Organization

During the final years of the nineteenth century, a change was made in the direction of finance capitalism. **Finance capitalism** is characterized by these conditions: investment banks and insurance companies dominate industry, large aggregates of capital are formed, ownership becomes separate from management, and the holding company appears.

The foremost product of finance capitalism is the **corporation,** a form of enterprise typically organized for large-scale production. To raise the huge sums of money needed for expansion, the owners of a company offer to sell stocks or bonds. **Stocks** are shares of ownership of the corporations. **Bonds** are promises to repay a loan with a set rate of interest. The buyers of shares or bonds become in effect the co-owners of the new organization. They may have as much or more power than the original owners, depending on the percentage of shares they own. Management and responsibility for operations are now carried out by executive managers hired by a centralized board of directors. The latter are elected at the annual stockholders' meetings, at which each share of stock corresponds to one vote.

The separation of ownership from management was designed to ensure that the profit motive does not become the prime concern of the managers, who are really salaried employees of the corporation. Their functions are to pursue the welfare of the corporation; the real owners—the shareholders—are, in effect, absentee owners.

The corporation is designated by the government as a legal entity. As such, it can acquire resources, own assets, manufacture and sell goods, extend credit or incur debts, sue and be sued, and perform other similar functions—all distinct from its owners, the shareholders. The limited liability clause ensures that the shareholders lose only their investment and are liable for nothing else if the corporation becomes bankrupt.

The corporation has become by far the most effective form of business organization because of its ability to raise capital. By pooling the savings of thousands of households, corporations acquire large sums of capital to buy raw materials and machinery and to pay for production. The shareholders also have advantages: they need not be concerned with managing the enterprise, investments may be spread among a number of corporations, and they can be easily disposed of.

Corporations are stable in the sense that they are not subject to death or disease of the owners in the same way sole proprietorships or partnerships are. An ill or inefficient manager is simply replaced. This "immortality" allows long-range planning and growth to take place. Corporations also offer certain tax advantages, because the rate of taxation is different for corporations than for individuals. The government offers corporations many tax advantages and breaks, so much so that this government largesse has been characterized as "corporate welfare" (Barlett & Steele, 1998, 36–40). Hoping to create jobs, the federal government offers many incentives, from tax abatements to price supports, from lucrative government contracts to outright grants. The same is true of state and local governments, which practically bribe corporations to locate in their geographic areas.

The very success of the corporate form of organization has led to some abuse. In the late nineteenth century, when corporations were coming into their own, they fueled economic expansion at great costs to small businesses. Monopolies and trusts came to replace the small entrepreneur and became the most powerful segment of the economy. In a **monopoly,** one firm produces the entire market supply of a specific product; **trusts** are mergers of corporations for the purpose of cornering a market. The early "captains of industry" (also remembered, perhaps more accurately, as the "robber barons") built huge industrial empires: Rockefeller in oil, Carnegie in steel, Armour and Swift in meat packing, Vanderbilt and Stanford in railroads, Morgan in banking, and Henry Ford in automobiles. So powerful were the heads of these empires that Henry Ford could single-handedly decide to raise the price of his car and, in addition, to make all Model Ts in black only. When told by his managers that people complained about the lack of choice in colors, he is reported to have said, "I don't care what you give them as long as it is black." The end result was that these corporations acquired such market power that they were able to set prices at will and totally destroy competition. Eventually, the power of monopolies and trusts grew to such an extent that reformers began to perceive them as social problems to be eradicated. Reformers began to talk of "trust-busting," or breaking up the enormous concentrations of economic power, and finally the government stepped in. Regulatory legislation was passed in the form of the Sherman Antitrust Act of 1890, prohibiting monopolistic activities in restraint of trade, and later the Federal Trade Commission Act of 1914 was passed, prohibiting unfair competition.

At present, corporations represent about 20 percent of all businesses, but corporate sales represent almost 90 percent of all business revenues. This high industrial concentration is called **oligopoly**. The pros and cons of oligopoly continue to be debated among economists and in the media. On the one hand, those who defend the large size and power of the corporations argue that modern technological and scientific advances require sophisticated machinery and teams of specialized personnel to operate it. The tremendous outlays of capital necessary to finance such projects are available only from large corporations, which can afford pilot plants and sales campaigns and are better able to absorb failures. On the other hand, critics maintain that large size and great power make it impossible for smaller firms to compete, leading to high prices, price fixing, and monopoly. An even greater danger may be the political power that large corporations wield as a result of the creation of interest groups and political action committees (PACs) (see Chapter 16), which may be able to alter the political decision-making process for their own benefit.

Corporations are powerful not only because some have been allowed to grow to gigantic proportions but also because they can own stock in other corporations, giving them an inordinate amount of control. Executive officers in one corporation are frequently members of the board of directors of other corporations, a condition called **interlocking directorates**, which also can lead to abuse. The small investor who owns a hundred or so shares in a corporation is virtually powerless in corporate affairs. On the other hand, a well-paid top manager of a corporation can afford to purchase large blocks of stock. Owning even less than 1 percent of a corporation the size of General Motors may in effect allow such a shareholder to be in control of millions of dollars. In addition, some corporations are able to engage in unethical behavior that is profitable to top administrators and financially detrimental to their employees and shareholders. An example in the recent past was provided by Enron, a corporation whose business dealings had to be investigated by Congress.

The power of the corporations does not go unchallenged, nor is it monolithic. Business cycles and unforeseen events can alter the powerful status of a corporation. Government intervention and consumer lobbying have similar effects. The government, for instance, had instituted an antitrust suit against the Microsoft Corporation and tried to determine whether it was a monopoly. Rival manufacturers had accused Microsoft of using its market power to bully them to shield its monopoly in operating system software from the challenge of other Internet software. Shifts of the economy away from manufacturing, as well as global competition, have of late eroded the power of many corporate giants; but, others have risen to take their place.

From Competition to Advertising

The oligopolistic nature of corporations has also changed the classical capitalist idea that the consumer is king in a free market, in which many producers compete for the consumer's business by offering high quality at low prices. When a small number of corporations have a lion's share of the market, there is little need for competition. Instead, to increase their profits, corporations spend large sums of money for advertising, hoping to sway the consumer into buying essentially the same products as the ones their competitors offer.

Advertising creates an artificial demand for products for which there is no real need. Anyone who has strolled through the malls of American cities is aware of the myriad products displayed for sale in stores, many of which fill no conceivable need. Advertising ensures that a desire for those products is created nonetheless. The public is saturated with advertising until it becomes convinced that the new product is indispensable. Another ploy used by manufacturing corporations to increase their profits is planned obsolescence, which means that products are deliberately built shoddily so that they must be replaced more often.

Advertising has been immensely successful as a method of increasing consumption—so much so that it has become a profitable industry in its own right. People in capitalist societies are willing to spend much more money on the often frivolous goods they are convinced they need than on taxes, which would allow the government to provide much-needed public services. It is a situation that has prompted some economists critical of these facets of capitalism to describe life in capitalist societies as offering private affluence but public squalor. They say that, for instance, fine automobiles are available to those who can afford them, but mass transit systems for those who cannot pay for private automobiles are sorely inadequate. However, this is only one side of the story: government is generally ineffective in providing well for public needs, and the capitalist ideology has convinced most people that individual effort will bring them personal affluence; thus, they are less concerned about public needs.

■ Diversification and Multinationalism

Whether it is good or bad, ethical or unethical, the fact is that most corporations have attempted to become even larger. Two ways in which they have been doing so is through diversification and multinationalism. **Diversification** is a corporation's acquisition of controlling shares in other corporations, often in totally different industries. A cosmetics company may also own a company—or a controlling share of a company—that produces movies and another that manufactures drugs. Diversification is a result of mergers and takeovers, some of which occur without the approval of the company being acquired. This procedure has been criticized because it results in the growth of a corporation without having to produce anything.

Multinationalism refers to the fact that, instead of merely exporting their products to foreign lands, some corporations move the production process itself into other countries. Moving the industrial process abroad is successful for corporations because labor is cheaper than in the United States and markets are vastly expanded. Therefore, profits increase. But both American workers and ultimately the host nations are suspicious of multinationals, whose profits are often greater than the national budgets of the host nations. Such profits and the fact that the corporations virtually control thousands of jobs give them excessive power, casting them in the light of exploiters. On the other hand, it has been shown that direct foreign investment raises demand for American goods and services and creates jobs and wealth at home. Such direct investment more than doubled in the years 1992 to 1995, as most of the world competed for American capital to finance their own economies. Even Japan, which had steadfastly refused to open its market to America, has had to relent because Japanese consumers want to eat at McDonald's, buy at Toys 'R' Us, and shop at the Gap. It seems, then, that in spite of the feeling that multinationalism is a form of economic colonialism, many products of American business are very popular. American corporations have become models for many countries that send their students to learn business methods and management skills at American universities (Myerson, 1995, E1, E14).

A side effect of multinationalism that worries Americans is the fact that a growing number of developing nations have become proficient in mass production at much lower wages than American workers demand. For instance, U.S. wages are several times higher than Taiwan's or South Korea's and about seven times higher than Mexico's. As a result, many U.S. companies are having their products manufactured overseas or, because they cannot compete with foreign companies, are replacing workers with lower-paid, part-time employees for whom they need not pay benefits. The reasons for this situation will be discussed later in the chapter.

■ The Nature of Work in the Industrial Society

In all societies, except the very simplest ones, obtaining the necessities for survival has meant that individuals have had to work. Workers are employed in one of three sectors of the economy. The **primary sector** deals with the extraction and processing of raw materials and includes such activities as agriculture, fishing, mining, and forestry. The **secondary sector** is concerned with manufacturing and constructing, or turning raw materials into finished products, such as producing automobiles, building homes, or packaging foods. The **tertiary sector** involves services, such as repairing automobiles, remodeling homes, providing education, or healing the sick members of a society (see Table 17.1 for changes in sectors).

Shifting Sectors

Historically, a dramatic switch has occurred when societies have become industrialized. In the first stages of industrialization, the large majority of workers are employed in the primary sector. As an example, in the early years of this country, almost 95 percent of

Although the union movement has declined in the United States, some unions still have enough power to bend employers to their will.

TABLE 17.1 Total Employment and Projected Change by Broad Occupational Group, 2004–14 (Employment in Thousands)

Occupational group	Employment, 2004	Percent change, 2004–14
Total, all occupations	145,612	13.0
Professional and related occupations	28,544	21.2
Service occupations	27,673	19.0
Office and administrative support occupations	23,907	5.8
Sales and related occupations	15,330	9.6
Management, business, and financial occupations	14,987	14.4
Production occupations	10,562	−0.1
Transportation and material moving occupations	10,098	11.1
Construction and extraction occupations	7,738	12.0
Installation, maintenance, and repair occupations	5,747	11.4
Farming, fishing, and forestry occupations	1,026	−1.3

Production occupations, as well as farming, fishing, and forestry (primary and secondary sector occupations) are declining, while professional and service occupations (tertiary sector) are increasing.

Source: http://www.bls.gov/oco/cg/indchar.htm

workers were employed in agriculture. It took that many people to provide enough food for the nation. By 1900, only 38 percent of the workforce were in farming. Today, only approximately 2 percent are still engaged in farming. Farming is now so efficient that very few people are needed to grow enough food for the whole population and for export.

As industrialization progresses, employment shifts from one sector to the next. From the turn of the century until the middle of it, the secondary sector showed a steady increase—from 35.8 percent in 1900 to 40.3 percent in 1950. As of 1950, the secondary sector has been declining—from 40.3 to 30 percent in 1982 and to below 20 percent as of 1997. The tertiary sector, on the other hand, has seen a spectacular spurt in growth—from 26.6 percent in 1900 to 62.1 percent in 1975 and 78 percent of GDP as of 2006 (Glushko & Saxenian). Obviously, in this latest stage of industrialization, the great majority of workers are employed in the tertiary sector of the economy. In contrast, blue-collar workers employed in the primary sector shrunk from 37.6 percent in 1900 to 4.5 percent in 1975 and 13 percent in 2002.

Professionalization

The shift into the tertiary sector has resulted in important changes in the occupational structure. More people are becoming professionals, managers, or technicians, and there is less need for unskilled or semiskilled occupations. Consequently, there have been changes in the stratification system, causing chronic unemployment for the segment of the population that is unable to attain professionalization.

Professions are more than specialized occupations. They require both theoretical knowledge and training in an art or a science. A carpenter needs training, but a physician needs to possess a body of theoretical knowledge in addition to training. Because of their long years of specialization, professionals are able to exert a great degree of autonomy over what they

Box 17.1 Machines: The Next Laborers

Economic systems generally last many generations in every society—sometimes even for hundreds or thousands of years. This was the case when hunting and gathering was the way our early ancestors survived, and this was also true when agriculture added trade and commerce and then turned to an industrial system as the primary economic engine. In each case, the change caused social unrest as people learned new skills and procedures and had to adjust to a new way of life (this chapter notes some of the changes in the wake of urbanization and industrialization).

In the last couple of centuries, however, the rate of change has dramatically increased so that there is a constant flow of new inventions, mainly revolving around more and more complex machines. When industry began to replace agriculture as the primary economic instrument, farmers ventured into cities where the factories were being built. This move gave rise to urbanization, or the tremendous growth of cities relative to rural areas. Of course, these movements are never wholesale: we still need agriculture, and there are still rural areas. Nor do these movements occur at the same rate around the world: Western societies are now predominantly urban, but many underdeveloped or developing societies are not.

Mechanization is a phenomenon that has been going on for several centuries, but, as noted, it has become much more sophisticated and rapid. As economies become global, it is more difficult for our industries to compete because labor is so much cheaper in developing nations. This reality has given rise to outsourcing, meaning that American firms either build factories in other nations or send out raw material to be produced abroad. This, of course, displaces American workers. Another way in which firms try to compete is by hiring immigrant laborers, many of them in the country illegally, because they, too, work for much lower wages than American workers. Now all workers are being threatened because in many industries they can be substituted by machines. Some employers have come to the conclusion that even cheap labor is not cheap enough.

One example is provided by the Florida orange industry (in the United States, even farming has become an industry). Because of global competition from countries such as Chile, Mexico, China, and others, orange growers find that even using illegal Mexican immigrants to harvest oranges is too expensive when compared with what a machine can do. A machine called a canopy shaker shakes loose 36,000 pounds of oranges from 100 trees in 15 minutes, dropping them into a large storage car. The same harvest would have taken four hand-pickers all day long. These workers would have had to stand on top of 16-foot ladders, with sacks slung around their backs, plucking oranges at a rate of 70 to 90 cents per 90-pound box, for a total of less than $75 a day. Moreover, competition is such that a pound of frozen concentrate from Brazil can be brought into the United States for 75 cents, while a Florida grower would have to charge 99 cents.

Because of the savings in labor, time, and money, the search for machines goes on. There are ways of drying and harvesting grapes mechanically, cherries are being knocked off trees onto conveyor belts, strawberries are being moved on mobile conveyor belts from the fields to storage bins, and mechanical cutters are being used for leaf lettuce and spinach. In the orange-growing industry, mechanical harvesting is continuing to improve, and it is estimated that within five years, 100,000 of the 600,000 acres of oranges in the state of Florida will be harvested by machines.

On the one hand, mechanization in this industry will displace workers. These workers are poorly paid, however, and many leave in search of better income anyway. Economists think that looking for more lucrative work may eventually benefit the displaced workers. And some workers will learn how to operate the machines, increasing their income in this way. Still, when the problems of outsourcing and labor-saving machines are multiplied across the economic spectrum, the problem of displaced workers remains unresolved.

(Eduardo Porter, 2004. "In U.S. Groves, Cheap Labor Means Machines," *New York Times*, March 22, p. 1, A17)

do. Professionals also establish associations that regulate the credentials of their members and maintain certain codes of behavior and ethics.

Professions have consistently increased in prestige and are the highest-paid occupations in the tertiary sector. As a result, there has been a tendency to professionalize any occupation that lends itself to it. Professionalization has not been very successful in the first two sectors of the economy, but it has been very successful among the white-collar workers of the tertiary sector.

■ The Corporate Bureaucracy

Industrial production involves a complex machine technology, an executive and administrative bureaucracy including a white-collar labor force, and the wielders of the machines themselves, the blue-collar labor force. In Chapter 4, we saw the goals of a pure bureaucracy and the way a bureaucracy works in reality. At the height of the industrial era, the corporate bureaucracy was a pyramid consisting of the following divisions.

The Executive

A chief executive officer (CEO) must be able to break all emotional bonds that might stand in the way of a career and must have personality traits that include self-discipline, ability to submit to authority, emotional and intellectual "cool," the capacity to sublimate immediate goals for future benefits, and an unusual amount of ambition and desire for success. In addition, such a person has to possess an element of ruthlessness to overcome possible obstacles, must have a great deal of self-confidence, and must be able to make rapid decisions that are adhered to, for better or for worse.

While the CEO must keep one finger in every pot of the organization, there are three general functions that every executive must fulfill: (1) establish organizational policy, (2) see that favorable relations exist between the organization and outside forces, and (3) be in charge of the operation and organization of the industrial plant.

Anxiety. Much has been made of the strains suffered by executives in their roles as corporate leaders, and the proverbial executive ulcer appears in countless jokes. Some of the difficulty encountered by executives on the way up may be due to the inability to adjust from the role of a subordinate with drive and ambition to that of ultimate decision maker and leader. A new executive may also experience feelings of loneliness and depersonalization as an object of envy and fear on the part of subordinates. And, of course, the feeling of responsibility, the knowledge that his or her actions will bear directly on the welfare of the organization and sometimes on that of the community, is not an easy burden to bear.

On the other hand, top executives are extremely well remunerated for their efforts. The difference between the average worker's salary and that of the average CEO is continually increasing: in 1960, it was a multiple of 41; in 1991, it was 93 (Kinsley 1991, 41). From 1990 to 2003, CEO pay rose by 313 percent, and corporate profits rose by 128 percent. In 2005, chief executives of large companies made 262 times the average worker's annual pay (**http://money.cnn.com/2006/06/21/news/companies/ceo_pay_epi/index.htm**; accessed 5/25/2007). This averaged to an annual pay of $10,982,000 for a CEO of a company with at least $1 billion in revenue. The average worker, on the other hand, made $41,861 in 2005. At least the gap between large-company CEOs and workers that year was slightly less than in 2003, when it had been greater than 300 to 1.

In the 1990s, the executives did make their companies profitable, creating one of history's greatest bull markets and so enriching their shareholders. During those heady days, it was not unusual for some CEOs to earn $100 million in a year. Beginning in 2000, however, the economy slowed and stocks fell, some drastically. While shareholders lost an average 12 percent of their portfolios, chief executives received an average 22 percent raise in salary and bonuses. In 2005, for instance, the CEO of United Health Group had gains on stock options valued at $1.6 billion, while the CEO of Exxon Mobil received a retirement package that averaged $144,000 a day (Trigaux, 2006; accessed 5/25/2007).

The generosity with which American CEOs are rewarded has created a lot of controversy, especially as the global economy spawns an increasing number of mergers between American and foreign companies. Some economists perceive American-style pay as a mechanism for jump-starting economic performance. In fact, these experts maintain that the vibrant performance of the American economy and the stock market in the 1990s is attributable to the motivation of high-paid American CEOs. Chief executives in the United States, somewhat like professional athletes, have short careers, and performance bonuses and incentives tied to a rising stock price incite them to stellar performances, which in the end add value to the company. (This, however, is not always the case. There have been many instances of CEOs who have been fired for poor performance, yet who left with very generous severance and bonus packages.) Other economists view the high salaries and perks, especially in comparison to those paid by other nations, as leading to increasing greed and excess.

The American form of management has advantages and disadvantages. The high salaries and perks tend to isolate the CEO from subordinates, and even from the public at large, leading to some wrong decisions. The American automobile industry, for instance, lost a large amount of world market share, mainly to the Japanese, because it kept producing automobiles that the public no longer wanted. On the other hand, greed is a tremendous motivating force and may spur CEOs to extraordinary performance. In the latest mergers between American and foreign companies, the latter seem to accept the American way.

Middle Management: White-Collar Workers

Between the position of corporate managers and that of the industrial workers who actually produce the goods, we find the vast limbo of the middle section of the industrial bureaucracy, consisting of executive vice presidents, specialists, office workers, and foremen. This rung of the hierarchy is proving to be the most obsolete in the new economic era and will probably be gradually phased out.

Industrial Workers

The last group in the corporate bureaucracy of the industrial system consists of those who actually turn the wheels of the system, the industrial, or blue-collar, workers. This class of workers evolved in an interesting way, and they are currently at a critical stage of development. Trends point to the necessity of their transformation into a more skilled, automated, responsible, and creative workforce.

Before the changes introduced by industrialization, most people in Western societies lived and worked on farms. It was a subsistence type of livelihood, except for the landowners, who could afford education and interests that went beyond sheer physical labor. Of course, societies also needed craftspeople and artisans: individuals who could make shoes, sew clothing, make furniture, and work in stone and metals. These individuals had a loftier position in the stratification system than the peasants who worked the soil, and the more talented acquired fame as what we would now call artists. By the tenth century, such individuals were organizing themselves into a variety of **guilds** (kinds of labor unions), of which the merchant and craft guilds had mostly economic objectives. Craft guilds were occupational associations established by the artisans in specific fields. The guilds restricted membership, requiring an apprenticeship period before an artisan could become a journeyman. In turn, the journeyman had to produce a "masterpiece" before he could be judged a master craftsman. In the guild system, an apprentice was taken into his master's home and clothed and fed along with the master's family. Though apprentices may have been exploited and

Box 17.2　**Methods of Production: Craft, Mass, and Lean**

Labor productivity in the United States had been on a steady upward move from the time the Industrial Revolution gained a foothold in the New World. For instance, in America's most important industry, the automobile industry, the first cars were produced by the craft method; that is, each car was made to order. With this method, factories were turning out only a few hundred cars a year, costs were high and did not decrease when volume increased, consistency and reliability were unequal, and the small craft shops could not afford the systematic research that would lead to technological advances. More important, with this method only the very wealthy could afford cars.

Mass production all but banished the craft method. This technique revolved around the idea of complete interchangeability of parts and the ease of fitting parts to each other. To speed up the process on the assembly line, Henry Ford assigned each worker only one task, which the worker performed while standing next to a moving line. Ford also designed machine tools that would perform only one task, thus avoiding the need to readjust tools to do a variety of tasks. In this way, Ford could use untrained, inexpensive labor, instead of the high-cost, highly skilled labor needed for the craft method. He also hired large numbers of "rework men," whose job it was to patch up defective cars. Because the latter were untrained and unmotivated, Ford had to increase the numbers of industrial, manufacturing, and product engineers. But while Ford and the founder of General Motors, William Durant, succeeded very well with their mass-production technique in the factory, they never managed to organize efficiently the bloated engineering, manufacturing, and marketing complex. This feat was accomplished by later General Motors presidents, but on the basis of creating specialized and decentralized departments, each of which knew little about the functioning of the others. There was a complete division of labor, in other words.

The new system of "lean" production that Americans began to embrace in the 1980s derives from the experience of the Japanese. Following World War II, Japanese labor unions succeeded in winning an agreement in which employees were guaranteed lifetime employment and a pay scale based on seniority instead of job function. In return, employees agreed to be flexible in the work assignments they accepted and committed to helping the company find new and more efficient production methods. In this situation, the system worked out by Toyota has become a model for all of Japan's lean production method. The scores of engineering and production specialists used by the mass-production method were never used by the Japanese: instead, they trained workers to do the specialists' work. Workers were organized into teams, each with its own leader, and were told to decide together how best to perform the necessary operations, thus foregoing the need for a foreman. Slowly, additional responsibilities were added to the teams, and each worker could stop the assembly line if a problem appeared that the worker could not resolve. Moreover, each error had to be traced back to its cause, and a solution had to be devised so that it would never recur. The result is that while in mass-production plants, 25 percent of total work hours and 20 percent of plant area are dedicated to fixing errors that occur on the assembly line, Toyota's assembly plants have virtually no rework areas and perform almost no rework. Yields approach 100 percent and the line almost never stops.

There are many more steps in the system of lean production—as well as in the way suppliers are used, and especially in the relationship of manufacturer and consumer—but in a nutshell, the goals of lean production are these: (1) whereas mass producers set limited goals—a certain number of defects, a maximum level of inventories—lean producers set their goals on perfection—zero defects, zero inventories, and continually declining costs; (2) lean production's main objective is to push responsibility far down the organizational ladder; and (3) the career path in lean production leads to a broadening of professional skills applied in a team setting instead of an attempt to climb upward in a rigid hierarchy with growing proficiency in a narrow area of specialization.

It appears that lean production combines the best features of craft production and mass production: the ability to reduce costs per unit, improve quality and respond rapidly to consumers' wishes while providing employees with challenging work. Although lean production has not been quickly or painlessly adopted, "it will supplant mass production and the remaining outposts of craft production in all areas of industrial endeavor and become the standard global production system of the 21st century. As a result, the world will be a different and better place" (Womack et al., 1990, 38).

may have gone hungry (depending on the master's personality and circumstances), they were made to feel protected and all their needs were provided for.

In the early stages of industrialization, work was done in the home, with merchants providing the raw material and paying for the finished product. This system was called the **cottage** or **putting-out system** (see Chapter 10). Although there was pressure to produce more, the workers remained basically in control of how and when to work, establishing their own hours and employing members of their family or apprentices as helpers. In addition, they were free to cultivate plots of land for additional revenue. In both the guild and the cottage systems, individual artisans produced the whole product and later an entire facet of the production process. They could see what they were making and could feel pride in a job well done.

The Factory System

The factory system, the next step in the progress of industry, changed all that. Workers were herded into a central building together with tens or hundreds of others. They were told exactly how much to produce in a specific amount of time, when to come to work, when to go home. The hours were long (a 12- or 14-hour day was not unusual), the environment was unpleasant—lacking in the most primitive hygiene facilities—and the pay was minimal. The entire family, dragged from a rural locale to the dirty and crowded city, found that it had to run the machines to eke out a meager livelihood.

Most important, however, was the change in how a worker produced goods. No longer responsible for the whole article, each worker now repeated the same routine action endlessly all day, often without really understanding its relation to the finished product.

The relationship between employee and employer also underwent a drastic change. The employer was now among the owners of the means of production, the "bourgeoisie" in Marxist terms, and the employee was a member of the "proletariat," or industrial workers. The employer felt no moral obligation or responsibility toward the employees and in a business slump had no qualms about firing or laying off workers. They were no more than names in a payroll ledger, unlike the apprentices to a master craftsman of former times. Working conditions in factories began to be characterized by impersonality and anonymity, features that persist to the present.

Conditions in the urban centers, meanwhile, were appalling. Workers could no longer supplement their livelihood by hunting or growing things. The owners and managers of industry were able to amass fortunes in those early days of capitalism, unhampered by government regulations, but not much of this wealth trickled down to the workers. The workers' wages always seemed to lag behind prices, forcing them to live in substandard conditions. They had no medical care, even for the numerous industrial accidents that occurred in the unsafe factories of the day. The worst trauma of all was the complete lack of security that workers experienced. The capitalistic system was unstable and subject to deep business cycles, and workers never knew when they would be laid off.

Inevitably, workers realized that they must organize, that no individual or chance circumstance would eliminate the hardships and injustices of their condition. Their only salvation lay in unity of purpose. However, it was not until the twentieth century that the goal of organized and peaceful industrial relations was reached.

■ The American Labor Movement

The labor movement in the United States had made only sporadic attempts at organization before the Civil War. The establishment of national labor organizations occurred in the

Conflicts between labor and management are usually resolved through grievance procedures and other processes of collective bargaining. On occasion, however, labor unions feel the need to strike in order to achieve a desired goal.

period following the Civil War and up to Roosevelt's New Deal during the Great Depression. It was a difficult struggle: the effort to join together nationally for the purpose of collective bargaining had many obstacles to overcome.

In the United States, workers had been a scarce commodity, but increasing mechanization was displacing artisans and skilled workers. The growing concentration of industry and the separation of ownership from the management of industry in the growth of the corporation produced feelings of anonymity and destroyed feelings of loyalty. The consequent depersonalization led to an indifferent attitude on the part of all concerned. The American labor force was a heterogeneous lot, representing different ethnic, cultural, religious, and racial backgrounds that were usually mutually incompatible and suspicious of each other. In addition, American workers were not keenly aware of their status as a social class. They believed the ideology of unlimited opportunity and viewed their status as transitional, only a step in their ascent to riches and power. Thus, they were unwilling to organize into a group they would soon abandon. Finally, the federal system of government stood in the way of effective organization: if workers organized in one state, the industry involved would move to another. The mood of the day was inimical to labor, too. The heroes of the day were the captains of industry, whose rags-to-riches stories fascinated the public.

In spite of these obstacles, in 1869 workers organized themselves into the Knights of Labor, and later, in 1886, into the American Federation of Labor (AFL). Under the leadership of Samuel Gompers, the AFL grew, and by 1920 four of the five million unionized workers were members of the AFL. In its early days, the AFL was interested principally in organizing skilled workers, so most of its member unions were craft unions. In a craft, or **horizontal**, union, each skill is organized into a separate entity. The workers in the building industry, for instance, are divided into carpenters, plumbers, bricklayers, and painters, and each group has its own union. The opposite form of union organization is represented by the United Mine Workers, who belong to an industrial, or **vertical**, union. In this form, all the workers are organized into one union regardless of the tasks they perform in their industry.

One labor leader committed to the industrial type of union who has come down in history as a hero of labor was the president of the United Auto Workers, Walter Reuther.

Although initially the government supported the opposition of business to unionization, eventually laws were passed that were interpreted as an admission on the part of government that workers had the right to organize and join unions. During the presidency of Franklin Delano Roosevelt, one of the worst periods of economic activity in the history of the United States, unionization was encouraged because it was thought that it would give workers additional purchasing power—through higher wages—and, thus, stimulate the stagnant economy. Legal sanctions for worker organization were also provided by the National Industrial Recovery Act of 1933, which prohibited employers from interfering with the process of unionization. This legislation was superseded by the Wagner Act of a few years later. The provisions for the protection of the workers encompassed in the Wagner Act were closely followed by the Social Security Act of 1935. This last piece of legislation was a clear attempt on the part of the government to alleviate the insecurity associated with the lot of the industrial worker, and it signaled an attitude of concern for public welfare.

Collective Bargaining

The most fundamental function that the union performs for the worker is collective bargaining. This process has become an accepted institution in our society. Although conflicts between labor and management crop up periodically, most solutions take place within the framework of collective bargaining. Some aspects of collective bargaining are employed every day, as workers air their complaints through what are called grievance procedures. These procedures generally involve the services of a shop steward or chairperson elected by the workers, who is given a degree of immunity from layoffs to remain loyal to the workers. The presence of the shop steward has done much to alleviate the problem of powerful and authoritarian foremen and bosses and helps explain the tremendous unionization that has occurred in the mass-production industries.

The Labor Movement Today

Like other sectors of society, organized labor is not free from strife and problems. It suffers from the same ailments as big business and big government. Its leadership has at times been corrupt, seeking power and financial perks at the expense of the workers it represents. Consequently, the government has had to take steps and intervene in its affairs.

In 2006 around 12 percent of employed wage and salary workers—about 15.4 million persons—belonged to or were represented by unions. The great majority belonged to those affiliated with the AFL-CIO, such as the Teamsters, the United Auto Workers, the Communications Workers, and so on. The rest belonged to independent unions not affiliated with the AFL-CIO, such as the National Education Association, the Nurses' Union, and the United Mine Workers. Workers in the public sector have a high rate of unionization, whereas those in agriculture, finance, insurance, real estate, and service industries have low rates. More men than women belong to unions because they tend to work in industries with high unionization. For the same reason, more blacks than whites are unionized and more urban residents than rural residents. Finally, union members earn more: in 2006, unionized, full-time, wage and salary workers had usual median weekly earnings of $833 against a median of $642 for nonunionized workers (Table 17.2).

Decline of Unionism

The degree of unionization in the private sector has declined since 1965, while union growth in the public sector has increased. After reaching a membership of almost 25 percent of the

TABLE 17.2   Median Weekly Earnings of Full-Time Wage and Salary Workers by Union Affiliation and Selected Characteristics in 2006

Age and Sex	Total	Members of Unions[1]	Represented by Unions[2]	Nonunion
Total, 16 years and over	$671	$833	$827	$642
Men, 16 years and over	742	887	883	717
Women, 16 years and over	600	758	753	579

[1]Data refer to members of a labor union or an employee association similar to a union.

[2]Data refer to members of a labor union or an employee association similar to a union as well as workers who report no union affiliation but whose jobs are covered by a union or an employee association contract.

Note: Beginning in January 2006, data reflect revised population controls used in the household survey. Estimates for the above race groups (white, black or African American, and Asian) do not sum to totals because data are not presented for all races. In addition, persons whose ethnicity is identified as Hispanic or Latino may be of any race and, therefore, are classified by ethnicity as well as race. Data refer to the sole or principal job of full- and part-time workers. Excluded are all self-employed workers regardless of whether or not their businesses are incorporated.

Source: **http://www.bls.gov/news.release/union2.t02.htm**. Accessed 5/25/2007.

total workforce in the mid-1950s, union membership has declined to the current 12 percent (Figure 17.1). There are a number of reasons for this decline. While mass production, heavy industry, transportation, public utilities, and construction remain heavily unionized, jobs in this sector of the economy are declining, as we saw at the beginning of this discussion. Domestic output has been changing from manufactured goods, industries that were heavily

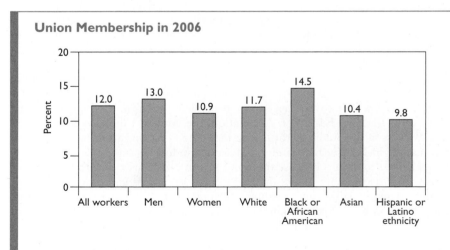

FIGURE 17.1   Union membership of wage and salary workers by demographic group, 2006
Source: **http://www.bls.gov/opub/ted/2007/jan/wk4/art05.htm**. Accessed 5/25/2007.

unionized, to services, which were sparsely unionized. Professional, technical, and white-collar workers, besides identifying with management, usually benefit from the same wage increases as their blue-collar counterparts. In the trade and service industries, employees are too diffused in location for effective unionization, and professional and technical workers are inclined to join professional associations instead of labor unions. In addition, a substantial increase in the labor force within the past several decades has consisted of women, part-time workers, and young people. These groups are difficult to unionize because they tend to change jobs fairly frequently. In addition, consumer demand has favored foreign-manufactured goods, which are cheaper, and foreign competition in industries such as automobiles and steel has further reduced the unionized workforce.

The leadership of organized labor may be a further factor in the decline of labor unions. There are fewer dedicated individuals and more bureaucrats, who display a greater interest in running the organization than in recruiting new members. A number of labor leaders gave all organized labor a bad name by their ties to organized crime. Finally, it may be that part of the reason for the unions' decline is their success: unions were able to gain sizable wage advantages over nonunion workers. Hence, they prompted many employers to use nonunion labor or to move plants to regions of the United States that were not heavily unionized (such as the South and Southwest) and abroad. In short, their success in raising wages may have ultimately affected the employment opportunities in the union sector as against the nonunion sector. That may explain instances in which workers themselves voted to remain nonunionized.

■ American Labor and the Global Economy

The American work force faces great challenges. The transition into the tertiary sector was supposed to move the economy from dirty, heavy industry to clean, well-lit offices. Not all workers, however, made this transition smoothly. Of all new jobs created in the past decade, 88 percent were in the service industries. Wages in this sector have been well below average manufacturing wages. At the same time, unskilled workers, particularly those lacking even a high school diploma, experience high unemployment, even though that rate has been fairly low compared to rates in other countries. In reality, there are vast differences among workers in different types of jobs, in different industries, and in different regions of the country. The pay of the least-skilled workers has stagnated or actually declined, while workers with more education and skills have enjoyed increased earnings. This is creating a widening gap in incomes and is effectively killing the "American dream," or the ability of working-class people to enter the middle class and a comfortable standard of living. One of the reasons for this situation has been a decrease in productivity.

Productivity is the amount, in dollars, that a worker produces in a given hour. The worker could be using computers, or complex machinery, or a hammer and wrench, or a telephone, or one's brain and hands. A worker can be working alone or in a team or on an assembly line. The important thing is that to flourish, an economy needs to have rising productivity. Technological innovations produced such rising productivity from about the end of the nineteenth century to about the 1970s. In tandem with productivity, the pay of American workers rose, so that they could afford private housing, more than one vehicle per family, and a college education for their children. In the 1970s, however, productivity began to decline. While the annual productivity growth rate had been 3.2 percent in the period 1948–1966, it had declined to 1.2 percent in the period 1990–1997. The slowing of labor

Box 17.3 Globalism and Its Foes

The 1990s saw phenomenal growth in the spread of capitalism around the globe. Former communist and socialist economies abandoned command forms or nationalization of industries to pursue the free market and engage in free trade. Generally referred to as "globalism" or "globalization," the movement has found a welcome in many economies and cultures of nations around the world. While economists and politicians have sung globalization's praises, however, ordinary people here and abroad have looked at the movement with a much more critical eye. This criticism came to public attention when it erupted in violence at such events as a meeting of the World Trade Organization (WTO), a meeting of the World Bank and the International Monetary Fund (IMF), and at one of the meetings of leaders of the Group of Eight in Genoa.

Who are the violent protesters, and what do they want? As to who they are, no one could have predicted in the past that this unusual combination of groups would ever agree on anything. The protesters, in fact, consist of religious groups who complain that the poorest nations of the world are excessively burdened with international debt and should obtain debt forgiveness. They protest against the World Bank and the IMF because these institutions are the leading lenders to those countries.

Another group of protesters are environmentalists, who complain that the spread of free-market capitalism is damaging the environment and contributing to the greenhouse effect. They also believe that the poor nations are being depleted of their natural resources. They are protesting against the World Bank for funding projects that contribute to environmental degradation and against the IMF for offering some governments aid if they decrease their spending on protecting the environment.

A third group of protesters are students, who are concerned with the poor working conditions in overseas factories producing articles for American companies. They accuse the World Bank and the IMF of standing behind the interests of corporations rather than of workers and of forcing companies in developing countries to accept investment by multinational corporations.

Organized labor is also part of these protesting groups. The AFL-CIO, the United Steelworkers of America, and the Teamsters, all claim that global trade will have a negative impact on workers in wealthy, industrial societies. They demand stricter trade and labor standards to be enforced around the globe. They want the WTO to change certain trade rules and the IMF to stop encouraging poor nations to develop export-oriented industries at the expense of American labor.

Finally, a number of ad hoc coalitions, such as Global Exchange, 50 Years is Enough, and the Ruckus Society insist that globalization works against native cultures, increasing social injustice and poverty. They protest against the World Bank and the IMF because they see these institutions as the chief instruments of capitalist expansion, working in tandem with the big corporations (Kahn, 2000, A5).

It is too early to know whether this motley crew of protesters will succeed as a social movement or disperse after a few instances of headline grabbing. What is becoming clearer, however, is that many people around the globe perceive the United States as an imperialistic power. Perhaps they admire the successes of capitalism and the free market economy, and perhaps they envy them. While Americans believe they are spreading democracy and human rights around the world, many in the world believe they are spreading economic and cultural domination.

productivity was a worldwide phenomenon, but it had been greater in the United States than in other industrialized countries. It had been a major factor in the stagnation of American paychecks.

Finally, America's accustomed role as the world's economic leader was seriously threatened by competition from Europe and Asia in the 1980s. The United States had for years indulged in excessive consumption and low national savings, as well as decreased productivity. Many American plants were old and inefficient. If corporations were to rebuild these plants, it would be at a tremendous cost. Coupled with the expense of employing only organized labor, the cost would prevent these corporations from competing in a world market.

American corporations solved these challenges in two ways. First, they used some surgical procedures, such as reengineering their work. They cut costs by laying off employees or used cheaper labor by employing part-time or temporary workers. They adopted new technologies and management styles. Many shifted their way of doing business to be more in step with the emerging high technologies. Secondly, they sought potential markets in new places. Often this included moving manufacturing abroad, or *global sourcing*. Global sourcing allows the creation of world capital markets, meaning that companies can build plants anywhere in the world, wherever it is cheapest or where the workers are the best skilled. Over the last several decades, the capital investments of American firms abroad grew by a much higher percentage than their domestic investments. Foreign operation of American-owned firms accounted for more than $1 trillion in sales per year. Profits earned by American firms in the United States dropped by 21 percent between 1989 and 1990, but the overseas profits of American-owned firms surged by 15 percent. General Motors, Ford, IBM, DEC, and Coca-Cola were only some of the corporations that earned most of their 1990 profits outside the United States (Reich, 1991, 21). In other words, American firms had discovered that they could make higher profits by producing their goods abroad, using cheap and more skilled labor than American workers, and selling products directly on the world market.

Today, the American economy and the economies of other nations are linked by a number of so-called *flows*. One is the **goods and services flow**, also called trade flow, by which is meant that the United States exports goods and services to other nations and imports goods and services from other nations. **Capital and labor flow**, also called resource flow, means that American firms establish production facilities in foreign countries and foreign firms establish production facilities in the United States. At the same time, labor also flows, in that many workers immigrate into the United States every year, and some American workers move to other countries to work. **Information and technology flows** refer to the fact that the United States transmits information to other countries and receives information from other countries regarding products, prices, investment opportunities, interest rates, etc. Similarly, technology created in the United States is used in other countries, and American firms use technology developed abroad. Finally, in **financial flows**, money is transferred between the United States and other countries for such purposes as paying for imports, buying assets, paying interest on debt, and providing for foreign aid.

As noted, the extent of these flows has greatly increased in the past several decades. Such an increase in the volume of international trade has been more significant for other countries, but the United States has also profited from the growth of exports and imports, allowing the nation to remain the world's leading trading nation. An overview of international trade includes the facts that: as of the summer of 2007 we had a trade deficit in goods and services of $57.6 billion; imports decreased to $195.9 billion and exports increased to $138.3 billion (see Figure 17.2 U.S. Census Bureau. **http://www.census.gov/indicator/www/ustrade.html**). We import some of the same goods that we export, that is, automobiles, computers, chemicals, telecommunications equipment, semiconductors, etc. The import and export of goods and services occurs with other industrial nations rather than with developing nations; and our most important trading partner is Canada: in 2007 total trade with Canada accounted for 18.4 percent.

International trade and an open economy allow the United States to specialize, that is, to focus on industries whose products are exportable and away from industries whose products can be imported. This kind of specialization on an international scale increases the productivity of the nation, and, thus, its standard of living. In spite of this reality, neither governments nor individuals or special interest groups are always in favor of free trade.

Governments have traditionally imposed a variety of protective tariffs, import quotas, licensing requirements, and export subsidies in attempts to impede imports and boost exports. Governments impose these barriers to free trade usually in response to political

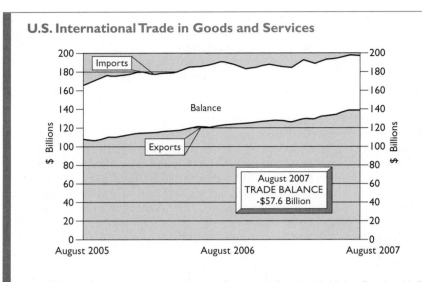

FIGURE 17.2   U.S. International Trade in Goods and Services Highlights October 11, 2007
Source: **http://www.census.gov/indicator/www/ustrade/html.** Accessed 10/18/2007

pressures by domestic industries, which are temporarily hurt by free trade. Protectionism plays well with some segments of the labor force and industry, but economists maintain that consumers and the entire nation are better served when trade remains unimpeded.

The trend around the world has been toward a decrease in protective tariffs and other impediments. Many nations have entered into agreements to reduce trade barriers. Among the most important ones are the General Agreement on Tariffs and Trade (GATT) and the World Trade Organization (WTO), both of which have been positive forces in liberalizing world trade. The WTO, however, has been a source of controversy in that critics are worried that the rules established to expand international trade and investment will lead firms to evade national laws, especially those that protect workers and the environment.

Another way that nations have sought to reduce protectionism has been through the creation of regional free-trade zones, or trade blocs. One of the most effective has been the European Union (EU) comprising 25 European nations, which has achieved greater productivity, output, and faster economic growth for the members. Another is the North American Free Trade Agreement (NAFTA), a trading bloc formed by the United States, Canada, and Mexico, according to which most trade barriers will be eliminated by 2008. Although critics of NAFTA were fearful that American workers would lose their jobs as firms relocated in Mexico to take advantage of lower wages and weaker environmental regulations, in effect the employment rate has risen in the United States, and it is generally felt that the standard of living has improved in all three countries.

After a painful transitional period, the American economy seemed to regain its edge worldwide. The 1990s saw full employment and a rising stock market. Profitability returned to the old corporations, and a myriad of new, highly lucrative companies were created in the new high technology field. Beginning in 2000, however, the economy slowed for a variety of reasons, which are reviewed in the next chapter.

The Chapter in Brief

To sustain life, people need a constant supply of food, sufficient shelter, and clothing for protection from the elements. These goods are scarce and require effort to obtain. The institution of the economy consists of the patterns of behavior that revolve around obtaining the scarce resources necessary for survival.

Essentially, societal members must decide what to produce, how to distribute and exchange what is produced, and in what manner to consume it. These decisions are made either by relying on custom and tradition, by the command of a leader or group of leaders, or by the functioning of a market dependent on supply and demand and on prices, profits, and losses. Most modern economies use a variety of these methods in decision making. Resources include labor, land, capital, entrepreneurship, and technology. Resources are versatile but finite; they must be conserved.

Modern industrial economies are characterized by (1) large amounts of capital; (2) extreme specialization and division of labor, which are methods for producing more goods with less effort; and (3) the use of money as the chief medium of exchange. Economic systems are both social and cultural systems legitimized by an ideology accepted by most people as valid. Capitalism, socialism (in both democratic and nondemocratic forms), and communism are the three ideologies underlying most of the modern industrial economies.

The corporation is a form of business enterprise that originated in the middle of the nineteenth century and provided the economy with a tremendous boost. Essentially, this form of business organization makes great sums of money available with diminished risks for individuals. The corporation has made finance capitalism—characterized by the dominance of investment banks and insurance companies, by tremendous aggregates of capital, by separation of ownership from management, and by holding companies—become prevalent.

The trend has been toward ever-greater concentrations of economic power, called oligopoly, in the hands of corporations, some of which are highly diversified and multinational. While the concentration of power leads to the formation of powerful pressure groups and to unfair competition with smaller firms, it also provides the sophisticated machinery and specialized personnel required for modern technological and scientific advances.

The corporation has given rise to a bureaucracy of managers and white-collar workers, who have become a definite force in the social life of the nation and around whom a fictional mythology and scientific research have developed. Corporate CEOs are extremely well-remunerated and some have engaged in forms of white-collar crime. It is felt that a reorganization of the corporate form of management is essential.

The remaining rung on the industrial ladder belongs to the blue-collar workers who run the machines and the assembly lines to turn out the finished products of industry. Their destinies have been traditionally separate from the rest of the industrial personnel.

The American economy, in which a modified version of capitalism called a mixed market prevails, is characterized by a workforce that is employed largely in the tertiary sector. That is, it supplies services instead of extracting raw materials (the primary sector) or turning them into finished products (the secondary sector). This shift in sectors has resulted in changes in the occupational structure of the society as well as in the stratification system. The changes consist of a trend toward professionalization of jobs that can be upgraded, whereas the unskilled or undereducated become the permanently unemployed or underemployed.

Organization of labor in the United States began in the late nineteenth century and did not flourish again until the passage of legislation acknowledging government's responsibility for the welfare of workers. The labor movement saw a further reawakening during the tenure of President Franklin Roosevelt, who encouraged unionization in the belief that it would give workers increased purchasing power, which in turn would stimulate the economy.

Today, organized labor is experiencing declining growth, partly as a result of the decline of the secondary sector and the growth of the tertiary sector, whose workers have traditionally avoided unionization, and partly because of other factors. American labor is now competing with better-educated, better-trained, and more disciplined foreign labor, just as the American economy is challenged by sharp competition from abroad.

Beginning in the 1970s, productivity in the United States began to decline. In addition, American industrial machinery and plants were old. Declining productivity results in a stagnating economy. To counteract this and other factors, American firms reengineered their work, cut costs by laying off employees or using part-time workers, and began to move manufacturing abroad, engaging in global sourcing. This method became so successful that we have effectively moved toward a global type of economy, in which goods and services, capital and labor, information and technology, and finances flow from the United States to other nations and back again.

International trade has been very profitable for all involved, especially for the industrial nations. International trade and an open economy allow the United States to specialize, focusing on specific products, and, thus, increase productivity. However, many segments of the population believe that open international trade allows American jobs to go abroad, and, consequently, they pressure the government to impede it. The government does this by imposing various tariffs and other trade barriers. Economists have shown that protectionism is detrimental in the long run, so governments have done away with most trade barriers. Instead, nations have entered into agreements such as GATT and WTO, both of which have additionally liberalized trade barriers. In addition, nations have tried to reduce protectionism by creating regional free-trade zones, such as the European Union and the North American Free Trade Agreement (NAFTA). These trading blocs have been successful in spite of fears that they would hurt American workers. There are vocal critics, however, who claim that economic globalism leads to exploitation of workers and weakened environmental regulations.

Terms to Remember

capital All material objects made by humans. One of the factors of production.

capitalism An economic system in which property belongs to private individuals; production is engaged in for a profit motive; and prices, wages, and profits are regulated by supply and demand, as well as competition. The welfare of the individual is the chief concern.

factors of production Labor, land, capital, entrepreneurship, time and technology, or the basic elements that are combined in the production of goods and services.

finance capitalism Capitalism associated with a later stage of industrialism in which business organizations are characterized by (1) dominance of investment banks and insurance companies, (2) large aggregates of capital, (3) ownership separate from management, (4) appearance of the holding company, and (5) appearance of the corporation.

industrial capitalism Capitalism associated with an early stage of industrialism in which business organizations were concerned mainly with manufacturing, mining, and transportation.

labor A human resource. One of the factors of production.

land Natural material things such as land, minerals, water. Another of the factors of production.

monopoly A situation in which one firm produces the entire market supply of a specific product.

multinational corporations Corporations that extend production to foreign nations at great profit to themselves (because labor is cheap and markets are expanded) but at the risk of being perceived as threats to the hosts.

oligopoly A condition of high industrial concentration in which a small number of corporations dominate an entire industry, effectively preventing price competition.

opportunity cost The sacrifice involved in making an economic choice.

production-possibility limits The optimum amount of production that a society can attain. Each society faces a production-possibility frontier beyond which it cannot produce.

resources Everything that is needed for the production of goods and services.

Suggested Readings

Barlett, Donald L., and James B. Steele. 1992. *America: What Went Wrong?* Kansas City, MO: Andrews & McMeel. Two Pulitzer Prize-winning journalists turn their investigative lens to the economic effects the past generation of Presidents and members of Congress have had on the nation. The authors conclude that the latter have been changing the American economy, by design and default, to favor the privileged, the powerful, and the influential at the expense of everyone else.

Friedman, Thomas L. 2005. *The World Is Flat: A Brief History of the Twenty-First Century.* New York: Farrar, Strauss and Giroux. The award-winning *New York Times* columnist explains the convergence of technology and events that has led to globalization. The world is flat because manufacturing and services can flow from one country to the next, allowing people of different countries to create wealth for their societies. A clear narrative that includes successes as well as failures and discontents that globalization evokes.

Galbraith, John Kenneth. 1992. *The Culture of Contentment.* New York: Houghton Mifflin. An influential liberal economist critiques the state of the American economy in the 1980s, blaming much of the trouble on the nonintervention—or selective intervention—of the government so that public needs are neglected at the expense of benefits accruing to the few. The author concludes that we have unleashed capitalism only to have it succumb to its own self-destructive tendencies.

Levitt, Steven D., and Stephen J. Dubner. 2005. *Freakonomics.* New York: William Morrow/HarperCollins. Neither a conventional economics book nor a run-of-the-mill social science book, but a new and different way of looking at everyday matters.

Levy, Frank. 1999. *The New Dollars and Dreams.* New York: Russell Sage Foundation. This book is an update of a 1987 book. The author analyzes the performance of the American economy since World War II, when steadily rising living standards were a fact. He then explains what has happened since the 1970s, in which productivity slowed and incomes began to stagnate, and what happened in the 1990s to prompt an economic recovery.

Luttwak, Edward. 1999. *Turbo-Capitalism: Winners and Losers in the Global Economy.* New York: Harper-Collins. The author characterizes the state of today's American economy as turbocharged, that is, overheated by the abolition of anticompetition laws and regulations, by the technological innovations brought on by the computer revolution, and by privatization and removal of most import barriers. Although turbo-capitalism is superior to the communist and socialist economic formulations, it has some corrosive effects on society.

Porter, Michael E., 1998. *The Competitive Advantage of Nations.* NY: The Free Press. The author has examined 10 economies and shows that productivity is central to a nation's competitive market position.

Web Sites of Interest

http://www.bea.doc.gov/
Web site of the U.S. Bureau of Economic Analysis. Offers various overviews of the U.S. economy.

http://www.bls.gov
Web site of the U.S. Department of Labor. Everything you want to know about American labor.

http://www.whitehouse.gov/fsbr/esbr.html
The briefing room in the White House dedicated to economic statistics.

http://www.firstgov.gov
All the federal agencies that make up the government of the United States.

http://www.usinfo.state.gov
The web site has several informative segments regarding what is a market economy and about international economy and trade.

http://www.fms.treas.gov/
Web site of the U.S. Department of the Treasury with the latest profile of the economy.

http://www.commerce.gov/
Web site of the U.S. Department of Commerce with information about the state of the economy.

Principles of Economic Behavior: Microeconomics and Macroeconomics

IN THIS CHAPTER, YOU WILL LEARN

- *the difference between microeconomics and macroeconomics;*
- *who are the participants in the market system;*
- *what is the essence of the price system;*
- *what are the market forces;*
- *the need for a public sector and for government intervention in the economy;*
- *about the economic goals of the society;*
- *the instruments at the government's disposal for intervening in the economy and the reason for their imperfect functioning;*
- *the major economic problems faced by the economy, and how the American economy responds to them.*

Economics is sometimes called the "dismal science," and many do not consider it a science at all. In fact, the predictive power of economics is weak, and much of its success is predicated on a positive psychology. Economists have learned much about the functioning of the economy, however, and they know which specific actions will have which economic result.

The Small Picture and the Large Picture

The analysis of an economic system is done on two levels: microeconomics and macroeconomics. **Microeconomics** is the study of individual behavior in the economy, as well as of specific markets. It deals with the details, the behavior of individual components of the economy, such as, for instance, what determines the price of a single product or why single consumers or firms act as they do.

When we look at the economy from the micro point of view, in other words, we look at single trees, not at the forest. We want to know how an individual, or a company, behaves in the economy. What do individuals do when they lose their jobs? How do they respond to various incentives and opportunities? Why do they buy certain goods and not others? What is the price of a specific product? What are the expenses of a particular firm? What is the income of a given household?

Macroeconomics deals with the national economy as a whole, that is, with the large picture, or the forest. In analyzing the economy in macro terms, we look at such national goals as maintaining full employment, limiting inflation, stabilizing the economy, and pursuing economic growth; we look at output, income, price level, foreign trade, and government policies. In short, we want to know how the economy as a unit is working, and we want to see how to improve it. Of course, the division into macro- and microeconomics is simply a matter of convenience, a way of dividing a huge amount of information to make it more amenable to analysis. In reality, we are looking at the same institution.

■ Market Mechanisms

It is one thing to describe the American economy as a mixed-market economy based on the principles of classical capitalism as outlined by Adam Smith, and another thing to know the mechanisms by which such a system functions. How is it, for instance, that the correct amount of a given product is manufactured? What happens if too much of a certain item is produced? Who tells companies what to make and when to make it? Where do consumers get the income to buy the products made by companies? What is the role of government? These and many more questions suggest themselves when a clear explanation of the working of the American economy is required.

Who Makes Decisions?

In a market economy, decisions about what to produce are made by consumers. The more consumers want a certain product, the more they are willing to spend for it. The more they are willing to pay for it, the more producers are eager to manufacture it, for large sales will increase producers' profits. Therefore, it is basically a **price system** that decides which goods and services are going to be produced. If consumers are willing to pay a price, producers are willing to make the item. The price system acts as a mechanism of social control—it controls what will be produced in the society. Note, however, that the price system does not necessarily reflect consumer needs, but rather consumer wants.

Who Participates in the Economy?

Three groups in society participate in economic, or market, transactions: households, firms, and central authorities. The **household** is defined as all the people who live under one roof and make financial decisions as a unit. Households are called consumers because they behave with a singleness of purpose, as if they were individuals. Households make two basic decisions: how to spend their income and how to sell their labor (or exploit their land or invest their capital, the other factors of production) to obtain income.

In the economic system we call a market system, consumers, through their actions, make the ultimate decisions as to what is to be produced and in what quantities. If women buy enough of a certain garment, you may be sure that more similar garments will be produced.

The **firm** is defined as the unit that decides how to use labor, land, and capital, and which goods and services to produce. It buys some factors of production from households (it hires labor, for instance) and uses the factors to produce goods and services, which it then sells back to other households, to other firms, and to central authorities. The firm's purpose is to produce as much as possible so that profits are high.

The **central authorities** are defined as all public agencies, government bodies, and other organizations under the control of the various levels of government that exercise control over the behavior of households and firms. The central authorities are generally referred to simply as the government. *Central* authorities do not act as a unit, or as if they were single individuals; on the contrary, they have many objectives.

Markets

A market, in an economic sense, is an abstraction. It may be defined in terms of a geographic area (worldwide or only several blocks wide) over which buyers and sellers negotiate the exchange of specific commodities. For example, "the sugar market" refers to the demand for, the supply, and the price of sugar on a worldwide level. Markets may be distinguished into **product markets,** in which firms sell their production of goods and services, and **factor (or resource) markets,** in which households sell the factors of production (land, labor, capital) that they control.

The Circular Flow

When it becomes clear what consumers want, business firms, looking for profits, begin to produce it. To maximize profits, they produce as much as possible for as little as possible—they

The stock market is the most abstract representation of a market: instead of apples or onions, shares in companies are bought and sold, at prices established by the laws of supply and demand.

try to reduce their production costs. In this process, they are able to employ more workers, and workers flock to jobs in specific industries because of the higher incomes they can earn.

A successful business firm soon attracts rivals eager to make profits, too. Here the role of competition comes in, with the ultimate effect of flooding the market with the desired goods or services. When there are more products than consumers willing to buy them, prices are forced down. This means that profits also go down for the manufacturers, but production will continue for a time, even for smaller profits. The business firm is always motivated by the thought of profit. However, it performs the important social function of organizing productive activity in the most efficient way, and it directs productive resources where consumer demand is strongest. As Adam Smith thought, greed is indeed the "invisible hand" that underlies business, but what strange consequences it has!

Who obtains the goods and services that business firms produce? Those households and firms that have both the desire for them and the income to pay for them. Here the circular nature of the process becomes obvious: Consumers earn money by selling their labor to business firms; in effect, consumers contribute to the production of the goods they want to consume. The income they earn depends on the importance of their contribution to the production process and the price other consumers are willing to pay for the products. Finally, the amount of income consumers earn determines how much they can actually buy of the goods and services they want. Because of scarcity, the price of some goods and services is so high that some consumers can buy only small quantities of the products or are eliminated altogether. The price system, then, also rations products among consumers on the basis of who is able to pay the most for a specific product.

The activities just described may be seen as a **circular flow** from product markets to factor markets and back again. Households want unlimited commodities but have only limited resources (income) with which to buy them. They must make choices as to which products to buy in the product market. Their choices affect the prices of products and act as signals to firms as to which goods and services consumers want. Firms affect prices, too, because they also make choices about which products they produce (those that provide them with the largest profit). In addition, firms must buy factors of production in amounts dependent on production decisions, which in turn depend on consumer decisions. They must buy labor, for instance, from households, and pay for it according to the demand for specific skills. Payments for labor provide households with income, which goes to pay for some of their many demands. In short, firms and households are bound together in an unending and unbroken circle (Figure 18.1).

Withdrawals and Injections. The circular flow of payments and incomes would be a completely closed system were it not for two important exceptions. First, neither households nor firms spend all of their incomes to buy goods and services and factors of production from each other. Households pay income taxes and save some of their income for future expenditures. This means that some of the household's income goes to the government, some is kept, and only some goes to firms. The same is true of firms: They must pay taxes, they save or invest for future expansions, and only some of their income goes back to households to buy labor or to other firms to buy some factors of production. Therefore, the circular flow of income is

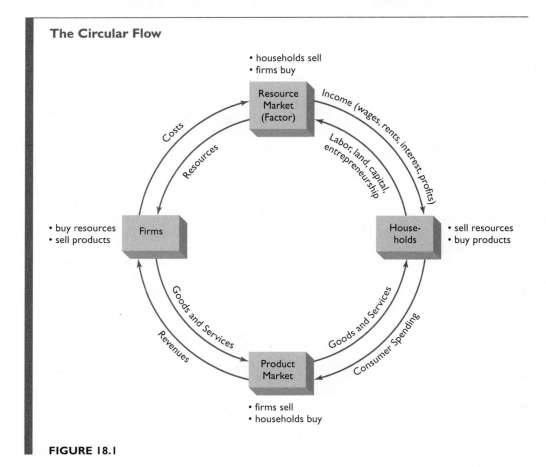

The Circular Flow

- households sell
- firms buy

Resource Market (Factor)

Income (wages, rents, interest, profits)

Costs

Resources

Labor, land, capital, entrepreneurship

Firms

- buy resources
- sell products

House-holds

- sell resources
- buy products

Goods and Services

Revenues

Goods and Services

Consumer Spending

Product Market

- firms sell
- households buy

FIGURE 18.1

interrupted by **withdrawals,** also called leakages, consisting of income received by households that is not returned to firms and income received by firms that is not returned to households or other firms. Second, the government also buys goods and services from firms, and firms sell to other firms. These exceptions are called **injections** into the circular flow of income. Injections are incomes received by firms that do not originate from the spending of households and incomes received by households that do not originate from the spending of firms.

■ Market Forces

The overall goal of all economic activities is to satisfy human needs in the face of scarcity. Specifically, each participant tries to maximize something in the marketplace. Consumers try to maximize their happiness by offering their labor or other resource on the market and obtaining the most satisfying combination of income or goods and services. Firms try to maximize their profits by using the most effective resources to manufacture the most profitable products. Government agencies are responsible for maximizing the general welfare of the population (that is, the society in general) by using resources to produce public goods and services and for redistributing income more equitably.

However, the participants are not entirely free to pursue their goals. All three participants are affected by money in the form of prices (for goods and services) and incomes (for labor). What consumers buy and the quantity they buy depend to a large degree on the price of the products and services and on their income. What firms produce and the quantity and variety of resources they employ in the production process depend to a large degree on the prices of resources and of labor. Even government agencies are stymied in their actions by a budget and by the prices of resources and products. Prices, then, affect all participants; when prices change, so does the behavior of consumers, firms, and government agencies.

Demand, Supply, and Price

The exchanges that take place in each market each day are so numerous and complicated in a society such as the American one that patterns of interaction are difficult to trace. It is easier to illustrate the behavior of a single individual, a consumer, knowing that such behavior must in reality be multiplied millions of times.

Every consumer disposes of a certain amount of purchasing power—has some income—that will be used to buy things according to specific needs, desires, taste, and so on. Out of this combination of factors, economists can identify the consumer's demand for any product. **Demand** is expressed as consumers' willingness and ability to buy a specific product at a given price. A consumer who needs some new shirts, and has set apart $100 to buy them, may decide to buy five shirts if they cost $20 each, three shirts if they cost $30 each, and only two shirts if they cost $50 each. The consumer's demand consists of these various combinations of quantities and prices. Economists illustrate demand with a graph in which the combinations of prices and quantities appear in the shape of a curve, the **demand curve.** The demand curve shows at a glance the inverse relationship between price and quantity demanded for any product. This can be called the **law of demand,** and it states that consumers will buy more of a product when it is offered at a low price and less of it when it is offered at a high price. The market demand curve is determined by adding the individual demand curves of each consumer.

The other side of this coin, which works exactly the same way, is the concept of market supply. **Market supply** represents the combined willingness and ability of firms (businesses or producers) to supply specific products (such as wheat or cars or shirts) at specific prices.

A supply curve is plotted in the same way as a demand curve except that now the relationship between price and quantity supplied is positive. In other words, as price increases, the quantity supplied increases, whereas as price falls, the quantity supplied decreases. This relationship may be called the **law of supply**, and it states that firms will produce and offer for sale more of their product at a high price than they will at a low price.

Demand and supply curves simplify the analysis of market action. They show at a glance the flow of resources, products, and money among the participants in the market. And they illustrate the quantity of goods and resources being exchanged in each market, as well as the prices at which they are bought and sold.

Equilibrium and Price Elasticity

In some situations neither a surplus nor a shortage occurs: the quantity demanded and the quantity supplied are in balance. This happens because the price at which producers are willing to sell and the price at which consumers are willing to buy coincides. Economists call this the **equilibrium** price and quantity (Figure 18.2).

People increase or decrease their purchases according to changes in price. This situation is described by economists as the **price elasticity** of demand. By elasticity, economists mean responsiveness. If consumers buy substantially more of a certain product in response to a small downward change in price, demand is said to be elastic. However, if consumers buy very little of a certain product in spite of its lowered price, demand is said to be inelastic.

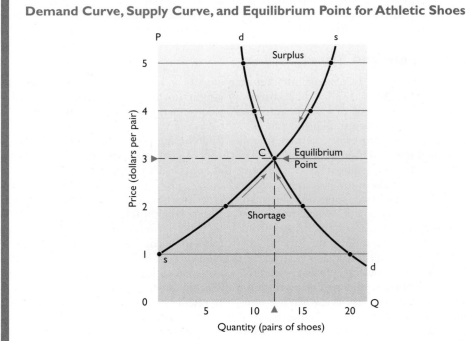

Demand Curve, Supply Curve, and Equilibrium Point for Athletic Shoes

FIGURE 18.2

The price elasticity of demand can be defined with mathematical precision. It is the percentage change in quantity demanded divided by the percentage change in price.

The Principle of Laissez-Faire and Public Needs.   The actions that take place in the marketplace have intrigued economists and laypersons alike. Without any fixed program, plan, or direction, both the content and the flow of goods and services between consumers and businesses take place and the prices at which products are exchanged are set. In short, both content and flow, as well as prices, are determined by the independent actions of individual buyers and sellers who do not even need to know how the market works. All they have to do is act on their personal desires, abilities, and incomes.

The mechanism of the market has many advantages or it would not have persisted these many years. It allows individuals to feel free from constraint. It permits each participant to maximize his or her goals, whether these be profits or satisfaction. Of course, each participant derives only as much profit and satisfaction as may be obtained from the products or resources each possesses. The participant with more income can obtain more products, and the one with more talent or skills or diligence can obtain more income. The mechanism of the market is such, in other words, that it enables an economy to function allowing all persons to derive some satisfaction. At the same time, society's scarce resources are used in the production of the goods and services for which there is greatest demand as expressed by the prices that participants are willing to pay. Finally, the economic output is distributed on the basis of the amount of purchasing power each participant is willing and able to part with in exchange for a particular product.

Because the market works so well without intervention, the policy that has been derived from it is precisely one of "leaving things alone." The policy was first formulated by Adam Smith and has since been referred to in its French translation as the "laissez-faire" doctrine.

One of the externalities in the economy consists of the constant need to repair the streets and roads of our cities. Repairing the street in front of our house contributes to our satisfaction, but we do not like to pay for it, and our neighbors may refuse to pay for repairs altogether. Therefore, we must rely on the local government to collect taxes from us and all our neighbors and then to pay for the needed repairs with these public funds.

This doctrine holds that the government should stay out of the economy, and it has long been a staple of pure capitalism and conservative politics.

Leaving things alone, however, does not always work to the advantage of a majority. For example, the market mechanisms make no provision for the production of public goods—highways, police and fire protection, and so on—from which everyone also derives benefits, but for which nobody wants to pay. Moreover, the mechanisms work to the advantage of those who already possess some resources with which to maximize satisfaction or obtain more profits. The market mechanisms favor individuals who have inherited particularly large fortunes or particularly good genes. In this respect, the market system perpetuates inequality.

Those who are in control of a significant proportion of productive resources are able to change the results of market transactions to serve their own interest. If one firm produces the vast majority of refrigerators in the country, that firm can control supply and pretty much set prices without worrying about the other participants in the market. This is why the government has had to interfere in the role of regulator of the free-market economy.

■ A Macroview

Adam Smith would be horrified to know that today Americans expect their government to provide full employment, maintain price stability, protect the environment, build and maintain—and continually improve—schools and highways, care for the sick, support the needy, enforce laws, regulate commerce, and do a myriad of other things. Smith envisioned government as providing for the nation's defense and hardly anything more.

The public sector—economic activities in which the government engages for the public good—has grown to such proportions that government spending now accounts for approximately one-third of all expenditures, and the government employs one out of every four workers. The reason is, of course, that the well-being of the people is served by the public sector in ways that the private sector cannot do. The results achieved in the private sector through market mechanisms are not totally consonant with societal goals. Therefore, market economies, including the American market economy, have had to accept the intervention of public power to make significant alterations in the functioning of the economy.

Unfortunately, the public sector is hampered by large, self-perpetuating bureaucracies that become so entrenched that it is difficult to dismiss employees for incompetence or eliminate agencies whose missions have been fulfilled. Consequently, when the government provides services, these tend to be inferior (and slower and more expensive) than those provided by the private sector. Yet we know we need a public sector because, in trying to attain a certain standard of living, we have certain economic goals in mind.

The Public Interest: Socioeconomic Goals

The goals of a society are not easily defined. This is particularly true in a nation like the United States of more than 300 million individuals with varied cultural experiences and distinct expectations. In addition, it is not easy to separate economic goals from other social goals, since the achievement of many economic goals leads directly to improved social conditions. Nonetheless, most Americans would agree that the predominant goals of the society include the following:

1. Full employment
2. A desirable mix of economic output

3. High as well as equitably distributed incomes
4. Reasonable price stability
5. Adequate economic growth

It is true that in a free society even what represents the public interest is a matter of debate. In the United States, politics colors our perception of the public interest. In a general way, liberal Democrats have maintained that there is a need for intervention by the government in the interest of the people. Conservative Republicans have leaned toward the view of leaving things alone, or the classic laissez-faire attitude. But probably liberals and conservatives alike would agree that most of the goals listed need some help from the government (public policy) to be achieved.

Full Employment

The concept of full employment refers specifically to the ability of the economy to utilize all individuals who are ready and willing to work. In gathering data about employment, only those working in exchange for pay are counted as employed. Those who are out of work but looking for a job are considered unemployed, but both categories of persons are part of the labor force. Students and those keeping house are not counted as either employed or unemployed. They are not considered to be part of the labor force. The goal of full employment is not total employment (zero unemployment), because there is always a segment of the labor force that is changing jobs. The goal of full employment is in reality a low rate of unemployment, approximately between 4 and 5 percent. The Bureau of Labor Statistics does a monthly nationwide random survey to estimate the size of the civilian labor force and the number of the unemployed. On this basis, it calculates the unemployment rate. For instance, to figure the 1997 unemployment rate, the number of unemployed persons, 6.7 million, divided by 136 million, the number of persons constituting the total civilian labor force, producing the rate of 4.9 percent. This rate is very good compared to those of other industrialized countries (Table 18.1).

The Great Depression, still vivid in the memories of many Americans, was historically the most dramatic case of massive unemployment. It resulted from insufficient demand, so that the economy's productive capacity failed to be utilized. The market did not reach an equilibrium, which resulted in disaster for a large part of the American population. The market failure prompted the government to intervene, following the theories of British economist John Maynard Keynes, by making up the difference between aggregate demand and potential output in the public sector. That is, the government became an active participant in the market, increasing demand sufficiently to coincide with supply.

Since the Depression, the government has acknowledged its responsibility for achieving full employment as expressed by the Employment Act of 1946. It does this through a large number of regulatory, fiscal, and monetary policies that we discuss later.

Desirable Mix of Output

Related to the goal of full employment is the goal of wanting to achieve the economy's production possibilities (trying to utilize the labor of those willing to work by producing as many goods and services as possible). The concern with output, however, has broader implications, including a preoccupation with the quantity and quality of what is produced. The difficulty lies in determining the exact quantity and quality of output that a majority of the population would consider desirable or beneficial. One way of measuring or defining the "correct" mix of output has been proposed by a government agency, the Department of

TABLE 18.1 Unemployment Rates in Ten Countries, Civilian Labor Force Basis, Approximating U.S. Concepts, 2005–2007

Period	United States	Canada	Australia	Japan	France	Germany	Italy	Netherlands	Sweden	United Kingdom
2005	5.1	6.0	5.1	4.5	9.9	11.2	7.8	5.2	7.7	4.8
2006	4.6	5.5	4.9	4.2	9.7	10.3	6.9	4.4r	7.0	5.5
2007	4.5	5.4	4.5	4.0	9.1	9.2r	6.2r	4.0	6.3	5.5

r = revised.
Data used to calculate these unemployment rates come mainly from national statistical sources but also from the Organization for Economic Cooperation and Development and the Statistical Office of the European Communities.

Source: U.S. Department of Labor, Bureau of Labor Statistics, October 5, 2007.

Health and Human Services, which has formulated a number of so-called **social indicators.** Social indicators are helpful in measuring the level of real benefits to the people that results from a given level of output. The indicators include indexes that measure the quality of housing, air, education, television viewing, and so on. As helpful as they may be, social indicators are too numerous (there are 165) and subjective.

An alternative is to focus on the process by which output is determined, the argument being that the correct mix is the one the population desires as expressed by the market mechanisms. However, note that the market is not democratic, in the sense that it does not work equally well for all. It works for the greatest good of those with the largest purchasing power. Because purchasing power is unequal, public policy is again called on to redistribute it through taxes and subsidies.

Government intervention is also called for in instances where no market demand exists for a particular good or service, yet the need exists. For instance, there is a need for protection from fires or criminal activity. Not all individual consumers are able or willing to pay for such protection, but all benefit from the service.

Finally, government action is justified in the attempt to control **externalities,** or the side effects of the market system that may be characterized as negative: congestion, pollution, urban decay, and so on. There is, of course, no demand for those externalities in the market system but, unfortunately, there is an eternal supply of them. Therefore, they must be controlled outside the system, in the public sector.

High and Equitably Distributed Incomes

The economic goal of high and equitably distributed incomes is related to both of the preceding ones; more income derives from more output, and output depends on the efficient utilization of all available resources. In a market economy, incomes are distributed according to the contribution that individuals make to production or to the sale or investment of other factors of production they own. People's wages are related to the value they add to total output, or their **marginal productivity.** Some people's contributions to productivity are very difficult to define and measure. In such cases, incomes are determined by social and institutional factors and by such considerations as how much money is needed to attract them away from other employment.

The question of the justice of the distribution of income is more political than economic, but once the distinction between efficiency and equity of the system is made, public policy can be used to maintain the one while achieving the other. However, public policy has so far failed in this endeavor. The income gap between the rich and the poor increased in the United States in the period between 1969 and 1996. The lowest 20 percent of families, or one-fifth, received only 3.4 percent of total income in 2005, whereas they had received 5.6 percent in 1969. On the other hand, the income share received by the highest 20 percent rose from 40.6 to 50.4 percent. The top 5 percent of families, who had received 15.6 percent of total before-tax income in 1969, increased their share of income to 22.2 percent in 2005 (Table 18.2).

Reasonable Price Stability

The public interest is best served by preserving the stability of prices, first, because stable prices make the planning of production and consumption easier, and second, because of the effect of changing prices on the distribution of income. Prices and income do not rise in unison. The income of some people rises faster than the prices they pay for their consumer

TABLE 18.2 Share of Aggregate Income Received by Each Fifth and Top 5 Percent of Households, All Races: 2000 to 2005 (Households as of March of the following year)

Year	Number (thousands)	Share of aggregate income					
		Lowest fifth	Second fifth	Third fifth	Fourth fifth	Highest fifth	Top 5 percent
2005	114,384	3.4	8.6	14.6	23.0	50.4	22.2
2004	113,343	3.4	8.7	14.7	23.2	50.1	21.8
2003	112,000	3.4	8.7	14.8	23.4	49.8	21.4
2002	111,278	3.5	8.8	14.8	23.3	49.7	21.7
2001	109,297	3.5	8.7	14.6	23.0	50.1	22.4
2000	108,209	3.6	8.9	14.8	23.0	49.8	22.1

Source: **http://www.census.gov/hhes/www/income/histinc/h02ar.html.** Accessed 6/2/2007.

Box 18.1 **Income Inequality: Will the Rich and the Poor Always Be with Us?**

As well as the market economy works, it has not been able to determine how to distribute incomes equitably so as to avoid having poverty in a society that also has individuals with immense wealth. Inequality has been a problem for societies for thousands of years. In democratic societies, inequality has depended largely on the political administration in power: the more conservative the administration, the more inequality. For instance, the end of the nineteenth century was called the Gilded Age, because the government had minimum taxation levels, did not regulate the nascent industrial system, and relied on charitable programs rather than on government social programs to help those in need. John D. Rockefeller was considered the richest man in the United States (he was one of the so-called robber barons mentioned in Chapter 17). In 1895, Rockefeller declared an income of $1.25 million. This represented 7,000 times the average per capita income in the country.

As the Great Depression ravaged the country, the government stepped in to correct some of these dramatic inequalities. From 1929 to 1947, aided by World War II, there was a large increase in the American middle class: the wages of production workers in manufacturing rose by 67 percent, while the richest 1 percent of Americans actually lost 17 percent of their income. In the postwar era, 1947 through 1973, the economic boom was shared by all: wages rose 81 percent, and the wealthiest 1 percent increased their income by 38 percent. The next period, 1973 through 1980, was an era of stagflation in which all lost ground: wages fell by 3 percent and the richest 1 percent lost 4 percent of their income. As of 1980, a new gilded age seems to have appeared, in line with modern conservatism which was gaining political power with the election of Ronald Reagan. While real wages for the middle and working classes began to fall, the income of the richest 1 percent climbed to sometimes astronomic proportions (Krugman, 2006; A19). For example, in 2006 one hedge fund manager earned $1.7 billion, which is more than 38,000 times the average income, and he is not unique. A true gilded age for some individuals is moderated, however, by government intervention in the guise of progressive taxation, estate taxes, social security, Medicare and Medicaid, and other social insurance programs that offer a safety net to those less fortunate (Krugman, 2007, 20).

It appears that because of differences in talent, hard work, background or education, and sheer luck, some individuals will always do better than others in the hierarchy of economic success. However, dramatic and gigantic differences among people and their lifestyles do not bode well for a harmonious society.

goods, whereas other people must pay higher prices for consumer goods faster than their income rises. When an economy is growing, even stable prices sometimes result in inequities. Increased production means that people receive higher paychecks, but only if the price of the product they are manufacturing is not lowered; but, with an increase in supply, the price is usually lowered.

Inflation. Price levels, as we noted previously, are partly determined by the decisions about production and expenditures that are made by individual consumers and firms. If they decide to use more of their purchasing power or to use it more rapidly, demand will go up. If the demand cannot be matched by an increase in supply, prices for the insufficient products or services will rise. This situation is called **inflation** and requires public policy for correction. Prices sometimes rise as a result of changes in supply that are not triggered by increased demand, as happened in the 1970s, when a cartel of oil-producing nations set the price of oil at high levels. In that case, it was also up to public policy to alter either the structure or the behavior of the market (the price of oil was brought down drastically, partly by the greed of the nations that overproduced and partly by government policies aimed at cutting consumer demand and encouraging domestic production).

Deflation. Situations in which prices go down do exist. They were common in the Great Depression and occurred in the case of the price of oil, as already noted. Price drops are

During the Great Depression of 1929—when a lack of demand produced a decline of productivity and resulted in epidemic rates of unemployment—the government had to step in first of all to save people from hunger, and secondarily to invest in the economy to increase demand and so stimulate productivity. This eventually led to a resumption of employment by creating jobs. Government has been a major player in the economy ever since.

called **deflation**. They appear to be beneficial to the consumer, but they force producers to lay off or fire workers who are no longer needed for production. Therefore, they too are subject to public policy.

Adequate Growth

The goal of adequate growth reflects a concern with the standard of living, since economic growth implies the expansion of production possibilities. The ultimate goal of an economy is to produce enough goods and services—food, housing, clothing, education, freedom from heavy labor—for many and not just for the few. At the same time, with population growth, economic growth is needed simply to maintain present living standards. Hence, the goal of "adequate growth" must include sufficient growth to maintain current standards of living in spite of a growing population. If an improvement in the standard of living is wanted, adequate growth must also include a desire to increase the amount of goods and services available to the average person. In economic terms, the gross national product (GNP) per capita (meaning for each individual) must be increased.

The gross national product, as well as the currently more commonly used gross domestic product, or GDP, are ways of calculating the output of the economy. The **gross national product** is the total output produced by the factors of production (land, labor, capital) and entrepreneurship of Americans, regardless of where these resources are located—in the United States or abroad. The **gross domestic product** consists of the total output of goods and services produced within the limits of the United States, by American or foreign-supplied resources, as well as all income earned. In other words, the cars produced by a Japanese-owned Honda plant in the United States would be counted in the American GDP, but the profits from an American-owned Ford plant in France would be excluded from it. Those profits would be included in the GNP. GDP and GNP figures do not differ by a great deal, however. They represent simply two different ways of measuring the economy.

It is difficult to determine how much of an increase of the GNP or of the GDP can be considered adequate. For example, the GNP has more than doubled since the 1950s, yet polls continue to show that people are no more satisfied with what they have now than they were then. The consensus seems to be that a growth rate of 4 percent is desirable, a rate that would double real GNP every 18 years.

Raising GNP and GDP per capita involves increases in productivity. The stock of capital equipment must be expanded so the labor force can avail itself of more plants and equipment. Public policy here is most likely in the form of government intervention to stimulate increased investment.

The quality, and not just the quantity, of capital and labor resources is important in economic growth. Investing in improved machinery and equipment obviously increases production possibilities. Similarly, the quality of the labor force affects economic growth in the sense that the more educated and highly skilled the labor force is, the more productive it can be. Investment in human capital is just as important as investment in physical capital. The public interest is served when government encourages research and development of technology, and if it subsidizes efforts at increasing the quantity and quality of education and training of the labor force.

The United States has been very successful when judged on the basis of its GDP. In fact, its GDP as of 2006 was $12.98 trillion, a sum that translates into $43,500 per capita. A number of developed countries have similarly stellar GDPs: Japan, with approximately $4.9 trillion, Germany with $2.89 trillion, the United Kingdom with $2.34 trillion. The developing countries, on the other hand, tell a vastly different story. Burkina Faso, one of the poorest countries of the world, has a GDP of $18.94 billion, with a per capita GDP of $1,300. Such gross economic inequities create problems in the world arena, as we see in the next chapter (CIA, The World Factbook: **http://www.cia.gov/library/publications/the-world-factbook/fields /2001.html.** Accessed 10/18/07).

In conclusion, economic goals seem to require at least a degree of government intervention for achievement. Such intervention, however, is not without side effects, the most dangerous of which is the inordinate growth of government itself. An increase in government power threatens freedoms that have traditionally belonged to the states and/or individuals. In more practical terms, it produces competition between the private and the public sectors, whereas ideally the two should complement one another.

We need public policy, even to mediate among the economic goals, which at times conflict with one another. Public policy must seek to achieve the most useful of the conflicting goals, but we should be aware that public policy cannot be perfect. It is in the hands of people, subject to human weaknesses. Therefore, it is not always used in the public interest but may be diverted to the private interest of those who hold power.

■ Instruments of Public Policy

Exactly what kinds of policies does the government use to alter market behavior in its attempt to achieve the economic goals that the market mechanisms alone are unable to achieve? In general terms, the most frequent instruments include fiscal actions, monetary actions, and direct regulation.

■ Fiscal Policy

Fiscal policy may be defined as the use of public expenditures and taxation powers by the government to change the outcomes of the economy. Fiscal policy consists of decisions by the government about how much and whom to tax and whether and how to spend tax revenues. The power to tax and spend revenues was given to Congress by the Constitution of the United States in Article I. As a result, the federal government now collects and spends billions of dollars every year.

The money turned over to the government in taxes has as its chief result the transfer of buying power from the private to the public sector. The public sector then acquires greater influence over **aggregate demand**, which is the total planned or desired spending in the economy as a whole in any given period. Further, in deciding to spend or not to spend tax revenues, the government affects the level and mix of output, redistributes incomes, and affects price stability and growth. While some segments of the population believe that the government spends too much on certain benefits, others believe it does not spend enough. For instance, a substantial minority of people cannot afford health care insurance. Their supporters believe that the government ought to provide such insurance to all, not just to those over 65 who can benefit from Medicare. However, conservatives in Congress maintain that it is better if the government stays out of health care. Currently, presidential candidates are debating the issue.

Fiscal policy alters economic outcomes in two ways: if the government decides to spend a lot, the GDP goes up; if it chooses to spend little, both aggregate demand and output are small. The government's purchasing power derives from revenues and credit. In this, the government resembles other market participants. However, the government has one advantage: it can increase its income (revenues) by raising taxes. Being able to levy taxes makes it possible for the government to affect not only the level of GDP but also its content. If the government levies taxes on consumers, obviously consumers will have less purchasing power, while the government will have more. If it levies taxes on businesses, they will have less potential for investment and the government will have more. If the government cuts taxes, consumers have more purchasing power, which raises demand, thus stimulating the economy.

The Function of Price and Employment Stabilizers

Fiscal policy is most often referred to in its function of **stabilization,** as a tool for achieving and maintaining full employment and stable prices. When the government engages in expenditures, it expands aggregate demand and so brings the economy back toward a position of full employment. Government spending also results in more consumer spending because the money the government spends ends up being some consumers' income; it is then put back into circulation to pay for goods and services the consumers need and want. Government spending, then, has the effect of higher consumption and ultimately translates into higher aggregate demand. This process is called the **multiplier effect.**

Government spending and the multiplier effect stimulate business and investment because both actual sales and sales expectations are raised. When firms invest, aggregate demand is again expanded, and full employment becomes once more a reality (this is called **induced investment**).

Fiscal policy is also used to curb excessive aggregate demand. In this situation, consumers and firms speed up their rate of spending, using credit to bolster their purchasing power. The results are decreases in supply and consequently higher prices for goods and services—in short, inflation. Here, government action is the reverse of that needed to stimulate aggregate demand. That is, the government reduces its spending, leading to negative multiplier effects. Ultimately, the result is a drop in sales and incomes. Consumers also curb their spending in this situation, and prices drop as goods remain on the shelves instead of being sold. In addition, the government can raise taxes, taking away even more purchasing power from consumers, businesses, or both.

The Federal Budget

As observed above, in its function of stabilizing the economy, the government periodically is called upon to spend either more or less, as the situation demands. As a result, the federal budget is often out of balance. When the government must spend more, its expenditures are likely to be larger than its revenues, and it is said to engage in **deficit spending.** The government then is forced to borrow money to make up the difference between expenditures and receipts. When it borrows money, either from the private sector or from the banking system, the Federal Treasury issues—that is, sells—bonds, thus establishing the public debt.

When it spends less than it takes in in revenues, the government has a budget surplus. This is indeed a rare occurrence, but we were in such a situation through most of the 1990s. If it is to be effective in its fiscal policy, however, the government must be free to intervene in either way in the economy. The achievement of a balanced budget in any given year, then, really is not something the public should expect. However, excessive debt, carried over a prolonged time, is a drag on the economy.

In the current administration, the government is running a huge deficit. Partly as a result of a sharp economic slowdown in 2000, partly because of the aftershocks of the September 11, 2001 terrorist attack and the two military actions in Afghanistan and Iraq,

TABLE 18.3   Budget Totals (Dollar amounts in billions)

	2006	2007	2008	2009	2010	2011	2012
Budget Totals:							
Receipts	2,407	2,574	2,659	2,803	2,954	3,095	3,300
Outlays	2,655	2,779	2,918	3,016	3,078	3,184	3,267
Deficit(−)/Surplus	−248	−205	−258	−213	−123	−89	33
Gross Domestic Product (GDP)	13,065	13,722	14,453	15,222	16,004	16,809	17,646
Budget Totals as a Percent of GDP:							
Receipts	18.4%	18.8%	18.4%	18.4%	18.5%	18.4%	18.7%
Outlays	20.3%	20.2%	20.2%	19.8%	19.2%	18.9%	18.5%
Deficit(−)/Surplus	−1.9%	−1.5%	−1.8%	−1.4%	−0.8%	−0.5%	0.2%

Source: Mid-Session Review Budget of the U.S. Government, Fiscal Year 2008, Office of Management and Budget, July 11, 2007.
http://www.whitehouse.gov/omb/budget/fy2008. Accessed 9/23/07.

and partly as a result of tax cuts that were intended to stimulate the economy, the government was running a deficit of $445 billion in 2004. Because budget deficits are funded with borrowed money, future generations will have to pay interest on this debt. As of the spring of 2007, the government had taken in $2.574 trillion in revenues, and spent $2.779 trillion, thus creating a shortfall of approximately $205 billion (Table 18.3).

Fiscal Decision Making

Fiscal policy decisions are made jointly by Congress and the President and are implemented by the executive branch. The budget is not newly established each year, however. Rather, many decisions about expenditures are built in or carried over from previous years. These are called **uncontrollable expenditures,** and they have the effect of limiting current expenditures.

The portion of the budget that consists of current decisions about spending or non-spending is referred to as **discretionary spending.** The discretionary spending in any given year is smaller than it could be because of the uncontrollable expenditures built into the budget. On the other hand, uncontrollable expenditures also act as automatic, built-in stabilizers. For instance, unemployment insurance benefits, which have been part of the budget since 1935, automatically increase in a year when unemployment is high. As a result, federal spending is increased, as it ought to be when aggregate demand is too low to employ the available work force (Figure 18.3).

■ Monetary Policy

Fiscal policy is one alternative open to government in its attempts to change the outcomes of the economy to correspond to the public interest. Another is monetary policy, which avails itself of the influence of income and credit available to individuals and firms. Specifically, monetary policy refers to the use of money and credit controls to affect economic outcomes.

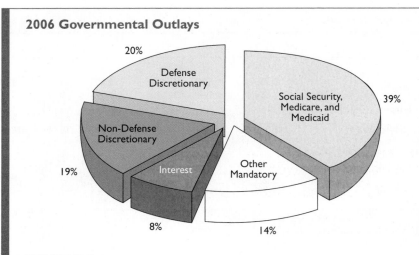

FIGURE 18.3

Source: Budget of the U.S. Government, Mid-Session Review, Fiscal Year 2007. **http://www.whitehouse.gov/omb/budget/fy2007/pdf/07rusr.pdf**

Banks

As noted previously, all market activity depends on the transfer of purchasing power between consumers and firms in what is called the circular flow. Purchasing power, in the form of cash or checks, is related directly to the supply of money in the economy. Commercial banks can affect the supply of money by extending credit. They do this simply by adding to a borrower's checking account, whether that borrower is an individual consumer or a business firm. The borrower uses this credit as if it were cash to buy goods and services. Sellers of goods and services do not care whether what they sell is being paid for with a buyer's savings or with a bank's money. Banks, by lending money, are able to expand the supply of money in the economy.

This ability, however, is not unlimited. A bank must keep some reserves in case some of its customers want to withdraw or transfer their holdings. As part of its regulatory function, the government makes certain that some reserves are kept aside for such eventualities. Banks try to calculate how much they need in reserve and use their excess reserves to make loans and thus expand the money supply.

What determines a bank's ability to make loans is the **reserve ratio,** or the proportion of deposits that must be retained for withdrawal, transfer, and government regulation. The lower the ratio of reserves to deposits, the greater is the bank's ability to increase the money supply available to the market.

Interest Rates

The desire of consumers and/or firms to borrow money varies. Sometimes banks can pick and choose those to whom they want to lend. At other times, there are few takers. The decision about whether or not to borrow is affected by the cost of borrowing or the **rate of interest**. Obviously, when interest rates are low, more consumers and firms want to borrow money. Consequently, by raising or lowering interest rates, banks are able to stimulate greater or lesser borrowing, again affecting the amount of purchasing power in the circular flow.

Regulating Banks

Because of the enormous effect the banking system has on the economy, it is in the public interest to have some control of it. The government influences the terms and amount of credit that banks make available by regulating the number of banks in existence, the ratio of their reserves, and the rate of interest they can charge.

The government also tries to prevent banks from failing, as panics resulting from failures have in the past led to great economic disruptions. Bank behavior is regulated by a number of government agencies. The **Federal Reserve Bank** is the most important public agency regulating banks and the money supply. Its chief function is in controlling bank reserves in the expansion or contraction of the money supply. The Federal Deposit Insurance Corporation protects depositors in case of bank failure against losses of up to $100,000.

The Federal Reserve

The role of the Federal Reserve Bank (called "the Fed" for short) is that of principal regulator of the money supply. It tries to regulate the supply of money in such a way as to avoid either insufficient or excessive spending in order to ensure the smooth working of the circular flow. This regulatory function is performed by either reducing excess bank reserves or by raising interest rates, by which actions the Federal Reserve diminishes the ability of banks to make loans and in so doing expand the money supply. On the other hand, by increasing excess bank reserves or lowering interest rates, the opposite effect is obtained.

One of the tools at the disposal of the Fed is the authority to establish minimum reserve requirements for all member banks. That is, banks must set aside the percentage of reserves that the Fed requires and can use only the remainder to make loans. The Fed also acts as a central or banker's bank, from which member banks can borrow upon presenting some collateral (in the form of government bonds or promissory notes). The Fed, however, also charges an interest rate—called the **discount rate**—for lending to member banks.

The most important tool for altering the flow of reserves into and out of banks is the Fed's ability to buy and sell government securities, a procedure called **open-market** operations. In buying securities, the Fed increases the amount of money in circulation. This raises bank reserves, expanding lending capacity. Open-market buying also lowers interest rates, again encouraging increased borrowing. In selling securities, a reduction in reserves results—with its attendant reduction in lending capacity and an increase in interest rates.

Monetary policy is effective in stabilizing the economy as long as two conditions are met. First, interest rates must be responsive to alterations in bank reserves. However, banks may not find it profitable to make loans below a specific rate of interest and will not lower interest rates even if the Fed supplies them with reserves. Second, debt and expenditure decisions must be responsive to interest-rate changes. In a slack period, firms have little incentive to expand production capacity and do not seek low interest rates. They do not borrow in spite of "cheap money."

Monetary policy is formulated and implemented by the Federal Reserve System, an independent and autonomous agency. Its decisions are not subject to either congressional or presidential review. The system consists of 12 regional banks and is coordinated by its board of governors (whose members are appointed by the president).

■ Incomes Policy

In addition to the monetary and fiscal policies that it utilizes to direct the economy toward the fulfillment of the economic goals of the society, the government also disposes of a large number of other regulatory powers. One such regulatory intervention, called **incomes policy,** became important during the 1960s and 1970s when two economic problems—inflation and unemployment—coexisted. The fiscal and monetary policies used to prevent these problems had been found guilty of creating one at the expense of the other. When aggregate demand is restricted to keep prices down, unemployment is often created. When aggregate demand is increased to achieve full employment, prices are pushed up, creating inflation. The conflict between full employment and inflation has been shown by the so-called **Phillips curve,** which illustrates that lower rates of unemployment are generally accompanied by higher rates of inflation. This problem is also called the full employment–inflation trade-off.

Incomes policy tries to use wage and price controls to direct economic outcomes. All government action, of course, has some effect on wages and prices, but such action is indirect because it goes through the market process and is, therefore, subject to the laws of supply and demand.

Incomes policy, however, attempts to change market outcomes in a direct fashion, by either establishing or limiting specifically determined wages and prices. The decisions of incomes policy affect the distribution of income, because prices are a basic determinant of the incomes of people who supply capital for production, and wages are the basic determinant of the incomes of people who supply labor for production.

Incomes policy is used when monetary and fiscal policies fail to achieve the goals of full employment and reasonable price stability. Of course, incomes policy has certain drawbacks. It tends to change the responsiveness of the market to demand-and-supply conditions. It may also lead to inequality of income distribution, because some groups are always behind others in wages, prices, or productivity. As a result, it is only used selectively.

■ Economic Problems and Government Response

The most pressing economic problems that the governmental actions described above try to solve or mitigate include the following.

Depression or Severe Recession

When both the output and the levels of employment are seriously lowered, the prescription is to expand aggregate demand. Spending may be stimulated by cutting taxes, increasing government expenditures, and expanding the money supply. Both the public and the private sectors must be involved, but the important point is that a variety of actions within the monetary and fiscal spectrum should produce a rapid stimulus. The problem is that some of these solutions cannot always be used. When the government is running a huge deficit, it cannot afford to increase its spending or cut taxes, actions that decrease its revenues.

Excessive Demand and Inflation

In this situation, public policy must aim to restrain aggregate demand until supply catches up. The actions here should include a reduction in the money supply, a reduction in government spending together with an increase in tax rates, and perhaps a temporary freeze or a price and wage control program.

Inflation and Unemployment

This is the most difficult situation to be repaired by a formulation of policy. In fact, if aggregate demand is stimulated to reduce unemployment, prices are pushed up, creating inflation. If inflationary pressures are alleviated through fiscal and monetary restraints, unemployment becomes a more severe problem.

This situation, unfortunately, is not unusual. It is a situation that demands finesse, or "fine-tuning," to resolve. It requires that those in charge of setting public policy use a mix of policies in different sectors of the market, perhaps decreasing demand in some industries while stimulating it in others, or even changing the structure of supply.

The situation of inflation with unemployment is aggravated by a noncompetitive market, where there is a concentration of power in a few corporations, or by labor unions. With lack of competition, prices and wages will go up with demand in spite of production or labor capacity. In such instances, incomes policy, or even antitrust action, may be necessary in coordination with monetary and fiscal policies.

This condition, coupled with a decline in the economy's aggregate output, is called **stagflation**. Stagflation was prevalent in the decade of the 1970s when there was stagnation, or contraction, in the economy's aggregate output and inflation, or increase, in the general price level. For instance, in 1975 inflation was at 8.9 percent, and unemployment had jumped to 8.5 percent. A policy objective had to be found that would increase the aggregate supply, a move that would both lower inflation and increase output and employment. This policy was derived from the theory of supply-side economics, discussed below.

■ Business Cycles

Macroeconomics is particularly concerned with business cycles, the periodically alternating waves of economic expansion and contraction that have characterized the American economy. The upswings and downswings are measured in terms of total output. In an upswing there is an increase in the volume of goods and services produced. In a downswing, the total volume of production declines. Of course, such changes in production are reflected in changes in employment—in an upswing, there is full employment; in a downswing, there is unemployment.

The U.S. economy has been plagued by business cycles in spite of the fact that its track record looks spectacular; for instance, in 1929, the GDP was $822 billion (in 1996 dollars). In 2006, it was more than $13 trillion (Bureau of Economic Analysis, 2006). However, this growth has not been even or constant; on the contrary, the growth of the U.S. economy has been a series of steps forward, interrupted by stumbles and setbacks. To try to combat the effects of such setbacks, a number of theories have been offered purporting to explain how the economy really works, the idea being that once we know exactly how the economy functions, we can act to prevent some happenings and encourage others.

Demand-Side Theories

Government intervention in the affairs of the economy did not occur before the Great Depression of the 1930s. Up to that time, classical economists had thought that the dominant feature of the industrial era—that is, growth—would continue unperturbed, at most with short-lived dislocations to which the economy was supposed to "self-adjust." The coming of the Depression in spite of the optimism of the classical economists destroyed their credibility, and their theories were replaced by those of economist John Maynard Keynes.

The Keynesian Revolution. In his denunciation of classical theory, Keynes asserted that, on the contrary, the private economy was inherently unstable and the invisible hand of the marketplace would actually magnify small disturbances in output, prices, or unemployment. This inherent instability of the marketplace, according to Keynes, could be stabilized only by the intervention of government. The Depression was not a unique event but a situation that would recur if societies continued to rely on the market mechanism alone. Thus, Keynes argued, societies cannot afford to wait for some mechanism to self-adjust but must "prime the pump" by buying more output, employing more people, providing more income transfers, and making more money available. Then, when the economy takes off again and perhaps overheats, government must again take the initiative to cool it down with higher taxes, reductions in spending, and making less money available. Keynesian theory did pull the country out of the Depression and, thus, became a mandate for government policy, although other demand-side, monetarist, and supply-side theories compete with it.

Monetarism. Another demand-side theory focuses on the role of money in financing aggregate demand. It is thought that because money and credit affect the ability and willingness of people to buy goods and services, if the correct amount of money is not available, it means that aggregate demand is too great or too small. Thus, a change in the money supply may be needed to move the aggregate demand curve to the desired position. Economist Milton Friedman is associated with this explanation.

Supply-Side Theories

A different explanation of the business cycle is provided by supply-side theories. These claim that a decline in aggregate supply may be responsible for downturns by causing output and employment to decline. Failure to achieve full employment, for instance, may result from the unwillingness of producers to provide more goods at existing prices. The option here is to find and implement policies that would reduce the costs of production or otherwise stimulate more output at every price level.

Eclectic Theories

Some macro explanations of business cycles blame neither the demand side nor the supply side but affirm that both supply and demand can cause us to achieve or defeat policy goals. These explanations draw from both sides of the market.

In essence, there are three policy options for counteracting business cycles: shift the aggregate demand curve by finding and using policy tools that stimulate or restrain total spending; shift the aggregate supply curve by finding and implementing policies that reduce the costs of production or stimulate more output; or do nothing, and let the market take its course.

Historically, all three policy options have been used. During and after the Great Depression, fiscal policy was used by the government to alter economic outcomes through the use of tax and spending powers. This policy is still an integral feature of modern economic policy. Monetary policy, in which money and credit are used to alter economic outcomes, has been and continues to be used by the Fed, as we saw in the preceding segment. Whereas both fiscal and monetary policies focus on the demand side of the market, supply-side policies attempt to shift the aggregate supply curve.

Theory and Reality

In theory, every combination of economic problems has a solution in a combination of economic policies. In reality, however, the economic goals are not always achieved. The United States has maintained a high growth rate and attained a high standard of living. The American per-capita income is one of the highest in the world. Still, as we have seen, the economy is subject to periodic slowdowns or recessions. The society is intermittently plagued by high unemployment rates, particularly among some segments of the population. There is price instability, especially in a constant upward direction, meaning inflation. Incomes never seem to keep up with prices. There is widespread dissatisfaction among some groups with the way income is distributed in the market system. Complaints are also being voiced against the quality of output. In short, there is a substantial gap between the potential of the economic system and the reality.

There are numerous reasons why the policies evolved by government do not work as efficiently as they should (remember the fallacy of the Phillips curve). First, there are problems in measurement. Economic phenomena are not highly visible. It takes some time before a jump in prices or an increase in unemployment becomes alarming.

In the second place, there are difficulties with interpretation. Even when everyone realizes that unemployment is increasing, the reason is not always immediately apparent. Policy makers prefer to be sure of a problem before acting. Consequently, by the time action is begun, the problem is more serious and requires more drastic steps. Sometimes it is too late to repair the damage.

Third, there are problems of implementation. If, for instance, the President and the Council of Economic Advisers become aware that the rate of spending is slowing down and that a tax cut would stimulate demand, they cannot implement such a tax cut with one swift stroke. Rather, they must wait for Congress to authorize the action. The tax proposal must first go through committees in both the House and the Senate, a lengthy and complicated procedure. As a result, there is always the possibility that a needed policy will not be implemented at all or will be implemented so late that the condition that prompted it no longer exists. Such an action could have the opposite effect on the economy.

Box 18.2 Old and New Economies

As a human institution, the economy is indeed pivotal, for it provides a pattern for individuals in societies of how to best procure the necessities of life. For thousands of years, these necessities were provided for minimally by hunting and gathering. Then, about ten thousand years ago, a great breakthrough occurred with the discovery and invention of agriculture. This innovation dramatically transformed groups of people: They became settled, developed surpluses, organized themselves in social groups that eventually became nations, built cities, and began to fight wars to conquer more land. Success in agricultural economies meant owning land, gold, and natural resources.

A second breakthrough that transformed economies, and societies, was industry. Industrialization was followed by urbanization, and a great transformation from Gemeinschaft to Gesellschaft societies (see Chapter 4). People moved to cities, left extended families behind, had to deal with other people whom they did not know, and obeyed laws enforced by impersonal institutions. Success in an industrial economy depended on owning industrial machinery and producing articles for mass consumption.

Now, according to a number of commentators, we are witnessing a third breakthrough: we are able to create wealth, not by growing things, not by making things, but by *knowing* things. Two books, one by a historian, one by an economist, discuss the new economy and its impact on society, its values, and its moral codes, as well as the changes it forces on social organization.

Francis Fukuyama, the historian, notes that the innovations that came with industrialization, that is, the factory system, the division of labor, and bureaucracy could not help but transform the moral rules that governed social interaction. In addition, Protestantism, coinciding with the emergence of capitalist ideas, also had transformative powers on societies. It justified the profit motive, for instance, and assured the emerging middle class that their wealth was a sign of God's approval.

How is the new economy transforming our lives? Unlike in the industrial system in which goods were produced under a hierarchical system, with orders from above, information does not rely on chains of command and formal rules. It depends on knowledge and mental dexterity. Women possess these talents in equal measure; hence, they have entered the work force in droves. No longer dependent on men for support, many women have opted to remain single, to have children out of wedlock, or to divorce if their marital relationship is unsatisfactory.

In addition, highly educated workers can easily move from job to job, improving their situation each time. Frequent moving, however, makes for an unsettled existence and is hard on intimate relationships. Sometimes spouses need to work in different cities; this does not bode well for family life.

The information economy emerged at about the same time that American society was becoming characterized by extreme individualism. The generations that matured from mid-twentieth century on have been called the "me" generations, and their increased self-interest has been bolstered by the information economy. In fact, the two are mutually reinforcing. The negative aspect, according to Fukuyama, is that the focus on the individual in the new economy fosters social distrust, both in the public and private arenas. This distrust may be linked to rising rates of crime, illegitimacy, and family dissolution, or what Fukuyama calls the "Great Disruption" that may eventually undermine the success attained by the economy. In the author's view, however, all will turn out well because we are biologically programmed to seek moral rules and social order (Fukuyama, 1999).

Lester Thurow is more pragmatic: he is interested in discovering how to build wealth in the new economy. He wants to know how one creates wealth by using only knowledge, rather than land, gold, or industrial processes, as in previous economic systems. Thurow also suggests that what we are witnessing now was last seen during the second industrial revolution. At that time, corporate research laboratories led to technological advances and electrification permitted a whole new group of industries to emerge—telephones, movies, etc.—as well as altering the production processes of the older economy.

To build wealth in the new economy, Thurow sets forth a number of rules whose gist is that businesses must learn to produce more with less; that they must be willing to destroy the old even while it is still successful, so that the new can become successful; that entrepreneurs must use imaginative ways to take advantage of shifting demographics and other social changes; that they must foresee situations of deflation, when prices go down because of too much supply or lower production costs; they must be creative in destroying old patterns of powerful vested interests to introduce new patterns; that creativity must be coupled with order because chaos leads to more chaos, while too much order stifles creativity; that for a knowledge-based economy to be successful, large public investments in education, infrastructure, and research and development are necessary; that the idea of a career with one company, or even in one field, must be forgotten, as employees must be ready to learn new skills and be flexible in the kinds of jobs they obtain.

Problems with the new economy will be difficult to eradicate. For one thing, technology is creating a global economy that is displacing the old national economies. Governments can no longer control such an economy as they could national economies, yet no one wants to establish a global government. Consequently, for a certain time the economy will remain largely unmanaged, allowing corporations to expand while they move to the most advantageous locations. This creates competition among nations and rising economic inequalities among countries, firms, and individuals—not a good situation in terms of political stability.

Thurow concludes that old modes of operating have been made obsolete to the point that individuals, firms, and nations must change. Individuals are exhorted to acquire skills and more skills. "The economic prospects of those without skills are bleak." He repeats that old business firms must be able to seize new opportunities even if it means destroying existing profitable activities. And nations that invest in education, infrastructure, and research and development are the ones that will eventually end up on top (Thurow, 1999).

■ Fitting into the Global Economy

As noted in the preceding chapter, the United States, stuck with its older mass-production system, has had to face the long-run problems of slow productivity growth and stagnant real incomes because it had allowed its once highly productive industrial system to decay. Well into the 1980s, it continued to produce mediocre-quality, standardized goods and services with nearly obsolete mass-production methods, while other economies, with better schooling and training systems and a more productive workplace organization, captured many of its world, and some of its domestic, markets. To reverse this economic decline, economists have felt that it was essential for a reorganization and rethinking to take place.

Such a reorganization has, in fact, taken place. In the old economic order, which came to an end around 1970, productivity depended on the success of the core corporation, a hierarchical structure that has been described in the preceding chapters: a pyramid with a managerial class at the top and production workers at the bottom. The goal of this kind of structure was the production of high-volume goods, and the more successful the corporation was at it, the better it was for everyone along the pyramid. As corporations became multinational, however, a reaction occurred, especially in Europe and Japan, which set out to compete with the United States. Their success created a new economic form of organization, which can be described as a spider web instead of a pyramid. Productivity is no longer dependent on high-volume goods, but on high-value goods created by people with new skills. These people are classified as "symbolic analysts" because of their ability to manipulate symbols such as data, words, visual representations, and so on. They include entertainers, top corporate executives, engineers, consultants, lawyers, and investment bankers. The American economy has been employing more symbolic analysts and fewer unskilled industrial workers.

While the symbolic analysts prosper in a world without economic borders, the uneducated and unskilled do not. The other types of work of the future, in addition to symbolic analysis, are "routine production services" consisting of blue-collar work and lower-level management, and "in-person services," exemplified by jobs such as physical therapist and security guard.

In the 1990s, productivity had a resurgence, but at a cost. While we were again competitive on the world market, the victory had been won at the price of massive downsizing, waves of layoffs, stagnating or limited wage increases, replacement of full-time workers by part-time or temporary workers, and more work heaped on employees. The economy

Box 18.3 Computers and Humans: The New Division of Labor

Commenting on the new economy, two eminent economics professors examine the new labor market, asking whether computers will become so important in business that they will eliminate humans. They answer this question in the negative, maintaining that computers help to create jobs even as they destroy them. What computers do is shift work away from routine tasks toward tasks that require thinking and communicating in a complex manner. Even in jobs in the service economy, workers have been put behind desks and have to use cognitive skills that computers themselves do not have: think of the waiter who handles your restaurant bill. Computers enhance productivity in many jobs, even though they may eliminate some other jobs, mainly blue-collar and clerical work that used to require moderate skills and pay middle-class wages. The problem, then, according to these economists, is not that computers take away jobs from humans, but that there are few properly trained workers in the labor market. Those blue-collar and clerical workers who have been displaced by computers have not been adjusting to the requirements of the new jobs that offer higher pay. This fact has created a division between workers who can earn good salaries in the computerized economy and those who cannot. The solution is obvious but difficult to attain—education that would prepare people for jobs that involve extensive problem solving and interpersonal communication. Some corporations have begun such training, but, according to the authors, there is a need for a radical educational reform if we want to have a successful work force in the new computerized economy (Levy & Murnane, 2004).

Computers themselves are changing in ways that are unexpected and surprising. First of all, the Internet has become so ubiquitous and approachable from so many instruments, and is able to supply so many things to so many people, that it is supplanting the activities of the desk PC. The two companies that have been responsible for providing operating systems—Microsoft and Apple—are working on developing new operating systems that will reflect the influence of the Internet. Another Internet startup company, Joost, is working on building a global television network. It will provide television shows from around the world, sending them to global viewers through the Internet. Their spokespeople maintain that eventually television as we know it will become obsolete: The software this company is planning to produce will reside in a variety of platforms, embedded in a television set or in a box on top of it, in a mobile phone, or in some future alternative device. In short, the global economy is advancing.

experienced a boom of five years' duration, making it one of the longest periods of growth since World War II. This prolonged boom made some economic commentators hope that perhaps business cycles would no longer be a part of the economic pattern. Because even midsize companies in the Midwest were beginning to enter the global economy, it was believed that the economy would be protected to an extent from dramatic swings.

With the beginning of the new century, however, the American economy began to cool. At first, this cooling off was attributed to a stock market that was grossly overpriced, particularly in the technological sector. It soon became apparent, however, that a downturn in the business cycle was inevitable and that a recession was looming. Other pressures on the economy came with the terrorist attacks of September 11, 2001, whose effects will undoubtedly be felt for many years to come. Toward the end of the first decade of the new century still more problems besiege the economy: The war in Iraq seems to have no end in sight and is costing the American public a tremendous amount of money that would be better spent on domestic needs; the price of oil has become sky high, yet it will take a long time for us to develop other ways of living without depending on fossil fuels; the housing market, after climbing for several years, has come tumbling down as problems with mortgages given to people unable to afford them plague credit markets; issues surrounding the inability of the government to continue funding important programs such as social security and Medicare; fears of how global warming and climate change will affect us, and much more. Consequently, now, more than ever, Americans must be vigilant about the health of this important institution.

The Chapter in Brief

The allocation of resources in a market economy proceeds according to the decisions made by households, firms, and central authorities about the production, sales, and purchases of goods and services. Decisions made by households and firms are said to be in the private sector; those made by central authorities are in the public sector.

At first, the mechanism that made the market function was little understood. Now we know that it is basically a price system that determines which goods and services are to be produced; that is, producers, looking for profits, make commodities they think people want at prices they think people will pay. If these prices are low enough, people will buy more of the product, and vice versa. Although business firms are motivated by profits, they perform the important social function of organizing productive activity in the most efficient way and directing productive resources where consumer demand is strongest.

The goods and services produced by firms go to consumers who have the desire for them and the income to pay for them. The income to pay for goods and services, in turn, is derived from consumers selling their labor (or other resources) to firms. Households and firms, then, are bound together in an unending circular flow interrupted only by withdrawals (income received by households and firms that is not returned to firms but goes for paying taxes or savings) and by injections (income received by firms that does not originate from households and income of households that does not come from firms).

The goals in a market economy are to maximize consumer happiness, the profits of firms, and the general welfare. However, participants in the market are constrained from pursuing their goals by prices and incomes. What firms produce depends on the prices of resources and labor. What consumers buy depends on their incomes and prices of goods. Prices affect all participants in the market—when prices change, so does behavior. What takes place in the market is an exchange process: energy and labor flow in one direction, and money in wages and salaries flows in the opposite direction. These two sides are defined as supply and demand: what one gives in the exchange is supply, what one gets is demand. Each participant is at one time on both sides of the exchange.

Aggregate demand is expressed as people's willingness and ability to buy a specific number of products at a specific price. Aggregate supply represents the combined willingness of individuals or firms to supply specific resources or products at a price consumers are willing to pay. Demand and supply curves simplify the analysis of market action because they show at a glance the flow of resources, products, and money passing among the market participants.

There is only one price and one quantity at which both buyers and sellers agree—when quantity supplied equals the price buyers are willing to pay. This point is called the equilibrium point. Demand is subject to price elasticity: If consumers buy more of a product because of a decrease in price, demand is said to be elastic. If consumers buy little of a product, even if its price has been drastically reduced, demand is said to be inelastic. Revenues fall when demand is inelastic and rise when demand is elastic.

The amazing thing about the market mechanism is that without a planned, fixed program, both the content and the flow of goods and services are determined and prices are set. The advantage of a market system is that it allows individuals freedom from constraint and allows each participant to maximize his or her goal. The disadvantage is that the mechanism is not equitable because the participants with more income can get more products, and those with more talent can get more income. Because of these inequities, and because there is no market for some products that benefit the public, the government must intervene in the economy.

In the view first formulated by Adam Smith, the free market worked quite efficiently without intervention. Therefore, Smith advocated leaving things alone, or laissez-faire: the government was enjoined to stay out of the economy. However, because the market makes no provision for the production of public goods and services—highways, police and fire protection, control of pollution, and so on—and favors those born with more talent or inherited fortunes (and because the free market does not work quite as well as Smith thought), the government has had to play an increasingly large role as an equalizer and regulator.

In contemporary societies, government intervention in the economy is accepted because people expect the economy to reach certain goals. In the United States, these goals include full employment, the right mix of output, high incomes equitably distributed, reasonable price stability, and sufficient economic growth. These goals, although not universally accepted, are generally considered to be in the public interest, and public power is needed to achieve them. Public power is vested in the public sector, which means the government. The government has three principal policies with which it controls the economy: fiscal, monetary, and incomes.

Fiscal policy involves the use of public expenditures and taxation power to change the outcomes of the economy. Fiscal policy alters such outcomes in two ways: if the government spends a lot, total output goes up; if it chooses not to spend, both aggregate demand and output are small. When the government engages in more spending, it stimulates more consumer spending, a process called the multiplier effect. Fiscal policy is considered a stabilizer, a tool for achieving and maintaining full employment and stable prices in situations where the market alone cannot prevent these dysfunctions.

Fiscal policy is also used to curb excessive demand. In this situation, the government can reduce its spending, raise taxes, or both. These actions result in a drop in sales and incomes and a reduction of the purchasing power of consumers, firms, or both. In its function as stabilizer, the government often engages in deficit spending, making it necessary to establish a public debt through the selling of bonds. Sometimes the government also experiences a budget surplus, but a balanced budget is really not as important as many believe it to be.

Monetary policy refers to the use of money and credit to control economic outcomes. Commercial banks are responsible for putting money—purchasing power—or credit into the circular flow. The government can control how much money the banks are putting into the flow by regulating the amount of reserves banks must keep on hand and the rates of interest they charge. Government even regulates the number of banks in existence. The most important public agency regulating banks and the money supply is the Federal Reserve Bank, commonly called "the Fed."

Incomes policy uses wage and price controls to direct economic outcomes. It is necessary because of the stubbornness of a problem illustrated by the Phillips curve: lower rates of unemployment are usually accompanied by higher rates of inflation. Incomes policy is a direct attempt to establish or limit specifically determined wages and prices, thus affecting the distribution of income.

All three policies are important tools in the hands of the government. Unfortunately, they are very difficult to implement, as they need careful coordination and "fine-tuning." Coordination is endangered by difficulties of measurement, interpretation, and implementation.

Social scientists are describing the current phase of the economy as one in which technical and scientific experts are in great demand and will come to be the new aristocracy. The new strategic resource, which was formerly capital, is now knowledge and information. The problem is what to do with the blue-collar segment of the labor force that is no longer retrainable.

Terms to Remember

budget surplus A surplus that occurs when the government's revenues are greater than its expenditures.

central authorities All public agencies, generally referred to as "the government."

circular flow Movement from product markets to resource markets and back again, which is interrupted by withdrawals and injections.

deficit spending Spending that occurs when the government's expenditures are greater than its revenues.

discount rate The interest rate charged by the Federal Reserve Bank for lending money to member banks.

discretionary spending The portion of the federal budget that consists of current spending, rather than carryovers from previous years.

disposable income National income less taxes and plus welfare payments. What people really have to spend or to save.

equilibrium The price and quantity at which both buyers and sellers are compatible—the quantity supplied equals the price buyers are willing to pay.

factor or resource markets Markets in which households sell the factors of production that they control.

firms Units that decide how to use labor, land, and capital and which goods and services to produce.

fiscal policy The use of public expenditures and taxation powers by the government to change the outcomes of the economy.

full employment A low rate of unemployment, between 4 and 5 percent.

gross domestic product (GDP) The total output of goods and services produced within the confines of the United States, by American or foreign-supplied resources, as well as all income earned.

gross national product (GNP) per capita The total output or dollar value of the economy divided by the total population.

household All the people who live under one roof and who make financial decisions as a unit. Also called the consumer.

incomes policy An attempt to use wage and price controls to direct economic outcomes.

inflation A situation in which demand cannot be matched by an increase in supply, resulting in rising prices.

marginal productivity The value people's work adds to total output.

market demand The combined willingness of individuals and firms to buy a specific number of products at a specific price.

market supply The combined willingness of individuals or firms to supply specific resources or products at specific prices.

monetary policy The use of money and credit to control economic outcomes.

multiplier effect Government spending that produces more income, results in higher consumption expenditures, and translates into a higher aggregate demand.

Phillips curve A graphic illustration of the conflict between full employment and price stability: lower rates of unemployment are usually accompanied by higher rates of inflation.

product markets Markets in which firms sell their production of goods and services.

public sector Economic activity on the part of the government in the name of the people or for the public interest.

social indicators Ways of measuring the level of real benefits resulting from a specific level of output.

uncontrollable expenditures Expenditures from previous years that are built into the annual federal budget.

Suggested Readings

Berger, Peter L. 1991. *The Capitalist Revolution: Fifty Propositions about Prosperity, Equality, and Liberty.* New York: Basic Books. A well-known sociologist summarizes the reasons for the productivity of capitalism and its effects on personal liberty.

Harrison, Bennett. 1998. *Lean and Mean: Why Large Corporations Will Continue to Dominate the Global Economy.* New York: Guilford Press. An analysis of the role of large corporations in economic growth and technological innovations, as well as the advent of the temporary and part-time job.

Harrison, Lawrence E. 1992. *Who Prospers?* New York: Basic Books. This book is subtitled "How Cultural Values Shape Economic and Political Success." The author, a director of USAID missions in five Latin American countries, Associate, Academy for International and Area Studies, Harvard University, and a former visiting scholar at Harvard University's Center for International Affairs makes the point that a society's culture, particularly its values with respect to work, education, excellence, family, and community, can either facilitate or impede progress in the economic and political spheres, and explains why some societies have succeeded while others have failed.

Levy, Frank and Richard J. Murnane. 2004. *The New Division of Labor.* Princeton, NJ: Princeton University

Press. Two economists from prestigious universities take a comprehensive look at how technology is affecting the occupational distribution in the United States. They predict which skills are going to be valued in future labor markets; consequently, this should be a must-read for students preparing to enter the work force.

McConnell, Campbell R. and Stanley L. Brue. 2002. *Economics Principles, Problems and Policies*, 15th ed. New York: McGraw-Hill-Irwin. A clearly written, down-to-earth survey of economics, covering the points touched on in this chapter in much more detail.

Web Sites of Interest

http://www.whitehouse.gov/fsbr/esbr.html
The web site of the Economic Statistics Briefing Room offers access to federal economic indicators and links to information by other federal agencies about employment, income, money, prices, production, output, and so on.

http://www.bea.doc.gov/
This is the site of the U.S. Department of Commerce, Bureau of Economic Analysis. Its information focuses on national, regional, international, and industrial facets of the economy.

http://www.stat-usa.gov/
Another site of the Department of Commerce dealing with U.S. business, economy, and trade and with direct access to the federal government's information on the economy.

http://www.census.gov/econ/www
The Census Bureau offers a wealth of information on every aspect of the economy.

http://www.cia.gov/library/publications/
the-world-factbook/fields/2001.html
Part of the CIA World Factbook deals with the U.S. economy. It includes a current summary and all types of information on every aspect of the economy. Information on the economies of other nations is also available.

19

Nation among Nations: Perspectives on International Relations

IN THIS CHAPTER, YOU WILL LEARN

- the definition of international relations;
- theoretical perspectives used to analyze the international system;
- who are the participants in the international political system;
- the objectives of states, as evidenced by foreign policy and its instruments;
- that states attain objectives by means of diplomacy and of war;
- the importance of the concept of power, and how the "balance of power" has changed;
- what is the role of the United Nations.

It is common today to refer to the "global" economy, meaning that economic activities take place across national borders. It is not only in the economic arena that countries interact: they do so in countless ways and for countless reasons, and almost continuously. When we speak of international relations, then, we refer to this type of interaction. The interaction need not involve direct physical contact: it can be of an economic nature, as in trade; or center on the use of military force, as in war; or entail public and private diplomacy.

When individuals interact, they eventually create a social system. Similarly, interaction of one nation with another or others creates an international social system within a global framework. However, the global social system differs considerably from a societal social system. A society may consist of a number of racial and religious groups, as the United States does; but, it has a consensus on values to guide its behavior and harbors common goals for its future. No such consensus exists on a global level. In fact, quite the opposite may be true; the goals of one nation are not necessarily complementary or reconcilable with those of another nation. Also, within a society, we maintain order and prevent violence through a number of institutions derived from the pivotal institution of government. Yet no global

Scenes like these are unfortunately common in regions of the world involved in conflict. In this refugee camp in Sudan, the United Nations and other transnational organizations provide food, shelter, water, and lifesaving assistance to the more than one million persons displaced by the fighting in Darfur.

institution with similar functions exists. There is no central authority with a monopoly on power, as exists within a society. On a global level, anarchy of a sort prevails.

Added to these shortcomings of the international system is the rapidity with which change occurs in the world. There has been a fundamental transformation in the bases of power from Western Europe to the United States and the Soviet Union in this century. A number of nations have become independent from colonial empires. Another rearrangement has occurred with the fall of communism in the former Soviet Union. The distribution of power is continually fluctuating from one group of states to another, a process that in all probability will continue to take place in the future. Finally, the ongoing changes in technology, not least in the field of weapons, will continue to have an impact on nations.

The discipline of international relations is, therefore, a vast and complex field. It concerns activities as diverse as war and humanitarian assistance, trade and investment, tourism and the Olympic Games. The core of inquiry of this discipline consists of three questions: (1) How do states act, and particularly why do they act the way they do toward one another (what is their national interest as expressed by their foreign policies)? (2) How do states attain their goals and objectives (what are their capabilities in terms of power)? (3) What are the main characteristics of the interactions between states (diplomacy, aid, exchange, cooperation)? First, however, we should have well in mind what states are and how they sometimes differ from nations, and in what ways their geographic location and the resources at their disposal affect their role on the world stage.

■ Regions of the World

There are many ways of classifying the nations of the world, but the most common one is into regions. Therefore, before trying to answer the questions raised above, it is appropriate to present a brief run-through of the several regions of the world.

Europe

The European region consists of 38 countries with a total population of one-half billion people (Figure 19.1). Now that the distinctions between Eastern Europe and Western Europe have disappeared as a result of the fall of communism, the countries are politically, economically, and even culturally similar, though differences in languages and religion remain. The

Map of Europe

FIGURE 19.1

region exhibits the most advanced form of regional cooperation in a variety of economic and security organizations, such as the European Union (EU) and the North Atlantic Treaty Organization (NATO). The EU has adopted a single currency and is involved in a number of trade agreements that do away with tariffs and duties among the countries. Its original objective was to prevent wars among the countries, because Europe historically had been the site of numerous such conflagrations.

Europe is no longer the dominant power in the world, not even in the Western world, as it had been throughout several centuries. However, it is competing successfully on the world stage in economic and technological matters and offers its citizens a high quality of life in terms of wealth, life expectancy, and education. These items, as measured by the Human Development Index (HDI), show European nations to be consistently at the top.

The Former Soviet Union

The region that formerly comprised the Soviet Union is no longer monolithic, though at one time it encompassed one-sixth of the earth's landmass and was the only country that took up a whole world region, numbering 285 million in population (Figure 19.2). The breakup of

Map of the Former Soviet Union

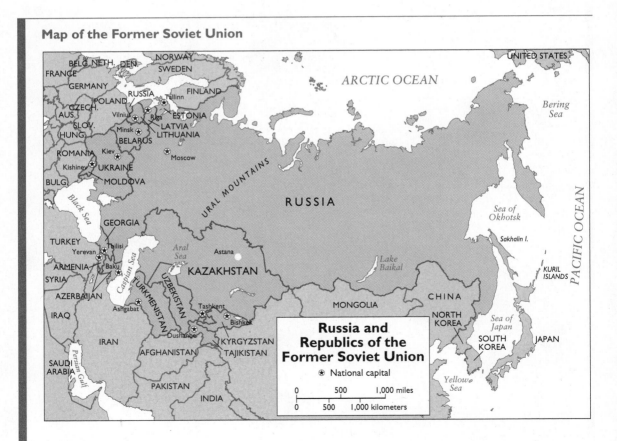

FIGURE 19.2

the Soviet Union in 1991 caused the 15 republics that made it up to become independent countries. Russia is the largest of these. Used to being a nuclear world power, Russia, which straddles Europe and Asia, has had difficulty adapting to democracy and capitalism after 70 years of communism.

The rest of the former Soviet Union consists of Slavic nations such as Ukraine and Belarus, whose populations are ethnically related to the Russians. Among the non-Slavic countries, the Baltic nations of Estonia, Latvia, and Lithuania, annexed by Stalin, have had deeper ties to Western Europe. The Asian nations of Armenia, Georgia, and Azerbaijan have fallen victim to much ethnic and religious violence as Christian and Muslim groups battle for dominance and smaller ethnic groups, the Chechens, Ingushis, and others, seek independence.

Central Asia is also home to five Islamic countries, of which the largest is Uzbekistan. These countries have closer ties to Turkic and Asiatic nations than to Russia, although they had been under Russian domination for a century and a half. Because of repressed resentment against the Russians, these countries sought independence immediately, but are now finding it difficult going because their economic ties had been predominantly with Russia.

After the fall of communism, then President Yeltsin declared the new government to be democratic. In spite of a constitution and some reforms, however, corruption became endemic and led to the emergence of a number of so-called oligarchs, persons who acquired great wealth by taking over formerly national industries at very low prices. The current President, Vladimir Putin, initially appeared to follow a democratic path. However, he soon began to centralize his power, first by stripping the oligarchs of their possessions, then by closing down a number of private media, newspapers and television stations that were opposed to some of his policies. Finally, following a horrific terrorist attack by Chechen guerrillas that killed more than 300 people, half of them schoolchildren on their first day of school, President Putin determined to strip Russian citizens of their right to elect their governors and their district representatives to Parliament. From then on, these officials have been appointed by the central government. The president explained that democracy "does not result in stability, but rather instability. It does not unify, but rather divides." He maintained that the ethnic and religious tensions among the non-Russian peoples that inhabit the rim of the country "can only be controlled by an iron hand from above" (Myers, 2004, Section 4, p. 1). These statements seem to predict a return to a rigid central authority, which is seen as the failure of the government to create a sense of national identity after the fall of the Soviet Union.

Additionally, Russia seems to have become a "corporate state," by which is meant a new hybrid of country and corporation that fuses the public and private sectors together to serve the central government. A deputy prime minister is also the chairman of the gigantic state gas monopoly Gazprom, and a deputy chief of staff is also the chairman of the state-owned oil company Rosneft, and so on.

Finally, relations between Russia and the United States are currently at a very low point. The American president has plans to build a network of radar and missile defenses in Poland and the Czech Republic, a plan that enrages the Russian president, who believes the system represents a threat to his country. In turn, he threatens to point Russian missiles at Europe. American officials have also criticized the Russian government for its poor human rights record. President Putin is at the end of his tenure as president, but he does not appear willing to let go of his power. The near future will tell how this debacle is concluded.

The Middle East

The Middle East consists of desert and semiarid grassland and is located at a point where northern Africa, southwest Asia, and southern Europe come together (Figure 19.3). It is a

Map of the Middle East

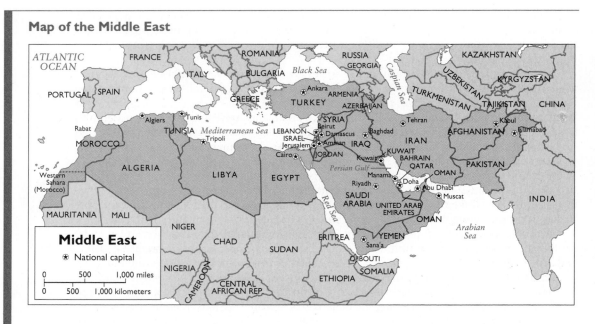

FIGURE 19.3

resource-poor area, except for a dramatic exception: some of the countries are rich in oil, the earth's most lucrative commodity. The oil-rich countries, such as Saudi Arabia, the United Arab Emirates, and Qatar, have high gross domestic products (GDPs) and are able to offer their residents a high standard of living (although the standard has declined in recent years as other problems have begun to plague these nations). However, the greatest part of the region, and especially nations such as Syria and Yemen, have very low GDPs and below-average quality of life.

The unifying factor in the region is Islam. Islam itself is not monolithic, however: there are divisions between Shiite and Sunni Muslims, as well as between conservative and more liberal Muslims. And of course, there is the state of Israel, whose citizens are predominantly Jewish and whose existence many Arab states resent.

This region has been, since the end of the colonial era, one of the most volatile in the world. There are disputes regarding borders, some of which had been drawn up by colonial powers. There are disputes regarding territory. There is hostility toward Israel, the only democratic and non-Muslim nation in the area, which was created by the United Nations to accommodate persecuted Jews from around the world. In addition, the rulers of some of the Muslim nations are autocratic and are viewed by a portion of their citizens as corrupt. Because the United States and its Western allies support their governments (we need their goodwill at least partly to obtain their oil), fundamentalist Islamic groups have emerged whose alleged goal is to destroy the West. Some of these groups have been engaged in terrorist activities, particularly against the United States: the bombing of the World Trade Center in New York, the bombing of the American embassies in Kenya and Tanzania, the bombing of the U.S.S. Cole, and the latest and most destructive act, the attack against the Twin Towers of the World Trade Center in New York City, as well as a partial destruction of the Pentagon by means of hijacked planes. These terrorist acts have resulted in the loss of thousands of lives and have prompted the United States to respond with military action.

The military action in Afghanistan rooted out the Taliban, a fundamentalist Islamist group that allowed terrorist groups such as al Quaeda to train in camps in their territory. However, the government that replaced the Taliban lacks sufficient authority to control the country, and United Nation forces are still deployed to keep an uneasy peace. Of late, there has been a resurgence of Taliban activity.

The military action in Iraq, on the other hand, has developed into a tragic misadventure for the United States, and its conclusion will not be known for a long time. The Republican administration in power during the 2001 terrorist attack convinced Congress that the leader of Iraq, Saddam Hussein, was harboring weapons of mass destruction, which he intended to deploy against the West in collusion with terrorist groups. Although the conquest of the country was swift, its occupation has been painful and unending. The population of Iraq consists of different sects of Islam that are hostile to one another. Additionally, there are problems of an economic nature that are not easily resolved in a nation unused to a democratic system of majority rule. The insurgency that developed targets not only the American military, but also the Iraqi population, which has been terrifically decimated. Here, too, the local government, although it was voted in by a democratic process, is unable to govern. The American public, having witnessed tragic losses of its servicemen and women and conscious of the cost of the war, has tired of and is anxious to end it. The problem remains how to end it.

Asia

Asia, particularly its eastern part, has seen phenomenal growth in the last several decades (Figure 19.4). Countries such as Japan have among the world's highest GDPs per capita. Even the smaller, newly industrialized countries—Taiwan, South Korea, Singapore, Malaysia, and the Special Administrative Region (SAR) of China, Hong Kong—have been so successful that they have been nicknamed the "little dragons." Their economies are export-driven and managed and for some time seemed invincible. The last years of the twentieth century, however, saw a retrenchment in these economies, coupled with a spectacular rise of China as an economic giant.

The three most important countries in the region are Japan, India, and China. Japan has a population of 127.5 million, crowded onto four small islands with very few natural resources. However, the country is culturally homogeneous, its people are highly educated, and hard work is a prevalent value. As a result, Japan was able to develop the world's second largest economy in the years following World War II.

Until recently, India had not been as lucky. It has a vast population—approximately 1 billion—but it has not succeeded in becoming industrialized fast enough. Although it has been a democracy since the departure of its colonial rulers, the British, it has experienced problems of caste differences and hostilities between the Hindu majority and the Muslim minority. It has not been able to provide its population with a good standard of living. Much of the country is still agricultural (subsistence agriculture, at that), and it lags in education.

Because of globalization, however, India has been discovered as an ideal nation for the outsourcing of key business processes. Finance and accounting functions, as well as marketing, are rapidly spreading to India from the United States as digital information and computer networks become common. A large segment of Indians speak English and

Map of Asia

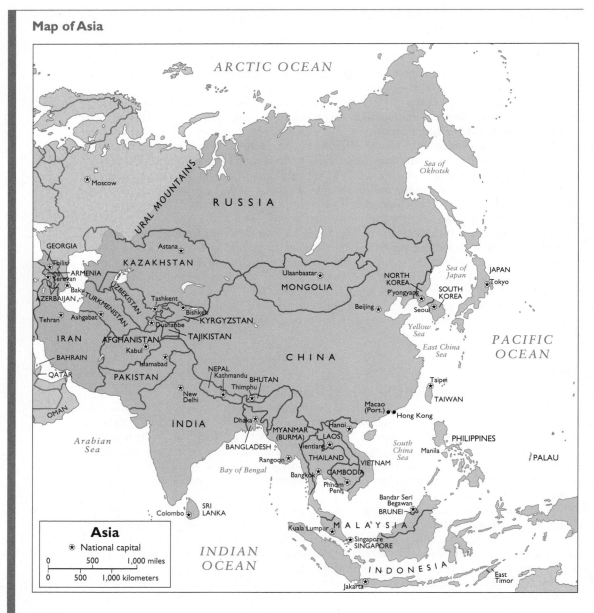

FIGURE 19.4

have better mathematics skills than Americans. Most important, they earn much less than Americans, making it profitable for American firms to employ them in what is called "offshoring." The city of Bangalore, in fact, has been dubbed the new Silicon Valley for its large number of computer-related companies.

The initial wave of offshoring has opened the way for the Indian economy in other ways: Indians have become major exporters of software services and software workers. Aided by a reduction in tariffs and easier consumer credit, the economy has been booming: It has had a growth rate of 8 percent between 2004 and 2007. Unfortunately, the booming economy is not able to overcome the problems of poverty, which are endemic because of the size of the population.

China has a population of 1.2 billion, fully one-fifth of the world's people. Having abandoned the communist-era centralized economy in favor of a liberalized command, or even market, economy, China has recently achieved the highest economic growth rates in the world: Its GDP has increased tenfold since 1978, and as of 2006, its economy is the second largest in the world. The government, however, has remained communist, and the split between a quasicapitalist economy and a repressive political system has resulted in difficulties for the Chinese. The population suffers from great inequities in income (economic development is centered in coastal areas while the interior remains agricultural and poor), problems of unemployment (workers laid off from state-owned enterprises, migrants from rural areas into cities), environmental damage, an aging population, and infractions of human rights.

Pacific Rim

The Pacific Rim is a small region of island nations with a total population of 28 million people. The region consists of Australia, New Zealand, Fiji, Micronesia, and Western Samoa (Figure 19.5). Australia is the largest of these nations in both population and territory. It enjoys a high GDP per capita, as well as a high standard of living overall. Most of these nations combine the cultures of indigenous people with those of European settlers, though the urban centers exhibit a predominantly European culture. Some of the indigenous people, particularly in Australia, are unhappy about the treatment they are still receiving. The economic growth of some of the East Asian countries has affected Pacific Rim economies positively.

Sub-Saharan Africa

Geographically, Sub-Saharan Africa is the largest of the world's regions, including 44 nations, most of which were created by colonial powers and do not correspond to ancient tribal borders (Figure 19.6, p. 545). Most of these countries have gained their independence only since the 1960s, and the job of building nations out of disparate tribes speaking hundreds of different languages has been very difficult. The area is plagued by the highest incidence of poverty, a short life expectancy, and some of the lowest living standards in the world. In the last 30 years, AIDS has become endemic, killing thousands and infecting thousands more. South Africa, the southernmost of the countries on the continent, had been a bastion of racism until 1994, when power was transferred to Nelson Mandela's African National Congress. Although progress in democratizing institutions has been made, economic and cultural problems still abound.

Latin America

Latin America includes the countries of Central America as well as the whole continent of South America (Figure 19.7, p. 546). It is a very large area in which the unifying motifs are the Spanish language and culture (with the exception of Brazil, which is Portuguese-speaking) and the Roman Catholic religion. This influence is the result of the conquest and settlement of the region by Spain and of the widespread annihilation of indigenous populations. The region has been plagued by political instability and has only in the recent past attained a

Map of the Pacific Rim

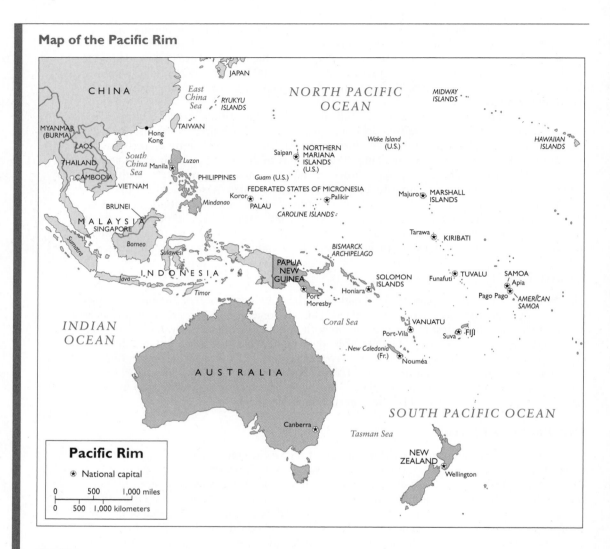

FIGURE 19.5

degree of democratization. Severe economic problems remain, however, in some countries more than in others. A deep gap exists between rich and poor, and resentments between the descendants of the white settlers and descendants of the indigenous peoples simmer just below the surface.

Anglo America

The continent of North America, containing the United States and Canada, is the wealthiest and politically most powerful region in the world. Although the North American Free Trade

Map of Africa

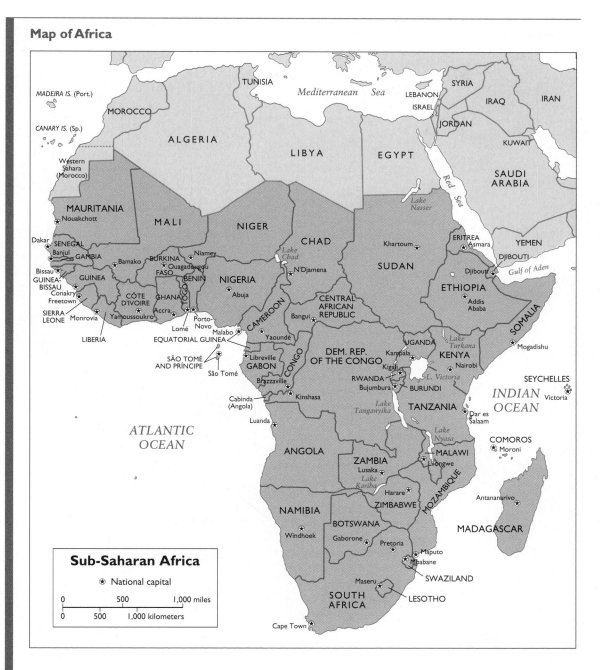

Sub-Saharan Africa

⊛ National capital

0	500	1,000 miles
0	500	1,000 kilometers

FIGURE 19.6

Map of Latin America

FIGURE 19.7

Agreement (NAFTA) includes Mexico, the latter has always had closer ties to Latin America; however, trade occurs on a large scale among these three nations. Enjoying many natural resources, fertile soils, a large population (more than 300 million for the United States, only 33 million for Canada), and political stability, the region exhibits one of the highest standards of living and life expectancy. Its mass culture appears to be a role model for the rest of the world, although the reputation of the United States has suffered as a result of the war in Iraq.

Other Ways of Classifying States

Until about 10 years ago, it was common to divide the countries of the world into those belonging to the First, the Second, and the Third World. The First World countries included the industrialized, capitalist nations such as the United States and Canada, Japan, Australia and New Zealand, and the nations of Western Europe. The Second World included all the socialist countries of the world, such as the former Soviet Union, China, Cuba, North Korea, the countries of Eastern Europe, and some African nations. The Third World included all the rest of the world, or countries that did not fit either one of the previous categories. These countries were large in number, counting among them almost two-thirds of the world. They were also referred to as the "developing" nations. Among them were Mexico, the nations of Central and South America, and the nonaligned communist nations of Asia and Africa.

Rich Nations, Poor Nations

With the dissolution of the Soviet Union, the Second World unraveled, so this classification lost much of its meaning. A more significant classification, therefore, is one into rich nations and poor nations. This classification is obtained by observing the gross domestic product per capita, that is, a country's yearly output of goods and services produced by economic activity, divided by its population. This is not exactly the most precise measure, as predominantly agricultural countries do not show up well in terms of wealth produced. But it gives a sufficiently clear picture showing countries stratified into high-income, middle-income, and low-income. Looking on a map, it is obvious that with a few exceptions the high-income countries are located in the northern regions. The middle- and low-income nations, on the other hand, are located in the southern regions (that is why this classification is also called the **North-South axis**). As shown on the maps above, the high-income regions are those of North America and Western Europe, as well as Australia and New Zealand. The middle-income countries are in Latin America, South Africa, and in those parts of North Africa that have oil, and the newly industrial nations of East Asia. The low-income countries are found in Africa and Asia. In terms of percentage of population, 56 percent of the more than 6 billion people who inhabit the earth live in the low-income regions, and only 15 percent live in the high-income regions.

The differences that exist between the rich and the poor nations of the world are a worrisome problem. According to the World Development Report of 2004, 2.1 billion of the 6 billion people in the world live on less than $2 a day. Another 1.1 billion people live on less than $1 a day. Of every 100 infants, 8 do not live long enough to see their fifth birthday. Of every 100 boys of school age, 9 do not attend school (and neither do 14 of every 100 girls). Poor people are also vulnerable to poor health, economic dislocations, natural disasters, and personal violence. The World Bank estimates that poverty reduction has occurred in China and the East Asia and Pacific regions, where the GDP per capita more than tripled, and the proportion of people in extreme poverty fell from 56 percent to 16 percent. However, in sub-Saharan Africa the GDP shrank by 14 percent, and poverty increased from 41 percent in 1981 to 46 percent in 2001. This means that 140 million people were added to those living in extreme poverty (World Development Indicators, 2004, 2). In 2005, sub-Saharan Africa was still experiencing extreme poverty and hunger: 41 percent of its residents were living on $1 a day or less. Thirty percent of children had no primary education. The attempt to halve the extent of hunger for children has been moving excruciatingly slowly. In spite of slight drops, the mortality of children under five is twice the rate of developed countries, while maternal health is a regional and global scandal, according to the report.

Finally, poor people lack political power, so that they are frequently on the receiving end of brutal civil conflicts. The rising disparities between the rich countries and the poor have awakened bitter resentment, as well as a sense of injustice in many, a situation that has already begun to explode and is a threat to the comfortable life of people in the wealthy nations.

■ Interaction among Nations

We see that the world is organized into regions containing nearly 200 nation-states. The behavior of each state toward another depends on the historical framework of international systems of the past. History illustrates that any given policy or action is shaped by the prevailing beliefs of the period, that is, by ideologies and the world views of the participants. It is also important to remember that both beliefs and world views change over time. Obviously, then, there is a clear link between theory (what is believed), policy (how leaders say they ought to behave as a result of the belief system), and practice (how policies are actually carried out by policymakers).

Theoretical Perspectives

International relations have been viewed through the lens of all the social sciences. Scholars, however, like all people, have different perceptions of reality. Consequently, they have analyzed events and behavior from different points of departure. An awareness of these differences is important in judging their conclusions.

Realism

The prevalent perspective among American scholars for much of this century has been realism. Realism is based on the assumption, first, that the essence of politics is the struggle for power and, by extension, that international politics is best understood as the study of the conflicts that arise as a result of this struggle. Scholars who subscribe to this view, popularized by Hans Morgenthau of the University of Chicago, approach international relations primarily in terms of disturbances to the system: wars, revolutions, and natural disasters. They seek to establish causes and foresee consequences of these power struggles. The issues of war and security affairs are considered of utmost importance and referred to as "high politics," as opposed to such matters of "low politics" as economic, social, and cultural interactions. The key concept in this perspective is power and the fact that each nation, in the absence of any central authority, must provide for its own security by using its power. This, of course, leads to escalation, because all other nations will behave in the same way. In the realist view, however, national survival and the national interest are primary political virtues, superseding personal morality or any other consideration.

The second assumption of realism is that states are the principal or most important actors in international relations and that they act as a unit; that is, that the state (the abstract embodiment of the nation) speaks with one voice and has one policy at a given time on any specific issue. This is an idealized version of reality because governments are not always stable, legitimate, and competent, and they never speak for all the people of the nation.

The third assumption is that the state is a rational actor. In establishing foreign policy, then, the decision-making process begins with a statement of objectives and considers all feasible alternatives in terms of the state's capabilities, the likelihood of attaining the objectives, and the costs and benefits entailed in each alternative. Decision makers then select the alternative that maximizes benefits and minimizes costs. In reality, it is doubtful that most decision-making processes follow such rational procedures.

Contemporary Perspectives

While realism held sway, theoretical perspectives that were opposed to it were dubbed idealistic. Beginning in the late 1950s, international relations were increasingly marked by the emergence of behavioral or scientific approaches—the scientific method was applied to international relations just as it had been to the other social sciences. The controversy between these new approaches and the older, traditional ones raged for a number of years and was never really resolved. Most contemporary scholars have attempted to transcend the controversy by selecting elements of each theoretical approach where they best fit. Contemporary approaches tend to look at international relations from the standpoint of pluralism, globalism, and neorealism.

Pluralism. Pluralism assumes that actors other than the state are important entities in international relations and cannot be ignored. International organizations and multinational corporations, with their own bureaucracies, have considerable influence in determining which issues are most important politically, particularly in an increasingly interdependent world economy. In addition, pluralists disagree that the state is a unitary actor. The state is composed of individual bureaucracies, interest groups, and individuals, all of whom try to formulate or influence foreign policy. They also challenge the notion that the state is a rational actor. They note that often policies are suggested to enhance the power, prestige, and standing of a group at the expense of others and with disastrous consequences for the foreign policy of the nation. Finally, pluralists reject the idea that the agenda of international politics is dominated by military and security issues; rather, they believe that agenda to be extensive, including economic and social welfare issues.

Globalism. Globalism assumes that the starting point of analysis for international relations is the global context within which states and other entities interact. They maintain that to explain behavior, one must first understand the essence of the global environment in which behavior occurs. Globalists also believe that it is necessary to view international relations from a historical perspective. For example, a study of the rise of capitalism in sixteenth-century Western Europe shows that its development, changes, and expansion have led to the establishment of a world capitalist system that affects the behavior of all states, even though some states benefit from capitalism and others do not.

Globalists also focus their analysis on state and nonstate actors as mechanisms of domination. In other words, they look at how some states, social classes, or elites benefit from the capitalist system at the expense of others and how dependency relations among northern industrial states (North America, Western Europe, Japan, and even the former Soviet Union and Eastern Europe) and the poor, underdeveloped, industrially deficient countries (Latin America, Africa, and Asia) initially developed and are maintained.

Finally, globalists stress to a great extent the critical importance of economic factors as an explanation for the dynamics of the international system. In fact, to globalists, economics is the key to understanding the development, evolution, and functioning of the contemporary world system. It should be obvious that the perspective has many Marxist features, but many globalists profess to be non-Marxists (Viotti & Kauppi, 1987, 6–10).

Neorealism

The neorealist perspective accepts some of the premises of realism. For instance, neorealists agree that international relations are faced with three problems: anarchy, order, and constraints. The fact that there is no central authority to govern the international system (that it is, in fact, in a situation of quasi-anarchy) forces the states into a "security dilemma." States feel impelled to arm themselves for protection, but this does not make them more secure because other states do the same thing. They also agree that states have sought to impose order on the anarchy, cooperating to prevent conflicts, so that rules of behavior do exist and some cooperation on an economic level is also a reality. Finally, the problem of constraint is that interdependence dictates that no state can act without taking the consequences of its actions for other states into consideration. Given that the competing factors of anarchy and order are dominant characteristics of the international system and that constraint on the part of the state is the prevailing reality, neorealists maintain that the role of power in international relations is of fundamental importance.

■ Participants in the International System

In the framework of the above cautionary statements, we may refine the definition of international relations as being a discipline concerned with actors (states, governments, leaders, diplomats, peoples, or even multinational corporations) trying to achieve specific goals (objectives, purposes), using particular means (foreign policy, diplomacy, and other instruments) dependent on their power or capability (Sondermann et al., 1970, 5).

Actors in International Relations

The most significant actor in the international relations system is the state (see Chapter 14). The origins of the state hark back to the Protestant Reformation and especially to the Treaty of Westphalia (1648), which established that the power of the state superseded the power of the Catholic Church as well as that of the Holy Roman Emperor or, for that matter, of any individual. After the treaty, the European state became the dominant actor on the world stage and the agent of the new economic and political ideas.

The State and the Nation

As noted previously, a state is defined as a unit consisting of a population that occupies a definite territory, that is subject to a sovereign government, and that has a regime recognized as legitimate by other states. The state and the nation, then, are not quite the same thing, and it is more accurate to speak of a nation-state or a national state. A nation is a large social grouping whose people share common customs, language, heritage, and a sense of group identity. A nation may be split and living under the jurisdiction of several

Box 19.1 The Emergence of the State

Before the Treaty of Westphalia (1648), political organization was twofold: on a macro level, covering vast areas of the earth, it was universal, and on a micro level—a village or town—it was local. The most universal political organization was the Roman Empire. After its collapse, other universal organizations emerged: the empires of Charlemagne, the Holy Roman Empire, and the Austro-Hungarian Empire in the west; the Byzantine and Ottoman empires in the east; the Russian empire to the north; the Chinese Empire in Asia; and the Aztec and Inca empires in the as yet undiscovered western hemisphere. Individuals, however, believed they owed their allegiance not to any of these empires, but rather to tribal, village, provincial, and family groups.

During the Middle Ages in Europe, the overarching universal authority was that of the Roman Catholic Church, to which even kings were subordinate. But this authority began to unravel when economic necessities required larger political units to function more efficiently, and improved transportation and communication made people more aware of the possibility of trade and commerce with others. Gradually, monarchs incorporated local feudal and church power centers into their kingdoms. The impact of the Renaissance (roughly 1350–1550) also detracted from the power of the church. The Renaissance was a secular movement of cultural reawakening that began in Italy and

in which the educated elites looked back to the days of glory of Greece and Rome. The final blow to the authority of the church came with the Protestant Reformation, a movement sparked by Martin Luther, who questioned the need for intermediaries between God and the people. By the middle of the sixteenth century, nearly one-fourth of the people of Western Europe had converted to Protestantism. Particularly painful for the Catholic Church was the break from it of King Henry VIII of England, who established a national Protestant religion, the Church of England, with himself at its head. On the surface, the reason for the break was the king's desire for a divorce (which he could not obtain from the Catholic Church). In reality, it was a struggle over the power of the church, the wealth it controlled, and its ability to command the loyalty of the king's nobles. Henry won the support of the new merchant classes by redistributing the country's wealth. Newly powerful, the merchant class now had a stake in preserving the state (represented by the monarch). England subsequently became one of the first nation-states to make the transition from a feudal system dominated by a landed aristocracy and a weak king, to a capitalist system dominated by those who controlled commerce and manufacturing (the advent of the Industrial Revolution coincided with these events) and a strong monarch.

different states (such as the Albanians living in Kosovo or the Kurds living in Turkey and Iraq) or a nation may have no state (such as the Palestinians now and the Jews before the establishment of Israel), or a state may have many nations living within its boundaries (as was the case in the former Soviet Union, among other pluralist societies). The first European states were true nation-states because the population of each was really a nation. But the population of a modern state is more likely to consist of a number of nations that reside within its boundaries because of migration, war, colonialism, or a combination of these factors.

Central to the conception of the state is its sovereignty, and it is because a state is sovereign that it can govern and represent all the people within its own borders. Two other characteristics of states are the presence of armed forces and recognition by other states. Because states are sovereign, they must protect their borders and populations. The armed forces, which states use both defensively and offensively according to their national interest, are organizations trained to inflict violence. Wars and the threat of wars have largely determined territory, defined borders, preserved political independence, and given birth to new states.

Once it is felt that a state has control over the people within its boundaries, other states give it their recognition. This involves an exchange of ambassadors and agreements. Because

The terrorist attack on the United States in September 2001 forced American foreign policy into a crisis response: the military action that eliminated the Taliban regime in Afghanistan—haven to many terrorists—and the ongoing debacle in Iraq.

recognition means acceptance of a state as a legitimate political entity, it is not always given. Israel has existed as a state since 1948, but of the Arab states, only Egypt and Jordan formally recognize it.

Nonstate Actors

In addition to states, actors in the international system include intergovernmental organizations (IGOs), which are voluntary associations of sovereign states organized for the pursuit of a variety of purposes. IGOs range in importance from the United Nations and the European Economic Community to the Permanent International Committee on Canned Food. Some IGOs have an almost universal membership: the United Nations, the World Bank, the International Monetary Fund, and so on. Most of them are regional, however, such as the Organization of American States (OAS) and the Arab League. There are also regional military alliances such as the North Atlantic Treaty Organization (NATO). Their functions may be political, economic, or social. Their day-to-day business is carried out by their bureaucracies, and their decisions are negotiated by government representatives, including foreign and defense ministers, who are assigned to them.

Other actors in the system include nongovernmental organizations (NGOs), also called transnational actors. NGOs are characterized by having headquarters in one country but operations in two or more countries; they perform their functions across national borders. Finally, another kind of NGO consists of multinational corporations, large firms that control plants and offices in many countries, in which they sell their goods and services. The size of the multinationals is one reason why they are listed as actors in the international system (their gross annual sales rival the gross national products of many nations). Another reason is the fear of some social commentators that they will render the nation-state obsolete. The global economy that the multinationals are introducing will tie nations to one another with material benefits, making the territorial state outdated and irrelevant.

Finally, the last several decades have seen the emergence of "national liberation" groups that purport to be working to overthrow repressive governments or governments seen as unjust. These groups use violent tactics, but because they do not involve a large number of people, they have seldom succeeded as revolutionary movements. The best-known of these was the Palestine Liberation Organization (PLO). This group was considered a terrorist group that claimed to speak for the Palestinian people and to work for the establishment of a Palestinian state. Even though it was not a state, the PLO had been recognized as the legitimate representative of the Palestinians, and it had been granted observer status at the United Nations, where it attended the meetings of the nonaligned countries. After the death of its leader, Yasser Arafat, elections were held in the Palestinian territories, and one group, Hamas, was elected to the premiership, while the position of president went to the leader of Fatah, Arafat's group. The two groups have been attempting to form a unity government, but the differences between them have led, thus far, to conflict and bloodshed.

Terrorist Groups

A more serious threat is posed by terrorist groups, which are becoming increasingly influential on the international scene. Some terrorist organizations, which call themselves guerrillas, attempt to establish independent states or secede from current states, and they do so with a mixture of public diplomacy and terror tactics. Other groups seem to have more ambiguous goals. The destruction in the wake of the September 11, 2001 attacks in New York, as well as a number of other terrorist attacks around the world, are examples of the violence of which such organizations are capable.

Terrorist groups differ from the national liberation organizations in that they do not organize the masses on a large scale; they tend to originate in cities, are led by anonymous leaders, hide in urban environments, and engage in sporadic violence. Both start out from positions of weakness, but terrorist groups hope to frighten their perceived enemy into making concessions.

Terrorism is resorted to by angry individuals who want to publicize their grievances. Such groups as the Party of God, the Iranian-sponsored organization that has taken Americans hostage in Lebanon, and alQaeda, use acts of highjacking, assassination, kidnapping, bombing of public buildings, and attacks on embassies to compel states to take notice and sometimes to negotiate with them.

■ The Goals of States

What do states want? We have already mentioned that a common objective of states is national security. However, states can attain only a degree of security, not total security. Not even the great powers are masters of their fate.

Security is broken down into several categories. First, there is simply a state's physical survival. An example in recent years of a state that has had to worry about its very survival is Israel. Surrounded by Arab states sworn to annihilate it, Israel has been forced to be extremely vigilant, and its policy makers consequently sometimes exaggerate in some of the actions they take as a result of the tensions produced by the state's vulnerability.

Following the September 11, 2001 terrorist attacks, the United States has also had to worry about its security. The worry has still not produced a significant program of defense, as it is very difficult in a free society to design a foolproof method of ensuring security.

National security is more commonly interpreted as referring to the preservation of a state's territorial integrity. Because of conflicts in the past, the borders of many states have shifted. Poland's borders have moved westward, as did those of the former Soviet Union. Conflicts concerning territory are frequent among states. China would like to reclaim some territory that was taken away from it by the Russian czars in the nineteenth century, but the present Russia refuses to give it back. Some of the new postcolonial nations would like to restore ethnic unity, but others feel it is to their benefit to defend the territory they acquired from their colonial predecessors. The Albanian majority in the Yugoslav province of Kosovo would like to become independent, but the Serbian majority in Yugoslavia will not part with its territory.

National security is also interpreted as meaning political independence, a state's freedom from foreign control, the preservation of its political and economic systems, and the maintenance of the values, patterns of social relations, lifestyles, and other features of a nation's character. The United States became involved in the two world wars and later in the Cold War primarily because its leaders felt that a Europe dominated by antidemocratic powers was a threat not only to the security of this nation but also to the kind of world environment in which the United States could freely exist and flourish. It did not want to see democracies extinguished by totalitarian states; democracy was a value it wanted to preserve not only for its own nation but also for the world as a whole.

National prestige, usually related to military power, is another objective of states. In this regard, the stalemate of the Vietnam War and the seizure of the U.S. embassy by Iran were severe blows to our prestige. Currently, our reputation is being tarnished by the Iraq war.

Economic security—wealth and prosperity—has been a goal not only of Western nations, which as a rule have attained such security, but also of the former Soviet Union and the less developed countries. The latter pursued a policy of nonalignment during the Cold War years to attract assistance from both superpowers. With the coming of détente, the demands of these nations have escalated, and it may well be that confrontations between the "have" and "have-not" states regarding a redistribution of wealth will increase in the future.

Finally, the protection or the promotion of an ideology is also an objective of some states. The United States has engaged in war, both "hot" and "cold," in defense of the democratic ideology. Revolutionary regimes, such as those of the former Soviet Union and China, have also sought to expand their influence and power under the banner of the communist ideology. Although most ideologies have been secular, under the Ayatollah Khomeini of Iran a religious ideology was promulgated. Islamic fundamentalism, with the aim of restoring traditional religious values throughout the Arab world and of destroying secular Western values in the Middle East and West Asian regions, continues to express itself in terrorist actions against Western targets. The result is that conflicts between states of differing ideologies are exacerbated.

The Competition of Objectives

It should be obvious that of the number of objectives listed above—and it is only a partial list—some are incompatible with others, or come at the expense of others. One such conflict is between security and economic welfare or, as economists say, guns and butter. Clearly, if a nation spends more on building arms, it has less to spend on building schools, hospitals, and highways, or on eradicating poverty. And if citizens must pay more taxes for the same purpose, they have less money with which to buy housing or education for their children. The argument about which should have priority goes on in most nations; how it is resolved depends a great deal on a nation's tradition and self-image. For instance, the former Soviet Union, having been subject to aggression, has been more willing to spend money on armaments. Western powers, particularly the United States and Great Britain, less subject to aggression, tend to give priority to domestic affairs.

Related to the above is the question of whether democratic values should be sacrificed in the name of security. During the Cold War, Senator Joseph McCarthy engaged in a "witch hunt" against Americans whom he considered to be communist sympathizers. His actions ruined careers and lives and certainly infringed on the victims' civil and human rights. In the 1960s and 1970s, both the executive branch and the Central Intelligence Agency were involved in activities that were unconstitutional—in addition to being undemocratic—to preserve security (the CIA planned a number of assassinations of leaders in other countries and helped overthrow a legitimately elected government in Chile).

As a result of the terrorist threat, the current administration of the United States has also been accused of violating the civil rights of some of its citizens with the excuse of doing it in the name of national security.

In the name of national security and welfare, the United States also allied itself with a number of nondemocratic states, either to contain communism or to continue to have access to oil. Here, too, decisions must be made about which is the most vital objective, and these decisions are often agonizing and divisive. The question of "what price security?" is a very delicate and difficult one. Policy makers must constantly grapple with exactly the right mixture of goals and the means of achieving them and must decide on the nation's degree of commitment to them.

■ Means of Achieving Goals: Foreign Policy

Many of the goals that nation-states attempt to reach are inherent in each nation's foreign policy. A nation's foreign policy consists of the actions the government takes to achieve certain goals in its relations with other nations. These actions may span a wide variety of activities, from informal negotiations to declarations of war, from exchanges of scholars or artists to trade boycotts. The actions may be taken in the economic, political, cultural, or military sphere. In other words, a nation, through its foreign policy, pursues its own self-defined national interest, but each nation's interest differs from, and sometimes conflicts with, the interests of other nations. Political scientists have tried to uncover a pattern, a guiding principle, or a common goal that characterizes the foreign policies of all nations. What they have found is the primacy of **power** in dictating foreign policy.

As noted above, nations pursue a variety of goals. Some goals are competitive, others absolute; some are clearly defined (shared by an overwhelming majority of a nation's people), others diffuse (changing with the mood or course of events); some may be declaratory (what a nation says), others action-oriented (what a nation does); some may be static (interested in preserving the status quo), others dynamic (looking for change). In short, no single concept explains the nature of national interest, and the goals of nations are subject to constant change (Stoessinger, 1975, 27–29).

Foreign policy, therefore, does not lend itself to easy definitions. Although a definitive concept of foreign policy cannot be formulated, the themes of struggle for power and concern for order are apparent in the relationships of nations around the world.

The United States maintains diplomatic relations with almost all of the approximately 200 nations of the world. American foreign policy as it relates to each of these countries is more or less custom-made. The United States tries to be aware of each country's individual values, interests, goals, and capabilities and to act in accordance with them. Relations are constantly affected by internal affairs, our own as well as those of other nations, and by external conditions that influence internal affairs. Americans have numerous commitments and agreements with other nations; often, we cannot act alone but must act in unison with others. As a result of the complexity of foreign relations, each nation has developed a large and complicated bureaucratic structure that gathers intelligence, researches, and analyzes foreign policy in every specific detail.

Types of Foreign-Policy Decisions

Foreign-policy decision making is essentially in the hands of individuals. Individuals are pressured and influenced by other individuals, by psychological factors, or by specific conditions present at the time; they are also limited by the organizational context in which they must operate. This context may be differentiated into three types.

General foreign-policy decisions are those that are expressed in policy statements and in direct actions. An example was the American policy of containment following World War II. The policy was expressed in presidential addresses and writings but also in actions, such as

The U.S. Department of State has the primary responsibility for administrative foreign policy decisions, although other agencies share in such decision making. As Secretary of State during part of the Bush Administration, Condoleezza Rice has had an arduous task in carrying out foreign relations policies in a politically unstable world.

the Vietnam War (the United States wanted to contain the spread of communism in Asia). It may be directed to the whole international community or refer to one specific action. It tends to be vague and is usually expressed in public statements, only sometimes backed up by definite planning. Public policy statements are not always truthful but may be designed to obtain particular effects. Neither are they always necessarily consistent. Consequently, it is not always easy to determine the general foreign policy of a nation-state.

Another type of foreign-policy decision is administrative. **Administrative decisions** are made by the government bureaucracy whose members are in charge of foreign affairs. In the United States, the Department of State has this primary responsibility, but other agencies such as the military and intelligence agencies, and the Department of Commerce, may all share in the administrative decisions that affect foreign policy. Whereas general foreign policy is determined by political leaders, bureaucrats implement policy through administrative decisions on some occasions.

The third type of foreign-policy decision is the **crisis decision**. A crisis in foreign policy occurs when one state feels that a certain situation will mark a turning point in its relationship with one or more other states in the international community. The need for a decision is perceived as urgent. Decision makers are forced to consider a number of alternatives, and one or more of the states involved feel that some crucial goals are threatened by the crisis. Crisis decisions are usually made with a combination of general and administrative personnel. The three types of foreign policies are deeply intertwined; often, one results from and in turn affects another. A recent example of a crisis decision was the administration's choice to respond militarily to the terrorist attack on the United States, first by the military action in Afghanistan and then by the overthrow of the dictator of Iraq and the subsequent occupation of the country.

Goals of American Foreign Policy

The goals of U.S. foreign policy can be said to include the following: First, the central goal is to protect the nation's physical security. This is a primary goal of every nation's foreign policy, but the United States has been more successful in it than most. In fact, since the War of 1812, no foreign armies have occupied the continental United States. In contrast, the nations of continental Europe were overrun twice in the twentieth century and repeatedly in the nineteenth century. However, the threat of terrorism may change the state of our security.

A second goal is to protect the physical security of the principal allies of the United States. For instance, since World War II, the United States has committed itself to protect the nations of Western Europe (through NATO), as well as to protect nations on other continents: Japan, South Korea, and Israel.

A third goal is to protect the economic security of the nation. This means that the United States must be able to buy the resources that it needs from nations willing to sell and sell manufactured goods or agricultural products to nations willing to buy. Selling abroad is more difficult than it might appear because products from the United States compete with domestic production, so their purchase may be against the self-interest of the buying nation. Yet foreign markets are in the self-interest of the United States.

Another goal, developed in the post–World War II era, was called containment, and meant an effort to limit the spread of communism. Whenever a conflict arose anywhere in the world that had links to the Soviet Union or China, American foreign policy dictated some type of intervention. However, as the communist threat has disappeared, the question of containment has become moot.

Finally, the oldest goal of American foreign policy has been to keep foreign powers out of North America and South America, and the Caribbean. First articulated in 1823, the Monroe

Doctrine was a warning to the European states to stay out of Latin America, which was considered to be in the American sphere of influence. The doctrine has been challenged in a number of Central American nations whose authoritarian regimes the United States had supported and in which Soviet-armed native guerrillas fought against the central governments.

■ The Role of Ideology

Foreign policy begins where domestic policy ends, but domestic policy deeply affects a nation's foreign policy. U.S. domestic policy is governed by the American historical experience, which has been revolutionary and guided by ideas of freedom. Therefore, self-determination, majority rule, and the right of dissent have been major concepts of American ideology. Because Americans once fought a revolutionary war, they are sympathetic to revolutionary causes; because they once were a colony, they officially decry colonialism; because they were once an underdeveloped country, they engage in aid to less developed nations; because they are a constitutional democracy, they align themselves with other such nations and oppose governments that rule by totalitarian or dictatorial means; finally, because they link democracy and freedom to love of peace, they attribute warlike expansionist tendencies to tyrannies and dictatorships. At least, such is the official version of American ideology.

Clearly, Americans do not always act according to such an ideology, either in domestic or in foreign policy making. Still, they are so committed to this official version that they can never act solely in the national interest or only for the economic well-being of the nation. Public opinion at home and expectations abroad do not allow it.

The difficulty of conducting foreign affairs lies in the fact that other nations subscribe to different ideologies, some of which conflict to a greater or lesser extent with the American ideology, while others have totally different emphases. To export and superimpose the American ideology on others violates the very principles of that ideology (although the United States attempts to do so and has done so.) At the same time, international relations in a world of conflicting ideologies present grave dangers.

■ Who Makes Foreign Policy Decisions?

Foreign policy decisions, as we have seen, are not made by one branch of government or by one agency alone. Rather, they result from the involvement of the White House, the foreign policy bureaucracy, Congress, and public opinion.

The most important decision maker in foreign policy is the president. Surrounded by his staff, the National Security Council (NSC) consisting of the president, the vice president, the secretary of state, and the secretary of defense, as well as by the director of the Central Intelligence Agency (CIA) and the chair of the Joint Chiefs of Staff (who are advisers to the NSC), the president is thought to be able to make the best decisions in the national interest.

Even though the president is powerful in decision making, he must also pay attention to the influence of the foreign policy bureaucracy, such as the State Department, the Defense Department, the intelligence community, and other federal agencies. These entities, staffed by career bureaucrats trained in foreign relations, offer advice to the president on issues of foreign policy, and they actually implement the decisions the president and Congress make.

The influence of Congress over foreign policy decision making has varied through American history. In times when the United States was not threatened from abroad, Congress dominated foreign policy, but in times when threats were feared, Congress deferred to the president. Congress affects foreign policy by passing substantive legislation (for instance, funding specific foreign policy ventures and not others or regulating trade), by passing procedural legislation (i.e., passing bills that change the procedure that the executive branch uses to make decisions). Finally, members of Congress can attempt to change the climate of opinion in the country by writing opinion editorials, giving speeches, appearing on television talk shows, and so on, to affect some specific aspect of foreign policy.

To a certain degree, the public can have an impact on foreign policy, also. First, individuals can vote for presidential and congressional candidates who share their view on foreign policy. And secondly, they can join interest groups who lobby government for some particular foreign policy action: human rights, the environment, immigration, etc. Polls seeking the electorate's opinions on specific foreign policy actions also affect decisions.

■ Instruments of Foreign Policy

What are the tools with which foreign policy accomplishes its goals? Among the most essential are the United Nations, foreign aid, collective security, the military establishment, and propaganda.

The United Nations

The United Nations (UN) was founded in 1945 for the purpose of establishing a community of nations, a world body able to take collective action in defense and pursuit of peace and human dignity. Unfortunately, the UN has not had much success in keeping the peace. This lack of success can be partially blamed on the organization's structure. The 15-member Security Council cannot act over the veto of any of its five permanent members, although the General Assembly, to which all member nations belong, can act when the Security Council members fail to reach unanimity. The UN has functioned as an effective force in some instances but has been ineffective in others (see Figure 19.8).

The United States intended to use the UN as the key instrument of American foreign policy, particularly to play the balance-of-power role: the United States could influence other nations without really intervening in their affairs. For instance, during the Korean War, the United States was able to use its own troops in Korea under the pretext that they represented the official UN peacekeeping force. Shortly after the Korean War, however, the United States was no longer able to control the admission of new members to the UN. At this time, membership rose from about 60 to 130 nation-states (today, it stands at more than 185). The influence of the United States in the UN has lessened, and the atmosphere in the UN has changed from a pro-Western to a neutralist and sometimes an anti-Western stand. Nonetheless, the UN does provide a forum for discussions that sometimes help to defuse tensions. In addition, the economic, social, and health agencies of the UN have improved living conditions for many people around the world.

Although everyone agrees that the United Nations needs to be reformed, it is becoming clear that the reforms sought by Third World countries differ substantially from those sought by the industrialized nations, particularly the United States. The East–West conflicts typical of the Cold War era are giving way to the North–South struggles of the developed and developing nations. In fact, while the developing nations would like the reforms to include an upgrading of the authority of the General Assembly, gaining additional representation on the Security Council, curtailing the veto rights of the five major powers, and expanding UN

The United Nations System

Principal Organs

Trusteeship Council

Security Council

General Assembly

Economic and Social Council

International Court of Justice

Secretariat

Subsidiary Bodies

Military Staff Committee

Standing Committee and ad hoc bodies

International Criminal Tribunal for the former Yugoslavia (ICTY)

International Criminal Tribunal for Rwanda (ICTR)

UN Monitoring, Verification and Inspection Commission (Iraq) (UNMOVIC)

United Nations Compensation Commission

Peacekeeping Operations and Missions

Programmes and Funds

UNCTAD United Nations Conference on Trade and Development

ITC International Trade Centre (UNCTAD/WTO)

UNDCP[1] United Nations Drug Control Programme

UNEP United Nations Environment Programme

UNICEF United Nations Children's Fund

UNDP United Nations Development Programme

UNIFEM United Nations Development Fund for Women

UNV United Nations Volunteers

UNCDF United Nations Capital Development Fund

UNFPA United Nations Population Fund

UNHCR Office of the United Nations High Commissioner for Refugees

WFP World Food Programme

UNRWA[2] United Nations Relief and Works Agency for Palestine Refugees in the Near East

UN-HABITAT United Nations Human Settlements Programme

Research and Training Institutes

UNICRI United Nations Interregional Crime and Justice Research Institute

UNITAR United Nations Institute for Training and Research

UNRISD United Nations Research Institute for Social Development

UNIDIR[2] United Nations Institute for Disarmament Research

INSTRAW International Research and Training Institute for the Advancement of Women

Other UN Entities

OHCHR Office of the United Nations High Commissioner for Human Rights

UNOPS United Nations Office for Project Services

UNU United Nations University

UNSSC United Nations System Staff College

UNAIDS Joint United Nations Programme on HIV/AIDS

Other UN Trust Funds[7]

UNFIP United Nations Fund for International Partnerships

UNDEF United Nations Democracy Fund

Subsidiary Bodies

Main committees

Human Rights Council

Other sessional committees

Standing committees and ad hoc bodies

Other subsidiary organs

Advisory Subsidiary Body

United Nations Peacebuilding Commission

Functional Commissions

Commissions on:
Narcotic Drugs
Crime Prevention and Criminal Justice
Science and Technology for Development
Sustainable Development
Status of Women
Population and Development
Commission for Social Development
Statistical Commission

Regional Commissions

Economic Commission for Africa (ECA)

Economic Commission for Europe (ECE)

Economic Commission for Latin America and the Caribbean (ECLAC)

Economic and Social Commission for Asia and the Pacific (ESCAP)

Economic and Social Commission for Western Asia (ESCWA)

Other Bodies

Permanent Forum on Indigenous Issues (PFII)

United Nations Forum on Forests

Sessional and standing committees

Expert, ad hoc and related bodies

Related Organizations

WTO World Trade Organization

IAEA[3] International Atomic Energy Agency

CTBTO Prep.Com[5] PrepCom for the Nuclear-Test-Ban-Treaty Organization

OPCW[5] Organization for the Prohibition of Chemical Weapons

Specialized Agencies[6]

ILO International Labour Organization

FAO Food and Agriculture Organization of the United Nations

UNESCO United Nations Educational, Scientific and Cultural Organization

WHO World Health Organization

World Bank Group
IBRD International Bank for Reconstruction and Development
IDA International Development Association
IFC International Finance Corporation
MIGA Multilateral Investment Guarantee Agency
ICSID International Centre for Settlement of Investment Disputes

IMF International Monetary Fund

ICAO International Civil Aviation Organization

IMO International Maritime Organization

ITU International Telecommunication Union

UPU Universal Postal Union

WMO World Meteorological Organization

WIPO World Intellectual Property Organization

IFAD International Fund for Agricultural Development

UNIDO United Nations Industrial Development Organization

UNWTO World Tourism Organization

Departments and Offices

OSG[3] Office of the Secretary-General

OIOS Office of Internal Oversight Services

OLA Office of Legal Affairs

DPA Department of Political Affairs

DDA Department for Disarmament Affairs

DPKO Department of Peacekeeping Operations

OCHA Office for the Coordination of Humanitarian Affairs

DESA Department of Economic and Social Affairs

DGACM Department for General Assembly and Conference Management

DPI Department of Public Information

DM Department of Management

OHRLLS Office of the High Representative for the Least Developed Countries, Landlocked Developing Countries and Small Island Developing States

DSS Department of Safety and Security

UNODC United Nations Office on Drugs and Crime

UNOG UN Office at Geneva

UNOV UN Office at Vienna

UNON UN Office at Nairobi

Published by the United Nations Department of Public Information

06-39572—August 2006—10,000—DPI/2431

NOTES: Solid lines from a Principal Organ indicate a direct reporting relationship; dashes indicate a non-subsidiary relationship.

1 The UN Drug Control Programme is part of the UN Office on Drugs and Crime
2 UNRWA and UNIDIR report only to the GA.
3 The United Nations Ethics Office and the United Nations Ombudsman's Office report directly to the Secretary-General
4 IAEA reports to the Security Council and the General Assembly (GA).
5 The CTBTO Prep.Com and OPCW report to the GA.
6 Specialized agencies are autonomous organizations working with the UN and each other through the coordinating machinery of the ECOSOC at the intergovernmental level, and through the Chief Executives Board for coordination (CEB) at the inter-secretariat level.
7 UNFIP is an autonomous trust fund operating under the leadership of the United Nations Deputy Secretary-General. UNDEF's advisory board recommends funding proposals for approval by the Secretary-General.

FIGURE 19.8 The United Nations System, Principal Organs

The United Nations has been most successful in helping people displaced by wars and conflicts, but not in preventing such wars and conflicts.

economic and social programs, the industrialized nations are aiming to curb the growth of these programs, streamlining the bureaucracy, and eliminating the waste, duplication, and general inefficiency, mismanagement, and fraud rampant in the body (Branigin, 1992).

Foreign Aid

As a major power in the international arena, the United States began early to exert influence through its economic position. The economic instruments of foreign policy may take the form of grants and loans. They may also consist of the development and maintenance of an institution that replaces the gold standard and supplies a nation with the currency needed to engage in trade on an international level.

Shortly after joining the UN, the United States found itself committed to giving military aid to several nations. Although this action was initiated by a crisis—Great Britain had pulled out of Greece and Turkey, leaving these regimes vulnerable to communist guerrilla forces—it was understood that this was part of our commitment to rebuild and defend nations that wanted to develop democratic systems and to ward off communist takeovers. The Marshall Plan, set up to aid in the recovery of post–World War II Europe, had essentially the same purpose.

It is difficult to know for sure whether the spread of communism was really impeded by American foreign aid. However, it is apparent that foreign aid has constituted a hefty proportion of the gross national product of many Third World nations. It is generally agreed that the policy of offering economic aid has indeed helped to prevent revolutionary movements, whether in Europe, the Middle East, or Latin America. Monetary relationships among nations have also been positively affected by economic assistance.

Collective Security

Collective security is a concept that was first embodied in the Covenant of the League of Nations and has been retained in the Charter of the United Nations. Its basic tenets are that:

(1) all nations reject the use of force except in self-defense; (2) all agree that an attack on one is an attack on all; (3) all nations pledge to join together to halt aggression and restore peace and agree to supply the material or personnel necessary to achieve that goal; and (4) a military force, composed of representatives of member nations, will defeat any aggressors and restore peace.

The idea of collective security resembles that of a police force involved in domestic law enforcement. In the United States, for instance, the criminal laws consider that a criminal commits a crime not just against another individual or individuals, but against the society (that is why in court proceedings it is "the people versus the defendant"). Moreover, individuals cannot resort to violence except in self-defense, and people collectively support the police through taxes.

Although this concept works domestically, it has not been a great success internationally. The essence of the problem is the unwillingness of countries to subordinate their sovereignty to collective action. Individual governments maintain their right to view conflict in the narrow terms of their national interest. They either support or oppose UN actions based on their ethnocentric point of view. In short, collective security exists only as a goal, not as a reality.

The Military

Because military commitments around the world have come to play such a significant role in foreign policy, the original separation of the military from the political sphere has undergone a transformation. Before World War II, the size and readiness of a standing army were important. Since then, military effectiveness has been measured in terms of technology. The nation with the most sophisticated technology can swing the most threatening stick in the international arena. Consequently, defense spending has continually escalated. The United States was producing, for a long time, large amounts of arms both for its own stockpiles and for export to other countries. As a side effect, the development of a large defense industry has improved the American balance of trade. The military is also an instrument of foreign policy because the nations that buy from the United States are dependent on American technology for their defense.

Assured Destruction Capability. During the Cold War, the military was considered a particularly important instrument of foreign policy because the United States had been involved in an arms race with the Soviet Union, and there had been a perpetually present danger of nuclear war. The basis of the American strategic policy was to deter nuclear attack by **assured destruction capability**—in short, the United States kept other nations from attacking it because these nations knew that the United States had the means to destroy them. Although this may have been a logical line of defense, the assured destruction capability of both the United States and the Soviet Union was sufficient to destroy the two nations, or any others, 10 or 20 times over.

De-escalation. Intermittent negotiations regarding the possibility of disarmament had long been going on, but it has been difficult to achieve any unanimity. In 1963, President John Kennedy revealed an agreement with the Soviet Union to ban nuclear testing in the air, under water, and in outer space. Although more than 100 nations signed this agreement, France and the People's Republic of China, both atomic powers, did not. A similar thing occurred with the Nonproliferation Treaty of 1969, which was signed by over 60 nations but which several prominent nations failed to sign. The two superpowers finally agreed to decrease the constant escalation of military armament by signing agreements reached at the Strategic Arms Limitation Talks (SALT I and SALT II). The SALT II agreement, which had been tacitly observed by both sides since 1979, limited the number and types of strategic weapons. The Intermediate-Range Nuclear Forces Treaty of 1987 had eliminated all U.S. and Soviet missiles with ranges between 500 and 5,000 kilometers. In January 1993, as a last act of his presidency, President George H. W. Bush and Russia's President Boris Yeltsin signed the Strategic Arms Reduction Treaty, calling for a two-thirds reduction in the strategic nuclear arsenals of the United States and Russia by the year 2003. Each side would be limited to 3,000 to 3,500 warheads, a dramatic decrease from the previous figures of approximately 11,000. In 1995, the Clinton administration made the Nuclear Non-Proliferation Treaty (NNPT) a bulwark of its foreign policy. Although this treaty is considered to be a positive step in the direction of slowing, if not stopping, the spread of nuclear weapons, there is no guarantee that it will succeed. In fact, a number of states have either succeeded or are trying to achieve nuclear capability. (In the recent past, India and Pakistan have achieved nuclear capability, while North Korea and Iran are working at it.) The current presidents of Russia and the United States have signed a new treaty on missile defenses. According to the treaty, both nations will cut their nuclear arsenals by two-thirds, to approximately 2000 strategic nuclear warheads over the next 10 years. President Bush commented that this treaty "will liquidate the legacy of the Cold War," and will start a new era of US-Russian relationship. At the same time, the President has proposed to build a national missile defense (NMD) to defend the United States against attack by long-range ballistic missiles. The proposal, of course, has both supporters and critics. Supporters believe such a system would shield the country from its enemies. The critics maintain, first, that we do not know whether such a system is even viable, and second, that it would threaten nations such as Russia and China, who would lack similar systems and be at a disadvantage. Consequently, those nations could refuse to get rid of the nuclear weapons they currently possess and begin stockpiling additional weapons, which in the end could endanger the United States more.

Ironically, during the Cold War, in spite of an atmosphere of hostility, there was a measure of structure, predictability, and hierarchy that kept the proliferation of nuclear weapons in check. Today, the much more fragmented and fluid world order may lead to new incentives toward proliferation, as more and more states (not to mention terrorist groups) decide that it is to their advantage to possess nuclear weapons.

The importance of the military has consequences in the domestic arena, too. The military establishment has become an important force in our society. Billions of dollars are appropriated for the military yearly, and a large bureaucracy and an important industry depend on it. Science has been harnessed into its service, as the military draws from universities, individual scientists, laboratories, aerospace industry contractors, and individual research firms.

The so-called military-industrial complex—an elite decision-making group not necessarily holding political office—was described as early as the Eisenhower administration. Its existence, of course, is not consistent with democratic principles. At the same time, a nation that engages in world politics must be able to show that it can at all times defend its sovereignty. To that purpose, any defense technology is eagerly sought and developed, which further expands the military-industrial complex.

Propaganda

As noted previously, propaganda is a means of spreading an ideology or a doctrine to convince people that it is right or correct for them. When propaganda becomes part of an attempt to capture power by an individual or group, there is a tendency to stretch the truth or to state outright falsehoods about alternative ideologies or doctrines. The United States, no less than other nations, has established a number of agencies for the express purpose of propagating the message that it has the "right" ideology.

One agency dedicated almost entirely to propaganda is the United States Information Agency (USIA). Representatives of this agency may be found in the major American embassies and missions in the larger urban centers around the world. Its best-known activity is the broadcasting of the Voice of America, which offers not only interesting and useful programs to listeners but also subtle messages regarding the virtues of the United States. The State Department, which runs embassies and consulates in most foreign countries, helps the USIA and is engaged in propaganda activities through its public relations department.

The Central Intelligence Agency (CIA) is responsible primarily for the collection and evaluation of information on activities in foreign countries, but it also disseminates propaganda. For instance, in the past, it had been known to subsidize organizations and publications that counter communist propaganda. In recent times, the CIA has suffered a tarnished image. First, it was discovered that it allowed some of its operatives to sell secrets to other governments for several years. Then, it was blamed for not foreseeing the terrorist attacks on New York and Washington, DC. Since then, it has undergone a thorough reorganization and is again considered to be of strategic importance to the United States.

The White House is equally adept at propaganda production. It may be said that every statement made by the president is made with the intention of enhancing the American image. The Departments of Defense, Labor, and Agriculture are also active in propaganda activities, conveying the basic message that American technological superiority is due in no small way to the democratic political system and the capitalist economic structure.

■ Diplomacy and Diplomats

One definition of diplomacy is that it is the conduct of international relations by negotiation (Stoessinger, 1975, 251). The purpose of diplomacy is for each nation to pursue its national goals to its best advantage without offending any other nation. Diplomacy is not used to achieve order or peace exclusively. Sometimes it is used to intensify a struggle between two nations. Usually, however, the use of diplomacy implies that nations attempt to settle their differences by peaceful means. Diplomacy is an old procedure and a major tool used in the achievement of political order.

Diplomacy and the diplomat have been altered quite radically in recent years. In the old form of diplomacy, diplomats had large powers of discretion, whereas today they tend to be little more than messengers. Often, diplomats are ignored while heads of state deal directly with one another. The various summit conferences are illustrations of the new methods: heads of state discuss their differences with the world as their audience. In the end, it seems that although summit meetings may be helpful in specific circumstances, they seldom resolve basic differences. The consummate diplomat of the last 50 years in the United States has been Henry Kissinger, Secretary of State during the Nixon administration.

Treaties and Alliances

Probably the most important instruments of foreign policy—in the sense that the United States has come to rely on them rather heavily—are the defense treaties and security arrangements with various nations that were formulated during the late 1940s and 1950s. These arrangements, multilateral or bilateral, were initially intended to give physical expression to the policy of containment. They were meant to encircle the Soviet and Chinese spheres of influence by a chain of nations with which the United States had treaties pledging mutual defense. The arrangements were so worded that an attack on one nation would be considered an attack on the United States, as well as on all the other member nations.

Defense treaties, especially long-term ones, tend to improve relations among member nations and benefit foreign policy. For example, NATO, which includes 26 nations among which are Belgium, Canada, Denmark, Germany, France, the United States and Great Britain (as well as a number of new members from the former Eastern bloc such as the Czech Republic, Hungary, and Poland) has a common structure of military and civilian bureaucracies (Figure 19.9). In addition, troops of one member country are stationed in some of the other member countries, and a great deal of information and technological skill is exchanged. Nonetheless, the mutual defense alliances have always fallen short of policy makers' expectations. For one thing, these alliances tend to be so vague that not all members always agree on the type of action that can be termed aggression. For another, the United States seems always to be the most eager of the member countries to enter into and live up to alliances. Although the United States would certainly go to the aid of any member country, the same cannot be said of other countries coming to the aid of the United States. At the same time, the alliances in the period after World War II have been positive in that they have permitted the United States to play a greater role in intervening in crisis situations. They may have kept some nations—Germany and Japan, for instance—from developing their own nuclear capabilities.

The fact that alliances have significant shortcomings has given the United States the justification for building sufficient weapon arsenals to be able to act alone, if necessary. In short, involvement in world affairs carries with it the need for military preparedness, which

The 26 NATO Member Countries

Belgium	Hungary	Portugal
Bulgaria	Iceland	Romania
Canada	Italy	Slovakia
Czech Rep	Latvia	Slovenia
Denmark	Lithuania	Spain
Estonia	Luxembourg	Turkey
France	The Netherlands	United Kingdom
Germany	Norway	United States
Greece	Poland	

FIGURE 19.9

Source: **http://www.nato.int/structur/countries.htm**: accessed 7/10/2007.

means maintaining a large military establishment. The administration of George W. Bush has been accused of arrogance in neglecting or ignoring historical alliances and proceeding to act alone on some vital world issues, in particular the overthrow of Saddam Hussein and the consequent debacle in Iraq.

Morality in Foreign Policy

Although the essence of foreign policy is to serve a nation's interest and preserve its survival, the idea has long prevailed that such a policy must also be "moral." Morality, of course, is a relative term, and interpretations of what is moral change with time and place. It is difficult, therefore, to make definitive statements about a moral foreign policy.

The United States has frequently condemned other nations for denying human rights to some of their citizens. China, as one example, responds repeatedly that such condemnation is equivalent to interfering with its domestic affairs. Is China right? Is the United States right? Are both nations right in each context? Is it advisable to strive for morality in foreign policy? Is it possible?

From experiences of the past and from viewing the current situation around the world, it becomes clear that morality should play a role, but it is uncertain that it ever will. In the concrete application of foreign policy, morality does not offer sufficient guidance. It is impossible to speak in terms of right versus wrong because each culture interprets right and wrong differently. More often, the application of foreign policy becomes a matter of one right versus one wrong; that is, each situation is dealt with individually. In a world that frequently seems to operate on individual and national greed, it becomes necessary to choose the lesser of two evils rather than the good as opposed to the evil. In such a world, morality is more often a matter of esthetics or rhetoric and only seldom a prescription for behavior.

■ Power

As has been said repeatedly, international relations occur within the framework of the important concept of power. Power has already been discussed both as a sociological concept and as a political instrument of control within a nation. In an international context, the nature of power has additional features and must be viewed in a wider perspective.

In the context of international relations, power may be defined as the "capacity of a nation to use its tangible and intangible resources in such a way as to affect the behavior of other nations" (Stoessinger, 1975, 25). At first sight, it may appear that a nation has power in proportion to its capabilities. However, this notion is incomplete. It is more correct to say that a nation's power is influenced by both psychological factors—how other nations view it, or how it thinks other nations view it—and relational factors—how much power it has in relation to other nations. When two nations have exactly the same capabilities, neither has power over the other and a stalemate exists.

In the past, geography played a strategic role in determining the power of nations. Today this role has been greatly reduced because of the sophistication of modern arms. A nation's power may now be determined by the possession of natural resources, particularly if these are accompanied by advanced technology and a strong economy, but natural resources alone do not justify a nation's power.

Population may be a factor in a nation's power, depending on whether it is harnessed profitably by the state to develop a modern industrial base. The type of government has bearing on national power, but it does not follow that democratic nations are the most powerful.

Psychological attributes such as a perception of national character and morale are equally important in determining national power. These attributes are derived from the culture, the historical experience, and the social structure of nations. Nationalism and particularly the development of an ideology are profound influences on a nation's power. Finally, a nation's leadership, especially the image of leadership that is projected around the world, is yet another source of power.

Power, then, is a function of neither size nor capability alone. There have been many instances of small and relatively poor nations successfully holding off, or even defeating, a superpower. Psychological factors, especially the will of the people and the use the government makes of it, are important sources of national power.

The central role of power in defining national interest is denied by some political scientists who maintain that power is only one factor in the determination of national interest. The goals of all nations are not necessarily competitive. Some nations actually encourage the acquisition of power by other nations or at least express a preoccupation for the welfare of other nations. The goals of some nations are absolute and not competitive. Switzerland, for example, does not try to compete with any other nation; it simply looks out for its own self-interest. Power and morality are both factors that enter into the determination of national interest, with one predominating over the other at different times. Sometimes nations have enough power to be able to afford to act morally, and at other times nations may lose some of their power by acting immorally.

■ The Balance-of-Power System

No matter how one approaches the analysis of international relations, one is forced to return to the role that power plays in them. Because of a lack of a central authority to make political decisions internationally, states must find some other regular pattern of behavior through which to coexist and resolve conflict, cooperate and coordinate their activities, defend their borders, or act as aggressors. The exterior forms of interaction occur through the traditional means of diplomacy, war, trade, or intervention. Underlying these formalities, however, there has always existed a balance-of-power system whose characteristics have varied through the centuries.

The Multipolar System

The balance-of-power system originated in the ruins of the feudal system in Europe. We saw earlier that the Peace of Westphalia allowed kings and princes to repudiate the authority of the Church and the emperor, substituting the idea of the sovereign and independent state to which the population within its territory owed its sole allegiance. The concept of sovereignty meant that, regardless of its size, military power, or geographic location, each state considered itself equal to any other state. For approximately 150 years, sovereignty was represented by a hereditary monarchy. After the French Revolution (1789), the concepts of nationalism and self-determination emerged and eventually triumphed, so that many groups of people and a number of principalities in Italy and Germany, feeling that they constituted separate nations, established nation-states. Still, the balance-of-power system prevailed. In Europe in that period, it was a multipolar system in which four or more major powers competed with one another and formed shifting alliances to avoid any one of them becoming stronger than any other. This system brought a measure of peace to the continent between 1815 and 1914. However, the big powers did exercise control over smaller powers, settling disputes, intervening in their affairs, and changing territorial boundaries.

The government leaders of the major industrial democracies, the so-called G8, meet annually to attempt to solve some of their own domestic economic and political issues, as well as those of the international community.

The World Wars

By the turn of the nineteenth century, the multipolar balance of power was beginning to disintegrate. Diplomacy failed to prevent the outbreak of World War I in 1914. The war had a number of consequences, but, most important, it demonstrated how badly the balance-of-power system had been undermined. After the war there was an attempt to institutionalize the balance of power in the newly formed League of Nations, through a system of "collective security" in which every country would be legally obliged to come to the aid of any other country that was being attacked. However, a number of states—Nazi Germany, fascist Italy, and communist Russia—repudiated the system at the same time that a worldwide depression demoralized Western society and cast doubts on its ability to solve its problems.

The remaining powers were distrustful of one another, which led two archenemies, Russia and Germany, to sign a nonaggression pact in 1939. Germany promptly initiated a *Blitzkrieg*, or lightning war, that brought it victory over Poland, Norway, Denmark, Holland, France, and the Balkans, initiating World War II. Eventually, Germany turned against Russia, allowing Britain and then the United States to win the war as allies of Russia.

The Bipolar System

Following World War II, the balance of power shifted again. The United States emerged from the war as a military and economic superpower. The Soviet Union, although it had suffered the greatest damage in the war, emerged as the chief rival of the United States. The Soviet–American confrontation, known as the Cold War, was based on a variety of economic and political interests. The vacuum created by the collapse of the multipolar system was taken up by the new bipolar system, in which most of the world politics was centered on the two superpowers. The Cold War resulted in the doctrine of containment, which led the United States into a war in Korea, into the Cuban missile crisis, and into the war in Vietnam, which became traumatic for the United States. A reassessment of the need to contain communism allowed President Richard Nixon to improve relations with the Soviet Union and China, resulting in the policy of détente. Based on the French word meaning a "release of tension," this policy broke the ice between the two superpowers and China, foreshadowing the eventual turn of events—amicable relations among the three nations.

A New Multipolar World

The balance of power has again changed, and it is no longer bipolar. Other actors who were not part of either pole have gained ascendancy in world politics. China's alliance with the Soviet Union has of course ceased to exist with the breakup of the latter nation. Europe and Japan have made phenomenal economic recoveries and follow foreign policies that favor their own national interests, which sometimes diverge from those of the United States. However, the determining factor was the breakup of the Soviet Union into Russia and a number of independent nations. Some of these nations, should they become nuclear powers, would present a clear and open danger to the rest of the world.

What does the future hold in store relative to the balance of power and American foreign policy? This is, of course, a matter of speculation because there are no certainties as far as human behavior is concerned. Some political scientists maintain that we are moving toward a world system in which national sovereignty disintegrates and greater control is taken by a supranational international organization, which, in an extreme case, could result in a world government. In this case, power would be unipolar. Such a system would have advantages and drawbacks, but it does not seem to be our immediate fate.

We live in a world much changed since the end of World War II. The dropping of the atomic bomb on Hiroshima in 1945 not only ushered in the atomic age, with its threat of self-destruction, but also divided the world into those who have nuclear arms and those who do not. The knowledge that the fate of the world hangs in the balance has so far kept the "have" states from unleashing a holocaust, but the world lives in an uneasy truce as long as it is known that they might unleash it. There has been a tremendous growth in economic interdependence, especially since the United States led a move toward the removal of tariffs and trade restrictions. Monetary relations have also been troubled, especially because of the massive loans made to the less developed countries, which those countries cannot repay on schedule. Finally, a fundamental reality in the world today is that a substantial majority of people and countries are poor. Particularly problematic is the inequity with which wealth is distributed. Issues of war and peace and power and lack of it will have to be framed within this overarching context, and American foreign policy will have to set a new course in an attempt to address the problem.

The Chapter in Brief

Interaction between and among states is the basic definition of international relations, a subdiscipline of political science. The discipline is analyzed from a variety of theoretical levels that result in a multiplicity of conclusions. Most scholars agree that the most important participants in the international system are states, that states attempt to attain specific objectives by means of foreign policies and diplomacy, and that underlying the international system is power under-stood as military strength. Power in this context is defined as the capacity of a nation to use its tangible and intangible resources in such a way as to affect the behavior of other nations. The power of a nation is not always dependent on its capabilities. National power is influenced by both psychological and rela-tional factors—how others view a nation and how powerful one nation is in relation to others.

Foreign policy is intended to protect and promote national independence, honor, security, and well-being. It is designed to pursue national interest as it is defined by each nation. Some political commentators believe that the pursuit of power is the central concern of national interest. Others suggest that national inter-est is determined by both power and morality. The goals that nations seek may be divided into those that are competitive or absolute, those that are clearly defined or diffuse, those that are declaratory or action-oriented, and those that are static or dynamic. The nature of national interest is not explained by sin-gle-factor concepts.

Foreign policy is made by individuals who are pressured and influenced by others, by psychological factors, and by specific conditions and are limited by the organizational context in which they operate. There are three types of foreign policy decisions: (1) general foreign policy decisions, expressed in policy statements and direct actions; (2) administrative decisions made by the governmental bureaucracy; and (3) crisis decisions made when one state feels that a specific situation marks a turning point in its relation-ships with one or more other states.

Foreign policy is affected by domestic policy. American domestic policy is guided by the democratic ideology, including revolutionary ideals and the con-cept of freedom. Although Americans do not always act according to this ideology, they are officially com-mitted to it. The problematic aspect of foreign policy is that other nations subscribe to other ideologies, some of which conflict with the American ideology.

The instruments of foreign policy include the United Nations, foreign aid, collective security, the military, and propaganda. The United Nations is not powerful enough because most decisions that affect world peace are made by the governments of the major powers. American aid to nations around the world may have helped contain communism and has definitely helped the economies of various nations. Treaties and security arrangements improve relations between and among nations, but they are never really totally dependable. The United States pro-fesses to want to halt the production of arms, but weapons production and stockpiling have escalated for a long time. Now there are some signs that the arms race is abating. The arms race had spiraled because each power must keep up with the technol-ogy of other powers if possession of nuclear arms is to act as a deterrent to mutual destruction. Propa-ganda—a means of spreading an ideology to con-vince others of its rightness—sometimes leads us to stretch the truth or to direct it at our own citizens. Many government agencies and departments are engaged in propaganda.

Diplomacy is the conduct of international relations by negotiation. Its purpose is the pursuit of national goals without offending any nation. Diplomacy is an old procedure, although it has changed in character in the last century. The power of diplomacy is limited because there are fundamental differences among the major powers and because diplomats in democratic countries are unsure of their roles.

A balance of power was maintained for several hundred years after the creation of nation-states by a system of shifting alliances that ensured that no single state or coalition would become stronger than any other. This multipolar balance of power began to decline at the turn of the nineteenth century, and fol-lowing World War II a bipolar system—with the United States and the Soviet Union as its poles—took its place. Today, the balance of power is again shift-ing, but it is not yet clear in what direction.

Terms to Remember

administrative foreign policy Decisions made by the government bureaucracy.

assured destruction capability A policy designed to deter others from attacking the United States because of

the knowledge that the United States has the means to destroy any nation that attacks it.

containment American foreign policy in the period following World War II, attempting to contain what were perceived as the imperialist goals of the Soviet Union.

crisis foreign policy Urgent decisions made when one state feels that a situation will mark a turning point in its relationship with another state. Crisis decisions are a combination of general and administrative decisions.

détente Foreign policy dependent on peaceful negotiations rather than containment.

diplomacy The conduct of international relations by negotiation.

foreign policy Goals intended to protect and promote national independence, national honor, national security, and national well-being.

general foreign policy Decisions expressed in policy statements and direct actions.

Monroe Doctrine Foreign policy in the guise of a warning to the European states to stay out of Latin America, which was considered to be in the American sphere of influence.

Suggested Readings

Evans, Graham, and Jeffrey Newnham. 1998. *Dictionary of International Relations*. New York: Penguin. An introduction to the terminology of foreign relations and a clear explanation of the increasing jargon of international relations, with many cross-references.

Kershaw, Ian. 1999. *Hitler: 1889–1936*. New York: W. W. Norton. A new biography of the charismatic man who led Europe almost to the brink of total chaos, focusing on the attraction he had for his country.

Kissinger, Henry. 1994. *Diplomacy*. New York: Simon & Schuster. The former secretary of state under President Nixon traces the evolution of diplomacy over the past 300 years.

Lake, Anthony. 2000. *Six Nightmares: Real Threats in a Dangerous World and How America Can Meet Them*. Boston: Little, Brown. An examination of security threats facing the United States in the current century, by a former national security adviser.

Mazower, Mark. 1999. *Dark Continent: Europe's Twentieth Century*. New York: Alfred A. Knopf. Today's Europe presents a picture of peace and abundance, but the first half of the twentieth century showed an altogether different picture of the continent: it was the site of war, destitution, and various attempts to destroy and exterminate whole populations. How to reconcile the incompatible views of the same place, why Europe failed to develop in the pattern of nineteenth-century rationalism, and what a different path its history might have followed, are the subjects of this book.

Ziegler, David W. 1993. *War, Peace, and International Politics*, 6th ed. New York: HarperCollins. Some of the burning issues the author pursues here include: Can the United States continue to be the world's police force? Can we ensure our economic well-being? What is the role of the United States in the new world order?

Web Sites of Interest

http://www.aei.org/default.asp?filter
This is the site of the American Enterprise Institute for Public Policy Research (AEI). It is one of America's oldest (since 1943) and largest think tanks, and it offers much research on domestic and international political issues.

http://www.unicef.org/
One of the most important United Nations agencies, this site often focuses on social changes on a worldwide scale.

http://www.cia.gov/cia/publications/factbook/index.html
Much information on many nations of the world is offered on this site of the Central Intelligence Agency.

http://www.cfr.org
The Council on Foreign Relations offers news and discussions on issues of international import. It also has links to other sites of interest.

http://www.first.sipri.org/
This site is called Facts on International Relations and Security Trends. It offers services to politicians, researchers, and the interested public on issues of international relations. It also offers an integrated database from research institutes around the world.

The Constitution of the United States of America

Preamble

We the people of the United States, in order to form a more perfect Union, establish justice, insure domestic tranquility, provide for the common defense, promote the general welfare, and secure the blessings of liberty to ourselves and our posterity, do ordain and establish this Constitution for the United States of America.

Article I

Section 1. All legislative Powers herein granted shall be vested in a Congress of the United States, which shall consist of a Senate and House of Representatives.

Section 2. The House of Representatives shall be composed of members chosen every second year by the people of the several States, and the electors in each State shall have the qualifications requisite for electors of the most numerous Branch of the State Legislature.

No person shall be a Representative who shall not have attained to the age of twenty-five years, and been seven years a citizen of the United States, and who shall not, when elected, be an inhabitant of that State in which he shall be chosen.

(Representatives and direct taxes shall be apportioned among the several States which may be included within this Union, according to their respective numbers, which shall be determined by adding to the whole number of free persons, including those bound to service for a term of years, and excluding Indians not taxed, three-fifths of all other Persons.) (The previous sentence was superseded by Amendment XIV, section 2.) The actual enumeration shall be made within three years after the first meeting of the Congress of the United States, and within every subsequent term of ten years, in such manner as they shall by law direct. The number of Representatives shall not exceed one for every thirty thousand, but each State shall have at least one Representative; and until such enumeration shall be made, the State of New Hampshire shall be entitled to choose three, Massachusetts eight, Rhode Island and Providence Plantations one, Connecticut five, New York six, New Jersey four, Pennsylvania eight, Delaware one, Maryland six, Virginia ten, North Carolina five, South Carolina five, and Georgia three.

When vacancies happen in the representation from any State, the Executive Authority thereof shall issue writs of election to fill such vacancies.

The House of Representatives shall choose their Speaker and other officers; and shall have the sole power of impeachment.

Section 3. The Senate of the United States shall be composed of two Senators from each State, *(chosen by the Legislature* thereof). *(The preceding five words were superseded by Amendment XVII, section 1.)* for six years; and each Senator shall have one vote.

Immediately after they shall be assembled in consequence of the first election, they shall be divided as equally as may be into three classes. The seats of the Senators of the first class shall be vacated at the expiration of the second year, of the second class at the expiration of the fourth year, and of the third class at the expiration of the sixth year, so that one-third may be chosen every second year; *(and if vacancies happen by resignation, or otherwise, during the recess of the Legislature of any State, the Executive thereof may make temporary appointments until the next meeting of the Legislature, which shall then fill such vacancies.) (The words in parentheses were superseded by Amendment XVII, section 2.)*

No person shall be a Senator who shall not have attained to the age of thirty years, and been nine years a citizen of the United States, and who shall not, when elected, be an inhabitant of that State for which he shall be chosen.

The Vice President of the United States shall be President of the Senate, but shall have no Vote, unless they be equally divided.

The Senate shall choose their other officers, and also a President pro tempore, in the absence of the Vice President, or when he shall exercise the office of President of the United States.

The Senate shall have the sole power to try all impeachments. When sitting for that purpose, they shall be on oath or affirmation. When the President of the United States is tried, the Chief Justice shall preside: and no person shall be convicted without the concurrence of two-thirds of the members present.

Judgment in cases of impeachment shall not extend further than to removal from office, and disqualification to hold and enjoy any office of honor, trust or profit under the United States; but the party convicted shall nevertheless be liable and subject to indict-ment, trial, judgment and punishment, according to law.

Section 4. The times, places and manner of holding elections for Senators and Representatives, shall be prescribed in each State by the Legislature thereof; but the Congress may at any time by law make or alter such regulations, except as to the places of choosing Senators.

The Congress shall assemble at least once in every year, and such meeting shall *(be on the first Monday in December,) (The words in parentheses were superseded by Amendment XX, section 2)* unless they shall by law appoint a different day.

Section 5. Each House shall be the judge of the elections, returns and qualifications of its own members, and a majority of each shall constitute a quorum to do business; but a smaller number may adjourn from day to day, and may be authorized to compel the attendance of absent members, in such manner, and under such penalties as each House may provide.

Each House may determine the rules of its proceedings, punish its members for disorderly behavior, and, with the concurrence of two-thirds, expel a member.

Each House shall keep a journal of its proceedings, and from time to time publish the same, excepting such parts as may in their judgment require secrecy; and the yeas and nays of the members of either House on any question shall, at the desire of one-fifth of those present, be entered on the journal.

Neither House, during the session of Congress, shall, without the consent of the other, adjourn for more than three days, nor to any other place than that in which the two Houses shall be sitting.

Section 6. The Senators and Representatives shall receive a compensation for their services, to be ascertained by law, and paid out of the Treasury of the United States. They shall in all cases, except treason, felony and breach of the peace, be privileged from arrest during their attendance at the session of their respective Houses, and in going to and returning from the same; and for any speech or debate in either House, they shall not be questioned in any other place.

No Senator or Representative shall, during the time for which he was elected, be appointed to any civil office under the authority of the United States, which shall have been created, or the emoluments whereof shall have been encreased during such time; and no person holding any office under the United States, shall be a member of either House during his continuance in office.

Section 7. All bills for raising revenue shall originate in the House of Representatives; but the Senate may propose or concur with amendments as on other bills.

Every bill which shall have passed the House of Representatives and the Senate, shall, before it become a law, be presented to the President of the United States; if he approves he shall sign it, but if not he shall return it, with his objections to that House in which it shall have originated, who shall enter the objections at large on their journal, and proceed to reconsider it. If after such reconsideration two-thirds of that House shall agree to pass the bill, it shall be sent, together with the objections, to the other House, by which it shall likewise be reconsidered, and if approved by two-thirds of that House, it shall become a law. But in all such cases the votes of both Houses shall be determined by yeas and nays, and the names of the persons voting for and against the bill shall be entered on the journal of each House respectively. If any bill shall not be returned by the President within ten days (Sundays excepted) after it shall have been presented to him, the same shall be a law, in like manner as if he had signed it, unless the Congress by their adjournment prevent its return, in which case it shall not be a law.

Every order, resolution, or vote to which the concurrence of the Senate and House of Representatives may be necessary (except on a question of adjournment) shall be presented to the President of the United States; and before the same shall take effect, shall be approved by him, or being disapproved by him, shall be repassed by two-thirds of the Senate and House of Representatives, according to the rules and limitations prescribed in the case of a bill.

Section 8. The Congress shall have power
To lay and collect taxes, duties, imposts and excises, to pay the debts and provide for the common defense and general welfare of the United States; but all duties, imposts and excises shall be uniform throughout the United States;

To borrow money on the credit of the United States;

To regulate commerce with foreign nations, and among the several States, and with the Indian tribes;

To establish a uniform rule of naturalization, and uniform laws on the subject of bankruptcies throughout the United States;

To coin money, regulate the value thereof, and of foreign coin, and fix the standard of weights and measures;

To provide for the punishment of counterfeiting the securities and current coin of the United States;

To establish post-offices and post-roads;

To promote the progress of science and useful arts, by securing for limited times to authors and inventors the exclusive right to their respective writings and discoveries;

To constitute tribunals inferior to the supreme Court;

To define and punish piracies and felonies committed on the high seas, and offenses against the law of nations;

To declare war, grant letters of marque and reprisal, and make rules concerning captures on land and water;

To raise and support armies, but no appropriation of money to that use shall be for a longer term than two years;

To provide and maintain a navy;

To make rules for the government and regulation of the land and naval forces;

To provide for calling forth the militia to execute the laws of the Union, suppress insurrections and repel invasions;

To provide for organizing, arming, and disciplining the militia, and for governing such part of them as may be employed in the service of the United States, reserving to the States respectively, the appointment of the officers, and the authority of training the militia according to the discipline prescribed by Congress;

To exercise exclusive legislation in all cases whatsoever, over such district (not exceeding ten miles square) as may, by cession of particular States, and the acceptance of Congress, become the seat of the Government of the United States, and to exercise like authority over all places purchased by the consent of the Legislature of the State in which the same shall be, for the erection of forts, magazines, arsenals, dockyards, and other needful buildings;—And

To make all laws which shall be necessary and proper for carrying into execution the foregoing powers, and all other powers vested by this Constitution in the Government of the United States, or in any department of officer thereof.

Section 9. The migration or importation of such persons as any of the States now existing shall think proper to admit, shall not be prohibited by the Congress prior to the year one thousand eight hundred and eight, but a tax or duty may be imposed on such importation, not exceeding ten dollars for each person.

The privilege of the writ of habeas corpus shall not be suspended, unless when in cases of rebellion or invasion the public safety may require it.

No bill of attainder or ex post facto law shall be passed.

No capitation, or other direct, tax shall be laid, unless in proportion to the census or enumeration herein before directed to be taken. *(Modified by Amendment XVI.)*

No tax or duty shall be laid on articles exported from any State.

No preference shall be given by any regulation of commerce or revenue to the ports of one State over those of another: nor shall vessels bound to, or from, one State, be obliged to enter, clear, or pay duties in another.

No money shall be drawn from the Treasury, but in consequence of appropriations made by law; and a regular statement and account of the receipts and expenditures of all public money shall be published from time to time.

No title of nobility shall be granted by the United States: and no person holding any office of profit or trust under them, shall, without the consent of the Congress, accept of any present, emolument, office, or title, of any kind whatever, from any king, prince, or foreign state.

Section 10. No State shall enter into any treaty, alliance, or confederation; grant letters of marque and reprisal; coin money; emit bills of credit; make anything but gold and silver coin a tender in payment of debts; pass any bill of attainder, ex post facto law, or law impairing the obligation of contracts, or grant any title of nobility.

No State shall, without the consent of the Congress, lay any imposts or duties on imports or exports, except what may be absolutely necessary for executing its inspection laws: and the net produce of all duties and imposts, laid by any State on imports or exports, shall be for the use of the Treasury of the United States; and all such laws shall be subject to the revision and controul of the Congress.

No State shall, without the consent of Congress, lay any duty of tonnage, keep troops, or ships of war in time of peace, enter into any agreement or compact with another State, or with a foreign power, or engage in war, unless actually invaded, or in such imminent danger as will not admit of delay.

Article II

Section 1. The Executive power shall be vested in a President of the United States of

America. He shall hold his office during the term of four years, and, together with the Vice President, chosen for the same term, be elected, as follows

Each State shall appoint, in such manner as the Legislature thereof may direct, a number of electors, equal to the whole number of Senators and Representatives to which the State may be entitled in the Congress: but no Senator or Representative, or person holding an office of trust or profit under the United States, shall be appointed an elector.

(The Electors shall meet in their respective States, and vote by ballot for two persons, of whom one at least shall not be an inhabitant of the same State with themselves. And they shall make a list of all the persons voted for, and of the number of votes for each; which list they shall sign and certify, and transmit sealed to the seat of the Government of the United States, directed to the President of the Senate. The President of the Senate shall, in the Presence of the Senate and House of Representatives, open all the certificates, and the votes shall then be counted. The person having the greatest number of votes shall be the President, if such number be a majority of the whole number of electors appointed; and if there be more than one who have such majority, and have an equal number of votes, then the House of Representatives shall immediately choose by ballot one of them for President; and if no person have a majority, then from the five highest on the list the said House shall in like manner choose the President. But in choosing the President, the votes shall be taken by States, the representation from each State having one vote; A quorum for this purpose shall consist of a member or members from two-thirds of the States, and a majority of all the States shall be necessary to a choice. In every case, after the choice of the President, the person having the greatest number of votes of the electors shall be the Vice President. But if there should remain two or more who have equal votes, the Senate shall choose from them by ballot the Vice President.) (This clause was superseded by Amendment XII.)

The Congress may determine the time of choosing the electors, and the day on which they shall give their votes; which day shall be the same throughout the United States.

No person except a natural born citizen, or a citizen of the United States, at the time of the adoption of this Constitution, shall be eligible to the office of President; neither shall any person be eligible to that office who shall not have attained to the age of thirty-five years, and been fourteen years a resident within the United States.

In case of the removal of the President from office, or of his death, resignation, or inability to discharge the powers and duties of the said office, the same shall devolve on the Vice President, and the Congress may by law provide for the case of removal, death, resignation or inability, both of the President and Vice President, declaring what officer shall then act as President, and such officer shall act accordingly, until the disability be removed, or a President shall be elected. *(This clause has been modified by Amendments XX and XXV.)*

The President shall, at stated times, receive for his services, a compensation, which shall neither be increased nor diminished during the period for which he shall have been elected, and he shall not receive within that period any other emolument from the United States, or any of them.

Before he enter on the execution of his office, he shall take the following oath or affirmation: "I do solemnly swear (or affirm) that I will faithfully execute the office of President of the United States, and will to the best of my ability, preserve, protect and defend the Constitution of the United States."

Section 2. The President shall be Commander-in-Chief of the Army and Navy of the United States, and of the militia of the several States, when called into the actual service of the United States; he may require the opinion, in writing, of the principal officer in each of the executive departments, upon any subject relating to the duties of their respective offices, and he shall have power to grant reprieves and pardons for offenses against the United States, except in cases of impeachment.

He shall have power, by and with the advice and consent of the Senate, to make treaties, provided two-thirds of the Senators present concur; and he shall nominate, and by and with the advice and consent of the Senate, shall appoint ambassadors, other public ministers and consuls, judges of the Supreme Court, and all other officers of the United States, whose appointments are not herein otherwise provided for, and which shall be established by law; but the Congress may by law vest the appointment of such inferior officers, as they think proper, in the President alone, in the courts of law, or in the heads of departments.

The President shall have power to fill up all vacancies that may happen during the recess of the Senate, by granting commissions, which shall expire at the end of their next session.

Section 3. He shall from time to time give to the Congress information of the state of the Union, and recommend to their consideration such measures as he shall judge necessary and expedient; he may, on extraordinary occasions, convene both Houses, or either of them, and in case of disagreement between them, with respect to the time of adjournment, he may adjourn them to such time as he shall think proper; he shall receive ambassadors and other public ministers; he shall take care that the laws be faithfully executed, and shall commission all the officers of the United States.

Section 4. The President, Vice President and all civil officers of the United States, shall be removed from office on impeachment for, and conviction of, treason, bribery or other high crimes and misdemeanors.

Article III

Section 1. The judicial power of the United States, shall be vested in one Supreme Court, and in such inferior courts as the Congress may from time to time ordain and establish. The judges, both of the Supreme and inferior courts, shall hold their offices during good behavior, and shall at stated times, receive for their services, a compensation, which shall not be diminished during their continuance in office.

Section 2. The judicial power shall extend to all cases, in law and equity, arising under this Constitution, the laws of the United States, and treaties made, or which shall be made, under their authority; to all cases affecting ambassadors, other public ministers and consuls; to all cases of admiralty and maritime jurisdiction; to controversies to which the United States shall be a party; to controversies between two or more States; between a State and citizens of another State; between citizens of different States; between citizens of the same State claiming lands under grants of different States, and between a State, or the citizens thereof, and foreign states, citizens or subjects. *(This section is modified by Amendment XI.)*

In all cases affecting ambassadors, other public ministers and consuls, and those in which a State shall be party, the Supreme Court shall have original jurisdiction. In all the other cases before mentioned, the Supreme Court shall have appellate jurisdiction, both as to law and fact, with such exceptions, and under such regulations as the Congress shall make.

The trial of all crimes, except in cases of impeachment, shall be by jury; and such trial shall be held in the State where the said crimes shall have been committed; but when not committed within any State, the trial shall be at such place or places as the Congress may by law have directed.

Section 3. Treason against the United States, shall consist only in levying war against them, or in adhering to their enemies, giving them aid and comfort. No person shall be convicted of treason unless on the testimony of two witnesses to the same overt act, or on confession in open court.

The Congress shall have power to declare the punishment of treason, but no attainder of treason shall work corruption of blood, or forfeiture except during the life of the person attainted.

Article IV

Section 1. Full faith and credit shall be given in each State to the public acts, records, and judicial proceedings of every other State. And the Congress may by general laws prescribe the manner in which such acts, records and proceedings shall be proved, and the effect thereof.

Section 2. The citizens of each State shall be entitled to all privileges and immunities of citizens in the several States.

A person charged in any State with treason, felony, or other crime, who shall flee from justice, and be found in another State, shall on demand of the Executive authority of the State from which he fled, be delivered up, to be removed to the State having jurisdiction of the crime.

(No person held to service or labor in one State, under the laws thereof, escaping into another, shall in consequence of any law or regulation therein, be discharged from such service or labor, but shall be delivered up on claim of the party to whom such service or labor may be due.) (This clause was superseded by Amendment XIII.)

Section 3. New States may be admitted by the Congress into this Union; but no new State shall be formed or erected within the jurisdiction of any other State; nor any State be formed by the junction of two or more States, or parts of States, without the consent of the Legislatures of the States concerned as well as of the Congress.

The Congress shall have power to dispose of and make all needful rules and regulations respecting the territory or other property belonging to the United States; and

nothing in this Constitution shall be so construed as to prejudice any claims of the United States, or of any particular State.

Section 4. The United States shall guarantee to every State in this Union a Republican form of government, and shall protect each of them against invasion; and on application of the Legislature, or of the Executive (when the Legislature cannot be convened) against domestic violence.

Article V

The Congress, whenever two-thirds of both Houses shall deem it necessary, shall propose amendments to this Constitution, or, on the application of the Legislatures of two-thirds of the several States, shall call a convention for proposing amendments, which, in either case, shall be valid to all intents and purposes, as part of this Constitution, when ratified by the Legislatures of three-fourths of the several States, or by conventions in three-fourths thereof, as the one or the other mode of ratification may be proposed by the Congress; provided that no amendment which may be made prior to the year one thousand eight hundred and eight shall in any manner affect the first and fourth clauses in the Ninth Section of the First Article; and that no State, without its consent, shall be deprived of its equal suffrage in the Senate.

Article VI

All debts contracted and engagements entered into, before the adoption of this Constitution, shall be as valid against the United States under this Constitution, as under the Confederation.

This Constitution, and laws of the United States which shall be made in pursuance thereof; and all treaties made, or which shall be made, under the authority of the United States, shall be the supreme law of the land; and the judges in every State shall be bound thereby, any thing in the Constitution or laws of any State to the contrary not withstanding.

The Senators and Representatives before mentioned, and the members of the several State Legislatures, and all executive and judicial officers, both of the United States and of the several States, shall be bound by oath or affirmation, to support this Constitution; but no religious test shall ever be required as a qualification to any office or public trust under the United States.

Article VII

The ratification of the Conventions of nine States, shall be sufficient for the establishment of this Constitution between the States so ratifying the same.

Done in convention by the unanimous consent of the States present the Seventeenth day of September in the year of our Lord one thousand seven hundred and eighty seven and of the independence of the United States of America the Twelfth. In witness whereof we have hereunto subscribed our names.

George Washington, *President and Deputy from Virginia*;

New Hampshire: John Langdon, Nicholas Gilman;

Massachusetts: Nathaniel Gorham, Rufus King;

Connecticut: Wm. Saml. Johnson, Roger Sherman;

New York: Alexander Hamilton;

New Jersey: Wil. Livingston, David Brearly, Wm. Paterson, Jona. Dayton;

Pennsylvania: B. Franklin, Thomas Mifflin, Robt. Morris, Geo. Clymer, Thos. FitzSimons, Jared Ingersoll, James Wilson, Gouv. Morris;

Delaware: Geo. Read, Gunning Bedford Jun., John Dickinson, Richard Bassett, Jaco. Broom;

Maryland: James McHenry, Daniel of Saint Thomas' Jenifer, Danl. Carroll;

Virginia: John Blair, James Madison Jr.;

North Carolina: Wm. Blount, Rich'd. Dobbs Spaight, High Williamson;

South Carolina: J. Rutledge, Charles Cotesworth Pinckney, Charles Pinckney, Pierce Butler;

Georgia: William Few, Abr. Baldwin;

Attest: William Jackson, *Secretary*.

Amendment I

Congress shall make no law respecting an establishment of religion, or prohibiting the free exercise thereof; or abridging the freedom of speech, or of the press; or the right of the people peaceably to assemble, and to petition the Government for a redress of grievances.

Amendment II

A well-regulated Militia, being necessary to the security of a free State, the right of the people to keep and bear arms shall not be infringed.

Amendment III

No soldier shall, in time of peace be quartered in any house, without the consent of the owner, nor in time of war, but in a manner to be prescribed by law.

Amendment IV

The right of the people to be secure in their persons, houses, papers, and effects, against unreasonable searches and seizures, shall not be violated, and no warrants shall issue, but upon probable cause, supported by oath or affirmation, and particularly describing the place to be searched, and the persons or things to be seized.

Amendment V

No person shall be held to answer for a capital, or otherwise infamous crime, unless on a presentment or indictment of a Grand Jury, except in cases arising in the land or naval forces, or in the militia, when in actual service in time of war or public danger; nor shall any person be subject for the same offense to be twice put in jeopardy of life or limb; nor shall be compelled in any criminal case to be a witness against himself, nor be deprived of life, liberty, or property, without due process of law; nor shall private property be taken for public use, without just compensation.

Amendment VI

In all criminal prosecutions, the accused shall enjoy the right to a speedy and public trial, by an impartial jury of the State and district wherein the crime shall have been committed, which district shall have been previously ascertained by law, and to be informed of the nature and cause of the accusation; to be confronted with the witnesses against him; to have compulsory process for obtaining witnesses in his favor, and to have the assistance of counsel for his defense.

Amendment VII

In suits at common law, where the value in controversy shall exceed twenty dollars, the right of trial by jury shall be preserved, and no fact tried by a jury shall be otherwise reexamined in any court of the United States, than according to the rules of the common law.

Amendment VIII

Excessive bail shall not be required, nor excessive fines imposed, nor cruel and unusual punishments inflicted.

Amendment IX

The enumeration in the Constitution, of certain rights, shall not be construed to deny or disparage others retained by the people.

Amendment X

The powers not delegated to the United States by the Constitution, nor prohibited by it to the States, are reserved to the States respectively, or to the people.

Amendment XI

The Judicial power of the United States shall not be construed to extend to any suit in law or equity, commenced or prosecuted against one of the United States by citizens of another State, or by citizens or subjects of any foreign state.

Amendment XII

The Electors shall meet in their respective States and vote by ballot for President and Vice-President, one of whom, at least, shall not be an inhabitant of the same state with themselves; they shall name in their ballots the person voted for as President, and in distinct ballots the person voted for as Vice-President, and they shall make distinct lists of all persons voted for as President, and of all persons voted for as Vice-President, and of the number of votes for each, which lists they shall sign and certify, and transmit sealed to the seat of the Government of the United States, directed to the President of the Senate;—the President of the Senate shall, in the presence of the Senate and House of Representatives, open all the certificates and the votes shall then be counted;—The person having the greatest number of votes for President, shall be the President, if such number be a majority of the whole number of Electors appointed; and if no person have such majority, then from the persons having the highest numbers not exceeding three on the list of those voted for as President, the House of Representatives shall choose immediately, by ballot, the President. But in choosing the President, the votes shall be taken by States, the representation from each State having one vote; a quorum for this purpose shall consist of a member or members from two-thirds of the States, and a majority of all the States shall be necessary to a choice. (*And if the House of Representatives shall not choose a President whenever the right of choice shall devolve upon them, before the fourth day of March next following, then the Vice-President shall act as President, as in the case of the death or other constitutional disability of the President.) (The words in parentheses were superseded by Amendment XX, section 3.)* The person having the greatest number of votes as Vice-President, shall be the Vice-President, if such number be a majority of the whole number of Electors appointed, and if no person have a majority, then from the two highest numbers on the list, the Senate shall choose the Vice-President; a quorum for the purpose shall consist of two-thirds of the whole number of Senators, and a majority of the whole number shall be necessary to a choice. But no person constitutionally ineligible to the office of President shall be eligible to that of Vice-President of the United States.

Amendment XIII

Section 1. Neither slavery nor involuntary servitude, except as a punishment for crime whereof the party shall have been duly convicted, shall exist within the United States or any place subject to their jurisdiction.

Section 2. Congress shall have power to enforce this article by appropriate legislation.

Amendment XIV

Section 1. All persons born or naturalized in the United States, and subject to the jurisdiction thereof, are citizens of the United States and of the State wherein they reside. No State shall make or enforce any law which shall abridge the privileges or immunities of citizens of the United States; nor shall any State deprive any person of life, liberty, or property, without due process of law; nor deny to any person within its jurisdiction the equal protection of the laws.

Section 2. Representatives shall be apportioned among the several States according to their respective numbers, counting the whole number of persons in each State, excluding Indians not taxed. But when the right to vote at any election for the choice of Electors for President and Vice-President of the United States, Representatives in Congress, the executive and judicial officers of a State, or the members of the Legislature thereof, is denied to any of the male inhabitants of such State, being twenty-one years of age, and, citizens of the United States, or in any way abridged, except for participation in rebellion, or other crime, the basis of representation therein shall be reduced in the proportion which the number of such male citizens shall bear to the whole number of male citizens twenty-one years of age in such State.

Section 3. No person shall be a Senator or Representative in Congress, or elector of President and Vice-President, or hold any office, civil or military, under the United States, or under any State, who, having previously taken an oath, as a member of Congress, or as an officer of the United States, or as a member of any State legislature, or as an executive or judicial officer of any State, to support the Constitution of the United States, shall have engaged in insurrection or rebellion against the same, or given aid or comfort to the enemies thereof. But Congress may by a vote of two-thirds of each House, remove such disability.

Section 4. The validity of the public debt of the United States, authorized by law, including debts incurred for payment of pensions and bounties for services in suppressing insurrection or rebellion, shall not be questioned. But neither the United States nor any State shall assume or pay any debt or obligation incurred in aid of insurrection or rebellion against the United States, or any claim for the loss or emancipation of any slave; but all such debts, obligations and claims, shall be held illegal and void.

Section 5. The Congress shall have power to enforce, by appropriate legislation, the provisions of this article.

Amendment XV

Section 1. The right of citizens of the United States to vote shall not be denied or abridged by the United States or by any State on account of race, color, or previous condition of servitude.

Section 2. The Congress shall have power to enforce this article by appropriate legislation.

Amendment XVI

The Congress shall have power to lay and collect taxes on incomes, from whatever source derived, without apportionment among the several States, and without regard to any census or enumeration.

Amendment XVII

Section 1. The Senate of the United States shall be composed of two Senators from each State, elected by the people thereof, for six years; and each Senator shall have one vote. The electors in each State shall have the qualifications requisite for electors of the most numerous branch of the State legislatures.

Section 2. When vacancies happen in the representation of any State in the Senate, the executive authority of such State shall issue writs of election to fill such vacancies: Provided, That the Legislature of any State may empower the Executive thereof to make temporary appointments until the people fill the vacancies by election as the Legislature may direct.

Section 3. This amendment shall not be so construed as to affect the election or term of any Senator chosen before it becomes valid as part of the Constitution.

Amendment XVIII

Section 1. After one year from the ratification of this article the manufacture, sale, or transportation of intoxicating liquors within, the importation thereof into, or the exportation thereof from the United States and all territory subject to the jurisdiction

thereof for beverage purposes is hereby prohibited.

Section 2. The Congress and the several States shall have concurrent power to enforce this article by appropriate legislation.

Section 3. This article shall be inoperative unless it shall have been ratified as an amendment to the Constitution by the legislatures of the several States, as provided in the Constitution, within seven years from the date of the submission hereof to the States by the Congress.

Amendment XIX

Section 1. The right of citizens of the United States to vote shall not be denied or abridged by the United States or by any State on account of sex.

Section 2. Congress shall have power to enforce this article by appropriate legislation.

Amendment XX

Section 1. The terms of the President and Vice President shall end at noon on the 20th day of January, and the terms of Senators and Representatives at noon on the 3rd day of January, of the years in which such terms would have ended if this article had not been ratified; and the terms of their successors shall then begin.

Section 2. The Congress shall assemble at least once in every year, and such meeting shall begin at noon on the 3d day of January, unless they shall by law appoint a different day.

Section 3. If, at the time fixed for the beginning of the term of the President, the President elect shall have died, the Vice President elect shall become President. If a President shall not have been chosen before the time fixed for the beginning of his term, or if the President elect shall have failed to qualify, then the Vice President elect shall act as President until a President shall have qualified; and the Congress may by law provide for the case wherein neither a President elect nor a Vice President elect shall have qualified, declaring who shall then act as President, or the manner in which one who is to act shall be selected, and such person shall act accordingly until a President or Vice President shall have qualified.

Section 4. The Congress may by law provide for the case of the death of any of the persons from whom the House of Representatives may choose a President whenever the right of choice shall have devolved upon them, and for the case of the death of any of the persons from whom the Senate may choose a Vice President whenever the right of choice shall have devolved upon them.

Section 5. Sections 1 and 2 shall take effect on the 15th day of October following the ratification of this article (Oct., 1933).

Section 6. This article shall be inoperative unless it shall have been ratified as an amendment to the Constitution by the Legislatures of three-fourths of the several States within seven years from the date of its submission.

Amendment XXI

Section 1. The eighteenth article of amendment to the Constitution of the United States is hereby repealed.

Section 2. The transportation or importation into any State, Territory, or Possession of the United States for delivery or use therein of intoxicating liquors, in violation of the laws thereof, is hereby prohibited.

Section 3. This article shall be inoperative unless it shall have been ratified as an amendment to the Constitution by conventions in the several States, as provided in the Constitution, within seven years from the date of the submission hereof to the States by the Congress.

Amendment XXII

Section 1. No person shall be elected to the office of the President more than twice, and no person who has held the office of President, or acted as President, for more than two years of a term to which some other person was elected President shall be elected to the office of the President more than once. But this Article shall not apply to any person holding the office of President when this Article was proposed by the Congress, and shall not prevent any person who may be holding the office of President, or acting as President, during the term within which this Article becomes operative from holding the office of President or acting as President during the remainder of such term.

Section 2. This article shall be inoperative unless it shall have been ratified as an amendment to the Constitution by the Legislatures of three-fourths of the several States within seven years from the date of its submission to the States by the Congress.

Amendment XXIII

Section 1. The District constituting the seat of Government of the United States shall appoint in such manner as the Congress shall direct:

A number of electors of President and Vice President equal to the whole number of Senators and Representatives in Congress to which the District would be entitled if it were a State, but in no event more than the least populous State; they shall be in addition to those appointed by the States, but they shall be considered, for the purposes of the election of President and Vice President, to be electors appointed by a State; and they shall meet in the District and perform such duties as provided by the twelfth article of amendment.

Section 2. The Congress shall have power to enforce this article by appropriate legislation.

Amendment XXIV

Section 1. The right of citizens of the United States to vote in any primary or other election for President or Vice President, for electors for President or Vice President, or for Senator or Representative in Congress, shall not be denied or abridged by the United States or any state by reason of failure to pay any poll tax or other tax.

Section 2. The Congress shall have the power to enforce this article by appropriate legislation.

Amendment XXV

Section 1. In case of the removal of the President from office or his death or resignation, the Vice President shall become President.

Section 2. Whenever there is a vacancy in the office of the Vice President, the President shall nominate a Vice President who shall take the office upon confirmation by a majority vote of both houses of Congress.

Section 3. Whenever the President transmits to the President pro tempore of the Senate and the Speaker of the House of Representatives his written declaration that he is unable to discharge the powers and duties of his office, and until he transmits to them a written declaration to the contrary, such powers and duties shall be discharged by the Vice President as Acting President.

Section 4. Whenever the Vice President and a majority of either the principal officers of the executive departments or of such other body as Congress may by law provide, transmit to the President pro tempore of the Senate and the Speaker of the House of Representatives their written declaration that the President is unable to discharge the powers and duties of his office, the Vice President shall immediately assume the powers and duties of the office as Acting President.

Thereafter, when the President transmits to the President pro tempore of the Senate and the Speaker of the House of Representatives his written declaration that no inability exists, he shall resume the powers and duties of his office unless the Vice President and a majority of either the principal officers of the executive department or of such other body as Congress may by law provide, transmit within four days to the President pro tempore of the Senate and the Speaker of the House of Representatives their written declaration that the President is unable to discharge the powers and duties of his office. Thereupon Congress shall decide the issue, assembling within forty-eight hours for that purpose if not in session. If the Congress, within twenty-one days after receipt of the latter written declaration, or, if Congress is not in session, within twenty-one days after Congress is required to assemble, determines by two-thirds vote of both houses that the President is unable to discharge the powers and duties of his office, the Vice President shall continue to discharge the same as Acting President; otherwise, the President shall resume the powers and duties of his office.

Amendment XXVI

Section 1. The right of citizens of the United States, who are 18 years of age or older, to vote shall not be denied or abridged by the United States or any state on account of age.

Section 2. The Congress shall have the power to enforce this article by appropriate legislation.

Amendment XXVII

Section 1. No law, varying the compensation for the services of the Senators and Representatives shall take effect until an election of Representatives shall have intervened.

References

Abramson, Jill. 1998. "The Business of Persuasion Thrives in Nation's Capital." *The New York Times*, September 29, pp. 1–22,23.

Administration on Aging. "Profile of Older Americans: 2000," p. 10. *http://www.aoa.gov/aoa/stats/profile/ default.htm*. Accessed 8/11/2001.

Administration on Aging. "Life Expectancy by Age Group & Race in Years, 1997." Facts and Figures: Statistics on Minority Aging in the U.S.—The Many Faces of Aging. *http://www.aoa.gov/minorityaccess/ stats.html*. Accessed 8/27/2001.

Adorno, T. W., Else Frenkel-Brunswik, Daniel J. Levinson, and R. Nevitt Sanford. 1950. *The Authoritarian Personality*. New York: Harper & Brothers.

Alba, Richard D. 1990. *Ethnic Identity: The Transformation of White America*. New Haven, CT: Yale University Press.

Albrecht, Stan L. 1980. "Reactions and Adjustments to Divorce: Differences in the Experiences of Males and Females." *Family Relations*, January, pp. 59–68.

Alexander, Herbert E. 1980. *Financing Politics: Money, Elections, and Political Reform*. Washington, DC: Congressional Quarterly Press.

Allman, William. 1994. "A Family Legacy for Lucy." *U.S. News & World Report*, April 11, p. 55.

Allport, Gordon. 1954. *The Nature of Prejudice*. Reading, MA: Addison-Wesley.

American Anthropological Association. 1996. "Statement on Race." *American Association of Physical Anthropologists (AJPA)* 101, pp. 569–570. Now available at *http://www.aaanet.org*.

Americans for Divorce Reform. *http://www. divorcereform@usanet*.

American Religious Identification Survey (ARIS). (2001). Graduate Center Survey of Religion in America. Complements US Census. October.

Andrews, P. 1993. "Fossil Evidence on Human Origins and Dispersal." In Russell L. Ciochon and John G. Fleagle, *The Human Evolution Source Book*. Englewood Cliffs, NJ: Prentice-Hall, pp. 3–11.

Angier, Natalie. 1991. "A Potent Peptide Prompts an Urge to Cuddle." *The New York Times*, January 22, pp. B5, B8.

Angier, Natalie. 1995. "If You Are Really Ancient, You May Be Better off." *The New York Times*. June 11, pp. 1 & 5E.

Angier, Natalie. 1997. "Sexual Identity Not Pliable After All, Report Says." *The New York Times*. March 14, 1997, pp. 1, A10.

Archdeacon, Thomas J. 1983. *Becoming American: An Ethnic History*. New York: Free Press.

Atchley, Robert C. 1982. "Retirement: Leaving the World of Work." *Annals*, 464, November, pp. 120–131.

BBC News. 2007. "'Altruistic' Brain Region Found." *http://newsvote.bbc.uk/mpapps/pagetools/print/news/ bbc.co.uk/1/hi/health/6278907. stm*.

Barlett, Donald L., and James B. Steele. 1998. "Corporate Welfare." *Time*. November 9, pp. 36–40.

Barna Research Group. 2004. "Beliefs: Heaven and Hell." *http://www.barna.org/FlexPage.aspx?Page= Topic&TopicID=3*. Accessed 7/13/04.

Basow, Susan. 1992. *Gender Stereotypes and Roles*, 3rd ed. Belmont, CA: Brooks/Cole.

Baylor Institute for Studies of Religion. 2006. *American Piety in the 21st Century*. September.

Bearak, Barry. 1998. "Caste Hate, and Murder, Outlast India's Reforms." *The New York Times*, September 19, p. A3.

Becker, Howard S. 1963. *Outsiders: Studies in the Sociology of Deviance*. New York: Free Press.

Bell, Daniel. 1987. "The World and the United States in 2013." *Daedalus* 116(3): 1–31.

Bellah, Robert N. 1970. *Beyond Belief*. New York: Harper & Row.

Bellah, Robert N., Richard Madsen, William M. Sullivan, Ann Swidler, and Steven M. Tipton. 1985. *Habits of the Heart*. Los Angeles: University of California Press.

Belsky, Jay, and Laurence D. Steinberg. 1978. "The Effects of Day Care: A Critical Review." *Child Development* 49: 929–949.

Bem, Sandra L. 1981. "Gender Schema Theory: A Cognitive Account of Sex Typing." *Psychological Review* 88: 354–364.

Bem, Sandra L. 1983. "Gender Schema Theory and Its Implications for Child Development." *Signs* 8: 598–616.

Bem, Sandra L. 1985. "Androgyny and Gender Schema Theory: A Conceptual and Empirical Integration." In T. B. Sonderegger, ed., *Nebraska Symposium on Motivations: Psychology of Gender*. Lincoln: University of Nebraska Press.

Besharov, Douglas, and Peter Germanis. 2001. *Rethinking WIC: An Evaluation of the Women, Infants, and Children Program*. Washington, DC: AEI Press.

Bierman, Jeffrey A. 1990. "The Effect of Television Sports Media on Black Male Youth." *Sociological Inquiry* 60 (Fall): 413, 427.

Blake, Judith, and Kingsley Davis. 1964. "Norms, Values, and Sanctions." In Robert E. L. Faris, ed., *Handbook of Modern Sociology*. Chicago: Rand McNally, p. 456.

Blau, Peter M., and Otis Dudley Duncan. 1967. *The American Occupational Structure*. New York: Wiley.

Blau, Peter M., and Marshall W. Meyer. 1971. *Bureaucracy in Modern Society*. New York: Random House.

Blood, Robert O., Jr., and Donald M. Wolfe. 1960. *Husbands and Wives: The Dynamics of Married Living*. Glencoe, IL: Free Press.

Blumer, Herbert. (1946) 1969. "Collective Behavior." In Alfred McClung Lee, ed., *Principles of Sociology*. New York: Harper & Row.

Blumer, Herbert. 1951. "Social Movements." In Alfred McClung Lee, ed., *Principles of Sociology*. New York: Barnes & Noble.

Blumstein, P. W., and Pepper Schwartz. 1977. "Bisexuality: Some Social Psychological Issues. *Journal of Social Issues* 33(2): pp. 30–45.

Bonner, Raymond, and Ford Fassenden. 2000. "Absence of Executions: A Special Report. States With No Death Penalty Share Lower Homicide Rates." *The New York Times*, September 22, p. A1.

Boswell, John. 1989. *The Kindness of Strangers*. New York: Pantheon.

Bowles, Samuel, and Herbert Gintis. 1976. *Schooling in Capitalist America: Educational Reform and the Contradictions of Economic Life*. New York: Basic Books.

Bradsher, Keith. 1995a. "America's Opportunity Gap." *The New York Times*, June 4, Section 4, p. 4.

Bradsher, Keith. 1995b. "Low Ranking for Poor American Children." *The New York Times*, August 14, p. A7.

Bramlett, Matthew D., and William D. Mosher. 2002. "Cohabitation, Marriage, Divorce and Remarriage in the United States." National Center for Health Statistics. *Vital and Health Statistics* 23(22): 23.

Branigin, William. 1992. "North vs. South at the U.S." *The Washington Post National Weekly Edition*, December 14–20, pp. 10–11.

Broderick, Carlfried B. 1993. *Understanding Family Process: Basics of Family Systems Theory*. Thousand Oaks, CA: Sage.

Brody, Jane E. 1983. "Divorce's Stress Exacts Long Term Health Toll." *The New York Times*, December 13, p. C1.

Bronner, Ethan. 1998. "Winds of Change Rustle University of Chicago." *The New York Times*, December 28, pp. 1, 18.

Browne, Malcolm W. 1992. "2 Skulls in China: Evidence of Early Humans Outside of Africa?" *The New York Times*, June 4, p. A7.

Bumpass, Larry, and James A. Sweet. 1995. "The Changing Character of Stepfamilies: Implications of Cohabitations and Nonmarital Childbearing." *Demography* 32(3): 425–436.

Bumpass, Larry, and Hsien-Hen Lu. 2000. "Trends in Cohabitation and Implications for Children's Family Contexts." Unpublished manuscript, Center for Demography, University of Wisconsin, Madison, WI.

Bureau of Economic Analysis. 2006. *http:// www.bea.gov/national/xls/gdplev.xls*.

Bureau of Justice Statistics/Capital Punishment/ Summary findings, 2004. *http://www.ojp.usdoj.gov/bjs/cp.htm*.

Bureau of Justice Statistics Publications. 2005. *Family Violence*. NCJ207846. June.

Bureau of Labor Statistics. 2006. *http://stats.bls.gov/cpsaatab.htm*.

Butterfield, Fox. 2004. "With Longer Sentences, Cost of Fighting Crime Is Higher." *The New York Times*, May 3, p. A18.

Cairncross, Frances. 2004. "Forever Young." *The Economist*, March 27, pp. 3–4.

Caplow, Theodore. 1968. *Two Against One: Coalitions in Triads*. Englewood Cliffs, NJ: Prentice-Hall.

Carey, Benedict. 2007. "Do You Believe in Magic?" *The New York Times*, January 23, pp. D1, D6.

Carroll, Sean B. 2005. *Endless Forms Most Beautiful*. New York: Norton.

Centers for Disease Control and Prevention (CDC). 2007. "A Glance at the HIV/AIDS Epidemic" Revised June 2007. *http://www.cdc.gov/hiv/resources/factsheet/ataglance.htm#3*.

Center on Budget and Policy Priorities. 2006. "The Number of Uninsured Americans Is at an All-Time High." August 29. *http://www.cbpp.org/8-29-06health.htm*.

Chen, M. Keith. 2007. "Prison Conditions: Gently Does It." *The Economist*, July 26.

Cherlin, Andrew J. 1981. *Marriage, Divorce, Remarriage*. Boston: Harvard University Press.

Cherlin, Andrew J. 1987. "Don't Fear the 'Depopulation' Bomb." *Christian Science Monitor*, January 5, p. 16.

Chodorow, Nancy. 1978. *The Reproduction of Mothering*. Berkeley, CA: University of California Press.

CIA. 2007. *http://www.cia.gov/library/publications/the-world-factbook*. Accessed 10/20/2007.

Cloward, Richard A., and Lloyd E. Ohlin. 1960. *Delinquency and Opportunity: A Theory of Delinquent Gangs*. New York: Free Press.

Cohen, Albert K. 1955. *Delinquent Boys: The Culture of the Gang*. New York: Free Press.

Cohen, Patricia. 2004. "Forget Lonely. Life Is Healthy at the Top." *The New York Times*, May 15, p. A17.

Cohn, Werner. 1958. "The Politics of American Jews." In Marshall Sklare, ed., *The Jews: Social Patterns of an American Group*. Glencoe, IL: Free Press.

Coleman, James S. 1966. *Equality of Educational Opportunity*. Washington, DC: U.S. Government Printing Office.

Coleman, James S. 1981. *High School Achievement: Public, Catholic, and Private Schools Compared*. New York: Basic Books.

College Board Research, Educational Testing Service, 2001. *http://www.etc.org/research/newpubs.htm*. Accessed 8/15/04.

Collins, Randall. 1979. *The Credential Society: An Historical Sociology of Education and Stratification*. New York: Academic Press.

Conant, Jennet, and Pat Wingert. 1987. "You'd Better Sit Down, Kids." *Newsweek*, August 24, p. 58.

Cooley, Charles Horton. 1909/1910. *Social Organization, A Study of the Larger Mind*. New York: Scribner's.

Cooley, Charles Horton. (1909) 1964. *Human Nature and the Social Order*. New York: Schocken, p. 152.

Cowley, Geoffrey. 1998. "Wilson's World." *Newsweek*, June 22, pp. 59–61.

CNNMoney.com. 2006. "CEO Paycheck: $24,000 a Day." June 21 (by Jeanne Sahadi, CNNMoney senior writer).

Creveld, Martin van. 2007. *The Changing Face of War: Lessons of Combat from the Marne to Iraq*. New York: Ballantine Books.

Crossette, Barbara. 1992. "Population Policy in Asia is Faulted." *The New York Times*, September 16, p. A7.

Crossette, Barbara. 2001. "Against a Trend, U.S. Population Will Bloom, U.N. Says." *The New York Times*, February 28, pp. A1, A5.

Dahl, Robert A. 1956. *A Preface to Democratic Theory*. Chicago: University of Chicago Press.

Dahl, Robert A. 1967. *Pluralist Democracy in the United States*. Chicago: Rand McNally, p. 24.

Dahl, Robert A., and Charles E. Lindblom. 1976. *Politics, Economics, and Welfare*. Chicago: University of Chicago Press.

Davidson, James D. 2004. "American Catholics and American Catholicism: An Inventory of Facts, Trends and Influences: *http://www.be.edu/bc.org/research/rap/church-in-america/davidson.html*.

Davis, Kingsley. 1947. *Final Note on a Case of Extreme Isolation*. New York: John Wiley.

Davis, Kingsley, and Wilbert Moore. 1945. "Some Principles of Stratification." *American Sociological Review* 10: 242–249.

DeWitt, Karen. 1994. "Wave of Suburban Growth Is Being Fed by Minorities." *The New York Times*, August 15, pp. 1, 12.

Domestic Violence Statistics. American Bar Association, Commission on Domestic Violence. Survey of Recent Statistics. *http://www.abanet.org/domviol/statistics.html*. Accessed 10/20/2007.

Donnerstein, Ed, Ron Slaby, and Leonard Eron. 1993. "The Mass Media and Youth Aggression." *Violence and Youth*. Washington, DC: American Psychology Association.

Dowd, James J. 1980a. "Exchange Rates and Old People." *Journal of Gerontology* 35: 596–602.

Dowd, James J. 1980b. *Stratification Among the Aged*. Monterey, CA: Brooks/Cole.

Dreifus, Claudia. 1998. "Tracing Evolution of Cosmos from Its Simplest Elements." *The New York Times*, April 28, p. B15.

Dunn, Judy, and Robert Plomin. 1990. *Separate Lives: Why Siblings Are So Different*. New York: Basic Books.

Durkheim, Emile. (1897) 1951, 1966. *Le suicide: Etude de Sociologie*. J. A. Spaulding and George Simpson, transl. New York: Free Press.

Durkheim, Emile. (1912) 1947. *The Elementary Forms of Religious Life*. Reprinted Edition. New York: Free Press.

Dye, Thomas R., and L. Harmon Zeigler. 1984. *The Irony of Democracy: An Uncommon Introduction to American Politics*. Monterey, CA: Brooks/Cole.

Dye, Thomas R., and L. Harmon Zeigler. 1993. *The Irony of Democracy: An Uncommon Introduction to American Politics*, 9th ed. Belmont, CA: Wadsworth.

Eakin, Emily. 2001. "Tilling History with Biology's Tools." *The New York Times*, February 10, pp. A15–17.

Ebenstein, William. 1973. *Today's Isms*, 7th ed. Englewood Cliffs, NJ: Prentice-Hall.

Eckholm, Erik. 2007. "Childhood Poverty Is Found to Portend High Adult Costs." *The New York Times*, January 25, p. A15.

Eckholm, Erik. 2007. "In Turnabout, Infant Deaths Climb in South." *The New York Times*, April 22, pp. 1–20.

Economist,The. 2004. "Forever Young: A Survey of Retirement." March 27, pp. 3–18.

Edmonston, Barry, and Thomas M. Guterbock. 1984. "Is Suburbanization Slowing Down? Recent Trends in Population Deconcentration in U.S. Metropolitan Areas." *Social Forces* 62(4): 9005–9025.

Edsall, Thomas B. 2007. "Party Boy: Why the GOP's Future Belongs to Rudy." *The New Republic*, May 21, pp. 26–32.

Egan, Timothy. 1998. "From Adolescent Angst to Shooting Up Schools." *The New York Times*, June 14, pp. 1, 20.

Ehrenreich, Barbara. 1989. *Fear of Falling: The Inner Life of the Middle Class*. New York: Pantheon.

Elkind, David. 1981. *The Hurried Child: Growing Up Too Fast Too Soon*. Reading, MA: Addison-Wesley.

Engels, Frederick. 1902 (First published 1884). *The Origin of the Family, Private Property and the State*. Ernest Untermann, transl. Chicago: C. H. Kerr & Company.

Ericksen, Julia A. 1999. *Kiss and Tell: Surveying Sex in the Twentieth Century*. Cambridge, MA: Harvard University Press.

Erikson, Erik H. 1963. *Childhood and Society*. New York: W. W. Norton.

Erikson, Erik H. 1968. *Identity, Youth and Crisis*. New York: W. W. Norton.

Erikson, Kai T. 1964. "Notes on the Sociology of Deviance." In Howard Becker, ed. *The Other Side: Perspectives on Deviance*, New York: Free Press.

Etzioni, Amitai. 1975. *A Comparative Analysis of Complex Organizations*, rev. ed. New York: Free Press.

Ewing, Charles P. 1995. *Kids Who Kill*. New York: Avon.

Fearon, James D., and David D. Laitin. 2002. "Ethnicity, Insurgency and Civil War." *American Political Science Review* 97(1), 75–90.

Ferguson, Thomas, and Joel Rogers. 1986. *Right Turn: The Decline of the Democrats and the Future of American Politics*. New York: Hill and Wang.

Fisher, Claude. 1984. *The Urban Experience*. New York: Harcourt Brace Jovanovich.

Flanigan, William H., and Nancy Zingale. 1998. *Political Behavior of the American Electorate*, 9th ed. Washington, DC: Congressional Quarterly Press.

Ford, Clelland S., and Frank A. Beach. 1951. *Patterns of Sexual Behavior*. New York: Harper & Row.

Franklin, Clyde W. II. 1988. *Men and Society*. Chicago: Nelson Hall.

Fratkin, Elliot. 1997. *Aarial Pastoralists of Kenya*. New York: Prentice Hall.

Frazier, Franklin E. 1966. *The Negro Family in the United States*. Chicago: University of Chicago Press.

Friedrich, Carl J., and Zbigniew Brzezinski. 1966. *Totalitarian Dictatorship and Autocracy*. New York: Praeger.

Friedrich, Carl J., Michael Curtis, and Benjamin R. Barber. 1969. *Totalitarianism in Perspective: Three Views*. New York: Praeger.

Frieze, I., and S. J. Ramsey. 1976. "Nonverbal Maintenance of Traditional Sex Roles." *Journal of Social Issues* 32: 133–141.

Frieze, I., J. Parsons, P. Johnson, D. N. Ruble, and G. Zellman, eds. 1978. *Women and Sex Roles*. New York: Norton.

Fukuyama, Francis. 1999. *The Great Disruption: Human Nature and the Reconstitution of Social Orders*. New York: Free Press.

Gallup/CNN/USA Today Poll, September 8–10, 2000. *The New York Times*, October 29, p. 5.

Gallup Poll, May and October 2003.

Gallup Poll, 2006. "Estimating Americans' Worship Behavior." January 3.

Gans, Herbert J. (1962) 1982. *The Urban Villagers: Group and Class in the Life of Italian-Americans*. New York: Free Press.

Gee, Henry. 2002. "Touma'A: Face of the Deep." *Nature*, 115, pp. 195–199.

Gelles, Richard J., Murray A. Straus, and Suzanne K. Steinmetz. 2006. *Behind Closed Doors: Violence in the American Family*. New Brunswick, NJ: Transaction Publishers.

Gerth, H. H., and C. Wright Mills, eds. 1946. *From Max Weber: Essays in Sociology*. New York: Oxford University.

Gilligan, Carol. 1982. *In a Different Voice: Psychological Theory and Women's Development*. Cambridge, MA: Harvard University Press.

Giniger, Seymour, Angelo Dispenzieri, and Joseph Eisenberg. 1983. "Age, Experience, and Performance on Speed and Skill Jobs in an Applied Setting." *Journal of Applied Psychology* 68: 469–475.

Gladwell, Malcolm. 1998. "Do Parents Matter?" *The New Yorker*, August 17, pp. 54–64.

Gladwell, Malcolm. 2006. "Here's Why." *The New Yorker*, April 10, p. 80–82.

Glaeser, Edward L. 2005. "Inequality." Harvard Institute for Economic Research. July.

Gleick, Elizabeth. 1995. "Rich Justice, Poor Justice." *Time*, June 19, p. 42.

Glock, Charles Y., and Rodney Stark. 1965. *Religion and Society in Tension*. Chicago: Rand McNally.

Glueck, Sheldon, and Eleanor Glueck. 1956. *Physique and Delinquency*. New York: Harper & Row.

Glushko, Bob, and Anno Saxenian. 2006. "The Information and Services Economy." University of California at Berkeley, School of Information. Fall.

Goffman, Erving. 1961. *Asylums: Essays on the Social Situation of Mental Patients and Other Inmates*. Garden City, NY: Anchor.

Goldberg Steven. 1977. *The Inevitability of Patriarchy*. London: Temple Smith.

Goldberg, Steven. 1989. "The Theory of Patriarchy: A Final Summation." *International Journal of Sociology and Social Policy* 9(1): 16–18.

Goldman, Ari L. 1991. "Portrait of Religion in U.S. Holds Dozens of Surprises." *The New York Times*, April 10, pp. 1, A11.

Goleman, Daniel. 1989. "Sad Legacy of Abuse." *The New York Times*, January 24, pp. A1, A22.

Goleman, Daniel. 1992. "New Storm Brews on Whether Crime Has Roots in Genes." *The New York Times*, September 15, B5, B8.

Goleman, Daniel. 2006. *Social Intelligence*. New York: Bantam.

Goode, William J. 1963. *World Revolution and Family Patterns*. New York: Free Press.

Goode, E. 1990. *Deviant Behavior*, 3rd ed. Upper Saddle River, NJ: Prentice-Hall.

Goode, Erica. 2001. "With Fears Fading, More Gays Spurn Old Preventive Message." *The New York Times*, August 19, pp. 1, 30.

Goodheart, Adam. 2004. "Change of Heart." *AARP*, May/June, pp. 37–41, 75.

Goodman, Walter, 1992. "Seeking Traces of the First Americans." *The New York Times*, October 20, p. B4.

Gottman, J. M. 1978. "Megalopolitan Systems Around the World." In L. S. Bourne and J. W. Simmonds, eds., *Systems of Cities: Readings on Structure, Growth, and Policy*. New York: Oxford University Press.

Graham, John. 2004. "How Long Do Stars Usually Live?" *Scientific American*, March 29. www.sciam.com/article. Accessed 6/5/04.

Greenfield, Liah. 1992. *Nationalism: Five Roads to Modernity*. Cambridge, MA: Harvard University Press.

Gregor, A. James. 1968. *Contemporary Radical Ideologies*. New York: Random House.

Grusky, David B., and Robert M. Hauser. 1984. "Comparative Social Mobility Revisited: Models of Convergence and Divergence in 16 Countries." *American Sociological Review*, 49: 19–38.

Gutman, Herbert G. 1976. *The Black Family in Slavery and Freedom, 1750–1925*. New York: Pantheon Books.

Hall, Trish. 1991. "Breaking Up Is Becoming Harder to Do." *The New York Times*, March 14, pp. B1–B4.

Harlow, Harry. 1966. "Learning to Love." *American Scientist* 54: 224–272.

Harris, Fred. 1986. *America's Democracy: The Ideal and the Reality*, 3rd ed. Glenview, IL: Scott, Foresman.

Harris, Judith Rich. 1999. *The Nurture Assumption*. New York: Touchstone.

Harris Poll #59, October 15, 2003. Taylor, Humphrey, "While Most Americans Believe in God, Only 36% Attend a Religious Service Once a Month or More Often." *http://www.harrisinteractive.com/harrispoll/index*. Accessed 8/12/04.

Harrison, Algea O., et al. 1990. "Family Ecologies of Ethnic Minority Children." *Child Development* 61: 347–362

Harvey, David. 1973. *Social Justice and the City*. Baltimore, MD: Johns Hopkins University Press.

Harvey, David. 1984. *The Limits to Capital*. Chicago: University of Chicago Press.

Harvey, David. 1985. *Consciousness and the Urban Experience*. Baltimore, MD: Johns Hopkins University Press.

Hauser, Robert M., and David L. Featherman. 1977. *The Process of Stratification: Trends and Analysis*. New York: Academic Press.

Haviland, William A. 1995. *Anthropology*, 7th ed. New York: Harcourt Brace College Publishers.

Hayden, Thomas. 2002. "A Theory Evolves." *U.S. News & World Report*. July 29, pp. 43–50.

Hayden, Thomas. 2004. "Jawboning Evolution." *U.S. News & World Report*, April 5, p. 72.

Headland, Thomas, and Lawrence Reid. 1989. "Hunter Gatherers and Their Neighbors from Prehistory to the Present." *Current Anthropology* 30: 43–66.

Herberg, Will. 1960. *Protestant, Catholic, Jew*. Garden City, NY: Doubleday (Anchor Books).

Herbert, Bob. 1999. "Addicted to Violence." *The New York Times*, April 22, p. A31.

Herbert, Wray. 1982. "Sources of Temperament: Bashful at Birth?" *Science News*, January 16, p. 36.

Hertz, Tom. 2006. "Understanding Mobility in America." *Center for American Progress*, April 26.

Hetherington, E. Mavis and John Kelly. 2002. *For Better or for Worse: Divorce Reconsidered*. New York: Norton.

Hite, Shere. 1981. *The Hite Report on Male Sexuality*. New York: Knopf.

Hofstadter, Richard. 1954. *The American Political Tradition*. New York: Vintage.

Holzer, Harry J., Peter Edelman, and Paul Offner. 2006. *Reconnecting Disadvantaged Young Men*. Washington, DC. *http://www.urban.org/url.cfm?ID=900956*.

Hoover, Kenneth, and Todd Donovan. 1995. *The Elements of Social Scientific Thinking*, 6th ed. New York: St. Martin's Press.

Horn, Jack C., and Jeff Meer. 1987. "The Vintage Years." *Psychology Today*, 21(5): 76–90.

Horn, Joseph M., Robert Plomin, and Ray Rosenman. 1976. "Heritability of Personality Traits in Adult Male Twins." *Behavior Genetics*, January, pp. 17–30.

Hoyenga, K. B., and K. Hoyenga. 1979. *The Question of Sex Differences: Psychological, Cultural, and Biological Issues*. Boston: Little, Brown.

Human Development Report 2006. "Beyond Scarcity: Power, Poverty, and the Global Water Crisis." United Nations Development Programme.

Hunt, Morton, and Bernice Hunt. 1980. "Another World, Another Life" In *Family in Transition*, Arlene Skolnick and Jerome H. Skolnick, eds. Boston: Little, Brown.

Hurley, Dan. 2004. "On Crime as Science (A Neighbor at a Time)." *The New York Times*, January 6, pp. D1, D2.

Irving, Carl. 1990. "Sociologist Refutes Midlife Crisis." *The (Cleveland) Plain Dealer*, October 25, p. 11E.

Jacquet, Constant H., and Alice M. Jones. 1991. *Yearbook of American and Canadian Churches*. Nashville, TN: Abingdon Press.

Jencks, Christopher, Marshall Smith, Henry Acland, Mary Jo Bane, David Cohen, Herbert Gintis, Barbara Heyns, and Stephan Michelson. 1972. *Inequality*. New York: Basic Books.

Jencks, Christopher. 1979. *Who Gets Ahead? The Determinants of Economic Success in America*. New York: Basic Books.

Jencks, Christopher. 1994. *Homeless*. Cambridge, MA: Harvard University Press.

Jolly, Clifford J., and Randall White. 1995. *Physical Anthropology and Archaelogy*, 5th ed. New York: McGraw-Hill.

Juel-Nielson, Neils. 1980. *Individual and Environment: Monozygotic Twins Reared Apart*. New York: International Universities Press.

Kahn, Joseph. 2000. "Globalism Unites a Many-Striped Multitude of Foes." *The New York Times*, April 15, p. A5.

Kaiser, Charles, 1997. *The Gay Metropolis*. Boston: Houghton Mifflin, Introduction.

Keller, Helen. 1903. *The Story of My Life*. New York: Doubleday, Page & Co., p. 24.

Keller, Susanne. 1963. *Beyond the Ruling Class*. New York: Random House.

Kennedy, Ruby Jo Reeves. 1944. "Single or Triple Melting Pot? Intermarriage Trends in New Haven, 1870–1940." *American Journal of Sociology* 49: 331–339.

Kerckhoff, Alan C., Richard T. Campbell, and Idee Winfield-Laird. 1985. "Social Mobility in Great Britain and the United States." *American Journal of Sociology* 91: 281–308.

Killian, Lewis M. 1964. "Social Movements." In Robert E. Faris, ed., *Handbook of Modern Sociology*. Chicago: Rand McNally.

Kinsey, Alfred C., Wardell B. Pomeroy, and Charles E. Martin. 1948. *Sexual Behavior in the Human Male*. Philadelphia: Saunders.

Kinsey, Alfred C., Wardell Pomeroy, Charles E. Martin, and Paul Gebhard. 1953. *Sexual Behavior in the Human Female*. Philadelphia: Saunders.

Kinsley, Michael. 1991. "TRB." *The New Republic*, January 21, pp. 4, 41.

Knudson, M. 1990. "Hear America Swinging?" *Baltimore Sun*, February 19, pp. 1A, 7A.

Kohlberg, Lawrence. 1963. "The Development of Children's Orientation Toward a Moral Order: I. Sequence in the Development of Moral Thought." *Human Development*. 6: 11–33.

Kohlberg, Lawrence. 1969. "Stage and Sequence: The Cognitive-Developmental Approach to Socialization." In D. A. Gloslin, ed., *Handbook of Socialization Theory and Research*. Chicago: Rand McNally, pp. 347–480.

Kohlberg, Lawrence. 1981. *The Philosophy of Moral Development: Moral Stages and the Idea of Justice*. New York, Harper & Row.

Kohn, Melvin. 1977. *Class and Conformity: A Study in Values*, 2nd ed. Homewood, IL: Dorsey Press.

Kolata, Gina. 1998. "Scientists Brace for Changes in Path of Human Evolution." *The New York Times*, March 21, pp. 1–12.

Konner, Melvin. 1988. "The Aggressors." *The New York Times Magazine*, August 14, pp. 33–34.

Kornblum, William, and. T. M. Williams. 1978. "Life-Style, Leisure, and Community Life," in D. Steet and Associates, eds., *Handbook of Contemporary Urban Life*. San Francisco: Jossey-Bass.

Kosmin, B., Mayer Egon, & A. Keyser. 2001. *American Religious Identification Survey*. New York: The Graduate Center of the City University of New York. (October).

Kozma, Anna-Liza. 1997. "Gender Foretells Arguments' Results: Women Lose." *The (Cleveland) Plain Dealer* (originally from the *Chicago Tribune*), March 4, p. 4E.

Kristof, Nicholas. 1991. "China. The End of the Golden Road." *The New York Times Magazine*, December 1, pp. 53, 87.

Krugman, Paul. 2006. "Wages, Wealth and Politics." *The New York Times*, August 18, p. A19.

Krugman, Paul. 2007. "Gilded Once More." *The New York Times*, April 27, p. 20.

Lane, Robert E. 1962. *Political Ideology: Why the American Common Man Believes What He Does*. New York: Free Press.

Lasswell, Harold, and Abraham Kaplan. 1950. *Power and Society*. New Haven: Yale University Press.

Laumann, Edward O., John H. Gagnon, Robert T. Michael, and Stuart Michaels. 1994. *The Social Organization of Sexuality: Sexual Practices in the United States*. Chicago: University of Chicago Press.

Lehmann-Haupt, Christopher. 1996. "How Did Man Get So Bad? By Looking to the Apes." *The New York Times*, October 10, p. B6.

Lemonick, Michael D. 1994. "One Less Missing Link." *Time*. October 3, pp. 68–69.

Lenski, Gerhard. 1966. *Power and Privilege: A Theory of Social Stratification*. New York: McGraw-Hill.

Lenski, Gerhard. 1970, 1987. *Human Societies*. New York: McGraw-Hill.

Leonhardt, David. 2001. "For the Boss, Happy Days Are Still Here." *The New York Times*, April 1, Section 3, pp. 1, 8.

Levi-Strauss, Claude. 1971. "The Family." In *Family in Transition*, Arlene S. Skolnick and Jerome H. Skolnick, eds. Boston: Little, Brown.

Levine, Richard. 1991. "Economic Troubles and Service Cuts Reduce the Lure of New York City." *The New York Times*, April 1, p. A9.

Levy, Frank, and Richard J. Murnane. 2004. *The New Division of Labor*. Princeton, NJ: Princeton University Press.

Lewin, Tamar. 2001. "Study Says Little Has Changed in Views on Working Mothers." *The New York Times*, September 10, p. A20.

Lewin, Tamar. 2006. "At Colleges, Women Are Leaving Men in the Dust." *The New York Times*, July 9, pp. 1, 19.

Liazos, Alexander. 1972. "The Poverty of the Sociology of Deviance: Nuts, Sluts, and Perverts." *Social Problems*, 20: 103–120.

Linden, Eugene. 1992. "Too Many People." *Time*, Fall (Special Issue), p. 64.

Lino, Mark. 1999. "Expenditures on Children by Families: 1998 Annual Report." Washington, DC: U.S. Department of Agriculture, Center for Nutrition Policy and Promotion.

Lipset, Seymour Martin. 1963. *Political Man*. Garden City, NY: Doubleday.

Lipset, Seymour Martin. 1976. "Equality and Inequality." In Robert K. Merton and Robert Nisbet, eds. *Contemporary Social Problems*, 4th ed. New York: Harcourt Brace Jovanovich.

Lipset, Seymour Martin, and Reinhard Bendix. 1959. *Social Mobility in Industrial Society*. Berkeley: University of California Press.

Lofland, John. 1981. "Collective Behavior: The Elementary Forms." In N. Rosenberg and R. H. Turner, eds., *Social Psychology: Sociological Perspectives*. New York: Basic.

Lofland, John. 1985. *Protest: Studies of Collective Behavior and Social Movements*. New Brunswick, NJ: Transaction.

Lofland, Lyn. 1973. *A World of Strangers*. New York: Basic.

Lombroso, Cesare. 1911. *Crime: Its Causes and Remedies*. Boston: Little, Brown.

Lowi, Theodore J. 1979. *The End of Liberalism: Ideology, Policy and the Crisis of Public Authority*, 2nd ed. New York: Norton.

Luepnitz, Deborah. 1979. "Which Aspects of Divorce Affect Children?" *The Family Coordinator* 28 (January), pp. 79–85.

Lyall, Sarah. 2004. "Britain Cracks Down on Nasties Like the 'Neighbor from Hell.'" *The New York Times*. April 2, pp. 1, A6.

MacIver, Robert. 1947. *The Web of Government*. New York: Macmillan.

Mannheim, Karl. 1936. *Ideology and Utopia*. New York: Harcourt Brace.

Marquardt, Elizabeth. 2006. *Between Two Worlds: The Inner Lives of Children of Divorce*. New York: Three Rivers Press.

Martin, Steven. 2006. "Trends in Marital Dissolution by Women's Education in the United States." *Demographic Research*, 13 December. *http://www. demographicresearch.org*. Accessed 7/11/07.

Marx, Gary T. 1967. *Protest and Prejudice*. New York: Harper & Row.

Marx, Karl, and Friedrich Engels. 1964. *On Religion*. New York: Schocken Books.

Maslow, Abraham. 1968. *Toward a Psychology of Being*, 2nd ed. New York: Van Nostrand.

Mauss, Armand L. 1975. *Social Problems of Social Movements*. Philadelphia: Lippincott.

McCready, William C., and Andrew M. Greeley. 1976. *The Ultimate Values of the American Population*. Beverly Hills, CA: Sage Publications.

McElvaine, Robert S. 2000. *Eve's Seed: Biology, the Sexes and the Course of History*. New York: McGraw-Hill.

McGoldrick, Monica, and Betty Carter, eds. 1988. *The Changing Family Life Cycle: A Framework for Family Therapy*. New York: Gardner Press.

McGuire, Meredith B. 1987. *Religion: The Social Context*, 2nd ed. Belmont, CA: Wadsworth.

McNeil, Donald G. Jr. 2004. "When Real Food Isn't an Option." *The New York Times*, May 23, Section 4, pp. 1, 12.

McPherson, Miller, Lynn Smith-Lovin, and Matthew E. Brashears, 2006. "Social Isolation in America: Changes in Core Discussion Networks Over Two Decades." *American Sociological Review*, 71(3), June, pp. 353–374.

McWhorter, John. 2001. "Against Reparations." *The New Republic*, July 23, pp. 32–38.

Mead, Margaret. 1935. *Sex and Temperament in Three Primitive Societies*. Magnolia, MA: Peter Smith.

Mead, Margaret. (1949) 1970. *Male and Female*. London: Penguin Books.

Mehrabian, A. 1971. "Verbal and Nonverbal Interaction of Strangers in a Waiting Situation." *Journal of Experimental Research in Personality* 5: 127–138.

Merton, Robert K. 1938. "Social Structure and Anomie.*" American Sociological Review* 3: 672–682.

Merton, Robert K. 1968. *Social Theory and Social Structure*, 2nd ed. New York: Free Press.

Mills, C. Wright. (1956) 1958. *The Power Elite*. New York: Oxford University Press.

Minerbrook, Scott. 1992. "A Tale of Two Suburbias." *U.S. News & World Report*. November 9, pp. 32, 40.

Moffet, Robert K., & Jack F. Scherer. 1976. *Dealing with Divorce*. Boston: Little, Brown.

Money, John, and Anke Erhardt. 1972. *Man and Woman, Boy and Girl*. Baltimore: Johns Hopkins Press.

Murdock, George Peter. 1945. "The Common Denominator of Cultures." In Ralph Linton, ed., *The Science of Man in the World Crisis*. New York: Columbia University Press, pp. 123–142.

Murdock, George Peter. 1957. "World Ethnographic Sample." *American Anthropologist* 59: 664–687.

Murdock, George Peter. 1965 (originally 1949). *Social Structure*. New York: Free Press.

Murray, Christopher J. L., Sandeep C. Kulkarni, Catherine Michaud, Niels Tomijima, Maria T. Bulzacchelli, Terrell J. Iandiorio, and Majid Ezzati. 2006. "Eight Americas: Investigating Mortality Disparities Across Races, Counties, and Race-Counties in the United States." *PLoS Med* 3(9): e260. DOI: 10.1371/journal.pmed .0030260. (September 12).

Myers, David. 2004. *Psychology*, 7th ed. New York: W. H. Freeman & Co.

Myerson, Allen R. 1995. "American Money Makes the Whole World Sing." *The New York Times*, December 17, pp. E1, E14.

Nagourney, Adam. 2006. "Internet Injects Sweeping Change into U.S. Politics." *The New York Times*, April 2, pp. 1, 17.

Narayan, Shoba. 1998. "Lessons from an Arranged Marriage." *New Woman*, January.

NASA/Goddard Space Flight Center. "New Image of Infant Universe Reveals Era of First Stars, Age of Cosmos, and More." February 2, 2003. *http://www.gsfc. nasa.gov/topstory/2003/0206mapresults.html*.

Nash, Madeleine J. 1993. "How Did Life Begin?" *Time*, October 11, pp. 69–74.

National Center for Health Statistics. 2006. Vital Statistics. *http://www.cdc.gov/nchs/vitalstats.htm*. Accessed: 6/12/07.

National Clearinghouse on Child Abuse and Neglect. 2004. "Child Abuse and Neglect Fatalities: Statistics and Interventions." *http://nccanch.acf.hhs.gov*. Accessed 12/11/04.

National Law Center for Homelessness and Poverty (NLCHPI), 2004. "2004 Appropriations Fail to Keep Pace with Increasing Homelessness." January 23.

Neergard, Lauran. 2006. "Where You Live Linked to Life Expectancy." *Houston Chronicle*. *http://www. houstonchronicle.com/section:national news.htm*.

Nisbet, Robert A. 1970. *The Social Bond*. New York: Knopf.

O'Dea, Thomas F. 1966. *The Sociology of Religion*. Englewood Cliffs, NJ: Prentice-Hall.

O'Dea, Thomas F., and Janet O'Dea Aviad. 1983. *The Sociology of Religion*, 2nd ed. Englewood Cliffs, NJ: Prentice-Hall.

Owen, D. R. 1972. "The 47 XYY Male: A Review." *Psychological Bulletin*, 78, 209–233.

Palen, J. John. 2002. *The Urban World*, 6th ed. New York: McGraw-Hill.

Palmore, Erdman. 1977. "Facts on Aging." *Gerontologist*, 17: 315–320.

Park, Robert Ezra. 1967. "The Urban Community as a Spatial Pattern and a Moral Order." In R. H. Turner, ed., *Robert E. Park on Social Control and Collective Behavior*. Chicago: University of Chicago Press.

Parrillo, Vincent N. 1990. *Strangers to These Shores*, 3rd ed. New York: Macmillan.

Patterson, Gerald R. 1980. "Children Who Steal." In *Understanding Crime: Current Theory and Research*. Travis Hirschi and Michael Gottfredson, eds. Beverly Hills, CA: Sage.

Patterson, Orlando. 2006. "A Poverty of the Mind." *The New York Times*, March 26, p. 13.

Pear, Robert. 1993. "Poverty in U. S. Grew Faster Than Population Last Year." *The New York Times*, October 5, p. 10.

Pear, Robert. 1998. "Number on Welfare Dips Below 10 Million." *The New York Times*, January 21, p. 12.

Pew Forum Resources. 2006. *Religion and World Affairs*. *http://pewforum.org/worldaffairs*. Accessed 5/9/2007.

Pew Global Attitudes Project. 2002. "What the World Thinks in 2002." December 4. *http://www.people-press. org*. Accessed 6/6/04.

Pew Research Center for the People and the Press. 2004. "GOP The Religion-Friendly Party . . ." *Survey Reports*. Released August 24, 2004. Accessed 9/15/2007.

Pew Research Center for the People and the Press. 2005. "GOP Makes Gains Among the Working Class, while Democrats Hold Onto the Union Vote." August 2.

Pew Research Center for the People and the Press. 2007. Survey Reports. "Summary of Findings: Public Knowledge of Current Affairs . . . " April 15. *http://people-press.org/reports/print/php3?PageID=1137.* Accessed 5/23/2007.

Phillips, Kevin. 1990. *The Politics of Rich and Poor: Wealth and the American Electorate in the Reagan Aftermath*. New York: Random House.

Piaget, Jean. 1950. *The Psychology of Intelligence*. London: Routledge & Kegan Paul.

Piaget, Jean. 1954. *The Construction of Reality in the Child*. New York: Basic Books.

Piketty, Thomas, and Emmanuel Saez. 2006. "The Evolution of Top Incomes: A Historical and International Perspective." National Bureau of Economic Research. January. *http://www.nber.org/papers(*W11955).

Pillard, R. C., and J. D. Weinrich. 1986. "Evidence of Familial Nature of Male Homosexuality." *Archives of General Psychiatry* 43: 808–812.

Piven, Frances Fox, and Richard A. Cloward. 1995. "Collective Protest: A Critique of Resource-Mobilization Theory." In Stanford M. Lyman, ed., *Social Movements*. New York: New York Unversity Press.

Police Executive Research Forum. 2006. "Violent Crime in America: 24 Months of Alarming Trends." October. *http://www.policeforum.org*.

Pope, Justin. 2004. "Study Finds More College Students But Not More Graduates." *Plain Dealer*, May 27, A6.

Popenoe, David. 1995. *Sociology*. Englewood Cliffs, NJ: Prentice-Hall.

Population Reference Bureau. 2001. *2001 World Population Data Sheet*. Washington, DC: U.S. Government Printing Office.

Prewitt, Kenneth, Sidney Verba, and Robert H. Salisbury. 1987. *An Introduction to American Government*, 5th ed. New York: Harper & Row.

Putnam, Robert D. 2000. *Bowling Alone: The Collapse and Revival of American Community*. New York: Simon and Schuster.

Qian, Zhenchao. 1998. "Changes in Assortive Mating: The Impact of Age and Education, 1970–1990." *Demography* 35(3): 279–292.

Quirk, Matthew. 2007. "The Mexican Connection." *The Atlantic*, April, p. 26.

Radelet, Michael L., and Ronald L. Akers, 1996. "Deterrence and the Death Penalty: The Views of the Experts." *Journal of Criminal Law and Criminology*, 87: 1–16.

Raudenbush, Stephen, and Felton Earls. 1997. "Neighborhoods and Violent Crime: A Multilevel Study of Collective Efficacy." *Science*, August 15, pp. 918–924.

Reich, Robert B. 1991. "Up the Workers." *The New Republic*, May 13, pp. 21–25

Relethford, John H. 2000. *The Human Species*. Mountainview, CA: Mayfield Publishing.

Rincon, Paul. 2 Jan 2004. BBC Online. 31 Mar 2004. *http://news.bbc.co.uk/1/hi/sci/tech/3361925.stm*.

Roberts, Sam. 2007. "51% of Women Are Now Living Without Spouse." *The New York Times*, January 16, p. A15.

Robinson, Randall. 2001. *The Debt: What America Owes to Blacks*. New York: Dutton/ Plume.

Rodriguez, Gregory. 1998. "Minority Leader." *The New Republic*, October 19, pp. 21–24.

Rogers, Carl R. 1961. *On Becoming a Person*. Boston: Houghton Mifflin.

Rymer, R. 1993. *Genie: An Abused Child's Flight from Silence*. New York: HarperCollins.

Safilios-Rothschild, Constantina. 1967. "A Comparison of Power Structure and Marital Satisfaction in Urban Greek and French Families." *Journal of Marriage and the Family* 30, pp. 527–531.

Safire, William. 1995. "News About Jews: The Dwindling Percentage." *The New York Times*, July 17, p. A11.

Salisbury, Robert H. 1969. "An Exchange Theory of Interest Groups." *Midwest Journal of Political Science* 13(February): 1–32.

Sampson, R. J., S. W. Raudenbush, and F. Earls. 1997. "Neighborhoods and Violent Crime: A Multilevel Study of Collective Efficacy." *Science*, August 15, pp. 918–924.

Samuelson, Robert J. 2001. "Indifferent to Inequality?" *Newsweek*, May 7, p. 45.

Sapir, Edward. 1949. *Selected Writings of Edward Sapir in Language, Culture, and Personality*, David G. Mandelbaum, ed. Berkeley: University of California Press.

Sapir, Edward. 1960. *Culture, Language and Personality: Selected Essays*. Berkeley: University of California Press.

Sapolsky, R. M., and L. J. Share. 2004. "A Pacific Culture Among Wild Baboons: Its Emergence and Transmission." *PLoSBiol*2(4): e106.DOI:10.1371/journal,pbio .0020106.

Sargent, Lyman T. 1969. *Contemporary Political Ideologies*. Homewood, IL: Dorsey.

Scanzoni, John H., and Maximiliane Szinovacz. 1980. *Family Decision Making: A Developmental Sex Role Model*. Beverly Hills, CA: Sage.

Schattschneider, E. E. 1942. *Party Government*. New York: Farrar & Rinehart, p. 1.

Schrof, Joanne M. 1994. "A Lens on Matrimony." *U.S. News & World Report*, February 21, pp. 66–69.*The New York Times*, January 25, pp. A1, A16.

Schwartz, John. 2007. "Of Gay Sheep, Modern Science and the Perils of Bad Publicity." *The New York Times*, January 25, p. A8.

Sengupta, Somini. 2001. "How Many Poor Children Is Too Many?" *The New York Times*, July 8, p. WK3.

Shea, Christopher. "Econophysics." *The New York Times*, December 11, 2005, p. B12.

Sheldon, William H. 1940. *The Varieties of Human Physique*. New York: Harper.

Sheldon, William H., et al. 1949. *Varieties of Delinquent Youth*. New York: Harper & Row.

Shils, Edward. 1961. "Mass Society and Its Culture." In N. Jacobs, ed., *Culture for the Millions*. New York: Van Nostrand Reinhold.

Shils, Edward. 1968. "The Concept of Ideology." In David L. Sills, ed. *The International Encyclopedia of the Social Sciences*. New York: Macmillan and Free Press.

Shorto, Russell. 1997. "Belief by the Numbers." *The New York Times Magazine*, December 7, pp. 60–61.

Shute, Nancy. 2001. "Where We Come From." *U.S. News & World Report*. January 29, pp. 34–41.

Simmel, Georg. (1905) 1956. *Conflict and the Web of Group Affiliation*. Kurt H. Wolff, transl. Glencoe, IL: Free Press.

Simpson, George E., and J. Milton Yinger. 1972. *Racial and Cultural Minorities: An Analysis of Prejudice and Discrimination*, 4th ed. New York: Harper & Row. (See also: 1985, 5th ed. New York: Plenum Press).

Smith, Adam. 1976. *The Wealth of Nations*. Chicago: University of Chicago Press.

Smith, Rupert. 2007. *The Utility of Force in the Modern World*. New York: Alfred A. Knopf.

Smith, Douglas A., and Patrick R. Gartin. 1989. "Specifying Specific Deterrence: The Influence of Arrest on Future Criminal Activity." *American Sociological Review* 54(1): 94–105.

Snarey, John. 1987. "A Question of Morality." *Psychology Today*, June, pp. 6–8.

Sondermann, Fred A., William C. Olson, and David S. McLellan. 1970. *The Theory and Practice of International Relations*, 3rd ed. Englewood Cliffs, NJ: Prentice-Hall.

Sowell, Thomas. 1983. *The Economics and Politics of Race: An International Perspective*. New York: Morrow.

Spencer, Herbert. 1873. *Descriptive Sociology*. Vol. I, New York: Appleton.

Spitz, Rene A. 1964. "Hospitalism." In Rose L. Coser, ed., *The Family: Its Structure and Functions*. New York: St. Martin's Press, pp. 399–425. Originally appeared in *The Psychoanalytic Study of the Child*, 1945, Vol. 1. New York: International Universities Press.

Stark, Rodney. 1985. *Sociology*. Belmont, CA: Wadsworth.

Stark, Rodney, and W. S. Bainbridge. 1985. *The Future of Religion: Secularization, Revival, and Cult Formation*. Berkeley: University of California Press.

Starrels, Marjorie. 1992. "Attitude Similarity Between Mothers and Children Regarding Maternal Employment," *Journal of Marriage and the Family* 54: 91–103.

Steinberg, Laurence, and Susan Silverberg. 1987. "Marital Satisfaction in Middle Stages of Family Life Cycle." *Journal of Marriage and the Family* 49 (4): 751–760.

Steinfels, Peter. 1998. "A Contrarian Sociologist of Religion Changes his Mind: Modernity Does Not Necessarily Lead to a Decline in Religion." *The New York Times*, September 5, p. 11.

Stevens, William K. 1990, "New Eye on Nature: The Real Constant is Eternal Turmoil." *The New York Times*, July 31, pp. B5, B6.

Stolberg, Sheryl Gay. 1999. "Birth Rate at New Low as Teenage Pregnancy Declines." *The New York Times*, April 29, p. A22.

Stolberg, Sheryl Gay. 2001. "Researchers Find a Link Between Behavioral Problems and Time in Child Care." *The New York Times*, April 19, p. A18.

Stoessinger, John G. 1975. *The Might of Nations: World Politics in Our Time*, 5th ed. New York: Random House.

Subramanian, Sribala. 1995. "The Story in Our Genes." *Time*, January 16, pp. 54–55.

Suplee, C. 1991. "Brain May Determine Sexuality." *The Washington Post*, August 30, pp. A1, A13.

Sutherland, Edwin H. 1949, 1961. *White Collar Crime*. New York: Dryden.

Suttles, Gerald. 1970. *The Social Order of the Slum*. Chicago: University of Chicago Press.

Szinovacz, Maximiliane E. 1987. "Family Power." In *Handbook of Marriage and the Family*. New York: Plenum, pp. 652–693.

Tilley, Charles. 2006. *Why?* Princeton, NJ: Princeton University Press.

Thurow, Lester C. 1999. "Building Wealth." *The Atlantic Monthly*, June, pp. 57–69.

Tönnies, Ferdinand. (1887) 1957. *Community and Society*. New York: Harper Torchbooks.

Trigaux, Robert. 2006. "CEO Pay Eclipses Ridiculous." *St. Petersburg Times*, April 24, p. 1D.

Troidén, Richard R. 1988. *Gay and Lesbian Identity: A Sociological Analysis*. New York: General Hall, pp. 42–58.

Turnbull, Colin. 1973. *The Mountain People*. New York: Simon & Schuster.

United Nations. 2007. "Population and Vital Statistics Report." Series A. Vol. LIX, No. 1. Department of Economic and Social Affairs. January 1, Table 3, p. 16.

U.S. Bureau of the Census. 2003. Economic and Statistics Administration. U.S. Census Press Release, December 18.

U.S. Bureau of the Census. 2004. Historical Income Tables–Income Equality. Table IE-1. *http://www.census.gov/hhes/income/histinc/ei1.html*. Accessed 7/8/07.

U.S. Bureau of the Census. 2006. "Percent of the Total Population Who Are 65 Years and Over." 2006 Population Estimates, July.

U.S. Bureau of the Census. 2007. Current Population Reports. "Domestic Net Migration in the United States: 2000 to 2004." Issued April 2006.

U.S. Conference of Mayors, 2006. "Hunger and Homelessness Remains a Critical Issue for Families; Leading Causes Cited Are Unemployment, Mental Illness, and Lack of Affordable Housing." *http:www.usmayors.org/USCM/home.asp*.

U. S. Department of Education. 2006. "A Test of Leadership: Charting the Future of U.S. Higher Education." A Report of the Commission Appointed by Secretary of Education Margaret Spellings. Washington, DC. September.

U.S. Department of Health and Human Services, Administration for Children and Families. *http:// www.nccic.org/index.html*. Last updated June 28, 2006.

U.S. Department of Justice, Bureau of Justice Statistics, 2001. *Criminal Offenders Statistics*. "Recidivism."

U.S. Department of Justice, Bureau of Justice Statistics, 2001. *Criminal Offenders Statistics*, "Lifetime Likelihood of Going to State or Federal Prison."

U.S. Department of Labor. 2000. *Highlights of Women's Earnings in 2005*. May. Report 943, p. 1. *http://www.dol.gov/wb/factsheets/qf- laborforce-06.htm*.

Veblen, Thorstein. (1899) 1953. *The Theory of the Leisure Class*. New York: The New American Library.

Verba, Sidney, Kay Schlozman, and Henry Brady. 1995. *Voice and Equality*. Cambridge, MA: Harvard University Press.

Viotti, Paul R., and Mark V. Kauppi. 1987. *International Relations Theory*. New York: Macmillan.

Vogel, Dena Ann, Margaret A. Lake, Suzanne Evans, and Katherine Hildebrandt Karraker. 1991. "Children and Adults' Sex-Stereotyped Perceptions of Infants." *Sex Roles* 24: 605.

Wade, Nicholas. 1997. "Neanderthal DNA Sheds New Light on Human Origins." *The New York Times*, July 11, pp. 1, A14.

Wade, Nicholas. 2000. "DNA Tests Cast Doubt on Link Between Neanderthals and Modern Man." *The New York Times*, March 29, p. A16.

Wade, Nicholas. 2002. "Insight Into Human-Chimp Differences." *The New York Times*, April 12, p. A18.

Wade, Nicholas. 2003. "Why Humans and Their Fur Parted Ways." *The New York Times*, August 19, pp. D1, D4.

Wade, Nicholas. 2007. "Pas de Deux of Sexuality Is Written in the Genes." *The New York Times*. April 10, pp. D1, D6.

Wagley, Charles, and Marvin Harris. 1958. *Minorities in the New World*. New York: Columbia.

Wallerstein, Judith S., and Joan B. Kelly. 1983. "The Effects of Parental Divorce: Experiences of the Child in Later Years." In Arlene S. Skolnick and Jerome H. Skolnick, eds., *Family in Transition*. Boston: Little, Brown.

Wallerstein, Judith, and Sandra Blakeslee. 1989. *Second Chances*. New York: Ticknor & Fields.

Wallerstein, Judith. 1989. "Children after Divorce." *The New York Times Magazine*. January 22, pp. 19–44.

Wallis, Claudia. 1987. "Is Day Care Bad for Babies?" *Time* (June 22), p. 63.

Wartik, Nancy. 2004. "Hard-Wired for Prejudice? Experts Examine Human Response to Outsiders." *The New York Times*, April 20, p. D5.

Wattenberg, Ben J., and Karl Zinsmeister. 1986. "The Birth Dearth: The Geopolitical Consequences." *Public Opinion* 8 (December/January): 6–13.

Wattenberg, Martin P. 1994. *The Decline of American Political Parties*. Cambridge, MA: Harvard University Press.

Weber, Max. (1925) 1947. *Theory of Social and Economic Organization*. A. L. Henderson and Talcott Parsons, transl. New York: Free Press.

Weber, Max. 1957. *The Theory of Social and Economic Organization*. New York; Free Press.

Weber, Max. (1904–5) 1958. *The Protestant Ethic and the Spirit of Capitalism*. New York: Charles Scribner's Sons.

Weishaus, Sylvia, and Dorothy Field. 1988. "A Half Century of Marriage: Continuity or Change?" *Journal of Marriage and the Family* 50 (August), pp. 763–774.

Weiss, Kenneth R. 1989. "80–Year Tide of Migration by Blacks out of the South Has Turned Around." *The New York Times*, June 1, p. Y29.

Weitzman, Lenore J. 1985. *The Divorce Revolution: The Unexpected Social and Economic Consequences for Women and Children in America*. New York: Free Press.

White, E. B. 1949. *Here Is New York*. New York: Harper & Row, pp. 27–30.

Whiting, B. 1963. *Six Cultures: Studies in Child Rearing*. London: Wiley.

Whorf, Benjamin. 1956. *Language, Thought and Reality*. New York: Wiley.

Whyte, William H. 1989. *Cities*. New York: Doubleday.

Wilford, John Noble. 1992. "Jawbone Offers Clues in Search for 'Missing Link'." *The New York Times*, March 17, p. B5.

Wilford, John Noble. 1993. "Old Tablet From Turkish Site Shows Early Spread of Culture." *The New York Times*, November 9, p. B7.

Wilford, John Noble. 1997. "New Clues Show Where People Made the Great Leap to Agriculture." *The New York Times*, November 18, pp. B9, B12.

Wilford, John Noble. 1998. "Ancestral Humans Could Speak, Anthropologists' Finding Suggests." *The New York Times*, April 28, pp. 1, 17.

Wilford, John Noble. 1998. "Look Who's Talking. Don't Bother Listening." *The New York Times*, May 3, Section 4, p. 4.

Wilford, John Noble. 1999. "Discovery Suggests Man Is a Bit Neanderthal." *The New York Times*, April 25, pp. 1, 21.

Wilford, John Noble. 2000. "Skulls in Caucasus Linked to Early Humans in Africa." *The New York Times*, May 12, pp. 1, A28.

Wilford, John Noble. 2001. "The Family of Man Grows a Little Larger." *The New York Times*, March 25, p. 3.

Wilford, John Noble. 2003. "New Clue on Which Came First, Tools or Better Diets." *The New York Times*, October 21, Section F, 3.

Wilford, John Noble. 2004. "Less Jaw, Big Brain: Evolution Milestone Laid to Gene Flaw." *The New York Times*, March 25, pp. 1, A18.

Wilford, John Noble. 2004. "Fossils Found in Spain Seen as Last Link to Great Apes." *The New York Times*, November 19, p. A8.

Wilford, John Noble. 2007a. "Fossils Reveal Clues on Human Ancestor." *The New York Times*, September 20.

Wilford, John Noble. 2007b. "Lost in a Million-Year Gap, Solid Clue to Human Origins." *The New York Times*, September 18, p. D1, 4.

Williams, Robin, Jr. 1970. *American Society: A Sociological Interpretation*, 3rd ed. New York: Knopf.

Wilson, Edward O. 1980. *Sociobiology*, abridged ed. New York: Belknap Press.

Wilson, Edward O. 1998. "Back from Chaos." *The Atlantic Monthly*, March, pp. 41–62.

Wilson, Edward O. 1999. *Consilience: The Unity of Knowledge*. New York: Vintage.

Wilson, James Q., and George L. Kelling. 1982. "Broken Windows." *Atlantic Monthly*, March, pp. 29–38.

Wilson, William Julius. 1978. *The Declining Significance of Race*. Chicago: University of Chicago Press.

Wilson, William Julius. 1987. *The Truly Disadvantaged: The Inner City, the Underclass, and Public Policy*. Chicago: University of Chicago Press.

Wirth, Louis. 1938. "Urbanism as a Way of Life." *American Journal of Sociology* 44: 1–44.

Wolfe, Alan. 1998. "The Homosexual Exception." *The New York Times Magazine*, February 8, pp. 46–47.

Wolin, Sheldon S. 1980. "Foreword." In *Democratic Elitism: A Critique*, Peter Bachrach, ed. Lanham, MD: University Press of America.

Womack, James P., Daniel T. Jones, and Daniel Roos. 1990. "How Lean Production Can Change the World." *The New York Times Magazine*, September 23, pp. 20–23, 34–38.

Women's Bureau, U.S. Department of Labor, Bureau of Labor Statistics, Employment and Earnings. November 2005. *http://www.dol.gov/wb/stats/main.htm*. Accessed 8/8/07.

World Development Report, 2000–2001. Press Conference on 2001 World Indicators. April 29, 2001. *http://www.worldbank.org/ndr/2001/overview.html*.

World Development Indicators. 2004. World Bank Group. *http://worldbank.org/data/wdi2004/ index. htm*. Accessed 9/12/07.

World Net Daily. 2006.

World Resources 1996–1997. "The Urban Environment." New York: Oxford University Press.

Wrangham, Richard and Dale Peterson. 1996. *Demonic Males: Apes and the Origins of Human Violence*. New York: Houghton Mifflin.

Yardley, Jim. 2006. "First Comes the Car, Then the $10,000 License Plate." *The New York Times*. July 6, p. A4.

Yetman Norman R., and C. Hoy Steele, eds. 1971. *Majority and Minority*. Boston: Allyn & Bacon.

Yetman, Norman R. 1985. *Majority and Minority: The Dynamics of Race and Ethnicity in American Life*. Boston: Allyn & Bacon.

Zeller, Tom. 2000. "Calculating One Kind of Middle Class." *The New York Times*, October 29, p. 5.

Zernike, Kate. 2000. "Gap Widens Again on Tests Given to Blacks and Whites." *The New York Times*, August 25, p. A14.

Photo Credits

Index